Environmental Law

Lisa Johnson, PhD, JD

Frona Powell, JD

CENGAGE
Learning·

Australia • Brazil • Mexico • Singapore • United Kingdom • United States

Environmental Law
Lisa Johnson and Frona Powell

Vice President, General Manager,
Social Science & Qualitative Business:
Barbara Stephan

Product Director: Mike Worls

Product Manager: Steven Scoble

Content Developer: Ted Knight

Product Assistant: Ryan McAdams

Brand Manager: Robin LeFevre

Market Development Manager: Jeff
Tousignant

Marketing Coordinator: Christopher Walz

Art and Cover Direction, Production
Management, and Composition:
Lumina Datamatics, Inc.

Media Developer: Kristen Meere

Senior Intellectual Property Director: Julie
Geagan-Chevez

Intellectual Property Project Manager, Text
and Image: Anne Sheroff

Manufacturing Planner: Kevin Kluck

Cover Image(s): © Siede Preis/Photodisc/
Getty Images

For product information and technology assistance, contact us at
Cengage Learning Customer & Sales Support, 1-800-354-9706

For permission to use material from this text or product,
submit all requests online at **www.cengage.com/permissions**
Further permissions questions can be emailed to
permissionrequest@cengage.com

Library of Congress Control Number: 2014933480

Student Edition ISBN: 978-1-133-96158-1

Cengage Learning
20 Channel Center Street
Boston, MA 02210
USA

Cengage Learning is a leading provider of customized learning
solutions with office locations around the globe, including Singapore,
the United Kingdom, Australia, Mexico, Brazil, and Japan. Locate your
local office at: **www.cengage.com/global**

Cengage Learning products are represented in Canada by
Nelson Education, Ltd.

To learn more about Cengage Learning Solutions, visit
www.cengage.com

Purchase any of our products at your local college store or at our
preferred online store **www.cengagebrain.com**

Printed in the United States of America
Print Number: 01   Print Year: 2014

Contents

CHAPTER 3

Introduction to the Law of Property   68

Preface

Welcome to *Environmental Law*! This book will act as a useful guide as you learn about the many different sources of environmental law, the problems that it seeks to address, and the challenges that remain.

We, the authors, are professors with many years of experience in teaching undergraduates. The primary reason for undertaking this project is to help students understand this sometimes confusing area of law. To be sure, environmental law is not a perfectly uniform system of law. There are overlapping jurisdictional issues, and there are outright gaps. Federal, state, and sometimes international laws constitute a mishmash of a legal environment. However, every page in this book was written with the goal of making the study of this vast topic understandable and enjoyable.

Students who enroll in undergraduate and graduate environmental law courses often have never taken a prior legal studies class, and they are motivated more by their love for the natural environment than by any love of law. This book responds to those students' needs by making accessible the many legal issues that arise in the context of the natural environment, without sacrificing comprehensiveness. This book is easy to read, but thorough.

We recognize that one of the major challenges in learning about environmental law is that familiarity with the basics of law is essential to fully understand the substantive area of environmental law. With that in mind, we have included sufficient introductory materials, as well as ample content suitable for more advanced students. This text develops environmental literacy in a challenging and engaging way.

Environmental law is an ever-evolving field. Hot topics and issues change quickly. Questions concerning whether or how the environment can be restored or protected, who should pay for restoration, and whether environmental degradation should be permitted at all are the types of inquiries that this book can help answer. How? It allows readers to gain a clear understanding of the existing legal environment, as well as the possibilities that might be built from the existing legal foundations. Of course, besides evolving topics, the law itself also changes. Courts make new decisions that shape industry reactions, public expectations, and executive and legislative agendas. Executives change and policies change; legislatures continue their work even though their members change.

The first incarnation of this book, *Law and the Environment*, authored by Frona Powell, was published more than 15 years ago. The present text retains many of the key attributes of the original. For example, each chapter features excerpts from illustrative case opinions and accompanying questions for discussion. Of course, a lot has changed in 15 years. Accordingly, the text has been thoroughly updated and reorganized. The book also includes new features, including contemporary examples and problems, definitions of key terms right on the subject page, and Internet-based activities.

The contents address the basic foundations of U.S. law that are essential to understanding our legal system as it pertains to the natural environment. Though the book's primary focus is on federal law, it addresses other jurisdictions as well. For example, because federalism is a fundamentally important concept in many environmental statutory schemes, both state and federal roles are addressed. Likewise, because certain state claims are relevant in environmental law, state law issues of torts and contracts are addressed.

The book follows the development and application of environmental laws to the present day. Major federal statutes like the Clean Air Act, Clean Water Act, and CERCLA, which are designed to address the problems of national air, water, and land pollution, respectively, are clearly important sources of environmental law. However, to view environmental law as simply the study of statutes created by Congress unduly narrows the focus. In fact, environmental law is not limited to pollution control by statutory or concomitant regulatory mandates. Likewise, it is not limited to conceptualizing natural resources as items to be managed, protected, or conserved—as our major federal statutes attempt to do. Though those things are important, environmental law also includes the concepts of property rights and property ownership, and how those fundamental understandings of humans' relationships to the land affect our understanding and belief about what we can do to it.

Moreover, animals and ecosystems are legitimate stakeholders in their own environment. Historically, our laws have rarely focused on animals' interests in habitat, food and water sources, and freedom of movement. However, these ideas are not alien to persons interested in the environment, and some indications exist that our environmental laws are maturing sufficiently to conceptualize and include those interests in the context of environmental law. For too long, the field of "animal law" has been oddly separated from the field of "environmental law." Wild animals are part of the environment, so laws relating to animals are relevant in a study of environmental law as well. Of course, these areas are not always separated. For example, the Endangered Species Act is a major and well-known environmental law statute. However, the field of environmental law has had little to say about many animal-related issues, such as their lack of standing, their status as property, and their lack of recognized interests in their necessities of life (e.g., habitat). This book reunifies those important—and mutually dependent—issues. While the book is not focused on animal law-related issues per se, it does not ignore them, either. Though animal law is primarily a study in shortcomings, it is also an actively evolving area of law. A claim of environmental literacy must include familiarity with those issues as well.

In keeping with this broad definition of *environmental law*, this text examines all of these issues in a manner that allows readers to build their knowledge in a logical manner. Chapters 1 through 8 are best studied in the order in which they are presented, because each chapter builds upon the concepts presented in the preceding chapters. A student new to the study of law will be introduced to basic law and legal concepts in the first several chapters, while building an understanding of environmental law along the way; each chapter uses environmental law examples to illustrate the concepts it covers.

Chapter 1 introduces readers to the major concerns raised and addressed through environmental law, including ethics, history, and the challenges of valuation. Chapter 2 explains the legal system, including basic information regarding the sources of law, federal versus state jurisdiction, civil versus criminal law, the structure of the federal and state court systems, and the steps in civil litigation. Chapter 3 addresses the law of real property, including acquisition, scope, kinds of ownership, easements, and covenants. Chapter 4 discusses torts and the use of common law remedies for environmental harms. This chapter also addresses claims that are relevant to a plaintiff contemplating a lawsuit for environmental damage, such as trespass, nuisance, negligence, and strict liability. Chapter 5 concerns contracts, including the basics of contract formation. It also addresses the liability issues that arise in contracts related to the environment, such as third-party liability in the purchase of real property; the role of warranty, indemnification, and disclaimer; and the application of product liability theory. Chapter 6 focuses on land use regulations and the Bill of Rights. Specifically, it addresses zoning and various state approaches to land use regulations. Additionally, it introduces students to the major constitutional law issue of takings and the Fifth Amendment to the U.S. Constitution. Chapter 7 introduces constitutional law, including the Commerce Clause, the dormant commerce clause, the Supremacy Clause, federal preemption of state laws, and the property clause. Chapter 8 lays out the principles of administrative law, including the delegation doctrine, the Administrative Procedure Act, rulemaking, and other powers of administrative agencies. It also discusses limitations on administrative agency power, such as judicial review, the Freedom of Information Act, and congressional oversight of administrative agency actions.

The next chapters cover several important statutory schemes. Chapter 9 addresses federal environmental policy, animals, and federal public lands. Specifically, it investigates the National Environmental Policy Act, the Endangered Species Act, and several public land acts, such as the Coastal Zone Management Act. Chapter 10 addresses air and water pollution, and includes overviews of the Clean Air Act and the Clean Water Act. Chapter 11 addresses toxic substances. Accordingly, it reviews the Federal Insecticide, Fungicide, and Rodenticide Act and the Toxic Substances Control Act. Chapter 12 addresses hazardous waste. The statutes reviewed in that chapter include the Resource Conservation and Recovery Act and the Comprehensive Response, Compensation, and Liability Act. Chapter 13 expands the field to international law, discussing the nature of international law, the sources of international environmental law, environmental issues related to trade, extraterritorial application of U.S. domestic law, and legal actions by foreign citizens in U.S. courts.

We hope that you enjoy your journey through *Environmental Law*!

About the Author(s)

Lisa Johnson, PhD, JD, is an Associate Professor at the University of Puget Sound's School of Business and Leadership. She has extensive education and teaching experience in environmental law and policy, and animal law and political theory. She is a fellow at the Oxford Centre for Animal Ethics.

Frona Powell, JD, is an Associate Professor Emeritus of Business Law at Indiana University's Kelley School of Business. Her research interests include environmental law and real estate law.

Environmental Law, Ethical Perspectives, and Disciplinary Intersections

Here's a good idea!

This is a "bare bones" outline of the chapter. Expand this outline with more detailed notes as you read the chapter. This will allow you to create a study guide as you work. This good study habit will help you learn the material, retain important points, and make efficient use of your time.

Learning Objectives

After reading this chapter, you will have an understanding of the origins of environmental law in the United States. Additionally, you will understand how ethical perspectives can affect environmental values, which can lead to policies and laws with different—and at times inconsistent—goals. You will examine disciplinary intersections with environmental law. Specifically, after reading this chapter, you should be able to answer the following questions:

1. How did environmental law develop in the United States?
2. What is environmental law?
3. What differing ethical perspectives exist that might lead to different points of view concerning humankind's relationship to the natural environment?
4. How do other disciplinary perspectives interface with environmental law?

▦ Introduction to Environmental Law

Today environmental law is a well-established, well-defined area of law. However, just 50 years ago, that was not the case. Indeed, just a few generations ago, actions that despoiled the environment—whether taken by industry or individuals in pursuit of profit—were often unquestioningly accepted as part of humans' relationship to the natural world. As the environment became more degraded, however, and as television technology allowed people to view larger parts of the world, people began to question the legitimacy of such a relationship with the environment. Questions became concern. Concern became organized **grassroots efforts**. Grassroots efforts led to legislative and policy changes, and to many of our first successes in protecting parts of our environment and some species of animals.

What types of things does environmental law currently seek to address? Parts of the environment are relatively easy to identify as falling under the purview of environmental law. For example, most people would probably agree that the environment includes the natural world, such as fields, forests, rivers, oceans, seas, sand dunes, animals, plants, and riparian areas. However, some people might be surprised to know that environmental law also has something to say about the built environment. Areas of concern to environmental law include things like green space in cities, public parks, dams, bridges, roads, buildings, malls, sidewalks, parking lots, and schools. Environmental law can address matters relating to environmental health—both human health and the health of the natural environment—in all of these areas. We need environmental law to protect and conserve the environment, and to redress prior damage to the environment. Environmental law often tries to answer questions concerning who should pay for damage done to the environment, as well as who should pay to prevent future harm to it.

Laws evolve to reflect society's current goals and values. No area of law more vividly illustrates this fact than environmental law. Historically, environmental law has been both proactive and reactive. That is, those who have sought change in the laws related to the environment are either trying to anticipate environmental issues that have not yet become problematic—which is a **proactive** approach, or create law that will correct or respond to an environmental problem that already exists or prevent a problem that has already occurred from reoccurring in the future—which is a **reactive** approach.

An example of proactive lawmaking can be seen in our efforts to codify **sustainability**. For example, some states and local jurisdictions have **statutes** or city **ordinances** that require government offices to purchase only post-consumer-waste recycled paper products. For example, as noted in the box titled "Proactive Environmental Lawmaking?," the City of Honolulu is required to purchase recycled paper products (from toilet paper to copy paper) per local ordinance.[1] Honolulu's requirement that the city procure recycled paper products when it purchases paper products is an example of a proactive environmental law, because it is primarily concerned with the sustainable use of natural resources, rather than attempting to rectify a prior environmental harm. Of course, prior environmental harm might be the catalyst for such a law, but prior acts are not **redressable** through such a law. In other words, this type of law does not create a cause of action for damages done to the environment in the past. It does, however, create a mandate governing future actions. A proactive approach to environmental problems can prevent future damage that might have occurred if the law had not been passed.

As an example of reactive lawmaking, consider the Love Canal hazardous waste catastrophe. In the late 1970s, residents of Love Canal, New York, discovered that their homes were built on 20,000 tons of toxic waste, which had been buried in an environmentally unsound manner. The steel drums that held the hazardous waste materials had rusted, and the waste had begun to seep to the surface. Persons who lived in Love Canal as children remembered playing with "hot rocks," or clods of material that would burn their hands when picked up. Pets that lived in Love Canal experienced burned paws. Children who lived there mysteriously fell ill. Eventually, the residents of Love Canal organized. Their ordeal eventually led Congress to pass a new federal statute. This statute,

grassroots efforts: Actions organized at the community level to address a problem or concern of importance to that community.

proactive: Anticipatory; acting in advance to address an expected challenge or issue.

reactive: Responding to something that happened in the past.

sustainability: Use of resources in a manner that does not permanently deplete them.

statute: A law enacted by a legislative body.

ordinance: A statute-like law enacted by a municipality.

redressable: Capable of being rectified or remedied.

---

[1] Revised Ordinances of Honolulu 1990, ch. 1, art. 12, § 1-12.3; available at http://www1.honolulu.gov/council/ocs/roh/ (last visited October 16, 2013).

the Comprehensive Environmental Response, Compensation, and Liability Act (**CERCLA**), imposed liability on specific parties associated with hazardous waste sites and also established a means to remediate such sites.

■ *Proactive Environmental Lawmaking?*

Required procurement of recycled paper products.

(a) [...] when procuring a paper product, the city shall procure only a recycled paper product. Revised Ordinances of Honolulu 1990, ch. 1, art. 12, § 1-12.3(a)

Questions for reflection:

1. Research your city's ordinances. Does your city mandate recycling or other sustainable practices?

2. What are some reasons that a mandate for recycling might be opposed?

3. What other types of laws could a city institute to engage in proactive environmental lawmaking?

Of course, sometimes laws are created to address a new environmental situation that has not yet been considered by our legal system. For example, the phenomenon of global warming or climate change caused or exacerbated by human actions is a relatively new concept. Of course, it is not surprising that no environmental law to address global warming was created before the phenomenon itself was identified. Furthermore, only recently has it been generally accepted that human beings contribute to the global warming phenomenon. Though we may have heard about global warming for the past few decades, our legal system does not move swiftly. As we know, law evolves in response to society's current goals and values. The word *evolves* correctly describes how law changes, denoting a slow adaptation to new circumstances rather than a rapid conversion. Discussions about whether and how human law might be crafted to address and mitigate global warming are only just now coalescing into laws enacted by our different systems of government—local, state, and federal—to address it. An interesting **jurisdictional** question exists with this particular example. Because global warming is by definition a global phenomenon, and because our systems of law are limited by specific jurisdictional boundaries, humanity will have to work together to transcend existing political and jurisdictional boundaries if we hope to create laws that will truly mitigate global warming.

These examples—sustainability-related laws, CERCLA, and the challenges presented by global environmental concerns—are each addressed in greater detail in subsequent chapters. They are offered here only as examples of the nature of environmental law. In short, environmental law exists to correct old harms, prevent new harms, and address emerging issues.

This chapter should help you understand some of the sticking points associated with the creation of environmental law and associated environmental policy, including the very real challenges presented when people hold legitimately different opinions related to environmental goals and objectives, varied conceptualizations of what the environment is or should be, and tradeoffs inherent in environmental decision making. Consider the questions presented in the box titled "An Environmental Dilemma: How 'Clean' Is Clean?"

CERCLA: The "Superfund" statute, which addresses hazardous waste sites.

jurisdictional: Relating to authority to apply or enforce a law.

■ *An Environmental Dilemma: How "Clean" Is Clean?*

Most people would agree that living in a clean and healthy environment is desirable. However, difficulties often arise when we have to decide what "clean environment" means. How "clean" is clean? How "healthy" is healthy? If scientists believe that a certain level of pollution in the air is not problematic for 99% of the human population, is that clean enough? What if you happened to be in the 1% of persons who suffered respiratory distress as a result of this contaminant?

Should the environment be protected in its natural state? Or should it be actively used— mined, forested, dammed—providing we do it sustainably? Whose interests should be paramount? Those of the people who live on the land? Those of the businesses that need to use environmental resources? Those of the animals that rely upon the land as habitat? Indeed, in the latter group, to what extent do our laws recognize nonhuman interests? In addition, though this concern may seem mundane, an underlying question always exists in our current conceptualization of environmental law and its intersecting disciplines: Who should bear the costs of decisions made about our environment?

As an example, suppose that a city decides to reclaim land contaminated by hazardous waste. Such a decision involves some weighty concerns. For example, if the land is to be remediated and converted to use as a public park, how will the project be paid for? The remediation of **brownfields** (abandoned hazardous waste sites) can run into the millions of dollars. Of course, there is also a cost to leaving the brownfield unremediated. Specifically, it poses continuing dangers to the health of both humans and wildlife. It also imposes costs through diminished aesthetic value, which may reduce the value of surrounding properties and diminish the area's sense of community. If the company that originally placed the hazardous waste on the land no longer exists, or if the person or persons who made the decision to pollute the land are no longer alive, is it fair to ask taxpayers to pay for the remediation of the land from public coffers? Finally, consider the tradeoffs that will occur as a result of pursuing this project. If the government's limited pot of money is used for environmental remediation, then some other projects may have to be forgone or postponed until a future date.

To get more information and perspectives on these issues, spend some time engaging with the following activity box. Watch one or several videos available through the Environmental Protection Agency link and answer the questions presented in the activity box.

brownfields: Abandoned hazardous waste sites.

■ ACTIVITY BOX   *Superfund Redevelopment Videos*

Visit the Environmental Protection Agency's Superfund Redevelopment Videos webpage: http://www.epa.gov/superfund/programs/recycle/info/video.html

Choose and watch one video; then answer the following questions:

1. In the video that you watched, how was the redeveloped site formerly used? What is it used for now? What are the differences between then and now?
2. What are the benefits of using redeveloped Superfund sites for public purposes?
3. Do you believe that remediated Superfund sites are safe for use for public purposes, such as soccer fields and parks? Why or why not?
4. Imagine that you are a member of a city council, and you are deciding whether the city will remediate and develop an existing brownfield site. What types of issues and concerns should you consider before making a decision?

Many questions about how we use the law to protect the environment will become apparent as you read this text—and you will realize that many of these questions do not have easy answers. The tensions reflected in such questions are everpresent when decisions are made about the environment. This is true in situations where an environmental problem is being remedied, where a direct conflict exists between parties with adverse interests related to the environment, and where a proactive approach is being taken to an emerging environmental issue or challenge.

How are such tensions resolved? What balancing of interests is appropriate? As discussed in Chapter 2, the United States has an adversarial legal system. This means that if an environmental dispute must be resolved through a formal dispute resolution method such as a trial, there are clear winners and losers. Consider whether such an outcome is an appropriate or desirable goal in matters relating to the environment, keeping in mind that unanimously agreed-upon resolutions are rare in matters of environmental controversy.

This book will help you learn about the tools that are commonly used to make decisions relating to the environment. These tools include the relevant laws relating to the environment, the manner in which those laws are applied, and the policies and regulations associated with those laws. Additionally, this book provides disciplinary context regarding decision making about the environment. For example, you will learn to consider not just what the law is, but also the social, economic, and political forces at play in environmental issues. Although decisions about the environment are often influenced by legal constraints and analysis, they also are often informed by ethical analyses and policy considerations. Even if clearcut answers cannot be expected in most environmental controversies, understanding the larger context in which environmental law is created can be useful when addressing past harms, planning for sustainability, and dealing with emerging environmental problems at their onset.

The law reflects choices made by our three branches of government: the legislative, judicial, and executive branches. It also reflects decisions made by administrative agencies. Thus, a basic understanding of our system of government is important when learning how laws affecting the environment fit together. Chapter 2 addresses the U.S. system of government, focusing on the important roles of each of the branches of government and the roles of administrative agencies. For now, however, it is enough to know that the people have a voice in our system of government. That voice is represented through the persons who are elected to office. Lawmakers and policy makers are influenced by many factors, including their constituents' priorities and interests, political interests and machinations, ethical perspectives, economic considerations, individual worldviews, science, and perceptions of risk. Of course, not all policy decisions are affected by each of these issues every time. Unfortunately, some policy makers seem to rely too much on one factor and not enough on the others. For example, imagine a politician who made all environmental decisions based solely upon scientific evidence. Would that be sufficient? What if science conflicted with the religious beliefs of the people who lived on the land involved? Which interest should be the overriding concern?

Several recurrent themes become apparent when you study environmental law. These themes include:

1. All living beings share or compete for resources. Consider whether *share* or *compete* is the correct verb. A hint of your worldview concerning humans'

relationship to the natural environment and to each other might be revealed when you consider whether you believe that we "share" resources or "compete" for resources. Who has the legal authority to make decisions about **transboundary** resources or animals? Gray whales, for example, are a highly migratory species. During their annual migration, they use the Pacific migratory corridor that extends through the waters of Canada, the United States, and Mexico. If one country makes a decision about its waters that will negatively affect the gray whale, should others have a voice in that decision? If so, who? Just the one country? All three countries? The entire world?

Notice, too, that when we discuss what the law is (e.g., "Who has the legal authority to make decisions … ?"), we are discussing **positive law**. In contrast, when we discuss what the law should be (e.g., "Which entities should have a voice … ?"), this is a **normative** consideration. This book focuses on positive law, but it also addresses competing normative claims. Both are important in environmental law.

2. Historically, there has been a tension between "doing business" and protecting or conserving the environment and natural resources. Does this tension have to exist? In Western countries, environmental costs associated with doing business have traditionally been externalized. Advocates of traditional business values and practices maintain that social responsibility (such as environmental concerns) should not be permitted to hinder business pursuits, and claim that corporations owe duties only to their shareholders. As succinctly stated by Milton Friedman, "[T]he social responsibility of business is to increase … profits."[2] The traditional Western approach seeks the greatest profit for business while externalizing negative environmental and social consequences.[3] At the opposite end of the continuum, advocates of corporate social responsibility argue that environmental attributes without traditional market value nevertheless have importance. When those attributes are damaged by business, that damage should be treated as part of the cost of doing business and captured by "green" accounting practices, rather than externalized and ignored as if it did not exist. **Green accounting** is an accounting method that incorporates **negative externalities** by valuing the damage to natural amenities and resources and treating it as a business cost. Traditional accounting models do not account for this damage. Green accounting has become popular as a public policy tool, but can also be applied by private industry.

In fact, many businesses are practicing environmental corporate social responsibility. These businesses do not see the tension between profit and environmental protection as irreconcilable. Instead, they hope to create businesses whose practices do not harm the environment and are profitable and sustainable over the long term. However, other businesses continue to externalize negative environmental costs and effects, per the traditional Western business model. In many ways, U.S. laws support this status quo. For example, traditionally organized U.S. corporations have a fiduciary relationship to its shareholders to maximize profits. Some state laws now recognize "benefit corporations," which permits or recognizes other appropriate corporate duties. However, if a traditionally organized corporation diverts money to

transboundary: Crossing jurisdictional boundaries.

positive law: Human-made law that actually exists.

normative law: What the law should be; a value-based statement about the law.

green accounting: An accounting method that attempts to include negative environmental externalities in the financial operation of a business or other institution.

negative externality: A negative impact on a third party.

---

[2] Milton Friedman, *The Social Responsibility of Business Is to Increase Its Profits*, N.Y. TIMES MAGAZINE 122–26 (September 13, 1970).
[3] L. Newton, BUSINESS ETHICS AND THE NATURAL ENVIRONMENT (2005).

projects related to environmental corporate social responsibility, does it violate that duty? Are our laws sufficient to dissuade a corporation that decides to use natural resources without concern for long-term sustainability because it wishes to make a fast profit?

Consider the standard types of environmental costs of doing business. For example, air pollutants pouring forth from smokestacks and industrial effluents discharged into our waterways are common. If the businesses engaged in those behaviors have obtained permits to discharge their pollutants, there is nothing illegal in those practices. Traditionally, these types of negative externalities, which are costs to our environment, are not attributed to their creators, because businesses do not capture or reflect those environmental costs in their bottom lines. However, that does not mean that the negative externalities disappear. Indeed, all who see or use the polluted environment experience the degradation. When environmental costs are externalized in this way, businesses can profit from the degradation and the harm to the environment often goes unremediated. Specifically, the business does not have to pay for the damage it does, and the cost of the product to the consumer does not reflect the costs to the environment (the negative externalities) incurred in its production. In this system, only internalized costs—things like cost of raw materials, labor, overhead, advertising, and so on—are captured in a product's price.

At the most basic level, the tension between business and the environment exists because business often involves extracting natural resources and polluting, whereas environmental protection often involves efforts to preserve or conserve those resources and avoid or remediate that pollution. Disagreements abound concerning the appropriate role for business vis-à-vis just about everything that falls under the umbrella of social responsibility, including environmental responsibility that exceeds the minimum requirements established by law. The debate between advocates of "profit only" business models, which externalize all environmental costs, and advocates of environmentally socially responsible business conduct, which seeks to recognize negative externalities as costs of doing business, will not likely be resolved any time soon.

3. Uncertainty. We learn a lot from different academic disciplines. For example, science can teach us about nature. However, even though we might like to think otherwise, science cannot explain everything. When creating law to address an environmental problem, we want to do the right thing—but guarantees are in short supply when it comes to environmental science. Even when we think that we have a good understanding of certain natural functions and processes, the fact is that we simply do not know everything about our natural world that might be helpful when creating laws to protect it. Thus, we can never be entirely certain that a law (and its implementation) will have the intended or desired effects.

The **precautionary principle** is the viewpoint that decision makers should err on the side of caution when their decisions will affect the environment. "Better safe than sorry" might be a good way to state the crux of this principle. For example, if the environmental consequences of a particular course of action cannot be undone, and if we do not know all of the consequences of that particular course of action, then the decision makers should err on the side of caution rather than taking risks. Nevertheless, lack of scientific certainty about environmental protection should not be used to avoid or delay actually taking measures to protect the environment.

precautionary principle: The idea that decision makers should err on the side of caution when their decisions will affect the environment.

The precautionary principle has been incorporated into some international environmental agreements, such as the Rio Declaration on Environment and Development of 1992 (**Rio Declaration**),[4] Convention on International Trade in Endangered Species of Wild Fauna and Flora (**CITES**),[5] and the **Cartagena Protocol on Biosafety**.[6] Even prior to these treaties, the Montreal Protocol on Substances That Deplete the Ozone Layer (**Montreal Protocol**) included similar language ("precautionary measures"). The following box shows how the precautionary principle has been inserted into these agreements.

■ *Examples of the Precautionary Principle in Action*

Here are some examples of how the precautionary principle appears in international environmental agreements:

The Rio Declaration:
In order to protect the environment, the precautionary approach shall be widely applied by States according to their capabilities. Where there are threats of serious or irreversible damage, lack of full scientific certainty shall not be used as a reason for postponing cost-effective measures to prevent environmental degradation. (Principle 15)

The Cartagena Protocol on Biosafety:
Reaffirm[s] the precautionary approach contained in Principle 15 of the Rio Declaration on Environment and Development. (Preamble)

CITES:
When considering proposals to amend the Appendices, the Parties shall, in the case of uncertainty, either as regards the status of a species or as regards the impact of trade on the conservation of a species, act in the best interest of the conservation of the species. (Annex 4, paragraph A)

Rio Declaration: An international agreement on principles guiding sustainable development.

CITES: An international agreement relating to trade in endangered plants and animals.

Cartagena Protocol on Biosafety: An international agreement related to the protection of biological diversity in the face of potential risks associated with the genetic modification of organisms made possible by modern technology.

Montreal Protocol: A treaty that phases out the production of ozone-depleting substances.

Additionally, when considering uncertainty as a recurrent theme in the study of environmental law, we must keep in mind that viewing nature through the disciplinary lens of science does not allow us to see everything. As noted, science does not yet tell us everything there is to know about the environment. But even if it did, would that be enough? Consider this chapter's Case Study regarding the Kashia Pomo and the potential clear-cutting of the Pomo Valley for a vineyard. If the decision to clear-cut is environmentally "safe," because it will not drive an endangered species into extinction, for example, should that be the final word on the matter? Among the things that remain unexamined

---

[4] Rio Declaration on Environment and Development, Report of the United Nations Conference on Environment and Development, U.N. Doc. A/CONF.151/6/Rev.1 (1992), 31 I.L.M. 874.

[5] Convention on International Trade in Endangered Species and Wild Fauna and Flora, Mar. 3, 1973, 993 U.N.T.S. 243, T.I.A.S. No. 8249, 12 I.L.M. 1085.

[6] Cartagena Protocol on Biosafety to the Convention on Biological Diversity, January 29, 2000, 39 I.L.M. 1027. This is not a comprehensive list of international agreements that have incorporated the precautionary principle into their texts. Review the following article for a more thorough discussion: J. Hepburn, *The Principle of the Precautionary Approach to Human Health, Natural Resources and Ecosystems*, retrieved from http://www.worldfuturecouncil.org/fileadmin/user_upload/papers/CISDL_P3_PrecautionaryPrinciple.pdf (last visited October 16, 2013).

when viewing such matters through a purely scientific lens are the values of persons who might rely upon that forest for spiritual reasons. In addition, even if a species is not endangered thereby, certainly other inhabitants of the forest—plants and animals—will lose their homes and their lives as a result of a decision to proceed with the clear-cut and the planting of a vineyard.

▪ **Historical Viewpoint:** *Scientific Uncertainty and the Case of the Snail Darter*

The snail darter is a small fish that was listed as endangered under the Endangered Species Act (ESA) in the early years of that statute. When this fish was discovered in the Little Tennessee River, the Tellico Dam project was halted, even though it was already substantially underway. Indeed, more than $100 million of taxpayer money had been expended when the case of the snail darter was brought forward. However, completion of the dam would have so disrupted the habitat of the snail darter that the fish would not have been able to survive if the project had been completed. In *Tennessee Valley Authority v. Hill*, 437 U.S. 153 (1978), the U.S. Supreme Court confirmed that the ESA did not permit any exceptions to the protection afforded to species listed as endangered.

Nevertheless, the Tellico Dam was eventually completed, utterly destroying the snail darter's habitat in the Little Tennessee River. Before its completion, some snail darters were moved to alternative suitable habitats. The snail darter story has a somewhat happy ending,

because these fish were subsequently discovered in other rivers (at the time the Tellico Dam was being built, though, its presence was not known in those other locations). Today, the snail darter is listed as threatened rather than endangered.

Questions for reflection:

1. Should the precautionary principle be incorporated into U.S. laws that exist to protect plants, animals, or the environment? What would the consequences have been in the Tellico Dam case if the precautionary principle had been the guiding principle in the ESA?

2. Besides science, what other disciplinary "lens" might have been illuminating in the case of the snail darter? Is there any other way to view this controversy besides the money that had already been spent on the dam versus the habitat preservation of the then-endangered snail darter?

4. Enforcement challenges. If a law is to be effective, it must not only exist, but it also must be capable of being monitored and enforced. Environmental law can be difficult to enforce, and violations of environmental law can be difficult to observe. Enforcement challenges include matters as mundane as lack of funding for enforcement officers, and as complex as constitutional barriers regarding the **standing** of a party who observes an environmental harm to bring a claim. (*Standing* is simply the right to bring a claim.)

Standing can be difficult to establish, particularly in environmental cases where the harm to the plaintiff may seem incidental or indirect. One way that lawmakers can overcome standing challenges is simply to include a **citizen suit provision** in the statute. A citizen suit provision is specific wording incorporated into a statute that essentially overrides or overcomes any objection on the basis of standing. In other words, a citizen suit provision typically allows anyone to bring a claim under the law containing such a provision without having to first show individual standing.

5. Intergenerational equity. **Intergenerational equity** is the idea that we have a duty to future generations to maintain the environment in a manner that will allow those future generations to enjoy, use, and benefit from it. This duty is based on the concept that the natural environment does not belong to any one generation. Instead, current generations may enjoy it and use it, providing that their enjoyment and use do not negatively affect future persons' use and enjoyment.

standing: The legal right to bring a lawsuit. The federal courts require that the citizen be able to prove injury in fact, a causal connection between the conduct that is the subject of the suit and the injury, and redressability of the injury by a court decision in the plaintiff's favor.

citizen suit provision: Statutory provision that allows any citizen to bring a legal action to enforce that statute or force a governmental entity to perform a nondiscretionary duty.

intergenerational equity: The concept that the current generation owes a duty to future generations to maintain the environment in a manner that will allow those future generations to enjoy, use, and benefit from it.

Do we have an obligation to maintain our environment for future generations? If we have such a duty, we may wish to consider from whence that duty arises. Also, if we have such a duty, what is the best way to express and implement it? Should we limit current business practices that may damage the environment for future generations, or forbid businesses whose actions may deplete natural resources so that future generations can never see or experience those natural resources? Additionally, do we have the duty to pay for cleanup of prior environmental damage and misdeeds, so that we leave the world in a better condition than we inherited it? The idea of sustainability inherently contemplates the interests of future generation. However, not everyone agrees that current actions should necessarily maintain sustainability for future generations. For example, if a business believes that serving its shareholders best means using natural resources in an unsustainable manner for a quick profit, then—in the absence of a law that bans such an activity—it will be allowed to do so.

6. Who pays? An ongoing and everpresent concern in environmental law is who should pay for environmental damages. Similarly, who should pay to protect the habitat of the animals and plants that need the habitat to survive? The **polluter pays principle** simply states that the actual polluter should bear the cost of pollution reduction or remediation of the damage. The concept underlying the polluter pays principle seems a fair idea, but what if the polluter cannot be reached? Often pollution occurred in prior generations, and the people who made the decisions that resulted in pollution are long gone. If the polluter is not available to pay—because the polluter is deceased or cannot be found, or the business is dissolved or insolvent—we have to move beyond the polluter pays principle. We must decide whether we wish to live with the pollution, simply maintaining the status quo, or if we should use our money— even though we did not generate the pollution ourselves—to collectively pay for the cleanup. Should public funds be expended for pollution cleanup, or should we rely on the private sector to undertake these projects? Likewise, if habitat must be protected to preserve or sustain an animal population, there must be a commitment from the people who are here now to agree to leave the habitat alone. See the following box for an example of a private company taking a novel approach to dramatically improving a degraded environment.

■ *ACTIVITY BOX   Rebuilding Detroit into a Farm*

Watch the video at http://www.cbsnews.com/video/watch/?id=50135788n
    Also, check out Hantz Farm's website at http://www.hantzfarmsdetroit.com/

Answer the Following Questions:

1. Based upon your knowledge of government processes, what do you think are some potential advantages to a private company, rather than a government, undertaking an environmental remediation project, such as has been proposed by Hantz Farms? What are the risks?

2. Who are the beneficiaries of the Hantz Farms projects? Should persons affected by these projects have input into the business's decisions? Why or why not?

polluter pays principle: Holds that the actual polluter should bear the cost of pollution reduction or remediation of the damage.

7. Bottom-up approach versus top-down approach. In environmental law, grassroots efforts really matter. This may be more true in environmental law than in any other area of law. Environmental law rarely comes from a "top-down"

mandate. Often, an environmental issue is first identified by concerned citizens, and that issue is pressed with the legislative body having jurisdiction over the area, or a lawsuit is brought by the people affected by the environmental issue. Whichever approach is used, grassroots efforts can matter greatly, because concerned citizens do have the power—as illustrated many times throughout our environmental legal history—to change the law.

Try to keep these recurring themes in mind as you move through the topics presented in this book. How you respond to each of these concerns, which are summarized in the box titled "Recurrent Themes in Environmental Law," might reveal your particular worldview about our relationship to the environment.

The rest of this chapter provides a brief history of the development of environmental law. It then introduces different worldviews and ethical perspectives illustrative of the human relationship to the environment, introduces important disciplinary intersections with environmental law, and discusses the potential trajectory of environmental law.

▪ *Recurrent Themes in Environmental Law*

Theme	Questions for Consideration	Examples
1. People share one world	Who has the legal authority to make decisions about transboundary resources, resources with common borders, shared resources, or unique resources?	Air pollution, highly migratory species (e.g., birds, whales), rivers that border or cross sovereign boundaries
2. Tension between business and environmental protection	Is tension between "doing business" and protecting the natural environment inevitable?	Consider the differences between high-polluting industries and individual companies committed to corporate environmental and social responsibility.
3. Uncertainty	Should we make irreversible decisions about the environment if we don't know everything about the environment? Should we make decisions that we cannot undo if we later find out that our science was wrong or incomplete? Should we delay protecting the environment just because we experience scientific uncertainty? Through what other lenses—besides that of science—can we view the environment?	How much habitat does a particular species need? If there are competing claims to land (e.g., development versus habitat preservation), and if our science informs us that a certain amount of habitat is sufficient, should we rely upon that assertion?
4. Enforcement challenges	How can barriers to the enforcement of environmental law be overcome? Barriers include lack of resources, poor understanding	What if you believed that a factory in another state was illegally dumping pollution into a river that you did not

(Continued)

Theme	Questions for Consideration	Examples
	about the importance of the natural world, inability to monitor violations of environmental law, and significant obstacles to pursuit of environmental claims by persons who might observe or know about the violations (e.g., lack of standing, lack of provable damage).	have any personal contact with? Do you think that you should be able to bring a claim against that business for violating the law?
5. Intergenerational equity	Does the current generation have a duty to future generations to maintain the environment in a manner that will allow those future generations to enjoy and use it?	If the current generation significantly contributes to the extinction of a particular species, such as the polar bear, has it violated a duty to future generations who will never be able to see a polar bear?
6. Who should pay?	Who should pay for environmental damages? Who should pay to protect the habitat of the animals and plants that need the habitat to survive?	Consider environmental harm from a business, such as the heavy metal contamination in the plume of the ASARCO plant in Ruston, Washington.
7. Bottom-up approach versus top-down approach	Grassroots efforts really matter in environmental law. If an environmental threat arose in your community, what would you do, if you discovered that no laws existed to prohibit the activity?	Mountaintop removal for coal mining in the Appalachians

▨ ▨ ▨ REVIEW AND STUDY QUESTIONS

1. Write a paragraph to describe what you believe constitutes the "human habitat." Compare your description to those of your classmates. How do they differ? Why might people have different ideas about what constitutes the human habitat?

2. Find a newspaper article that addresses environmental law. Summarize the environmental issue or dispute in the article. How is environmental law being used in this environmental dispute? Can environmental law solve the problem presented in the article? Why or why not?

3. Identify a grassroots environmental organization in your community. What are the goals of this organization? Are the goals of this organization supported by existing law? If not, could the grassroots organization's goals be incorporated into or implemented by law? In other words, what would those goals "look like" in law?

4. Identify matters that could be addressed by environmental law:

   a. In your community
   b. In your state
   c. In your region
   d. In your country

5. What is the difference between reactive and proactive approaches to environmental law?

6. Can you think of an emerging environmental issue that has not yet been contemplated or addressed by law? Should it be? Why or why not?

7. Describe the recurrent themes in environmental law as they relate to one issue of environmental importance or interest to you.

■ A Brief History of Environmental Law

Environmental law is a relatively new, though now well-established, area of law. This section discusses the history and development of environmental law. It focuses specifically on U.S. domestic federal law (law created in the United States by the U.S. government), as well as some key state laws related to environmental preservation and conservation. Additionally, this section addresses the history of some international environmental law, which is legal or law-like agreements (**soft law**) made between nation-states to regulate matters of importance to the signers of the agreement.

Of course, nations other than the United States have created environmental laws. Although this chapter does not dwell on foreign domestic law, it is addressed tangentially. The omission of a discussion of foreign domestic law should not be taken as an indication that foreign domestic environmental law is somehow unimportant. Indeed, foreign domestic environmental law, in some cases, is far more progressive than current U.S. laws. Consider the fact that 177 of the 193 UN member nations recognize the legal right to a healthy environment; 93 of those countries establish that right in their constitutions. For example, the South Korean constitution declares a "[r]ight to a healthy, pleasant environment; the state and all citizens have to make efforts to conserve the environment." Compare this to the environmental language in the U.S. constitution, which is nonexistent.

Environmental law has developed primarily from the "bottom up" rather than from the "top down." This means that people who have been affected by environmental issues—either positively or negatively—have been influential in garnering support for their causes and ultimately inserting that interest into lawmakers' or policy makers' agendas.

In the 19th century, concerns about the environment became apparent in the writings of persons such as George Perkins Marsh, John Burroughs, John Muir, and Henry David Thoreau. Marsh's *Man and Nature* (1864), for example, brought attention to the harmful impact that human beings often have on their natural environment. Marsh, a 19th-century U.S. senator from Vermont, argued that environmental degradation can lead to the collapse of civilizations. That same year, Congress passed a new type of law, which granted Yosemite Valley to California for the purpose of designating it as a public park. Though it was reacquired by the federal government in 1905, when Yosemite National Park was formed, this piece of early legislation reflected the times. Conservation and preservation were important to many people in the United States, and those working in our government and legal systems were trying to figure out the best ways to protect and conserve environmentally important lands. For example, in 1872, Congress set aside the land near the Yellowstone River headwaters to be used as a park. This, of course, became Yellowstone National Park, Wyoming, which was the first national park to be established in the United States. As the 19th century moved to a close, other natural areas became protected as well: Mount Rainier National Park, Sequoia National Park, and General Grant National Park were all established before 1900.

As another example of the influence of naturalists' writings, John Muir's work stimulated the passage of federal law that eventually established the U.S. Forest Service, which actually embraced conservation rather than Muir's preservationist

soft law: Rules that do not lack legal significance but are not necessarily binding.

ideal. This tension between the conservationist ideal and the preservationist vision continues to play out in our government's policies concerning the natural environment.

Nineteenth-century citizens organized and became actively engaged in restoration, conservation, and preservation efforts. For example, during the last quarter of that century, a group of citizens that included notable landscape architect Frederick Law Olmstead[7] focused its interest on reclaiming Niagara Falls, which had been badly damaged by industrial activities. In 1885, after 15 years of work, New York state passed laws that eventually led to the establishment of Niagara Falls State Park, which is the oldest state park in the United States. Additionally, naturalist and environmental writers of the time extolled the virtues of outside adventuring as a form of recreation. Groups such as the Appalachian Mountain Club and the Sierra Club were formed.

Lands and land use were not the only focus of lawmakers and the interested public during these early years. Federal and state governments also passed laws to conserve salmon fisheries, fur-bearing animals, wild bison (after their near extermination), wildlife, and "game" animals. For example, the Lacey Act, which was passed in 1900, made poaching animals or capturing prohibited animals and transporting them across state lines a federal offense. Its purpose was to conserve wildlife.

The 19th-century environmentalists did not work in a vacuum. They not only influenced the public with their writings, art, and opinions, but they also influenced each other. For example, Gifford Pinchot, the first chief of what would become the U.S. Forest Service, greatly admired Marsh's work. Additionally, Marsh's writings were instrumental in the move to establish public parks as a way to protect the land. Marsh's writings were published at the end of the Civil War, and the events of those times may have shaped his perception of the human impact on the natural world.

Marsh, Burroughs, Thoreau, and others were early writers who influenced the way people thought about the environment. John Muir was also instrumental in the development of a preservationist ethic, which is a different perspective than the conservationist ethic represented by Pinchot. However, while conservationists and preservationists wrote and debated the best way to interact with our natural environment, many early U.S. environmental laws concerned the protection of commerce, rather than protection of the environment for the environment's sake. (This is a theme that we still see today in environmental laws.) For example, when the many versions of the federal Rivers and Harbors Act were passed, the concern being addressed was that the rubbish and debris being dumped into rivers and harbors were causing difficulty for ships engaged in commerce to pass; this is a far cry from concern about the aesthetic value of the rivers and harbors, or of the pollution and habitat destruction caused by the dumping.

In the very early part of the 20th century, Theodore Roosevelt became the U.S. president. Conservation was an important part of his domestic policy. This commitment to conservation was apparent in the mandate of the first U.S. Forest Service, which we typically associate with Pinchot; the U.S. national parks reflected more of the preservationist ethic that we typically associate with Muir. This differing way of viewing humans' relationship to the land—conservation versus

---

[7] The Olmstead brothers (F.L. Olmstead's sons) were also landscape architects, whose insights and long-term outlook related to the importance of the natural environment can still be seen in places like Portland, Oregon's 40-mile loop.

preservation—was particularly well illustrated in the Hetch Hetchy controversy. Muir campaigned mightily to preserve the beautiful Hetch Hetchy Valley from being flooded to act as a water source for San Francisco. Despite his efforts, conservation, rather than preservation, eventually won the day. The Hetch Hetchy Valley was flooded to be used as a resource for Californians, rather than preserved in its awe-inspiring natural state.

In the middle and latter parts of the 20th century, federal and state governments adopted major legislation to address specific environmental problems or to address apparent problems that were not yet regulated. In other words, governments addressed environmental problems in both a reactionary manner and a proactive manner. Environmental laws were sometimes adopted following debate over how best to address particular environmental problems, or discussion about whether a problem should be addressed at all. Just like in the present, once environmental problems were identified, disagreements ensued over the prioritization of regulating those problems. Additionally, if a problem was identified and prioritized as one that should be addressed, questions concerning the costs and benefits of environmental protection often proved challenging. Those disagreements provided fertile ground for stalling or derailing the passage of laws, just as they do today.

Specific federal laws passed during the 20th century are addressed at length in subsequent chapters. Here we present a brief sketch that accurately characterizes the statutory nature of our modern federal and state governments' efforts to address environmental concerns. In some ways, this shift to a statutory scheme signified a move away from common law remedies, which could benefit single plaintiffs who chose to bring actions against specific defendants, toward a scheme that could benefit the general public. This is because statutory law applies broadly, sets minimum requirements and goals, and states policy. Additionally, environmental statutes created in the 20th century often included citizen suit provisions, which allow plaintiffs to bring suits against defendants who are violating the law, even if those plaintiffs would not otherwise be able to establish standing or injury.

The following box provides a snapshot of major federal statutory developments related to the environment. This is not a comprehensive list, but merely a sketch of some of the major federal environmental statutes passed during the 20th century. As you can see, these laws contemplate and address issues related to both pollution and natural resources.

■ *Major Federal Statutory Laws of the 20th Century*

1948: Federal Water Pollution Control Act
1955: National Air Pollution Control Act
1963: Clean Air Act (amended many times, including 1990)
1964: The Wilderness Act
1965: Solid Waste Disposal Act
1969: National Environmental Policy Act
1970: Wilderness Act
1972: Federal Water Pollution Control Amendments (FWPCA)

1972: Federal Insecticide, Fungicide, and Rodenticide Act (FIFRA)
1972: Marine Protection, Research, and Sanctuary Act
1972: Marine Mammal Protection Act
1972: Coastal Zone Management Act
1973: Endangered Species Act
1974: Safe Drinking Water Act
1976: Resource Conservation and Recovery Act

(Continued)

1976: Toxic Substances Control Act

1977: Clean Water Act (amended FWPCA of 1972)

1977: Surface Mining Control and Reclamation Act

1978: National Energy Conservation Policy Act

1980: Comprehensive Environmental Response, Compensation, and Liability Act

1986: Safe Drinking Water Act Amendments

1986: Emergency Planning and Community Right-to-Know Act

1986: Superfund Amendments and Reauthorization Act

1987: Water Quality Act (amended FWPCA of 1972)

1990: Clean Air Act Amendments

1990: Oil Pollution Act

1996: Food Quality Protection Act (amended FIFRA)

1996: Safe Drinking Water Act Amendments

Questions for reflection:

1. Can you identify events during these years that might have influenced the passage of these laws, based upon what you already know about history? For example, consider the fact that during the first Earth Day, in 1972, millions of people took to the streets to protest and demonstrate on behalf of the environment.

2. Could your exploration of other social, political, or economic events lead to additional insight relating to the passage of environmental laws? Think of a research topic related to (a) one major piece of federal legislation from this list and (b) social, political, cultural, or economic history.

This flurry of statute making—particularly the activity of the 1970s—was unique to its time period. We have not seen a similar volume of new statutes emerging from Congress to protect the environment before or since. However, during those years, the American public's concern about the problems associated with environmental pollution was high and highly visible. Additionally, as in the 19th century, significant writings influenced the public's perception by informing it of the environmental problems that existed, though often unrecognized as problems. For example, in the 1960s, Lake Erie, one of the Great Lakes, was dying, polluted by industry and raw sewage, with most of its beaches not suitable for swimming. *Time Magazine* described it as a "giant cesspool." Likewise, Lake Cuyahoga was described as a "constant fire hazard" because of the tremendous amount of industrial pollution deposited in it.[8] In fact, the Cuyahoga River spontaneously ignited in 1969, causing great concern and a public outcry. After all, what is more unnatural than a river catching fire? Widescale dumping of toxic chemicals in the Great Lakes had been a long-standing practice that was rarely questioned; certainly it was not questioned by industry, which largely equated pollution with progress and profit. This treatment of our natural environment reflected disregard for other life forms whose habitats were destroyed, and it also reflected little understanding of the absolute necessity of a healthy environment for our own survival.

Unlike the 19th century, during the 1960s people had access to televisions, though television was a relatively new invention. On their televisions, people were able to see—for the first time ever—the devastating effects on wildlife of these types of environmental disasters. Consider, for example, the oil spills first viewed by audiences in the 1960s via television broadcasts. An oil spill that coated the beaches near Santa Barbara, California, killed large numbers of land and ocean

[8] *America's Sewage System and the Price of Optimism*, TIME MAGAZINE, Aug. 1, 1969. Retrieved from http://www.time.com/time/magazine/article/0,9171,901182,00.html (last visited October 16, 2013).

animals, and people were able to see the devastation. The *Torrey Canyon*, an oil tanker, ran aground off of the coast of England, and 120,000 tons of oil were spilled. Because no plans had been made in anticipation of such an environmental disaster, the British prime minister decided to bomb the tanker to see if the oil could be burned off. Not only did that strategy not work, it compounded the environmental disaster exponentially. People watched their televisions in horror as newscasters showed seabirds, dead or dying, covered in oil and unable to fly. People who volunteered to help clean the seabirds described how the thick oil burned the skin of the birds so badly that it caused tremendous pain to those lovely animals. They described in graphic detail how they had to forcibly scrape the thick, heavy oil off by hand. These images burned in the minds of viewers, and they decided that something had to be done. Important questions were asked: Why wasn't there a plan for an environmental catastrophe? Should we be transporting oil in single-hulled ships through fragile ecosystems? Should we be interacting with the natural environment in such a destructive manner? Through television, people also saw their world for the first time, when the first moon landing was televised. Our world was indeed "one"—a beautiful blue globe that looked very small, fragile, and connected.

During those years, pollution was not the only thing on people's minds. The deadly effects of DDT, which was a common mosquito pesticide used in the United States in the 1940s, 1950s, and 1060s, were wreaking havoc on the environment. "Better living through chemistry" might have been the mantra of the day, but people were starting to lose faith and question the belief that the scientists had everything under control. The fact was (and is) that there are limits to our knowledge about how we interact with our natural world, and those limits were becoming increasingly difficult to ignore. In 1962, Rachel Carson's seminal book *Silent Spring* called attention to the negative effects of DDT and other pesticides that were harming our environment. Carson argued that humans were recklessly polluting the Earth with pesticides without understanding the ultimate effect of the chemicals. She expressed dismay that poisonous chemicals were used indiscriminately by those who were unaware of their potential for harm. She related the story of a friend who had witnessed birds dying terrible, spasmodic deaths from poisoning, immediately after DDT had been sprayed over a bird sanctuary. Carson also asserted that human beings were entitled to a safe environment. In part because of *Silent Spring*, in 1964 the Department of Agriculture convinced Congress to revise the existing pesticide registration system to permit the secretary of agriculture to refuse to register a new product or to cancel an existing pesticide registration. The burden of proof regarding safety and effectiveness of the pesticide was also placed on the registrant. In 1972, the existing pesticide law was rewritten, and the Federal Insecticide, Fungicide, and Rodenticide Act (FIFRA) was passed. (This law has been amended many times since its passage in 1972.) This is a direct and relatively recent example of how one person's writing influenced federal law, as we saw in the 19th-century examples.

Not only were laws changed, but public belief and opinion also began to recognize that indiscriminate use of pesticides in the environment was not a good thing. Regarding DDT, for example, wildlife biologists discovered that fish-eating birds were, essentially, being poisoned by their prey, which were loaded with DDT that had washed out to sea. Incorporation of the pesticide in the birds' eggs at Anacapa Island made the eggshells too fragile to support the successful incubation and development of chicks; this led to a dramatic decrease in the populations of certain species of predatory birds. Indeed, the scientists who visited Anacapa Island found only 2 live young out of 1,200 nesting attempts. The pesticide pollution thus proved lethal to those populations.

These and other events combined to create a climate of ecological concern that led in 1969 to the adoption of the National Environmental Policy Act (NEPA), which addressed the need for a national environmental policy. Also, in 1970, President Nixon created the Environmental Protection Agency (EPA), an independent agency charged with the mission of protecting human health and the environment. Before its creation, the federal government did not have a single administrator to address pollution problems. In 1971, the Environmental Protection Agency began the process of "delisting" DDT, effectively banning its use in the United States.

During the late 1960s and 1970s, the subfield of "environmental law" itself was born. Before this era, matters of law related to the environment were largely addressed through the common law. Suits were brought by individual plaintiffs who could establish standing against specific defendants for specific harms. While this method of dispute resolution is still viable, it may not be as effective as bringing a suit against a defendant for violating a statute. This is because many current statutes contain citizen suit provisions, set minimum acceptable standards for pollution emission, and can be used to address largescale damages to multiple plaintiffs. A person who practiced in the area of environmental law before 1970 or so would have drawn his or her arguments and causes of action primarily from tort and property law. Now, of course, environmental law is a well-established discipline. There is less outright borrowing from other areas of law, and more statutory laws that directly address matters of environmental concern.

Although the mid-20th century saw the enactment of a great number of statutes addressing environmental problems and concerns, not all goals that were set during that era were achieved. Additionally, lawmakers did not have perfect foresight concerning problems that should be addressed. Nevertheless, these statutes, and the growing public environmental consciousness that drove their creation, constituted significant progress toward environmental health. For example, in 1970, Congress enacted the Clean Air Amendments, now known as the Clean Air Act (CAA). The CAA created requirements for both stationary and mobile sources of pollution. At the time of its passage, it did not contemplate problems like ozone layer depletion or acid rain, but those and other issues were addressed in subsequent amendments. Consider also the example of the Clean Water Act (CWA). In 1972, Congress substantially amended the Federal Water Pollution Control Act to create the CWA, with the goal that all waters in the United States would be safe for swimming by 1983. This goal was not met, but the Clean Water Act certainly made substantial strides in regulating the waters of the United States. These and other examples of important federal legislation created during these heady "environmental years," together with goals aimed for but not yet achieved, are discussed in subsequent chapters.

In 1980, Congress responded to another environmental crisis—this time in Love Canal, New York—with the passage of the Comprehensive Environmental Response, Compensation, and Liability Act of 1980 (CERCLA). Also known as "Superfund," this law was created to govern remediation of brownfields and hazardous waste sites. Though the Superfund has been successful in remediating many sites nationwide, some argue that it has been hampered by funding challenges. Since 1995, the Superfund has not been funded; previously, it had been supported by taxes on the petroleum and chemical industries. Superfund site remediation is supposed to be done according to the polluter pays principle—but when the polluters cannot be found or are insolvent, then the Superfund itself must pay for the cleanup. Because the Superfund is no longer being funded, Congress must appropriate cleanup funds on a case-by-case basis.

Another major environmental disaster occurred in 1987, when the *Exxon Valdez* caused a massive oil spill in the formerly pristine Prince William Sound, Alaska. This disaster crippled the local economy and devastated the wildlife and ecosystem of the Sound. In response, CERCLA was amended in 1990 to add the Oil Pollution Act of 1990. This and other amendments addressed problems in the original act as well as new issues. Passage of major federal environmental statutes during the last half of the 20th century reflected public commitment to environmental protection and a desire to remediate an environment that had been harmed by industry during the early years of our country. Additionally, laws like the Endangered Species Act, Marine Mammal Protection Act, and Wild and Scenic Rivers Act were adopted or strengthened in order to protect public lands, wildlife, and wilderness areas. Laws protecting coastal zones and the oceans from pollution were also passed.

Today, environmental concerns often focus on global issues. Problems such as global warming, sustainable resource use, and transboundary environmental issues—such as pollution control and protection for highly migratory species—are major concerns. Though federal and state governments can only create laws that govern conduct within their respective jurisdictions, the fact remains that people are increasingly viewing the world as a single global environment, rather than a local area delimited by political boundaries. This has led to a number of international efforts for natural resource protection and use, as well as pollution control, mitigation, and remediation.

The remainder of this chapter discusses some of the questions that policy makers, environmentalists, business and industry leaders, and ultimately the average citizen must consider when contemplating present and future environmental challenges. As you consider the issues discussed here, bear in mind that there are no easy answers and many different responses to environmental policy concerns.

▪ ▪ ▪ REVIEW AND STUDY QUESTIONS

1. What is the difference between U.S. domestic federal law, state law, international law, and foreign domestic law? Identify environmental issues that would be an appropriate focus for each type of law.

2. Describe how writers can influence the development of environmental law. Can you identify a writer today who might influence the development of future environmental law?

3. Sketch and label a timeline of the most important developments in environmental law during the past two centuries in the United States.

4. Identify and describe an example of a bottom-up approach to the creation of specific environmental laws. Can you identify any grassroots movements today that may lead to the development of new environmental law?

5. What types of things do environmental laws attempt to accomplish? Why are the goals of environmental laws often different from one law to the next?

6. The Environmental Protection Agency's mission is to protect human health and the environment. How does this mission limit what the EPA might do? How does it create opportunities for this federal agency to proactively address environmental issues?

7. Identify an environmental issue that may not be adequately addressed through U.S. domestic federal law. How could this issue be addressed in law?

8. Can we interpret the flurry of statute making in the mid-20th century as reflecting confidence in government to solve or correct problems in the environment? Do we have the same confidence in our government today?

9. Draw a timeline of major influences on environmental law and consequences to environmental law from the 19th century to the modern era.

▪ Ethical Perspectives and Worldviews Concerning the Natural Environment

Law is a vehicle through which ideas about how human beings can or should relate to the environment can be implemented. How humans define and value the natural environment is therefore important to the creation of law, because definitions and valuations guide goals and policies. However, there are distinct disagreements about how to define the environment, and about whether the environment or its attributes can be valued in a manner that makes sense. Such disagreements arise from people's differing ethical and ecological perspectives and beliefs about the human relationship to the environment. Human beings, as a part of the natural world, depend on the planet for survival. However, sometimes people think of the environment as a separate "place" other than where humans live. Students sometimes comment that they have "no experience" with the environment. But, of course, you do! You live in the environment. A belief that human beings are somehow separate from the natural environment can be fostered by physical separation from the natural world, or cultural, societal, philosophical, or religious beliefs that human beings were placed in the world to dominate it. In such ways of thinking, the environment and all nonhuman inhabitants of the environment are "there" to be "used." Regardless of whether a person believes that he or she is part of the environment or a ruler over the environment, a safe and healthy environment is valuable to humans. Fouling the earth and polluting the air and water is like sitting on the limb of a tree while sawing it off at the trunk.

In the United States and western European culture, land has traditionally been viewed as a property interest, the utility of which can and should be maximized. Indeed, the legal recognition and protection of property rights serve an important economic function by creating incentives to use resources efficiently. The assumption in such a system is that an individual owner of land will endeavor to maximize the value of the land.

The notion that land and natural resource use should be maximized through private ownership most certainly spurred the territorial expansion and economic growth of the United States throughout the 19th and early 20th centuries. While there are many property rights advocates who continue to argue for this position, there are others who believe that profit maximization through use of private resources will ultimately result in catastrophic and possibly irreversible environmental degradation.

Worldviews

The U.S. legal system reflects primarily a rights-based worldview. The law protects civil rights and rights to property, for example. How does this orientation translate into environmental law? Our laws recognize that people generally have the right to do with their property whatever they wish to do with it. So, if someone owns a forest, that person has the right to cut down the trees, or keep and use the forest as he or she wishes, and forbid or permit others to access the area, unless some law restricts or compels particular behavior related to the forest. Not surprisingly, many people are very reluctant to allow laws that might restrict their abilities to do what they wish on and with their own property. This is a **rights-based worldview**.

rights-based worldview: Belief that one's individual rights to do as one wishes are of primary importance compared to any duties that one might have to the community.

Now let's compare the rights-based worldview with a **duty-based worldview**. Instead of a worldview in which people have the right to do with their land what they wish regardless of the consequences to other creatures or persons, and do not have affirmative duties to the community where that land exists, a duty-based perspective focuses primarily on what a person *should* do for the community or wider state.[9] Such a perspective recognizes the interconnectivity between human beings and the environment, as well as the interconnectivity between generations. For example, a duty-based approach in law might impose public service requirements on each member of society, according to which they would maintain common areas and use their land to meet common needs.

Ethical Perspectives

Many different ethical perspectives exist regarding the human relationship to the environment. Once we recognize those different perspectives, we can more easily understand how reasonable people can completely disagree about human interactions with the environment. In other words, different ethical perspectives can lead to very different opinions and conclusions about the same issue.

A helpful way to think about these different viewpoints is to arrange them on a continuum; The box titled "Continuum of Ethical Perspectives About the Environment" shows just such a continuum. On one end is the belief that we should create laws relating to the natural environment to ensure that the environment

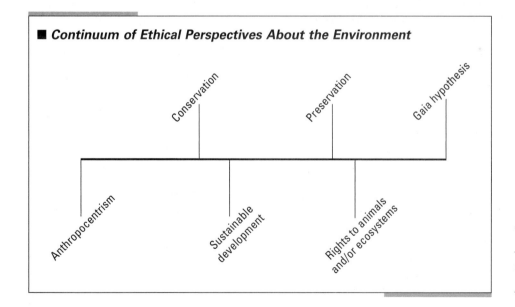

■ *Continuum of Ethical Perspectives About the Environment*

duty-based worldview: Belief that one's duties to the community are of primary importance compared to individual rights to do as one wishes.

---

[9] See C. G. Weeramantry, *Sustainable Development: An Ancient Concept Recently Revived* (presentation at the Global Judge's Symposium on Sustainable Development and the Role of Law, Johannesburg, South Africa, Aug. 18, 2002), in UNIVERSALISING INTERNATIONAL LAW 431 (2002).

serves our own self-interests above all else. This is an **anthropocentric view** of the environment. In its purest sense, the primary motivation for creating laws about the environment from the anthropocentric viewpoint is to ensure that human beings have the things they need and want. This viewpoint sees the environment primarily as something for humans to use, without any particular regard for sustaining natural resources for reasons unrelated to human interests. For example, a purely anthropocentric viewpoint could support a corporation's desire to clear-cut a forest for financial profit, because that viewpoint supports the idea that the trees are there primarily for human beings to use—in this example, for economic profit. At this most basic level, there is no recognition that other creatures have any right to their habitat and so humans have a duty to preserve it. In this worldview, the belief that habitat should be maintained is rooted in the understanding that the habitat is a resource for human beings to use, and if we are to continue using it, we must preserve some part of it. For example, a fishery that was completely depleted of fish would not be available for use in subsequent years. Therefore, the belief that the fishery should be sustained might be congruent with a purely anthropocentric viewpoint, even though no real consideration is given to needs or "rights" of the fish or other creatures that live in the fishery.

At the opposite end of the viewpoint continuum is the **Gaia hypothesis**, which holds that the planet Earth is a living, self-regulating organism. Taking that viewpoint, we might recognize that although human-made laws can help the Earth maintain its health, ultimately the Earth is not dependent upon human laws to survive. Instead, humans are simply a part of a system that is co-dependent with the Earth and all other species that live upon the Earth. The Earth will self-regulate to bring itself back to health when it has been damaged by overuse, pollution, or overpopulation. Note that the Gaia hypothesis does not necessarily impute a consciousness to this self-regulation in a metaphysical sense.

In between the purely anthropocentric and Gaia hypotheses are several viewpoints that probably are already familiar to you. For example, conservation was discussed earlier in the context of Gifford Pinchot's U.S. Forest Service policy.

Conservation is based on the belief that resources are there for human beings to use, but that we should use them wisely so they continue to be available to us to use in the future. Conservation strategies are often implemented in plans for sustainability. For example, if a tree is cut down, a new one must be planted. Laws related to fisheries, forests, wildlife, and drinking water are often conservationist or include conservation elements.

Sustainable development is very closely related to conservation. **Sustainable development** was defined in a United Nations report, published as *Our Common Future*, as "development that meets the needs of the present without compromising the ability of future generations to meet their own needs."[10] Laws related to sustainable development recognize that human development will occur, and hold that such development should be permitted provided it does not impinge on the ability of future generations to provide for themselves. For example, a growth management policy that permitted all trees in the state of New York to be cut down would not be sustainable, because that act would compromise the ability of future New York state residents to meet their needs.

anthropocentric view: Belief that human beings are the most important species on Earth.

Gaia hypothesis: Belief or theory that the Earth is a living, self-regulating organism.

conservation: Stance stressing wise use of natural resources so that they continue to be available for use in the future.

sustainable development: "Development that meets the needs of the present without compromising the ability of future generations to meet their own needs."

---

[10] United Nations General Assembly Resolution 42/187, *Report of the World Commission on Environment and Development*, Dec. 11, 1987. Retrieved from http://www.un.org/documents /ga/res/42/ares42-187.htm (last visited October 16, 2013).

A **preservation** viewpoint holds that the land and its resources should be protected, either in pristine state or managed to ensure a healthy but nondeveloped natural area. The land and animals are valuable for their own sake. Land need not be placed in productive use to be valuable. The Wilderness Act generally reflects a preservationist policy goal, because it seeks to maintain designated wilderness land with minimal human impact, including no roads.

An **animal rights** or an **ecosystem rights perspective** recognizes that animals or ecosystems have rights inherent to their own existence. An animal rights perspective holds that animals have the right to live without interference to them or to their habitats by human beings. An ecosystem rights perspective also holds that an ecosystem has a right to exist. For example, an animal rights perspective would recognize that an individual animal has both a right to life and a right to live without interference from human beings, whereas an ecosystem rights perspective would place the rights of the ecosystem above individual animals' rights. So, if an invasive species of animal caused harm to an ecosystem, then the interests of the ecosystem itself would take precedence over an individual animal's interests. In other words, an ecosystem rights perspective would support the removal of the invasive species (even though members of those species are individual animals or plants) so as to preserve the health of the overall ecosystem.

■ Applied Problem

Apply the different ethical perspectives and worldviews to the policy issue of human population. In recent decades, public environmental concerns have mounted as populations increase and humans' ability to modify and degrade the natural environment becomes more obvious. The fact is that the Earth's human population is growing rapidly, and even conservative estimates suggest that the carrying capacity of the planet may be exceeded in relatively shorter order, given our current trajectory. In 1800, the world population was about 957 million people. By 2050, the world population is expected to be more than 9 billion people. Many are concerned that the problems of population explosion are not getting the attention they deserve. Population and human consumption are the most significant causes of environmental degradation, but governments tend to focus on pollution problems as more easily addressed than those of population.

Questions for reflection:

1. Which worldview would support a population control policy, a rights-based view or a duty-based view? Why?
2. Which ethical perspective would support a population control policy? Why? Which ethical perspective would not support a population control policy? Why not?

Who Should Speak for the Environment?

Protection of the environment is an important goal, but who should represent the environment in the debate over competing values? In which forum should that debate be conducted? Obviously, a river cannot speak for itself—but does that mean that it does not have an interest in remaining free, flowing, and clean? Additionally, when competing values related to the environment are at issue, which environmental goals and perspectives should be represented? Are decisions about the environment most appropriately made by individual landowners who may wish to do different things on their individual parcels of land? Or should an overarching decision-making body look at the land and its resources as a whole, and make

preservation: Stance that the environment should be protected rather than used.

animal rights perspective: The belief that animals have the right to live without interference by humans.

ecosystem rights perspective: The belief that the ecosystem itself has the right to exist; does not necessarily hold that individual members of the ecosystem have rights.

planning decisions that are best for the greater good? Answers to these questions clearly affect our final decisions about what we should protect, and also feed the debates about the appropriate balance of competing interests in policy making.

Christopher D. Stone famously proposed that natural objects such as trees, mountains, rivers, and lakes should, like corporations, have certain legal rights.[11] That position was embraced by Justice Douglas in his dissent in *Sierra Club v. Morton*. Read Justice Douglas's dissent after reading Justice Stewart's opinion related to standing. Recall from earlier in this chapter that *standing* is the legal right to bring a lawsuit. If a person or legal entity like the Sierra Club has standing, it may obtain judicial review of federal agency action. As you read this case, consider the political and environmental implications of the dispute over whether the Sierra Club had standing to bring and maintain the lawsuit in the case. Also, this is a good opportunity to see the standing doctrine in action—as least as it was understood in 1972 when this case was decided.

Study Help: How to Read a Legal Case

We read cases to learn how the judges who decided the case came to their conclusions, and to learn about rules of law and specific holdings. Legal reasoning is often demonstrated in well-written opinions. From those writings, we can discern how judges apply the law. We can often learn the facts of the case from these opinions, too. The facts of the case often appear near the beginning. In Chapter 2, we will look closely at the different parts of a judicial opinion. For now, notice that the majority opinion appears first. If a dissent was written, it will follow the majority opinion. In the case excerpted here, Justice

Douglas's dissent appears after Justice Stewart's delivery of the majority opinion.

Although entire opinions do not appear in this book, they can easily be found online, or in Westlaw or Lexis Legal databases. Text contained within brackets has been added by the textbook authors to summarize parts of the court's opinion. Three centered asterisks (* * *) indicate that a comparatively large amount of text has been omitted from the excerpt. The cases are annotated to draw attention to the important language of the opinion for the purposes of learning to study law.

Sierra Club v. Morton

405 U.S. 727 (1972)

STEWART, Justice

The Mineral King Valley is an area of great natural beauty nestled in the Sierra Nevada Mountains in Tulare County, California, adjacent to Sequoia National Park. It has been part of the Sequoia National Forest since 1926, and is designated as a National Game Refuge by special Act of Congress. Though once the site of extensive mining activity, Mineral King is now used almost exclusively for recreational purposes. Its relative inaccessibility and lack of development have limited the number of visitors each year, and at the same time have preserved the valley's quality as a quasi-wilderness area largely uncluttered by the products of civilization.

The United States Forest Service, which is entrusted with the maintenance and administration of national forests, began in the late 1940s to give consideration to Mineral King as a potential site for recreational development. Prodded by a rapidly increasing demand for skiing facilities, the Forest Service published a prospectus in 1965, inviting bids from private developers for the construction and operation of a ski resort that would also serve as a summer recreational

(Continued)

---

[11] C. Stone. *Do Trees Have Standing?* 450 S. CAL. L. REV. 45 (1972).

area. The proposal of Walt Disney Enterprises, Inc. was chosen from those of six bidders, and Disney received a three-year permit to conduct surveys and explorations in the valley in connection with its preparation of a complete master plan for the resort.

The final Disney plan, approved by the Forest Service in January, 1969, outlines a $35 million complex of motels, restaurants, swimming pools, parking lots, and other structures designed to accommodate 14,000 visitors daily. This complex is to be constructed on 80 acres of the valley floor under a 30-year use permit from the Forest Service. Other facilities, including ski lifts, ski trails, a cog-assisted railway, and utility installations, are to be constructed on the mountain slopes and in other parts of the valley under a revocable special use permit. To provide access to the resort, the State of California proposes to construct a highway 20 miles in length. A section of this road would traverse Sequoia National Park, as would a proposed high-voltage power line needed to provide electricity for the resort. Both the highway and the power line require the approval of the Department of the Interior, which is entrusted with the preservation and maintenance of the national parks.

Representatives of the Sierra Club, who favor maintaining Mineral King largely in its present state, followed the progress of recreational planning for the valley with close attention and increasing dismay. … In June 1969 the Club filed the present suit in the United States District Court for the Northern District of California, seeking a declaratory judgment that various aspects of the proposed development contravene federal laws and regulations governing the preservation of national parks, forests, and game refuges, and also seeking preliminary and permanent injunctions restraining the federal officials involved from granting their approval or issuing permits in connection with the Mineral King project.

[The district court had granted the preliminary injunction, rejecting the government's challenge to Sierra Club's standing to sue. The Sierra Club relied on section 10 of the Administrative Procedure Act (APA), which provides: "A person suffering legal wrong because of agency action, or adversely affected or aggrieved by agency action within the meaning of a relevant statute, is entitled to judicial review thereof." In earlier cases, the Court had held that persons had standing to obtain judicial review of federal agency action under this section when they alleged that the challenged action had caused them "injury in fact," and the alleged injury was an interest "arguably within the zone of interests to be protected or regulated" by the statutes the agencies were claimed to have violated.

The Court of Appeals for the Ninth Circuit reversed the trial court's decision, and the Supreme Court granted Sierra Club's petition for writ of certiorari in the case.]

* * *

The injury alleged by the Sierra Club will be incurred entirely by reason of the change in the uses to which Mineral King will be put, and the attendant change in the aesthetics and ecology of the area. Thus, in referring to the road to be built through Sequoia National Park, the complaint alleged that the development "would destroy or otherwise affect the scenery, natural and historic objects and wildlife of the park and would impair the enjoyment of the park for future generations." We do not question that this type of harm may amount to an "injury in fact" sufficient to lay the basis for standing under section 10 of the APA. Aesthetic and environmental well-being, like economic well-being, are important ingredients of the quality of life in our society, and the fact that particular environmental interests are shared by the many rather than the few does not make them less deserving of legal protection through the judicial process. But the "injury in fact" test requires more than an injury to a cognizable interest. It requires that the party seeking review be himself among the injured.

The impact of the proposed changes in the environment of Mineral King will not fall indiscriminately upon every citizen. The alleged injury will be felt directly only by those who use Mineral King and Sequoia National Park, and for whom the aesthetic and recreational values of the area will be lessened by the highway and ski resort. The Sierra Club failed to allege that it or its members would be affected in any of their activities or pastimes by the Disney development. Nowhere in the pleading or affidavits did the Club state that its members use Mineral King for any purpose, much less that they use it in any way that would be significantly affected by the proposed actions of the respondents.

* * *

The requirement that a party seeking review must allege facts showing that he is himself adversely affected does not insulate executive action from judicial review, nor does it prevent any public interests from being protected through the judicial process. It does serve as at least a rough attempt to put the decision as to whether review will be sought in the hands of those who have a direct stake in the outcome. That goal would be undermined were we to construe the APA to authorize judicial review at the behest of organizations or individuals who seek to do no more than vindicate their own value preferences through the judicial process. The principle

(Continued)

that the Sierra Club would have us establish in this case would do just that. ...

... The judgment is

Affirmed.

DOUGLAS, Justice, dissenting.

I share the view of my Brother BLACKMUN and would reverse the judgment below.

The critical question of "standing" would be simplified and also put neatly in focus if we fashioned a federal rule that allowed environmental issues to be litigated before federal agencies or federal courts in the name of the inanimate object about to be despoiled, defaced, or invaded by roads and bulldozers and where injury is the subject of public outrage. Contemporary public concern for protecting nature's ecological equilibrium should lead to the conferral of standing upon environmental objects to sue for their own preservation. ... This suit would therefore be more properly labeled as *Mineral King v. Morton.*

Inanimate objects are sometimes parties in litigation. A ship has a legal personality, a fiction found useful for maritime purposes. The corporation sole—a creature of ecclesiastical law—is an acceptable adversary and large fortunes ride on its cases. The ordinary corporation is a "person" for purposes of the adjudicatory processes, whether it represents proprietary, spiritual, aesthetic, or charitable causes.

So it should be as respects valleys, alpine meadows, rivers, lakes, estuaries, beaches, ridges, groves of trees, swampland, or even air that feels the destructive pressures of modern technology and modern life. The river, for example, is the living symbol of all the life it sustains or nourishes—fish, aquatic insects, water ouzels, otter, fisher, deer, elk, bear, and all other animals, including man, who are dependent on it or who enjoy it for its sight, its sound, or its life. The river as plaintiff speaks for the ecological unit of life that is part of it. Those people who have a meaningful relation to that body of water—whether it be a fisherman, a canoeist, a zoologist, or a logger—must be able to speak for the values which the river represents and which are threatened with destruction.

I do not know Mineral King. I have never seen it nor traveled it, though I have seen articles describing its proposed "development" ... .

Mineral King is doubtless like other wonders of the Sierra Nevada such as Tuolumne Meadows and the John Muir Trail. Those who hike it, fish it, hunt it, camp in it, or frequent it, or visit it merely to sit in solitude and wonderment are legitimate spokesmen for it, whether they may be a few or many. Those who have that intimate relation with the inanimate object about to be injured, polluted, or otherwise despoiled are its legitimate spokesmen.

... [T]he problem is to make certain that the inanimate objects, which are the very core of America's beauty, have spokesmen before they are destroyed. It is, of course, true that most of them are under the control of a federal or state agency. The standards given those agencies are usually expressed in terms of the "public interest." Yet "public interest" has so many differing shades of meaning as to be quite meaningless on the environmental front. ...

[T]he pressures on agencies for favorable action one way or the other are enormous. The suggestion that Congress can stop action which is undesirable is true in theory; yet even Congress is too remote to give meaningful direction and its machinery is too ponderous to use very often. The federal agencies of which I speak are not venal or corrupt. But they are notoriously under the control of powerful interests who manipulate them through advisory committees, or friendly working relations, or who have that natural affinity with the agency which in time develops between the regulator and the regulated....

The Forest Service—one of the federal agencies behind the scheme to despoil Mineral King—has been notorious for its alignment with lumber companies, although its mandate from Congress directs it to consider the various aspects of multiple use in its supervision of the national forests.

The voice of the inanimate object, therefore, should not be stilled. That does not mean that the judiciary takes over the managerial functions from the federal agency. It merely means that before these priceless bits of Americana (such as a valley, an alpine meadow, a river, or a lake) are forever lost or are so transformed as to be reduced to the eventual rubble of our urban environment, the void of the existing beneficiaries of these environmental wonders should be heard.

Perhaps they will not win. Perhaps the bulldozers of "progress" will plow under all the aesthetic wonders of this beautiful land. That is not the present question. The sole question is, who has standing to be heard?

Those who hike the Appalachian Trail into Sunfish Pond, New Jersey, and camp or sleep there, or run the Allagash in Maine, or climb the Guadalupes in West Texas, or who canoe and portage the Quetico Superior in Minnesota, certainly should have standing to defend those natural wonders before courts or agencies, though they live 3,000 miles away. Those who merely are caught up in environmental news or propaganda and flock to defend those waters or areas may be treated differently. That is why these environmental issues should be tendered by the inanimate object itself. Then

(Continued)

there will be assurances that all of the forms of life which it represents will stand before the court—the pileated woodpecker as well as the coyote and bear, the lemmings as well as the trout in the streams. Those inarticulate members of the ecological group cannot speak. But those people who have so frequented the place as to know its values and wonders will be able to speak for the entire ecological community.

Ecology reflects the land ethic; and Aldo Leopold wrote in *A Sand County Almanac* (1949), "The land ethic simply enlarges the boundaries of the community to include soils, waters, plants, and animals, or collectively, the land."

That, as I see it, is the issue of "standing" in the present case and controversy.

▪ ▪ ▪ REVIEW AND STUDY QUESTIONS

1. Legal standing requires that in a suit by a citizen against a government officer, the citizen must show that the government's action invades or will invade a private legally protected interest. The issue of standing in *Sierra Club v. Morton* raised the important policy question of whether environmental groups should be permitted to use the courts to challenge proposed developments.

   In earlier cases, the court had (1) defined standing under the Administrative Procedure Act as "injury in fact," and (2) required that the injury be an interest "arguably within the zone of interests to be protected or regulated" by the statute the agencies were claimed to have violated.

   This case was important because it essentially adopted a broad definition of standing. Despite the fact that the majority ruled against the Sierra Club, it was not difficult for the club to establish standing under the holding in this case by alleging that it or its members would be affected in any of their activities by the proposed development. In other standing cases, which are discussed in subsequent chapters, the Supreme Court narrowed the test of standing, making it more difficult for environmental groups to meet this legal requirement.

   What are the practical effects of granting or limiting standing in such cases?

2. Justice Douglas, in his dissent in *Sierra Club v. Morton*, noted that one of the political issues in this case was "who should decide—the agency or the courts?" The Forest Service, which is entrusted with the maintenance and administration of national forests, had approved the Disney plan, and the state of California had proposed construction of a highway to facilitate its development.

   Why, then, should private environmental groups be permitted to challenge the decision of a government agency and elected officials? What is Justice Douglas's response to this question?

3. What would be the practical results of giving inanimate objects standing so that an object (for example, a tree or a mountain) could sue through a representative, a person, or an environmental group? What are the practical reasons for giving a corporation legal standing? Do you think similar reasons should apply to inanimate objects in environmental disputes?

4. Many people have urged that animals, such as the dolphin, should be given legal standing. One advantage of doing so is that damages for pain and suffering of the animal might be awarded in some cases. What ethical and social policy issues could be addressed by granting nonhuman animals standing in order for their injuries to be compensable?

▪ Economics and Regulation

Valuing the Natural Environment

Today, most people agree that protecting and preserving the environment are important policy goals. The more difficult policy issues often center on valuation of the natural environment, particularly when no market for the environmental attribute already exists. Valuation is often a necessary step when using economics-based policy analysis tools. Indeed, rational-choice economics has provided many methodological tools applicable to policy analysis. Among the most important are cost-benefit analysis (CBA), along with various methods of valuation, and statistical analysis. The U.S. federal government views CBA as a "primary tool" for regulatory analysis affecting public policy choices.[12] In simple terms, CBA is "add[ing] up all the gains from [a] policy alternative, subtract[ing] all the losses, and choos[ing] the alternative that maximizes net benefits."[13] It is used to show that costs of a policy can be justified by the benefits therefrom and to discover the alternative representing the most cost-effective choice. It recognizes that economic efficiency may not be the most important concern for every public policy objective, and that CBA cannot capture all benefits and costs.

The primary concept of CBA is the idea of opportunity costs, measured by willingness-to-pay (WTP) or willingness-to-accept (WTA). WTP "measures what individuals are willing to forgo to enjoy a particular benefit"; when used, it implies that individual preferences are the guiding factor in the analysis. Similarly, WTA compensation measures the opportunity cost of "not receiving the improvement."[14]

Methods used to determine values include revealed preference methods (e.g., actual market decisions made by market participants), direct and indirect uses of market data, stated preference methods (e.g., surveys concerning WTP), and benefit-transfer methods.[15] These are all different but not mutually exclusive methodological approaches to CBA. This chapter does not examine the steps involved in each.

Advocates of CBA argue that it is not a substitute for common sense.[16] Instead, it is a

> [f]ramework for organizing thoughts, or considerations: nothing more and nothing less. For any real world choice, there will always be some considerations that cannot be easily enumerated or valued, and where the analysis becomes quite conjectural. Benefit-cost analysis does not, and should not, try to hide this uncertainty. The sensible way to deal with uncertainty about some aspects of a benefit or a cost is to quantify what can be quantified, to array and rank nonquantifiable factors, and to proceed as far as possible.[17]

Unquantifiable elements, such as ecological or aesthetic concerns, are also presented in CBAs undertaken by the federal government, subject to ranking by the individual government analyst's professional judgment concerning the importance of these unquantifiable issues.[18]

CBA has not been used in questions concerning wildlife conservation to the extent it has been used in pollution control policy. Indeed, the shortcomings of

---

[12] Office of Management and Budget, *Circular A-4*, at 2 (Sept. 17, 2003). Retrieved from http://www.whitehouse.gov/sites/default/files/omb/assets/omb/circulars/a004/a-4.pdf (last visited October 16, 2013).
[13] E. M. Gramlich, A GUIDE TO BENEFIT-COST ANALYSIS 8 (Englewood Cliffs, NJ: Prentice-Hall, 1990).
[14] *Circular A-4, supra* note 13, at 18–19.
[15] *See id.* at 26–27.
[16] *See* Gramlich, *supra* note 14, at 5.
[17] *Id.*
[18] *See Circular A-4, supra* note 13, at 27.

CBA as applied to wildlife protection are many. The reasons that motivate wildlife protection are rendered meaningless in CBA. One study concluded that reducing the wildlife to economic value and monetary terms essentially "denigrate[s] the aesthetic, spiritual, and moral impulses that drive people to report large monetary values [non-use values] for animals."[19] Regarding non-use values, CBA loses information rather than generating information.[20] This is because CBAs focus primarily on use or consumption values, which are relatively easy to ascertain because they are based upon existing market values of animals or parts of animals. Non-use values can be obtained through contingent valuation. However, contingent valuations often indicate that non-use values are higher than use valuations for charismatic species like eagles, humpback whales, and gray wolves.[21] Irreversible loss, such as an extinction event, and its associated impact on humans, such as anxiety, are not reflected well in CBA or other economic analysis.[22] Economic analysis "misses the moral dimension of the reasons underlying why species are protected in the first place," because moral dimensions are often reflected not in consumption or use, but in the ways that humans do *not* use certain things.[23]

Indeed, conflicting ideologies exist concerning whether economic policy tools, such as CBA, should be relied upon at all by policy makers when evaluating the appropriate level or type of environmental protection. Some people believe that reliance upon such analyses by lawmakers or policy makers makes sound sense; others argue that reliance upon such tools seriously misses the point of the value of environment, which is often difficult or impossible to quantify in a manner with which everyone would agree. Valuation is suspect because many believe that the environment should exist for the sake of existing, and this "value" cannot be captured or even recognized by any rational economics tool that deals exclusively with objects that are quantifiable. Moreover, even if lawmakers or policy makers do use economic decision-making models or tools in connection with decisions about the environment, are the numeric comparisons generated by those models appropriate when prioritizing environmental concerns?

Consider, for example, what would most likely happen if a human baby fell down a well. People would spend virtually any amount of money to save that one child from a horrific demise. However, if we applied a CBA to the question of whether that one child should be saved or not, we might learn that the costs of saving the child outweigh the benefits of doing so. Of course, such an outcome would be repugnant to most people, because we feel that a child has intrinsic value that cannot be reduced to simple dollars and cents.

The same concern holds true for the environment. For example, if we knew that we must stop global warming to prevent the certain extinction of the wild polar bear population, we might wish to do so, regardless of the cost. However, a CBA to evaluate the undertaking of saving the polar bears might show that the

---

[19] Lisa Heinzerling, *Why Care about the Polar Bear? Economic Analysis of Natural Resources Law and Policy* (Georgetown Law and Economics Research Paper No. 1026288), at 3. Retrieved from http://papers.ssrn.com/sol3/papers.cfm?abstract_id=1026288 (last visited October 16, 2013).
[20] *Id.* at 4.
[21] *Id.* at 11.
[22] *Id.* at 24.
[23] *Id.*

polar bears should not be saved, because the costs will outweigh the apparent benefit. Such an analysis cannot adequately account for the intrinsic value of the polar bear; it can only reduce the value of the polar bear to human beings' conception of quantifiable value.

Although this debate continues, opposition to the use of CBA as a policy tool in deciding matters of environmental law has been mounting.[24] But, as noted earlier, CBA is the primary policy tool used by the U.S. federal government. In addition, when a CBA indicates that the costs of environmental protection outweigh the benefits, politicians and other policy makers who are not in favor of the particular environmental undertaking in question often find it a powerful tool to support their position. People who hear that "the costs outweigh the benefits" often do not realize that values relating to nonquantifiable issues, such as intrinsic value, or the value that the animal or natural object places upon its own life or existence, are not—and cannot be—included or reflected in such studies with any objective certainty. Thus, public opinion is often swayed because the public generally lacks a thorough understanding of the policy tools employed to make environmental decisions. For these reasons, to understand environmental law—that is, to participate in it, create it, and critique it—it is essential to be aware of what and how policy tools are being used in its development.

Market-Based Incentives versus Command and Control

Let us for the moment put to the side issues (like wildlife protection) that are difficult or impossible to evaluate with CBA, and turn to a consideration of pollution. The change of subject does not avoid the tough questions. One important aspect of the environment-related debate focuses on whether it is best to regulate pollution through **command and control** legislation, or to address the problem through other means such as **market-based incentives**.

Those who favor government regulation protecting the environment argue that there are external costs to the environment associated with some private actions. For example, air pollution produced by a manufacturing plant is a negative externality, or a negative social cost, associated with the manufacturing. These costs are not accounted for or recognized because those who bear the external costs (those who breathe air polluted by the plant) are not part of the transaction. In 1968, Garrett Hardin argued this point in his seminal essay, "The Tragedy of the Commons."[25] That essay's primary focus was the population challenges that we are continuing to grapple with today. However, the best-remembered point Hardin made in this article is that a grant of property rights can foster greater stewardship of a resource than it might receive if no one had property rights to it or an incentive to maintain it well. Since then, Elinor Ostrom's work has provided new insight into the management of common-pool resources. Ostrom, the recipient of a Nobel Prize in economics, used an Institutional Analysis and Development (IAD) framework to better understand the influences of collective action, trust, and cooperation in the management of the **commons** (a scarce resource available

command and control: Direct regulation that proscribes or permits (or mandates) certain behaviors.

market-based incentives: Regulations that encourage certain behavior through market action that rewards such behavior.

commons: A scarce resource available for use by all or many.

---

[24] *See, e.g.,* F. Ackerman & L. Heinzerling, *Pricing the Priceless: Cost Benefit Analysis of Environmental Protection,* 150 U. Pa. L. Rev. 1553–84 (2002).

[25] Garrett Hardin, *The Tragedy of the Commons,* 162 SCIENCE 1243–48 (Dec. 13, 1968).

for use by all or many, which belongs to no particular individual). Ostrom found that private ownership such as Hardin argued for was not always necessary, because people often manage the commons pretty well on their own. This result could be used to advocate against government control of the commons.

The decision to manage some common resources as **public goods** removes them from the arena of traditional market forces. If the market does not operate to determine the value of such goods, how does one assign value to them? Assigning value is a complex and controversial problem, as noted earlier. Nevertheless, determining the value of natural resources is important in deciding whether the benefit of a particular course of action is worth the cost of undertaking it. While it may be possible to assign an economic value to the Mineral King development project contemplated in *Sierra Club v. Morton*, for example, how should one determine the value of an unspoiled Mineral King Valley? One important legal issue that may arise under certain environmental laws is the valuation of natural resources for purposes of determining "natural resource damages." When the law mandates payment of money damages for harm to natural resources, should those damages be determined based only on the cost of restoration?

Future generations and the environment itself pay the costs of activities that pollute the environment (such as loss of plant and animal species), but they are not parties to or participants in the market that creates those costs. The externalization of these costs, and the failure by private actors to consider the environmental impact of their activities do not, however, automatically lead to the conclusion that regulation and public management are the only way to address this problem.

Some question whether the regulatory process effectively and efficiently achieves our environmental goals. Many critics argue that federal air and water pollution policy, which relies on technology-based command and control regulation, is simply too costly for the resulting benefits. They point to the economic costs of environmental regulation and challenge the idea that the current regulatory approach is the best way to expend scarce monetary resources.

Critics question the success of current regulatory programs and maintain that many regulations mandate solutions that may actually exacerbate environmental damage; for example, banning some types of packaging when production of the substituted packaging will result in more air and water pollution. They also argue that substituting regulatory bureaucracy for market mechanisms actually perpetuates environmental problems by impeding innovative solutions to environmental problems and punishing the economy. Governments are comprised of individuals acting in their own self-interests. Individuals act in their own self-interest even when they are part of a group.[26] Consequently, individual self-interests in politics will lead to inequitable distributions of wealth,[27] and economic efficiency will not be achieved when public goods are provided by governments.

public good: A resource that is available or common to all or many (nonexcludability) and use of which by an individual does not diminish its availability to others (nonrivalrous).

---

[26] M. Olson, THE LOGIC OF COLLECTIVE ACTION: PUBLIC GOODS AND THE THEORY OF GROUPS (2nd ed.) (Cambridge, MA: Harvard University Press, 1965).
[27] *See, e.g.,* J. B. Stevens, THE ECONOMICS OF COLLECTIVE CHOICE (Boulder, CO: Westview Press, 1993).

■ Applied Problem: Command and Control versus Market Incentives

Defenders of a regulatory approach to environmental policy making emphasize the successes of national environmental laws—and the environmental laws passed in the 1970s have indeed achieved some measurable successes. Some environmentalists argue that providing free-market incentives, such as permitting companies to purchase and sell pollution rights, is an inexpensive and effective way to reduce pollution. This free-market approach was adopted in part in the emissions trading program for sulfur dioxide emissions under the 1990 amendments to the CAA. Since then, state governments have enacted cap-and-trade regulatory schemes for volatile organic compounds (Illinois), carbon dioxide emissions (New York), and greenhouse gas emissions (regional).

Supporters argue that creating trading allowances, rather than simply imposing command and control regulations, ultimately achieves cost reduction by fostering the sales of emission permits and reduction of overall emissions. If a party can sell its permit, there is an incentive to reduce its emissions. In other words, if one no longer needs a permit, one can sell it. This is an incentive to clean up one's production methods.

Opponents argue that allowing pollution trading essentially grants a right to pollute at a certain level. Moreover, it creates a social justice issue by potentially concentrating high emissions in specific areas, thereby placing the negative externality burden of excessive pollution on certain vulnerable populations.

The debate about whether market-based incentives should replace command and control regulation of industrial pollution will likely continue as people search for ways to increase efficiency and achieve the greatest possible benefit from the money spent on environmental protection.

Questions for reflection:

1. To what extent should business bear the costs of environmental protection? Should an industry that is a primary source of pollution bear a substantial amount of the costs of controlling that pollution?
2. Does business itself have any ethical obligations to maintain a clean and safe environment, regardless of what the law mandates?
3. Could cap-and-trade emission schemes be useful on a worldwide scale to address global warming? Why or why not?

Problems Associated with Risk Management

In the United States, the system for making choices about environmental policy is essentially a political one, and decision making—whether by agencies or elected officials—is subject to direct political pressure. Environmental policy makers must consider both the costs and the benefits of environmental policies, as discussed earlier. However, they must also consider the politics of environmental protection.

Cost-benefit analysis is expressly mandated by some environmental laws. Risk assessment, a component of cost-benefit analysis, determines whether the cost of regulating a particular risk is acceptable based upon the nature and scope of that risk. While there may be a general awareness of the risks related to a particular hazardous substance, for example, in many instances it is difficult to assess the actual risks of such exposure. This is partly because of the complexity of the factors that may give rise to risk, partly because of the fact that the dangers associated with some risks—like exposure to toxic materials—may increase over time, and partly because of limited scientific knowledge about those effects.

Moreover, spending priorities are often dictated, at least in part, by an ill-informed public perception of environmental risks. For example, while the public greatly fears abandoned hazardous waste facilities, it is unconcerned about radon in homes. Risk assessment professionals, however, consider radon a far greater health hazard.

The problems regarding scientific uncertainty and risk assessment in environmental litigation are exemplified by the rules for evaluating the sufficiency of scientific evidence in complex toxic tort litigation. Under traditional tort law, a plaintiff in a civil suit who alleges that the defendant's wrongful action harmed the plaintiff must prove that the defendant's action was the "cause in fact" of the injury. Proof of scientific causation in such cases often requires the court to determine whether the scientific evidence introduced at trial is generally accepted, valid, and supports the argument in the case.

■ ■ ■ REVIEW AND STUDY QUESTIONS

1. How can conflicting ideologies concerning economic policy tools influence the likelihood of passage of environmental laws?

2. What are some difficulties with quantifying the value of the natural environment?

Who Should Regulate?

Another matter on which there is considerable disagreement is whether environmental goals can best be met through regulation at the state level or the federal level. In the debate on environmental policy making, the argument can be made that by decentralizing environmental decision making, local and state governments will be better able to respond to changing circumstances and new information. However, risks are inherent in the delegation of authority to local or state governments that may lack the resources, political will, and expertise to implement environmental programs. Indeed, some contend that working at both the local and the global levels is the best way to address environmental problems. This vision, which is in essence embraced by the European Union, is consistent with the potential globalization of the goals of cultural diversity protection, local community building, and individual empowerment and participation. Such a vision would allow for multilevel governance structures, which would do much to allay fears of one overwhelmingly dominant world order and lack of individual input and access to government. Nation-states would maintain their identity and legitimacy, albeit in a more integrated system of government.

Clearly, some environmental problems, such as air and water pollution, cannot be addressed solely at a local level, because air and water do not remain in one circumscribed jurisdiction. Therefore, this problem is more effectively handled at a higher level, such as the state or federal government.

Many federal environmental laws, such as the Clean Air Act, the Coastal Zone Management Act, and the Clean Water Act, have established a state-federal partnership scheme. For example, the Environmental Protection Agency establishes emission standards under the CAA, but states develop proposals for meeting those requirements, and they shoulder the monitoring and enforcement responsibilities. These are good examples of federalism in action. *Federalism* simply refers to a system of a government in which power is divided. In the United States, power is divided between the federal government and the state governments.

■ Law and the Future: Where Should We Go from Here?

A few generations ago, few people thought anything was wrong with pouring gasoline down a sewer drain or dumping batteries or paint cans in the trash. Recycling was practically unheard of. Today, many Americans are aware of and concerned about the environmental implications of these actions and many other everyday activities, in part because of federal environmental regulatory policy. The way we think about the environment has changed over the years. Our grassroots initiatives have led to laws to protect or sustain certain aspects of the environment, and behaviors that are less harmful to the environment have become routine. However, many areas of our environment are still under extreme pressure from overexploitation, pollution, and population pressure. Loss of habitat, extinction of species, air quality problems, traffic congestion, encroachment by development into rural lands, climate change, ocean health decline, and many other topics continue to demand our attention. Our law can do more.

Global environmental issues are increasingly important. Many environmental problems do not stop at national boundaries. Additionally, the global economy creates domestic concerns about the environmental impact of products imported into the American economy, such as pesticide contamination of imported foods. Specific concerns about global warming, nuclear radiation, and a myriad of other issues continue to grow as evidence of the harmful effects of human activity on the global environment mounts.

Public opinion will continue to play an important role in establishing international environmental policy and determining the costs that society is willing to bear to achieve environmental goals.

■ Conclusion

The purpose of this chapter is to highlight some of the important environmental policy thinking, problems, and goals that underlie our environmental laws and policy making, and to encourage you to think about various points of view concerning our natural environment. Subsequent chapters of this book examine how various environmental laws address particular environmental problems and issues. As you read those chapters, remember that these laws neither spring from nor exist in a vacuum. Legislators, courts, and agency officials adopt and implement laws and regulations in response to perceived harms and a determination that a particular approach will best address those harms. Ultimately, lawmaking is policy making. As you study environmental law in the following chapters, try to identify the environmental policy goals of each law. What environmental concerns does the law attempt to address? How likely is it that the law will achieve its environmental goals? Are there alternative approaches to solving this problem? What are the costs and the benefits of this approach to environmental policy making?

■ *Some Important Federal Environmental Acronyms*

Clean Air Act (CAA)—The Clean Air Act creates federal authority over and responsibility for air pollution. Among other things, the CAA directs the EPA to establish national ambient air quality standards, which are enforceable by the states through state implementation plans. The CAA was amended in 1977 and again in 1990 to address specific problems such as hazardous air pollutants and acid rain.

Clean Water Act (CWA)—The Clean Water Act protects surface water by controlling or preventing discharge of pollutants into those waters. The law was amended in 1987 to address water quality in areas where compliance with minimum discharge standards is insufficient to meet water quality goals.

Comprehensive Environmental Response, Compensation, and Liability Act of 1980 (CERCLA)—CERCLA, commonly known as Superfund, was enacted in 1980 to address the threat to human health and the environment posed by abandoned hazardous waste disposal sites. The law was substantially amended in 1986 by the Superfund Amendments and Reauthorization Act (SARA).

Endangered Species Act (ESA)—This 1973 Act prohibits the import, export, taking, or trading of any endangered species of fish or wildlife. The ESA protects both endangered and threatened species. Any person may petition to have a species removed from or added to the endangered or threatened species lists.

Environmental Protection Agency (EPA)—This federal agency was created in 1970. The EPA studies environmental problems and establishes and enforces U.S. environmental standards, including air and water pollution standards, toxic substances regulations, solid and hazardous waste rules, and pesticide and insecticide registration requirements.

Federal Insecticide, Fungicide, and Rodenticide Act (FIFRA)—First enacted in 1947 and substantially amended many times thereafter, this statute generally provides that a person may not distribute, sell, ship, or deliver a pesticide unless that pesticide is registered with the EPA. To become registered under the law, pesticides must be properly labeled and produce no unreasonably adverse effects on the environment.

National Environmental Policy Act (NEPA)—Adopted in 1970, this statute sets forth the general policy of the federal government concerning the environment, establishes the Council on Environmental Quality (CEQ), and requires federal agencies to consider the environmental impact of every major federal action significantly affecting the quality of the human environment.

Oil Pollution Act of 1990 (OPA)—This act establishes the federal liability scheme for vessels and facilities that spill oil on or into waters subject to United States jurisdiction.

Resource Conservation and Recovery Act (RCRA)—This law was enacted in 1976 to address problems associated with the generation and disposal of hazardous and solid wastes. RCRA, which applies mainly to active facilities, is designed to provide "cradle-to-grave" control of hazardous waste by imposing management requirements upon generators and transporters of hazardous wastes and upon owners and operators of disposal facilities. The law was substantially amended in 1984 by the Hazardous and Solid Waste Amendments (HSWA).

Safe Drinking Water Act (SDWA)—The SDWA was originally enacted in 1974 and has been amended a few times. Its purpose is to protect the quality of the nation's drinking water supply; it fulfills this purpose by requiring the EPA to establish maximum contaminant level goals and national primary drinking water regulations for certain contaminants found in public water systems.

Toxic Substances Control Act (TSCA)—Enacted in 1976, the TSCA has been amended several times. The TSCA places the responsibility on manufacturers to

(Continued)

provide data on the health and environmental effects of chemical substances and mixtures, and gives the EPA comprehensive authority to regulate the manufacture, use, distribution, and disposal of chemical substances. Other titles in the TSCA address specific problems: Title II of the TSCA is the Asbestos Hazardous Emergency Response Act, Title III is the Indoor Radon Abatement Act, and Title IV is the Lead-Based Paint Exposure Reduction Act.

Chapter 1 Case Study
Pomo Valley and the Kashia Pomo

Would you support clear-cutting the Pomo Valley for a vineyard? Review the following link: http://intercontinentalcry.org/lawsuit-filed-to-stop-clearcutting-of-sacred-redwood-forest/

Environmental groups have filed suit to stop the clear-cutting of the Pomo Canyon redwoods, held sacred by the Kashia Pomo, a Native American people. The clear-cut is planned as a way to make land for vineyards for wine production. This case study illustrates the tension between different worldviews and goals of law, and it provides a good focus for a discussion of environmental ethics, the importance of differing values, and the challenges of enforcement related to environmental law.

Now, assume that you are a policy maker, and your job requires you to vote whether to allow clear-cutting of this forest so the land can be used for a vineyard. Your scientific advisors indicate that the clear-cut will not harm the overall ecosystem of the forest or the overall wildlife habitats within it. However, this particular area of the forest is a sacred ground used for religious rituals and retreats, as noted earlier. The old trees and all parts of this ecosystem are sacred to the people who engage in religious practices there. Clear-cutting of this area would destroy the ability of those people to access the divine through their religious practices.

How should you vote? Should science prevail, or should the interests of the people who have historically used the land prevail? Couple these questions with a consideration of the political environment that you are navigating as a policy maker. How do your political allies' opinions become a part of this calculation? If you ignore your political allies, will that have negative repercussions for your professional future? What does the answer to this question tell you about self-interest and public policy?

Whose interests should dominate in this dispute? Why?

The American Legal System

Learning Objectives

After reading this chapter, you will have an understanding of the American legal system. Specifically, after reading this chapter, you should be able to answer the following questions:

1. What are the differences between civil and criminal law?
2. What are the sources of law?
3. What is the structure of the federal and state court systems?
4. What are the steps of civil litigation?

Here's a good idea!
This is a "bare bones" outline of the chapter. Expand this outline with more detailed notes as you read the chapter. This will allow you to create a study guide as you work. This good study habit will help you learn the material, retain important points, and make efficient use of your time.

▓ Introduction

The purpose of this chapter is to provide some general information about the American legal system and the rules applied by the courts in resolving civil disputes. Knowledge of the American legal system will help you understand how law affects the environment. Additionally, it will provide an orientation to help you understand the different sources of law discussed in this text. This chapter examines the sources of law, the state and federal court systems, and the steps in civil litigation.

When people think of environmental law, they often think of substantive law. *Substantive law* is law that addresses rights and obligations of people. However, procedural law is also very important. *Procedural law* consists of the legal rules for enforcing rights and duties or for redressing harms. To understand case opinions, one must also know the context of those decisions, including the procedures under which cases are heard.

■ Civil versus Criminal Cases

Civil law is the law under which an individual brings an action against another party (e.g., another person, government, business) for breach of legal duties owed to that individual. The **plaintiff** is the injured party. The **defendant** is the party alleged by the plaintiff to be responsible for the plaintiff's injury.

Civil cases can be based in common law, such as tort or contracts (and these common laws have often been codified or otherwise incorporated into state statutes); statutory law, such as the Clean Air Act or the Clean Water Act (which may also carry criminal penalties for violations); regulatory law, such as the rules and regulations promulgated by an administrative agency; and so on. *Civil cases* are any cases that are not criminal cases. An example of a civil suit is an action by a plaintiff against a defendant for harm caused to the plaintiff as a result of the defendant's negligence. Imagine, for example, that the defendant removed all of the soil and subsoil from its city lot, which caused the plaintiff's neighboring land to collapse due to lack of lateral support. (Negligence is a specific type of tort and is discussed in Chapter 4.) The legal remedy in civil cases is generally monetary. A **legal remedy** is simply the relief granted by a court to enforce a right or redress a violation of law. In some civil cases a court may order other kinds of relief, such as an **injunction**, which is a court order mandating certain behavior or action by the defendant or prohibiting the defendant from engaging in certain activity in the future.

In another kind of civil law case, a plaintiff challenges a law directly, or challenges an administrative agency's implementation of a statute or administrative rule. Examples include cases brought by plaintiffs to challenge agency rule making, as well as cases in which a petitioner challenges the legality of the statute itself. Such a plaintiff may file an action for **declaratory relief**, which requests that the court rule on the legality of the challenged statute or regulation.

To obtain **judicial review** of agency action, which is simply court review of an agency action, a plaintiff files a **petition** in a court under the relevant statute. Various legal doctrines, including standing and exhaustion of administrative remedies, may affect a court's willingness to grant judicial review in cases challenging agency action. **Standing** is the legal right to bring a claim. As discussed in more depth in Chapter 8, **exhaustion of administrative remedies** is required as well. Essentially, this means that a plaintiff must follow all procedural channels established by the agency and seek all possible relief from the agency itself before requesting review by the courts. In such cases, if judicial review is granted, the court reviews the decision of the administrative agency to determine whether the agency violated a provision of law in its interpretation or application of the statute or rule. Also, instead of challenging an agency rule directly, a person may choose to wait until an enforcement action is brought against him or her and then challenge the rule in that proceeding.

Noncivil legal actions brought by the government against an individual or entity fall into the category of **criminal law**. Criminal laws prohibit certain actions or conduct, because those actions or conduct threaten public safety and welfare; they also specify the punishment for such conduct. The prosecutor or district attorney prosecutes the defendant in a criminal case. The victim of a crime is a witness in a criminal case, rather than the plaintiff. This important distinction underscores the role of the government (i.e., the public in general) as the party injured by someone's commission of a criminal offense.

civil law: Law involving actions for breach of legal duties owed by private parties to other individuals. A civil lawsuit may be based on a statute or common law.

plaintiff: The party who brings a civil suit.

defendant: The party alleged by the plaintiff in a civil suit to be responsible for the plaintiff's injury.

legal remedy: Judicial remedy imposed by law.

injunction: A court order to refrain from or perform some activity.

declaratory relief: A court's ruling regarding the legality of a statute or regulation.

judicial review: Court review of the action of an agency or other governmental entity.

petition: A written application to a court by which a plaintiff commences a lawsuit.

standing: The legal right to bring a lawsuit.

exhaustion of administrative remedies: Doctrine requiring that a plaintiff use all procedural channels and seek all possible relief from an agency before seeking relief from the courts.

criminal law: Substantive law specifying what conduct constitutes a crime and the punishment for such conduct.

Criminal cases are brought in state or federal courts. If a defendant is accused of committing a federal crime, such as violating the Endangered Species Act in a criminal manner, the case will be heard in federal court. If a defendant is accused of committing a state crime (a criminal act that violates state law), the case will be heard in state court. It is important to note that many state environmental crimes are also crimes under federal environmental laws. This means that a particular environmental crime quite likely will involve violations of both state and federal law. In such instances, the case may be tried in either the state or the federal court system.

Criminal charges are most commonly brought against an individual defendant, but such charges may also be brought against a nonhuman person or entity, such as a corporation. Review Figure 2.1 for a comparison between criminal and civil law.

■ **FIGURE 2.1** *Comparison of Criminal and Civil Law*

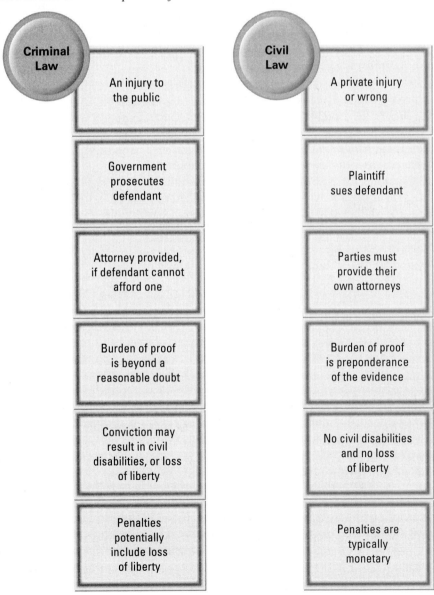

The differences between criminal and civil law include:

■ The party that may bring the lawsuit—the government brings a criminal case, but a plaintiff brings a civil case.

■ To whom the injury accrues—the government is the injured party in a criminal case, but the plaintiff is the one allegedly injured in a civil case.

■ The burden of proof—the standard is beyond a reasonable doubt in criminal cases, but by a preponderance of the evidence in a civil case.

■ The possible penalties—incarceration is a possibility in a criminal case, but not in a civil case. In a civil case, monetary damages (and possibly injunctive relief) are typically awarded to a successful plaintiff.

Sometimes a criminal and a civil case can arise from the same incident. This allows the government to bring a claim for injury to the public (for violating a criminal law), and a plaintiff to bring a claim for private injury. This does not violate the prohibition against double jeopardy, found in the Fifth Amendment to the U.S. Constitution, because the prohibition against double jeopardy applies only to being tried twice for the same criminal charge.

■ ACTIVITY BOX   EPA Enforcement Cases Map

Visit the Environmental Protection Agency's Enforcement Cases Map: http://www.epa.gov /enforcement/data/eoy2012/casemap.html
Enter your city or town into the search box.

1. Identify one civil and one criminal enforcement action related to environmental law in your community.
2. What are the benefits of making this information public through a website such as the EPA's Enforcement Cases Map?
3. Describe the differences between (a) what you thought about your community's compliance with environmental law and (b) what the EPA map revealed.
4. Imagine that you own a business identified by this map as having been the defendant in an environmental action (whether criminal or civil). Write a press release explaining to the community how your business will change to address this matter in the future and to improve public relations.

■ Sources of Law

The American system of government is a system of **federalism**, with a central government made up of three branches of government and many state governments. The federal government is comprised of the legislative branch (the U.S. Congress), the executive branch (the president and executive agencies), and the judicial branch (the federal court system). Additionally, each of the state governments is made up of a state legislative body (legislative branch), a governor (executive branch), and a state court system (judicial branch). Persons in the United States are subject to laws passed by both the federal government and the state governments that have jurisdiction over them, as well as political subdivisions within the state, such as counties and cities. Figure 2.2 shows that some powers are exclusive to the federal government, some are exclusive to the states, and some powers are shared.

federalism: A system of shared government, where power is divided between a central government and additional political units.

■ **FIGURE 2.2** *Federal and State Governmental Powers*

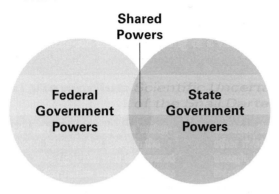

The scope of federal power is important in environmental law cases. The answers to important political and social policy questions often turn on whether federal environmental law preempts state law, and the federal government's ability to enact environmental laws under its commerce clause powers. These questions are examined in Chapter 7. For now, let's focus on the basic sources of law.

A *source of law* is simply a legitimate authority from whence we derive our law. For example, if your professor said, "Cell phones are banned in class," that would not be a law. It would simply be a rule of the class. Your professor does not have the authority to create law (though he or she can legitimately establish class rules). However, our branches of government do have the legitimate authority to create law.

■ Applied Problem

First, review Figure 2.2; then refer to Article I, section 8, of the U.S. Constitution. Also, reflect upon issues that you already know are under state purview. Make three lists:

a. Some of the responsibilities of the federal government
b. Some of the responsibilities of state governments
c. Some responsibilities that are shared between the state and federal governments

---

Constitutional Law

The foundational source of law in the United States is the **U.S. Constitution**, the document that created the structure of our government. Any powers not given to the federal government are reserved to the states, under the Tenth Amendment to the Constitution. However, per the **Supremacy Clause**, state laws may not conflict with federal laws. Under the express language of the Supremacy Clause, the Constitution is the supreme law of the land. This means that federal laws enacted by the federal government under its constitutional power take priority over state laws if those laws conflict.

The U.S. Constitution created three branches of the federal government: the legislative branch, the executive branch, and the judicial branch. The function of the legislative branch is to create law. Congress is the federal legislative branch; it creates statutes. Environmental law relies heavily upon federal and state statutes that have been passed by the federal and state legislative bodies to protect our environment or to place restraints on conduct that directly affects the environment.

U.S. Constitution: The supreme law of the United States.

Supremacy Clause: A portion of the U.S. Constitution that asserts the U.S. Constitution is the supreme law of the land.

Article I, section 8, of the U.S. Constitution enumerates specific powers of Congress. Another way to understand this is that Congress may not exercise any power that is not specifically given to it by the U.S. Constitution. If Congress passes a statute that exceeds its constitutional authority, that law can be struck down as exceeding the powers of Congress if it is challenged. Thus, it is important to recognize which powers Congress legitimately possesses. This allows informed persons to object when the lawmaking branch of our federal government exceeds its authority, and it allows informed persons to ask Congress to create and enact laws that are within its legitimate authority.

The president of the United States is the most visible member of the federal executive branch. The governor is the most visible member of a state's executive branch. The executive branch is charged with implementing and enforcing the law created by the legislative branch.

Our federal judicial system was also created by the U.S. Constitution, which established the Supreme Court and gave Congress the power to create additional courts as needed. Of course, today the federal court system is well developed and extensive.

Laws and legal doctrines that are stated in or derived from the U.S. Constitution are known as **constitutional law**. The Constitution and federal laws enacted in conformance with its provisions take priority over all other laws, such as when state laws conflict with federal laws. Under the principle of judicial review, the courts may declare any state or federal law unconstitutional if that law conflicts with provisions of the U.S. Constitution. If a law is declared unconstitutional by an appropriate court, then the law is null and void, meaning it no longer has the force of law. Each state's constitution similarly takes priority over conflicting laws of that state.

It is important to note that the only party that can violate a constitutional right is a government actor (a person or entity clothed with governmental authority). This government actor may be an individual human being (such as a police officer or an elected official), or a government entity (such as an executive agency).

Another important constitutional issue in environmental law cases is the scope of the Fifth and Fourteenth Amendment prohibitions against government taking of private property without just compensation. This issue is explored in Chapter 6. The **Bill of Rights**, the first 10 amendments to the Constitution, is also a basis for many constitutional challenges to state and federal environmental laws. The Bill of Rights contains specific language protecting against certain government actions that interfere with individual freedom. For example, in one case, the Dow Chemical Company argued that aerial photographs taken of its property by the EPA without a search warrant violated Dow's Fourth Amendment constitutional right against unreasonable searches and seizures.[1]

Additionally, the First Amendment is increasingly a focus in environmental law. The First Amendment to the Constitution, which protects freedom of speech, reads as follows:

> Congress shall make no law respecting an establishment of religion, or prohibiting the free exercise thereof; or abridging the freedom of speech, or of the press; or the right of the people peaceably to assemble, and to petition the Government for a redress of grievances.

Note that the First Amendment does not protect all types of speech. Generally, there are certain recognized types of speech. **Political speech**, for example, is the most highly protected form of speech; it is used to express opinions about

constitutional law: Laws and legal doctrines drawn or derived from the U.S. Constitution.

Bill of Rights: The common name for the first 10 amendments to the U.S. Constitution.

political speech: Speech used to express opinions about government.

[1] 476 U.S. 227 (1986).

government. **Commercial speech**, which is economic in nature, is less protected than political speech. Therefore, government can restrict it in certain circumstances. **Obscenity**, which is yet another type of speech, is not constitutionally protected. Government can create law to restrict or prohibit obscene speech.

Let's consider a case related to commercial speech. Recombinant bovine growth hormone (rbGH) is widely used in the dairy industry; when injected into dairy cows, this hormone stimulates the cows to produce more milk. In response to concerns by some consumers as to the safety of dairy products derived from rbGH-treated cows, some dairy producers wished to place labels on their products indicating that their products did not come from rbGH-treated cows. However, the Ohio Department of Agriculture adopted a rule that prohibited the use of labels such as "no hormones," "hormone free," "rbGH free," "no artificial hormones," and "bST free." Before the final rule went into effect, the International Dairy Foods Association and the Organic Trade Association sued. Among other things, the suit challenged the rule as an unconstitutional restraint on commercial speech. After the plaintiffs initially lost at the district court level, the case was appealed to the Sixth Circuit Court of Appeals. Read the following excerpt regarding the First Amendment and commercial speech.

> **commercial speech:** Speech that is economic or commerce-related.
>
> **obscenity:** A form of speech that is not constitutionally protected; speech that appeals primarily to prurient interest.

International Dairy Foods Association v. Boggs
622 F.3d 628, 2010 U.S. App. LEXIS 20184 (6th Cir. 2010)

II. Analysis

* * *

B. First Amendment Challenge to the Ban ...

The [plaintiffs] contend that the Ohio rule violates the First Amendment by placing a ... ban on ... claims such as "rbST free," "antibiotic-free," and "pesticide-free." Both sides agree that the ... claims at issue constitute commercial speech and are thus afforded less extensive protection under the First Amendment than noncommercial speech.... Under the commercial-speech framework, "[t]ruthful advertising related to lawful activities is entitled to the protections of the First Amendment," *In re R.M.J.*, 455 U.S. 191 ... (1982), but the government is "free to prevent the dissemination of commercial speech that is false, deceptive, or misleading," *Zauderer* [*v. Office of Disciplinary Counsel of the Supreme Court of Ohio*, 471 U.S. 626 (1985)] at 638.

... [B]ans on commercial speech are evaluated under a four-part analysis first set forth in *Central Hudson Gas & Electric Corp. v. Public Service Commission*, 447 U.S. 557, 100 S. Ct. 2343, 65 L. Ed. 2d 341 (1980). Pursuant to that analysis, a court first determines whether the speech concerns unlawful activity or is misleading. *Id.* at 566. If a court finds in the affirmative on either prong, the speech is not entitled to First Amendment protection, and the analysis ends.... But if the court finds that the speech is

entitled to First Amendment protection, it then makes three additional inquiries: (1) whether the asserted governmental interest is substantial, (2) whether the regulation directly advances that interest, and (3) whether the regulation is more extensive than necessary to serve the asserted interest.

* * *

1. Whether the ... Claims are Inherently Misleading

The district court in the present case concluded that the ... claims were misleading and therefore not entitled to any First Amendment protection. "Misleading advertising may be prohibited entirely," including where the speech is "inherently likely to deceive or where the record indicates that a particular form or method of advertising has in fact been deceptive." *In re R.M.J.*, 455 U.S. at 202-03. Where speech is only potentially misleading, however, the *Central Hudson* framework applies. *Id.* at 203. Under these circumstances, "the preferred remedy is more disclosure, rather than less." *Bates v. State Bar of Ariz.*, 433 U.S. 350, 374-75, 97 S. Ct. 2691, 53 L. Ed. 2d 810 (1977)....

The district court held that the composition claims were inherently misleading because "they imply a compositional difference between those products that are produced with rb[ST] and those that are not," in contravention of the FDA's finding that there is no

(Continued)

measurable compositional difference between the two. This conclusion is belied by the record, however, which shows that, contrary to the district court's assertion, a compositional difference does exist between milk from untreated cows and conventional milk ("conventional milk," as used throughout this opinion, refers to milk from cows treated with rbST). As detailed by the … parties seeking to strike down the Rule, the use of rbST in milk production has been shown to elevate the levels of insulin-like growth factor 1 (IGF-1), a naturally-occurring hormone that in high levels is linked to several types of cancers, among other things. [They] also point to certain studies indicating that rbST use induces an unnatural period of milk production during a cow's "negative energy phase." According to these studies, milk produced during this stage is considered to be low quality due to its increased fat content and its decreased level of proteins. The amici [friends of the court] further note that milk from treated cows contains higher somatic cell counts, which makes the milk turn sour more quickly and is another indicator of poor milk quality. This evidence precludes us from agreeing with the district court's conclusion that there is no compositional difference between the two types of milk.

In addition, and more salient to the regulation of composition claims like "rbST free," the failure to discover rbST in conventional milk is not necessarily because the artificial hormone is absent in such milk, but rather because scientists have been unable to perfect a *test* to detect it. As recognized by the State's brief in the district court, "given existing technology, it is currently impossible to test milk to determine whether the hormones present are natural hormones or recombinant hormones (such as rbST)." The State further conceded this point at oral argument, acknowledging that conventional milk "could" contain rbST, but that no test has been able to verify if this is in fact the case. This uncertainty is also implicit in the FDA's 1994 Guidance. There, the agency stated that "there [i]s no *significant* difference between milk from treated and untreated cows" because "[t]here is currently no way to differentiate analytically between naturally occurring bST and [r]bST in milk." 59 Fed. Reg. 6279, 6280 (emphasis added). The FDA thus appears to have left room for the fact that *some* compositional difference between the two types of milk may exist, leaving open the possibility that one day a method might exist to detect whether rbST is in fact present in conventional milk.

Taken collectively, this evidence points to two distinct types of milk. On the one hand is milk from cows never given rbST, which in turn cannot produce milk that has rbST as a matter of fact. The composition claim "rbST free" is therefore demonstrably true as applied to this milk. On the other hand, milk from cows treated with rbST might contain the artificial hormone, although there is currently no way to determine whether that is the case. But even if rbST is not present in conventional milk, there is still evidence that it contains increased levels of IGF-1 and might be compositionally of a lesser quality.

A compositional difference thus exists between the two types of milk, although the extent of this difference—namely whether conventional milk does in fact contain rbST—is still very much an open question. As such, the composition claim "rbST free" at best informs consumers of a meaningful distinction between conventional and other types of milk and at worst potentially misleads them into believing that a compositionally distinct milk adversely affects their health. Under these circumstances, we conclude that composition claims like "rbST free" are not inherently misleading. We must therefore apply the remaining three *Central Hudson* factors to assess the constitutionality of the Rule's prophylactic ban on the composition claims "rbST free" and "artificial hormone free."

* * *

2. The Remaining Central Hudson factors

Having determined that the composition claim "rbST free" is not inherently misleading, we must review the State's ban on such claims under the final three *Central Hudson* factors: (1) whether the State's asserted interest is substantial, (2) whether the regulation directly advances that interest, and (3) whether the regulation is no more extensive than necessary to serve the asserted interest. *See Central Hudson*, 447 U.S. at 566. All three of these factors must be met in order for the Rule to be upheld.…

Turning to the first factor, we note that the Rule's purported purpose is to prevent the use of "false or misleading" labeling. *See* Ohio Admin. Code § 901:11-8-01(A). The Processors [challengers] concede that this interest is substantial. But because the Rule is aimed at preventing consumer deception, the State bears the burden to "demonstrate that the harms it recites are real and that its restriction will in fact alleviate them to a material degree." *Ibanez v. Fla. Dep't of Bus. & Prof'l Regulation, Bd. of Accountancy*, 512 U.S. 136, 146, 114 S. Ct. 2084, 129 L. Ed. 2d 118 (1994).…

In the present case, the record of deception is weak at best. The only evidence that the State points to is the FDA's Interim Guidance and consumer comments that it received in response to the proposed Rule. But the

(Continued)

Guidance provides little support in this regard. The FDA suggests in the Guidance that the claim "rbST free" "*may imply a compositional difference*" between the two types of milk, 59 Fed. Reg. 6279, 6280 (emphasis added), but this statement does not establish that such a claim is necessarily misleading in every context. Furthermore, the FDA cited no evidence or studies in the Guidance to support its concerns regarding consumer confusion. The Guidance therefore does not constitute "evidence of deception" as required under *Ibanez*.

Also unhelpful are the consumer comments that the ODA received after issuing the proposed Rule. The State received approximately 2,700 comments, of which the Processors estimate that only 70 were in support of the Rule. We agree with the State that some of these comments demonstrate consumer confusion regarding the use of rbST in milk production. One commenter, for example, asserted that she needed "to know that the milk I drink has no added hormones," thereby indicating that she believed rbST to be present in conventional milk. But few if any of these commenters indicated that their confusion stemmed from the product labels. The commenter quoted above, for instance, was informed about rbST and milk production from conversations with her oncologist, not from reading the labels. Although there is not a "complete absence of deception" …, the proof falls far short of establishing that Ohio consumers have been misled by dairy-product labeling.

We need not address this issue further, however, because we conclude that the Rule does not directly advance the State's interest and is more extensive than necessary to serve that interest. These last two steps of the *Central Hudson* test are complementary. They involve "asking whether the speech restriction is not more extensive than necessary to serve the interests that support it." *Lorillard Tobacco Co. v. Reilly*, 533 U.S. 525, 556, 121 S. Ct. 2404, 150 L. Ed. 2d 532 (2001).… Accordingly, there must be a "reasonable fit between the legislature's ends and the means chosen to accomplish those ends, a means narrowly tailored to achieve the desired objective." … "[I]f there are numerous and obvious less-burdensome alternatives to the restriction on commercial speech, that is certainly a relevant consideration in determining whether the 'fit' between ends and means is reasonable." *City of Cincinnati v. Discovery*

Network, Inc., 507 U.S. 410, 417 n.13, 113 S. Ct. 1505, 123 L. Ed. 2d 99 (1993).

… [T]he potential consumer confusion created by the composition claim "rbST free" could be alleviated by accompanying the claim with a disclaimer informing consumers that rbST has yet to be detected in conventional milk. Examples of possible disclaimers include a statement regarding the lack of evidence that conventional milk contains rbST, or even the disclaimer already required by the Rule to accompany production claims: "The FDA has determined that no significant difference has been shown between milk derived from rbST-supplemented and non-rbST-supplemented cows."

… The claim "rbST free," when used in conjunction with an appropriate disclaimer, could assure consumers that the substance is definitively not in milk so labeled while also advising them that it has yet to be detected in conventional milk. There thus exists a method by which the potential difference between the two types of milk can be presented without also being deceptive.…

For these reasons, we conclude that the Rule's prophylactic ban of composition claims such as "rbST free" is more extensive than necessary to serve the State's interest in preventing consumer deception. This provision of the Rule therefore cannot withstand scrutiny under *Central Hudson*.

Questions for discussion:

1. As this case illustrates, courts have fashioned various tests for determining whether a law violates the First Amendment constitutional principles, depending upon the type of speech at issue. How can you tell that the speech at issue here was classified as commercial speech?

2. What are the elements of the test that was applied to the facts in this case to determine whether the proposed rule violated the First Amendment as it relates to commercial speech?

3. Why do you think Ohio imposed a rule that banned labels such as "hormone free" from products?

4. Do you believe that commercial speech should ever be banned? If so, why? If not, why not?

We will revisit the concept of constitutional law throughout this book, as the Constitution is a pervasive and important source of law. For example, in Chapter 7, we examine some of the issues that may arise regarding Congress's power to regulate interstate commerce under the **Commerce Clause** (one of the enumerated powers granted to Congress in Article I, Section 8).

Commerce Clause: A portion of the U.S. Constitution that gives Congress the power to regulate interstate commerce.

Treaties

Treaties are agreements between two or more nation-states. Under the Constitution, treaties made by the president with foreign governments and approved by the U.S. Senate by two-thirds vote are considered law. Moreover, a state or federal law may be invalid if it conflicts with the provisions of a duly enacted treaty.

Only the federal government may enter into a treaty. An individual state or local government may not enter into a treaty with a foreign nation. However, local governments can certainly adopt policies that mirror or support international treaties that the U.S. government has not ratified if those policies do not conflict with federal law. Consider the Kyoto Protocol, for example, which was intended to address climate change by creating binding obligations on industrialized nations to reduce greenhouse gas emissions. The Kyoto Protocol was ratified by more than 140 countries, but not by the United States. Because the United States did not ratify the Kyoto Protocol, the then-mayor of Seattle, Greg Nickels, launched the U.S. Conference of Mayors Climate Protection Agreement, through which each of the signatory mayors' respective cities commits to advancing the goals of the Kyoto Protocol. In 2005, when the agreement was originally introduced, 141 mayors signed (interestingly, the same number of countries that had then ratified the Kyoto Protocol). However, as of 2013, 1,060 mayors have signed, which represents almost 89 million Americans committed to reducing greenhouse gas emissions.

Notwithstanding such commitments, it is important to note that individual states and cities cannot adopt policies or laws that conflict with federal treaties or laws. For example, it would be unlawful for a city or for a state to unilaterally boycott another country's products.

Statutes

Statutes are laws passed by Congress or a state legislature. These laws become effective when signed by the executive. In the federal government, the executive is the President of the United States. The executive in each state is the governor.

A statute begins as a **bill**, which is a draft of a proposed law. In the federal government, a bill may be introduced in either the House of Representatives or the Senate (that is, either of the two houses of Congress). Once a bill is introduced, it is sent to the appropriate committee so that the members of the committee can discuss, accept, modify, table, or reject the bill. Once the bill passes the committee, it is sent to the full house on the side that it originated on. For example, if a bill originated in the House of Representatives, then after passing through the appropriate House committee, it goes to the full House of Representative for a vote. If the first house passes the bill, it is sent to the other house, where it goes through the same process: committee work and then a full house vote. Both the Senate and the House of Representatives may choose to work on the same bill at the same time, of course. Additionally, if either the House or the Senate votes down the bill, it does not go further.

If a bill passes in both houses of the legislature, it is sent to a joint committee comprised of both House of Representatives and Senate members. There, any differences between the House version of the bill and the Senate version of the bill are reconciled. After it passes the joint committee, it is sent to the full legislative body for a vote. If it passes, then it is sent to the executive for signature. At that point, the executive may choose to veto the bill, which means that the executive may reject the bill and thereby prevent its becoming law. At that point, the legislative body may overturn an executive veto by a two-thirds majority vote.

treaties: Agreements made between two or more nation-states.

statutes: Laws passed by the legislative branch of government.

bill: A draft of a proposed statute.

In the process of **codification**, individual statutes are arranged into an organized code. U.S. statutes are codified in the United States Code. Each state has its own code for state laws. If someone wishes to research a specific statute, they may find the exact language of the statute by looking in the appropriate code.

Local laws, called **ordinances**, are enacted by a legislative body, such as a city council, under authority of state law. Most states, for example, have statutes authorizing local governments to adopt a local zoning code. Under zoning ordinances, local governments, such as cities or counties, regulate land use within their jurisdictions. Some local governments have adopted ordinances to address specific environmental concerns.

Executive Orders

The Constitution does not give the executive branch any direction to make laws. However, executives, such as the president and the governors of the states, have the responsibility to enforce and implement the law. Furthermore, the executive may direct the executive branch as he or she sees fit, within the confines of constitutional authority (i.e., not exceeding constitutional authority). In some instances the executive may issue **executive orders** to the executive branch of government; these directives are legally enforceable if the order is justified on constitutional grounds. Environmental statutes generally empower administrative agencies to develop and promulgate rules and regulations for implementation and enforcement of those statutes. However, the president or governor can also empower an executive agency to promulgate regulations by executive order.

In 1996, a group of Chester, Pennsylvania, residents filed a civil rights complaint in a U.S. district court, accusing the state Department of Environmental Protection of allowing eight large waste treatment facilities to operate in three densely populated areas where African Americans made up a large portion of the population. This was one of the first environmental racism lawsuits in the nation. The plaintiffs cited Executive Order 12898, which calls for an end to "disproportionately high and adverse human health or environmental effects of its programs, policies, and activities on minority … and low-income populations" and the EPA's draft environmental justice strategy for Executive Order 12898 (issued in January 1995), which cited the City of Chester as a possible example of "environmental racism."[2] See the following box for an activity related to executive orders.

codification: The arrangement of statutes into an organized code.

ordinances: Local laws passed by a legislative body.

executive order: An order issued to the executive branch by the executive.

■ Historical Viewpoint

You can find executive orders issued between 1937 and 2012 at http://www.archives.gov/federal-register/executive-orders/disposition.html

1. Click on President Clinton's name. Find Executive Order 12898. The first section, § 1-101, introduces the order by mandating that "each Federal agency shall make achieving environmental justice part of its mission by identifying and addressing, as appropriate, disproportionately high and adverse human health or environmental effects of its programs, policies, and activities on minority … and low-income populations." Critique this directive. Is it broad enough? Too narrow? How could our law effectively address such

disparate-impact situations, which some have labeled "environmental racism"? In what ways are the powers of the executive branch limited in addressing this issue?

2. Click on "Search the Disposition Tables" on the left side of the screen. Click on "Text of Executive Orders" on the left side of the screen, then click on the link to "Proclamations and Executive Orders Chapter Index" in the bulleted list on the main screen. Click on chapter 40, "Protection of Environment." Select an executive order. Read it and summarize it. What was the purpose of the executive order? Is it still valid? What effect did this executive order have on our environment?

---

[2] *Chester Residents Concerned for Quality Living v. Seif*, No. 96-CV-3960.

Signing statements are common—and controversial—presidential decrees issued when a bill is signed into law (or vetoed). A signing statement essentially says that the law will be enforced to the extent that the executive branch believes the law to be constitutional. The executive branch is not charged with deciding "what the law is," because that has been the purview of the judicial branch since *Marbury v. Madison*.[3] Additionally, the executive branch is not charged with creating the law, because that is the role of the legislative branch. The executive branch *is* charged with enforcing and implementing the law. These different roles are the basis of our very important system of **checks and balances** on the powers of government branches.

Rules and Regulations

Most environmental law today consists of federal and state administrative rules and regulations, administrative decisions, and administrative policy implemented in enforcement actions. These administrative rules and regulations constitute a body of law known as **administrative law**. The *Federal Register* and the **Code of Federal Regulations (CFR)** contain these federal administrative rules and regulations; state administrative agency rules and regulations are codified at the state level.

In conformance with statutes creating and delegating to them such powers, agencies have the authority to adopt and implement administrative rules, to adjudicate disputes, and to impose sanctions for violations of their rules. The influence of agency action and administrative rule making is pervasive in the area of environmental law and regulation.

Administrative law has the force of law because the legislative body delegates some of its authority to the agency. An agency has the powers, express and implied, granted to it by the *enabling legislation*, the congressional statute that creates the agency. Chapter 8 examines administrative law principles and issues in more depth.

Common Law

Common law is judge-made law or case law. The common law originated in England and continues to evolve as judges write legal opinions on actual cases. In the United States, England, and other common law countries, judges are required to follow the previous decisions of other judges in their jurisdiction in similar cases. This is called the doctrine of **stare decisis**, which means "let the decision stand." However, every case is unique, and for this reason, common law permits a court to **distinguish** prior case law, thereby allowing common law to evolve.

In cases where public policy no longer supports application of a particular legal rule, courts also may modify or even abandon the common law rule altogether. An example of the ability of common law to evolve is *Prah v. Maretti*, 321 N.W.2d 182 (Wis. 1982), a nuisance case. Prah sued Maretti, alleging that the construction of Maretti's home would constitute a private nuisance because it would substantially obstruct Prah's solar collectors, which supplied energy for heat and hot water.

The district court granted summary judgment for Maretti. Under traditional American common law, in the absence of an easement a landowner has no legal right to unobstructed light and air from the adjoining land. However, the Wisconsin Supreme Court permitted Prah to pursue a nuisance claim in this case. The court

signing statement: A statement by the president relating to the bill being signed into law.

checks and balances: Political system in which each branch of government has specifically assigned powers and duties that constrain or limit the other branches' powers and duties; ensure that no branch becomes too powerful on its own.

administrative law: Rules and regulations promulgated by an administrative agency.

Code of Federal Regulations (CFR): Codification of the rules and regulations promulgated by administrative agencies.

common law: Judge-made law or case law.

stare decisis: Literally, "let the decision stand"; doctrine requiring judges to follow precedent in their jurisdictions in similar cases.

distinguish: To notice differences in the facts of a case that allow the court to change common law, apply it differently, or depart from stare decisis.

---
[3] 5 U.S. 137 (1803).

based its decision on its conclusion that policies supporting the original rule were no longer applicable. The court said:

> Courts should not implement obsolete policies that have lost their vigor over the course of the years. The law of private nuisance is better suited to resolve landowners' disputes about property development in the 1980s than is a rigid rule which does not recognize a landowner's interest in access to sunlight....

It also quoted with approval the following statement:

> Inherent in the common law is a dynamic principle which allows it to grow and to tailor itself to meet changing needs within the doctrine of stare decisis, which, if correctly understood, was not static and did not forever prevent the courts from reversing themselves or from applying principles of common law to new situations as the need arose. If this were not so, we must succumb to a rule that a judge should let others "long dead and unaware of the problems of the age in which he lives, do his thinking for him" (quoting Justice Douglas, 49 Columbia Law Review [1949]).

▓ ▓ ▓ REVIEW AND STUDY QUESTIONS

1. Identify and define six sources of law, and describe where those laws come from.
2. Are the following powers of the federal government, the state government, or both? How do you know?

   ▓ Make street repairs
   ▓ Enforce building codes
   ▓ Enact zoning laws to protect the environment
   ▓ Create national parks
   ▓ Declare war
   ▓ Make regulations pursuant to federal environmental statutes
   ▓ Pass laws for protecting the environment

3. Identify a specific statute designed to protect the environment. Research and describe how it became a law.
4. How do rules and regulations relate to statutes?
5. How do judges and court opinions create law? How does this judge-made law interact with statutes?
6. What environmental problem do you wish was addressed by law, or addressed better by law? What source of law would best address that problem? Why?
7. What is the appropriate relationship between a state government and the federal government? How does your answer inform your understanding of the concept of federalism?

▓ Structure of Court Systems

The federal court system is established by Article III of the U.S. Constitution. State court systems (and that of the District of Columbia) are established by state constitutions. The particular structures of these systems share fundamental common characteristics.

State Court Systems

The state court systems generally consist of three levels of courts: inferior courts, trial courts, and appellate courts. **Inferior courts** are minor courts with limited jurisdiction to resolve minor criminal matters and small civil disputes. Examples include municipal courts and small claims courts. In most cases, appeals from these courts of limited jurisdiction require a new trial (**trial de novo**) because the inferior courts do not keep a formal record of their proceedings.

inferior courts: Minor courts with limited jurisdiction.

trial de novo: New trial.

By far, the most legal business in this country takes place in state trial courts. A **trial court** is the entry-level court. That is, if a matter is litigated, it will start in trial court. In most states, there is at least one state trial court for each county, and larger counties may have many more.

The state trial court establishes the facts in a dispute and applies the law to the facts to reach a decision. In some cases, such as serious criminal offenses and certain kinds of civil cases, a party is entitled to a jury trial. In these cases, a jury determines the facts and applies the law to those facts as instructed by the trial court judge. A case that is tried without a jury, where the judge acts as both the finder of fact and the finder of law, is known as a **bench trial**.

What does it mean to "find the facts"? The fact-finder (either the jury or the judge) hears evidence produced by both sides during litigation. This evidence might include testimony of relevant parties; documentary, physical, and other evidence; and perhaps testimony of expert witnesses. It is important to realize that evidence is presented *only* at the trial-court level; this is why both sides strive to make their evidence complete and compelling. On the basis of the evidence presented, the jury then determines what actually happened; that is, what the facts are. Once the facts are determined, the law is applied to the facts.

There is no limit on the amount of civil damages that may be awarded by trial courts, which are **courts of general jurisdiction**, and there is no limit on the kinds of criminal cases the trial court may hear. State courts of general jurisdiction may hear all types of cases that the state has jurisdiction over. However, some states have also established separate divisions of trial courts to hear particular matters. These are known as **courts of limited jurisdiction**. State courts of limited jurisdiction, such as probate court, family law court, or juvenile court, may only hear cases involving their specific subject matters. In the state court system, courts of limited jurisdiction generally exist to expedite the litigation process and to encourage the development of subject matter expertise among the judges presiding over such courts.

Trial courts are known by many different names, which vary from state to state. For example, some state trial courts are known as circuit courts, superior courts, district courts, and particular county courts. Additionally, some localities have municipal courts.

All states have at least one **appellate court**, which in most states is called the state supreme court. Most states also have an intermediate level of appeals court that hears appeals from the state trial courts and determines whether there were any errors of law in the trial court proceedings. State appeals courts also hear appeals from state administrative agency decisions.

In general, an appeals court decides only questions of law, not questions of fact. A **question of law** is something that requires the application or interpretation of law to a specific set of facts. A **question of fact** is a question that the fact-finder decides in the litigation: specifically, what actually happened? The questions of fact are what the evidence presented by both sides during the litigation tries to answer. In reading appellate court decisions, keep in mind that the appeals court normally does not make factual findings; rather, it takes the facts as found by the trial court to be true. As a practical matter, this means that no new evidence is presented at the appellate court level.

The state supreme court is the ultimate interpreter of state law. State courts may also hear cases involving federal law, including questions of constitutional law, unless the federal courts have been given exclusive jurisdiction over the matter. For example, bankruptcy cases are heard exclusively in federal bankruptcy courts. The U.S. Supreme Court has the final word in cases involving federal law.

trial court: The court where evidence is submitted and questions of facts are resolved.

bench trial: A trial before a judge but no jury.

courts of general jurisdiction: Courts that have authority to hear all types of cases.

courts of limited jurisdiction: Courts that have authority to hear only limited or specific types of cases.

appellate court: A court that hears appeals.

question of law: A dispute or disagreement that requires the interpretation of law or application of a law to a specific set of facts.

question of fact: Question about the truth of a matter or what actually happened; evidence presented by both sides in a litigation tries to answer such questions.

One of the primary functions of a court is **statutory interpretation**. To apply the law to particular facts, a court is sometimes required to interpret the law. In environmental law cases, courts are often asked to interpret the meaning of statutory language. Sometimes the language itself is inherently ambiguous: for example, when is a person an "operator" for purposes of CERCLA, and thus subject to liability for cleanup costs under the Superfund law? In some instances, legislatures intentionally use ambiguous language in order to give courts the opportunity to give substance to the meaning of the statute through case-by-case adjudication. In other instances, legislators fail to address a particular problem, either because it is controversial, or simply because they did not foresee that particular issue. Additionally, sometimes statutes are just very poorly written. For all these reasons, the courts frequently must interpret the language of the statute in order to apply the law in a given case.

Courts follow certain rules of construction to interpret the meaning of particular words in a statute. These rules are applied in steps that can also be used when the court must interpret the language of a administrative rule or regulation. The first step is to apply the **plain meaning rule**, which requires a court to interpret and apply the statute according to the plain, accepted meaning of the language and words used in that law. If the meaning of the statute cannot be garnered from the plain meaning of the words, then the courts will take the second step and review the **legislative history** of the statute to ascertain legislative intent or purpose. The legislative history is often discerned by reviewing the legislative record that was made during debates surrounding the passage of the bill, before it became a statute. Sometimes, however, the legislative history is silent on the matter in question. That is, sometimes lawmakers simply did not address or put on the record the issue about which the court seeks clarification. When the meaning of the statute cannot be determined based upon the plain meaning of the words, and cannot be determined based upon legislative history, then courts may turn to the **general public purpose** of the statute, rely on **prior interpretations** of similar language in other cases, and invoke certain maxims of statutory interpretation.

Motion for Summary Judgment

At any point in the proceedings, either party may ask the court to grant it **summary judgment**. A party is entitled to summary judgment if there are no genuine issues of material fact and that party is entitled to judgment as a matter of law. In such cases, trial is unnecessary. The moving party may satisfy the first part of the test through its pleadings, discovery information, affidavits, and in some instances testimony at a hearing on the motion. One of the most important legal questions before a court that is determining whether to grant summary judgment is whether or not the facts are in dispute. If the facts are in dispute, summary judgment is inappropriate and should not be granted.

The grant of summary judgment is a final judgment that may be appealed by the losing party. In many cases, the issue on appeal of grant of summary judgment is whether the facts were in dispute. This requires the appeals court to consider all the material facts to determine whether a reasonable person could find for the appealing party.

Consider the following excerpt from a case in which the court goes through several of the steps described earlier to interpret the meaning of a rule or regulation. Additionally, summary judgment is illustrated in this case. The court first relates the facts of the case, then discusses summary judgment, and finally applies the steps of statutory construction.

---

statutory interpretation: The process by which a court determines the meaning of a law.

plain meaning rule: Doctrine according to which a court interprets and applies a statute according to the plain, accepted meaning of the language used in that law.

legislative history: Lawmakers' record concerning why a statute was passed or the meaning of the words in the statute.

general public purpose: The lawmakers' intended purpose for a law; investigated as the third step in statutory interpretation.

prior interpretations: Precedents.

summary judgment: Decision issued by a court when no genuine issues of material fact exist and a party is entitled to judgment as a matter of law.

Natural Resources Defense Council, Inc. v. United States Food and Drug Administration

2012 U.S. Dist. LEXIS 39457; 42 ELR 20073 (S.D.N.Y. 2012)

T.H. Katz, United States
Magistrate Judge

Background

I. Overview

For over thirty years, the FDA has taken the position that the widespread use of certain antibiotics in livestock for purposes other than disease treatment poses a threat to human health. In 1977, the FDA issued notices announcing its intent to withdraw approval of the use of certain antibiotics in livestock for the purposes of growth promotion and feed efficiency, which the agency had found had not been proven to be safe. The FDA issued the notices pursuant to 21 U.S.C. § 360b(e)(1), which states that

> [t]he Secretary shall, after due notice and opportunity for hearing to the applicant, issue an order withdrawing approval of an application … with respect to any new animal drug if the Secretary finds … (B) that new evidence not contained in such application or not available to the Secretary until after such application was approved, or tests by new methods, or tests by methods not deemed reasonably applicable when such application was approved, evaluated together with the evidence available to the Secretary when the application was approved, shows that such drug is not shown to be safe for use under the conditions of use upon the basis of which the application was approved.…

21 U.S.C. § 360b(e)(1) (B). Although the notices were properly promulgated and over twenty drug sponsors requested hearings on the matter, the FDA never held hearings or took any further action on the proposed withdrawals.

In the intervening years, the scientific evidence of the risks to human health from the widespread use of antibiotics in livestock has grown, and there is no evidence that the FDA has changed its position that such uses are not shown to be safe. In May 2011, after the FDA failed to respond to two Citizen Petitions urging the agency to follow through with the 1977 notices, Plaintiffs filed this action seeking a court order compelling the FDA to complete the withdrawal proceedings for antibiotics included in the 1977 notices. In December 2011, the FDA withdrew the original notices on the grounds that they were outdated, and it now argues that Plaintiffs' claim is moot.

II. Use of Antibiotics in Food-Producing Animals

Antibiotics, also known as antimicrobials, are drugs used to treat infections caused by bacteria. Although

antibiotics have saved countless lives, the improper use and overuse of antibiotics has led to a phenomenon known as antibiotic resistance. Specifically, the misuse of antibiotics creates selective evolutionary pressure that enables antibiotic resistant bacteria to increase in numbers more rapidly than antibiotic susceptible bacteria, increasing the opportunity for individuals to become infected by resistant bacteria. People who contract antibiotic-resistant bacterial infections are more likely to have longer hospital stays, may be treated with less effective and more toxic drugs, and may be more likely to die as a result of the infection. The FDA considers antibiotic resistance "a mounting public health problem of global significance." …

In the 1950s, the FDA approved the use of antibiotics to stimulate growth and improve feed efficiency in food-producing animals, such as cattle, swine, and chickens. Antibiotics used for growth promotion are typically administered through animal feed or water on a herd- or flock-wide basis. The approved doses of antibiotics for growth promotion are typically lower than the approved doses for disease treatment. The administration of "medically important" [The term "medically important antibiotics" refers to antibiotic drugs that are important for therapeutic use in humans.] antibiotics to entire herds or flocks of food-producing animals, at "subtherapeutic" levels, [The term "subtherapeutic" was commonly used in the 1960s and 1970s to refer to any use of antibiotics for purposes other than disease treatment and prevention, including growth promotion and feed efficiency in animals.…] poses a qualitatively higher risk to public health than the administration of such drugs to individual animals or targeted groups of animals to prevent or treat specific diseases.… Research has shown that the use of antibiotics in livestock leads to the development of antibiotic-resistant bacteria that can be—and has been—transferred from animals to humans through direct contact, environmental exposure, and the consumption and handling of contaminated meat and poultry products. Consequently, the FDA has concluded that "the overall weight of evidence available to date supports the conclusion that using medically important antimicrobial drugs for production purposes [in livestock] is not in the interest of protecting and promoting the public health." …

III. Penicillin and Tetracyclines

The present action pertains to the use of three different antibiotics in animal feed: penicillin and two forms of tetracycline—chlortetracycline and oxytetracycline

(Continued)

("tetracyclines"). Pursuant to the FDCA, any "new animal drug" that is introduced into interstate commerce must be the subject of an FDA approved new animal drug application ("NADA") or, with respect to generic drugs, an abbreviated NADA ("ANADA"). See 21 U.S.C. § 360b(b)-(c). Drug companies that submit NADAs/ANADAs are typically referred to as "applicants" or "sponsors." The FDA lawfully issued NADAs and ANADAs for penicillin and tetracyclines in the mid-1950s. Since that time, penicillin has been used to promote growth in chickens, turkeys, and swine, and tetracyclines have been used to promote growth in chickens, turkey, swine, cattle, and sheep.

In the mid-1960s, the FDA became concerned that the long-term use of antibiotics, including penicillin and tetracyclines, in food-producing animals might pose threats to human and animal health. As a result, in 1970, the agency convened a task force to study the risks associated with the use of antibiotics in animal feed. The task force was composed of scientists from the FDA, the National Institutes of Health, the U.S. Department of Agriculture, the Center for Disease Control, as well as representatives from universities and industry. In 1972, the task force published its findings, concluding that: (1) the use of antibiotics in animal feed, especially at doses lower than those necessary to prevent or treat disease, favors the development of antibiotic-resistant bacteria; (2) animals receiving antibiotics in their feed may serve as a reservoir of antibiotic pathogens, which can produce human infections; (3) the prevalence of bacteria carrying transferrable resistant genes for multiple antibiotics had increased in animals, and the increase was related to the use of antibiotics; (4) antibiotic-resistant bacteria had been found on meat and meat products; and (5) the prevalence of antibiotic resistant bacteria in humans had increased.... The task force made several recommendations, including that (1) antibiotics used in human medicine be prohibited from use in animal feed unless they met safety criteria established by the FDA, and (2) several specific drugs, including penicillin and tetracyclines, be reserved for therapeutic use unless they met safety criteria for non-therapeutic use....

In response to the findings of the task force, the FDA, in 1973, issued a regulation providing that the agency would propose to withdraw approval of all subtherapeutic uses of antibiotics in animal feed unless drug sponsors and other interested parties submitted data within the next two years "which resolve[d] conclusively the issues concerning [the drugs'] safety to man and animals ... under specific criteria" established by the FDA.... One of the most important of the human

and animal health safety criteria that the FDA established for drug safety evaluations under the regulation involved the transfer of antibiotic resistant bacteria from animals to humans. The FDA regulation required that "[a]n antibacterial drug fed at subtherapeutic levels to animals must be shown not to promote increased resistance to antibacterials used in human medicine." ... The other health safety criteria involved showing that use of antibiotics would not increase salmonella in animals, would not increase the pathogenicity of bacteria, and would not increase residues in food ingested by man, which may cause "increased numbers of pathogenic bacteria or an increase in the resistance of pathogens to antibacterial agents used in human medicine." ...

Over the next two years, the Bureau of Veterinary Medicine ("BVM"), a subdivision of the FDA, reviewed the data submitted by drug sponsors to support the subtherapeutic use of antibiotics. By April 20, 1975, all data concerning the safety and efficacy criteria for antibiotic drugs had been received.... The NAFDC sub-committee issued a report and recommendations on the subtherapeutic use of penicillin in animal feed, which the NAFDC adopted in 1977.... The NAFDC "recommended that FDA immediately withdraw approval for the subtherapeutic uses of penicillin, i.e., growth promotion/feed efficiency, and disease control." ... Similarly, the NAFDC sub-committee made certain recommendations regarding the use of tetracyclines in animal feed. Specifically, for tetracyclines, the sub-committee recommended that the FDA "(1) discontinue their use for growth promotion and/or feed efficiency in all animal species for which effective substitutes are available, (2) permit their use for disease control where effective alternate drugs are unavailable ..., and (3) control the distribution of the tetracyclines through ... a veterinarian's order to restrict their use." ... The NAFDC rejected the first two recommendations, but adopted the third recommendation.

* * *

IV. The 1977 NOOHs

After carefully considering the recommendations of the NAFDC and the NAFDC sub-committee, the Director of the BVM issued notices of an opportunity for hearing ("NOOHs") on proposals to withdraw approval of all subtherapeutic uses of penicillin in animal feed, ... and, with limited exceptions, all subtherapeutic uses of oxytetracycline and chlortetracycline in animal feed.... In the Penicillin Notice, the Director reported that "[n]one of the specified human and animal health safety criteria [for the subtherapeutic use of antibiotics

(Continued)

in animal feed] have been satisfied...." ... With respect to the transfer of antibiotic-resistant bacteria, the Director surveyed the available data and found that (1) the pool of bacteria carrying transferrable resistance genes was increasing; (2) the increase was due in part to the subtherapeutic use of penicillin in animal feed; and (3) antibiotic-resistant bacteria were transferred from animals to humans as a result of direct human-animal contact, the consumption of contaminated food, and the widespread presence of resistant bacteria in the environment.... Studies submitted by penicillin applicants and sponsors had failed to rebut [these] findings.... Based on this evidence, the Director of the BVM proposed to withdraw approval of all NADAs/ANADAs for the use of penicillin in animal feed on the grounds "that the[se] drug products are not shown to be safe...." ... The Director further cautioned that "[t]he evidence, in fact, indicates that such penicillin use may be unsafe...." ...

Similarly, the Director of the BVM announced health and safety concerns regarding the subtherapeutic use of tetracyclines in animal feed. The Director explained that "[e]vidence demonstrates that the use of subtherapeutic levels of the tetracyclines ... in animal feed contributes to the increase in antibiotic resistant *E. Coli* and in the subsequent transfer of this resistance to *Salmonella*. Further, some strains of *E. Coli* and *Salmonella* infect both man and animals.... Thus, the potential for harm exists...." ... The Director also noted that, in response to the 1972 FDA regulation announcing the health safety criteria for use of antibiotics in animal feed, the studies submitted by the holders of tetracyclines NADAs/ANADAs "were inconclusive because the studies were inappropriate." ... The Director concluded that he "is unaware of evidence that satisfies the requirements for demonstrating the safety of extensive use of subtherapeutic tetracycline-containing premixes...." ... Based on this evidence, the Director proposed to withdraw approval of certain NADAs/ANADAs for the subtherapeutic use of tetracyclines "on the grounds that they have not been show[n] to be safe...." ...

In response to the 1977 NOOHs, approximately twenty drug firms, agricultural organizations, and individuals requested hearings.... On November 9, 1978, the Commissioner of the FDA granted the requests for hearings, stating that "there w[ould] be a formal evidentiary public hearing on [the proposed withdrawals]." ... The Commissioner stated that a date for the hearing would be set "as soon as practicable." ... According to the statutory and regulatory scheme, at the hearing, the drug sponsors would have the burden of proving that the drugs were in fact safe....

V. The FDA's Actions Following the Issuance of the 1977 NOOHs

The Commissioner never set a date for the hearings on the BVM's proposal to withdraw approval of the use of penicillin and tetracyclines in animal feed. In the late 1970s and early 1980s, Congressional committees issued three reports that contained statements that the FDA interpreted as requests to postpone the withdrawal hearings pending further research.... Importantly, none of these recommendations was adopted by the full House or Senate, and none was passed as law.

Regardless of the legal effect of these Congressional statements, the FDA never held hearings on the proposed withdrawals, and instead engaged in further research on the risks associated with the subtherapeutic use of antibiotics in food-producing animals.

* * *

... The Commissioner explained that the 1977 NOOHs "represent[ed] the Director's formal position that use of the drugs is not shown to be safe" and that the Commissioner "concur[red]" with the decision of the Director.... In 2003, the FDA published a proposed rule that referenced the risks to human health from the subtherapeutic use of antibiotics in animal feed.... The FDA "(1) [c]oncluded that the risks were neither proved nor disproved, (2) did not deny there was some degree of risk, and (3) did not conclude that the continued subtherapeutic use of penicillin and tetracyclines in animal feed is safe." ... In 2004, the BVM, now known as the Center of Veterinary Medicine ("CVM"), sent letters to several manufacturers of approved animal feed products containing penicillin and tetracyclines, explaining that "[t]he administrative record does not contain sufficient information to alleviate the CVM's concerns about the use of [these] product[s] and [their] possible role in the emergence and dissemination of antimicrobial resistance." ... The FDA invited manufacturers to meet with the agency to discuss the agency's findings....

On June 28, 2010, the FDA released a non-binding Draft Guidance entitled The Judicious Use of Medically Important Antimicrobial Drugs in Food-Producing Animals ("2010 Draft Guidance").... In the Draft Guidance, the FDA reviewed recent scientific studies on the risks posed by the subtherapeutic use of antibiotics in animal feed, including a 1997 World Health Organization expert committee report that "recommended that the use of antimicrobial drugs for growth promotion in animals be terminated if these drugs are also prescribed for use as anti-infective agents in human medicine or if they are known to induce cross-resistance to antimicrobials used for human medical therapy." ... After

(Continued)

reviewing the scientific evidence, the FDA concluded that "the overall weight of evidence available to date supports the conclusion that using medically important antimicrobial drugs ... is not in the interest of protecting and promoting the public health." ... The FDA announced two non-mandatory principles to guide the use of antibiotics in animal feed: (1) "[t]he use of medically important antimicrobial drugs in food-producing animals should be limited to those uses that are considered necessary for assuring animal health[;]" and (2) "[t]he use of medically important antimicrobial drugs in food-producing animals should be limited to those uses that include veterinary oversight or consultation." ...

On December 16, 2011, nearly twenty-five years after their initial publication and during the pendency of this action, the FDA rescinded the 1977 NOOHs.... The FDA explained that it was rescinding the NOOHs because the "FDA is engaging in other ongoing regulatory strategies developed since the publication of the 1977 NOOHs" and that if the FDA were to move forward with the NOOHs it would need to "update the NOOHs to reflect current data, information, and policies" and "prioritize any withdrawal proceedings." ... The FDA noted that "although [it] is withdrawing the 1977 NOOHs, FDA remains concerned about the issue of antimicrobial resistance." ... The FDA explained that the withdrawal of the NOOHs "should not be interpreted as a sign that FDA no longer has safety concerns or that FDA will not consider re-proposing withdrawal proceedings in the future, if necessary." ...

VI. The Present Action

Plaintiffs filed the present action on May 25, 2011, alleging that the FDA's failure to withdraw approval of the subtherapeutic use of penicillin and tetracyclines pursuant to the 1977 NOOHs constituted an agency action unlawfully withheld or unreasonably delayed in violation of the ... FDCA [Federal Food Drug and Cosmetic Act].... Plaintiffs seek a Court order compelling the FDA to withdraw approval for the subtherapeutic use of penicillin and tetracyclines in animal feed, unless, after a hearing, the drug uses at issue are determined to be safe.... Plaintiffs further request that the Court set a deadline by which the FDA must hold hearings and issue a final decision on the withdrawals.... Plaintiffs maintain that under the FDCA, 21 U.S.C. § 360b(e)(1), once the FDA found that the subtherapeutic use of penicillin and tetracyclines in animal feed was not shown to be safe to humans, the agency was statutorily obligated to withdraw approval of those uses, unless the drug sponsors demonstrated the safety of the drugs. Defendants

contend that withdrawal was not legally required, and, in any event, the issue is now moot because the 1977 NOOHs have been withdrawn. Plaintiffs reply that the recent withdrawal of the NOOHs was in response to this litigation and has no bearing on the FDA's obligation to act.

Discussion

I. Legal Standard

A. Summary Judgment

A motion for summary judgment may not be granted unless the Court determines that there is no genuine issue of material fact to be tried, and that the facts as to which there is no such issue warrant judgment for the moving party as a matter of law.... The burden of demonstrating the absence of any genuine dispute as to a material fact rests upon the party seeking summary judgment, ... but once a properly supported motion for summary judgment has been made, the burden shifts to the nonmoving party to make a sufficient showing to establish the essential elements of that party's case on which it bears the burden of proof at trial.... Where, as here, a court considers cross-motions for summary judgment, the court applies the same legal principles and "must evaluate each party's motion on its own merits, taking care in each instance to draw all reasonable inferences against the party whose motion is under consideration." ...

Here, the parties do not dispute the essential facts. The only issue before the Court is the legal conclusion resulting from those facts.

II. Application

* * *

B. Legally Required Action

* * *

1. Statutory Interpretation

a. Legal Standard

In interpreting a statute, a court "must give effect to the unambiguously expressed intent of Congress." ... "To ascertain Congress's intent, [a court] begin[s] with the statutory text because if its language is unambiguous, no further inquiry is necessary." ... Statutory interpretation must take into account the "structure and grammar" of the provision.... "If the statutory language is ambiguous, however, [a court] will 'resort first to cannons [sic] of statutory construction, and, if the [statutory] meaning remains ambiguous, to legislative history'" to determine the intent of Congress.... If the

(Continued)

intent of Congress remains unclear, a court will defer to an agency's interpretation of the statute, so long as it is "reasonable." ...

b. Application: Findings Pursuant to § 360b(e)(1)

Here, the statute unambiguously commands the Secretary to withdraw approval of any new animal drug that he finds is not shown to be safe, provided that the sponsor of the animal drug has notice and an opportunity for a hearing. See 21 U.S.C. § 360b(e)(1). The statute does not explicitly state the order in which this process must occur. Defendants maintain that the Secretary can only issue a finding after a hearing, whereas Plaintiffs claim the Secretary makes a finding first, which then triggers the Secretary's obligation to provide notice and an opportunity for a hearing.

The Court finds that Plaintiff's interpretation provides a common sense reading of the statute based on its text and grammatical structure. The statute states that "[t]he Secretary shall, after due notice and opportunity for hearing to the applicant, issue an order withdrawing approval of a[] [NADA/ANADA] ... if the Secretary finds ... [that a drug is not shown to be safe]...." The "after due notice and opportunity for hearing" clause is setoff by commas and immediately precedes the words "issue an order withdrawing approval," indicating that the "notice" clause modifies the "issue an order" clause and not the findings clause. See United States v. Liranzo, 729 F. Supp. 1012, 1014 (S.D.N.Y. 1990) (interpreting a modifier to apply to the verb closest to it) (citing W. Strunk, Jr. & E.B. White, *The Elements of Style* 30 (3d ed. 1979)). Accordingly, the statute only requires the Secretary to give notice and provide an opportunity for a hearing before issuing an order of withdrawal and *not* before making findings. Under this reading, if the Secretary finds that an animal drug has not been shown to be safe, he is statutorily required to withdraw approval of that drug, provided that the drug sponsor has notice and an opportunity for a hearing.... If, after a hearing, the drug sponsor has not met his burden of proving the drug to be safe, the Secretary must issue a withdrawal order....

The text and grammar of other provisions within § 360b support this interpretation. For example, § 360b (d)(1) explicitly requires the Secretary to provide notice and an opportunity for a hearing before making findings regarding the approval or refusal of a NADA.... Section 360b(d) (1) reads: "If the Secretary finds, after due notice to the applicant ... and giving him an opportunity for a hearing, ... he shall issue an order refusing to approve the application." By placing the "notice" clause immediately after the phrase "[i]f the Secretary finds," § 360b(d)(1) clearly requires notice and an opportunity for a hearing prior to the issuance of findings by the Secretary. The fact that Congress used such language in § 360b(d)(1) and used different language in § 360b(e)(1) supports the Court's conclusion that notice and an opportunity for a hearing are not required before the Secretary makes findings under the latter provision....

Moreover, § 360b(e)(1) includes a specific note about the notice and hearing requirement when the Secretary finds that a new animal drug poses an imminent risk to humans or animals, which indicates that findings are made before a hearing. Specifically, the statute states that

> [i]f the Secretary (or in his absence the officer acting as Secretary) finds that there is an imminent hazard to the health of man or of the animals for which such drug is intended, he may suspend the approval of such application immediately, and give the applicant prompt notice of his action and afford the applicant the opportunity for an expedited hearing under this subsection....

21 U.S.C. § 360b(e)(1). This provision anticipates the Secretary making findings in advance of a hearing; otherwise, the clause requiring the Secretary to provide notice and an opportunity for an expedited hearing would be redundant and nonsensical. The Court cannot adopt such an interpretation.... Although the Secretary's authority to make a finding of imminent hazard "shall not be delegated," the fact that this finding is made before notice or an opportunity for a hearing are provided supports that findings pursuant to § 360b(e)(1) are made prior to a hearing. This interpretation is further buttressed by the statutory purposes underlying the FDA, the agency tasked with implementing § 360b(e)(1) and the FDCA. Specifically, the FDA "shall ... promote the public health by promptly and efficiently reviewing clinical research and taking appropriate action on the marketing of regulated products in a timely manner; [and] with respect to such products, protect the public health by ensuring that ... human and veterinary drugs are safe and effective[.]" 21 U.S.C. § 393(b)(1)-(2). According to its statutory mandate, the FDA is responsible for continuously monitoring regulated drugs and reviewing new studies of their effectiveness and safety. Given this regulatory structure, it seems clear that Congress intended the FDA to monitor approved animal drugs and issue findings when new evidence indicates that a drug is no longer shown to be safe, triggering the withdrawal process.

(Continued)

Accordingly, based on the text and grammar of § 360b(e)(1), as well as the structure of § 360b as a whole and the overriding purpose of the FDA, the Court finds that the plain meaning of § 360b(e)(1) requires the Secretary to issue notice and an opportunity for a hearing whenever he finds that a new animal drug is not shown to be safe. If the drug sponsor does not meet his burden of demonstrating that the drug is safe at the hearing, the Secretary must issue an order withdrawing approval of the drug.

This interpretation is consistent with how courts have interpreted 21 U.S.C. § 355(e), the human drug parallel to § 360b(e)....

Were the Court to conclude that § 360b(e)(1) is ambiguous as to when the Secretary makes findings, the Court would defer to the agency's reasonable interpretation of the statute. See *Chevron*, 467 U.S. at 842-43, 104 S. Ct. at 2781-82. Although in this litigation the FDA has maintained that findings pursuant to § 360b(e)(1) can only be made after a hearing, the agency's implementing regulation, 21 C.F.R. § 514.115, interprets § 360b(e)(1) to require the agency to make findings prior to a hearing. The regulation reads: "The Commissioner shall notify in writing the person holding [a NADA/ANADA] and afford an opportunity for a hearing on a proposal to withdraw approval of such [NADA/ANADA] if he finds ... that such drug is not shown to be safe...." ... The plain language of the regulation requires the Commissioner to provide notice and an opportunity for a hearing to a drug sponsor *after* making a finding that a drug has not been shown to be safe. It logically follows that findings are made by the Commissioner before a hearing. [fn. omitted] Accordingly, if the Court were to defer to the agency's interpretation of the statute it would reach the same conclusion: findings pursuant to § 360b(e)(1) are made before a hearing and trigger the withdrawal process.

Defendants, nevertheless, argue that the regulation does not mean what it says.

* * *

... [T]he Court cannot defer to Defendants' interpretation that the regulation creates a different set of findings based on a different standard.

* * *

Conclusion

For the foregoing reasons, Plaintiffs' Motion for Summary Judgment on their first claim for relief is granted and Defendants' Motion for Summary Judgment is denied. Defendants are hereby ordered to initiate withdrawal proceedings for the relevant NADAs/ANADAs. Specifically, the Commissioner of the FDA or the Director of the CVM must re-issue a notice of the proposed withdrawals (which may be updated) and provide an opportunity for a hearing to the relevant drug sponsors; if drug sponsors timely request hearings and raise a genuine and substantial issue of fact, the FDA must hold a public evidentiary hearing. If, at the hearing, the drug sponsors fail to show that the use of the drugs is safe, the Commissioner must issue a withdrawal order.

Questions for discussion:

1. Describe how the steps of statutory interpretation were applied in this case.

2. Are you surprised by the facts of this case? Why aren't the facts of this case (and other cases like it) more widely known to the public? Where is a court opinion, such as this one, found? Do you think that judicial opinions should be more widely available to the general public, rather than simply existing in specialized public records (e.g., court reporters, legal databases)? Why or why not?

3. Why were the plaintiffs entitled to summary judgment? What is the rule for summary judgment?

Maxims are rules of logic applied by courts when interpreting statutory language. For example, the U.S. Supreme Court, in *Babbitt v. Sweet Home*,[4] focused on the meaning of the word "harm" in the Endangered Species Act. In an earlier decision, the court of appeals had limited the meaning of the word *harm* by applying a statutory maxim: *noscitur et sociis*, which literally means "words are known by the company they keep." The Supreme Court rejected that interpretation, and upheld the Fish and Wildlife Service's definition of the word *harm* to include significant habitat modification that actually harms an endangered species. The Supreme Court relied on the "plain meaning" of the word *harm* and legislative history of the act in upholding the agency's interpretation in the *Babbitt* case.

maxim: A general statement of a rule of law.

Students are often surprised and dismayed to learn that the resolution of a legal dispute may depend on what a particular word in a statute means. However, when we think about the very great importance of a statute—a bona fide source of primary law—then we can recognize that each word in the statute matters a great deal. Because language is inherently ambiguous, lawmakers must be very careful when crafting the wording of statutes, as well as when creating the legislative records to support the passage of the statute, in the event that such a record is needed during future litigation on the point.

Another very important consideration is the jurisdiction of state courts. **Jurisdiction** is the power or authority of a court to hear a case. There are two kinds of jurisdiction:

1. **Subject matter jurisdiction**, which gives the court has the power to hear that type of case, and
2. either **personal (in personam) jurisdiction** over the defendant or **in rem jurisdiction** over property located within the state.

A court must have both kinds of jurisdiction to issue a valid decision binding the parties in a case.

Generally speaking, state courts have very broad subject matter jurisdiction. Keep in mind that all matters not constitutionally assigned to the federal government are reserved to the states to govern. This places entire swaths of legal terrain squarely within state court jurisdiction. Contracts, real and personal property law, torts, family law, probate, wills, and much of the criminal law, among others, are all matters of state law. Many other areas of law draw upon complementary or parallel state and federal laws: employment law, environmental law, constitutional laws, and many areas of regulatory law (e.g., insurance, banking, securities, etc.). However, some areas of law are strictly federal, such as bankruptcy law, copyright law, trademark and patents law, admiralty, and antitrust law, for example.

Having *personal jurisdiction* means that the court has authority over the particular defendant based on the residence, location, or activities of the defendant. State courts have jurisdiction over citizens of the state, those who are residents of the state, and those who are physically present in the state when process is served on them. In addition, a defendant can consent to personal jurisdiction. States have also enacted **long-arm statutes** that give courts in personam jurisdiction over out-of-state defendants in some situations. Under typical long-arm statutes, acts that may establish personal jurisdiction over nonresidents include:

▨ Doing business in the state

▨ Causing personal injury or property damage by an act or omission within the state

▨ Causing personal injury or property damage in the state by an occurrence, act, or omission done outside the state if the defendant regularly does or solicits business or derives substantial benefit from goods, materials, or services used, consumed, or rendered in the state

▨ Supplying or contracting to supply services in the state

▨ Owning, using, or possessing real property or a real property interest within the state

▨ Contracting to ensure or act as a surety on behalf of any person, property, or risk within the state

jurisdiction: The power or authority of a court to hear a case.

subject matter jurisdiction: Jurisdictional authority over a particular kind of case.

personal (in personam) jurisdiction: Jurisdiction over a person based on residency, consent, presence in a location, or a long-arm statute.

in rem jurisdiction: Jurisdiction over property located within a state.

long-arm statute: Law that gives the courts in a state personal jurisdiction over out-of-state defendants for certain acts done within the state.

■ Living in a marital relationship within the state notwithstanding subsequent departure from the state, as to all obligations for alimony, custody, child support, or property settlement, if the other party continues to reside in the state

Because it has *in rem jurisdiction*, a state court may determine rights in property located within the state, even though the persons affected by that determination are outside the state's *in personam* jurisdiction. An example of exercise of in rem jurisdiction is a quiet title case in which a state court determines title to land located within the state.

To exercise jurisdiction over a defendant, a state must also meet minimum constitutional **due process** requirements. The courts have held that the requirements of due process mandate that there be sufficient "minimum contacts" between the state and the defendant before the state can exercise jurisdiction over the defendant. In addition, the state must properly serve notice of the action to the defendant.

Venue, which differs from jurisdiction, refers to the particular physical location where a court exercises its jurisdiction. Under typical state venue statutes, a plaintiff can bring an action in either the county where a majority of the defendants reside or in the county where the cause of action arose.

Federal Court System

In the federal court system, the **U.S. district court** is the lowest court level. This is where trials begin and where all evidence is presented and heard. Unlike state court systems, all federal courts are courts of limited jurisdiction. This means that a plaintiff must establish a basis for federal court jurisdiction before the court can hear the case.

The two bases of federal court jurisdiction are federal question jurisdiction and diversity jurisdiction. As the name suggests, **federal question jurisdiction** arises when a plaintiff alleges that the case involves a substantial federal issue. Examples include questions arising under federal constitutional law, federal statutory law, treaties, federal regulatory law, or any federal law whatsoever. Federal question jurisdiction is exclusive only in those cases where the law so provides or requires. In many instances, federal and state courts have **concurrent jurisdiction** over a case or controversy. This means that a plaintiff may bring a case involving a federal question in either state or federal court, provided the plaintiff can obtain personal jurisdiction over the defendant. In some situations, a defendant may be entitled to remove a case from state to federal district court. **Removal** of a case simply means transferring it from a state court to a federal court or vice versa.

The second important basis of federal jurisdiction is **diversity jurisdiction**, which arises when a suit is between citizens of different states and the amount in controversy exceeds $75,000. Both of these elements are required for federal diversity jurisdiction to exist. For purposes of diversity, a corporation is considered a citizen of both its state of incorporation and the state of its principal place of business.

A U.S. district court functions like a state trial court, finding the facts and applying the law to those facts to reach a decision. As noted earlier, there are other specialized courts within the federal court system. These include the claims court, Court of International Trade, and tax courts. Generally, decisions by these courts are appealed to a federal appeals court.

due process: Constitutional requirement for notice and opportunity to be heard, to ensure fairness in legal proceedings.

venue: The particular physical location where a court exercises its jurisdiction.

U.S. district court: The trial court in the federal court system.

federal question jurisdiction: Federal court jurisdiction based on a substantial issue arising under the laws of the United States.

concurrent jurisdiction: A situation in which two or more legal authorities may exercise jurisdiction.

removal: Transfer of a case from a state to federal court, or vice versa.

diversity jurisdiction: Federal court jurisdiction that arises when citizens of different states present a substantial issue arising under the laws of the United States.

The federal circuit courts of appeals and the U.S. Supreme Court are the federal appellate courts. The function of the federal appeals courts is similar to that of a state appeals court. These courts do not conduct trials, but rather hear appeals from decisions of the federal district courts. There are 13 federal courts of appeals: 12 circuit courts representing 11 districts and the District of Columbia, plus a federal circuit court of appeals, which hears a variety of specialized appeals.

The U.S. Supreme Court functions primarily as an appeals court, although there are rare circumstances in which it may function as a trial court. For example, the Supreme Court has original and exclusive jurisdiction over suits between two or more states. It also has original, but not exclusive, jurisdiction over some other specific cases, including controversies between the United States (federal government) and a state.

Most of the appeals heard by the U.S. Supreme Court come from federal courts of appeals and state supreme courts. The vast majority of these cases reach the U.S. Supreme Court on **writ of certiorari**, which is a discretionary writ. The Court is not required to take a case submitted via writ, but decides whether or not it wants to hear the case. The U.S. Supreme Court's certiorari jurisdiction for appeals from a state supreme court (or the highest court in the state) arises when a person challenges the validity of a treaty or federal statute; alleges that a state statute conflicts with federal law; or claims a title, right, privilege, or immunity under federal law.

▤ ▤ ▤ REVIEW AND STUDY QUESTIONS

1. What is the difference between reviewing a case for errors of law, which is the focus of appellate courts, and hearing a case to determine questions of fact, which is the focus of a trial court?

2. U.S. district courts and state trial courts are both trial courts that may empanel juries. Why is it important for persons who are called for jury duty to report and make themselves available for jury duty? What other legal duties do we have in this society? What is the difference between a legal duty and a legal right?

▤ Steps in Civil Litigation: Civil Procedure

The Federal Rules of Civil Procedure establish the basic steps for civil lawsuits in federal court. Most states have adopted similar rules that are applicable in their respective courts. For example, the Oregon Rules of Civil Procedure are applicable in the Oregon state courts. A basic understanding of the steps in a civil lawsuit is important for all citizens; in addition, familiarity with the terms and concepts found in rules governing the conduct of civil cases will help in understanding the cases and decisions. The focus here is on civil litigation, rather than criminal litigation, because civil suits are far more common than criminal cases. Review Figure 2.3 for a flowchart concerning the most important stages and motions in a civil litigation.

The Adversary System

Both civil and criminal proceedings in the United States are based on the **adversary system**. This means each of the parties aggressively presents the facts in a

writ of certiorari: Discretionary writ by which the U.S. Supreme Court chooses which decisions from the state and federal appeals courts to review.

adversary system: Legal framework in which opposing parties present evidence in the way that is most favorable to their respective sides.

■ **FIGURE 2.3** *Schematic of Civil Litigation Progress through the Adversary System*

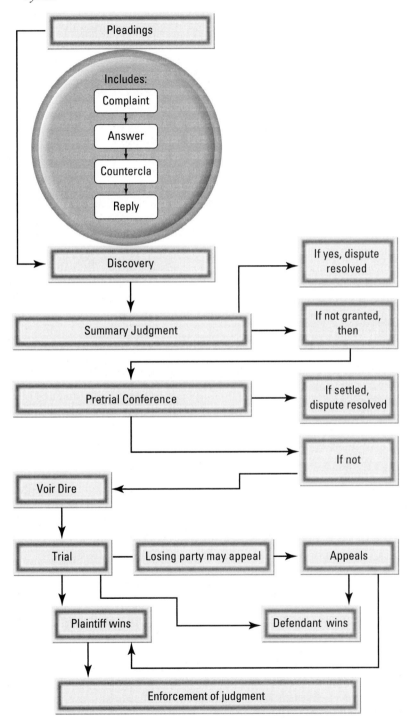

way that is most favorable to its side. Recall that the parties in a civil suit are plaintiff and defendant, whereas in a criminal suit, they are prosecutor and defendant. The judge, or in some cases a jury, acts as a neutral arbiter to resolve the dispute. A basic assumption of the adversary system is that by permitting the parties to present their best cases and to criticize the other's arguments, the facts will emerge.

Critics of the adversary system fear that too often an aggressive advocate can obscure rather than clarify the truth. Other problems are the substantial time and expense associated with pursuing litigation. Some cases take years to reach trial, and even longer to be resolved on appeal. Litigation can also be expensive: even if a person wins and is awarded court costs, that person may not be able to recover (be reimbursed for) expert witness fees and attorney's fees.

One way to avoid these serious problems is to avoid litigation altogether. Claims can be negotiated and settled early and out of court. Additionally, time and cost considerations also encourage **alternative dispute resolution (ADR)**, such as mediation and arbitration. ADR may be used instead of litigation if both parties agree to submit to that process.

Of course, there are time requirements to be met. The applicable statute of limitations requires claims to be brought within a statutorily specified length of time. If claims are not brought within the specified time, then they may not be brought at all (they are *barred*). Statutes of limitations vary based upon the type of claim and the jurisdiction where the claim will be brought. Additionally, the legal doctrine of **res judicata** prevents relitigation of an issue that has already been judicially decided.

Commencing the Action: The Complaint and Summons

A plaintiff begins a lawsuit by filing a **complaint**, which is a statement (1) alleging facts sufficient to show that the court has jurisdiction in the case, (2) summarizing the nature of the dispute and stating facts showing that the plaintiff is entitled to legal relief from the defendant, and (3) stating the remedy sought. The complaint is first filed with the court clerk, who assigns it a file and file number. A copy of the complaint, along with the summons, is then served on the defendant.

The **summons** notifies the defendant that it is being sued and must be served properly for the defendant to be legally notified of the suit. Statutes, court rules, and constitutional due process requirements set the standards for proper service. Personal delivery, service by registered mail, and in some instances service by publication, can constitute proper service under state and federal law.

The Answer and Counterclaim

Once the defendant is served with a copy of the complaint, the defendant files an **answer**, in which it admits or denies the allegation. The defendant may also file preliminary objections or motions; for example, a motion to dismiss for lack of jurisdiction or a motion to dismiss for failure to state a claim. The latter type of motion alleges that the complaint does not state a legal cause of action against the defendant, even if all of the allegations in the complaint are true. As part of the answer or separately, the defendant may file a **counterclaim** in which the defendant makes a complaint against the plaintiff.

In a civil lawsuit against a private party, the plaintiff has the burden of proving, by a **preponderance of the evidence**, facts sufficient to establish its case. The

alternative dispute resolution (ADR): Any form of dispute resolution that is not litigation.

res judicata: A doctrine that prevents matters that have already been decided from being relitigated.

complaint: A pleading that initiates a lawsuit.

summons: A notice of lawsuit served on the defendant.

answer: A pleading submitted by a defendant to admit and/or deny the allegations of a complaint.

counterclaim: A pleading through which the defendant files its own complaint against the plaintiff.

preponderance of the evidence: The burden of proof standard in a civil case.

preponderance of the evidence test is often described as a test requiring the plaintiff to prove that the facts are "more likely than not" true. The preponderance of the evidence test is much easier for the civil plaintiff to meet than the test of **beyond a reasonable doubt**, which is the standard in criminal cases. The defendant in a civil suit has the burden of proving any affirmative defenses by a preponderance of the evidence, and must prove the allegations of any counterclaim against the plaintiff by the same standard.

If the plaintiff is served with a counterclaim, the plaintiff must file a **reply**. A reply is like an answer, but it is filed by the plaintiff in response to a counterclaim, rather than by the defendant in response to a complaint.

The complaint, answer, counterclaim, and reply are the initial **pleadings**. The function of the pleadings is to define and limit the questions before the court in the case. Not only do the pleadings limit the scope of the dispute, they also provide notice of the other party's claims. This is important because the rules establish broad **discovery** mechanisms, through which parties can acquire information relevant to the dispute.

The modern rules of civil procedure substantially reduce the possibility of a surprise at trial because they make it difficult, and in many cases improper, to withhold relevant information from the other party in the litigation. Modern procedural rules are intended to ensure that both parties are as fully informed as possible, so that both can present their clearest and best cases. The **pretrial conference** between attorneys and judge helps the parties to clarify the issues in controversy and often leads to settlement negotiations.

Discovery mechanisms help the parties gather information relevant to the issues in dispute. Major discovery techniques include:

1. **Interrogatories**, which are written questions relevant to the dispute that the opposing party must answer.
2. **Motions for the production of real evidence**, under which a party is allowed to inspect and copy documents, books, papers, accounts, and other evidence in the possession of the opposition.
3. Requests for admissions, which are written requests that the other party admit the truth of a particular statement or confirm the genuineness of a document.
4. **Depositions**, which are statements made out of court but under oath; these statements are used to preserve and "freeze" the testimony of a witness.

These discovery methods are all tools that attorneys use to search for the facts of the case. However, they may also be used as weapons in attempts to delay the proceedings and increase the cost of litigation. When parties complain about being "papered to the wall" in civil litigation, they are referring to the voluminous discovery requests that are frequently generated by parties in major lawsuits.

After discovery, the trial itself will begin, unless a settlement is reached before trial.

Trial

If the judge denies preliminary motions and the case is not settled, the parties proceed to **trial**.

The trial process begins with selection of a jury through **voir dire**. During this procedure, the attorneys for both the plaintiff and the defendant ask potential jurors questions in an attempt to weed out unfavorably biased persons and empanel persons who might view their respective clients' arguments favorably.

beyond a reasonable doubt: The burden of proof standard in a criminal case.

reply: A plaintiff's answer to a counterclaim.

pleadings: The documents that define and limit the questions to be brought before the court; in civil litigation, the complaint, answer, counterclaim, and reply.

discovery: The process through which litigants acquire information relevant to the dispute.

pretrial conference: A meeting between the opposing attorneys and the judge before the trial.

interrogatories: Written questions relevant to the dispute served on the opposing party; one of several discovery mechanisms.

motion for the production of real evidence: Application to the court to allow one party to gain access to documents and other evidence in the possession of the opposing party; one of several discovery mechanisms.

deposition: An out-of-court statement made under oath; one of several discovery mechanisms.

trial: An examination of the issues between two parties by a court with appropriate jurisdiction.

voir dire: A jury selection process in which attorneys question potential jurors.

After the jury is empaneled, both sides put on their cases. As noted earlier, the plaintiff in a civil case must show by a preponderance of the evidence that the plaintiff's case has been established. If the plaintiff succeeds in doing so, the plaintiff wins. Again, keep in mind that our system is an adversary system. This means that there will be a winner and a loser as a result of the trial.

If the jury finds for the plaintiff, it may award damages, including **compensatory damages** to compensate the plaintiff for injuries incurred, and in some cases **punitive damages**, which are designed to punish intentional malicious wrongdoing by the defendant. Other remedies, such as an injunction ordering a party to refrain from or perform some activity, may be ordered by the judge in some cases.

■ ■ ■ REVIEW AND STUDY QUESTIONS

1. What is the difference between a summary judgment and a judgment rendered at the end of a trial?

2. Why might a losing party choose to appeal a trial court's decision? What are the consequences of an appeal to each of the parties?

3. Identify a case in which both a criminal and a civil case were brought based on the same incident. What are the benefits and drawbacks of a criminal and a civil case being brought against the same defendant for the same action? Why doesn't this violate the prohibition against double jeopardy?

Appeals

The appeals court is not a trial court, so it does not retry the facts. Rather, the appellate court considers whether errors of law at the trial-court level require it to reverse the trial court's decision, remand (return) the case to the trial court for further proceedings, or affirm the trial court's decision. Questions of law raised on appeal may concern such things as a trial judge's decision to grant or deny a motion to dismiss or motion for summary judgment, trial rulings on jurisdiction and service of process, or rulings on the admissibility of evidence during trial.

■ Conclusion

This chapter has provided general information about the American legal system, including identification of several sources of law, the structure of our court systems, important differences between civil and criminal cases, and steps in civil litigation. In addition, in studying this chapter you have examined general sources of law and the function of courts in interpreting and applying statutory law. Throughout the remaining chapters of this text you will read portions of court decisions addressing various issues of environmental law. Keep in mind that these cases not only contribute to a growing body of environmental law, they also represent the resolution of real disputes between real parties. As you read these cases, ask yourself these questions:

1. What were the facts in this case?

2. Who sued whom and why?

3. How did this case reach this court?

4. What were the legal issues before the court?

5. How did the court resolve those legal issues and what were its reasons for its decision in the case?

compensatory damages: Monetary awards that compensate the plaintiff for injuries.

punitive damages: Monetary awards designed to punish intentional malicious wrongdoing by defendant.

Study Help: Dissecting a Case Opinion

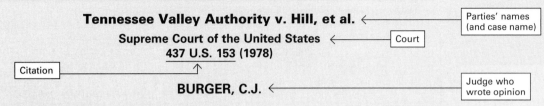

Tennessee Valley Authority v. Hill, et al. ← Parties' names (and case name)

Supreme Court of the United States ← Court
437 U.S. 153 (1978)

Citation

BURGER, C.J. ← Judge who wrote opinion

We begin with the premise that operation of the Tellico Dam will either eradicate the known population of snail darters or destroy their critical habitat. Petitioner does not now seriously dispute this fact.

Starting from the above premise, two questions are presented: (a) would TVA be in violation of the Act if it completed and operated the Tellico Dam as planned? (b) if TVA's actions would offend the Act, is an injunction the appropriate remedy for the violation? For the reasons stated hereinafter, we hold that both questions must be answered in the affirmative. ← Holding

It may seem curious to some that the survival of a relatively small number of three-inch fish among all the countless millions of species extant would require the permanent halting of a virtually completed dam for which Congress has expended more than $100 million.

> One would be hard pressed to find a statutory provision whose terms were any plainer than those in § 7 of the Endangered Species Act. Its very words affirmatively command all federal agencies "to *insure* that actions *authorized, funded*, or *carried out* by them do not *jeopardize* the continued existence" of an endangered species or *"result* in the destruction or modification of habitat of such species...." 16 U. S. C. § 1536 (1976 ed.). (Emphasis added.) This language admits of no exception. Nonetheless, petitioner urges, as do the dissenters, that the Act cannot reasonably be interpreted as applying to a federal project which was well under way when Congress passed the Endangered Species Act of 1973. To sustain that position, however, we would be forced to ignore the ordinary meaning of plain language. It has not been shown, for example, how TVA can close the gates of the Tellico Dam without "carrying out" an action that has been "authorized" and "funded" by a federal agency. Nor can we understand how such action will *"insure"* that the snail darter's habitat is not disrupted. Accepting the Secretary's determinations, as we must, it is clear that TVA's proposed operation of the dam will have precisely the opposite effect, namely the *eradication* of an endangered species.
>
> Concededly, this view of the Act will produce results requiring the sacrifice of the anticipated benefits of the project and of many millions of dollars in public funds. But examination of the language, history, and structure of the legislation under review here indicates beyond doubt that Congress intended endangered species to be afforded the highest of priorities.
>
> "The dominant theme pervading all Congressional discussion of the proposed [Endangered Species Act of 1973] was the overriding need *to devote whatever effort and resources were necessary* to avoid further diminution of national and worldwide wildlife resources. Much of the testimony at the hearings and much debate was devoted to the biological problem of extinction. Senators and Congressmen uniformly deplored the irreplaceable loss to aesthetics, science, ecology, and the national heritage should more species disappear." Coggins, Conserving Wildlife Resources: An Overview of the Endangered Species Act of 1973, 51 N. D. L. Rev. 315, 321 (1975). (Emphasis added.)

Statutory interpretation Two steps are plainly indicated: Plain meaning Legislative intent

The legislative proceedings in 1973 are, in fact, replete with expressions of concern over the risk that might lie in the loss of *any* endangered species. Typifying these sentiments is

(Continued)

the Report of the House Committee on Merchant Marine and Fisheries on H. R. 37, a bill which contained the essential features of the subsequently enacted Act of 1973; in explaining the need for the legislation, the Report stated:

> As we homogenize the habitats in which these plants and animals evolved, and as we increase the pressure for products that they are in a position to supply (usually unwillingly) we threaten their—and our own—genetic heritage." *The value of this genetic heritage is, quite literally, incalculable.*
>
> … From the most narrow possible point of view, *it is in the best interests of mankind to minimize the losses of genetic variations.* The reason is simple: they are potential resources. They are keys to puzzles which we cannot solve, and may provide answers to questions which we have not yet learned to ask. To take a homely, but apt, example: one of the critical chemicals in the regulation of ovulations in humans was found in a common plant. Once discovered, and analyzed, humans could duplicate it synthetically, but had it never existed—or had it been driven out of existence before we knew its potentialities—we would never have tried to synthesize it in the first place.
>
> Who knows, or can say, what potential cures for cancer or other scourges, present or future, may lie locked up in the structures of plants which may yet be undiscovered, much less analyzed? … Sheer self-interest impels us to be cautious. *The institutionalization of that caution* lies at the heart of H. R. 37...."
> H. R. Rep. No. 93-412, pp. 4-5 (1973). (Emphasis added.)

As the examples cited here demonstrate, Congress was concerned about the *unknown* uses that endangered species might have and about the *unforeseeable* place such creatures may have in the chain of life on this planet.

In shaping legislation to deal with the problem thus presented, Congress started from the finding that "[the] two major causes of extinction are hunting and destruction of natural habitat." S. Rep. No. 93-307, p. 2 (1973). Of these twin threats, Congress was informed that the greatest was destruction of natural habitats.

It is not for us to speculate, much less act, on whether Congress would have altered its stance had the specific events of this case been anticipated. In any event, we discern no hint in the deliberations of Congress relating to the 1973 Act that would compel a different result than we reach here.

One might dispute the applicability of these examples to the Tellico Dam by saying that in this case the burden on the public through the loss of millions of unrecoverable dollars would greatly outweigh the loss of the snail darter.[33] But neither the Endangered Species Act nor Art. III of the Constitution provides federal courts with authority to make such fine utilitarian calculations. On the contrary, the plain language of the Act, buttressed by its legislative history, shows clearly that Congress viewed the value of endangered species as "incalculable." Quite obviously, it would be difficult for a court to balance the loss of a sum certain—even $ 100 million—against a congressionally declared "incalculable" value, even assuming we had the power to engage in such a weighing process, which we emphatically do not.

Having determined that there is an irreconcilable conflict between operation of the Tellico Dam and the explicit provisions of § 7 of the Endangered Species Act, we must now consider what remedy, if any, is appropriate. It is correct, of course, that a federal judge sitting as a chancellor is not mechanically obligated to grant an injunction for every violation of law. [But] [o]nce Congress, exercising its delegated powers, has decided the order of priorities in a given area, it is for the Executive to administer the laws and for the courts to enforce them when enforcement is sought.

Here we are urged to view the Endangered Species Act "reasonably," and hence shape a remedy "that accords with some modicum of common sense and the public weal." *Post*, at 196. But is that our function? We have no expert knowledge on the subject of endangered species, much less do we have a mandate from the people to strike a

(Continued)

Common theme in environmental law (see Chapter 1): Risk

Common theme in environmental law (see Chapter 1): Precautionary principle

Checks and balances between judicial and legislative branches of government

Common theme in environmental law (see Chapter 1): Economic interest versus preservation

Statutory interpretation: Legislative intent & history

Separation of powers between judicial and legislative branches balance of equities on the side of the Tellico Dam. Congress has spoken in the plainest of words, making it abundantly clear that the balance has been struck in favor of affording endangered species the highest of priorities, thereby adopting a policy which it described as "institutionalized caution."

Our individual appraisal of the wisdom or unwisdom of a particular course consciously selected by the Congress is to be put aside in the process of interpreting a statute. Once the meaning of an enactment is discerned and its constitutionality determined, the judicial process comes to an end. We do not sit as a committee of review, nor are we vested with the power of veto. The lines ascribed to Sir Thomas More by Robert Bolt are not without relevance here:

> "The law, Roper, the law. I know what's legal, not what's right. And I'll stick to what's legal.... I'm *not* God. The currents and eddies [***147] of right and wrong, which you find such plain-sailing, I can't navigate, I'm no voyager. But in the thickets of the law, oh there I'm a forester.... What would you do? Cut a great road through the law to get after the Devil? ... And when the last law was down, and the Devil turned round on you—where would you hide, Roper, the laws all being flat? ... This country's planted thick with laws from coast to coast—Man's laws, not God's—and if you cut them down ... d'you really think you could stand upright in the winds that would blow then? ... Yes, I'd give the Devil benefit of law, for my own safety's sake." R. Bolt, A Man for All Seasons, Act I, p. 147 (Three Plays, Heinemann ed. 1967).

The function of the judiciary and the limits of the court

We agree with the Court of Appeals that in our constitutional system the commitment to the separation of powers is too fundamental for us to pre-empt congressional action by judicially decreeing what accords with "common sense and the public weal." Our Constitution vests such responsibilities in the political branches.

Affirmed. Powell, Blackmun, JJ., and Rehnquist, C.J., dissent. ← *Names of judges who dissented from the majority opinion*

Decision of the court

Questions for Reflection

1. Find a case opinion in this textbook. Identify the following parts of that opinion:

   a. The name of the judge who decided the case
   b. The case name
   c. The parties' names
   d. The citation
   e. The holding
   f. The court's reasoning
   g. The decision of the court

2. Why is it important to understand the court's reasoning in an opinion? Describe how that reasoning may be used by litigants who are involved in future environmental disputes relating to the same issue. Why might a party argue to "distinguish the facts" of a case, if the prior precedent was not favorable to the desired outcome of a current dispute? What effect would "distinguishing the facts" of a future case have in deciding that future case?

Introduction to the Law of Property

Here's a good idea!

There are many vocabulary words in this chapter. Make flashcards for each section. This will help you learn the words, which will make studying the concepts easier.

Learning Objectives

After reading this chapter, you will have an understanding of property law, including legal concepts related to the different types of property, acquisition of property, scope of interests, kinds of ownership, and easements and covenants. After reading this chapter, you should be able to answer the following questions:

1. What are the different categories of property?
2. How is property acquired?
3. What interests in property may be the subject of ownership interests?
4. What kinds of ownership interests exist in property?
5. How does property law relate to environmental law?

▪ Introduction

The sources of environmental law are varied and complex. One area of law with particular significance for the student of environmental law is the law of property. American property law consists essentially of common law, or judge-made rules, which reflect earlier English common law rules. Some of the traditional rules governing ownership of real and personal property have been superseded by environmental statutes or regulations. For example, a prior owner of contaminated property may be liable for the costs of cleaning up the property under federal Superfund law even though that owner long ago sold the property to another person.

Why should a student of environmental law be familiar with the common law rules governing property? First, many environmental cases discuss legal theories of property rights and describe ownership interests in property. A knowledge of some principles of property law and legal terms commonly used to describe ownership interests will help in understanding those cases. Keep in mind, however, that property rights are generally defined by state law, and specific property laws may differ from state to state.

Second, much of the debate over **regulatory takings** focuses on the problem of defining the appropriate scope of an owner's rights to develop and use its property for private gain. Under current law, statutes or regulations that restrict an owner's property rights may constitute a **taking** of property, and thus require the government to pay compensation. Environmental laws and regulations that limit an owner's rights to use its property (for example, by prohibiting development of property containing "wetlands") may be subject to legal attack on this basis.

Third, principles of American property law reflect underlying assumptions about the appropriate relationship between humans and the environment—the land, water, and other natural resources that support human life. These assumptions are increasingly being questioned, but they are still firmly embedded in our legal system. The way in which the law classifies ownership rights in these natural resources reflects society's understandings of those relationships. Furthermore, the law relating to property ownership rights reflects concepts of the value of land, air, and water.

At a fundamental philosophical level, property law consists of a system of legal rules defining the way we think about land and natural resources. As you learn about the principles of property law discussed in this chapter, consider the following questions:

- On what ethical, political, and social policy assumptions are these laws are based?
- Who makes the rules governing the rights of property owners?
- What are the environmental and economic implications of these rules?
- Should the greater society ever have a voice in how or to what extent a private landowner may use its land?
- Should private ownership in land override society's interests in protecting endangered species or maintaining a natural aesthetic?

■ The Nature of Property

Property is a legally protected expectation of deriving certain advantages from a thing.[1] There are various categories of property. For example, **personal property** is property that is not real property; it may be tangible or intangible. A **chattel** is personal property that is tangible and moveable. **Intellectual property** is a kind of intangible personal property consisting of creations of the mind. **Real property** is land or immovable objects attached to the land, such as a house or a forest. Real property is defined by the relationship between a person and a piece of the earth or something affixed to the earth. A person who is the owner of land has legal rights in relation to this real property, such as the right to possess it, to use it, to exclude others from it, and to transfer it by gift or sale to another.

A property owner may transfer all or some ownership rights to another. For example, the owner might agree to transfer possession to another for a specified period of time. The contract formalizing this agreement is called a **lease**. In this arrangement, the *tenant* (lessee) buys possession of the property but does not acquire other ownership rights, such as the right to sell the property to another person.

Property rights are protected by the law, but they are not unlimited. Property as a legal concept reflects society's notions of the appropriate relationship between human

regulatory taking: A regulatory restriction on an owner's use of property to the extent that all or nearly all economic value in the property is lost.

taking: A government seizure of privately owned property for public use.

property: A legally protected expectation of being able to draw an advantage from a thing.

personal property: Tangible or intangible property that is not attached to land.

chattel: An item of tangible, moveable personal property.

intellectual property: Intangible personal property consisting of creations of the mind.

real property: Land or immovable objects attached to the land.

lease: A contract for possession of property for a specified period of time.

---

[1] Jeremy Bentham/Etienne Dumont, Theory of Legislation (1840).

beings and things of the world. The debate about a private property owner's responsibility for protecting common environmental resources like wetlands or endangered species is essentially a debate about the nature of private ownership rights and duties.

Property is also an economic concept. As many economists and legal scholars have noted, private ownership of property creates incentives to use resources associated with that property efficiently. Imagine, for example, that you own a house. You have a financial interest in maintaining that house, so you might fix the sink if it leaks, or you might correct faulty wiring once you notice it. Now, imagine that the house was not owned by you, but rather was owned by every adult in the city in which you live. Anyone could stay in the house and use it as they wished. There would be little incentive for you—or for anyone else—to repair that house, because no person would derive economic benefit from doing so. Property ownership includes the right to exclude others. Rights that are exclusive and transferable are required for the efficient use of resources.[2]

How we define people's relationships with things raises a number of social policy questions. For example, one of the attributes of private ownership is the right to exclude others. Consider the social policies involved in laws regarding private property versus public property. **Private property** is owned by an individual, group of individuals, or a business. **Public property** is owned by a government entity. In the case of private property, the owner traditionally has the right to use the property as it chooses, as long as that use does not constitute a **nuisance**. However, today, many federal and state laws limit a private owner's use of land. For example, a private owner of a wetland may not destroy the habitat of an endangered species. Additionally, local zoning law restricts how one may use one's land, such as constraining an owner's right to build certain kinds of structures on the property or use the property in certain ways.

private property: Property owned by an individual, group of individuals, or a business.

▩ ▩ ▩ REVIEW AND STUDY QUESTIONS

1. How do you feel about the government imposing restrictions on the use of private property? What benefits and drawbacks result from such restrictions?

2. Identify examples of real property and personal property. Why might these distinctions be important?

3. How have concepts of property differed in different places or different times?

4. Consider Justice Scalia's comments about the nature of property in *Lucas v. South Carolina Coastal Council*, 505 U.S. 1003, 112 S. Ct. 2886 (1992): "[F]or what is the land but the profits thereof[?]" (quoting 1 E. Coke, INSTITUTES, ch. 1, § 1 (1st American ed., 1812)). What does Justice Scalia mean by this statement? Do you agree with this assessment? What are the political and environmental implications of this statement?

public property: Property owned by a government entity.

nuisance: An unreasonable interference with the use and enjoyment of another's property.

▩ Legal Categories of Property

Traditional property law characterizes property in different ways, and these classifications are not mutually exclusive. As noted earlier, one important distinction is between real or personal property. The earth's crust and things firmly attached to it (e.g., a house, trees) are considered real property. Personal property includes all

---

[2] Richard Posner, Economic Analysis of Law (Little, Brown & Co., 1973). Posner also argues that universality is an additional criterion of an efficient system of property rights.

other objects and rights capable of being owned. The distinction between real property and personal property may be important for a number of legal reasons. For example, the rules governing transfer of real property differ from those governing the sale of personal property.

It is not always simple to make the distinction between real and personal property. Property may be characterized differently depending on when that determination is made. For example, trees growing naturally on land will be treated as part of the real property; once they are harvested, however, they become movable personal property. A stone in the ground is real property until it is quarried; it then becomes personal property. If it is used to build a house, it becomes part of the structure and thus part of the real property.

A **fixture** is personal property that has been attached to or integrated into real property in such a manner that it is treated as real property. Whether a particular item will be treated as real property depends on the intention of the parties, the degree of attachment of the item, and the degree to which the property has been adapted to the use of the item. The distinction may be important in determining whether an item passes with the real property upon sale. Whether an item is a fixture may also determine liability under some environmental laws.

fixture: Personal property that has been attached to or integrated into real property in such a manner that it is treated as real property.

■ Historical Viewpoint

In *U.S. EPA v. New Orleans Public Service, Inc.*, 826 F.2d 361 (5th Cir. 1987), the question of whether an electric transformer containing PCBs became a fixture when installed in a brewery ultimately determined whether an electric utility was liable for improper storage, marking, and disposal of PCBs under the Toxic Substances Control Act (TSCA). In that case, an administrative law judge held that New Orleans Public Service, Inc. (NOPSI) violated the TSCA by improperly disposing of electrical transformers containing PCBs. The utility appealed.

NOPSI had purchased three 5,000-pound, 1250-KVA transformers containing PCBs from General Electric. The transformers were installed in the Jackson Brewery Building in New Orleans in 1963 and were an integral element in the electrical service furnished by NOPSI to the building. The transformers were bolted to the floor and connected with wires to the electrical system of the building.

In 1978, the building was sold to the American Can Company. The transformers were in place and were used until electrical service was discontinued in 1979. In 1982, the building was sold to an investment company for conversion into a retail mall for shops and restaurants. The sale included all attachments, improvements, and components of the building. While a demolishing company was removing the transformers from the building, oil containing PCBs was spilled.

In rejecting NOPSI's argument that it was not responsible for proper disposal of the transformers, because they were component parts of the brewery building, the administrative law judge said that the parties themselves regarded the transformers as movables. On appeal, the court disagreed, holding that the transformers were component parts of the building rather than movables. The court determined that NOPSI was not liable for PCB contamination because under state statute, the transformers were "electrical installations."

If you purchased a building in which a potentially hazardous item had been stored, what would you want to do to minimize your liability exposure?

Property also may be classified as tangible or intangible. **Tangible property** has a physical existence, like land or goods. As noted earlier, tangible personal property is also referred to as *chattels*. **Intangible property** has no physical existence. An **easement**, which is a right to use another's property for a certain purpose, or a contract right are considered intangible.

Also as noted earlier, property may be classified as public or private. This classification is based on the concept of ownership: Property owned by an individual, group of individuals, or a business is considered private property, whereas public

tangible property: Property that has a physical existence.

intangible property: Property that does not have a physical existence.

easement: A right to use another's property.

property is owned by a government entity (e.g., a municipal city hall building or park). This distinction may be important in environmental law because public property may be exempt from some environmental laws and regulations.

The distinction may also protect common environmental resources such as natural waterways. The **public trust doctrine** recognizes that the public has a permanent interest in things that are common property, such as air, running water, the sea, and the shores of the sea. This doctrine, which was first recognized in ancient Rome, found its way into the customs and laws of most European nations, including England, during the Middle Ages. Under the doctrine, public trust resources are preserved for the benefit of all. Title to such property vests in the state and is not subject to private ownership.

A notable decision recognizing the public trust doctrine in the United States is the 1882 Supreme Court decision in *Illinois Central Railroad Co. v. Illinois*, 146 U.S. 387 (1892). In that case, the Illinois legislature had granted more than 1,000 acres of submerged land—essentially the entire commercial waterfront of Chicago—to the Illinois Central Railroad. Four years later, the legislature repealed the grant and declared the original grant invalid. The railroad appealed.

The U.S. Supreme Court upheld the state's claim that it could revoke the grant. According to the Court, the state held title to the submerged land "in trust for the people of the state, that they may enjoy the navigation of the waters, carry on commerce over them, and have liberty of fishing therein, freed from the obstruction or interference of private parties."[3] Following the public trust doctrine, the Court held that the state legislature lacked the power to convey a natural resource like Chicago's harbor into private hands. It said that "[t]he state can no more abdicate its trust over property in which the whole people are interested … than it can abdicate its police powers in the administration of government…."[4]

The public trust doctrine is traditionally associated with the beds of navigable waters, and it is most commonly applied in cases where states have attempted to transfer land underneath navigable waters within their borders to private parties. Such grants are unenforceable under the public trust doctrine. A private owner cannot acquire rights to public property under other common law legal doctrines, either.

Furthermore, the traditional definition of land underlying navigable waters has been challenged by some environmentalists as too narrow. Changing theories of navigability have been used to expand the doctrine to include waters that otherwise might not have met the traditional definition of public trust property. There is also pressure by some environmentalists to expand the public trust doctrine beyond submerged lands to include resources essential to maintain the general health of natural systems. Thus, this legal doctrine may be important in future environmental cases.

In *Lake Michigan Federation v. U.S. Army Corps of Engineers*, the Court struck down a proposal to landfill a portion of Lake Michigan in order to expand the campus of Loyola College in Chicago. The Court struck down the project under the public trust doctrine despite express approval by the state legislature. The Court said:

> Three basic principles can be distilled from this body of public trust case law. First, courts should be critical of attempts by the state to surrender valuable public resources to a private entity…. Second, the public trust is violated when the primary purpose of a legislative grant is to benefit a private interest…. Finally, any

public trust doctrine: A legal recognition that the public has permanent interests in certain things as common property.

[3] 146 U.S. at 452.
[4] *Id.* at 453.

attempt by the state to relinquish its power over a public resource should be invalidated under the doctrine.[5]

▪▪▪ REVIEW AND STUDY QUESTIONS

1. How do trees become personal property? When are corn, wheat, or other crops real property? What are some practical reasons why these legal distinctions matter?

2. How do trees become real property? When are corn, wheat, or other crops personal property?

▪ Acquisition of Property

Discovery, Conquest, Capture, Creation, Finding

The law recognizes different ways in which a person may acquire a property right in real property or in personal property. These include acquisition by discovery, conquest, capture, bequest, creation, purchase, gift, and adverse possession. **Discovery** is the finding of unknown or uncharted territory. **Conquest** refers to taking possession of enemy territory through force. Those who settled North America in the past four or so centuries found natural resources that seemed unlimited. As the federal government acquired vast areas of new lands, it adopted the policy of transferring those lands to private owners for private development and settlement. The Homestead Act of 1862 permitted settlers to enter and gain title to public land by building a home on it and cultivating the land. Many landowners today trace their ownership rights to such early land grants.

Under traditional common law, a person can obtain property rights over wild animals by capture. This **rule of capture**, which evolved in a time when people relied on hunting and fishing for their livelihood, recognizes that a person who captures a wild animal owns that animal. The capture rule reflects the legal assumption that animals, like other natural resources, should be utilized to improve human welfare. The rule of capture also applies in various ways, according to state law, to oil and minerals.

Although society continues to recognize the right of humans to acquire animals as property, there are some in America today who challenge traditional attitudes about the appropriate relationship between animals and humans. The use of animals in experiments, for purposes of fashion, or for entertainment is considered inhumane, and many people have demanded that the law be changed or applied to stop those who continue to use animals for such purposes. Many believe that animals should possess legal rights suitable to their own needs and capabilities, such as the right to be free from cruel and inhumane treatment, the right to move their bodies, or the right to live their lives free from interference by humans.

The following case is an example of application of the traditional rule of capture. As you read this case, consider how the court's interpretation of the law of capture reflected America's economic, social, and ecological values in 1881.

discovery: The finding of unknown or previously uncharted territory.

conquest: Taking possession of enemy territory through force.

rule of capture: Doctrine holding that the first person to capture a natural resource owns that natural resource; also applies in various ways, according to state law, to oil and minerals.

---

[5] 742 F. Supp. 441, 21 ELR 20111, 20112 (N. D. Ill. 1990).

Ghen v. Rich

8 F. 159 (D. Mass. 1881)

United States District Court, District of Massachusetts

Nelson, J.

[The plaintiff brought this case to recover the value of a fin-back whale. The whale was killed by the plaintiff, but was found 3 days later on the beach 17 miles from the spot where it was killed, and was sold by the finder to the respondent.]

* * *

... The facts, as they appeared at the hearing, are as follows:

In the early spring months the easterly part of Massachusetts Bay is frequented by the species of whale known as the fin-back whale. Fishermen from Province-town pursue them in open boats from the shore, and shoot them with bomb-lances fired from guns made expressly for the purpose. When killed they sink at once to the bottom, but in the course of from one to three days they rise and float on the surface. Some of them are picked up by vessels and towed into Provincetown. Some float ashore at high water and are left stranded on the beach as the tide recedes. Others float out to sea and are never recovered. The person who happens to find them on the beach usually sends word to Province-town, and the owner comes to the spot and removes the blubber. The finder usually receives a small salvage for his services. ... Each boat's crew engaged in the business has its peculiar mark or device on its lances, and in this way it is known by whom a whale is killed.

The usage on Cape Cod, for many years, has been that the person who kills a whale in the manner and under the circumstances described, owns it, and this right has never been disputed until this case....

It was decided by Judge Sprague, in *Taber v. Jenny*, 1 Sprague, 315, that when a whale has been killed, and is anchored and left with marks of appropriation, it is the property of the captors; and if it is afterwards found, still anchored, by another ship, there is no usage or princi-ple of law by which the property of the original captors is diverted, even though the whale may have dragged from its anchorage....

* * *

I see no reason why the usage proved in this case is not as reasonable as that sustained in the cases cited. Its application must necessarily be extremely limited, and can affect but a few persons. It has been recognized and acquiesced in for many years. It requires in the first taker the only act of appropriation that is possible in the nature of the case. Unless it is sustained, this branch of industry must necessarily cease, for no person would engage in it if the fruits of his labor could be appropri-ated by any chance finder. It gives reasonable salvage for securing or reporting the property. That the rule works well in practice is shown by the extent of the industry which has grown up under it, and the general acquiescence of a whole community interested to dis-pute it.... If the fisherman does all that it is possible to do to make the animal his own, that would seem to be sufficient....

[Judgment entered for plaintiff.]

Questions and Comments for Discussion

1. To what extent do the business interests of whalers affect the court's decision in this case? How would you balance the economic and environmental con-siderations raised by this case if it were to be decided today?

2. The law of capture, which provides that the taking of a wild animal vests property rights in the hunts-man, was recognized in early Roman law. Although American law still follows the English common law rule of capture, the government today regulates the taking of some wild animals and protects endangered species. Do you think that such regu-lation adequately reflects a changing view of ani-mal life or humans' relationship to animals?

3. To what extent should the federal government be able to regulate the taking of wild animals by an owner on the owner's private property? What are the ecological and ethical implications of your answer?

4. Whales occupy a unique political status. Since the signing of the International Convention for the Regulation of Whaling in 1946, whales have come under the global jurisdiction of the International Whaling Commission (IWC), a body established by this treaty to conserve and manage them. In the spring of 1993, both houses of Congress unani-mously adopted a resolution calling for the United States to oppose "any resumption of commercial whaling." However, with a permit, whales can still be captured for use in a display as "entertainment" animals, and they can still be used in scientific research. Discuss whether whales enjoy adequate legal protection.

Creation is the production of personal property. If an individual produces personal property, he or she gains title in it, unless that individual is producing it as an employee. In that situation, the employer owns it. This is true for intellectual property as well.

A person who finds personal property may or may not gain ownership of that property. A finder of personal property may claim ownership of the **found property** if it is **abandoned property**, that is, property in which the owners intended to relinquish ownership. However, **lost** or **mislaid property** still belongs to the owner who lost or mislaid it, and once the rightful owner demands its return, the finder must return it. A final categorization of found personal property is a **treasure trove**, a collection or cache of money or precious metals. As with all found personal property, state law determines whether the finder may keep a treasure trove.

Acquisition of Title to Real Property

Title is a legal term describing ownership rights in real property. As noted previously, private individuals first acquired title to land in the United States from the government or, in some cases, from another country that held the land prior to acquisition by the United States. In 1823, the U.S. Supreme Court, in *Johnson v. M'Intosh*, 21 U.S. 543, refused to recognize that the plaintiffs' purchase of land from the Piankeshaw Indians conveyed title to the property. The Court said:

> However extravagant the pretension of converting the discovery of an inhabited country into conquest may appear; if the principle has been asserted in the first instance, and afterwards sustained; if a country has been acquired and held under it; if the property of the great mass of the community originates in it, it becomes the law of the land, and cannot be questioned. So, too, with respect to the concomitant principle, that the Indian inhabitants are to be considered merely as occupants, to be protected, indeed, while in peace, in the possession of their lands, but to be deemed incapable of transferring the absolute title to others. However this restriction may be opposed to natural right, and to the usages of civilized nations, yet, if it be indispensable to that system under which the country has been settled, and be adapted to the actual condition of the two people, it may, perhaps, be supported by reason, and certainly cannot be rejected by Courts of justice.

Acquisition of Title by Purchase, Gift, or Bequest

Most people who own real property have acquired title by **purchase** of the property from its prior owner. The formal requirements for transfer and recording of ownership of real estate vary by state. Real property may also be acquired by **gift**, when the owner delivers a deed to the recipient without accepting consideration for it. The owner of real property may also dispose of it through a will by **bequest**, although this type of disposition is subject to some restrictions. To be effective, the will containing the bequest must be drawn and executed in accordance with the statutory requirements of the state in which the real property is located.

How real property has been acquired may be important for purposes of establishing liability under some environmental laws. For example, the Comprehensive Environmental Response, Compensation, and Liability Act (CERCLA) imposes liability for cleanup costs of contaminated property on the owner of the property, but in some circumstances exempts those who have acquired the property through gift or will. In CERCLA, the term "contractual relationship," for purposes of establishing

creation: The production of personal property.

found property: Personal property that has been abandoned, lost, or mislaid by the original owner and is discovered by another.

abandoned property: Property over which the original owner has completely relinquished ownership and control.

lost property: Property involuntarily left where the owner is unlikely to find it.

mislaid property: Property left in a place that the owner then forgot or could not find again, although the owner intended to be able to retrieve the item.

treasure trove: A collection or cache of money or refined precious metals.

title: The right of ownership in property.

purchase: An exchange of something of value for title to property.

gift: A free, voluntary transfer of an ownership interest between a donor who intends to deliver the ownership interest and actually delivers the interest, and a recipient who accepts the interest.

bequest: A transfer of personal property by will; an inheritance or legacy.

liability of property owners under the Act, excludes those who acquired property by inheritance, so long as the property on which the hazardous substance is located was acquired after the disposal or placement of the substance.[6] Additionally, title may be an issue in cases where property is taken for public use, and the owner is entitled to just compensation.

Acquisition of Real Property by Adverse Possession

State laws also recognize that a person may acquire property by **adverse possession**. Under this doctrine, if a person occupies land and maintains open and continuous possession for a statutorily specified period of time, the person may acquire title to the land in a **quiet title action**. While the exact requirements differ from state to state, the essential elements of adverse possession are: (1) that the possession is hostile and under some claim or right (that is, against the owner's interest), (2) it is actual possession, (3) it is open and notorious (obvious to others), (4) it is continuous, and (5) it is exclusive. In some states, the person claiming title by adverse possession must also have paid the taxes on the property. Likewise, the length of time for which an adverse possessor must hold the property differs from state to state.

■ Evolution of Law: Adverse Possession in Colorado?

In 2007, a Boulder, Colorado, adverse possession case attracted nationwide attention due to perceived unfairness of the Colorado law. The adverse possession was successful for the trespassers—a retired judge and his attorney wife—much to the chagrin of the property's former owners, a couple who had hoped to build a house on it in retirement. The former owners lost about a third of the lot in the adverse possession case. Read an article about it at http://articles.latimes.com/2007/dec/03/nation/na-land3.

The Colorado legislature changed the adverse possession law in response to this case, requiring the adverse possessors to believe in good faith that the property is theirs, and requiring that such belief must be reasonable.

Questions for reflection:

1. What are the limits of real property ownership?

2. Do you agree with adverse possession laws? Why or why not?

3. Is it reasonable that an owner should have to "use" land, or risk losing it through adverse possession?

4. What can people who wish to preserve land in its natural state do to prevent an adverse possession action?

5. In the 2007 Colorado case, the adverse possessors were following the law. In fact, they won their case and successfully claimed title to one-third of their neighbor's lot. Why do you think that public opinion expressed outrage rather than support?

---

adverse possession: Means of acquiring title to land by openly taking possession of and using another's property for a certain period of time.

quiet title action: A proceeding to establish title to land by bringing into court all who have claims to the title to the property.

Under the general common law rule, a person cannot acquire title by adverse possession to property owned by the state. Why should this be so? A number of states have changed the common law rule, either by legislation or court decisions. A few permit title to government land to be acquired by adverse possession using the same requirements as for private lands; others permit it only if the adverse possession continues for a period much longer than in the case of private lands.

---

[6] § 101(35)(A).

Under the public trust doctrine, however, such claims to title may still be subject to legal challenge.[7]

■ *Acquisition of Property by Category*

How may each type of property be acquired?

	Real Property	Personal Property
Discovery	Yes	No
Conquest	Yes	No
Capture	No	Yes
Creation	No	Yes
Found (abandoned, lost, mislaid, treasure trove)	No	Yes
Purchase	Yes	Yes
Gift	Yes	Yes
Bequest	Yes	Yes
Adverse possession	Yes	No

■ ■ ■ REVIEW AND STUDY QUESTIONS

1. Discovery and conquest have both been recognized by American courts as methods of acquiring property. The United States acquired title to lands in America from native peoples already living here, under the theory of conquest. What are the ethical and social implications of such theories of property acquisition?

2. Animals are categorized as personal property in our legal system. However, movements are afoot to change that categorization to something that better represents the fact that animals are living, intelligent beings that fundamentally differ from other chattels, such as a table. Some terms that have been suggested are "legal persons" (such as a ship or a corporation) and "living property." How would a change in legal classification affect the methods by which animals can be acquired and owned? What other changes would result from the shift in legal concept from property to something else? (Hint: Keep in mind that slaves were once understood to be personal property.)

3. Under the doctrine of adverse possession, plaintiffs have to establish that their possession of the disputed property was hostile and under claim of right, actual, open and notorious, continuous, and exclusive. What kinds of proof would plaintiffs need to establish these elements in a case like this?

4. What is the rationale for the doctrine of adverse possession? Should the law permit a person to acquire title to property under this doctrine? What implications does this doctrine have for the environment?

5. Acquisition of title by adverse possession can be traced to the Middle Ages. In a society that lacks a recording system, the doctrine permits owners to prove title through possession. Today the doctrine is applied primarily in title and boundary dispute cases where building encroachments are discovered. How might these disputes be settled without resort to the concept of adverse possession?

---

[7] *See generally* John R. Call, *Adverse Possession of Public Land: A Look at the Recommendation of the Public Land Law Review Commission*, 1971 LAW & SOC. ORD. 131; Elmer M. Million, *Adverse Possession against the United States—A Treasure for Trespassers*, 26 ARK. L. REV. 467 (1973).

■ Scope of Interests in Real Property

The owner of real estate not only owns the surface of the earth, but also has rights in the air above the surface and in the soil and minerals below the surface. While the common law rule is a simple one, a number of legal questions may arise in its application:

- What limits should be placed on ownership of air rights to accommodate air travel?
- Who owns minerals and resources, such as gas and oil, that may migrate under the earth?
- To what extent may one owner block access to the sunlight of another?
- Does an owner of property own geothermal energy beneath the property's surface?

Air Rights

Under traditional common law rules, a person owns property "to the sky," and has the right to exclude others from its airspace. Invasion of that airspace by another constitutes trespass. Thus, if a person shoots at ducks and other waterfowl flying over the plaintiff's land, and the shot falls on the plaintiff's land, there is a trespass.[8] In modern times, the courts have had to balance this common law rule against the public necessity for air travel.

In one famous case, *United States v. Causby*, 328 U.S. 256 (1946), the U.S. Supreme Court held that there was an unconstitutional taking of the plaintiffs' property when airplanes flew close enough over the chicken farm owned by the plaintiffs to barely miss the tops of trees. However, the Court acknowledged in that case that a person's air rights are not unlimited. The Court recognized a need to balance competing interests without defining the precise limits of air ownership rights beyond the immediate reaches of the enveloping atmosphere. The Supreme Court said that a "landowner owns as least as much of the space above the ground as he can occupy or use in connection with the land."[9] However, the common law rule that ownership of the land extended to the periphery of the universe has no place in the modern world, according to the Court. It said:

> While the owner does not in any physical manner occupy that stratum of airspace or make use of it in the conventional sense, he does use it in somewhat the same sense that space left between buildings for the purpose for light and air is used. The superadjacent airspace at this low altitude is so close to the land that continuous invasions of it affect the use of the surface of the land itself.[10]

Who owns outer space? Many private companies are preparing commercial ventures for outer space. To circumvent potential problems, countries like the United States and Russia have signed treaties providing that no one owns outer space. But there is no agreement as to where a country's airspace ends and outer space begins.

---

[8] *Whittaker v. Stangvick*, 100 Minn. 386, 111 N.W. 295 (1907).
[9] 328 U.S. at 264.
[10] *Id.* at 265.

■ Mars Property

Consider Mars One, which is a nonprofit company that plans to establish a permanent colony on Mars by 2023 (see the company website: http://mars-one.com/en/). If Mars One succeeds in establishing a settlement, will the company be able to claim ownership of Mars, or at least the area of the settlement, under a theory of conquest? Discovery? Creation? Adverse possession? What problem of jurisdiction arises when attempting to assert a legal claim for property on Mars? Why does this matter?

As society becomes more and more complex, and industry and technology expand, courts rely more on nuisance theories to balance the rights of defendants and plaintiffs in air rights cases. In the following case, a court was asked to determine whether an electric utility's use of its airspace for a 600-foot stack could be enjoined (that is, legally prevented) under a nuisance theory because it interfered unreasonably with the plaintiff's air rights.

General Aviation, Inc. v. Cleveland Electric Illuminating Co.
2 ERC 1328 (N.D. Ohio 1971)

Pattisti, J.

This suit has been brought to prevent interference with plaintiff's airport operations by a 600-foot stack being constructed by the defendants.

Lost Nation Airport has been maintained by the plaintiff, General Aviation, as a private airport since 1931. Seventeen years later, in 1948, the Cleveland Electric Illuminating Company (CEI) acquired land nearby, in Eastlake, Ohio, and a few years later built an electric generating plant, whose 307-foot stacks made it necessary to alter approach and landing patterns at the airport. CEI now is constructing an addition to this plant, and air pollution control standards require a 600-foot stack. Despite $72,000 being spent by the defendants for lighting, this stack will have a detrimental impact on the airport, interfering in particular with instrument landings on three of its runways.

The plaintiff, claiming that the height and location of the stack make it a nuisance, that it constitutes an extraordinary structure in the area, and further, that it violates navigable airspace assigned to General Aviation by the Federal Aviation Authority, wants CEI to provide two Localizer-Type Directional Aids (LDAs). These, plaintiff contends, would minimize, but not eliminate, the effects of the stack upon instrument approaches to runways 5 and 9.

Superficially, at least, the nuisance argument is a seductive one—but on closer examination is not really relevant to this case. Essentially the law of nuisance will apply when one landowner so uses his property that he interferes with his neighbor's right to the quiet enjoyment of his own land. Here, however, the direct effect of the stack is upon the plaintiff's flights over the defendants' land. Granted that this in turn has a substantial detrimental effect upon the operations at the airport itself, it would seem, nevertheless, that the connection is too remote to give rise to an action for nuisance.

That the stack is extraordinary in the area is, in one sense, incontrovertible; it will rise to the height, perhaps, of a fifty-story skyscraper. In essence, however, the difference between the 600-foot stack and its 307-foot predecessors will be one merely of degree. The new structure may restrict operations at the airport, as did the construction of the earlier ones, but this inconvenience must not be equated with hazard, since there has been no showing that in this case there will be increased danger resulting from the new stack. Since anyone proposing to use Lost Nation Airport will be guided by maps and charts showing the new stack, it would seem that plaintiff's specter of danger to the public at large is as intangible as the very air. Thus it is not to this alleged hazard, but rather to questions of possible interference with specific property rights enjoyed by the plaintiff that this court must address itself.

At common law the extent of a landowner's rights in his property was defined as: "Cujus est solum, ejus est usque ad coelum,"—Ownership of land extends as high as the sky. It has been only with the development of air travel in this century that the blitheness of this maxim has been questioned, and the absurdity of its full

(Continued)

implications recognized by the courts…. The question of what constitutes the "immediate reaches" of the atmosphere has been the subject of endless legal nit-picking—but perhaps the simplest formula is the one provided by the Court in *Causby*: "The landowner owns at least as much of the space above the ground as he can occupy or use in connection with the land." …

The extent of the defendants' estate in the property, then, is subject to change as dictated by circumstances. Had marshy land or building codes restricted construction to one-story structures, that height would have demarcated the height of CEI's property interest; on the other hand, construction of a skyscraper on previously vacant land may raise that frontier to the very edge of the upper atmosphere. The defendants, then (to repeat) have title not only to the surface of their property, but as much of the airspace above the surface as they [actually] use….

It is concluded, then, that the plaintiff has no rights in or to defendants' land. Like the airport-respondent in *Griggs v. Allegheny County*, 369 US. 84 (1961), the plaintiff was obligated to purchase any necessary land or to obtain easements from neighboring landowners, and as in *Griggs*, … "it did not acquire enough."

Accordingly, plaintiff General Aviation's prayer for injunction is hereby denied, and its complaint is dismissed.

Questions and Comments for Discussion

1. Traditional common law theories, such as trespass and nuisance, have prohibited air and water use by a landowner if that use unreasonably harms the interests of a neighboring property owner. However, these theories have generally been found inadequate in dealing with the massive problems of air and water pollution. As a result, Congress has enacted federal legislation to regulate discharge of pollutants into air, land, and water. These laws are examined in detail in subsequent chapters of this text. However, nuisance laws are still useful. Consider the 2013 case against Huy Fong Foods, Inc., manufacturer of srirachi sauce. The residents of Irwindale complained that Huy Fong Foods created a public nuisance, due to the smell associated with creating the sauce. A judge ordered a partial shutdown of the plant. Read the story here: http://articles.latimes.com/2013/nov/29/local/la-me-1128-sriracha-20131129

What are the benefits and drawbacks of using nuisance law to address an environmental problem? In what ways is statutory law better?

2. What alternatives might the parties have pursued to avoid the problems addressed by this case?

3. In a part of its opinion not reproduced here, the *General Aviation* court discussed the fact that the defendants could not have obtained a "prescriptive easement" (a right to use another's property acquired under a theory similar to that of adverse possession). Discuss the merits of adverse possession. Does it serve the same purpose that it might have served when no reliable system of recording existed to determine who owned property?

Like mineral rights, air rights may be sold separately from surface rights. Sale of a condominium, for example, may involve the sale of a unit of airspace described as a subdivision of air lots, or may involve a survey showing the dimensions of the unit, or may utilize a floor plan showing the location of each unit. Condominium owners establish their rights and duties in the condominium by agreement, and they should be particularly careful to address their rights if the air lots infringe on others' lots as a result of settling or natural disaster.

Mineral (Subsurface) Rights

Just as an owner owns its property "to the sky," so traditional common law provides that an owner also owns the property "to the depths." Thus, an owner may sell or lease subsurface mineral rights in its property, and may be entitled to damages if another trespasses on those rights. In one unusual case, the opening to an underground cave was located on one person's property, but the cave extended under a considerable portion of a neighboring landowner's property. The owner of the property on which the entrance was located, and who had been conducting tours of the cave for a fee, sued to claim title to the entire cave and its cavities under the theory of adverse possession. But the Indiana Supreme Court held that the plaintiff had not established the elements of adverse possession. Consequently, under common law rule, the court held that the neighboring owner could prohibit others from exploring the caverns under his property, even though the owner had no access to the cave from the surface.[11]

If an owner sells mineral rights to its property, the purchaser may use the surface to tunnel below it to mine the minerals. The provisions of the lease or mineral deed should be carefully drafted to clarify the rights and responsibilities of each of the parties. Strip-mining is of particular environmental concern because this method entails bulldozing, dynamiting, and shoveling off soil and vegetation, with serious damaging consequences. Similarly, so-called mountain top removal—blasting away the tops of mountains in order to scoop coal out—is extremely damaging to all aspects of the environment.

Both state and federal governments have passed strip-mining controls. The Mining and Minerals Policy Act of 1970, 30 U.S.C. § 21, declares that it is the policy of the United States to foster and encourage private enterprise in the development of economically stable mining and mineral industries, and the development of methods of disposal, control, and reclamation of mineral waters and mineral land so as to lessen the effects of mining on the environment. In 1977, Congress passed the Surface Mining Control and Reclamation Act (SMCRA).[12] Among other things, the SMCRA is designed to ensure that surface coal mining operations are conducted in a manner that protects the environment and the public interest through effective controls. The SMCRA imposes regulatory restrictions on strip-mining and requires that the land be restored to approximately its original state. Despite the detailed provisions of the SMCRA, some have suggested that common law remedies are more effective than public law in this area because of enforcement problems.

Another legal question regarding an owner's rights "to the depths" of its property concerns **lateral support**. The common law rule holds that someone who is excavating soil on its own property owes a duty to an adjoining property owner to exercise at least ordinary care to investigate the effects of that action. An owner has an absolute duty to support a neighbor's property in its natural state. The common law rule has been modified by statutes that apply to certain types of excavations.

Oil and natural gas tend to collect in underground reservoirs under land with different ownership. However, these resources may then migrate, making ownership difficult to determine. States that follow the **ownership in place theory** have adopted the position that a landowner owns the oil beneath its land in the same way it owns coal or other minerals.[13] Other states are **nonownership theory** states; they take the position that because oil may move when wells are drilled, the landowner does not own the oil until it has taken possession of the oil through pumping. But all oil states follow the rule of capture, which provides that a person owns all the oil and gas produced by a well on its land, even if some of those resources have migrated to that well from a neighbor's property. This rule is subject to regulation, and oil and gas leases vary considerably in their terms and conditions from state to state.

lateral support: The upholding of land by the land next to it.

ownership in place theory: Doctrine that a landowner owns the oil beneath the landowner's land.

nonownership theory: Doctrine that a landowner does not own oil until the landowner has taken possession of the oil.

---

[11] *Marengo Cave Co. v. Ross*, 212 Ind. 624, 10 N.E.2d 917 (1937).

[12] 30 U.S.C. § 1201 *et seq.* (1977).

[13] Arkansas, Kansas, Mississippi, Ohio, Pennsylvania, Texas, and West Virginia are ownership states.

Right to Light

In an earlier agrarian society in a country with vast open spaces, ownership of light rarely was a legal issue. The question of who owns the right to light has arisen more frequently in modern times, as many environmentalists and property owners promote solar energy as a solution to dwindling energy resources.

Under the common law **doctrine of ancient lights**, anyone who used the light for an uninterrupted period of 20 years was entitled to protection of that use. Historically, however, American courts rejected that rule, perhaps because of its impact on development. The case of *Fontainebleau Hotel Corp. v. Forty-Five Twenty-Five, Inc.*, arose when the Fontainebleau luxury hotel undertook construction of a 14-story addition that would block the sun for part of the day over the sunbathing areas of a neighboring hotel, the Eden Roc. Eden Roc sued to stop construction of the addition and the trial court found for Eden Roc. However, the Florida district court of appeals held that there was no legal basis for enforcing the neighboring hotel's right to light. That court said: "No American decision has been cited, and independent research has revealed none, in which it has been held that—in the absence of some contractual or statutory obligation—a landowner has a legal right to the free flow of light and air across the adjoining land of his neighbor."[14]

Parties may avoid the common law rule by contracting for the right to light, and in some states a person may acquire the right by easement or covenant. In addition, many states have enacted statutes that change the common law rule and protect the right to light under some circumstances. For example, Wyoming has adopted a statute providing that the first user of light for solar energy purposes acquires the right to continued use of the light. Other states have adopted **solar easement laws**, and still other states encourage zoning as a means to address solar access considerations. Finally, some state courts have utilized common law nuisance theory to provide protection for solar access rights. Legislation to protect solar access may avoid the time and expense associated with litigating individual cases under a nuisance theory. However, legislating such rights may deter commercial development and encourage takings (regulatory takings) litigation. Also, such legislation does not permit a court to develop a case-specific remedy in individual cases.

doctrine of ancient lights:
Doctrine that anyone who used light for an uninterrupted period of 20 years was entitled to protection of that use; historically rejected by American courts.

solar easement laws:
Statutes that permit the execution and recognition of easements for solar access.

■ *Right to Light?*

In *Prah v. Maretti*, 321 N.W.2d 182 (Wis. 1982), an owner of a solar-heated residence maintained that his neighbor's proposed construction of a residence would interfere with his access to light. In holding that the plaintiff could maintain a nuisance action in that case, the Wisconsin Supreme Court said:

> This court's reluctance in the nineteenth and early part of the twentieth century to provide broader protection for a

landowner's access to sunlight was premised on three policy considerations. First, the right of landowners to use their property as they wished, as long as they did not cause physical damages to a neighbor, was jealously guarded....Second, sunlight was valued only for aesthetic enjoyment or as illumination. Since artificial light could be used for illumination,

(Continued)

---

[14] 114 So. 2d 357 (Fla. Dist. Ct. App. 1959).

loss of sunlight was at most a personal annoyance which was given little, if any, weight by society. Third, society had a significant interest in not restricting or impeding land development....This court repeatedly emphasized that in the growth period of the nineteenth and early twentieth centuries change is to be expected and is essential to property and that recognition of a right to sunlight would hinder property development....

... These three policies are no longer fully accepted or applicable. They reflect factual circumstances and social priorities that are now obsolete.

First, society has increasingly regulated the use of land by the landowner for the general welfare.... Second, access to sunlight has taken on a new significance in recent years. In this case the plaintiff seeks to protect access to sunlight, not for aesthetic reasons or as a source of illumination but as a source of energy. Access to sunlight as an energy source is of significance both to the landowner who invests in solar collectors and to a society which has an interest in developing alternative sources of

energy.... Third, the policy of favoring unhindered private development in an expanding economy is no longer in harmony with the realities of our society.... The need for easy and rapid development is not as great today as it once was, while our perception of the value of sunlight as a source of energy has increased significantly. [For these reasons, the court held that the plaintiffs could maintain a nuisance action under these facts.][15]

Questions and Comments for Discussion

1. In *Prah v. Maretti*, the court said that the policy of favoring unhindered private development in an expanding economy is "no longer in harmony with the realities of our society." What did the court mean by this statement? What are the policy implications of preventing construction of a neighboring residence that would block another homeowner's access to sunlight?

2. What kinds of problems arise in a government's attempt to legislate a right to light by statute or zoning ordinance?

3. Who should decide the question of right to light—the courts through common law or the legislature?

Water Rights

The right to water is an increasingly valuable part of real estate ownership. Under traditional common law principles, water rights will depend on the type of water body involved and where the water is located. The states have adopted different rules to determine ownership rights in water. Most states west of the Mississippi River follow the **prior appropriation doctrine**, characterized by the notion that "first in time is first in right." Most states east of the Mississippi River follow a **riparian rights doctrine**, characterized by the requirement of reasonable use by riparian owners. (A **riparian owner** is a person who owns property adjacent to a waterway.) These

prior appropriation doctrine: Common law doctrine concerning determination of water rights which essentially declares "first in time, first in right," regardless of riparian owner status; followed primarily in states west of the Mississippi.

riparian rights doctrine: Common law doctrine concerning determination of water rights, which requires "reasonable use" and declares that only riparian owners may assert those rights; followed primarily in states east of the Mississippi.

riparian owner: A person who owns property adjacent to a waterway.

---

[15] 321 N.W.2d at 235–37.

common law doctrines reflect different attitudes about an owner's right to exploit water as a resource and the difference in availability of water resources.

There are major differences between the riparian and prior appropriation rights concepts. First, the distinguishing features of the common law riparian rules are equality of rights and reasonable use. Unlike the prior appropriation doctrine, there is no priority of rights under the riparian doctrine. Second, as noted earlier, to be a riparian owner, by definition, one must own riparian land (land abutting the water of a river, lake, or stream). To be a prior appropriator, a person need not own land. This person must only (1) have an intention to "appropriate" water, which means to divert the water from the source of supply; (2) put the water to beneficial use; and (3) follow any necessary legal or administrative procedures for establishing its right.

The reason why the two different doctrines arose is obvious: The western states that adopted the appropriation doctrine are states where water sources are scarce. The prior appropriation doctrine contemplates the best economic use of this natural resource. It also encourages use of the resource to protect the right to appropriate.

As a result of the widespread concern over the limits of the basic water supply, and the pressure to protect it from waste and pollution, state and federal laws governing a property owner's right to water continue to multiply. The Clean Water Act and other similar laws represent government's attempts to protect public water resources. These environmental laws affect a water owner's or user's common law rights and obligations. Several states, particularly in the west, have established state regulations governing private water rights and separate "water courts" to adjudicate those rights.

▪ ▪ ▪ REVIEW AND STUDY QUESTIONS

1. How might our society be different if ownership interests could not be asserted or granted in air, minerals, light, or water?

2. Why do you think that different theories of water rights developed for lands east of the Mississippi as compared to lands west of the Mississippi? Should water rights laws be harmonized nationwide? Why or why not?

3. How far below the earth's surface should a landowner own or have exclusive rights to? How far above the earth's surface should rights extend?

4. Consider changing concepts of private development in light of an increasing concern over environmental impact, population growth, species protection, and other environmental concerns. What are the benefits and drawbacks of making decisions about the environmental impact at the local level? The state level? The federal level? Should private parties (e.g., neighboring landowners) ever be permitted to prevent construction of a neighboring structure, if that structure negatively infringes upon their access to light, to a view, or to some other environmental amenity?

5. Traditionally, land use is regulated through zoning, building codes, and planning commissions. What are the benefits and drawbacks of this regulatory structure?

6. Aesthetic restrictive covenants can be written into parcel deeds for subdivision developments. Consider the benefits and drawbacks to including the following kinds of limitations in such covenants: right to light, landscaping constraints, building height, setback requirements.

7. How broadly should courts construe the "beneficial use" requirement of the prior appropriation doctrine? Imagine a drought year, in which wildlife near a waterway need the water to survive, but an owner of water rights under prior appropriation must use the water or risk losing it. Should courts recognize an exception to the beneficial use requirement in such situations?

■ Ownership Concepts

Present Estates in Land

In this chapter we have examined the nature and scope of real property. This section examines the kinds of ownership rights a person may acquire in real property, and the legal relationship between those who share property interests in land. These basic concepts will help in understanding some of the legal issues in cases involving the rights and responsibilities of property owners under environmental laws.

The rights of ownership that a person may have in real property may be present or future, vested or contingent. An **estate** in land is a feudal concept. In the Middle Ages, people were classified into estates, such as clergy, nobility, and commoners. Today, the term describes the kind of ownership interests a person may have in real property. This is why real property is sometimes called *real estate*. Legally, the term is used to describe a kind of interest in real property. The simplest and most complete estate in land is called a **fee simple absolute**; this is what "owning" real property means to the average person.

A person may grant some ownership rights to another while retaining an interest in the property. For example, an owner may convey property to another on the condition that the property be used for a particular purpose. The words "to the City of Tacoma, so long as it uses the property for a public park," is an example of such a conveyance. This grant creates what is called a **fee simple defeasible**; it is "defeasible" (subject to revocation or being undone) because the grantor will recover ownership rights in the property upon breach of the condition.

The nature of ownership rights under such conditional land grants has been the subject of litigation under the National Trails System Act Amendments of 1983. This law represented efforts to preserve shrinking miles of rail track by converting unused rights of way to recreational pathways. Several provisions in various laws promote the conversion of abandoned railroad lines to trails (called "Rails to Trails" projects). In one case, plaintiffs in Vermont who claimed (under state law) a reversionary interest in a railroad right of way adjacent to their land brought a quiet title action (to establish legal title to property), alleging that upon abandonment of the railroad's easement through their property, the right of way had reverted to them by operation of state property law. The State of Vermont argued, among other things, that the land could not revert while it was still being used for a public purpose. In the final hearing of this case, *Preseault v. Interstate Commerce Commission*, 494 U.S. 1 (1990), the Supreme Court upheld the constitutionality of the federal "Rails to Trails" statute, but avoided deciding whether an unconstitutional taking of the petitioner's property had occurred.

Life Estates

A **life estate** arises when one person grants to another an ownership interest in real property which is measured by the life of that (or another) person. "To Davis, for life," creates a life estate, with Davis's life as the "measuring life," and entitles Davis to ownership rights during his life. At Davis's death, the property will automatically revert to the grantor or grantor's heirs (the **grantor** is the person who conveyed the life estate). Like the fee simple absolute and fee simple defeasible, the life estate is a present estate in land, and the grantor retains a future

estate: An ownership interest in real property.

fee simple absolute: The most comprehensive estate in land, which conveys to the grantee complete ownership of the property.

fee simple defeasible: A fee simple qualified by language that will cause the fee to end if and when a certain event happens.

life estate: An ownership interest in real property measured by a specified person's life.

grantor: Person who conveys an interest in real property to another.

interest (a reversion or **remainder** interest) in the property. A person who has a remainder interest in real property is known as the **remainderman**.

A **life tenant**, like a tenant under a lease, has a duty to keep the property in good repair. As a general rule, the life tenant may act as a fee simple owner, but may not act in a way that would diminish the market value of the remainder. If it does so, it may be liable for waste. Thus, a life tenant, like a tenant under a lease who improperly stores hazardous materials on the leased property, would be liable to the grantor for damages if the property's value were substantially diminished as a result of environmental contamination. A life tenant may transfer his or her interest in the property. However, keep in mind that a life tenant—and all other types of estate ownership—may not transfer any interest greater than what the owner actually has. So, it would be impossible for a life tenant to transfer the property in fee simple absolute, simply because the life tenant does not own that interest.

Future Interests in Land

Land interests are not limited to present time; they may be divided into present and future interests. The defeasible fee discussed earlier is an example of an estate in land under which it is possible that ownership of the property will return to the grantor in the future; this is an example of a future interest in property. In the case of the defeasible fee, that future interest is only a possibility: If the **grantee** and its successors comply with the conditions of the grant, the land will not revert to the grantor. Other types of future interests, however, are based on certainties. For example, a remainder interest may be given to another living person. "To Davis for life, and then to Beth," creates in Beth (or her heirs) the certainty of future ownership in the property.

Kinds of Ownership

Not infrequently, environmental issues arise in the sale and purchase of real property, especially commercial property. The owner of real property may be liable under state and federal laws for the costs of cleaning up hazardous substances found on the property, even if the owner did not cause or contribute to that contamination. It is not unusual for more than one person to hold an ownership interest in real property. For this reason, it is helpful for the student of environmental law to be familiar with these basic forms of multiple ownership.

The **tenancy in common** is the most common type of joint ownership in land. Usually a grant will be construed to be a tenancy in common rather than a joint tenancy. A grant "To Smith and to Jones" creates a tenancy in common. Under a tenancy in common, co-tenants have an equal right to the possession and use of the entire property even though they may hold unequal shares. They may also be jointly liable as owners of property under environmental laws regulating the manufacture and storage of hazardous materials.

A tenant in common may sell, lease, or mortgage his undivided interest in the property, and upon his death, his interest passes to his heirs. Whether the parties are tenants in common may be significant in cases determining ownership interests. For example, when two or more persons participate in the location of a mining claim, a tenancy in common arises. Each locator has the same rights (and presumably duties) in respect to her share as a tenant, but she holds her interest

remainder: A future interest in property.

remainderman: A person who has a remainder interest in real property.

life tenant: A person who owns a life estate.

grantee: Person to whom a legal interest in real property is conveyed or transferred.

tenancy in common: Form of real property co-ownership in which the parties hold separate undivided interests in the property.

independently of the other and may transfer, devise, or encumber it separately without the consent of the other co-tenants.

Unlike the tenancy in common, the **joint tenancy** is characterized by a **right of survivorship**. A grant of land "To Smith and to Jones as joint tenants with rights of survivorship" creates a joint tenancy. Unlike the tenancy in common, under a joint tenancy with rights of survivorship, upon the death of one tenant, ownership automatically vests in the other joint tenant or tenants.

Another form of joint tenancy, recognized by about half the states, is called a **tenancy by the entirety**. This tenancy arises only between husband and wife, and can be terminated only by joint action of the husband and wife. The ownership interest of a spouse may become an issue in the determination of liability under some environmental laws.

In some western states, property owned by husband and wife is called **community property**. Community property states classify property in different ways, but generally distinguish between property that was acquired during the marriage and property acquired by gift or inheritance or accumulated prior to marriage.

Another form of shared ownership of real property is a **condominium** arrangement. The purchaser of a condominium purchases the living space in a unit. He or she also purchases an interest in the common areas of the condominium (including the land under the structure) as a tenant in common. The rights and duties of the condominium purchaser are set out in the master deed and the bylaws to the condominium corporation, and states have enacted statutes that also govern those rights and duties. An association of condominium or homeowners may, if it is a separate legal entity, acquire an interest in real property.

Landlord and Tenant Law

The relationship between landlord and tenant is determined not only by contract law but also by the law of property. A *lease* is both a conveyance of a possessory interest in real property by the owner to another (the conveyance of an "estate") and a contract specifying certain particular rights and duties with regard to the property. The estate concept is utilized in property law to define the possessory interest transferred from the owner to the tenant. There are four basic kinds of tenancies:

■ The **estate for years**, which has a definite beginning and a definite end

■ The **periodic tenancy**, which lasts for a period of time and is automatically renewed until either party gives notice that it will end

■ The **tenancy at will**, which is characterized by an indefinite duration

■ The **tenancy at sufferance**, which arises when a person in possession refuses to leave after its right to possession has ended

Although a lease may arise from an informal arrangement between the parties, it is always best to state the terms of the lease in a clear and specific writing. The terms are critical in determining the rights and duties of the parties, and these lease terms may be especially important when leased commercial property becomes subject to a cleanup action under federal or state hazardous waste laws or a suit for damages under state nuisance law. Indemnity issues, warranties, and exculpatory clauses in the lease may ultimately determine the liability between the landlord and tenant in such cases.

joint tenancy: Form of real property co-ownership that includes a right of survivorship.

right of survivorship: Interest in real property such that upon the death of a co-owner, the ownership interest of the deceased automatically vests in the other owner(s).

tenancy by the entirety: Form of real property ownership by husband and wife.

community property: System of property ownership by husband and wife that exists in some but not all states.

condominium: A type of shared ownership of real property.

estate for years: A type of tenancy that has a definite beginning and ending.

periodic tenancy: A type of tenancy that lasts for a period of time and is automatically renewed until either party gives notice that it will end.

tenancy at will: A type of tenancy characterized by an indefinite duration.

tenancy at sufferance: A type of tenancy that arises when a person in possession refuses to leave after its right to possession has ended.

The landlord-tenant relationship involves both property and contract principles. In environmental cases, landlord-tenant issues may arise in determining each party's relative rights and duties regarding contaminated property under hazardous or toxic waste laws. In such cases, the terms of the lease may be critical in determining the relative liability of the parties, although such terms are not effective in relieving a party of liability to the government.

Partition and Waste   If all tenants have the equal right of possession to the property, what happens in a property dispute between co-owners? In such cases, the co-owners may agree upon, or a court may order, a division of the property called a *partition*. **Partition** is an actual geographical division of the property and results in former co-owners becoming separate owners of adjoining parcels of land. If it is impossible to physically divide the land, the property may be sold and the proceeds divided.

Waste occurs when a land possessor causes permanent injury to the property that diminishes the value of the property to the landowner. A person entitled to property under the terms of a lease is obligated to use the property in a way that preserves its value. If a tenant of commercial property permitted the property to become contaminated with hazardous materials, the tenant could be held liable for the owner's loss of value in the real estate under the theory of waste. The tenant may also be liable for the costs of cleaning up the property as an "owner or operator" under federal environmental laws.

Ownership for Investment Purposes

Persons who invest in property for business purposes have many options to limit their liability exposure through careful creation of the business organizational form that they establish. Note that for purposes of environmental law, joint ownership of property carries with it **joint and several liability**, which means that all responsible parties, together or independently, are liable for the full amount of damages until the total amount of damages is paid.

Partnership   Investors often choose to own real property through partnerships for various business reasons, such as tax purposes. The law defines a **partnership** as an association of two or more persons formed to carry on a business for profit. Each partner is a co-owner of partnership property and holds the property as a tenant in partnership; this tenancy has the characteristics of a joint tenancy. If a partner dies, the ownership of partnership property belongs to the remaining partners. However, a partner's interest in the partnership, which is that person's share of profits and surplus in the partnership, can pass to his or her heirs and may be subject to the claims of creditors. Partnerships can be risky for general partners, due to their unlimited liability exposure, but the partnership still remains a common form of business.

Corporations   Unlike a partnership, a **corporation** is a legal entity separate and distinct from its shareholders. More complicated than a partnership, a corporation is formed when parties file articles of incorporation and obtain a corporate charter. A corporation's directors must conduct business under procedures set out in its articles and charter, as well as in applicable federal and state statutes. The major advantage of the corporate business form is that the corporation, as a legal entity separate from its shareholders, is liable for its own contracts and torts; the shareholder's liability is limited to its investment in the corporation.

partition: A physical division of co-owned property whereby co-owners become adjoining landowners or neighbors.

waste: An unlawful act or breach of duty by a tenant that results in permanent injury to the leased property.

joint and several liability: Liability of all responsible parties, together or independently, for the full amount of damages until the total amount is paid.

partnership: An association of two or more persons formed to carry on a business for profit; examples of business forms in partnership include general partnership, a limited partnership, or a limited liability partnership (LLP).

corporation: A legal entity separate and distinct from its shareholders (owners).

A corporation may purchase and hold real property in its own name, and a corporation may be liable for harm caused by environmental contamination of its property or for the costs of cleanup. Several important issues involving corporate liability for environmental contamination have emerged in recent years. One debated issue is the extent to which persons who are corporate officers or directors should be personally liable for the environmental wrongs caused by their actions in that capacity. Another question is the extent to which a corporation should be able to discharge its liability for environmental harm through bankruptcy. Additional questions concern whether a corporation may limit its liability by forming subsidiary corporations, and whether a corporate successor may be liable for the environmental harms caused by its corporate predecessor.

The principle of limiting liability through incorporation is vital to capital formation. Without protection from liability, investors would be unlikely to purchase stock. It is common for corporations to create subsidiaries to engage in different specialized activities, especially if the corporate activity carries with it a high risk of potential liability, such as the generation and disposal of hazardous waste. In the corporate parent-subsidiary relationship, the corporate parent generally controls the actions of the subsidiary. If the subsidiary is found liable for environmental harms, may the parent corporation be held liable as well? The courts are not quick to disregard corporate form, but they have also consistently construed federal hazardous waste laws broadly. As a result of these conflicting policies, the courts' decisions in such cases have not been uniform.

One corporation may purchase the assets of another, either directly or through merger. General common law principles establish when a successor corporation is deemed to have purchased (or otherwise taken on) the liabilities of its predecessor. In cases involving potential liability under CERCLA, some courts have been willing to extend successor liability beyond that which would arise under traditional common law.

Corporations may be subject to both criminal and civil penalties under federal and state environmental laws.

■ *ACTIVITY BOX*   *EPA Criminal Enforcement*

Select a video related to environmental crimes committed by a corporation from http://www2.epa.gov/enforcement/criminal-enforcement-videos

Review signs of environmental violations at http://www2.epa.gov/enforcement/criminal-enforcement-signs-environmental-violations

Also, check out the general criminal investigations website at http://www2.epa.gov/enforcement/criminal-enforcement

Answer the following questions:

1. Based upon your knowledge of property ownership, who should be liable when a corporation commits an environmental crime? Remember that a corporation has no "body" to incarcerate, because it is a fictitious person in law. However, it is a separate "person" in law, distinct from its directors, employees, and shareholders.

2. When prior generations of landowners who committed environmental crimes can no longer be found or who have died, who should pay for the environmental damage?

3. Besides "command and control" legislation that sets minimum standards for environmental behavior, what types of incentives could be established to encourage landowners—including business landowners—to practice environmentally responsible behavior on their land?

Limited Liability Company   The **limited liability company (LLC)** business form embodies the positive attributes of the corporate form (e.g., limited liability for owners) without the negative sides of it (e.g., double taxation). Because of its flexibility and ease of formation, the LLC is a very popular option.

▓ ▓ ▓ REVIEW AND STUDY QUESTIONS

1. The fact that ownership can be divided as to time probably is not a new concept, but it raises questions about the relatively unlimited right of an owner of property to do with it as he or she wishes. For example, an owner may wish to tie up the use of specific property indefinitely, by building a large structure on it. The owner may wish to create a defeasible fee, which imposes a condition upon the use of land into the indefinite future. Should a landowner be permitted to tie up the use of land for a specific purpose for a period longer than his or her own life? Why or why not? How might our society change if a time limit was placed upon how long an individual person could use the land, after which time the land must be returned to its natural state?

2. Should the holder of a life estate be treated as an owner for purposes of enforcing environmental laws? What about the holder of a remainder interest?

3. Should a landlord be liable for an environmental violation on its land if that land is rented by a tenant that commits the violation? Why or why not? Consider the public policy implications of your response.

▓ Easements and Covenants

limited liability company (LLC): A distinct legal business structure that limits liability exposure of its owners, while offering favorable tax treatment and flexibility in the creation of the operating agreement.

easement appurtenant: An easement that benefits a particular possessor or tract of land.

easement in gross: An easement that belongs to the public regardless of whether the holder owns adjacent property.

express easement: An easement created by a specific grant.

implied easement: An easement that arises out of necessity.

A person may acquire other interests in real property, including nonpossessory interests. An *easement* is a nonpossessory interest that gives the holder certain rights in the land owned by another. An easement may be valid indefinitely, may have terms, or may end through operation of law. The owner of an easement is entitled to use and enjoy the land on a limited basis and is entitled to protection from third parties as to that use and enjoyment. An easement may be conveyed.

Easements are characterized in different ways. An easement that benefits a particular possessor or tract of land is called an **easement appurtenant**. An easement that belongs to the public regardless of whether the holder owns adjacent property is called an **easement in gross**. An easement may also be characterized as *affirmative* (giving the owner of the easement a right to use another's land) or *negative* (giving the owner of the easement the right to prevent another from using its property; for example, to prevent the blockage of sunlight).

An **express easement** may be created by a specific grant, which must comply with all requirements established by the state for conveyance of an interest in land. Easements may also arise by implication. An **implied easement** includes one that arises from necessity. In one case in which a court enjoined the use of a lagoon on another's property as part of a final sewage treatment process, the court affirmed a finding that the defendant had not acquired a perpetual easement to use the lagoon. The court said that an implied easement must be continuous, apparent, permanent, and necessary. According to the court, "the necessity should be judged by whether an alternative would involve disproportionate expense and inconvenience, or whether a substitute can be furnished by reasonable labor or expense."[16]

---

[16] *Gulf Park Water Co. v. First Ocean Springs Dev. Co.,* 530 So. 2d 1325 (Miss. 1988) (quoting *Fourth Davis Island Land Co. v. Parker,* 469 So. 2d 516, 520–21 (Miss. 1985)).

Easements may also arise by prescription. Obtaining an **easement by prescription (prescriptive easement)** is similar to obtaining title to property through adverse possession, discussed in an earlier section of this chapter. The easement must have been used for the appropriate period under law (ranging from 5 to 20 years depending on the state), and the use must have been adverse, open and notorious, and continuous and exclusive. In one case, *McCullough v. Waterfront Park Association, Inc.*, 630 A.2d 1372 (Conn. App. Ct. 1993), the Connecticut Court of Appeals held that a homeowner's association had acquired an easement to waterfront property owned by the defendant under this theory.

In the following case, the Oregon Supreme Court held that the public may acquire a right to use property under the English doctrine of "custom," a concept with some similarities to the prescriptive easement.

easement by prescription (prescriptive easement): An easement obtained through use and that meets statutory requirements similar to those required to establish adverse possession.

State ex rel. Thornton v. Hay
462 P.2d 671 (Or. 1969)

Goodwin, J.

William and Georgianna Hay, the owners of a tourist facility at Cannon Beach, appeal from a decree which enjoins them from constructing fences or other improvements in the dry-sand area between the sixteen-foot elevation contour line and the ordinary high-tide line of the Pacific Ocean.

The issue is whether the state has the power to prevent the defendant landowners from enclosing the dry-sand area contained within the legal description of their ocean-front property.

The state asserts two theories: (1) the landowners' record title to the disputed area is encumbered by a superior right in the public to go upon and enjoy the land for recreational purposes; and (2) if the disputed area is not encumbered by the asserted public easement, then the state has power to prevent construction under zoning regulations made pursuant to ORS 390.640.

* * *

The land area in dispute will be called the dry-sand area. This will be assumed to be the land lying between the line of mean high tide and the visible line of vegetation....

Below, or seaward of, the mean high-tide line, is the state-owned foreshore, or wet-sand area, in which the landowners in this case concede the public's paramount right, and concerning which there is no justiciable controversy. The only issue in this case, as noted, is the power of the state to limit the record owner's use and enjoyment of the dry-sand area, by whatever boundaries the area may be described.

The trial court found that the public had acquired, over the years, an easement for recreational purposes to go upon and enjoy the dry-sand area, and that this easement was appurtenant to the wet-sand portion of the beach which is admittedly owned by the state and designated as a "state recreation area."

Because we hold that the trial court correctly found in favor of the state on the rights of the public in the dry-sand area, it follows that the state has an equitable right to protect the public in the enjoyment of those rights by causing the removal of fences and other obstacles....

In order to explain our reasons for affirming the trial court's decree, it is necessary to set out in some detail the historical facts which lead to our conclusion. The dry sand area in Oregon has been enjoyed by the general public as a recreational adjunct of the wet-sand or foreshore area since the beginning of the state's political history. The first European settlers on these shores found the aboriginal inhabitants using the foreshore for clam-digging and the dry-sand area for their cooking fires. The newcomers continued these customs after statehood. Thus, from the time of the earliest settlement to the present day, the general public has assumed that the dry-sand area was a part of the public beach, and the public has used the dry-sand area for picnics, gathering wood, building warming fires, and generally as a headquarters from which to supervise children or to range out over the foreshore as the tides advance and recede. In the Cannon Beach vicinity, state and local officers have policed the dry sand, and municipal sanitary crews have attempted to keep the area reasonably free from man-made litter.

Perhaps one explanation for the evolution of the custom of the public to use the dry-sand area for recreational purposes is that the area could not be used

(Continued)

conveniently by its owners for any other purpose. The dry-sand area is unstable in its seaward boundaries, unsafe during winter storms, and for the most part unfit for the construction of permanent structures. While the vegetation line remains relatively fixed, the western edge of the dry-sand area is subject to dramatic moves eastward or westward in response to erosion and accretion. For example, evidence in the trial below indicated that between April 1966 and August 1967 the seaward edge of the dry-sand area involved in this litigation moved westward 180 feet. At other points along the shore, the evidence showed, the seaward edge of the dry-sand area could move an equal distance to the east in a similar period of time.

* * *

The disputed area is *sui generis*. While the foreshore is "owned" by the state, and the upland is "owned" by the patentee or record-title holder, neither can be said to "own" the full bundle of rights normally connoted by the term "estate in fee simple." ...

In addition to the *sui generis* nature of the land itself, a multitude of complex and sometimes overlapping precedents in the law confronted the trial court. Several early Oregon decisions generally support the trial court's decision, i.e., that the public can acquire easements in private land by long-continued [use] that is inconsistent with the owner's exclusive possession and enjoyment of his land....

A second group of cases relied upon by the state, but rejected by the trial court, deals with the possibility of a landowner's losing the exclusive possession and enjoyment of his land through the development of prescriptive easements in the public.

In Oregon, as in most common-law jurisdictions, an easement can be created in favor of one person in the land of another by uninterrupted use and enjoyment of the land in a particular manner for the statutory period, so long as the use is open, adverse, under claim of right, but without authority of law or consent of the owner.... In Oregon, the prescriptive period is ten years.... The public use of the disputed land in the case at bar is admitted to be continuous for more than sixty years. There is no suggestion in the record that anyone's permission was sought or given; rather, the public used the land under a claim of right. Therefore, if the public can acquire an easement by prescription, the requirements for such an acquisition have been met in connection with the specific tract of land involved in this case.

The owners argue, however, that the general public, not being subject to actions in trespass and ejectment, cannot acquire rights by prescription, because

the statute of limitations is irrelevant when an action does lie.

While it may not be feasible for a landowner to sue the general public, it is nonetheless possible by means of signs and fences to prevent or minimize public invasions of private land for recreational purposes. In Oregon, moreover, the courts and the Legislative Assembly have both recognized that the public can acquire prescriptive easements in private land, at least for roads and highways....

* * *

Because many elements of prescription are present in this case, the state has relied upon the doctrine in support of the decree below. We believe, however, that there is a better legal basis for affirming the decree. The most cogent basis for the decision in this case is the English doctrine of custom. Strictly construed, prescription applies only to the specific tract of land before the court, and doubtful prescription cases could fill the courts for years with tract-by-tract litigation. An established custom, on the other hand, can be proven with reference to a larger region. Ocean-front lands from the northern to the southern border of the state ought to be treated uniformly.

The other reason which commends the doctrine of custom over that of prescription as the principal basis for the decision in this case is the unique nature of the lands in question. This case deals solely with the dry-sand area along the Pacific shore, and this land has been used by the public as public recreational land according to an unbroken custom running back in time as long as the land has been inhabited.

A custom is defined in [*Bouvier's Law Dictionary*] as "such a usage as by common consent and uniform practice has become the law of the place, or of the subject matter to which it relates."

* * *

The custom of the people of Oregon to use the dry-sand area of the beaches for public recreational purposes meets every one of Blackstone's requisites. While it is not necessary to rely upon precedent from other states, we are not the first state to recognize custom as a source of law....

[I]n support of custom, the record shows that the custom of the inhabitants of Oregon and of visitors in the state to use the dry sand as a public recreation area is so notorious that notice of the custom on the part of persons buying land along the shore must be presumed. In the case at bar, the landowners conceded their actual knowledge of the public's long-standing use of the dry-sand area, and argued that the elements of consent present in the relationship between the landowners and the public precluded the application of the

(Continued)

law of prescription. As noted, we are not resting this decision on prescription, and we leave upon the effect upon prescription of the type of consent that may have been present in this case. Such elements of consent are, however, wholly consistent with the recognition of public rights derived from custom.

Because so much of our law is the product of legislation, we sometimes lose sight of the importance of custom as a source of law in our society. It seems particularly appropriate in the case at bar to look to an ancient and accepted custom in this state as the source of a rule of law. The rule in this case, based upon custom, is salutary in confirming a public right, and at the same time it takes from no man anything which he has had a legitimate reason to regard as exclusively his. … [T]he decree of the trial court is affirmed.

Questions and Comments for Discussion

1. The court said that to recognize a custom as law, the custom must (1) be ancient; (2) be a right exercised without interruption; (3) be peaceable and free from dispute; (4) be reasonable; (5) be of certain limit; (6) be obligatory (not left to the option of each landowner); and (7) not be repugnant to or inconsistent with other customs or laws. Why did the court adopt this custom theory entitling the public to ownership rights in this case rather than the theory of prescriptive easement?

2. Identify a property interest that could be claimed in your town based upon "custom."

Grant of an Express Easement

A property owner may expressly grant to another the right to use its property for a particular purpose. For example, it is common for a utility or pipeline company to obtain a right of way on another's property for placement of its equipment. In such cases, the rights of the parties will be determined in large part by the actual language in the granting instrument. In *Chevron Pipe Line Co. v. De Roest*, 858 P.2d 164 (Or. Ct. App. 1993), the plaintiff was the owner and operator of an interstate petroleum products pipeline that crossed the defendant's property. The plaintiff sought an order enjoining the defendant from placing fill material over the pipeline and requiring the defendant to remove fill material and heavy equipment he had placed there, allegedly in violation of the plaintiff's easement.

The defendant's predecessors had conveyed a 16.5-foot easement across their land to the plaintiff's predecessor, the Salt Lake Pipe Line Company, for purposes of transporting liquid petroleum products from a refinery in Salt Lake City, Utah. The conveyance granted to the plaintiff:

the right of way from time to time to lay, construct, reconstruct, replace, renew, repair, maintain, operate, change the size of, increase the number of, and remove pipe lines and appurtenances thereof, for the transportation of oil, petroleum, gas, gasoline, water or other substances, or any thereof, and to erect, install, maintain, operate, repair, renew, power lines and appurtenances thereof on a single line of poles or underground, as Grantee from time to time and place to place may elect, with the right of ingress and egress to and from the same, over and through, under and along that certain parcel of land….

The conveyances reserved to the defendant's predecessor:

the right to use and enjoy said premises, provided that Grantor shall not construct or maintain the whole or any part of any structure on said strip of land or in any manner impair or interfere with the present or prospective exercise of any of the rights therein granted.

The slope of the land made it less than desirable for the defendant's proposed use of the property, so over the years he filled the upper portion of his property with fill material of various kinds (dirt, concrete, and asphalt) and created two terraces which, at the higher edge, covered the plaintiff's pipeline to a depth of 22.55 feet. The plaintiff contended that the presence of the fill and equipment impaired its access to the pipeline and therefore violated the easement's restriction on the defendant's use of the property. It asked the court to require the defendant to stop parking equipment on the easement and to remove the fill to a depth of not more than five feet above the pipeline. In the plaintiff's view, the placement of fill on the pipeline was a per se interference with the plaintiff's right to install, replace, and repair the pipe, and thus a violation of the easement.

The court of appeals, however, concluded that the trial court correctly rejected an absolute restriction on the servient tenant's (defendant's) right to use the property. According to the court, "[t]he right of the easement owner, and the right of the land owner, are not absolute, irrelative, and uncontrolled, but are so limited, each by the other, that there may be a due and reasonable enjoyment of both." In view of all the circumstances, the court held that the defendant's use of his property did not interfere with the plaintiff's use of the easement in a manner not contemplated by the parties at the time the easement was granted.

As this case indicates, the language of the granting instrument determines the relative rights and duties of the parties. In addition, easements in gross (easements that do not belong to any person by virtue of ownership of appurtenant land), granted for commercial or public purposes, are transferrable. The express easement, as an interest in land, should be recorded so that future owners are on notice of its existence.

Restrictive Covenants

A **restrictive covenant** is a voluntary restriction on land use created by contract. The covenant is unique because it not only binds the parties to the contract, but also binds later owners of the land. Unlike an easement, which is an interest in land, the **covenant** is a contractual promise that passes with the land. And unlike the defeasible fee, which terminates if the promise is not kept, breach of a restrictive covenant results in damages or an action for injunctive relief.

restrictive covenant: A contractual promise that passes with the land.

covenant: A contractual agreement to do or refrain from doing something that binds owners of the land subject to it.

Covenants are created by a document, usually a deed, which spells out restrictions on land use or refers to another plan or document containing detailed restrictions on land use. Covenants "run with the land," which means that they apply to subsequent purchasers of the property; they are commonly used in residential development projects to control the physical appearance of property. Some contain specific restrictions based on aesthetics (limiting, for example, the kind of fences or roofs to be constructed in the neighborhood), and may address environmental concerns such as the right to light. Even if a restrictive covenant does not mention solar devices, design review requirements, height restrictions, setback and yard requirements, and other restrictions may affect residential solar designs.

▨ ▨ ▨   REVIEW AND STUDY QUESTIONS

1. Covenants stated in clear and unambiguous language are generally enforceable. How can covenants address environmental concerns, such as permitting or prohibiting the use of lawn pesticides within subdivisions?

2. To what extent should courts look to ancient and accepted custom as a source of a rule of law? Does such a stance open courts to a criticism that they are acting as legislators?

■ Conclusion

This chapter has introduced some fundamental concepts of property law that are useful in discussion of environmental law issues. The concept of property is ultimately a discussion of the relationship between human beings and other things. As such, it is not a static legal concept, but rather reflects economic, social, and political considerations. As those considerations change, so the law of property changes.

The rules governing ownership of property, characterization of property, and estates in land have come down to us from earlier times. As times have changed, so have these concepts. The evolution of the law of property has been accomplished to a great extent by the courts, through common law decision making. However, as federal and state legislatures become increasingly active in passing laws to protect the environment, property rights are more affected by statutory and administrative regulations.

The traditional common law of property does not always promote an ecologically sound perspective on the relationship between humans and their environment. Certainly, the legal concept of property and the nature of ownership rights have great implications for the environment. Some have even suggested that society should reconsider the legal concept of ownership. From a legal perspective, the proper balance between a government's right to regulate land, air, and water and individuals' right to use and enjoy their property is a constitutional issue of great significance.

Chapter 3 Case Study Adverse Possession after the Crash: A Question of Ethics

After the mortgage crisis of 2008, many houses were abandoned by owners who were unable to pay their mortgages. This created opportunities for persons to engage in adverse possession of houses—sometimes worth millions—simply by laying claim to a houses under the laws of the state in which it is located.

You can read one such story at http://abcnews.go.com/Business/texas-man-claims-mansion-16/story?id=14099714 and get another view of the situation at http://realestate.msn.com/can-you-get-a-house-for-free.

Do a Google search using the terms "adverse possession" and "news" to find additional stories.

Questions for discussion:

1. Do adverse possession laws take unfair advantage of the owner of the property? Does the answer to that question depend upon whether the owner is a natural person or a bank? Why?

2. Should adverse possession rely upon an antiquated notion that land must be "used" to be valued? If adverse possession laws did not exist, is there any danger in allowing land to remain unused or houses to sit vacant?

3. Adverse possessors are called *squatters*. Discuss the difference in connotations between those two words. How do words "matter" in law, particularly in terms of classifying issues to analyze in law?

4. Can adverse possession be used to protect property, or must it exist in contravention to preservation of property (e.g., adverse possession rewards those who "use" property)?

Common Law Remedies in Tort for Environmental Harms

Here's a good idea!

This is a "bare bones" outline of the chapter. Expand this outline with more detailed notes as you read the chapter. This will allow you to create a study guide as you work. This good study habit will help you learn the material, retain important points, and make efficient use of your time.

Learning Objectives

After reading this chapter, you will have an understanding of common law tort remedies—as opposed to statutory remedies—for environmental harms. You will be able to distinguish between intentional torts, negligence, and strict liability, and you will understand the application of each category of tort to various types of civil wrongs. After reading this chapter, you should be able to answer the following questions:

1. How do common law remedies apply to environmental harms?
2. What are the differences between intentional torts, negligence, and strict liability?
3. How are common law remedies applied to environmental harms today?
4. What are the strengths and weaknesses of the common law in addressing environmental harm?

■ Introduction

This chapter addresses common law tort theories that protect and restrict ownership rights in real property. Specifically, this chapter focuses on four common law tort theories that plaintiffs often use to recover damages for environmental harm to their property or person: trespass, nuisance, negligence, and strict liability.

First, recall that *common law* refers to judge-made law, and judge-made law continuously evolves. Judges rely upon precedent when making decisions about legal matters, but a judge can also distinguish the case at bar to depart from precedents and decide an issue in a novel or unique way. So, when we say that this chapter addresses common law theories, we are saying that it focuses on the specific type of law known as common law, rather than, say, statutory law or administrative rules and regulations.

A **tort** is a civil wrong against a person or a person's property. A person injured as a result of the tortious act of another is entitled to a legal remedy. In most instances, this means that the plaintiff is entitled to money damages. In cases where money damages are inadequate compensation, the court may issue an **injunction**, which is a court order requiring the defendant to do something or refrain from doing something. Note, too, that when we say that a tort is a civil wrong, we are saying that it is not a criminal wrong.

Recall from Chapter 2 that the differences between civil law and criminal law are many. As noted in Chapter 2, the differences between criminal and civil law include:

- The parties who may bring the lawsuit. The government brings a criminal case, but a plaintiff brings a civil case.
- Who is the injured party. The injury accrues to the government in a criminal case, but it accrues to a plaintiff in a civil case.
- The burden of proof. The standard is beyond a reasonable doubt in criminal cases, but by a preponderance of the evidence in a civil case.
- Potential penalties. Incarceration is a possibility in a criminal case, but not in a civil case. In a civil case, monetary damages are typically the result of a successful lawsuit.

This chapter discusses common law tort theories, which have evolved through judicial decision making in individual cases. Tort actions are private civil actions. That is, they are actions brought by one person against another person or legal person. All human beings are persons, and entities such as corporations are legal persons.

Common law rules tend to be flexible, as the courts apply them to the unique circumstances of each specific case. Common law decision making depends on the particular facts of the case. Because common law is implemented on a case-by-case basis, it has often been criticized as being too slow or too uncertain to resolve the technologically induced problems of environmental pollution. To some extent, this criticism is justified, and as a result both the federal and state governments have adopted laws and administrative rules and regulations to address pollution in a broader statutory and regulatory framework.

Many federal and state statutes do not permit individuals to recover damages for personal injuries or property damages.[1] Consequently, individuals continue to rely on common law tort theories like trespass, nuisance, negligence, and strict liability to recover damages for environmental harms to their property or person.

As courts apply these common law tort principles to the facts in individual cases, they also create environmental policy to respond to societal conditions and changes. In this way, and as noted earlier, the common law continues to evolve. One 19th-century jurist put it this way:

> It is one of the great merits and advantages of the common law, that, instead of a series of detailed practical rules, established by positive provisions, and adapted to the precise circumstances of particular cases, which would become obsolete and fail, when the practice and course of business, to which they apply, should cease

tort: A civil wrong or injury.

injunction: A court order requiring the defendant to do or refrain from doing something.

---

[1] Under the Comprehensive Environmental Response, Compensation, and Liability Act (CERCLA) (42 U.S.C. § 9601 *et seq.*), the recoverable costs and damages are limited to a broad range of expenses associated with Superfund cleanup activity.

or change, the common law consists of a few broad and comprehensive principles, founded on reason, natural justice, and enlightened public policy, modified and adapted to the circumstances of all the particular cases which fall within it. These general principles of equity and policy are rendered precise, specific, and adapted to practical use, by usage, which is the proof of their general fitness and common convenience, but still more by judicial exposition; so that, when in a course of judicial proceeding, by tribunals of the highest authority, the general rule has been modified, limited and applied, according to particular cases.[2]

Some examples of the evolutionary nature of the common law include the 20th-century modification of traditional trespass theory to define the scope of liability in airborne pollution cases, as well as the recognition of a plaintiff's right to recover damages for emotional distress absent physical injury in pollution and product liability cases. More recently, we have seen evolution in nuisance law in the 21st-century's Supreme Court decision that effectively bars of the use of federal nuisance law to address climate change.[3]

■ Tort Law

punitive damages: A monetary award designed to punish a defendant and deter it from similar actions in the future.

recklessness: Conduct demonstrating a conscious disregard for a known risk of probable harm to others.

intentional tort: Tort resulting when a person acts with a desire to cause harm or with knowledge that such harm is substantially certain to follow as a result of those actions.

negligence: Failure to maintain the standard of care in a legal duty to another (usually the duty to act with reasonable care), which results in a breach of the duty that actually and proximately causes actual injury.

strict liability: Liability resulting from activities that cause harm to others, even if no intent or negligence exists.

Tort liability is based on the concept that a person may be liable for breach of a legal duty owed to another. A person who commits a tort is a *tortfeasor*; the tortfeasor is the defendant in a civil action in tort. Tort law reflects a balance between protecting personal interests and recognizing the demands of a complex industrial society. Tort law differs from criminal law in that it is designed to compensate tort victims rather than to punish wrongdoers. However, in some cases, a plaintiff may recover **punitive damages**, which is a monetary award designed to punish the defendant for its wrongdoing and deter the defendant from similar actions in the future. Punitive damages may be awarded, for example, when the defendant is judged to have acted recklessly. **Recklessness** is conduct by a defendant that demonstrates a conscious disregard for a known risk of probable harm to others. Generally, however, damages in tort simply compensate the victim. For example, actual damages may include those for physical injury, medical expenses, lost pay and benefits, and intangible harms such as pain and suffering or emotional distress.

There are different ways to classify torts. One distinction is based on the level of fault by the wrongdoer. **Intentional torts** arise when a person acts with desire to cause harm or with knowledge that such harm is substantially certain to follow as a result of those actions. **Negligence** is conduct that falls below established legal standards, with the most common standard being a person's duty to act with reasonable care. Negligence may also be established by proof that a defendant breached other legal duties, such as a duty imposed under state or federal law. Under principles of **strict liability**, a defendant may be liable for some activities that result in harm to others, even though that defendant did not act intentionally or negligently in causing such harm.

---

[2] *Norway Plains Co. v. Boston & Maine R.R.*, 67 Mass. 263, 267 (1854).

[3] *American Electric Power Co. v. Connecticut*, 549 U.S. 497, 131 S. Ct. 2527 (2011). *See also Native Village of Kivalina v. ExxonMobil Corp.*, 696 F.3d 849, 856 (9th Cir. 2012) (barring federal nuisance claims under "displacement theory" as articulated in *American Electric Power Co. v. Connecticut:* "'The test for whether congressional legislation excludes the declaration of federal common law is simply whether the statute speak[s] directly to [the] question at issue.' AEP, 131 S. Ct. at 2537").

This chapter primarily addresses intentional torts, negligence, and strict liability. Notably, some torts do not fit exclusively in any particular classification. For example, nuisance may be an intentional tort, negligence, or a strict liability tort. Additionally, the same facts in any given case may support more than one theory or cause of action, though the plaintiff would not be entitled to separate damages under each theory.

When dealing with intentional torts, it is very important to note that intent in law is not the same thing as motive. **Intent** in law means that a person has (or should have) knowledge that harm is substantially certain to follow a particular action. In other words, intent does not require that a person intend to cause harm. Although a person may in fact intend or decide to cause harm, that motive is not determinative of whether legal intent exists or not. *Intentional* denotes a deliberate act, including knowing with a substantial certainty that the action will result in the harm.

Likewise, it is very important to remember that "accidents" are not the only things that give rise to a cause of action for negligence. If the five elements of negligence—(1) duty of care, (2) breach of the duty of care, (3) actual causation, (4) proximate causation, and (5) actual injury—are present and proven, then negligence will be found. Note that no element of accident exists in this analysis. In many cases of negligence, the defendant had good intentions (or at least lacked bad ones) but simply failed to maintain the standard of care. Negligence is discussed in detail later in this chapter.

This chapter discusses several torts that are relevant in the context of environmental law. Though the focus today is often on statutory schemes like the Clean Air Act or the Clean Water Act, common law is also an important source of law for addressing environmental harms. Indeed, some scholars believe that common law is superior to regulatory approaches in addressing environmental harms, given the ability to customize it and adapt it to particular situations, and its potential for incremental change.[4] The top-down approach of establishing national statutory schemes, in a "one size fits all" approach, takes away the possibility of a locality-driven response to environmental challenges.

However, common law adjudication only addresses past harms by providing compensation for injuries actually incurred. It does not regulate pollution proactively. The "command and control" approach to regulation of air and water pollution in the Clean Water Act and the Clean Air Act, for example, potentially counters that shortcoming in the common law.

▪ *ACTIVITY BOX* **Tort Law in China**

Visit the Environmental Protection Agency's China Environmental Law Initiative:

▪ http://www.epa.gov/ogc/china/initiative_home.htm
▪ http://www.epa.gov/ogc/china/legal_resources.htm

Review the many resources on those pages, while considering the following questions:

1. Identify new developments in Chinese environmental law.
2. What are some difficulties in adoption of common law remedies to address environmental harms in China?

intent: Knowledge that harm is substantially certain to follow a particular action.

---

[4] *See, e.g.,* S.J. Eagle, *Common Law Environmental Protection: The Common Law and the Environment,* 58 CASE W. RES. L. REV. 583, 620 (2008).

3. Tort law places power in the hands of individuals to bring claims against tortfeasors. Consider the differences between the systems of government in the USA and in China. How might structural differences in government and the legal systems assist or detract from an individual's ability to maintain a clean environment?

■ Trespass

Trespass is an intentional, voluntary intrusion on or invasion of the tangible property of another that interferes with the possessor's right of exclusive possession of the property. A wrongful intrusion by a person onto the land of another constitutes **trespass to land**, an early common law tort consisting of an action that violates a person's right to exclusive possession of property. Trespass also occurs if one causes a thing or another person to do so. An intrusion can also constitute a nuisance if it interferes with the plaintiff's use and enjoyment of its property. For example, gasoline leaks from a service station that contaminate a neighboring property constitute both trespass and nuisance.[5]

A person may be liable for either negligent or intentional trespass. Thus, if construction activities on private property result in a landslide that causes damage to neighboring property, a trespass has occurred.[6] A person may also be liable if he or she intentionally or negligently remains on the land of another or fails to remove from the land a thing that he or she is under a duty to remove.

Under traditional common law, if a person intentionally interfered with another's exclusive right of possession of property without a privilege to do so, he or she was liable for trespass without proof of actual damages. For purposes of trespass law, proof that the defendant knew or should have known that a particular result was substantially certain to follow from his or her action constitutes intention. If a city closes a sewage overflow valve and knows that the blockage will cause some sewage backup, the city may be liable under the theory of intentional trespass to a homeowner who suffers damages.[7]

Historically, many courts distinguished between trespass and nuisance by applying a "dimensional test." Under the dimensional test, whether an intrusion constituted trespass or nuisance depended on the size of the intruding agent. If the intruding agent could be seen by the naked eye, it was considered trespass. If it could not be seen, it was considered indirect and less substantial, and consequently a nuisance. By limiting liability for trespass to the intrusion of an observable object, the rule limited the scope of a defendant's liability for trespass. But modern courts have modified the rule in airborne pollution cases.

The Oregon Supreme Court first discarded the dimensional test in *Martin v. Reynolds Metals Co.*[8] In that case, the court held that a trespass had occurred when certain fluoride compounds from the manufacturing process of the defendant's aluminum reduction plant became airborne and settled upon the plaintiff's land. This was so even though the fluoride compounds took the form of gases and particulates invisible to the naked eye, the court said. *Martin* was one of the first cases

trespass: Intentional, voluntary intrusion on or invasion of the tangible property of another without permission or privilege.

trespass to land: Intentional, voluntary intrusion on or invasion of the land owned by another without permission or privilege.

---

[5] *Martin v. Reynolds Metals Co.*, 342 P.2d 790 (Or. 1959).
[6] *County of Allegheny v. Merrit Constr. Co.*, 454 A.2d 1051 (Pa. Super. Ct. 1982).
[7] *Dial v. City of O'Fallon*, 411 N.E.2d 217 (Ill. 1980).
[8] 342 P.2d 790 (Or. 1959).

to depart from the traditional common law rule of trespass to land that required a physical invasion of an object observable with the naked eye.

It is quite possible that in an earlier day, when science had not yet peered into the molecular and atomic world of small particles, the courts could not fit an invasion through unseen physical instrumentalities into the requirement that a trespass can result only from a direct invasion. In more modern times, of course, most people know that invisible particulate matter can have profoundly deleterious effects on property.

In the *Bradley* case, the Washington Supreme Court followed the Oregon court's reasoning in *Martin v. Reynolds Metals* and held that an intentional trespass had occurred in an airborne pollution case. The court also recognized that public policy required the modification of traditional common law trespass to incorporate a balancing test like that of nuisance law.

Bradley v. American Smelting & Refining Co.
709 P.2d 782 (Wash. 1985)

Callow, J.

[This case came before the state court on certification from the U.S. District Court for the Western District of Washington.]

* * *

The parties have stipulated to the facts as follows: Plaintiffs Michael O. Bradley and Marie A. Bradley, husband and wife, are owners and occupiers of real property on the southern end of Vashon Island in King County, Washington. The Bradleys purchased their property in 1978. Defendant ASARCO, a New Jersey corporation doing business in Washington, operates a primary copper smelter on real property it owns in Ruston, which is an incorporated municipality surrounded by the city of Tacoma, Washington.... [P]laintiffs brought this action against defendant alleging a cause of action for intentional trespass and for nuisance.

Plaintiffs' property is located some 4 miles north of defendant's smelter. Defendant's primary copper smelter (also referred to as the Tacoma smelter) has operated in its present location since 1890. It has operated as a copper smelter since 1902, and in 1905 it was purchased and operated by a corporate entity which is now ASARCO. As a part of the industrial process of smelting copper at the Tacoma smelter, various gases such as sulfur dioxide and particulate matter, including arsenic, cadmium and other metals, are emitted. Particulate matter is composed of distinct particles of matter other than water, which cannot be detected by the human senses.

[The court noted that these emissions were subject to regulation under the Federal Clean Air and state statutes, and that the smelter was in compliance with those laws. The parties had stipulated that some particulate emissions of both cadmium and arsenic from the Tacoma smelter continued to be deposited on the plaintiffs' land, but that there was no proof of actual damages to the plaintiffs or their property as a result of the emissions.]

* * *

... The issues present the conflict in an industrial society between the need of all for the production of goods and the desire of the landowner near the manufacturing plant producing those goods that his use and enjoyment of his land not be diminished by the unpleasant side effects of the manufacturing process. A reconciliation must be found between the interest of the many who are unaffected by the possible poisoning and the few who may be affected.

* * *

... The defendant cannot and does not deny that whenever the smelter was in operation the whim of the winds could bring these deleterious substances to the plaintiffs' premises. We are asked if the defendant, knowing what it had to know from the facts it admits, had the legal intent to commit trespass.

* * *

The defendant has known for decades that sulfur dioxide and particulates of arsenic, cadmium and other metals were being emitted from the tall smokestack. It had to know that the solids propelled into the air by the warm gases would settle back to earth somewhere. It had to know that a purpose of the tall stack was to disperse the gas, smoke and minute solids over as large an area as possible and as far away as possible, but that while any resulting contamination would be diminished

(Continued)

as to any one area or landowner, that nonetheless contamination, though slight, would follow …:

> Intent … is broader than a desire to bring about physical results. It must extend not only to those consequences which are desired, but also to those which the actor believes are substantially certain to follow from what he does.… The man who fires a bullet into a dense crowd may fervently pray that he will hit no one, but since he must believe and know that he cannot avoid doing so, he intends it.…

* * *

We find that the defendant had the requisite intent to commit intentional trespass as a matter of law.

* * *

> Trespass is a theory closely related to nuisance and occasionally invoked in environmental cases. The distinction between the two originally was the difference between the old action of trespass and the action on the case: if there was a direct and immediate physical invasion of plaintiff's property, as by casting stones or water on it, it was a trespass; if the invasion was indirect, as by the seepage of water, it was a nuisance.
>
> Today with the abandonment of the old procedural forms, the line between trespass and nuisance has become "wavering and uncertain." …
>
> The first and most important proposition about trespass and nuisance principles is that they are largely coextensive. Both concepts are often discussed in the same cases without differentiation between the elements of recovery.…
>
> It is also true that in the environmental arena both nuisance and trespass cases typically involve intentional conduct by the defendant who knows that his activities are substantially certain to result in an invasion of plaintiff's interests. The principal difference in theories is that the tort of trespass is complete upon a tangible invasion of plaintiff's property, however slight, whereas a nuisance requires proof that the interference with use and enjoyment is "substantial and unreasonable." … [citing W. RODGERS, ENVIRONMENTAL LAW § 2.13, at 154-57].
>
> We hold that the defendant's conduct in causing chemical substances to be deposited upon the plaintiffs' land fulfilled all of the requirements under the law of trespass [citing *Martin v. Reynolds Metals Co.*, 221 Or. 86, 342 P.2d 790 (1959)].

* * *

> Under the modern theory of trespass, the law presently allows an action to be maintained in trespass for invasions that, at one time, were considered indirect and, hence, only a nuisance. In order to recover in trespass for this type of invasion, a plaintiff must show 1) an invasion affecting an interest in the exclusive possession of his property; 2) an intentional doing of the act which results in the invasion; 3) reasonable foreseeability that the act done could result in an invasion of plaintiff's possessory interest; and 4) substantial damages to the *res* [the property] [citing *Borland v. Sanders Lead Co.*, 369 So. 2d 523 (Ala. 1979)].

When airborne particles are transitory or quickly dissipated, they do not interfere with a property owner's possessory rights and, therefore, are properly denominated as nuisances.… When, however, the particles or substance accumulates on the land and does not pass away, then a trespass has occurred.… While at common law any trespass entitled a landowner to recover nominal or punitive damages for the invasion of his property, such a rule is not appropriate under the circumstances before us. No useful purpose would be served by sanctioning actions in trespass by every landowner within a hundred miles of a manufacturing plant. Manufacturers would be harassed and the litigious few would cause the escalation of costs to the detriment of the many. The elements that we have adopted for an action in trespass … require that a plaintiff has suffered action and substantial damages. Since this is an element of the action, the plaintiff who cannot show that actual and substantial damages have been suffered should be subject to dismissal of his cause upon a motion for summary judgment.

[Author's note: Following certification, the U.S. District Court found that under the principles articulated by the Washington court in this case, the plaintiffs were not entitled to recover damages for trespass because they could not prove that they had incurred "substantial damages."]

Questions and Comments for Discussion

1. The *Bradley* court concluded that the defendant had the requisite intent to commit intentional trespass, and that an intentional deposit of microscopic particulates, undetectable by the human senses, gives rise to a cause of action for trespass as well as a claim of nuisance. The defendant had the requisite intent to commit intentional trespass as a matter of law because it knew that airborne pollution would result from its operation. Importantly, this is true even though the defendant may not have desired that effect. The traditional rule that intentional trespass should not require proof of actual damages was rejected in airborne pollution cases. The court's decision limited the concept of liability for defendants like American Smelting. The court said that a cause of action under such circumstances also requires proof of actual and substantial damages. How did the court's decision change the traditional common law tort of trespass? What policy concerns did the court cite to support this change?

(Continued)

2. As this case suggests, the "intention" of the defendant may be a factor in determining whether trespass has occurred. Under the Restatement of Torts, a defendant may be liable in trespass if it intentionally enters land of another, regardless of whether it actually causes harm to the interest of the plaintiff. Intention is proved by "desiring to bring about a certain result or with knowledge that the result is substantially certain to follow." Negligence is a breach of duty (in most cases, failing to use reasonable care.) Actual harm is a required element of a cause of action for reckless or negligent trespass. The traditional rule that intentional trespass was actionable without proof of damage recognized the value people place on being able to exclude others from their property, regardless of whether another's presence causes actual harm. How realistic is the distinction between intentional and negligent trespass? Why should a defendant be liable for intentional trespass if it causes no harm to the plaintiff?

3. *Bradley* illustrates some of the limitations of common law adjudication in airborne pollution cases. Suppose that the plaintiffs had been able to prove substantial damages to their property. Should they then be entitled to continuing damages or an injunction closing the plant? What would be the impact of permitting individual plaintiffs to sue manufacturers for airborne pollution under a continuing trespass theory? Consider that allowing parties to sue under a continuing trespass theory would increase litigation and potential damages in such cases.

4. What are the relative advantages and disadvantages of adopting a regulatory strategy to address the problems of air pollution rather than establishing such policy through common law case adjudication? Do you agree with those who have criticized common law adjudication as too slow and imprecise to be an effective way of establishing environmental policy? Or do you believe that common law provides a better scheme for addressing environmental harm than the "top-down" approach of national or state statutory and regulatory approaches? Remember that regulatory schemes permit a comprehensive approach to pollution, and pollution itself is a problem that affects people far beyond the source of the pollution.

5. The *Bradley* case came before the Washington State Supreme Court on certification from the U.S. District Court. The federal court must defer to the state court's opinion on a question of state common law like trespass. Discuss how the concept of federalism helps or hinders efforts to protect the environment in both common law and statutory law approaches.

6. The defendant in *Bradley* had the requisite intent to commit intentional trespass as a matter of law because it knew that airborne pollution would result from its operation. This is so even though the defendant may not have desired that effect. Explain the difference between intent as a matter of law, and the use of the word *intent* in everyday parlance.

■ *ACTIVITY BOX   Asarco Smelter, Ruston*

Visit the Environmental Protection Agency's Asarco Smelter-Ruston webpage: http://yosemite.epa.gov/r10/cleanup.nsf/sites/asarco#Study%20Area%20Zones

Also, Google "Asarco remediation Tacoma" to find video footage on YouTube of the smelter being demolished.

Consider the following questions:

1. Why did the residents of Tacoma and Ruston gather to watch the demolition of the Asarco smelter? Why did they cheer when it was demolished, especially in light of the fact that the smelter represented jobs for several generations of people?

2. If common law tort remedies were not available in cases such as the Asarco Smelter-Ruston situation, could local people ensure that businesses (often global businesses) did not contaminate their land and move on, with little or no responsibility to clean up the damage?

3. What are the drawbacks to common law remedies in mass tort cases, such as the one involving the Asarco plant in Tacoma?

4. How did the *Bradley* decision limit liability for defendants like American Smelting and Refining? Consider how allowing parties to sue under a continuing trespass theory would affect litigation and potential damages.

■ Nuisance

Nuisance is an unreasonable activity or condition on the defendant's land that substantially or unreasonably interferes with the plaintiff's use and enjoyment of his or her property. Nuisance law protects these rights and does not require a physical invasion of the property.

To recover damages for nuisance, a plaintiff must prove that the defendant's activities were "unreasonable" and that those activities "substantially interfered" with the plaintiff's enjoyment of his or her property. This requires the court to engage in a balancing test to determine whether a nuisance has occurred. As the court's opinion in *Bradley v. American Smelting & Refining* suggests, nuisance and trespass theories overlap in some cases, and plaintiffs seeking to recover damages for pollution of land, air, and water may use both theories.

Whether the defendant's activity is unreasonable for purposes of nuisance law depends on whether the activity is customary for the area, whether it causes observable effects most would find unpleasant, whether there are better methods for carrying on the activity, whether the activity has value to the defendant and society, and whether the defendant's activity began before the plaintiff's occupation of his or her land. Like the reasonableness test, the requirement of "substantial harm" to the plaintiff's use and enjoyment of his or her land in nuisance cases depends upon consideration of a number of factors. These include the value of the plaintiff's loss, whether there is observable damage to the property, and whether the harm is intermittent or unremitting.

Typical nuisance-causing agents include noise, dust, smoke, odors, and airborne or waterborne contaminants. Nuisance law has been used by plaintiffs seeking to recover damages for environmental harm like the contamination of groundwater by neighboring landfill operations, and for injury caused by noise, dust, and hazardous particulates deposited on land by incinerator and oil refinery operations. Nuisance law has also been utilized by some courts in right-to-light cases.

The successful plaintiff in a nuisance action may recover damages (measured by the loss of the value of the property), or may seek an injunction ordering the defendant to cease the activities that cause the nuisance. An injunction is subject to the court's discretion and requires the court to balance the hardship that would accrue to the plaintiff if the injunction is not issued against the defendant's hardship if it is. In the following 1970 airborne pollution case, the question of remedy was a central issue. Consider the limitations of the law of nuisance in controlling the general problems of air and water pollution, and the court's view of its role in making policy decisions about how best to address these problems.

In *Boomer v. Atlantic Cement Co.*, note that an injunction would have shut down the plant—and that closure would have had tremendous economic ramifications. As noted previously, the *Boomer* case was decided the same year that the Clean Air Act was enacted. Under the Clean Air Act, the Environmental Protection Agency or the state could enforce regulations to shut down the plant if it failed to meet legal standards, but the standards are technology-based standards, imposed by the state in implementation plans. Thus, a claim under the CAA requires a very different analysis than a common law nuisance analysis.

nuisance: Substantial or unreasonable interference with the plaintiff's use and enjoyment of its property.

Boomer v. Atlantic Cement Co.

26 N.Y.2d 219, 257 N.E.2d 870, 309 N.Y.S.2d 312 (1970)

Bergan, J.

Defendant operates a large cement plant near Albany. These are actions for injunction and damages by neighboring land owners alleging injury to property from dirt, smoke and vibration emanating from the plant. A nuisance has been found after trial, temporary damages have been allowed; but an injunction has been denied.

The public concern with air pollution arising from many sources in industry and in transportation is currently accorded ever wider recognition accompanied by a growing sense of responsibility in State and Federal Governments to control it. Cement plants are obvious sources of air pollution in the neighborhoods where they operate.

But there is now before the court private litigation in which individual property owners have sought specific relief from a single plant operation. The threshold question raised … on this appeal is whether the court should resolve the litigation between the parties now before it as equitably as seems possible; or whether, seeking promotion of the general public welfare, it should channel private litigation into broad public objectives.

A court performs its essential function when it decides the rights of parties before it. Its decision of private controversies may sometimes greatly affect public issues. Large questions of law are often resolved by the manner in which private litigation is decided. But this is normally an incident to the court's main function to settle controversy. It is a rare exercise of judicial power to use a decision in private litigation as a purposeful mechanism to achieve direct public objectives greatly beyond the rights and interests before the court.

Effective control of air pollution is a problem presently far from solution even with the full public and financial powers of government. In large measure adequate technical procedures are yet to be developed and some that appear possible may be economically impracticable.

It seems apparent that the amelioration of air pollution will depend on technical research in great depth; on a carefully balanced consideration of the economic impact of close regulation; and of the actual effect on public health. It is likely to require massive public expenditure and to demand more than any local community can accomplish and to depend on regional and interstate controls.

A court should not try to do this on its own as a by-product of private litigation and it seems manifest that the judicial establishment is neither equipped in the limited nature of any judgment it can pronounce nor prepared to lay down and implement an effective policy for the elimination of air pollution. This is an area beyond the circumference of one private lawsuit. It is a direct responsibility for government and should not thus be undertaken as an incident to solving a dispute between property owners and a single cement plant— one of many—in the Hudson River valley.

The cement making operations of defendant have been found by the court at Special Term to have damaged the nearby properties of plaintiffs in these two actions.… The total damage to plaintiffs' properties is, however, relatively small in comparison with the value of defendant's operation and with the consequences of the injunction which plaintiffs seek.

* * *

One alternative is to grant the injunction but postpone its effect to a specified future date to give opportunity for technical advances to permit defendant to eliminate the nuisance; another is to grant the injunction conditioned on the payment of permanent damages to plaintiffs which would compensate them for the total economic loss to their property present and future caused by defendant's operations. For reasons which will be developed the court chooses the latter alternative.

* * *

[T]echniques to eliminate dust and other annoying by-products of cement making are unlikely to be developed by any research the defendant can undertake within any short period, but will depend on the total resources of the cement industry Nationwide and throughout the world. The problem is universal wherever cement is made.

For obvious reasons the rate of the research is beyond control of defendant. If at the end of 18 months the whole industry has not found a technical solution a court would be hard put to close down this one cement plant if due regard be given to equitable principles.

On the other hand, to grant the injunction unless defendant pays plaintiffs such permanent damages as may be fixed by the court seems to do justice between the contending parties. All of the attributions of economic loss to the properties on which plaintiffs' complaints are based will have been redressed.

[The court then held that the injunction should "be vacated upon payment by defendant of such amount of permanent damage to the respective plaintiffs as determined by the" trial court.]

(Continued)

JASEN, J. (dissenting)

I agree with the majority that a reversal is required here, but I do not subscribe to the newly enunciated doctrine of assessment of permanent damages, in lieu of an injunction, where substantial property rights have been impaired by the creation of a nuisance.

* * *

The harmful nature and widespread occurrence of air pollution have been extensively documented. Congressional hearings have revealed that air pollution causes substantial property damage, as well as being a contributing factor to a rising incidence of lung cancer, emphysema, bronchitis and asthma.

The specific problem faced here is known as particulate contamination because of the fine dust particles emanating from defendant's cement plant. The particular type of nuisance is not new, having appeared in many cases for at least the past 60 years.... It is interesting to note that cement production has recently been identified as a significant source of particular contamination in the Hudson Valley. This type of pollution, wherein very small particles escape and stay in the atmosphere, has been denominated as the type of air pollution which produces the greatest hazard to human health. We have thus a nuisance which not only is damaging to the plaintiffs, but also is decidedly harmful to the general public.

I see grave dangers in overruling our long-established rule of granting an injunction where a nuisance results in substantial continuing damage. In permitting the injunction to become inoperative upon the payment of permanent damages, the majority is, in effect, licensing a continuing wrong. It is the same as saying to the cement company, you may continue to do harm to your neighbors so long as you pay a fee for it. Furthermore, once such permanent damages are assessed and paid, the incentive to alleviate the wrong would be eliminated, thereby continuing air pollution of an area without abatement....

Questions and Comments for Discussion

1. What do you think of the majority's decision to require payment of "permanent damages" to the plaintiffs in this case in lieu of an injunction? Do you agree with the dissenting judge's statement that this amounts to "licensing a continuing wrong"? How would you have balanced the equities in this case? Consider that an injunction would have shut down the plant, which would have caused great economic consequences and ramifications.

2. Note that the *Boomer* case was decided in 1970, the year that the modern Clean Air Act (CAA) was adopted. The CAA does not necessarily preempt common law actions for nuisance like the one in this case. Should plaintiffs be entitled to common law remedies in cases where defendants are in compliance with state and federal air quality regulations? What are the implications of your answer?

3. In another case,[9] the plaintiffs sued a solvent company, alleging contamination and pollution of their well water as a result of the defendants' improper handling of toxic chemicals and industrial waste at their facilities. The trial court dismissed the plaintiffs' claims for damages under a nuisance theory because no intrusion of contaminated water had occurred and there was no quantifiable damage based on the claim. The plaintiffs maintained that because the defendants had contaminated the groundwater, their property values had diminished, notwithstanding the fact that no contaminants had come or would come onto their property.

   Should the court hold that property owners who have only suffered a decrease in property values are entitled to damages under a nuisance theory? For what policy reasons do you think a court might be willing to permit recovery of damages in such cases?

Public Nuisance and Private Nuisance

public nuisance: A wrong that affects a large portion of the public by interfering with their common rights.

private nuisance: Substantial interference with the right of another to the use and enjoyment of its property.

A **public nuisance** affects a large portion of the public by interfering with their common rights. A **private nuisance** affects a private interest in the use and enjoyment of land. The difference between a public and private nuisance is a matter of degree. The same kind of activity that gives rise to an action for a private nuisance may also give rise to an action for public nuisance. But public nuisances cause a pervasive, widespread harm to many, whereas a private nuisance affects a narrower class of individuals. Under various state statutes, the government or private individuals may be authorized to bring an action to abate a public nuisance.

---

[9] *Adkins v. Thomas Solvent Co.*, 459 N.W.2d 22 (Mich. Ct. App. 1990), *rev'd & remanded*, 487 N.W.2d 715 (Mich. 1990).

In one California case, *Lincoln Properties, Ltd. v. Higgins,*[10] Lincoln Center, a shopping center in Stockton, California, asserted a public and private nuisance claim against tenants of Lincoln Center who operated dry cleaning establishments there. Tests conducted in 1985 and 1986 revealed that water in San Joaquin County wells adjacent to the shopping center had been contaminated by several hazardous chemical compounds used by the dry cleaners. Lincoln was statutorily liable for the contamination because it owned the property, and it sued the past and present owners of the dry cleaning facilities in an effort to force them to investigate and remediate the contamination and reimburse Lincoln for costs it had incurred.

The court agreed that the release of manmade carcinogenic chemical compounds in the soil and groundwater under Lincoln Center interfered with Lincoln's free use and comfortable enjoyment of its property and constituted both a public and private nuisance. It said that the nuisance affected a considerable number of persons, as it had forced the county to close four water supply wells. It also said that Lincoln had established a nuisance per se because the defendants' actions violated the discharge permit requirement of the county code. The court rejected the dry cleaners' argument that because their leases required them to use the premises only for conducting dry cleaning, Lincoln had authorized that activity in the lease.

Application of Federal Nuisance Law to Environmental Claims

Today, the use of federal nuisance law in the area of climate change litigation has been sharply curtailed by the U.S. Supreme Court. In 2011, the Supreme Court heard arguments in *American Electric Power Co. v. Connecticut.*[11] This suit, brought by several states, New York City, and several land trusts, sought to use federal nuisance law to curtail carbon dioxide emissions from the defendant utility companies. The court held "that the Clean Air Act and the EPA actions it authorizes displace any federal common law right to seek abatement of carbon-dioxide emissions from fossil-fuel fired power plants.... [E]missions of carbon dioxide qualify as air pollution subject to regulation under the [Clean Air] Act.... And we think it equally plain that the Act 'speaks directly' to emissions of carbon dioxide from the defendants' plants."[12]

Since then, the circuit courts of appeal have followed precedent. For example, in 2012, in *Native Village of Kivalina v. ExxonMobil,*[13] the Ninth Circuit Court of Appeals barred federal nuisance claims as articulated in *American Electric Power Co. v. Connecticut.*

Of course, federal nuisance claims could still be brought by plaintiffs whose claims are not "displaced" by a federal statutory scheme. However, in the context of climate change, this tort action has essentially been foreclosed.

Application of State Nuisance Law to Environmental Claims

Notwithstanding the various death knells for nuisance law—consider *Boomer*'s "permanent damages" strategy, as well as the more recent *American Electric Power Co. v. Connecticut* decision by the U.S. Supreme Court barring federal nuisance claims in climate change litigation—state nuisance law remains alive and well (as does federal

---

[10] 23 Envtl. L. Rep. 20665 (E.D. Cal. 1993).
[11] No. 10-174, 594 U.S. ___ (2011).
[12] *Id.* at 2537.
[13] 696 F.3d 849 (9th Cir. 2012).

nuisance law in areas where federal statutory schemes have not displaced it). Additionally, it's useful to remember that tort claims can be stacked, and they can also be brought in addition to claims of statutory violations. This simply means that a plaintiff may bring many tort claims against the defendant at a time. The plaintiff does not have to choose between competing tort claims or statutory claims.

A good example of this is *Ellis v. Gallatin Steel Co.*,[14] in which the plaintiff succeeded on claims under both state nuisance law and the federal Clean Air Act, resulting from the defendant's manufacturing activities that caused "fugitive dust" to migrate onto private land. This dust resulted in health problems, among other things. Not only were compensatory damages awarded under nuisance law, but punitive damages were awarded as well, for a total of almost $850,000. The court discussed the trial court's findings, which it affirmed, concerning the actions that gave rise to the nuisance suit:

> [T]he district court found that it operated its slag processing facility for seven years without air pollution controls sufficient to stop its air pollution, all the time knowing that its dust created a nuisance but refusing to take action until the district court ordered it. The court also found that Harsco built its slag pit in the open even though it knew explosions would result from rain hitting the molten slag and that the company neglected to cover the pit to stop the explosions until the court ordered the construction of a containment building. As to Gallatin, the district court found that it knew dust from its operations drifted onto plaintiffs' land but did not abate the nuisance.[15]

A defense to nuisance is "coming to the nuisance," a doctrine which asserts that the plaintiff should not be able to recover for injuries if the condition that created the nuisance was present before the plaintiff's alleged presence and injury. However, if the character of the area has substantially changed after the condition giving rise to the nuisance was established, then this defense will most likely not prevail.

■ Negligence

Negligence imposes liability on a person who breaches a legal duty to another. The elements of a negligence action are: (1) the defendant had a legal duty to the plaintiff; (2) the defendant breached that duty; and (3) the defendant's breach of duty was the actual cause and (4) proximate (legal) cause of (5) a legally recognizable injury to the plaintiff.

Unlike intentional torts such as assault, battery, and intentional trespass and nuisance, negligence does not require proof that the defendant intended to bring about a particular result. The essence of a negligence action is breach of legal duty by the defendant. Breach may occur either through the defendant's act or failure to act when it has a duty to do so.

The basic legal duty that each of us owes to others is the duty to act "with reasonable care." To determine whether a person has acted with reasonable care, the finder of fact (either a judge or jury) uses an objective standard of conduct: namely, whether the defendant acted or failed to act as a "reasonable person of ordinary prudence in similar circumstances" would have. This **reasonably prudent person standard** is a flexible standard that allows the fact-finder to consider all the circumstances surrounding a particular action. Defenses to negligence include assumption of the risk and contributory negligence or comparative fault.

reasonably prudent person standard: An objective standard of conduct against which actions are measured to determine negligence.

[14] 390 F.3d 461 (6th Cir. 2004).
[15] *Id.* at 471.

The law may impose special duties on people in some instances. Special duties may arise from a special relationship between the parties. For example, a contractual or agency relationship between the parties may impose a duty to disclose information, and the law has long imposed upon a common carrier or innkeeper a duty to protect passengers and guests against the foreseeable wrongful acts of others. Whether a defendant had a special duty to a plaintiff is a question of law.

Another important source of legal duties is federal and state laws. Under the theory of **negligence per se**, a person may be liable for injuries to another that result from violation of an environmental statute or regulation. Negligence per se requires proof that the harm the statute was designed to prevent occurred to a person whom the statute was intended to protect. To illustrate, assume that there is a law prohibiting the discharge of paint thinner into a public sewer system. If the defendant discharges paint thinner into a public sewer, he can be liable for damages that are foreseeable as a result of his negligence. He may also be subject to a civil or criminal penalty for violating state and federal hazardous waste laws. However, even if a plaintiff can prove breach of duty under a negligence per se theory, the plaintiff will not win the case unless she can prove that the breach of the duty was the actual cause of her injuries. Failure to comply with regulatory standards would be proof of negligence per se if the harm that occurred to the

Benefits and drawbacks of common law remedies as compared to statutory remedies

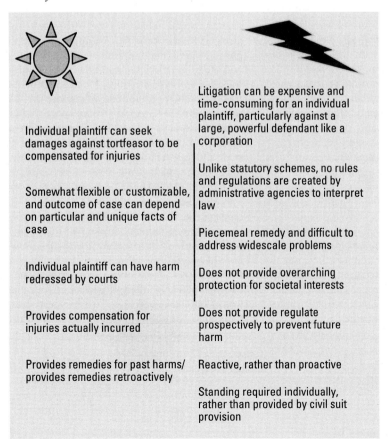

Individual plaintiff can seek damages against tortfeasor to be compensated for injuries	Litigation can be expensive and time-consuming for an individual plaintiff, particularly against a large, powerful defendant like a corporation
Somewhat flexible or customizable, and outcome of case can depend on particular and unique facts of case	Unlike statutory schemes, no rules and regulations are created by administrative agencies to interpret law
	Piecemeal remedy and difficult to address widescale problems
Individual plaintiff can have harm redressed by courts	Does not provide overarching protection for societal interests
Provides compensation for injuries actually incurred	Does not provide regulate prospectively to prevent future harm
Provides remedies for past harms/ provides remedies retroactively	Reactive, rather than proactive
	Standing required individually, rather than provided by civil suit provision

negligence per se: Negligence arising from a defendant's breach of a legal duty imposed by statute, ordinance, or administrative rule or regulation, which results in injury occurring to a person whom that statute was intended to protect.

plaintiff was the kind of harm the regulation was designed to prevent and the plaintiff was in the class of persons protected.

Negligence theory may be used by plaintiffs seeking to recover damages from defendants in environmental cases. In most cases, negligence is just one of several different theories argued by plaintiffs in such cases. In the following case, the court held that the plaintiff had satisfactorily stated a claim for negligence.

Newhall Land & Farming Co. v. Superior Court of Fresno County (Mobil Oil Corp. et al., real parties in interest)

19 Cal. App. 4th 334, 23 Cal. Rptr. 2d 377, 1993 Cal. App. LEXIS 1012 (1993)

Franson, J.

Newhall is the current owner of real property which was previously the site of a natural gas processing plant. Newhall filed an action against [defendants Amerada and Mobil Oil Corp.] to recover damages stemming from the contamination of the soil and groundwater which occurred while Amerada and Mobil were operating this gas plant between 1950 and 1970. Newhall purchased the property in 1984.

* * *

Mobil acquired the property in 1950 and built a natural gas processing plant on it. Mobil operated this gas plant until 1970 when it sold the property to Amerada. Amerada continued operating the gas plant for less than one year. Thereafter, the plant was partially dismantled and rendered inoperative.

In 1971, Amerada sold the property to a third party. In 1984, following several intervening owners, Newhall acquired the surface rights of the property. Newhall is a farming company and used water from this property in its farming operations.

During the time Mobil and Amerada operated the gas plant, they discharged hazardous substances onto the ground, knowing that these substances would pollute the soil and enter the groundwater. This discharge was expressly prohibited by three [California] statutes: ... When the property was sold, neither Mobil nor Amerada disclosed the existence of the contamination on the site.

When Newhall acquired the property, there was no visible evidence of these prior discharges. At that time, Newhall had no way of knowing and did not suspect that the property was contaminated. Newhall discovered petroleum staining of the soil when removing the remaining concrete foundations from the property in August 1989. Further environmental testing revealed other contamination in the form of heavy metals and other volatiles in the water table beneath the property.

These pollutants continue to move through the soil and into the groundwater, causing new damage each day. As a result of the contamination, Newhall has been unable to sell this property.

* * *

Newhall's cause of action is founded on negligence. "It is hornbook law that 'actionable negligence involves a legal duty to use due care, a breach of such legal duty, and the breach as the proximate or legal cause of the resulting injury....'" (*Felburg v. Don Wilson Builders* (1983) 142 Cal. App. 3d 383, 393 [191 Cal. Rptr. 92].)

* * *

... Here, Newhall has alleged: (1) the property's soil and groundwater have been contaminated with hazardous substances due to Mobil's and Amerada's unlawful discharges; (2) this condition has unreasonably affected the groundwater's use for domestic, industrial, agricultural and other beneficial use and thus, has materially lessened the value of the property; (3) Mobil and Amerada knew of this contamination but did not disclose the condition of the property to subsequent purchasers; (4) at the time Newhall acquired the property, it was unaware of the contamination. There was no visible evidence of contamination, and Newhall was not made aware of any facts or information which would have caused suspicion about or knowledge of contamination, and no such information was available to Newhall. Newhall also alleges it has been damaged in that it will incur costs to evaluate, test and remove the contamination, and further that it has not been able to sell the property due to the contamination.

Through these allegations, Newhall has covered all the elements ... necessary to state a cause of action except for the element of causation, i.e., that Newhall would not have purchased the property had the contaminated condition of the property been disclosed. It can be inferred that this is true.

Questions and Comments for Discussion

1. Summarize the facts in the *Newhall* case. Who was the plaintiff? Why did the plaintiff sue the

(Continued)

defendants? According to the plaintiff, what acts or omissions of the defendants constituted negligence? What might the defendants have done to avoid liability for negligence in this case?

2. What standard of care were the defendants required to meet in this case? Note that in general, a purchase/sale agreement does not create a special duty between buyer and seller. Most states, however, have imposed upon the seller of residential property a duty to disclose material defects in the property if they are known to the seller and not discoverable by the buyer. Whether this duty to disclose extends to sellers of commercial property is a policy question that is not settled.

Negligent or intentional misrepresentation, including misrepresentation through nondisclosure, may be a basis for recovering damages in tort or for rescinding a contract for the sale or lease of property. Fraud is an intentional tort, requiring proof of a false misrepresentation with intent to deceive. What kind of evidence might support such a theory in this case? What kind of evidentiary problems might arise for the plaintiffs in attempting to establish fraud under these facts?

As illustrated in the *Newhall Land* case, the five elements of negligence must all be present in order to state a claim for negligence. Again, these elements are: (1) duty of care, (2) breach of the duty of care, (3) actual causation, (4) proximate causation, and (5) actual injury. In other words, it is not enough for a plaintiff merely to prove breach of legal duty if it hopes to recover damages from the defendant under a negligence theory. The plaintiff must also prove the other elements, too. Here's how that works:

Duty of care: The plaintiff must first show that the defendant had a duty of care to the plaintiff. A duty of care is owed to persons within the foreseeable zone of danger.

Breach of the duty of care: The plaintiff must then show that the duty of care was breached. This is usually done by showing that the defendant's actions fell below the reasonably prudent person standard.

Actual causation: Next, the plaintiff must show that the defendant's breach of duty was the actual cause of the plaintiff's injuries. The requirement of actual causation (or "cause in fact") requires the plaintiff to prove an actual causal link between the defendant's action and the harm that occurred. Courts frequently employ a "but-for" test in determining actual causation. Under this test, a defendant's conduct is the actual cause of a plaintiff's injury if that injury would not have occurred *but for* the defendant's breach of duty. In other cases, especially those in which the defendant's conduct combined with other circumstances to cause the plaintiff's injury, courts may employ a substantial factor test. Under this test, a defendant's conduct is the actual cause if it was a substantial factor in bringing about the plaintiff's injuries.

Proximate causation: Next, the plaintiff must show that the defendant's actions were the proximate cause, or legal cause, of the injury. Tests of proximate cause include whether the injury was "foreseeable," or within the scope of foreseeable risk.

Actual injury: The injury to the plaintiff must be actual rather than speculative or potential.

Let's look a little more closely at the third element, actual causation. It may seem that the requirements to prove actual causation are fairly simple to meet. However, actual causation can be a very difficult element for the plaintiff to establish in environmental tort cases. Especially in toxic tort and pollution cases, the requirement to establish cause in fact may prevent plaintiffs from recovering damages because it is so difficult to prove a causal link between the defendant's activity and the personal injuries that a plaintiff alleges occurred as a result. Review the following case and see if you agree with the court's opinion.

Wilcox v. Homestake Mining Co.
2008 U.S. Dist. LEXIS 110321; 38 Envtl. L. Rep. 20270 (D.N.M. 2008)

Conway, J. E.

THIS MATTER comes before the Court … for Summary Judgment…. This "toxic tort" lawsuit arises from the alleged release of radioactive and other hazardous substances by Defendants from their uranium milling facility near Milan, New Mexico. Plaintiffs are residents or former residents of neighborhoods adjacent to the Homestake uranium milling facility. They contend that Defendants' release of these hazardous substances into their environment, including their drinking water, caused them to develop various cancers.

I. Background

[T]his Court … allow[ed] Plaintiffs … to "produce expert affidavits which make a prima facie showing of harmful exposure and specific causation for each injury the particular Plaintiff claims was caused by the Defendants' alleged contamination." … Defendants acknowledge receipt of Plaintiffs' affidavits from Inder J. Chopra, M.D.; Robert Peter Gale, M.D., Ph.D., D.Sc. (hon.), F.A.C.P.; F. Owen Hoffman, Ph.D.; and A. James Ruttenber, M.D. but contend that these affidavits "fail as a matter of law to make a prima facie showing of specific causation." … Defendants argue that

> Plaintiffs' expert affidavits fail to raise a factual issue on the essential "but for" element of proximate causation. The affidavits do not declare or even imply that, but for or without Homestake's conduct, any Plaintiff would not have experienced the claimed adverse health effects.

* * *

Acknowledging that causation is generally an element that requires determination by a jury, Defendants argue there are no facts presented that could allow a reasonable jury to find a sufficient causal connection between their actions and Plaintiffs' cancers…. Whereas causation must be proved by probability, … Defendants contend Plaintiffs offer only "mere speculation and conjecture—possibilities, not *probabilities*." …

In response, Plaintiffs do not dispute their burden. Plaintiffs admit they "must show that it is more probable

than not that (or to a reasonable degree of medical probability) Homestake's negligence contributed to the cause of the alleged injuries, such that had Homestake not been negligent, these Plaintiffs would probably be cancer free." … Their expert affidavits satisfy the but-for test for causation, according to Plaintiffs. They explain a three-step process. First, Plaintiffs' expert Dr. Owen Hoffman estimated the probability of causation for each of the remaining three Plaintiffs as follows: (1) Hartman's probability of causation is between 0.5% and 41%, (2) Serna's probability of causation is between 0.073% and 25%, and (3) Wilcox's probability of causation is between 3.3% and 80%…. Second, Dr. James Ruttenber avers that "the best approach to determining the contribution to the cause of cancer diagnosed in an individual is with estimates of cancer risk and assigned share." … Third, Drs. Inder Chopra and Robert Gale, relying on Drs. Hoffman and Ruttenber, testify that Plaintiffs' exposures to radiation were a "substantial factor" in each Plaintiff's development of cancer….

More specifically, Dr. Chopra's original affidavit states, "[i]n my opinion, Ms. Serna was thus exposed to potentially carcinogenic doses of radionuclides and her exposure was of sufficient magnitude, duration and intensity that it may have been a substantial contributing factor contributing to the onset, growth and/or progression of her thyroid cancer." … Dr. Chopra's supplemental affidavit states that Plaintiff Serna's "exposure to radiation from Homestake's operations was a contributing factor to her cancer." … Dr. Gale opines as to both Plaintiff Hartman and Wilcox that "[a]ssuming the medical records available to me are correct and complete and that no other parameter(s) unknown to me could, as a sole cause overwhelmingly explain each plaintiff having the cancer specified, I opine: to a reasonable medical probability exposure to ionizing radiations as a consequence of Defendants' operations was a substantial factor contributing to each plaintiff developing cancer." …

Plaintiffs freely acknowledge that the cause of cancer is unknown. They state that "[i]t is not necessary (nor is it possible) to opine that but for exposure at Homestake, [Plaintiffs] would never have suffered an

(Continued)

injury in the same category [i.e., cancer]." … As Defendants point out, "there are many other possible causes of Plaintiffs' cancers, including Plaintiffs' lifestyles, family histories, and other radiation exposure (e.g., medical and natural) to name a few." … Whereas Plaintiffs correctly contend they do not have to negate every potential cause in order to meet their burden of proving but-for causation, … Defendants allege that summary judgment is appropriate unless Plaintiffs' experts testify that radiation exposure as a result of Homestake's operations was a but-for cause of Plaintiffs' respective cancers….

II. Legal Standard

Summary judgment is appropriate "if the pleadings, the discovery and disclosure materials on file, and any affidavits show that there is no genuine issue as to any material fact and that the movant is entitled to judgment as a matter of law." …

* * *

III. Discussion

A. Defendants Rely Upon *June v. Union Carbide Corp.*

Defendants urge the Court to follow the reasoning of Judge Marcia S. Krieger of the Federal District Court of Colorado in *June v. Union Carbide Corp.*, [2007 U.S. Dist. LEXIS 95443,] 2007 WL 4224228 (D.Colo., Nov. 27, 2007), a toxic tort case involving facts similar to the present case as well as the same lawyers on both sides and the same experts who appear for the Plaintiffs in the present case. Judge Krieger granted summary judgment in favor of Defendants, holding that

> the opinions offered by the Plaintiffs' experts, Dr. Inder Chopra and Dr. Robert Gale, were insufficient to establish causation under Colorado law, because they offered no opinion that, 'but for' the exposure to radiation at Uravan, the Plaintiffs would not have become ill. Their opinions fell short in that they only opined that exposure to radiation was a substantial factor contributing to the [] Plaintiffs' injuries….

… Judge Krieger confirmed that Colorado law requires proof of but-for causation and held that the "substantial factor" test has not subsumed the but-for test for causation…. Judge Krieger further held that causation cannot be shown merely by showing exposure to hazardous substances at levels generally sufficient to cause the injuries alleged…. Specific evidence that exposure to the defendant's waste caused the plaintiffs' conditions is required….

Plaintiffs argue that *June* is distinguishable from the present case, but they do not present any facts to demonstrate how *June* is not analogous. Plaintiffs also claim that there is a different standard for causation under Colorado law versus New Mexico law; however, the but-for tests at issue in both *June* and this case are identical.

B. Standard for Causation Under New Mexico Law

New Mexico's Uniform Jury Instruction on causation provides

> An [act] [or] [omission] [or] [_____ (*condition*)] is a "cause" of [injury] [harm] [_____ (*other*)] if [, unbroken by an independent intervening cause,] it contributes to bringing about the [injury] [harm] [_____ (*other*)] [, and if injury would not have occurred without it]. It need not be the only explanation for the [injury] [harm] [_____ (*other*)], nor the reason that is nearest in time or place. It is sufficient if it occurs in combination with some other cause to produce the result. To be a "cause", the [act] [or] [omission] [or] [_____ (*condition*)], nonetheless, must be reasonably connected as a significant link to the [injury] [harm].

Although the but-for clause is bracketed in the latest version of this jury instruction, there is no indication in New Mexico case law that the but-for clause is no longer a required element of causation….

In fact, the New Mexico Court of Appeals specifically declined to relax the standard of causation to one "requiring proof of only a substantial possibility that the result complained of would have been avoided but for the tortious conduct." … Given that the substantial factor test has been described as "more lenient," *see, e.g., In re Hanford Nuclear Reservation Litigation*, 534 F.3d 986, 1010 (9th Cir. 2008), this Court will not substitute any causation standard in place of the but-for test absent some evidence that the New Mexico Supreme Court has adopted and approved the alternative standard. [The court included the following footnote: "It appears doubtful that Plaintiffs could satisfy the more lenient substantial factor test even if the Court were to apply it in place of the but-for test. As noted by the Ninth Circuit, applying Washington law, the applicable substantial factor causation "applies when there have been 'multiple, independent causes,' each of which alone is sufficient to cause the injury." … Based on facts similar to those in the present case, the Ninth Circuit held that cancers suffered by the plaintiffs, downwinders from the test site for the atomic bomb, could have been caused solely by their genetics or multiple other factors, and plaintiffs therefore could not show that their exposures alone would have been sufficient to cause their cancers."]

(Continued)

C. But-For Causation in the Context of a Toxic Torts

"To survive summary judgment on a toxic tort claim for physical injuries, [a plaintiff must] show that he was exposed to chemicals that could have caused the physical injuries he complains about (general causation), and that his exposure did in fact result in those injuries (specific causation)." *Golden v. CH2M Hill Hanford Group, Inc.*, 528 F.3d 681, 683 (9th Cir. 2008).... Assumptions as to the cause of a disease made for purposes of treatment does not establish causation....

Federal courts have noted the important role of causation in the area of toxic torts. *Rider v. Sandoz Pharmaceuticals Corp.*, 296 F.3d 1194, 1197 (11th Cir. 2002) ("[t]oxic tort cases, such as this one, are won or lost on the strength of the scientific evidence presented to prove causation"). Where the plaintiffs' alleged injuries are cancer-related, causation poses a particular problem for plaintiffs, since cancer frequently occurs in the absence of any toxic exposure and since it is generally very difficult, if not impossible, to scientifically trace an individual's cancer to a particular exposure. *See, e.g., In re Hanford Nuclear Reservation Litigation*, 534 F.3d 986, 1010-1011 (9th Cir. 2008) (rejecting the plaintiffs' request to apply the more lenient substantial factor test and recognizing that factors other than defendants' plutonium emissions, such as smoking and genetics, could have caused the plaintiffs to develop cancer even in the absence of any plutonium emissions).

D. Analysis of Plaintiffs' Expert Affidavits

The Court agrees with Defendants that Plaintiffs' expert affidavits do not establish a prima facie case of specific causation. Dr. Chopra's initial affidavit very clearly fails to meet the but-for test. Not only does Dr. Chopra indicate that Plaintiff Serna was exposed only to "*potentially* carcinogenic doses of radionuclides," but he also states that this exposure "*may have been* a substantial contributing factor contributing to the onset, growth and/or progression of her thyroid cancer." ... Dr. Chopra does not cure the deficiencies in his original affidavit with the supplemental language that Ms. Serna's exposure "was a *contributing factor* to her cancer." ... Nowhere in either of Dr. Chopra's affidavits does he indicate that but for Homestake's operations, Ms. Serna probably would not have developed cancer.

Dr. Gale's affidavit is similarly deficient. Initially, Dr. Gale states only that the exposure [of] Plaintiffs Hartman and Wilcox was, more likely than not, a substantial factor contributing to each plaintiff developing cancer." ... Thus, like Dr. Chopra's opinion, Dr. Gale's opinion does not meet the but-for threshold. Further,

Dr. Gale's opinion acknowledges that unknown parameters could be the but-for cause of these Plaintiffs' cancers.... By assuming at the outset that no other unknown factors could be the "overwhelming" cause of these Plaintiffs' cancers, Dr. Gale's opinion is reminiscent of the plaintiffs' expert in the Agent Orange toxic tort litigation brought by Vietnam veterans. There, the plaintiffs' causation expert Dr. Singer averred as follows:

> Assuming the truth of the affidavits submitted, and absent any evidence of pre-existing, intervening, or superseding causes for the symptoms and diseases complained of in these affidavits, it is my opinion to a reasonable degree of medical probability (that is, more likely than not) that the medical difficulties described by the affiants were proximately caused by exposure to Agent Orange.

... The court rejected Dr. Singer's opinion as to causation, holding that

> One need hardly be a doctor of medicine to make the statement that if X is a possible cause of Y, and if there is no other possible cause of Y, X must have caused Y. Dr. Singer's formulation avoids the problem before us: which of myriad possible causes of Y created a particular veteran's problems. To take just one of the diseases reported by plaintiffs in an undifferentiated form, and relied upon by Dr. Singer, hepatitis: this is a disease common in the civilian population and there is not the slightest evidence that its incidence is greater among those exposed to Agent Orange than those not exposed. It may well be that hepatitis among Vietnam veterans is greater than among those who did not serve there because of greater incidence of this problem in Vietnam resulting from drug abuse and generally unsanitary conditions. There is no showing that among Vietnam veterans the incidence of hepatitis is greater in those exposed to Agent Orange.... Dr. Singer's conclusory allegations lack any foundation in fact. His analysis, in addition to being speculative, is so guarded as to be worthless....

IV. Conclusion

Having reviewed the parties['] briefings and being otherwise fully informed, the Court determines there are no genuine disputes as to material issues of fact. Because Plaintiffs' experts are not able to testify that, more likely than not, Defendants' alleged negligence was a but-for cause of their cancers, Plaintiffs cannot meet their prima facie burden of demonstrating specific causation. Summary judgment should therefore be granted in favor of Defendants.

(Continued)

Questions and Comments for Discussion

1. Under the but-for test used in this case, the plaintiffs were unable to establish cause in fact. Problems of causation raise fundamental questions of risk assessment. Is it ever possible to establish causation beyond doubt using a but-for test? Courts are permitting plaintiffs to prove cause in fact by proving that the defendant's act or omission was a "substantial factor" in causing the plaintiff's injury. Do you think the substantial factor test unduly favors one side in toxic tort litigation?

2. In many environmental cases, proving that an injury occurred as a result of the defendant's activity or product may be extremely difficult. For example, what difficulties would a plaintiff who developed lung cancer after working in an asbestos plant for many years have in proving cause in fact? What kinds of evidence might the defendant introduce to raise doubt about cause in fact in such instances?

3. In another case, *Renaud v. Martin Marietta Corp.*,[16] the court held that community members had failed to show that a missile manufacturer had contaminated their drinking water to levels sufficient to cause injury, or that the contaminants caused their health problems. The court held that no reasonable juror could find, based on the expert opinions presented, that it was probable that community members had been exposed to the manufacturer's contaminants. The court held that circumstantial evidence only proved a possibility of exposure, and mere possibilities or conjecture cannot establish a probability. Community members' experts presumed exposure and testified that the injuries were consistent with such an exposure, but the court said that the evidence did not prove that community members had been exposed to the contaminants.

Let's now consider more closely the fourth element of negligence, proximate causation. Theoretically, every action by a person sets into motion an infinite chain of events that follow from that action. Like dropping a stone in a pool, "ripple" effects of the action spread out in all directions. For example, assume that the driver of a truck hauling toxic materials stops for lunch and spends 10 minutes longer than necessary at the lunch counter because a waitress arrived at work 10 minutes late. Three hours later, the driver's truck collides with another vehicle that suddenly pulls into his path. The crash results in a spill of toxic materials. Should the waitress be liable for negligence in causing the spill? Isn't it true that "but for" the fact that the waitress was late, the accident would not have occurred? If the waitress had been on time, the driver would have been 10 minutes farther down the road and would never have had the opportunity to collide with the other vehicle.

However, no one would seriously suggest that the waitress should be liable for the toxic waste spill in this example. It was simply not within the scope of foreseeable possibilities that late arrival at work would result in a toxic waste spill. This is the essence of the legal requirement of proximate cause in a negligence case. A defendant's liability is limited to results that were in the scope of the foreseeable risk created by its actions. Unlike actual causation, which is a question of fact, proximate cause is a question of law for the court.

Whether a manufacturer's negligent design and construction of a ship's steering gear system was the proximate cause of an oil spill was an issue in *In re Oil Spill by the Amoco Cadiz*.[17] In that case, the court ruled that the Amoco Corporation must pay the French government and other parties approximately $204 million in damages for a 1978 oil spill that damaged 180 miles of the Brittany coastline in France. In determining liability under a negligence theory, the court said that the failure of the steering gear system of the *Amoco Cadiz* was proximately caused by

---

[16] 749 F. Supp. 1545 (D. Colo. 1990).
[17] 954 F.2d 1279 (7th Cir. 1992).

the shipbuilder's improper design and construction and Amoco's negligence in failing to make repairs to the ship.

Applying the foreseeability test of proximate cause, one may conclude, as did the court in *Amoco Cadiz*, that it is foreseeable that negligence in the design and construction of a ship's steering gear and failure to repair the gear when it malfunctions could result in an accident that would lead to an oil spill. Another test that courts sometimes use to determine proximate cause is the reasonable and probable consequences test, under which a defendant is liable for the reasonable, natural, and probable consequences of its negligent act or omission.

Amoco Cadiz also illustrates the theory of negligence per se, because the court found that the flange assembly installed by the shipbuilder did not meet code requirements for high-pressure systems. Moreover, the court also found that Amoco was negligent in failing to reasonably perform its obligations to repair and maintain the steering gear, to properly train its crew, to provide the vessel with a redundant steering system with which to steer in the event of failure of the hydraulic system, and to fulfill its duty as the party who supervised and approved the design to ensure that the design and construction were properly carried out.

Finally, for a negligence claim to be successful, a plaintiff must have sustained actual—rather than speculative—injury. A plaintiff in a tort case is entitled to recover damages for physical injuries resulting from the defendant's negligent act or omission and for pain and suffering stemming from those physical injuries. But the law is unsettled on whether a plaintiff should recover damages for purely emotional injuries incurred as a result of the defendant's negligence. Part of the court's reluctance to permit recovery of emotional damages is a result of the fear of spurious claims and the difficulty of placing a monetary value on emotional injuries.

This becomes an issue in toxic tort cases where plaintiffs seek to recover damages because they suffered emotional injuries such as severe depression or anxiety as a result of exposure to toxic chemicals. In one such case, *Stites v. Sundstrand Heat Transfer, Inc.*,[18] the plaintiffs alleged that they suffered severe injuries from exposure to various toxic chemicals leaked from a manufacturing plant that the defendant operated in Dowagiac, Michigan. One of the chemicals used as a degreasing agent in the manufacturing process was trichloroethylene (TCE). The plaintiffs alleged that because of the defendant's failure to properly dispose of used TCE, the chemical had been entering the plaintiffs' drinking water for many years. They alleged that their prolonged and extensive exposure to the chemical caused them to suffer a depreciation in the market value of their property; loss of the use and enjoyment of the property; severe and permanent injury to their physical health; severe depression over fear of cancer; and humiliation, anxiety, mortification, anguish, emotional distress, outrage, and a loss of society and companionship from fellow family members, all of which were past, present, and future. On the defendant's motion for summary judgment, the court determined that the plaintiffs had failed to demonstrate the existence of sufficient facts indicating that they had a reasonable certainty of acquiring cancer in the future. However, it found the plaintiffs' fear-of-cancer claim more difficult to resolve. Michigan courts are lenient in finding allegations of physical harm sufficient to satisfy the requirement that plaintiffs' fears manifest themselves in the form of a definite and objective physical injury. The court said that a genuine issue existed as to whether some of the plaintiffs had experienced physical injury as a result of their fear of contracting cancer in the future. Consider the problem of proving injury in

---

[18] 660 F. Supp. 1516 (W.D. Mich. 1987).

this type of case. Should damages compensate for such intangibles as loss of quality of life?

In *Exxon Mobil Corp. v. Ford*,[19] a leak in a punctured line at an Exxon station caused gasoline to contaminate the groundwater with volatile organic compounds that are probable carcinogens. The court affirmed the jury's award of damages for emotional distress stemming from fear of cancer, holding that "the plaintiffs' alleged fear of cancer is a *present* harm, not a future one. Fear of cancer is a particularized type of emotional distress, not an attempt to circumvent the limitations on recovering for disease that may or may not develop in the future. Thus, while the fear must be reasonable … [the] reasonableness require[ment] … [does not require] the plaintiff to show that it is more likely than not that he or she will develop cancer."

The take-away point regarding actual injury is that the injury must be actual rather than speculative. In *Exxon Valdez v. Ford*, fear itself was recognized as injury.

◼ ◼ ◼ REVIEW AND STUDY QUESTIONS

1. What are the elements of trespass to land? What are the elements of nuisance? What are the elements of negligence? How would a plaintiff prove a claim for each?

2. What is the difference between negligence and negligence per se?

3. Do you agree that an intentional deposit of microscopic particulates, undetectable by the human senses, upon a person's property, should give rise to a cause of action for trespass? Why or why not?

4. The traditional rule that intentional trespass was actionable without proof of damage recognized the value that people place on being able to exclude others from their property, regardless of whether another's presence causes physical or actual damage. How is that principle still reflected in law today? Should it be? Why or why not?

5. Do you believe that statutory schemes such as the Clean Air Act or the Clean Water Act that seek to address environmental harms proactively are better at protecting the environment than common law approaches? Why or why not? See Box 4.3 for some points of comparison.

6. Explain the difference between trespass and nuisance. Is there a true difference in airborne pollution cases? Consider the holding in *Bradley*, which imposed a "substantial damages" test. Is the difference between trespass and nuisance that great?

7. Review the preceding *Amoco Cadiz* discussion. If you were an employer, what measures would you take to reduce liability exposure for negligence?

8. The issue on appeal in the *Stites* case was whether the trial court should have granted the defendant's motion for summary judgment. Recall that a motion for summary judgment requires the court to determine whether there is a dispute regarding material facts, and if not, whether the moving party is entitled to judgment as a matter of law. In the *Stites* case, the court declined to grant the defendant's motion for summary judgment as to the fear-of-cancer claim. What is the procedural effect of this decision?

9. Until fairly recently, most courts would not permit plaintiffs to recover for emotional injuries resulting from a defendant's negligence absent some physical impact or contact with the plaintiff's person. As the *Stites* and *Exxon Mobil* cases illustrate, many courts have abandoned this rule and permit recovery for emotional injuries alone; however, most still require, as a precondition of recovery, proof that some serious physical injury or symptoms resulted from the plaintiff's emotional distress. In cases like *Stites* or *Exxon Mobil*, what kind of evidence could a plaintiff submit to prove physical injury? What are the difficulties in proving such injuries? As a policy matter, should plaintiffs be entitled to recover damages for emotional distress and cancerphobia in toxic tort cases like this one? What are the consequences—to our courts, to business, and to society—of allowing such claims?

---

[19] 204 Md. App. 1 (Md. Ct. Spec. App. 2012).

Defenses to Negligence

As noted earlier, there are a number of defenses to tort actions. The defendant can argue that the facts as alleged by the plaintiff are not true, or the defendant can raise affirmative defenses.

Under traditional common law, a plaintiff in a negligence case could not recover damages if she was contributorily negligent herself or if she assumed the risk of injury. The doctrine of contributory negligence provides that a plaintiff who fails to exercise reasonable care for his own safety is barred from recovery if his own negligence was a substantial factor in producing his injury.

The doctrine of assumption of the risk affords another defense to liability. It provides that the plaintiff cannot recover damages under negligence if she has voluntarily undertaken a known risk. Assumption of the risk is allowed as a defense in a strict liability action, but contributory negligence is not.

A growing majority of states have discarded the traditional rule that contributory negligence and assumption of the risk are complete bars to recovery of damages by the plaintiff in negligence cases. Most states have adopted a comparative fault system that permits the fact-finder to determine the relative fault of the parties in a negligence action and to allocate damages to a plaintiff based on that determination.

The doctrines of contributory negligence and assumption of the risk are important in some environmental cases. If a plaintiff's own actions contribute to his exposure to hazardous materials, this may substantially limit his recovery of damages or bar recovery altogether.

In *Hull v. Merck & Co.*,[20] a supervisor for a fiberglass coating company was working on a project replacing fiberglass sewer lines at three chemical plants operated by Merck. A year after completing the contract, the employee suffered bone marrow depression and leukemia, which he said was caused by exposure to hazardous chemicals during the project. He sued Merck for $2.5 million plus punitive damages, alleging (among other things) that Merck had negligently failed to disclose the health dangers of the waste chemicals carried in its pipelines and failed to warn of the necessity for wearing protective gear during the replacement work. After being instructed that assumption of the risk would bar the employee's recovery under Georgia law, the jury ruled in favor of Merck and the employee appealed.

On appeal, the federal court of appeals said there was ample evidence to support a finding that the employee had assumed the risk of injury in this case. The court said that although the employee might not have had any knowledge of a specific carcinogenic risk posed by toluene (a toxic chemical in the pipeline), he knew from long experience that the handling of waste chemicals warranted protective measures. He also knew that Merck and his own company were supplying adequate safety gear, and despite this fact, and his substantial experience working with chemicals, he quit wearing any of the safety gear after a few days on the job. Under all the circumstances, according to the court, there was more than enough evidence to warrant the jury finding that Hull had assumed the risk by working around a continuing flow of waste chemicals during the replacement of the pipes.

Other defenses include discharge in bankruptcy (if the liability is a dischargeable debt), estoppel, laches, res judicata, and expiration of the statute of limitations.

---

[20] 758 F.2d 1474 (11th Cir. 1985).

■ Multiple-Party Toxic Torts Cases

A growing area of environmental litigation involves lawsuits by many persons exposed to toxic materials in the workplace or through the use of certain products or substances. These toxic tort cases create some unique problems. As a practical matter, the large number of plaintiffs suing a few defendants often results in difficult case management problems. There are usually complex issues of proof in such cases, particularly problems with establishing levels of toxicity and proving a causal link between the plaintiffs' injuries and exposure to the toxic substance. In some asbestos exposure cases, for example, long periods of time elapse between exposure and injury. Apportioning damages among the defendants in cases with multiple defendants may also be difficult.

In response to the complexity of such cases, courts have developed a procedural system to address some of the issues created by mass pleadings and multiple lawsuits. Rule 23 of the Federal Rules of Civil Procedure permits all persons who allege injury to be represented in a class action suit. In a class action suit, the class is represented in litigation by one member or a small portion of the class. Examples of class action mass tort cases include "Agent Orange" product liability litigation, asbestos litigation, radioactive waste litigation, and injuries related to global warming and drinking water contamination. Innovative procedural devices to facilitate multiple party litigation have been utilized in such cases.

One important development is recognition of industry-wide liability in some toxic tort or product liability cases. In cases where it is not possible for a plaintiff to prove which company within an industry produced the particular product causing injury, a court may apportion liability among all companies that *might* have produced the harmful product. This apportionment is usually based on market share throughout the industry at some point in time. Some courts have used this approach in lawsuits based on long-term exposure to asbestos.

■ Strict Liability

The previous sections have discussed how intentional or negligent behavior may result in liability for environmental harms caused to another. Under the theory of strict liability, a person who participates in certain harm-producing activities may be held liable for harm that results to others, even though that person did not intend to cause the harm, and even though he or she did everything possible to prevent the harm. **Strict liability** imposes liability on an individual or legal entity for the results of the defendant's actions regardless of negligence. Foreseeability is not a factor in strict liability cases, but courts recognize the defense that, looking back from the harm to the actor's conduct, it appears "highly extraordinary" that its actions should have brought about the harm.[21]

Imposition of liability under the theory of strict liability is a social policy decision. The rationale underlying strict liability is that the risk associated with some activities should be borne by those engaged in that activity rather than by the person who is exposed to the risk. Most courts hold that even if the other person is negligent, contributory negligence is not a bar to recovery under strict liability,

strict liability: Imposition of liability on an individual or legal entity for the results of its actions, regardless of negligence.

---

[21] RESTATEMENT (SECOND) OF TORTS § 435(2).

although assumption of the risk is generally a good defense in a strict liability action.

The justification for imposing strict liability upon defendants who engage in certain abnormally dangerous or ultrahazardous activities is that the person who voluntarily engages in that activity can ultimately pass the costs of liability on to other consumers, and in this way can spread the risk of liability for the activity. You may be aware of one class of activities for which strict liability is imposed: the manufacture or sale of defective or unreasonably dangerous products.

Certain environmentally dangerous activities, such as operating a hazardous waste landfill, may be designated an abnormally dangerous or ultrahazardous activity for which strict liability may be imposed. The decision to designate a particular activity as abnormally dangerous for purposes of this theory is an important policy decision for the courts. Imposing strict liability for certain activities will make conducting that activity riskier and more expensive for the operator. In some instances, people may be reluctant to engage in the activity at all.

Courts generally consider several factors when making the determination of whether an activity is abnormally dangerous or ultrahazardous for purposes of imposing strict liability. In *Indiana Harbor Belt Railroad Co. v. American Cyanamid Co.,*[22] the question before the court was whether a railway shipper of hazardous chemicals should be strictly liable for the consequences of a spill or other accident to the shipment en route. In deciding not to impose strict liability on the shipper of hazardous chemicals, the court reviewed section 520 of the *Restatement (Second) of Torts*, which lists factors to be considered in making that determination. The court said:

> The roots of section 520 are in nineteenth-century cases. The most famous one is *Rylands v. Fletcher* ... (1868), but a more illuminating one in the present context is *Guille v. Swan*, 19 Johns (N.Y.) 381 (1822). A man took off in a hot-air balloon and landed, without intending to, in a vegetable garden in New York City. A crowd that had been anxiously watching his involuntary descent trampled the vegetables in their endeavor to rescue him when he landed. The owner of the garden sued the balloonist for the resulting damage, and won. Yet the balloonist had not been careless. In the then state of ballooning it was impossible to make a pinpoint landing.
>
> *Guille* was a paradigmatic case for strict liability. (a) The risk (probability) of harm was great, and (b) the harm that would ensue if the risk materialized could be, although luckily was not, great (the balloonist could have crashed into the crowd rather than into the vegetables). The confluence of these two factors established the urgency of seeking to prevent such accidents. (c) Yet such accidents could not be prevented by the exercise of due care; the technology of care in ballooning was insufficiently developed. (d) The activity was not a matter of common usage, so there was no presumption that it was a highly valuable activity despite its unavoidable riskiness. (e) The activity was inappropriate to the place in which it took place—densely populated New York City.... (f) Reinforcing (d), the value to the community of the activity of recreational ballooning did not appear to be great enough to offset its unavoidable risks.

To determine whether imposing liability under this theory for a shipper of hazardous materials was appropriate, the court in *Indiana Harbor* next examined the circumstances of the case in light of the *Restatement* factors. The court pointed out that a railroad network is a hub-and-spoke system, and the hubs are in metropolitan areas. It is unlikely that chemicals can be rerouted around all metropolitan

---

[22] 916 F.2d 1174 (7th Cir. 1990),

areas in the country except at prohibitive cost. Even if it would be feasible to reroute them, a carrier, rather than a shipper, would be better situated to do the rerouting. In any event, according to the court, rerouting is no panacea because it will often increase the length of the journey or compel the use of a poorer track, or both. This in turn increases the probability of an accident and perhaps even the consequences of an accident. After considering these and other factors, the court ultimately concluded that this was not an apt case for strict liability.

Courts have imposed strict liability for a variety of different environmental activities. A Florida appellate court held that fumigation is an ultrahazardous activity for which a fumigation company may be held strictly liable, regardless of any alleged negligence by a third party. In that case, the defendant fumigated two evacuated condominium buildings, but fumes entered a third building through a supposedly impenetrable fire wall. Residents in the third building were injured when they inhaled the fumes, and they sued the fumigator. The court held that because its conduct was an ultrahazardous activity, negligence by third parties (the architect and contractors who allegedly failed to construct a proper fire wall), would not permit the fumigator to avoid liability.[23]

Review the following excerpt from *In re Hanford Nuclear Reservation Litigation*. This excerpt sets forth the facts and the portion of the case in which the court discusses abnormally dangerous activity under strict liability.

In re Hanford Nuclear Reservation Litigation v. E.I. DuPont de Nemours & Co., General Electric Co., et al.

534 F.3d 986 (9th Cir. 2008)

Schroeder, Circuit Judge:

I. Introduction

The origins of this case trace back more than sixty years to the height of World War II when the federal government solicited Appellants E.I. DuPont de Nemours & Co. [and other defendants] to operate the Hanford Nuclear Weapons Reservation ("Hanford") in southeastern Washington. The Hanford Reservation was a plutonium-production facility that helped make the atomic bomb that dropped on Nagasaki, Japan in World War II.

A regrettable Hanford byproduct was the radioiodine emitted into the surrounding area. The plaintiffs in this litigation are over two thousand residents who now claim that these emissions, known as 1-131, caused various cancers and other life-threatening diseases.... After almost two decades of litigation, which already has included two appeals to this court, the parties in 2005 agreed to a bellwether trial. The trial was designed to produce a verdict that would highlight the strengths and weaknesses of the parties' respective cases.... The

purpose of the trial was to promote settlement and bring long-overdue resolution to this litigation.

Before us on appeal is a litany of issues stemming from the bellwether trial....

... Defendants argue that even if they are not immune, they are not strictly liable for any 1-131 emissions, because the amounts of the emissions were within federally-authorized levels; the plutonium-production process was not an abnormally dangerous activity that would create strict liability; and even if it were, Defendants qualify for the "public duty" exception to strict liability. The district court held that none of Defendants' contentions were sufficient to relieve them of strict liability for the injuries they caused. We agree.

* * *

II. Background

The United States government constructed Hanford during World War II to manufacture plutonium for military purposes. The facility was a component of the Army Corps of Engineer's secret Manhattan Project,

(Continued)

---

[23] *Old Island Fumigation Inc. v. Barbee*, 604 So. 2d 1246 (Fla. Dist. Ct. App. 1992).

with the primary objective of developing an atomic bomb. In 1942, the Army Corps began hiring civilian contractors to help build and operate the Hanford facility. It first recruited the University of Chicago Metallurgical Laboratory ("Met Lab") to design the process and equipment to produce plutonium. It then solicited E.I. DuPont de Nemours & Co. ("DuPont") to actually run the facility. It is apparent the government itself did not have the expertise or resources to operate Hanford.

DuPont initially refused. The government, however, persisted and implored DuPont to run the plutonium-production facility, because, as the government provided in DuPont's contract, the project was of the "utmost importance" and was "necessary in facilitating the prosecution of the war." DuPont eventually acquiesced, stating it would run the facility out of patriotic considerations. It accepted only one dollar as payment for its services. Several years later, the Hanford facility successfully produced the plutonium that was used in 1945 to drop the atomic bomb on Nagasaki and effectively end World War II. (The bomb dropped on Hiroshima was uranium-based, not plutonium-based).

As part of the plutonium-production process, the Hanford facility emitted 1-131, a fission byproduct known as radioiodine. I-131 was known at the time to have potential adverse health effects on humans. Accordingly, the Met Lab scientists set tolerance doses for human exposure. For example, the Met Lab determined that the human thyroid should not absorb more than one rad per day for those individuals subject to continuous exposure in the area. A rad is a measurement of the amount of radioiodine absorbed into an organ or tissue. On the basis of these safe exposure limit estimates, the Met Lab approved a detailed operating procedure that would ensure that the plutonium was produced within those emission limits. The key to decreasing 1-131 emissions was to allow for longer cooling times of the uranium slugs used to produce the plutonium. This strategy, however, often conflicted with the federal government's orders to increase plutonium production.

On September 1, 1946, DuPont transferred its duties to General Electric ("GE"), which also agreed to earn no profit from its work. GE ran the Hanford facility through the Cold War. During the period of its operation, GE asked the federal government to increase cooling times to allow for lower emissions of 1-131. By this time, Congress had established the Atomic Energy Commission ("AEC") ... and GE was bound by its determinations. The AEC denied the request for longer cooling times, and GE continued to produce plutonium

consistent with government demands. By the 1950s, however, significant improvements were made to the production process, and I-131 emission levels dropped.

In 1987, the United States Department of Energy ("DOE") created the Hanford Environmental Dose Reconstruction Project ("HEDR"), overseen by the Center for Disease Control and Prevention. The underlying purpose of the HEDR was to estimate and reconstruct all radionuclide emissions from Hanford from 1944 to 1972 in order to ascertain whether neighboring individuals and animals had been exposed to harmful doses of radiation. Of particular concern to the HEDR were the estimated doses of 1-131 received by the thyroid glands of humans, principally through consumption of milk from cows that ingested contaminated vegetation on neighboring farms and pastures. The HEDR concluded that 1-131 emissions peaked during the period from 1944 to 1946, when an estimated 88% of Hanford's total iodine emissions occurred. HEDR explained that in later years, emissions declined because of technological advances. In 1990, the Technical Steering Panel of HEDR released a report entitled Initial Hanford Radiation Dose Estimates that publicly disclosed for the first time that large quantities of radioactive and nonradioactive substances had been released from Hanford, beginning in the 1940s.

This disclosure sparked a blaze of litigation. Thousands of plaintiffs filed suit pursuant to the Price-Anderson Act, ... which had been amended in 1988 to provide exclusive federal jurisdiction over all claims arising from a nuclear incident, otherwise known as public liability actions. The PAA allowed the plaintiffs to sue private parties, such as DuPont, and to consolidate the claims in federal district court.... While Congress wanted to ensure that victims of nuclear incidents recovered compensation, it also included government indemnification provisions in the PAA to give private parties an incentive to participate in the nuclear industry....

The PAA provides that although federal courts have exclusive and original jurisdiction over claims stemming from nuclear incidents, the substantive rules of decision are provided by the law of the state in which the nuclear incident occurs.... Plaintiffs therefore brought tort claims under Washington law, asserting that because Defendants were engaged in an abnormally dangerous activity, they were strictly liable for any Hanford-caused radiation illness.

* * *

... In a published order, the [lower] court ... ruled that plutonium production at Hanford was an abnormally

(Continued)

dangerous activity warranting strict liability under Washington law....

* * *

... Defendants argue that Plaintiffs may not proceed under a strict liability theory, because [among other arguments made by plaintiffs,] ... the plutonium-production process was not an abnormally dangerous activity under Washington law ...

* * *

IV. Strict Liability

Defendants next argue that the district court erred as a matter of Washington state law in holding Defendants strictly liable for any 1-131 emissions from the Hanford facility. Defendants challenge that ruling ... [by arguing that] the Hanford activity did not meet the "abnormally dangerous activity" test that warrants strict liability....

* * *

B. Abnormally Dangerous Activity.

... Defendants contend that operating the Hanford facility does not constitute an "abnormally dangerous activity" under Washington law. We review *de novo* the question of whether an activity is abnormally dangerous, ... and we affirm.

Washington has adopted the Restatement (Second) of Torts, sections 519 and 520, which outline the strict liability regime for abnormally dangerous activities.... Section 519 provides:

(1) One who carries on an abnormally dangerous activity is subject to liability for harm to the person, land, or chattels of another resulting from the activity, although he has exercised the utmost care to prevent such harm.

(2) Such strict liability is limited to the kind of harm, the risk of which makes the activity abnormally dangerous.

Section 520 lists the factors to be used when determining what constitutes an abnormally dangerous activity:

(a) Whether the activity involves a high degree of risk of some harm to the person, land or chattels of another;

(b) Whether the gravity of the harm which may result from it is likely to be great;

(c) Whether the risk cannot be eliminated by the exercise of reasonable care;

(d) Whether the activity is not a matter of common usage;

(e) Whether the activity is inappropriate to the place where it is carried on; and

(f) The value of the activity to the community.

... A court does not have to weigh each of the elements listed in § 520 equally.... One factor, alone, however, is generally not sufficient to find an activity abnormally dangerous....

Defendants argue that at the time of the emissions in the 1940s, they did not know the risks that were attributable to radioiodine exposure, and therefore § 520's factors (a)-(c) cannot be weighed against them. Any possible injury from radiation, however, need not have been actually known by Defendants at the time of exposure in order to impose strict liability. Under Washington law, if the actual harm fell within a general field of danger which should have been anticipated, strict liability may be appropriate. Whether an injury should have been anticipated does not depend on whether the particular harm was actually expected to occur.... It is sufficient that "the risk created [be] so unusual, either because of its magnitude or because of the circumstances surrounding it...."

There is no question that Defendants should have anticipated some of the many risks associated with operating a nuclear facility, creating plutonium, and releasing 1-131 into the atmosphere. It is exactly because of these risks, and the potential exposure to liability arising from them, that the government contracted with Defendants to limit liability in case of an accident. For these same reasons, the Met Lab scientists recommended dosage limits.

We agree with the district court that Defendants' conduct at Hanford was an abnormally dangerous activity under the § 520 factors. There was a high degree of risk to people and property associated with the Hanford facility and the gravity of any harm was likely to be great.... Regardless of Defendants' efforts to exercise reasonable care, some 1-131 would be released, and developing plutonium is hardly an activity of common usage. While the value to the community at large, i.e., the nation, of developing an atomic bomb was perceived as high and there is pragmatically no very appropriate place to carry on such an activity, the § 520 factors on balance support holding that Defendants' activities were abnormally dangerous.

Questions and Comments for Discussion

1. What are the economic implications for industry if strict liability is imposed on an activity? Who ultimately bears the cost of that increased liability?

2. Do you think the fact that DuPont and GE were only paid $1 or less should mitigate their liability in this type of case? Why or why not?

▓ Remedies

The purpose of tort law is generally to compensate the plaintiff for injuries suffered as a result of the defendant's wrongful act or omission. The issue of appropriate remedies for an injured plaintiff in a tort case raises other difficult issues. For example, is money a fair or adequate compensation for injury? If not, is anything else better? What public policy consequences flow from other options besides monetary damages for civil injuries?

Compensatory damages (that is, money paid to compensate the injured plaintiff) may include sums for property damage, injuries to the plaintiff's health, pain and suffering, and other foreseeable losses. Punitive damages may be awarded in cases where the defendant's behavior is egregious. As noted earlier in this chapter, punitive damages are designed to punish flagrant wrongdoers and to deter them and others from engaging in similar conduct in the future.

In some cases, plaintiffs also may seek the equitable remedy of an injunction, which is a court order requiring the defendant to cease some action or, less commonly, to do some act. In environmental cases, innovative remedies, such as requiring monitoring or installation of particular control technologies, are sometimes fashioned through the court's power to issue injunctive orders.

■ *Practice worksheet*

The first row has been completed as an example.

Common law	List the elements	Provide an example
1. Trespass to land	Intentional, voluntary intrusion on tangible property of another, without permission	Chemicals leaking onto a neighboring property
2. Nuisance		
3. Negligence		
4. Negligence per se		
5. Strict liability		

▓ Conclusion

This chapter focused on several important tort theories that plaintiffs may use to recover damages as a result of environmental harm to their person or property. Tort law liability ranges from actions to recover damages for intentional torts, as in cases of intentional trespass or nuisance; to actions under negligence theory, based on breach of a legal duty; to strict liability actions, which impose liability without fault in cases where the defendant was engaged in an abnormally dangerous or ultrahazardous activity. The elements of these actions differ, and a plaintiff may argue that he or she is entitled to recover damages under many or all of these theories in the same case.

Chapter 4 Case Study Activity

In this activity, you have an opportunity to review the elements of each common law theory discussed in this chapter and apply each to the facts of a case.

In the following case, residents who lived near a corporation's chemical waste burial site brought a class action against a chemical corporation to recover damages for personal injuries and property damage. The plaintiffs alleged that they were entitled to damages under the legal theories of strict liability, common law negligence, trespass, and nuisance. The plaintiffs also sought punitive damages from the defendants, to punish the defendant for its wrongful acts and to deter it (and other similarly situated actors) from engaging in wrongful conduct in the future. As you read the facts of this case, review the elements of each of the legal theories discussed. After you have read the case, answer the "Questions for Discussion" that follow it.

Sterling v. Velsicol Chemical Corp.

647 F. Supp. 303 (W.D. Tenn. 1986)

Horton, District Judge.

This class action lawsuit was originally filed by plaintiffs against Velsicol Chemical Corporation in the Circuit Court of Hardeman County, Tennessee, on December 4, 1978.

Plaintiffs are a class of persons who owned property or lived within a three mile radius of the northern most boundary line of a 242 acre chemical waste burial site in Hardeman County, Tennessee, owned and operated by Velsicol from late 1964 until it was closed as hazardous in 1973 by order of the State of Tennessee. Plaintiffs in this class action seek damages for personal injury and damages to their property allegedly suffered when water in their home wells became contaminated by hazardous chemicals which escaped from Velsicol's burial site.

* * *

Plaintiff's Contentions

The substance of plaintiffs' claims is that they have suffered physical injury, bodily harm, mental and emotional anguish, property damage, and loss and destruction of an entire community and a way of life, all proximately resulting from Velsicol's grossly negligent selection, implementation, operation and burial of more than 300,000 fifty-five gallon drums filled with ultrahazardous chemical waste, and hundreds of boxes of ultrahazardous dry chemical waste on its burial site which adjoined plaintiffs' homes and property. Plaintiffs contend Velsicol was grossly negligent in the selection and implementation of its chemical waste burial site, in the manner in which it containerized chemical waste, in its burial operations, and in allowing ultrahazardous and highly toxic chemical waste to escape from the burial site, infiltrate into and contaminate their underground well water.

Plaintiffs contend that as a result of their drinking, bathing, cooking, canning, cleaning, breathing steam from hot water, and otherwise using their home well water contaminated by hazardous chemicals from Velsicol's burial site, over a period of years, ... they have suffered severe and permanent physical injuries, mental and emotional anguish, and damage to and loss of their property.

* * *

Strict Liability Theories

... [T]he rule of law from *Rylands v. Fletcher* allows for the imposition of liability for damages proximately caused by the defendant's dangerous, nonnatural use of land regardless of the standard of care defendant utilized in conducting that activity. Generally, modern courts have applied this strict or absolute liability to activities "variously characterized as 'perilous,' 'ultra or extra-hazardous,' or 'abnormally dangerous.'" ... "The judicial rationalization seems to be that one who conducts a highly dangerous activity should prepare in advance to bear the financial burden of harm proximately caused to others by such an activity." ...

* * *

Conclusion

[After reviewing Tennessee cases indicating that strict or absolute liability was an accepted theory of recovery under Tennessee law, the court continued:]

As noted earlier, no Tennessee cases were found expressly adopting *Rylands v. Fletcher*.... However, the

(Continued)

cases discussed herein lead to the inescapable conclusion that under Tennessee law, Velsicol would be subject to strict or absolute liability for the non-natural, ultrahazardous and abnormally dangerous activities it conducted which gave rise to this action. The facts in the present case align squarely with both the application and the rationale underlying the rule of strict or absolute liability as that doctrine is viewed by Tennessee courts.

* * *

… The Court holds that the creation, location, operation and closure of the toxic chemical dump site by defendant was and is an inherently and abnormally dangerous activity.

Moreover, the Court concludes that Velsicol's activity on the farm was not only ultrahazardous activity, but also abnormally dangerous activity and therefore the defendant is strictly liable for any damages that have occurred. This conclusion is made for … the following reasons:

1. There was a high degree of risk of some harm to the person, land or chattels of others …;

2. There was a likelihood that the harm that results would be great, such as the increased risk of many diseases including cancer, and the destruction of plaintiffs' quality of life;

3. The inability to eliminate the risk by the exercise of reasonable care;

4. The extent to which the activity at the dump was not a matter of common usage and as a means of disposal and violated the state of the art;

5. The inappropriateness of the location of the dump where it was carried out; and

6. The extent to which its value to the community (none) was outweighed by its dangerous attributes (great).

Common Law Negligence

… Velsicol is clearly guilty of negligence … for the following reasons:

1. … [T]here was a duty, a standard of conduct, imposed by law on Velsicol to protect others from unreasonable harm arising from the dumping of the chemicals on its farm; and

2. The … defendant breached that duty by its failure to do the following:

    a. Defendant failed to investigate the geological makeup or strata under the dumpsite prior to its purchase or operation;

    b. Defendant failed to investigate the hydrological, or water bearing zones under the dumpsite prior to its purchase or operation;

    c. Defendant failed to hire knowledgeable persons to investigate the … area under the dumpsite …;

    d. Defendant failed to install proper monitoring procedures in and around the dumpsite …;

    * * *

    i. Defendant failed in the selection, location, operation and maintenance of the dumpsite under the prevailing state of the art for such operation during the entire length of time the dumpsite was open …; … [and]

    k. Defendant failed to take steps in 1967 to halt the leakage that was already occurring from the dumpsite….

* * *

Trespass

* * *

Actual trespass is not an issue in this case. Velsicol admits the movement of certain chemicals from its dump site through the local aquifer and "onto property owned by various plaintiffs and into the sphere of influence of various wells constitutes a trespass under Tennessee law." …

In general, Tennessee trespass law as applied to the present case allows for the recovery of damages caused by admitted "incursion" of Velsicol's chemical waste onto property owned by various plaintiffs within the designated area surrounding Velsicol's Chemical waste burial site….

* * *

Nuisance

The doctrine of nuisance applies to this case. The Court finds Velsicol has interfered with plaintiffs' right to the use and enjoyment of their property—whether owned or leased—by the creation of a nuisance….

Occasionally, a nuisance proceeds from a malicious desire to do harm, but usually a nuisance is intentional in the sense that the defendant has created or continued the condition causing the nuisance with full knowledge that the harm to the plaintiffs' interest is substantially bound to follow therefore. A nuisance may also result from conduct which is merely negligence, to-wit: a failure to take precautions against a risk apparent to a reasonable man. Finally, a nuisance may occur when a defendant carries on in an inappropriate place an abnormally dangerous or hazardous activity….

(Continued)

* * *

Punitive Damages

… The principal requirements for the recovery of punitive damages are:

(1) Proof of an independent cause of action, since there is no cause of action for punitive damages only.…

(2) Proof of actual or compensatory damages.…

(3) Evidence that the defendant's wrongful act was characterized by either willfulness, wantonness, maliciousness, gross negligence or recklessness, oppression, outrageous conduct, insult, indignity, or fraud.…

* * *

The Court concludes that Velsicol's actions in creating, maintaining and operating its chemical waste burial site, with superior knowledge of the highly toxic and harmful nature of the chemical contaminants it disposed of therein, and specifically its failure to immediately cease dumping said toxic chemicals after being warned by several state and federal agencies several years prior to the final cessation of such abnormally hazardous and harmful activity, constituted gross, wilful and wanton disregard for the health and well-being of the plaintiffs, and therefore is supportive of an award of punitive and exemplary damages.

* * *

[The Court held that five representatives of the class of plaintiffs were entitled to recover compensatory damages totaling $5,273,492.50 and that the corporation was liable to the class as a whole for punitive damages in the amount of $75,000,000. On appeal the appellate court upheld liability but ordered the trial court to recompute the damage award based on its instructions.]

Questions for Discussion

1. *Sterling v. Velsicol* presents an opportunity to review the elements of each common law theory discussed in this chapter and to apply it to the facts of this case. What tests of actual causation (cause in fact) and proximate cause did the plaintiffs have to meet to be successful in this case? How might plaintiffs in a similar case prove causation at trial?

2. What are the economic and environmental effects of declaring that the creation, location, operation, and closure of a toxic chemical dump site like that of the defendant Velsicol is an inherently and abnormally dangerous activity? Do you agree that a nonnegligent operator should incur liability under this theory even though a plaintiff might be negligent in exposing herself to risks associated with the site? Why or why not?

3. The court enumerated a number of other reasons why the defendants were liable for negligence under the facts of this case (which were omitted from the excerpt of the opinion). Can you think of other reasons a plaintiff might allege that an owner or operator of a toxic dump site breached a duty of reasonable care? Should the owner/operator be liable under a theory of negligent or intentional failure to disclose hazardous materials in the dump to adjoining landowners? What are the policy implications of your answer to this question?

Contracts and Environmental Harms

Here's a good idea!

This is a "bare bones" outline of the chapter. Expand this outline with more detailed notes as you read the chapter. This will allow you to create a study guide as you work. This good study habit will help you to learn the material, retain important points, and make efficient use of your time.

Learning Objectives

After reading this chapter, you will have an understanding of some contract law issues that arise in environmental law cases. Additionally, you will understand the basic contract and tort principles underlying product liability law. Specifically, after reading this chapter, you should be able to answer the following questions:

1. What is contract law and how does it arise in environmental cases?

2. What are warranties, indemnification agreements, and disclaimers?

3. What contract and tort theories support claims for product liability?

▮ Introduction to Contract Law

This chapter examines some contract law issues that may arise in environmental law cases, examines warranties and disclaimers as they apply to environmental issues, and discusses basic contract and tort principles underlying product liability law.

Contract issues may be important in allocating liability for environmental harm—for example, when a buyer of real property sues to recover damages for breach of contract from the seller or seeks to rescind the contract because the property is contaminated with hazardous materials. In such cases, warranties, indemnification clauses, and disclaimers in the contract may determine the seller's liability or the purchaser's right to rescind. Similar issues may arise in actions between landlord and tenants based on covenants (promises) in the lease.

This chapter also examines legal principles useful to plaintiffs that hope to recover damages arising from the purchase and use of environmentally unsafe products. Under principles of contract law, such as breach of express and implied warranties, as well as the principles of negligence and strict liability discussed in Chapter 4, plaintiffs have recovered damages for injuries they received as a result of exposure to products containing toxic and dangerous substances like lead, asbestos, and harmful chemicals.

The chapter further addresses techniques of contract interpretation, as well as defenses in contracts cases and defenses to product liability claims.

▨ Contract Law

A **contract** is "a promise or set of promises for the breach of which the law gives a remedy, or the performance of which the law in some way recognizes as a duty."[1] Another (shorter) way of putting this is that a contract is a legally enforceable promise or set of promises.

Contract law principles have evolved through common law decision making. Contract law is state law rather than federal law. Two types of law govern contracts. The common law governs contracts for services and contracts that the **Uniform Commercial Code** (**UCC**) does not govern. The UCC is a model statute that has been adopted in full or in part by most states. When individual states adopt the UCC into their statutory schemes, the UCC becomes state law. The UCC governs certain types of contracts. For example, it governs contracts for the sale of goods valued at more than $500 and the sale of goods between merchants.

Under broad principles of contract law, a private party is able to create a private, enforceable law that governs its relationship with another party. The law ensures that these private agreements are enforceable in order to preserve stability in contracting and to protect commercial enterprise.

Common law courts have both developed and clarified the basic elements of an enforceable contract. These elements include (1) an offer and (2) an acceptance (3) supported by consideration (4) by parties who have the capacity to contract and (5) make the agreement for a legal purpose. All elements are required for formation of a valid contract. If all five elements are not present, the contract is not valid. Let's quickly review each of these elements, so you know what to look for in a contracts analysis.

The first two elements (offer and acceptance) are together known as *mutual assent.* These elements have somewhat different interpretations depending on whether common law or the UCC governs the contract in question. For example, a common law contract offer must be definite and certain. A common law contract acceptance must be a mirror image of the offer. However, in contracts governed by UCC Article 2, any manner that shows intent to contract will be deemed valid mutual assent. This means that the acceptance does not have to be a mirror image of the offer, and the offer need not contain all terms in definite and certain language. The only essential element in a UCC contract is quantity, because other terms—price, time for delivery, and so on—can be determined by the "gap fillers," which are unique to the UCC.

The element of consideration is the same for both types of contracts. *Consideration* is simply a bargained-for exchange: something that imposes legal detriment on each party. It is something of legal value given in exchange for an act or a promise. For example, money given in exchange for services is valid consideration. Money for goods is also valid consideration.

Capacity is the idea that the parties to the contract have the ability to understand or comprehend what they are doing and agreeing to. Capacity can be affected or

contract: A legally enforceable promise.

Uniform Commercial Code (UCC): A model statute, which has been adopted in full or in part by most or all states, that governs certain types of contracts.

---

[1] RESTATEMENT (SECOND) OF CONTRACTS § 1 (1981).

compromised by things like mental infirmity, intoxication, age, or other factors that interfere with or diminish the party's ability. Some of these, such as age, are general legal limitations on capacity rather than party-specific factors.

Finally, to be valid, a contract must be for a legal purpose. A contract created between parties for a purpose that is not legal is not a valid contract. This is because the courts will not step in to enforce an illegal act (in violation of public law).

If a contract is deemed valid, the parties thereto must perform unless there is a valid defense to or reason for nonperformance. A nonexhaustive list of defenses includes unconscionability, nonvoluntariness, mistake, and misrepresentation or fraud.

Courts may refuse to enforce a contract provision that is unconscionable. As a defense against the requirement to perform under a contract, **unconscionability** is generally defined as a contract provision that is both procedurally and substantively unfair. A court may also set aside a contract if it finds that a party did not voluntarily enter into the agreement; evidence of coercion or duress is often proffered in such cases. A party who was mistaken about an important fact, or who entered into the agreement because of **misrepresentation** or **fraud**[2] by the other party, is entitled to rescind the contract. See *Garb-Ko Inc. v. Lansing-Lewis Services, Inc.* later in this chapter for a case that addresses mutual **mistake** as a defense to performance. (See questions 2 and 3 following that case for a further exploration of mistake, misrepresentation, fraud, and rescission.) To gain **rescission** for misrepresentation, the plaintiff must prove that (1) there was an untrue assertion, presented as fact, that was (2) material or fraudulent; (3) the plaintiff actually relied on the assertion; and (4) the plaintiff's reliance was reasonable.

A particular problem in misrepresentation cases is whether nondisclosure constitutes misrepresentation. Today, most states impose upon the seller of residential property a duty to disclose known material defects that the purchaser does not know about, or could not discover in the exercise of reasonable care. There is some question, though, as to whether this duty extends to sellers of commercial property. Obviously, these decisions have important implications for cases involving sale of contaminated property.

Some types of contracts must be in writing to be enforceable against the defendant. Specifically, contracts governed by the Statute of Frauds must be in writing. Such contracts include those regarding any interest in real property, promises to pay the debts of another, any contract that cannot be fully performed within one year, and any contract in consideration of marriage. Other types of contracts are not required to be in writing to be enforceable against a breaching party; these contracts may be valid even if they are simply oral.

Of course, in many disputes concerning liability for environmental contamination of real property, the parties have entered into a written contract, either for sale or lease of the property, that contains the express terms and conditions of their agreement. As a general rule, a contract only binds the parties who entered into the agreement. Parties may choose to allocate liabilities for environmental harms between the parties to the contract, but this allocation does not affect their liability to noncontracting parties (e.g., liability to the government under CERCLA or to other persons).

The issue in the following case involved the liability of a contracting party to a third party who was not a party to the original contract. Generally, only a party to a contract may sue another contracting party for damages as a result of breach of contract, as the *Lincoln* case illustrates.

---

[2] *Fraudulent misrepresentation*, which is a misrepresentation made with intent to deceive, is also a basis for liability under the common law of intentional torts.

unconscionability: A defense to performance of a contract based on procedural and/or substantive unfairness. An *unconscionable* contract is one that "no man in his senses … would make … and … no fair and honest man would accept …" (*Hume v. United States*, 132 U.S. 406, 10 S. Ct. 134, 33 L. Ed. 393 (1889)).

misrepresentation: An assertion not in accord with the facts.

fraud: The use of deception to acquire money or property; in this context, the basis for a defense to performance of a contract.

mistake: A defense to performance of a contract based upon ignorance of an important fact not caused by neglect of a legal duty.

rescission: Cancellation of a contract and placement of party in position he was in prior to the formation of the contract cancelled.

Lincoln Alameda Creek v. Cooper Industries, Inc.
829 F. Supp. 325 (N.D. Cal. 1992)

[This action involves a complaint brought by Mary Orsetti against Beta Associates ("Beta").] Orsetti is seeking indemnification or contribution from Beta for alleged negligence, breach of warranty, and misrepresentation in their preparation of a ground contaminants investigation. The matter is now before the court on Beta's motion to dismiss the complaint and for summary judgment .... After careful consideration of the parties' submissions and arguments, the court GRANTS Beta's motion for summary judgment.

* * *

Mary Orsetti entered into an agreement with the plaintiff, Lincoln Alameda Creek ("Lincoln"), for the sale of a piece of property located at 29990 Union City Boulevard, Union City, California. According to the agreement, Lincoln's purchase was conditioned upon its approval of the condition of the soils, sub-soils, and groundwater of the property. In October, 1986, Lincoln hired Beta, an environmental consultant, to perform a subsurface soil and groundwater contaminants investigation of the property in order to assist Lincoln in deciding whether to purchase it. This contract between Beta and Lincoln was an oral contract.

* * *

The report was completed on November 21, 1986 and was given to Lincoln. Lincoln did not discuss with Beta their intention that the report would be for the benefit of anyone other than Lincoln. Beta was also not informed that Mary Orsetti would review or rely on the report. Beta did not have a contract with Orsetti, and did not give Orsetti any express warranty.

The report stated that Beta's analysis of the land did not reveal any of the "constituents of concern" and therefore they felt the property was clear of contamination. The sale of the land was subsequently completed. Lincoln is presently involved in litigation with Orsetti for the alleged contamination of the property. Orsetti brought this **third-party complaint** against Beta for its alleged negligence, breach of warranty, and misrepresentation in the preparation of the ground contamination report. Orsetti is seeking **indemnification** and compensatory damages from Beta.

Beta's motion for summary judgment turns on the following issues: (1) whether Beta owed Orsetti any duty of care in the preparation of the report, (2) whether

Orsetti was a third-party beneficiary of the contract between Lincoln and Beta and (3) whether Beta committed any fraud or misrepresentation to the damage of Orsetti.

* * *

III. Intended Beneficiary Argument

In order to recover under a theory of breach of contract and warranty, Orsetti must be an intended beneficiary of the contract between Beta and Lincoln. "For a third party to qualify as a beneficiary under a contract, the contracting parties must have intended to benefit that third party, and their intent must appear from the terms of the contract." ... The third party beneficiary must show that the contract was made "expressly" for her benefit.... Therefore, Orsetti must show that the contract between Beta and Lincoln was clearly intended to inure to her benefit.

... The contract [between Beta and Lincoln] was oral and its relevant terms have been provided. According to [the evidence], Orsetti was not an intended beneficiary. Beta and Lincoln never discussed the report being produced for the benefit of Orsetti, nor did they intend it to benefit her.

From the available facts, therefore, it is clear that the contract was not made "expressly" for her benefit.... Even if she now says she relied on the contamination report, she has not presented any facts to prove that Lincoln and Beta intended for her to rely on it.

Orsetti also argues that Beta's agreement to test her property included a "warranty of workmanlike service that is comparable to a manufacturer's warranty." ... [However,] Beta and Orsetti do not have a contractual relationship. Since there is no contract between Beta and Orsetti, a warranty cannot be implied.

Accordingly, Beta's motion for summary judgment regarding the breach of contract and warranty cause of action is GRANTED.

Questions and Comments for Discussion

1. Who were the parties to the original contract? Under what theory did Orsetti, the original defendant, argue that she was entitled to damages from Beta for breach of warranty under the contract?

(Continued)

2. There may be circumstances in which the performance of a contract is intended to benefit a person not a party to the contract. In such instances, the **third party** may be entitled to enforce the contract. For example, the benefit to a third person may be an essential part of an insurance contract. As the court's decision in *Lincoln Alameda Creek* indicates, whether a third party can enforce a contract depends on whether that party was an intended beneficiary of the contract. When a third party's benefit is merely an unintended byproduct of the contract, the third party is called an **incidental beneficiary**. Incidental beneficiaries do not acquire the right to enforce the original contract. In other words, for a third person to have the right to enforce the contract, that person must prove intent to benefit him or her. In *Lincoln Alameda Creek*, the owner of the property was unable to prove that she was an intended beneficiary of the contract between the purchaser and its environmental consultant.

Note that the purchaser (Lincoln Properties) might have a cause of action against the consultant under negligence theory or breach of contract. What would the buyer have to prove to be successful in such a case?

Techniques of Contract Interpretation

Contract interpretation is a process by which a court determines the meaning of the language in a contract. Courts are often required to interpret contracts. Words are inherently vague, and contract language, like all language, may be ambiguous. Contracts may be ambiguous because of inconsistent language within the contract itself or because the circumstances that actually occurred were outside the contemplation of the parties. As a result, courts are frequently called upon to give meaning to contract language within the context of a specific dispute.

Courts attempt to interpret contract language in light of the parties' intentions. Courts first rely on the express language of the contract. In determining intention, a court may also rely on dictionary definitions, under the theory that the parties should be bound by the common or "plain meaning" of the words they use. Courts also sometimes employ rules and legal maxims as an aid to contract interpretation. One rule of contract interpretation—especially important in insurer liability cases—is that in interpreting standardized form contracts, courts generally construe ambiguity of language against the drafter of the contract. This means that ambiguities in standardized insurance contracts will be construed against the insurer. In addition, if language is reasonably susceptible to two interpretations, the interpretation that favors public interest will be preferred.

third-party complaint:
A complaint filed by a defendant against another person other than the plaintiff.

indemnification: Reimbursement for costs or damages incurred.

third party: One who is not party to a transaction, but might be affected by it.

incidental beneficiary: A third party who does not acquire the right to enforce a contract because the contract was not designed or intended to benefit the third party, even though benefit to that third party may be byproduct of the contract.

▨ Assessing Environmental Damage to Real Property before Contracting to Purchase

All Appropriate Inquiries and Due Diligence

Prospective purchasers of industrial or commercial property routinely undertake an investigation to ascertain the existence of any environmental hazards on the property. Such knowledge is essential for determining the value of the property and assessing potential liabilities for future environmental cleanup costs. Perhaps the strongest incentive for conducting an environmental audit prior to purchase is the "innocent landowner" defense available under the Comprehensive Environmental Response, Compensation, and Liability Act, commonly known as CERCLA. One of the few defenses under CERCLA available to an owner or operator of contaminated property is proof that, at the time the owner acquired the property, the owner "did not know and had no reason to know" that any hazardous substance had been disposed of or released onto the property.[3]

Because a significant number of environmental contract disputes involve questions of CERCLA liability, it is helpful to first summarize some key provisions of that law. As noted in Chapter 1, CERCLA was originally enacted in 1980 to address the problem of abandoned hazardous waste disposal sites. CERCLA mandates cleanup of these sites and allocates responsibility for cleanup costs to various "responsible parties." Responsible parties may also be liable for any necessary response costs incurred by others, damages for injury to natural resources, and the costs of certain monitoring and health studies. Most courts have held that liability between responsible parties under CERCLA may be allocated by agreement (although such agreements cannot limit a party's liability to the government, as noted earlier); consequently, contract language may be critical in determining and allocating responsibility between the parties for cleaning up hazardous waste sites under CERCLA.

In 2002, the Small Business Liability Relief and Brownfield Revitalization Act was passed, which amended CERCLA. Among other things, it clarified protection from liability for potentially responsible parties. Any government purchaser of property or any purchaser of commercial property or property that will become commercial property who may wish to claim a defense under CERCLA, including that of innocent landowner, should undertake "all appropriate inquiries" (AAI).

The Environmental Protection Agency (EPA) defines AAI as "the process of evaluating a property's environmental conditions and assessing potential liability for any contamination."[4] In 2006, the EPA's final rule set forth requirements for AAI, the objectives of AAI, the definition of "environmental professional," and specific activities required for conducting the inquiries. Persons who have complied with AAI criteria and who did not themselves contaminate the property may be protected from CERCLA liability. As noted, a property owner's ability to successfully assert a defense to CERCLA liability is a major incentive to undertake AAI. CERCLA itself is not specific about what constitutes environmental due diligence. However, compliance with the AAI rule allows landowners to assert that they have performed due diligence and are entitled to CERCLA liability protection.[5]

---

[3] "All Appropriate Inquiries" final rule. Retrieved May 30, 2013, from http://www.epa.gov/brownfields/aai/aai_final_factsheet.pdf
[4] *Id.*
[5] J.K. Warren, *EPA's All Appropriate Inquiry Rule: When Is Enough, Enough?* Retrieved May 30, 2013, from http://www.apps.americanbar.org/buslaw/newsletter/0045/materials/pp5.pdf

■ **ACTIVITY BOX   How Much Diligence Is Due?**

If you were considering the purchase of commercial property, but you wanted to ensure that you could assert the innocent landowner defense if the property was discovered to be contaminated, you would want to ensure that due diligence was performed before you actually purchased the property. Examine the "All Appropriate Inquiries Rule" at http://www.epa.gov/brownfields/aai /aai_final_factsheet.pdf

Identify three activities or inquiries that must be undertaken. Then, write a paragraph for each that describes specifically how an environmental professional hired to perform AAI would find this information. After completing this activity, consider the following questions:

1. Do you think that AAI is sufficient for determining whether or not a parcel of real property is contaminated? If you think it is not sufficient, how could it be improved?

2. What are the benefits and drawbacks of AAI from an individual landowner's (or potential landowner's) perspective? What are the benefits and drawbacks of AAI from a public policy perspective?

Third-Party Environmental Consultants in the Purchase of Real Property

Environmental consultants contract with various parties to assess the environmental condition of real property being considered for purchase or sale. Contracts between environmental consultants and either the prospective property owners or the actual property owners are private enforceable law between the parties to the contract. Clearly, a professional duty of care is owed to the prospective or actual property owners by the environmental consultants who are hired, to ensure that the assessment meets the standard of care to be expected from a professional environmental consultant. However, environmental consultants are increasingly finding that they are also being sued for the work that they have performed—and in some cases held liable—by third parties.[6] (Recall that *third parties* are persons who are not parties to the original contract.)

In the following case, a purchaser of real property brought a claim against an engineering firm that had been hired by the prior owner of the property to investigate the presence of mercury contamination. The engineering firm was a third party, because the contract for purchase of the property was between the current and prior owners. The engineering firm contracted only with the prior owner, not the current owner (the purchaser of the property), but the current owner still brought suit against the firm. The engineering firm claimed that it owed no duty to prospective purchasers and asked this court for summary judgment. As you will read, the court denied the firm's summary judgment request. It held that the firm owed a duty to the purchaser, who had relied upon a review of the firm's report to the prior owner under New Jersey state law (the Environmental Cleanup Responsibility Act, or ECRA), because it was foreseeable that a purchaser would rely on that report in making the decision to purchase the property for residential use.

---

[6] J. Schneider, *The Expanding Liability of Environmental Consultants to Third Parties*, 13 VILL. ENVTL. L.J. 235 (2002).

Grand Street Artists v. General Electric Co.

19 F. Supp. 2d 242, 1998 U.S. Dist. LEXIS 17327 (D.N.J. 1998)

Ackerman, D.J.

This matter comes before the court upon a motion for summary judgment by the defendant, Jenny Engineering Corp ("Jenny") on several counts [including] ... negligence,... contribution ..., [and] indemnification .... Jenny's motions on the negligence, contribution, and indemnification claims are DENIED ....

I. Background

In 1993, a partnership formed by artists, Grand Street Artists ("GSA"), purchased the premises at 720-732 Grand Street, Hoboken, New Jersey which had been formerly used for industrial purposes by the defendant Quality Tool & Die Co. ("Quality"). GSA envisioned the building of "customized urban homes" to serve the dual purpose of providing housing to their families and spaces in which they could work. Thus, GSA intended to convert the premises into residential condominium units and working lofts, but were forced to evacuate when mercury contamination was discovered.... Thereafter, the plaintiffs ... brought suit ... alleging violations of ... CERCLA [and New Jersey state statutes] ..., and common law claims for strict liability, negligence,... public nuisance and punitive damages....

Before 1954, the Grand Street buildings were owned by either GE or Cooper-Hewitt. Between 1954 and September 1988, Quality operated a tool and die business on the premises. At the end of that period, defendant John Pascale, in his capacity as Quality's principal, decided to terminate operations and to sell all machinery. That decision is where much of this story begins. When John Pascale shut down operations, he did so without following New Jersey's hazardous waste statute, the Environmental Cleanup Responsibility Act ("ECRA") and thus, in a way which was technically improper.... Among other things, an owner who decides to terminate operations must notify the New Jersey Department of Environmental Protection ("DEP") and then submit to an extended ECRA process. At the end of this process, the DEP must give its approval to either a negative declaration stating that the property is not contaminated or to a cleanup plan.... By not participating in the ECRA process, John Pascale did not properly shut down operations in September 1988.

Contemporaneously with the termination of operations, John Pascale and his son David were engaged in a protracted legal battle for control of the company.... [Eventually] the New Jersey Supreme Court returned control of the company to David Pascale .... For purposes of the instant motion, this see saw battle meant that John Pascale controlled Quality from March 1987 to November 1988—the time when operations were discontinued. Upon his return, David learned of Quality's noncompliance with ECRA and in March 1989, Quality hired Jenny to provide "technical assistance" in the ECRA process. Because Quality's decision to comply with ECRA came one year after the actual shut down, Jenny expressed its concern about incurring legal liability for this failure....

* * *

On April 23, 1990, Quality submitted an ECRA-1 General Information Statement and an ECRA-2 Site Evaluation Submission. Quality answered "No" to the question of whether the "transaction initiating ... ECRA review" involved a sale.... Indeed, there is no question that it was the "cessation of operations" that triggered ECRA. Shortly after making its submissions, the DEP informed Quality that its ECRA-2 submission was incomplete because its answers regarding history, prior ownership and use did not cover the period between 1940 and 1950. With Jenny's help, Quality filed a letter on June 18, 1990 with the DEP indicating that prior to 1950 the building had been operated by GE and Cooper-Hewitt and that the two companies manufactured light bulbs at the site.... The ECRA filing made no mention of any mercury contamination.

Quality terminated Jenny on October 9, 1992 and hired a new environmental consultant to complete the ECRA process.... In his letter informing Jenny to stop work, David Pascale expressed that based upon a "turnover in personnel" at Jenny, he lacked confidence in Jenny's ability to complete the project.... Thereafter, on December 15, 1992, Quality filed its ECRA "negative declaration affidavit." ...

Based upon Quality's "negative declaration affidavit," there is no question that Quality was seeking DEP approval of its "cessation of operations" and thus, informed that the DEP that there were no potential

(Continued)

sellers or buyers. The DEP reviewed the submissions and granted its approval in February 1993, but limited its approval to the "cessation of operations." …

Beginning in at least 1993, GSA began considering the purchase of the premises and it decided to retain Rogers Environmental Management, Inc. ("REM"), an environmental consulting firm to conduct a "Due Diligence Pre-Purchase." This "Due Diligence Pre-Purchase" involved an examination of the premises to determine whether they could be safely converted to residential use…. As part of its due diligence, REM reviewed Quality's ECRA case file and concluded that the level of contamination met current "Cleanup Standards." … REM advised GSA that the property was suitable for development as a residential project. In August 1993, Quality sold the premises to GSA. GSA alleges that it relied upon this recommendation when it purchased the premises. In 1996, after mercury was discovered, the DEP rescinded its approval.

In the instant case, the plaintiff has brought a negligence claim against the defendant Jenny on the ground that the ECRA submissions were "materially false and misleading" in that they [failed] to identify the mercury contamination. According to plaintiffs, Jenny should have discovered the "48 year history of mercury-related manufacturing operations" and the "pervasive[]" mercury contamination. Thus, plaintiffs contend, Jenny breached a "duty of due care which it owed to plaintiffs by failing to conduct its environmental audit … in an independent manner and in accordance with generally accepted standards … ." …

Jenny argues that it … owed no duty to prospective purchasers. Additionally, it argues that because it did not have a duty, it cannot be held liable for contribution or indemnification….

* * *

III. Discussion

A. Plaintiffs' Negligence Claim

The question here is whether a defendant/environmental consultant who provides ECRA assistance to an owner who wishes to cease operations owes a duty to a plaintiff who has relied upon a review of the owner's ECRA submissions in making the decision to purchase the premises and convert them for residential use…. Ultimately, the "question of whether a duty exists in a particular case is a question of fairness and policy that implicates many factors." … Among these factors, the foreseeability of injury

to others from defendant's conduct is the most important….

In the instant case, plaintiffs contend that Jenny owed a "duty of care to the … prospective purchasers of the Premises, to file ECRA submissions that were truthful, accurate and complete and to perform its professional environmental consulting services in a reasonably competent manner" …. Plaintiffs allegedly breached that duty when it assisted Quality in filing ECRA submissions which were "materially false and misleading" in that they failed to disclose any mercury contamination on the premises…. In order to determine whether defendants owed a duty to prospective purchasers, the court must first consider the foreseeability of injury.

Although it is well settled that an environmental consultant must conform to a standard of care possessed by members of the profession in good standing, it only owes a duty to those persons who fall normally and generally within a zone of risk created by the tortious conduct and are therefore foreseeable…. This does not "require a specific forecasting of particularly identifiable victims … ." … "That a plaintiff may be found within a range of harm emanating from tortfeasor's activities is more significant than whether the parties stand in a direct contractual relationship." …

… [T]his court must focus upon the "objective purpose" of Jenny's services. On that issue, there is much dispute between the parties.

* * *

… When an environmental consultant agrees to assist an owner in ECRA compliance, the underlying purpose of the consultant's work is to facilitate a particular transaction whether that be the cessation of operations or the sale of the property. By design, ECRA has rendered the clean-up of hazardous waste a byproduct of the transaction. In the instant case, the DEP's February 1993 approval of the negative declaration permitted Quality to shut down operations, but it did not authorize a sale of the premises.

Here, plaintiff wants to argue that the legislative purpose of ECRA—to protect the public from the risk of hazardous and toxic substances—is enough to establish a duty to any member of the public…. Following plaintiff's interpretation, any environmental consultant who performed ECRA related services would be liable to any member of the community, especially prospective purchasers, for any harm caused by contamination not discovered during the

(Continued)

ECRA process. The court finds this view to be somewhat overbroad because it confuses the underlying purpose of Jenny's services with ECRA's precatory mission of eradicating hazardous waste. While there is overlap between the two, they are not necessarily interchangeable. The proper analysis of Jenny's liability must employ a more precise definition of the underlying purpose of Jenny's services.

In the instant case, Quality hired Jenny in March 1989 because it wanted to properly cease operations. The question then becomes whether it is foreseeable that prospective purchasers will rely upon ECRA submissions in deciding whether to purchase premises. Certainly, there is nothing in the record which indicates that Quality informed Jenny that it intended on selling the premises. However, there is some indication that Jenny knew that the premises would be sold once the ECRA process was completed.... According to Syed Pasha, a "former Senior Geologist for Jenny and the person principally responsible for the environmental consulting services rendered," it was his "understanding" that after the ECRA process was completed, Pascale would sell the premises....

Although Quality's ECRA submissions were not triggered by a sale of the premises, given the structure of ECRA and the ECRA process, it was foreseeable that prospective purchasers would rely upon the ECRA submissions. Practically speaking, whether an owner is ceasing operations or selling the premises, the necessary steps prescribed by ECRA are identical.... In many circumstances, the cessation of operations is just the first step in an attempt to sell the premises.... From the structure of ECRA, Jenny should have known its work would have been used by others interested in purchasing the premises. These ECRA submissions are public filings which were easily accessible to prospective purchasers. Thus, it was foreseeable that a potential purchaser would look to the prior ECRA submissions in considering whether to enter into the transaction.

In its brief, Jenny has argued that it could not anticipate the prospect of liability to purchasers who intended to convert the premises for residential purposes because the DEP guidelines differed as to premises which were to be used for residential purposes in contrast to those applicable where operations at a former industrial site are shut down. That argument is not persuasive. While the DEP might have imposed different standards of approval when the premises were converted for residential purposes, the process for compliance was the same.

Therefore, it was foreseeable that a prospective purchaser would examine the results of a previous ECRA submission even if that prior application process had only resulted in an approval for cessation of operations. As I have already noted, to establish a duty, there need not be a "specific forecasting of particularly identifiable victims or a precise prediction of the exact harm." ... Here, it was foreseeable that Quality would eventually sell the premises and that Jenny's services would be used for that purpose. It was not necessary for Jenny to know of an actual sale or that the premises would be converted for residential use.

* * *

Jenny has also raised a number of fairness and policy arguments. First, it argues that by finding a duty to "remote and future purchasers," the court will "affect an equally inefficient allocation of professional responsibilities." ... According to Jenny, "[f]uture purchasers regardless of the number of real estate transactions occurring before them, will be permitted to assert claims against environmental professionals" and will expose environmental professionals to an unlimited class of plaintiff[s] and limitless liability.... Initially, I note that the plaintiffs in this case are not "remote." They are the ones who purchased the premises, a purchase which I have already held, was foreseeable. The court's finding of a duty does not extend beyond "those persons who fall normally and generally within a zone of risk created by the tortious conduct" and therefore, plaintiff's argument fails.... That the magnitude of the liability may be great does not by itself provide enough of a reason for not finding a duty. Environmental harm is often substantial.

* * *

Questions for Discussion

1. Why was the defendant found to owe a duty of care to a party with which the defendant did not contract? Do you think that a third party should owe a duty to a party with whom it has never contracted? What are the public policy reasons supporting this finding?

2. Why did the court call the plaintiff's argument that a duty under New Jersey ECRA should be owed to any member of the public "overbroad"? If the court had adopted this argument, what would be the consequences for environmental consultants?

▨ ▨ ▨ REVIEW AND STUDY QUESTIONS

1. Draw up a table to compare and contrast common law contracts with UCC contracts. Which type of law is most important in contracts involving real property? Why?

2. What are the elements of a valid contract? Identify one contract that you are party to. Is it a valid contract? How do you know? (Remember to use all the elements of contract formation when answering this question.)

3. Compare the holdings in *Lincoln Alameda Creek* with those in *Grand Street Artists*. Why were different outcomes reached in those cases?

4. What is the difference between an intentional third-party beneficiary and an incidental third-party beneficiary? Imagine that you are writing a contract and wish to address both of those types of beneficiaries. Write sample clauses using the specific language that you would include in the contract to identify intentional third-party beneficiaries and to limit liability to incidental third-party beneficiaries.

5. If you were an environmental consultant, how would you limit your liability to third parties?

6. Should the duty to disclose known material defects in the sale of real property be imposed on sellers of commercial and industrial real property? Are there reasons to hold sellers of commercial property to a different standard than sellers of residential property? Why or why not?

▨ Warranty, Indemnification, and Disclaimer

Purchasers of property with suspected environmental problems not only routinely demand an environmental assessment of the property before proceeding to closing, as discussed in the preceding section, but they also demand contract warranties that the property is in compliance with current state and federal law. A **warranty** is a contract promise that any assertion or statement made in the agreement is true (that is, fact). A contracting party may warrant, for example, that no federal or state environmental cleanup actions are pending against the property at the time of sale.

Purchasers of real property also often seek **indemnification agreements**, which ostensibly will protect the purchaser from liability for specified areas of concern. In an indemnification agreement, one person promises to reimburse another person, or hold that person harmless, for loss or damage. These agreements, assigning liability and costs associated with cleanup and remediation of a site, are increasingly important for purchasers of commercial real estate.

Just as a buyer may want to protect himself from potential liability in the purchase of contaminated property, so a seller may attempt to insulate himself from liability in the sale of the property through express contractual disclaimers. A **disclaimer** is a statement in a contract that one party will not be liable for damages to the other for breach of contract under certain circumstances.

As part of a sales agreement, a purchaser will attempt to negotiate comprehensive environmental warranties and representations, while the seller will seek to limit or extinguish those warranties. The courts and the EPA have recognized that the enforcement of such agreements helps facilitate the purchase and sale of commercial property in the face of uncertain environmental liabilities. For this reason, a majority of courts permit private parties to allocate the risk of CERCLA cleanup costs between the parties by contract, although a minority of courts prohibit contractual allocation of environmental liability under any circumstances. Those courts that recognize and enforce such agreements hold that the agreements are only sufficient to allocate liability between parties to the

warranty: A contractual promise that an assertion or statement is true.

indemnification agreement: Agreement by which one person promises to reimburse another person, or hold that person harmless, for loss or damage.

disclaimer: Contract provision whereby one party denies responsibility for certain events or occurrences.

agreement. Contractual warranties and indemnification agreements are not enforceable against the government and would not affect a party's liability to the government under CERCLA. This means that the parties responsible for cleanup cannot escape liability to the government simply by contracting with another party. Regardless of whether or not CERCLA violations are present, buyers and sellers of real property will try to allocate the risk of environmental cleanup costs should contamination be detected.

Warranty

A warranty may be express or implied. An **express warranty** is one that is actually set out in words (*expressed*) in the contract. An **implied-in-fact warranty** is one that is not stated in actual words but is implied by the intention and conduct of the parties. For example, a court might find that the seller implicitly warranted that the property was in compliance with all local and state environmental laws at the time of sale because this was the intention of the parties, even though the parties did not include an express warranty to that effect in their contract. A warranty may also be implied in law. An **implied-in-law warranty** is one that is not expressly or implicitly intended by the parties, but is imposed on the parties by law for public policy reasons. Later sections of this chapter discuss the law-imposed implied warranty of habitability in the sale of residential property, and the implied warranties of merchantability and of fitness in the sale of goods.

The importance of environmental warranties in the sale of real estate has grown in direct response to the potential liability of landowners under CERCLA. The cost and time required to clean up hazardous waste contamination are significant, and in many (if not most) cases, cleanup costs will far exceed the purchase price of the property. Potential CERCLA liability has significantly affected the previously less complicated transfer or lease of property, land, and buildings.

Indemnification Agreements

Under CERCLA, a person may by agreement be held harmless or indemnified by another party. Section 107(e)(1) provides:

> (1) No indemnification, hold harmless, or similar agreement or conveyance shall be effective to transfer from the owner or operator of any vessel or facility or from any person who may be liable for a release or threat of a release under this section, to any other person the liability imposed under this section. Nothing in this subsection shall bar any agreement to insure, hold harmless, or indemnify a party to such agreement for any liability under this section.[7]

The apparently contradictory language of this section and other CERCLA sections has given rise to conflicting interpretations of the enforceability of indemnity clauses in CERCLA cases.[8] The majority rule is the Ninth Circuit's decision in *Mardan Corp. v. C.G.C. Music, Ltd.*,[9] where the court held that releases and indemnity agreements were permissible under CERCLA, and thus would constitute a bar to subsequent suits for contribution. However, a series of cases have prohibited

express warranty: A warranty explicitly set out in words in the contract.

implied-in-fact warranty: A warranty not stated in words within a contract but implied by the intent and conduct of the parties.

implied-in-law warranty: A warranty imposed by law; not expressly or implicitly intended by the parties.

---

[7] 42 U.S.C. § 9607(e)(1) (1980).
[8] *See, e.g., Fina v. ARCO*, 200 F.3d 266 (5th Cir. 2000), in which indemnification agreements were held inapplicable to CERCLA claims.
[9] 600 F. Supp. 1049 (D. Ariz. 1984), *aff'd*, 804 F.2d 1454 (9th Cir. 1986).

private parties from distributing environmental liability by contract, even among themselves,[10] though such approach has been criticized by some courts and scholars. Nevertheless, *Mardan* is still followed.[11] Even assuming that courts permit contractual distribution of response costs under CERCLA, other issues remain. For example, what laws should govern the interpretation of the indemnification contract? The *Mardan* court held that state law should apply to interpretations, but some courts have held that federal common law should apply to contracts allocating CERCLA response costs.

Let's review the concepts discussed in this section by examining a case in which several of these issues were addressed. In the *Wilder* case, a seller owned a large tract of farmland, which was sold to The Nature Conservancy, an environmental organization. The seller had expressly warranted in the contract that the land was not contaminated; however, the land was in fact contaminated with petroleum. The Nature Conservancy won a judgment against the seller for breach of contract. In this case, the seller argued that the Thompson Drainage and Levee District had failed to properly maintain a pump house and storage tank, leakage from which led to the contamination of the property. Essentially, the seller was asking that the Thompson Drainage and Levee District indemnify it for the judgment rendered against it in the earlier suit. This court held that the seller could not invoke noncontractual indemnity to shift the risk that it had assumed in the contract.

Wilder Corp. of Delaware v. Thompson Drainage & Levee District

658 F.3d 802, 2011 U.S. App. LEXIS 19655, 41 ELR 20310 (7th Cir. 2011)

Posner, Circuit Judge.

This appeal from the grant of summary judgment to the defendant in a diversity suit governed by Illinois law tests the outer limits of the common law doctrine of indemnity.

The word "indemnity" is from a Latin word that means "security from damage." The most common form of indemnity in modern life is an insurance contract: A is harmed by conduct covered by an insurance contract issued by insurance company B; the contract secures A from the harm by shifting its cost to B. But indemnity is not limited to insurance contracts (indemnity provisions are frequently found in other

contracts ...)—or, more to the point, to contracts, period. For there is a tort doctrine of indemnity, which shifts the burden of liability from a blameless tortfeasor (which sounds like an oxymoron, but we're about to see that it isn't) to a blameworthy one.... The tort doctrine is sometimes called "implied indemnity" to distinguish it from contractual indemnity, but a clearer term is "noncontractual indemnity."

To illustrate: an employee, acting within the scope of his employment (whether or not with the authorization, or to the benefit, of his employer) negligently injures a person. The victim sues the employer, the employer being strictly liable for the employee's tort under the doctrine of respondeat superior. After paying

(Continued)

---

[10] *AM International, Inc. v. International Forging Equipment*, 743 F. Supp 525 (N.D. Ohio 1990), *rev'd in part*, 982 F.2d 989 (6th Cir. 1993).

[11] *See, e.g., In re Glazier Group (T-Bone Restaurant LLC & Strip House Las Vegas, LLC v. General Electric Capital Corp.)*, 2012 Bankr. LEXIS 5559, 2012 WL 6005764 (Bankr. S.D.N.Y. Nov. 30, 2012).

a judgment to, or settling with, the victim, the employer, being itself blameless (respondeat superior is as we just said a doctrine of strict liability) turns around and sues the employee to recover the cost of the judgment or settlement, the employee being liable to the employer for that cost under the doctrine of non-contractual indemnity. This may seem a roundabout alternative to a rule that only the employee is liable. But it is more than that. The employee often will be judgment-proof. In that event the employer won't be able to shift its liability to him, and so the employee will be undeterred, to the detriment of the employer, whom respondeat superior will stick with liability for the employee's tort. This prospect gives an employer an incentive to try to prevent its employees from committing torts. The employer may screen applicants for employment more carefully, or monitor their performance at work more carefully, than it would do had it no back-up liability for its employees' torts.... Or it might try to reduce the number of negligent injuries inflicted by its employees by reducing the scale or scope of its activity; a reduction in output is one way of reducing potential tort liability....

The twist in this case is that the party seeking indemnity (the plaintiff, Wilder) is trying to shift liability not for a tort but for a breach of contract.

Wilder owned 6600 acres of farmland, on which it grazed cattle, in Fulton County, southwest of Peoria; Fulton is a rural county bounded by the Illinois River. In 2000 Wilder sold the land for $16.35 million to The Nature Conservancy, the well-known environmental organization, which wanted to restore Wilder's land to its pre-twentieth century condition as an ecologically functional floodplain (that is, land adjacent to a body of water, in this case the Illinois River, that overflows from time to time, soaking the land, creating wetlands that preserve biodiversity). The Conservancy claims that its restoration project is one of the largest such projects in the United States.... (What had been Wilder's land now constitutes more than half of Emiquon Natural Wildlife Refuge.)

Wilder expressly warranted in the contract of sale that there was no contamination of the land by petroleum. But the land was contaminated by petroleum, though there is no indication that Wilder knew this and we'll assume it didn't.

Six years later the Conservancy, having discovered the contamination, sued Wilder in an Illinois state court for breach of warranty. The federal district court to which Wilder removed the case (the parties being of diverse citizenship) gave judgment for the Conservancy, awarding it some $800,000 in damages, though some of this amount reflected a separate breach of Wilder's contract with the Conservancy—its failure to clean up "sewage lagoons" in which it had deposited waste generated by its cattle.

Wilder appealed the judgment, unsuccessfully.... It had already brought the present suit, a companion suit, against the local drainage district. Illinois drainage districts are public corporations directed and empowered to minimize damage from the overflow of waters that collect on agricultural land.... To facilitate the drainage of excess water, the district had long ago obtained a right of way on the land later bought by Wilder and had built a pump house on the land to pump excess surface waters into the Illinois River. To have at hand fuel for the pumps, the drainage district stored petroleum both in storage tanks that it owned in the vicinity, of which at least one was on or under the land Wilder sold to The Nature Conservancy, and in the pump house itself. (The Conservancy, wanting to restore the land as wetlands, turned off the pumps.)

Wilder asks that the drainage district be ordered to indemnify it for the money it's had to pay the Conservancy as damages for its breach of warranty. It claims to be entitled to indemnity because, it argues, negligent maintenance by the drainage district of the pump house and the storage tanks was the sole cause of the contamination of the Conservancy's (formerly Wilder's) land. It argues that it should have been allowed to conduct discovery to try to prove that it was indeed blameless and the district at fault.

The Nature Conservancy's suit against Wilder was a contract suit rather than a tort suit. The warranty on which the suit was based was, as we noted, imposed in the contract of sale, not by law, as in the case of implied warranties. Granted, Wilder's denial that it contributed to the petroleum contamination is not inconsistent with its having lost the suit brought by the Conservancy, because liability for breach of contract is strict. As Holmes explained in The Common Law 300 (1881), "in the case of a binding promise that it shall rain to-morrow, the immediate legal effect of what the promisor does is, that he takes the risk of the event, within certain defined limits, as between himself and the promisee. He does no more when he promises to deliver a bale of cotton." But the blameless contract breaker ("blameless" in the sense that his breach was involuntary) cannot invoke noncontractual indemnity to shift the risk that he assumed in the contract.

The reasons are several. One is to head off the avalanche of litigation that might be triggered if an

(Continued)

involuntary contract breaker could sue anyone for indemnity who a court might find had contributed to the breach....

... Although the drainage district may not have known that Wilder had executed a warranty that would make it liable for any negligent leakage by the district, it would or should have known that it would be liable, if it created a nuisance on Wilder's land, to whoever owned the land when the nuisance materialized. But the defense against a suit brought not by the owner but by a guarantor would be more complicated than defending a nuisance case. For suppose, confident that it could shift the cost of any judgment obtained by The Nature Conservancy to the drainage district, Wilder had not put up a strong defense on the damages phase of the Conservancy's suit; then in Wilder's suit against the district for indemnity, the district would have to litigate the adequacy of Wilder's defense in the earlier suit. A further complication is that Wilder sold the land for a use that was likely to make petroleum contamination a far more serious problem than if the land had remained ranchland.

* * *

To impose noncontractual indemnity in this case would have the ... perverse consequence of making the drainage district an insurer of Wilder's contract with The Nature Conservancy. One generally can't insure against a breach of contract, because of moral hazard (the tendency of an insured to be less careful about preventing the harm insured against than if it were not insured).... Yet Wilder seeks to make the drainage district the insurer of Wilder's breach of contract—and an involuntary insurer at that, as the district couldn't have prevented Wilder from warranting that the land it was selling to the Conservancy was uncontaminated, though it might have been able to intervene in the Conservancy's suit against Wilder to protect its interests.

We acknowledge that as between Wilder and the drainage district, the latter was in a better, and probably the only, position to prevent the contamination. And so Wilder can appeal to the principle, which underlies the tort doctrine of indemnity along with many other tort doctrines, that liability for inflicting a harm should come to rest on the party that could, at the lowest cost, have prevented the harm in the first place.... The pump house, and the petroleum-storage tank or tanks on the property, were outside Wilder's control. It had no right to oversee their maintenance. It might therefore seem to have a

compelling argument for shifting liability for the contamination from its own shoulders to those of the district.

* * *

Had Wilder refused to give The Nature Conservancy a warranty against petroleum contamination, the Conservancy would doubtless have sued the drainage district for committing the tort of nuisance .... It was Wilder's choice to shoulder the risk of liability for petroleum contamination, and it would have been compensated in advance by getting a higher price for the land—it wouldn't have given such a dangerously broad warranty for nothing. One cannot be heard to complain when a risk materializes if one took it voluntarily because paid one's price for taking it.

* * *

... Wilder could have protected itself against the drainage district's negligence by a subrogation clause in its contract with The Nature Conservancy, failed to, and has only itself to blame for that failure....

Questions for Discussion

1. What should a seller of real property do to protect itself from liability for claims of environmental contamination? What should a seller of real property *not* do?

2. What public policy reasons can you think of to support the court's position of not allowing a noncontractual indemnification claim, such as that attempted by Wilder, to stand? If noncontractual indemnification was permitted, what would be the consequences?

3. Precise and comprehensive writing is important when drafting a contract. This precision should extend to including a description and summary of the reasons for the agreement and the limitations to the agreement. Terms and conditions should be defined clearly.

   Specific issues that should be addressed in a contract include substances, wastes, materials covered, laws and regulations covered, known or suspected risks, permits, properties or conditions covered or excluded, parties, specific term of the agreement, law to apply in any such dispute, dispute resolution mechanisms, nature of the obligations and specific costs covered by the agreement, and trigger for the duty to defend or indemnify. Can any contract can be written to absolutely protect against liability? Why or why not?

Disclaimers of Liability and the "As Is" Clause

Contract disclaimers of environmental liability in the sale of commercial property are generally enforceable as long as they are negotiated by the parties in good faith and as long as the parties have actual notice of their contents. However, courts always retain the power to declare a contract provision unenforceable if they find that the clause violates public policy or is unconscionable. *Public policy* is a broad term describing a court's or legislator's view of policy that is in the best interests of the public and society in general. It may be manifested in statute or by judicial determination. Some contractual disclaimers, such as disclaimers of implied warranties in the sale of residential property, may be unenforceable because they are not in the best interests of the public.

In the following case, a plaintiff purchaser sought to enforce a contract for the sale of commercial property after the property was discovered to be contaminated. The seller sought to rescind the contract on the basis that the parties had been mutually mistaken about the contamination on the property and because the seller was obligated under state and federal law to bear the cost of cleaning up the property. The buyer relied on an as-is provision in the contract in arguing that the contract was enforceable.

Garb-Ko Inc. v. Lansing-Lewis Services, Inc.
423 N.W.2d 355 (Mich. Ct. App. 1988)

E.M. Thomas, J.

Plaintiff appeals as of right from the trial court's order denying specific performance of a sales contract against defendants …. We affirm.

This case presents an anomalous situation in which the seller seeks to rescind a contract for the sale of land based on a defect in the property discovered after the sales agreement was entered into. Garb-Ko and Action Auto, the parent company of Lansing-Lewis Services, Inc., entered into a buy-sell agreement on or about February 11, 1985, by which plaintiff was to purchase a gas station and automotive parts store in East Lansing from defendants for $320,000. The buy-sell agreement contained an "as is" clause. The site was to be used for a 7-Eleven store. The property has seven underground storage tanks which hold four thousand to six thousand gallons of gasoline each.

Garb-Ko did not inquire into the environmental condition of the property or the integrity of the gasoline tanks prior to making the offer to purchase. Action Auto subsequently learned that the gasoline storage tanks on the property might be leaking and contaminating the ground and groundwater. Neither party was aware of any contamination on the property at the time the buy-sell agreement was executed. Garb-Ko was informed of the contamination on the property in

a letter dated April 5, 1985, and given the option of terminating the agreement or providing Action Auto with full indemnification for all costs and penalties arising out of any gasoline storage leakage and proceeding with the sale. Garb-Ko did not agree to indemnify the sellers for the costs and expenses arising out of the contamination and did not accept the seller's offer to terminate the agreement. …

* * *

A bench trial was held on December 23, 1985, to determine whether specific performance of the buy-sell agreement should be ordered. The court found that a mutual mistake affecting a basic, material assumption of the contract had occurred and that it would be unreasonable and unjust to enforce the terms of the buy-sell agreement.…

A contract may be rescinded because of a mutual mistake of the parties; however, this equitable remedy is granted only in the sound discretion of the trial court. … The determination whether plaintiffs are entitled to rescission involves a bifurcated inquiry: (1) was there a mistaken belief entertained by one or both of the parties to a contract? and (2) if so, what is the legal significance of the mistaken belief? …

In its opinion and order, the trial court found that the parties had clearly entered into the buy-sell

(Continued)

agreement under a serious mistake of fact since, at the time the agreement was signed, neither party was aware of the gasoline leakage. We agree.

A contractual mistake "is a belief not in accord with the facts." … This mistake must relate to a fact in existence at the time the contract is executed.… The testimony at trial clearly revealed that there had been a large gasoline leak on the property that could result in contamination of both soil and groundwater. The testimony also indicated that none of the contracting parties were aware of that fact at the time they executed the buy-sell agreement.…

* * *

Here, the mutual mistake relates to a basic assumption of the parties upon which the contract was made. Additionally, this mistake materially affects the agreed performance of the parties. In any commercial real estate sale, the parties assume and desire that the sale will result in a complete transfer of rights, obligations, and responsibilities. The purchaser does not want the seller involved in, or disrupting, the new business in any way. Likewise, the seller desires to sever all ties with the property and any obligations. Under the common law, a sale of property resulted in such a transfer of rights and obligations. However, environmental-protection statutes have altered the common law and made previous owners of sites liable for environmental contamination.… Under these laws, a previous owner may be required to conduct a site investigation and cleanup and would have a continuing liability after contaminated property is sold. It is this continuing responsibility for the land in question which requires us to affirm the trial court's ruling rescinding the buy-sell agreement and denying plaintiff's request for specific performance of the agreement.

We are not persuaded by plaintiff that the "as is" clause contained in the buy-sell agreement controls and bars rescission of the contract. Paragraph 11 of the buy-sell agreement states:

> PURCHASER HAS PERSONALLY EXAMINED THIS PROPERTY AND AGREES TO ACCEPT SAME IN ITS PRESENT CONDITION EXCEPT AS MAY BE SPECIFIED HEREIN AND AGREES THAT THERE ARE NO OTHER ADDITIONAL WRITTEN OR ORAL UNDERSTANDINGS.

Under this clause, the risk was clearly allocated to the purchaser. 1 Restatement Contracts, 2nd, § 152 … states that when a legally significant mutual mistake has occurred, the contract is voidable by the adversely affected party, unless he bears the risk of the mistake. However, the purchaser is not the adversely affected party; thus, the "as is" clause holds no significance. Here, due to the state and federal environmental-protection statutes which impose continuing liability after the sale of the land on defendant sellers for contamination that occurred while defendants owned the property, it is clear that they are the adversely affected party. The "as is" clause of the buy-sell agreement would not operate to relieve defendant sellers of their liability under these statutes. Had plaintiff agreed to indemnify Action Auto for all costs and penalties arising out of any gasoline storage leakage, rescission possibly would not have been granted. However, since plaintiff did not do so, defendant sellers remain the adversely affected party having incurred the "burden" imposed by law of cleaning up the contamination. The contract is voidable ….

In this case, equity requires that we affirm the trial court's ruling. Defendants have a continuing obligation and responsibility for the contaminated property. One expert estimated that the cost of cleanup could be anywhere from $100,000 to $1,000,000. In order to contain further cleanup costs and third-party claims arising from use of the contaminated land, defendants need control over the use of the property. Sale to plaintiff would not give them such control.

Indeed, this case is unique since rarely does a purchaser of property, after discovering that the property is contaminated, request that the sale continue and ask the court to order specific performance of the contract. However, due to the continuing nature of the obligation and responsibilities defendants have over the environmental contamination of the property, we conclude that the trial court did not err in ordering rescission of the contract and denying plaintiff's request for specific performance.

Affirmed.

Questions and Comments for Discussion

1. Who sued whom in this case and why? Who wanted to enforce the contract? Generally, if a party breaches a contract, it is obligated to pay damages to the other party. In this case, the buyer sought the equitable remedy of **specific performance**. This remedy is appropriate in cases where contract damages are inadequate to compensate a contracting party for breach. Under this remedy, a court may order the breaching party to actually perform the contract. The

(Continued)

remedy is particularly appropriate in cases where the contract involves the sale of unique property like real estate.

2. As the court indicated in this case, a court may set aside a contract on the basis of mutual mistake if it finds that (1) both parties were mistaken about a basic assumption on which the contract was made; (2) the mistake had a material effect on the agreed exchange of performance; and (3) the mistaken party did not bear the risk of the mistake. A party may "bear the risk" of the mistake if it agrees to accept the property "as is." As in this case, however, a court may refuse to enforce an as-is clause if it finds that enforcement is inappropriate or that the clause was not intended to apply under the particular circumstances of the case. When would enforcement be inappropriate? Explain.

3. A party may also rescind a contract if it can show that it entered into the contract because the other party misrepresented an important fact about the property. *Misrepresentation* is defined as a false assertion purported to be fact. Under this theory, a false assertion of material "fact" can be the basis of rescission if the other party actually and reasonably relied on the misrepresentation. Misrepresentation that is intentionally and knowingly made to deceive another is called *fraud* and may be the basis for contract rescission as well as an action for damages for intentional tort. An innocent and negligent misrepresentation may also be the basis for contract rescission if it concerns a material fact and the other party actually and justifiably relied on the misrepresentation. A buyer may be entitled to rescind a contract for the purchase of real property if the seller misrepresented the property as not environmentally contaminated when in fact it was. What type of evidence might be useful to show that a seller misrepresented the presence of environmental contamination on property?

Implied Warranties of Habitability

Most states have recognized an **implied warranty of habitability** in the sale of new residential property. Under this theory, a builder-vendor who sells a new home impliedly warrants that the home will be habitable and fit for occupation. Similarly, most states recognize an implied warranty of habitability in residential leases. Under these implied warranties, a purchaser or tenant of residential property may be entitled to damages or rescission if the property is uninhabitable because of the presence of environmental hazards like radon gas, asbestos, or formaldehyde. Specific remedies for breach of the implied warranty of habitability include damages, termination of the lease, rent abatement, and rights to repair and deduct the cost of repairs from the rent.

The doctrine of **caveat emptor** ("let the buyer beware") in real property transactions has largely been usurped by implied warranties. A type of implied warranty of habitability is an implied warranty of quality, which is recognized in the majority of states and is applicable to the sale of new homes. Accordingly, the doctrine of **caveat venditor** ("let the seller beware") in the sale and lease of residential property is more clearly expressed in our laws today.

Implied warranties of habitability do not guarantee perfection. Such warranties only protect against latent defects.

Residential and Commercial Leases

Historically, a lease agreement between a landlord and a tenant was viewed primarily as a conveyance of real property. This relationship has changed dramatically, and the relationship now is more typically characterized as a contractual one. Under modern contract law, doctrines such as unconscionability and the implied warranty of habitability are applied to the sale and lease of residential property. These doctrines are used to protect tenants as well as to ensure that

specific performance: Remedy whereby a defendant is ordered to perform the contract according to its terms.

implied warranty of habitability: Warranty implied in law that a living structure will be habitable and fit for occupation.

caveat emptor: "Let the buyer beware"; maxim expressing a warning and expectation that a buyer will examine or test the potential purchase before consummating the transaction.

caveat venditor: "Let the seller beware"; maxim expressing that a seller must meet its heightened legal and contractual obligations.

policies underlying the enactment of public health and safety laws, such as environmental laws, are met.

Landlord–tenant obligations arise under contract (the lease), the law of property (e.g., common law rights under the leasehold estate, such as right of possession), and the principles of tort law. Landlords must meet the requirements of the lease, including the requirements of any implied warranties, such as the implied warranty of habitability. Additionally, landlords have a duty to use reasonable care in the maintenance of the leased property, including a duty to repair. Moreover, a number of statutes and ordinances may apply in landlord-tenant cases, such as building codes and specific environmental codes, such as those related to lead-based paint in the cases that follow.

Just as the implied warranty of habitability in the sale of new property is generally limited to sales of new residential property, so implied warranties of habitability are generally limited to leases of residential property. However, the same policies that underlie protection of tenants in residential property often apply to the sale and lease of commercial property as well. For example, an employee who works in a "sick" building (a building with hazards that may affect the health of those working within it) may reasonably argue that the landlord or builder should be liable for damages under the theory that the commercial landlord also impliedly warrants that the building is safe for human habitation. Considering the trend toward expanding liability of the owner or **lessor** of residential property under these theories, it is certainly possible that courts will expand protection of commercial tenants.

Most cities and states have adopted housing codes that impose duties on the landlord with respect to conditions of the property. These codes commonly require that the property meet minimum standards of cleanliness, safety, and sanitary conditions. Violation of such standards may give rise to an action for breach of an implied warranty of habitability.

Some states have also recognized that specific environmental hazards may pose a risk to tenants and have enacted laws designed to protect tenants from those hazards, such as those posed by lead-based paint. Title X of the Housing and Community Development Act of 1992 requires sellers of pre-1978 housing units to disclose to prospective buyers or tenants any known lead hazards.

lessor: A person who leases a property to another; commonly referred to as a landlord.

In the following two cases, the tenants sued their landlords for personal injuries sustained by tenants' children, who ingested lead-based paint. Why did these cases result in different outcomes?

Hardy v. Griffin
569 A.2d 49 (Conn. Super. Ct. 1989)

Demayo, Judge.

The plaintiff, Patricia Hardy, brought this action on behalf of her six-year-old child, Verron Hardy, claiming that he suffered severe and permanent brain damage from his exposure to, and ingestion of, lead-based paint.

From about November 1, 1984, to August 1, 1986, the plaintiff occupied a housing unit at 18 Arthur Street in New Haven. During this time, Verron was found to have abnormally high levels of lead in his blood. The named defendant and the defendant Leona A. Griffin were the owners of 18 Arthur Street and leased the premises to Patricia Hardy.

(Continued)

In this case of first impression, the plaintiff has claimed damages on a theory of strict liability because of the defendants' alleged violation of both state statutes and a city ordinance. The failure to keep the premises free of lead-based paint is claimed to be the violation....

The defendants have denied any knowledge of the existence of such paint, suggesting that if there were any, it existed prior to their purchase of the property. They further deny the use of any lead-based paint on the premises.

From the evidence the plaintiff presented at trial, the court concludes that Verron suffers from lead paint poisoning and that this condition was a result of his exposure to the lead-based paint present at 18 Arthur Street.

The named defendant admitted that in January, 1987, he received a notice from the city of New Haven advising him of the presence of lead paint at 18 Arthur Street. On prior occasions, he had been put on notice that repairs to this unit were required. The plaintiff testified that she had seen Verron eating paint chips, which prompted her to have him tested for the presence of lead in his blood. She also stated that the apartment was painted by the defendants but that the previous coat of paint was not scraped. This underlying coat was described as "thick, chipped and peeling."

The named defendant's suggestion that someone "set him up" by spraying on lead paint is entitled to no credence. As for the testimony offered by the defendants that Verron was observed eating paint out of a can, their own evidence as to the dates of the termination of the manufacture and sale of lead-based paint in Connecticut renders this event, even if it is accepted by this court as having occurred, to be of dubious significance.

In support of the strict liability theory, the plaintiff cites General Statutes sec. 47a-8 and the New Haven Code of General Ordinances. Section 47a-8 provides as follows: "The presence of paint which does not conform to federal standards as required in accordance with the Lead-Based Paint Poisoning Prevention Act ... or of cracked, chipped, blistered, flaking, loose or peeling paint which constitutes a health hazard on accessible surfaces in any dwelling unit, tenement or any real property intended for human habitation shall be construed to render such dwelling unit, tenement or real property unfit for human habitation and shall constitute a noncompliance with subdivision (2) of subsection (a) of section 47a-7." Section 47a-7(a)(2) imposes an affirmative duty upon landlords to "make all repairs and do whatever is necessary to put and keep the premises in a fit and habitable condition. ..." The New Haven Code of General Ordinances sets a stricter standard than the federal standards referred to in sec. 47a-8.

The plaintiff cites *Panoroni v. Johnson*, 158 Conn. 92, 256 A.2d 246 (1969). In that case, the Supreme Court stated: "The violation of an ordinance enacted for the protection of the public is negligence as a matter of law." *Panoroni* also involved the New Haven housing code, and the court found that the plaintiff there was a member of the class for whose protection the New Haven code was enacted. This court similarly concludes that the plaintiff in the present case is a member of the class for whose protection the provision of the housing code referred to above was enacted.

The defendants' breach, therefore, of the duty imposed by the New Haven Code of General Ordinances to maintain rental premises free of lead paint (or not to rent premises containing lead paint) renders them liable for the injuries incurred by Verron Hardy. On the facts here, the court further finds that the defendants are liable for Verron's condition by virtue of their negligent failure to keep the premises free of lead paint and because they rented the premises when they should have known of the presence of lead paint.

In view of [experts'] testimony, there is little doubt that Verron is severely and permanently mentally disabled as a result of lead poisoning, causing behavioral and learning abnormalities. He has a marked inability to concentrate and to organize his thoughts. It is unlikely he will be able to graduate from high school.

... Verron's loss of earning capacity over his life expectancy [has been computed by an expert in economics]. The court accepts his lowest computation, which presumes Verron will complete the eighth grade, as the most realistic. The court sees little likelihood that he will enter and complete high school. Wright's computation for the completion of eight grades is $828,626.

In view of the foregoing, judgment may enter for the plaintiff to recover from the defendants the sum of $828,626, plus attorney's fees of $100,000 and costs.

Szewczuk, et al. v. Stellar 117 Garth, LLC, et al.
2012 U.S. Dist. LEXIS 188143 (S.D.N.Y. 2012)

Honorable Paul A. Crotty, United States District Judge:

Plaintiffs bring this action on behalf of themselves and as natural guardians of Benedicta Szewczuk ("Benedicta") ... against Stellar 117 Garth, LLC [and other defendants] ... (collectively "Defendants"), seeking damages arising from alleged exposure to lead paint in an apartment owned and managed by Defendants. Plaintiffs assert that Benedicta's alleged exposure to lead paint in the apartment caused her to suffer brain dysfunction. They contend that Defendants did not take proper measures to remove the lead paint, and that Plaintiffs were forced to vacate their apartment as a result of the allegedly dangerous condition. On November 9, 2009, Plaintiffs filed their Amended Complaint asserting claims for breach of the warranty of habitability and constructive eviction; damage to personal property; interference with use of personal property; and intentional infliction of emotional distress.

* * *

Background

In October of 2000, Plaintiffs leased apartment 3G at 117 Garth Road, Scarsdale, New York (the "Building"). ... Stellar Management purchased the Building on May 18, 2005.... [S]hortly thereafter, Stellar Management began demolition work in apartments on Plaintiffs' floor.... Szewczuk testified in his deposition that during the summer of 2005, there was often dust and debris from the demolition throughout the Building and that this dust, along with paint chips, were tracked into the Apartment....

Plaintiffs allege that prior to the demolition work, Benedicta was exposed to lead in the Building and in the Apartment. At her first annual physical examination in early 2004, Benedicta was found to be underweight and undersized, and was diagnosed with failure to thrive.... Blood tests conducted on January 8, 2004 indicated that Benedicta had a blood lead level of 7 micrograms per deciliter.... A second blood sample was taken on August 22, 2005, and showed Benedicta's blood lead level had decreased to 6 micrograms per deciliter.... Szewczuk testified that, according to these reports, blood lead levels of zero to 9 micrograms per deciliter are considered normal for children ages 0 through 16.... In addition, Friend testified that no doctor has ever told her that Benedicta's blood lead levels

were outside the normal range.... Nor has Friend ever asked Benedicta's doctors whether any of Benedicta's health issues were caused by exposure to lead.... Both Szewczuk and Friend testified that they never saw Benedicta ingesting paint chips in the Building or the Apartment.... Friend also testified in her deposition that she had "never seen [Benedicta] chew on a molding or anything like that." ...

On December 9, 2005, testing conducted by Defendants revealed lead-based paint in another apartment in the Building.... On January 18, 2006, Stellar Management sent Plaintiffs a letter stating that they received notice of peeling paint in the Apartment, and requesting that Plaintiffs contact them to schedule an access date for testing.... Sultan Ibric, Defendants' superintendent, vaguely recalled that Plaintiffs had contacted him in late 2005 or early 2006 regarding peeling and chipped paint in their Apartment ....

On February 15, 2006, Stellar Management determined that lead abatement work in the Apartment was necessary, and Plaintiffs agreed to allow them to send a third party vendor to test the Apartment for lead.... [I]mmediately thereafter, on March 6, 2006, Plaintiffs filed an application for rent reduction with the New York State Division of Housing and Community Renewal ("DHCR")....

On March 13, 2006, Exclusive Testing Labs, Inc. ("ETL") inspected the Apartment for lead-based paint. ... ETL observed lead-based paint throughout the Apartment; but it noted that all paint was intact and posed no danger.... Its report stated: "When a positive component is intact and is showing no signs of deterioration, it will not present a hazardous situation (except for friction surfaces)." ...

On April 17, 2006, Stellar Management notified Plaintiffs of their option to remain in the Apartment or temporarily move to another apartment in the Building during the lead abatement.... On May 16, 2006, Plaintiffs advised Stellar Management that the proposed renovation dates were not convenient for them, and that any work in the Apartment would have to wait three and one half months, until August, 2006.... Plaintiffs vacated the Apartment with all of their belongings in August, 2006, and Stellar Management proceeded to perform lead abatement work.... Szewczuk and Friend both testified that none of their furniture or property was damaged due to the lead or abatement work in the Building.... Following the abatement, ETL returned to

(Continued)

the Apartment on August 28, 2006 to perform a lead wipe clearance and visual inspection, and found that any lead present was within acceptable limits....

On October 5, 2006, approximately two months after Plaintiffs vacated the Apartment, the DHCR awarded Plaintiffs a rent reduction to one dollar per month based on Plaintiffs' March 6, 2006 application....

* * *

In support of their motion for summary judgment, Defendants offer the opinions of Dr. Shlomo Shinnar ("Dr. Shinnar"), a specialist in neurology, pediatrics, and epidemiology at the Albert Einstein College of Medicine, and Dr. Thomas Boland ("Dr. Boland"), a psychologist with a specialty in pediatrics at the Cornell University Medical College....

Dr. Shinnar examined Benedicta on June 10, 2010 and reviewed Benedicta's medical and school records, as well as the record in this case.... Dr. Shinnar concluded that there was no evidence in the records provided by Benedicta's mother that Benedicta had elevated blood lead levels.... He also reported that "[t]here has never been an association between" Benedicta's blood lead levels and any of her alleged deficiencies.... Dr. Shinnar further opined that Benedicta has normal cognition, development, and behavior, and that she has "an entirely normal neurological examination." ...

On September 1, 2010, Dr. Boland performed a psychological evaluation of Benedicta and John Paul on behalf of Defendants, concluding that both scored within the average to above average range "in all major domains." ... Dr. Boland concluded that, since the highest recorded blood lead levels for Benedicta and John Paul were 7 micrograms per deciliter and 2 micrograms per deciliter, respectively, and since there was no evidence of impaired functioning, Benedicta and John Paul did not have lead poisoning.... On September 7, 2010, Dr. Boland evaluated Szewczuk, and later evaluated Friend on September 27, 2010. Dr. Boland concluded that the results of these tests did "not indicate any objective evidence ... of clinically significant psychological impairment." ...

In opposition to Defendants' motion for summary judgment, Plaintiffs submit an affidavit from Dr. Theodore Lidsky, a psychologist specializing in neuroscience and neuropsychology.... Dr. Lidsky has evaluated "more than 1,000" lead poisoned children within the last ten years....

Dr. Lidsky examined Benedicta on November 3, 2010 and reviewed the record in this case, as well as Benedicta's medical and school records.... He observed that, while Benedicta had high overall verbal cognitive functioning and superior visual cognitive functioning, she showed impairments of visual attention, visuospatial construction, verbal memory and other functions.... He opined that Benedicta's records indicated brain dysfunction, and that "Benedicta's neuropsychological impairments are due to brain injury caused by lead." ...

* * *

Discussion

II. Breach of Warranty of Habitability and Constructive Eviction

New York Real Property Law § 235-b provides an implied warranty of habitability in residential leases: "[I]n every written or oral lease or rental agreement for residential premises the landlord or lessor shall be deemed to covenant ... that the premises ... are fit for human habitation ... and that the occupants ... shall not be subjected to any conditions which would be dangerous, hazardous or detrimental to their life, health or safety." ... Under section 235-b, a landlord's liability "is conditioned upon a showing that the landlord had notice of the defect and a reasonable time to repair." *Mahlmann v. Yelverton*, 109 Misc. 2d 127, 439 N.Y.S.2d 568, 571 (N.Y. Civil Ct., Queens Cty. 1980).

Defendants have established that there is no genuine issue of fact on Plaintiffs' warranty of habitability claim. Szewczuk alleges that in the summer of 2005, there was debris throughout the Building resulting from Defendants' demolition work. Defendants concede that there was lead-based paint present in the Building, and that abatement work was necessary in the Apartment. In February 2006, Defendants advised Plaintiffs that they would bring a third-party vendor into the Apartment to inspect and test the unit. ETL performed this inspection on March 13, 2006. ETL found lead paint on various surfaces in the Apartment, but it noted that any lead-based paint in the Apartment was intact, and therefore nonhazardous. ETL reported that "[w]hen a positive component is intact and is showing no signs of deterioration, it will not present a hazardous situation ... ." ... The report does not state that any lead dust was found in the Apartment. Defendants nevertheless scheduled lead abatement work in the Apartment, which was performed after Plaintiffs vacated the Apartment with all of their belongings in August, 2006.

In their opposition brief, Plaintiffs fail to address any of this evidence or show how the intact paint in the Apartment created a hazardous condition. To the extent

(Continued)

that Plaintiffs rely on Ibric's deposition testimony, in which Ibric stated that he "was told by the lead testing company that there is lead in [the] [A]partment," ... Ibric conceded that he "never looked at any results" and "was just told verbally." ... Thus, apart from their own deposition testimony, Plaintiffs cite no evidence on which a trier of fact could find that there was a hazardous condition in the Apartment itself. Such testimony, without more, is insufficient to defeat summary judgment.... Accordingly, Plaintiffs' claim for breach of the warranty of habitability is dismissed. [The court included the following footnote: "To the extent that Plaintiffs may have been seeking to recover for their and Benedicta's alleged personal injuries, the implied warranty of habitability does not provide such relief ... ."]

Nor do Plaintiffs point to any evidence in the record to show a genuine issue of fact in support of their claim for constructive eviction. A "constructive eviction exists where, although there has been no physical expulsion or exclusion of the tenant, the landlord's wrongful acts substantially and materially deprive the tenant of the beneficial use and enjoyment of the premises." *Barash v. Pennsylvania Terminal Real Estate Corp.*, 26 N.Y.2d 77, 83, 256 N.E.2d 707, 308 N.Y.S.2d 649 (1970). The record does not show how any action or inaction on the part of Defendants forced Plaintiffs to vacate the Apartment. Indeed, the record shows just the opposite. When notified of the possible presence of lead paint, Defendants arranged to have the Apartment tested and abatement work performed. Defendants gave Plaintiffs the option of temporarily relocating to another apartment within the Building. Contrast that with Plaintiffs' actions. Upon receiving notice of the presence of lead paint, Plaintiffs almost immediately filed for a rent reduction. Further, they delayed the beginning of abatement work for three and a half months until August 2006, at which time they moved out of the Building. As Plaintiffs fail to show any wrongful conduct on the part of Defendants that would constitute a constructive eviction, Defendants are entitled to summary judgment on this claim....

* * *

Conclusion

For the reasons stated, Defendants' motion for summary judgment is granted.

Questions and Comments for Discussion

1. What role do expert witnesses play in cases like this? How can a fact-finder (such as a judge in a bench trial or a jury in a jury trial) determine which expert is "right"?

2. The legal theory used in *Hardy v. Griffin* was negligence per se, discussed in Chapter 4. Under this theory, a defendant is liable for negligence if it breaches a statutory duty, and (1) the kind of harm the statute was designed to prevent, and (2) occurs to a person the statute was designed to protect. This theory provides additional incentives for landlords to comply with laws like those in effect in this case. What types of statutes exist in your community to protect residential tenants? How might a landlord violate those statutes? What type of harm would likely result?

3. According to a report by the Centers for Disease Control, some 57 million U.S. homes built before 1980 contain lead-based paint. About 4 million of those homes have young children who are at special risk because lead can cause mental retardation, learning disabilities, hyperactivity, attention deficit disorder, convulsions, lack of coordination, kidney damage, and even death. Some claim that minority communities are the hardest hit by the lead-paint situation. Some experts suggest that the best way to rid communities of lead-paint poisoning is through education. What policy arguments support holding landlords liable for young children's lead-paint exposure? What policies oppose holding landlords liable under a nondisclosure theory?

4. In other recent lead-abatement cases, plaintiffs have recovered money damages under various legal theories, including negligence, negligence per se for violation of state law, and breach of implied warranty of habitability. For a survey of cases, *see* Note, "Landlord Liability for Lead Poisoning of Tenant Children Caused by Defects in the Premises," 70 *U. Det. Mercy L. Rev.* 429–450 (1993).

5. Another potential source of lead in residential property is lead pipes. Before the 1920s, lead pipes were commonly used in homes. Lead leaching from copper pipes and soldered with lead is also another major source of water contamination. In 1991, the EPA issued a regulation requiring public water suppliers to monitor lead levels in the water supply by sampling and to minimize the corrosivity of the water to reduce lead levels. Amendments to the 1986 Safe Drinking Water Act banned the use of solder that contained more than 0.2% lead and other plumbing materials that contained more than 8% lead in residential plumbing systems. In your opinion, how effective are EPA rules and regulations that seek to address environmental harms that are "built in" to the human environment?

Expanding Landlord and Tenant Liability

As the *Szewczuk* case illustrates, courts have continued to abrogate the traditional doctrine of *caveat lessee* ("let the tenant beware") in landlord-tenant transactions. Under various statutory and common law theories, modern courts have held landlords liable for harm to the tenant that occurs as a result of environmental contamination or toxic substances on the property.

Under common law theories like negligence and nuisance, landlords may incur liability for the actions of their tenants. A landlord may be liable, under several tort theories, for its selection of the tenant and for the tenant's wrongdoing when the landlord continues to exercise control over the premises. In *State of New York v. Monarch Chemicals, Inc. et al.,*[12] the State of New York, the Town of Vestal, and three of the town's water districts brought an action to abate a nuisance caused by contamination of the soil and groundwater under premises owned by the defendant Knowles and leased by the defendant Monarch Chemicals. The government alleged that the tenant handled and stored dangerous chemicals on the site, and that these chemicals seeped into the public water supply. The owner moved to dismiss the complaint, claiming that he had engaged in no affirmative misconduct at the site. However, the court said that the record reflected the possibility that the owner knew of possible contamination at the site. The landlord's failure to take any precautions to prevent contamination of the groundwater was sufficient to support liability under a nuisance theory. According to the court, at the very least the plaintiffs had stated a valid cause of action against the owner respecting negligent maintenance of a nuisance.

Under CERCLA, both the landlord and tenant (as owner and operator) may be liable for the cleanup costs associated with disposal of hazardous substances on the property. Just as with disputes between buyers and sellers of contaminated property, in allocating responsibilities between landlord and tenant the court will consider express contractual agreements by the parties, as well as factors such as the amount and type of hazardous substances involved; the degree of the parties' involvement in the transportation, treatment, and storage of the substances; and the degree of care exercised by the parties with respect to the substances involved.

Avoiding Environmental Liability

As the previous discussion suggests, purchasers and sellers of real property, as well as lessors and lessees, should consider and address potential liability that may result from noncompliance with environmental laws or from environmental contamination of the property. This is especially true for those involved in the sale or lease of commercial property, which may have been contaminated as a result of prior manufacturing or industrial activity at the site or which may become contaminated through such activity. It is especially important for these commercial parties to consider and address all the potentially relevant environmental issues that may arise at such sites.

A prospective purchaser should make all appropriate inquiries into past ownership and use of the facility prior to purchase, thereby exercising due diligence in determining whether the property has been contaminated. The seller and buyer

---

[12] 90 A.D.2d 902, 456 N.Y.S.2d 867 (App. Div. 1982).

should also attempt to limit their respective liabilities through various contractual provisions. Typical contract representations, warranties, and indemnities include:

1. Warranties that the property and operations on the site comply with applicable environmental laws, regulations, and court or administrative orders
2. Warranties that there are no pending private or governmental claims relating to environmental conditions on the property
3. Warranties that necessary permits, licenses, and government approvals are in existence or will be obtained
4. A provision that the seller has made all relevant disclosures and exercised due care in discovering the existence of any environmental liabilities at the site

The seller may refuse to provide such warranties based on lack of knowledge of prior activity at the site, but may agree to give the buyer a reasonable period of time to evaluate potential liability before the buyer is obligated to proceed with the purchase. A seller may choose to provide that any representations or warranties are based solely upon the "seller's actual knowledge" and may wish to limit its representations to those activities occurring during its ownership of the property. The seller may also limit the time period for those representations and warranties, or limit the extent of its liability for breach of warranties or misrepresentation to a certain dollar amount. The seller should also seek a promise from the buyer that the buyer will use its best efforts to maintain and operate the premises in compliance with all applicable environmental laws.

Indemnification agreements often include promises to reimburse the other party for environmental liabilities, as well as attorneys' fees and litigation expenses. Indemnity agreements should include:

1. The length of time the agreement will be in effect
2. Provisions for notice of claims subject to the indemnity
3. Monetary limits on liability
4. Applicability of the indemnity agreement to acts of a seller's predecessors

The contract also may provide a **right of termination** if an environmental audit reveals problems. This right of termination may be triggered by the discovery (by either party) of environmental problems within a specified time. In some cases, a right of termination may be more narrowly defined to be exercisable in the event of triggering conditions such as a certain cost to correct, a certain length of time to remedy, or a particular kind of problem.

The concerns of the landlord and tenant are similar to those of buyers and sellers. Just as a purchaser should investigate the property prior to purchase, so a tenant should ensure that it is not leasing property with environmental liabilities. Before executing a lease, the tenant should seek a guarantee from the landlord that the property is free from environmental liabilities, and get a promise to indemnify the tenant for liability incurred as a result of preexisting contamination at the site.

The landlord should include lease provisions requiring the tenant to comply with all applicable laws and regulations, and specifying that failure to comply constitutes a material breach of the lease. The landlord that leases commercial property should review any activity or equipment on the property that might result in contamination or violation of applicable environmental laws. The landlord may require a security deposit to offset pollution cleanup expenses.

right of termination:
Express contractual provision giving a party the right to cancel the contract upon the occurrence of some specified event.

The landlord should retain the right to enter and inspect the property for contamination. The tenant should be required to notify the landlord of any significant release, environmental problems, or receipt of any notices of environmental liability. Finally, at lease termination, the tenant should be required to clean up any contamination and to return the property in a condition that complies with all laws.

The value of these contractual provisions is somewhat limited, as warranties and indemnification agreements are only as good as the contracting party's ability to pay. The protection afforded by these contractual devices is also often limited in time, as there may be a long latency period before environmental problems are discovered at the site. Furthermore, these contractual devices do not necessarily insulate the parties from most federal and state claims for cleanup and response costs.

■ ■ ■ ■ REVIEW AND STUDY QUESTIONS

1. What are the differences between warranties, indemnification agreements, and disclaimers?

2. The lack of predictability in construction and interpretation of contract warranties and indemnification clauses creates substantial problems in the sale and lease of industrial or commercial real property with suspected contamination. Identify three reasons why warranties and/or indemnification clauses should be upheld as to cleanup costs, and three reasons why they should not be. Which do you find the most persuasive position, from a viewpoint of utilitarianism?

3. Would you buy real property sold "as is"? Why or why not? What would you do first to ensure that the property was not contaminated with toxic waste or pollution?

4. In what way has statutory law changed common law regarding the sale of real property and the rights and obligations associated with the real property? Do you believe that the common law approach was better or worse than the statutory

approach? Which ethical perspective informs your position on this matter?

5. If you were a landlord, how would you ensure that you met your duties under the implied warranty of habitability? Could you ever be completely certain that the leased premises were habitable under the implied warranty? How could you protect your assets from future claims arising under the implied warranty of habitability?

6. Should a builder/vendor be able to disclaim the implied warranty of habitability? Why or why not? What are the public policy consequences of your answer?

7. How far should warranties extend? To subsequent purchasers? If so, to how many subsequent purchasers?

8. Landlords may be liable to their tenants for the presence of environmental hazards (such as lead-based paint), or liable for the actions of their tenants who cause pollution or toxic waste spills. What are the public policy consequences of this assignment of risk?

■ Product Liability Law

Product liability law refers to the body of legal rules that governs **damages** resulting from the sale of defective goods. These rules include negligence, breach of warranty, and strict liability theories. Breach of warranty is essentially a contract theory, whereas negligence and strict liability are tort theories. Under traditional common law negligence theory, a plaintiff is entitled to recover damages for injuries from exposure to a toxic substance if she can prove that the defendant breached a legal duty owed to her and that the breach resulted in her injuries.

product liability: Name for a group of theories used in cases where plaintiffs seek to recover for personal injury or property damage resulting from a defective product.

damages: Compensation in money for a loss or injury.

In addition, she must prove that the defendant's negligence actually caused her injuries, and that it was foreseeable such injuries would result.

In some product liability cases where the product has many component parts and a long chain of distribution, it may be difficult for the plaintiff to prove that the manufacturer was negligent. Under traditional common law doctrine, defenses such as contributory negligence and assumption of the risk also act as a complete bar to recovery.

Beginning in the early 1960s, courts began to compensate those injured by defective products under a strict liability theory. This theory is based on the assumption that sellers, manufacturers, and their insurers should bear the economic costs of defective products, and pass on those costs. The states' adoption of this theory underlies the huge number of product liability suits brought since then.

Strict liability is characterized as liability without fault. The injured consumer need not establish that the manufacturer or seller breached a duty of reasonable care in the manufacture, design, or sale of the product. Strict liability also recognizes that contract and negligence law are often inadequate protection from defective products. As the U.S. economy has become an increasingly corporate-based system, it is less likely that consumers can deal directly with manufacturers, protect themselves through contracts, or inspect the manufacturing process; they also generally lack the knowledge required to determine whether a process or product is defective or dangerous. Product liability law has thus shifted toward a caveat venditor ("let the seller beware") approach. Strict liability is based on the perception that sellers and manufacturers are better able to bear the economic costs associated with defective products than the injured consumer.

Product liability theories entitle a person to recover damages for injuries or property damage caused by toxic or hazardous products. By recognizing the right to sue under product liability theories, courts have permitted common law remedies to supplement federal laws regulating the manufacture, transportation, and disposal of toxic chemicals. Consequently, state common law and statutory product liability law act as additional incentives for manufacturers and sellers to ensure that products are environmentally safe.

Theories of Product Liability

Product liability law is concerned with compensating for personal injury or property damage caused by defective products. There is no single theory for plaintiffs to use, so they often rely on both contract and tort theories to recover damages. Product liability law is a complicated combination of contract law (implied and express warranties), negligence (including negligence per se based upon breach of statutory duties), and strict liability under the *Restatement (Second) of Torts* § 402A.

For example, a person injured by a defective product may argue that the defect constituted a breach of express or implied warranty. All states have adopted the UCC, which contains provisions recognizing an **implied warranty of merchantability** in the sale of goods, which only applies to those who are merchants with respect to goods of the kind sold. This implied warranty is created by operation of law and permits a plaintiff to recover damages if the product was sold by a merchant and is not fit for common, ordinary use. The seller may disclaim an implied warranty of merchantability or an **implied warranty of fitness** if the seller proceeds in a manner that is legally recognized as resulting in a valid disclaimer.

To be *merchantable*, goods must at least (1) pass without objection in the trade; (2) be fit for the ordinary purposes for which such goods are used; (3) be of even

strict liability: Product liability theory that holds the manufacturer, distributor, or seller of a defective product liable for physical harm or property damage suffered by the purchaser even though the manufacturer, distributor, or seller exercised all reasonable care in the preparation and sale of the product.

implied warranty of merchantability: An implied warranty that goods conform to the ordinary standard for usage (that they are "merchantable").

implied warranty of fitness: An implied warranty that goods are suitable for a particular purpose.

kind, quality, and quantity within each unit (case, package, or carton); (4) be adequately contained, packaged, and labeled; (5) conform to any promises or statements of fact made on the container or label; and (6) in the case of fungible goods, be of fair average quality. The most often emphasized, and therefore the most important of these, is the requirement that goods be fit for the ordinary purposes for which such goods are used.

A plaintiff may also rely on common law tort theories like negligence in maintaining an action against the seller or manufacturer of a defective product. Negligence theory applies in cases where the plaintiff claims that the manufacturer/seller failed to use reasonable care in the design, manufacture, inspection, or packaging of the product. A product may also be defective because the manufacturer/seller negligently failed to warn of dangers associated with the product.

Another theory of product liability is strict liability. As you will recall from Chapter 4, strict liability exists for injuries resulting from ultrahazardous or abnormally dangerous activities by a defendant, such as the operation of a hazardous waste landfill. Strict liability theory in defective product cases is based on *Restatement (Second) of Torts* § 402(a), which states:

> A seller engaged in the business of selling a particular product is liable for physical harm or property damage suffered by the ultimate user or consumer, if the product was in a defective condition unreasonably dangerous to the user or consumer or to his property.

Under this theory, a merchant/seller may be liable to a consumer injured by a defective product even though the seller exercised all possible care in the preparation and sale of the product.

Product liability actions have been brought by plaintiffs who allege they were injured by toxic or environmentally unsafe products. The courts have held asbestos insulation manufacturers strictly liable for damages for asbestosis and mesothelioma contracted by industrial asbestos workers. In *Borel v. Fibreboard Paper Products Corp.*,[13] evidence showed that the manufacturers not only failed to test their products for adverse effects, but also failed to avail themselves of scientific knowledge regarding the dangers of asbestos. According to the court of appeals, these dangers made the defendants' asbestos products unreasonably dangerous to the ultimate user and thus defective under Restatement of Torts § 402(a).

In an era of caveat emptor, laws governing suits for defective goods were to the advantage of sellers and manufacturers. Product liability law has changed this substantially, allowing consumers recourse against sellers and manufacturers for defective products that cause injury.

In the following case, peanut farmers brought claims against a pesticide manufacturer, arguing that the pesticide label contained false statements about the appropriate usage of the product. The farmers brought several tort claims, including claims for strict product liability, and also for breach of warranty. The pesticide manufacturer argued that the common law claims, including those for product liability, were preempted by federal statute (specifically, the Federal Insecticide, Fungicide, and Rodenticide Act or FIFRA). However, the U.S. Supreme Court held that FIFRA did not necessarily preempt state law claims. This was an important case, because it reversed a trend in the lower courts to bar common law claims for injuries arising under FIFRA, given the lower courts' mistaken reasoning that FIFRA preempted state law claims.

---

[13] 493 F.2d 1076 (5th Cir. 1973).

Bates v. Dow Agrosciences LLC
544 U.S. 431, 125 S. Ct. 1788 (2005)

Justice Stevens delivered the opinion of the Court.

Petitioners are 29 Texas peanut farmers who allege that in the 2000 growing season their crops were severely damaged by the application of respondent's newly marketed pesticide named "Strongarm." The question presented is whether the Federal Insecticide, Fungicide, and Rodenticide Act (FIFRA) … pre-empts their state-law claims for damages.

… Pursuant to its authority under FIFRA, the Environmental Protection Agency (EPA) conditionally registered Strongarm on March 8, 2000, thereby granting respondent (Dow) permission to sell this pesticide … in the United States. Dow obtained this registration in time to market Strongarm to Texas farmers, who normally plant their peanut crops around May 1. According to petitioners … Dow knew, or should have known, that Strongarm would stunt the growth of peanuts in soils with pH levels of 7.0 or greater…. Nevertheless, Strongarm's label stated, "Use of Strongarm is recommended in all areas where peanuts are grown," …. When petitioners applied Strongarm on their farms—whose soils have pH levels of 7.2 or higher, as is typical in western Texas—the pesticide severely damaged their peanut crops while failing to control the growth of weeds. The farmers reported these problems to Dow, which sent its experts to inspect the crops.

Meanwhile, Dow reregistered its Strongarm label with EPA prior to the 2001 growing season. EPA approved a "supplemental" label that was for "[d]istribution and [u]se [o]nly in the states of New Mexico, Oklahoma and Texas," … the three States in which peanut farmers experienced crop damage. This new label contained the following warning: "Do not apply Strongarm to soils with a pH of 7.2 or greater." …

… Dow filed a declaratory judgment action in Federal District Court, asserting that petitioners' claims were expressly or impliedly pre-empted by FIFRA. Petitioners, in turn, brought counterclaims, including tort claims sounding in strict liability and negligence. They also alleged … breach of warranty …. The District Court granted Dow's motion for summary judgment, rejecting one claim on state-law grounds and dismissing the remainder as expressly pre-empted by … [FIFRA], which provides that States "shall not impose or continue in effect any requirements for labeling or packaging in addition to or different from those required under this subchapter."

The Court of Appeals affirmed. It read [FIFRA] to pre-empt any state-law claim in which "a judgment against Dow would induce it to alter its product label." … The court held that because petitioners' fraud, warranty, and deceptive trade practices claims focused on oral statements by Dow's agents that did not differ from statements made on the product's label, success on those claims would give Dow a "strong incentive" to change its label. Those claims were thus pre-empted. … The court also found that petitioners' strict liability claim alleging defective design was essentially a "disguised" failure-to-warn claim and therefore pre-empted. … It reasoned: "One cannot escape the heart of the farmers' grievance: Strongarm is dangerous to peanut crops in soil with a pH level over 7.0, and that was not disclosed to them…. It is inescapable that success on this claim would again necessarily induce Dow to alter the Strongarm label." … The court employed similar reasoning to find the negligent testing and negligent manufacture claims pre-empted as well….

This decision was consistent with those of a majority of the Courts of Appeals,… as well of several state high courts,… but conflicted with the decisions of other courts … and with the views of the EPA …. We granted certiorari to resolve this conflict….

Prior to 1910 the States provided the primary and possibly the exclusive source of regulatory control over the distribution of poisonous substances. Both the Federal Government's first effort at regulation in this area, the Insecticide Act of 1910, 36 Stat. 331, and FIFRA as originally enacted in 1947, ch. 125, 61 Stat. 163, primarily dealt with licensing and labeling. Under the original version of FIFRA, all pesticides sold in interstate commerce had to be registered with the Secretary of Agriculture. The Secretary would register a pesticide if it complied with the statute's labeling standards and was determined to be efficacious and safe…. In 1970, EPA assumed responsibility for this registration process.

In 1972, spurred by growing environmental and safety concerns, Congress adopted the extensive amendments … that "transformed FIFRA from a labeling law into a comprehensive regulatory statute." *Ruckelshaus v. Monsanto Co.*, 467 U.S. 986, 991[, 81 L. Ed. 2d 815, 104 S. Ct. 2862] (1984). "As amended, FIFRA regulated the use, as well as the sale and labeling, of pesticides; regulated pesticides produced and sold in both intrastate and interstate commerce; provided for review, cancellation, and suspension of registration;

(Continued)

and gave EPA greater enforcement authority." ... The 1972 amendments also imposed a new criterion for registration—environmental safety....

Under FIFRA as it currently stands, a manufacturer seeking to register a pesticide must submit a proposed label to EPA as well as certain supporting data.... The agency will register the pesticide if it determines that the pesticide is efficacious (with the caveat discussed below),... ; that it will not cause unreasonable adverse effects on humans and the environment,... ; and that its label complies with the statute's prohibition on mis-branding,.... A pesticide is "misbranded" if its label contains a statement that is "false or misleading in any particular," including a false or misleading statement concerning the efficacy of the pesticide.... A pesticide is also misbranded if its label does not contain adequate instructions for use, or if its label omits necessary warnings or cautionary statements.... [Footnote by court: "A pesticide label must also conspicuously display any statement or information specifically required by the statute or its implementing regulations.... To mention only a few examples, the label must contain the name and address of the producer, the product registration number, and an ingredient statement...."]

Because it is unlawful under the statute to sell a pesticide that is registered but nevertheless misbranded, manufacturers have a continuing obligation to adhere to FIFRA's labeling requirements.... Additionally, manufacturers have a duty to report incidents involving a pesticide's toxic effects that may not be adequately reflected in its label's warnings ..., and EPA may institute cancellation proceedings,... and take other enforcement action if it determines that a registered pesticide is misbranded....

* * *

Although the modern version of FIFRA was enacted over three decades ago, this Court has never addressed whether that statute pre-empts tort and other common-law claims arising under state law. Courts entertained tort litigation against pesticide manufacturers since well before the passage of FIFRA in 1947,... and such litigation was a common feature of the legal landscape at the time of the 1972 amendments.... Indeed, for at least a decade after those amendments, arguments that such tort suits were pre-empted by [FIFRA] either were not advanced or were unsuccessful.... It was only after 1992 when we held in *Cipollone v. Liggett Group, Inc.*, 505 U.S. 504[, 120 L. Ed. 2d 407, 112 S. Ct. 2608], that the term "requirement or prohibition" in the Public Health Cigarette Smoking Act of 1969 included common-law duties, and therefore pre-empted certain tort claims against cigarette companies, that a groundswell of federal and state decisions emerged holding that [FIFRA] pre-empted claims like those advanced in this litigation.

This Court has addressed FIFRA pre-emption in a different context. In *Wisconsin Public Intervenor v. Mortier*, 501 U.S. 597, [115 L. Ed. 2d 532, 111 S. Ct. 2476] (1991), we considered a claim that [FIFRA] pre-empted a small town's ordinance requiring a special permit for the aerial application of pesticides. Although the ordinance imposed restrictions not required by FIFRA or any EPA regulation, we unanimously rejected the pre-emption claim. In our opinion we noted that FIFRA was not "a sufficiently comprehensive statute to justify an inference that Congress had occupied the field to the exclusion of the States." ... "To the contrary, the statute leaves ample room for States and localities to supplement federal efforts even absent the express regulatory authorization of [FIFRA]." ...

As a part of their supplementary role, States have ample authority to review pesticide labels to ensure that they comply with both federal and state labeling requirements.... Nothing in the text of FIFRA would prevent a State from making the violation of a federal labeling or packaging requirement a state offense, thereby imposing its own sanctions on pesticide manufacturers who violate federal law. The imposition of state sanctions for violating state rules that merely duplicate federal requirements is equally consistent with the text of [FIFRA].

* * *

... For a particular state rule to be pre-empted, it must satisfy two conditions. First, it must be a requirement "*for labeling or packaging*"; rules governing the design of a product, for example, are not pre-empted. Second, it must impose a labeling or packaging requirement that is "*in addition to or different from* those required under this subchapter." A state regulation requiring the word "poison" to appear in red letters, for instance, would not be pre-empted if an EPA regulation imposed the same requirement.

... Rules that require manufacturers to design reasonably safe products, to use due care in conducting appropriate testing of their products, to market products free of manufacturing defects, and to honor their express warranties or other contractual commitments plainly do not qualify as requirements for "labeling or packaging." None of these common-law rules requires that manufacturers label or package their products in any particular way. Thus, petitioners' claims for defective design, defective manufacture, negligent testing, and breach of express warranty are not pre-empted.

(Continued)

To be sure, Dow's express warranty was located on Strongarm's label.... But a cause of action on an express warranty asks only that a manufacturer make good on the contractual commitment that it voluntarily undertook by placing that warranty on its product.... Because this common-law rule does not require the manufacturer to make an express warranty, or in the event that the manufacturer elects to do so, to say anything in particular in that warranty, the rule does not impose a requirement "for labeling or packaging." ...

* * *

... A design defect claim, if successful, would surely induce a manufacturer to alter its label to reflect a change in the list of ingredients or a change in the instructions for use necessitated by the improvement in the product's design. Moreover, the inducement test is not entirely consistent with [FIFRA], which confirms the State's broad authority to regulate the sale and use of pesticides.... Under [FIFRA], a state agency may ban the sale of a pesticide if it finds, for instance, that one of the pesticide's label-approved uses is unsafe. This ban might well induce the manufacturer to change its label to warn against this questioned use. Under the inducement test, however, such a restriction would anomalously qualify as a "labeling" requirement. It is highly unlikely that Congress endeavored to draw a line between the type of indirect pressure caused by a State's power to impose sales and use restrictions and the even more attenuated pressure exerted by common-law suits. The inducement test is not supported by either the text or the structure of the statute.

Unlike their other claims, petitioners' fraud and negligent-failure-to-warn claims are premised on common-law rules that qualify as "requirements for labeling or packaging." These rules set a standard for a product's labeling that the Strongarm label is alleged to have violated by containing false statements and inadequate warnings.... [S]ome of [the courts of appeals] too quickly concluded that failure-to-warn claims were pre-empted under FIFRA ....

... [FIFRA] prohibits only state-law labeling and packaging requirements that are "*in addition to or different from*" the labeling and packaging requirements under FIFRA. Thus, a state-law labeling requirement is not pre-empted by [FIFRA] if it is equivalent to, and fully consistent with, FIFRA's misbranding provisions. Petitioners argue that their claims based on fraud and failure to warn are not pre-empted because these common-law duties are equivalent to FIFRA's requirements that a pesticide label not contain "false or misleading" statements,... or inadequate instructions or warnings.... We agree with petitioners insofar as we hold that state law need not explicitly incorporate FIFRA's standards as an element of a cause of action in order to survive pre-emption. ...

* * *

... "[B]ecause the States are independent sovereigns in our federal system, we have long presumed that Congress does not cavalierly pre-empt state-law causes of action." *Medtronic*, 518 U.S., at 485[, 135 L. Ed. 2d 700, 116 S. Ct. 2240]. In areas of traditional state regulation, we assume that a federal statute has not supplanted state law unless Congress has made such an intention "'clear and manifest.'" *New York State Conference of Blue Cross & Blue Shield Plans v. Travelers Ins. Co.*, 514 U.S. 645, 655[, 131 L. Ed. 2d 695, 115 S. Ct. 1671] (1995) (quoting *Rice v. Santa Fe Elevator Corp.*, 331 U.S. 218, 230[, 91 L. Ed. 1447, 67 S. Ct. 1146] (1947)); .... Our reading is at once the only one that makes sense of each phrase in [FIFRA] and the one favored by our canons of interpretation....

The long history of tort litigation against manufacturers of poisonous substances adds force to the basic presumption against pre-emption. If Congress had intended to deprive injured parties of a long available form of compensation, it surely would have expressed that intent more clearly.... Moreover, this history emphasizes the importance of providing an incentive to manufacturers to use the utmost care in the business of distributing inherently dangerous items.... Particularly given that Congress amended FIFRA to allow EPA to waive efficacy review of newly registered pesticides (and in the course of those amendments made technical changes to [FIFRA]), it seems unlikely that Congress considered a relatively obscure provision like [the one at issue in this case] to give pesticide manufacturers virtual immunity from certain forms of tort liability. Overenforcement of FIFRA's misbranding prohibition creates a risk of imposing unnecessary financial burdens on manufacturers; underenforcement creates not only financial risks for consumers, but risks that affect their safety and the environment as well.

Finally, we find the policy objections raised against our reading of [FIFRA] to be unpersuasive. Dow and the United States greatly overstate the degree of uniformity and centralization that characterizes FIFRA. In fact, the statute authorizes a relatively decentralized scheme that preserves a broad role for state regulation.... Most significantly, States may ban or restrict the uses of pesticides that EPA has approved ... ; they may also register, subject to certain restrictions, pesticides for uses beyond those approved by EPA ....

(Continued)

Private remedies that enforce federal misbranding requirements would seem to aid, rather than hinder, the functioning of FIFRA.... FIFRA contemplates that pesticide labels will evolve over time, as manufacturers gain more information about their products' performance in diverse settings. As one court explained, tort suits can serve as a catalyst in this process:

> "By encouraging plaintiffs to bring suit for injuries not previously recognized as traceable to pesticides such as [the pesticide there at issue], a state tort action of the kind under review may aid in the exposure of new dangers associated with pesticides. Successful actions of this sort may lead manufacturers to petition EPA to allow more detailed labeling of their products; alternatively, EPA itself may decide that revised labels are required in light of the new information that has been brought to its attention through common law suits. In addition, the specter of damage actions may provide manufacturers with added dynamic incentives to continue to keep abreast of all possible injuries stemming from use of their product so as to forestall such actions through product improvement." *Ferebee*, 736 F.2d, at 1541-1542.

Dow and the United States exaggerate the disruptive effects of using common-law suits to enforce the prohibition on misbranding. FIFRA has prohibited inaccurate representations and inadequate warnings since its enactment in 1947, while tort suits alleging failure-to-warn claims were common well before that date and continued beyond the 1972 amendments. We have been pointed to no evidence that such tort suits led to a "crazy-quilt" of FIFRA standards or otherwise created any real hardship for manufacturers or for EPA. Indeed, for much of this period EPA appears to have welcomed these tort suits....

In sum, under our interpretation, [FIFRA] retains a narrow, but still important, role. In the main, it pre-empts competing state labeling standards—imagine 50 different labeling regimes prescribing the color, font size, and wording of warnings—that would create significant inefficiencies for manufacturers.... The provision also pre-empts any statutory or common-law rule that would impose a labeling requirement that diverges from those set out in FIFRA and its implementing regulations. It does not, however, pre-empt any state rules that are fully consistent with federal requirements.

Questions and Comments for Discussion

1. Describe the lower courts' errors that the U.S. Supreme Court was attempting to correct in *Bates*.
2. A plaintiff wishes to bring a product defect claim under theories of tort and/or breach of warranty. How would you determine whether the claims were barred by preemption under FIFRA?
3. What public policy reasons did the court recognize as important in allowing common law claims to proceed when a federal environmental statute also regulates in the same field?

Defenses in Product Liability Actions

States have placed limits on the time within which a product liability action may be brought; these periods are set out in a **statute of limitations** and may vary from state to state. Time limits in product liability cases involving environmental hazards like asbestos may be critical in determining whether a plaintiff is entitled to recover damages for injuries caused by exposure to a toxic substance over a long period. In most states, the statute of limitations for negligence and strict liability is shorter than the UCC statute of limitations for express and implied warranty claims. However, the statute generally begins to run only after the defect is or should have been discovered. Consequently, the tort statute of limitations may be more advantageous to the plaintiff in some product liability cases than the longer contractual statute of limitations.

Some states have enacted specific statutes that address time limits on product liability suits. Some also have special time limits for delayed-manifestation injuries such as those resulting from exposure to asbestos. Finally, some states have adopted statutes establishing a "useful safe life" defense. Such statutes prevent the plaintiff from suing when the harm occurs after the product's useful safe life has passed.

statute of limitations: Law prescribing time limits on the right to bring certain legal actions.

Whether a particular defense to a product liability action will be permitted depends in part on the legal theory underlying the plaintiff's action. Traditional defenses include misuse of the product by the plaintiff, assumption of the risk by the plaintiff, or contributory negligence.

The traditional defenses of assumption of the risk and contributory negligence are discussed in Chapter 4. An example of application of the principle of contributory negligence is *Jones v. Owens-Corning Fiberglas Corp.*[14] In that case, the plaintiffs worked at the Babcock & Wilcox (B&W) plant in North Carolina. Both plaintiffs, Jones and Culverhouse, were long-term cigarette smokers and were exposed to asbestos on a daily basis at the B&W plant. They eventually developed asbestosis and lung cancer. After a trial, the jury awarded more than $1.3 million to each plaintiff. On appeal, however, the appellate court set aside the judgment and ordered a new trial. It said that Owens-Corning Fiberglas should have been allowed to introduce evidence that (1) the plaintiffs failed to exercise reasonable care under the circumstances in their use of asbestos-containing products because (2) they continued to smoke cigarettes after the hazards of cigarette smoking and the relationship between cigarette smoking and asbestos exposure became widely known; and (3) their smoking, combined with their exposure to asbestos-containing products, was a proximate cause of their injuries.

Product misuse occurs when a plaintiff uses the product in an unusual, unforeseeable way. Ignoring a manufacturer's instructions, mishandling the product, and using the product for purposes for which it was not intended may constitute product misuse. In some cases, however, if the defendant should have foreseen the misuse and failed to take reasonable steps to prevent it, the defendant may still be liable. The defense of product misuse is generally available under all product liability theories, including warranty, negligence, and strict liability cases.

In product liability cases, as well as other toxic tort actions where a plaintiff seeks to recover damages for injuries from a toxic substance, claims for injuries from exposure may include existing illnesses, increased risks of future illness, and costs for future medical surveillance. However, causation is often difficult to prove because of the difficulty in establishing a correlation between the physical injury and exposure to the substance. The plaintiff may have been exposed once or several times over an extended period of time, and often there is a long latency period between the exposure and development or manifestation of the disease. The testimony of medical experts is often necessary to establish a causal connection between exposure to a toxic substance and resulting injury or disease.

■ ■ ■ REVIEW AND STUDY QUESTIONS

1. Under which theories of law are product liability claims brought? Describe the benefits and drawbacks to this grab-bag approach to addressing injuries.

2. Which system is better: caveat emptor or caveat venditor? Support your position. Identify a contemporary example where one party was benefited or disadvantaged due to the modern caveat venditor approach to product liability.

3. Identify defenses that may be used in a product liability case. Can you think of any defenses that should be recognized but are not?

4. Do you think that sellers and manufacturers should bear liability for the products that they sell or make? Why or why not? What would be the public policy consequences of placing the risk of injury on the consumer only?

[14] 69 F.3d 712 (4th Cir. 1995).

■ Conclusion

This chapter has focused on some important issues of liability in environmental cases. Many liability issues arise regarding contracts for the sale or lease of real property, when the property turns out to be contaminated with toxic or hazardous materials. In these cases, contractual devices such as disclaimer clauses, warranties, and indemnification agreements may determine the parties' respective liability for costs of the cleanup mandated by federal and state governments.

Changing concepts of contract law in society have led courts to abandon traditional notions of caveat emptor in favor of a caveat venditor approach to the sale and lease of residential property. Under this newer policy, courts have recognized implied warranties of habitability in the sale and lease of residential property. A landlord or seller also may be liable to a purchaser for failing to disclose an environmental liability on the property or for negligently or innocently misrepresenting the environmental condition of the property. Breach of environmental laws (such as lead-abatement laws) may be the basis for tort liability of a landlord or a seller under the theory of negligence per se.

In product liability cases, plaintiffs may employ both contract law and tort law, including negligence law and principles of strict liability. Product liability law is important in environmental cases where consumers or employees sue the seller or manufacturer of products containing toxic or hazardous materials (for example, insecticides or pesticides).

Chapter 5 Case Study Activity

This case presents an opportunity to review the concepts of torts (from Chapter 4) and contracts (this chapter) together in one case.

In the following case, the plaintiffs lived near a hydraulic fracturing ("fracking") operation. Defendants had warranted, among other things, that the plaintiffs' drinking water would not be affected by the fracking. However, the plaintiffs' water became undrinkable and unusable for human consumption shortly after fracking commenced. The plaintiffs alleged that they were entitled to damages under several theories in tort, as well as under a breach of contract theory.

As you read the facts of this case, review the elements of each of the legal theories discussed. Read the case and answer the Questions for Discussion that follow it.

Roth v. Cabot Oil & Gas Corp.
2013 U.S. Dist. LEXIS 12261 (M.D. PA, 2013)

Opinion by John E. Jones III

Presently pending before the Court is the Motion to Dismiss ... filed by Defendants ...

* * *

III. Statement of Facts

* * *

Plaintiffs Frederick J. and Debra A. Roth are husband and wife and are the owners of property located ... in Springville, Pennsylvania ..., where they have resided

(Continued)

for more than thirty-five (35) years.... Defendant Cabot Oil and Gas Corporation ... engages in various oil and gas exploration and production activities in the Commonwealth [of Pennsylvania].... At all times relevant to this action, Defendants owned and operated several natural gas wells and engaged in natural gas exploration and production in ... Pennsylvania. [Some of] [t]hese [gas wells] (the "Wells") were located less than 1,000 feet from the Plaintiffs' Property and residence....

A representative of Cabot visited the Plaintiffs' Property in or about March of 2008 for the purpose of executing an oil and gas lease agreement ("Gas Lease") in order to obtain the legal right to drill on or near Plaintiffs' Property and extract natural gas from the Property.... Cabot's representative warranted the following to the Plaintiffs in negotiating the lease: that Cabot would test Plaintiffs' pond and water supplies prior to and after commencement of drilling operations to ensure that the water would not be adversely affected; that Cabot would timely and fully disclose the test results to Plaintiffs; that Plaintiffs' persons, property, and land resources would be undisturbed ... by said operations; that Plaintiffs' quality of life and use and enjoyment of the Property would not be disrupted or adversely affected; that if Cabot's operations do adversely affect the Property, Cabot would immediately disclose that information to Plaintiffs and take, at its sole expense, all steps necessary to return the Property to pre-drilling conditions; and that Cabot would remain at all times in compliance with all state and federal laws and regulations governing safe oil and gas drilling practices....

The Defendants' drilling operations involve a process known as hydraulic fracturing, sometimes referred to as hydro-fracturing or hydro-fracking, which discharge significant volumes of hydraulic fracturing fluids into underground shale formations in order to discharge the gas contained therein .... The fracking fluids used by the Defendants in their operations included diesel fuel, lubricating agents, barite, gels, pesticides, and defoaming agents .... In addition to these hazardous chemicals, other contaminants, such as gas, oil, brine, heavy metals, and radioactive substances naturally present in the shale formations, are dislodged during drilling operations.... In order to collect the discharged waste fluids, drilling muds, and other hazardous substances, the Defendants maintain large waste pits at the Wells....

The Defendants began drilling operations at the Wells near the Plaintiffs' Property in or about April of 2010 .... Prior to that time, the Plaintiffs' groundwater supply had always appeared clean, containing no visible gases, malodors, or off-tastes. ... The Plaintiffs had their groundwater supply tested before the commencement of drilling operations, and those tests revealed that the pre-drilling groundwater supply did not contain detectable levels of methane gas.... In August of 2010, the Plaintiffs began to notice that their groundwater supply had diminished in quality, containing excess sedimentation and appearing brown and cloudy.... The water supply likewise became malodorous, and in January of 2011, the Plaintiffs began to notice yellow and pink staining in their toilets from the polluted groundwater.... These issues continue to date.... Because of these issues, the Plaintiffs have ceased drinking from and no longer trust their water supply....

The Department of Environmental Protection ("DEP") has cited the Defendants on several occasions for noncompliance with state law as it governs oil and gas operations ... [including permitting hazardous wastewater to enter the soil and contaminate the groundwater; failing to dispose of drill fluids in a manner that prevents pollution of the waters, and spillage of one-half barrel of waste fluid directly on the surface; failing to prevent migration of gas or waste fluids into groundwater supplies; failure to report defective casing and cementing; leakage of diesel fuel onto a well pad, which had a breach in the perimeter berm; and failure to construct waste pits and tanks with sufficient capacity to contain pollutants]....

The DEP sampled the Plaintiffs' groundwater supply in January of 2011, approximately eight (8) months after the Defendants began their drilling activities.... The results of that sampling revealed that levels of dissolved methane in the Plaintiffs' groundwater supply were as high as 15.6 mg/L, rendering the water unsafe and unfit for human consumption.... The Plaintiffs believe and aver that the Defendants' noncompliance with the statutory and regulatory frameworks governing oil and gas drilling is responsible for allowing the methane and other harmful contaminants to enter the Plaintiffs' water supply. The Plaintiffs assert that as a result, they have suffered loss of value to their Property, loss of the use and enjoyment of their Property and its land resources, and loss to their quality of life. Plaintiffs also assert that they have suffered damage to appliances which use the contaminated groundwater supply and have had incurred substantial out-of-pocket expenses for water quality monitoring, water sampling, and alternative potable water supplies.

* * *

(Continued)

IV. Discussion

The Plaintiffs' Amended Complaint ... sets forth nine separate causes of action, [including] negligence ..., negligence per se ..., private nuisance ..., strict liability ... and breach of contract ....

* * *

B. Count II—Negligence

Pennsylvania common law requires a plaintiff to establish the following elements in support of a negligence claim: "(1) a duty or obligation recognized by the law, requiring the actor to conform to a certain standard of conduct; (2) a failure to conform to the standard required; (3) a causal connection between the conduct and the resulting injury; and (4) actual loss or damage resulting to the interests of another." ...

With respect to the first element, the Plaintiffs assert, and the Defendants apparently do not dispute, that the Defendants are under a legally cognizable duty to conform to certain standards of conduct. The laws and regulations of the Commonwealth of Pennsylvania establish that entities engaging in gas drilling operations must do so in a manner that would not jeopardize the health, safety, and well-being of the citizens of the Commonwealth.... It is indisputable then that the Defendants, as owners and operators of drilling wells, are subject to a certain and articulable standard of conduct, satisfying the first element.

Further, the Plaintiffs satisfy the second element by pleading that the Defendants have used improper drilling techniques and materials and that they have constructed (and failed to remedy) deficient and ineffective well casings and waste disposal pits in violation of this standard of conduct.... We thus find that the Defendants have satisfied their pleading burden by establishing that the Defendants breached the applicable standard of conduct.

We turn then to the element of causation. Pennsylvania law presumes that "a well operator is responsible for pollution of a water supply if ... (i) the water supply is within 1,000 feet of an oil or gas well; and (ii) the pollution occurred within six months after completion of drilling or alteration of the oil or gas well." ... The Plaintiffs have pled that the identified wells are located within 1,000 feet from their Property and thus satisfy the first element of the statutory presumption.... The Plaintiffs have likewise satisfied the second element by demonstrating that their injuries began in August of 2010, approximately three (3) months after drilling operations commenced and while drilling operations were ongoing.... The temporal and physical proximity of the Defendants' actions to the Plaintiffs' harm, in addition to the lack of contemporaneous and alternative sources of the contamination, permit the reasonable inference that the Defendants were responsible for that harm....

Lastly, we consider whether the Plaintiffs have satisfactorily pled an injury caused by the Defendants' conduct. The Plaintiffs' Amended Complaint contains numerous allegations with respect to the harms that they have suffered, including: contaminated groundwater unsafe for human consumption ..., loss of value to their property ..., and damage to appliances which utilize the groundwater. Most critically, the Plaintiffs have incurred and will continue to incur substantial costs for water sampling and testing, water quality monitoring, and water treatment systems, in addition to the costs of purchasing alternative water supplies....

* * *

C. Count III—Negligence Per Se

In addition to their negligence claim, the Plaintiffs also raise a claim of negligence per se, premised upon the Defendants' alleged violations of several state laws, including ... Pennsylvania Solid Waste Management Act ("SWMA"),... and the Pennsylvania Hazardous Sites Cleanup Act ("HSCA") ....

In order to state a claim based on negligence per se, a plaintiff must establish that: "(1) The purpose of the statute must be, at least in part, to protect the interest of a group of individuals, as opposed to the public generally; (2) The statute or regulation must clearly apply to the conduct of the defendant; (3) The defendant must violate the statute or regulation; [and] (4) The violation of the statute must be the proximate cause of the plaintiff's injuries." ....

The Plaintiffs here also assert a negligence per se claim based on the Defendants' alleged violations of the Pennsylvania Oil and Gas Act.... The Plaintiffs presently before the Court reside less than 1,000 feet from the Defendants' gas wells and allege numerous injuries as a result of the Defendants' violations of the Oil and Gas Act, thus falling directly within the particular group of individuals that the Act is intended to protect. We thus conclude that the Plaintiffs have satisfied the first element of a negligence per se action with respect to the HSCA, the SWMA, and the Oil and Gas Act.

We ... find that the Plaintiffs' Amended Complaint satisfies all elements of a negligence per se claim having the HSCA, SWMA, and Oil and Gas Act as a basis ....

* * *

(Continued)

D. Count IV—Private Nuisance

In Count IV, the Plaintiffs assert a claim for private nuisance, alleging that the Defendants have created and maintained a continuing nuisance in the area of the Wells by allowing the Wells to exist and operate in a dangerous and hazardous condition and causing the discharge of hazardous chemicals and combustible gases into the Plaintiffs' groundwater supply. The Pennsylvania Supreme Court has adopted Section 822 of the Restatement (Second) of Torts for determining the existence of a private nuisance. This Section provides that:

> One is subject to liability for a private nuisance if, but only if, his conduct is a legal cause of an invasion of another's interest in the private use and enjoyment of land, and the invasion is either (a) intentional and unreasonable, or (b) unintentional and otherwise actionable under the rules controlling liability for negligent or reckless conduct, or for abnormally dangerous conditions or activities.

Kembel v. Schlegel, 329 Pa. Super. 159, 478 A.2d 11, 14-15 (Pa. Super. Ct. 1984) (quoting Restatement (Second) of Torts § 822). The Restatement further provides that "[t]here is liability for a nuisance only to those to whom it causes significant harm, of a kind that would be suffered by a normal person in the community or by property in normal condition and used for a normal purpose." ... Invasions are "significant" if "normal persons living in the community would regard the invasion in question as definitely offensive, seriously annoying or intolerable."

* * *

As we have held previously, the Plaintiffs have adequately asserted that the Defendants' negligence has caused and continues to cause harm to their property. We thus consider whether the alleged injuries to the Plaintiffs rise to the level contemplated by the Restatement.

With respect to whether the alleged invasion is "definitely offensive, seriously annoying or intolerable," the Defendants contend that the Plaintiffs' injuries are speculative and merely "anticipated" as opposed to having been already realized. This contention is belied by the Plaintiffs' allegations that their water supply had already been contaminated as early as August of 2010 and that they have incurred costs for water sampling, water quality monitoring, and purchasing alternative potable water sources for consumption and other residential uses. These matters are a potentially serious inconvenience, and ongoing expenses to remedy them by the Plaintiffs could reasonably be deemed "seriously

annoying or intolerable." We conclude that ... the Plaintiffs have sufficiently alleged that the Defendants caused a substantial invasion to the Plaintiffs' interest in the private use of their Property causing a "seriously annoying or intolerable" nuisance and satisfying the second prong of the Restatement test....

* * *

H. Count VIII—Breach of Contract

In Count VIII, the Plaintiffs assert a claim for breach of contract against only Defendant Cabot. It has been held by Pennsylvania courts that gas leases are governed by general principles of contract law and interpretation.... Under Pennsylvania law, a plaintiff asserting a breach of contract claim must first establish the essential terms of the contract and then demonstrate that the defendant breached a duty imposed by one or more of those terms and that the plaintiff suffered damages as a result....

We must first consider, then, what essential terms make up the contract relative to the Plaintiffs' claims. In their Amended Complaint, the Plaintiffs assert that Cabot had the following obligations under the Gas Lease: to test Plaintiffs' domestic water supply prior to commencement of drilling operations and ensure that the water supply was not adversely affected; to return the water supply to pre-drilling quality in the event the operations were determined to have contaminated the water; to construct and install wells in a manner which would minimally affect the water supply; and to conduct operations in accordance with DEP regulations.... Cabot apparently agrees that the Gas Lease created these obligations but contends that inclusion of the phrase "on the premises" therein excludes harms resulting from subsurface drilling from these provisions.... Resolution of this issue thus turns on proper interpretation of the phrase "on the premises" as used within the Gas Lease.

When a written agreement is unambiguous, "its meaning must be determined by its contents alone." ...

We ultimately find that considering the agreement as a whole, rather than parsing the use of "premises" therein, clarifies the parties' intent in the use of the word throughout the Gas Lease.

The purpose of the Gas Lease as identified therein was for the lessor Plaintiffs to lease to lessee Cabot land identified as "the premises" for the purpose exploring for and ultimately withdrawing natural and other gas stored in the rock underlying the leased property .... It hardly seems logical that "premises" in paragraph 1, which defines the very property leased and the rights granted to Cabot, would include the subsurface area while, in subsequent paragraphs articulating Cabot's

(Continued)

remedial responsibilities, liability for operations "on the premises" would be limited to only surface operations. Despite its apparent desires, Cabot cannot selectively interpret the term "premises" to include subsurface areas in one provision but exclude subsurface areas in another for its own financial benefit. [The Court inserted the following footnote here: "Further, it is our supposition that had Cabot intended to immunize itself from any liability resulting from subsurface drilling, it would have expressly and unequivocally done so in the contract. While the benefit of hindsight might encourage Cabot to limit its contractual obligations, it is not this Court's prerogative to rewrite such exclusions into an otherwise well-drafted agreement."]

The remainder of our breach of contract inquiry is much simpler. The Plaintiffs, having established contingent obligations on the part of Cabot, must demonstrate that the contingent obligation became an affirmative one, that Cabot failed to satisfy the contractual obligation, and that the Plaintiffs suffered damages as a result.... Here, the Plaintiffs have alleged facts which establish that Cabot was responsible for contaminating its groundwater, thus triggering the remedial provisions and establishing an affirmative obligation for Cabot. The Plaintiffs have further alleged that Cabot has failed to satisfy those obligations by failing to return their groundwater to pre-drilling quality as required by the agreement and that they have incurred and will continue to incur substantial financial costs until and unless Cabot satisfies its contractual obligations. Thus, assuming the facts as pled to be true, the Plaintiffs have successfully pled that Cabot has breached the Gas Lease and that they have suffered damages as a result.

Questions for Discussion

1. *Roth v. Cabot Oil & Gas Corp.* presents an opportunity to review the elements of several common law tort theories discussed in Chapter 4 and to consider breach of contract claims as well. Consider why it makes sense for a plaintiff to argue several theories of tort and/or breach of contract in a complaint. It is useful to know that some of the *Roth* plaintiffs' claims were dismissed by the court, including the claims of trespass to land and misrepresentation claims.

2. What are the appropriate remedies for breach of contract when that breach has led to environmental contamination? Are those remedies adequate? Why or why not?

3. In situations where no specific landowner claims injury by environmental contamination caused by another party, should "the environment" or "nature" be able to bring a claim for its own damages? Such a claim could be brought by a guardian ad litem, for example. What are the consequences of barring such actions?

Land Use

Here's a good idea!

This is a "bare bones" outline of the chapter. Expand this outline with more detailed notes as you read the chapter. This will allow you to create a study guide as you work. This good study habit will help you to learn the material, retain important points, and make efficient use of your time.

Learning Objectives

After reading this chapter, you will have an understanding of land use regulations in the United States. Additionally, you will examine constitutional issues related to land use regulations. Specifically, after reading this chapter, you should be able to answer the following questions:

1. Under what power do the state and federal governments regulate land use?
2. What are specific types of state land use regulation?
3. What are the major constitutional issues related to land use regulation?

▮ Introduction

Local and regional land use regulations affect the environment. This chapter examines land use regulations and some of the legal issues that may arise in controlling land use to protect the environment.

Land use restrictions have prohibited construction and development in environmentally sensitive areas such as beachfronts, mountainsides, and floodplains. Proponents of such regulation note that it is necessary to protect the land through statutory schemes that can override an individual landowner's personal property rights to do with the land what it wishes. Because state police powers give the states the ability to regulate the health, welfare, and safety of their citizens, states have a duty to protect the natural environment, which is essential for human beings to live. More moderately stated, government has a valid interest in regulating how land is used. Opponents of land use restrictions argue that such regulations are beyond the scope of the government's police power; that regulations depriving owners of all economic use of their property constitute a "taking" of that property, which requires compensation; or that the regulation was established by a procedurally flawed process. Some view government regulation of land use as a fundamental interference with a landowner's liberty, freedom, and rights.

As you read this chapter, try to keep these larger issues in mind. Do you accept that government must protect the land in order to preserve it, even if that means prohibiting a landowner from doing with its land what it might otherwise wish to do? Or do you believe that land use regulations represent an overreach by government? Consider whether lands such as those found in Yellowstone National Park or Yosemite National Park would exist in their present condition without such protections. Where is your favorite natural area? Would it exist that way today without legal protections, or would a private landowner have grabbed it up for "development" without such protections?

■ Zoning

The term **zoning** describes local and regional regulations that control the use of land within a particular jurisdiction. Zoning laws usually take the form of *ordinances*, which are laws passed by local governments such as a city, town, or county. Zoning ordinances generally divide a community into different districts or *zones*, and designate types of structures and activities that are permitted or prohibited in each zone according to this classification. Zoning regulations also address such matters as building height, landscaping, setback requirements, and types of construction permitted within a particular zone. Some communities also address aesthetic issues, such as building exteriors, in their zoning codes.

History

Zoning is a principal tool of planning. However, it was not widely used by local governments until the 20th century.

Well before the 20th century—in 1632, to be precise—Cambridge, Massachusetts, enacted an ordinance that provided for the erection of buildings only upon the consent of the mayor. (This ordinance would be invalid today, because no standards for approval were included; it gave unfettered discretion to the mayor.) Between 1916 and 1926, zoning came of age through three significant occurrences. In 1916, New York City enacted a much-emulated comprehensive zoning ordinance, the purpose of which was to keep the garment district out of the Fifth Avenue shopping district. This was the first such ordinance in the United States. Until the 1920s, courts frequently struck down zoning ordinances unless they concentrated on prohibiting nuisance uses. Soon after New York City adopted that first comprehensive zoning ordinance, it was attacked in the courts under the theory that it encroached on constitutionally protected property rights. In 1922, the Department of Commerce published an initial draft of a "Standard State Zoning Enabling Act." Each state has since adopted a similar text into its statutes, thereby delegating to municipalities the police power to zone. Consequently, most land use regulation has been implemented by local governments. In 1926, the U.S. Supreme Court upheld comprehensive zoning in *Village of Euclid v. Ambler Realty Co.*[1] In that case, the Supreme Court recognized that the zoning process is a permissible exercise of the government's police power and that a decrease in land value as a result of zoning legislation does not necessarily constitute a taking of property requiring compensation under the Fifth and Fourteenth Amendments to the Constitution. The Court upheld the validity of zoning in general and of a comprehensive zoning ordinance in particular. After *Euclid*, a validly enacted ordinance may still be held unconstitutional as applied to a particular tract of land, but this determination is made on a case-by-case basis. Also after *Euclid*, comprehensive zoning ordinances were enacted throughout the country and became the primary means of land use control by local government.

zoning: Term describing local and regional land use regulations controlling the use of land within a particular jurisdiction.

---

[1] 272 U.S. 365 (1926).

Authority to Zone under Police Power

The *Euclid* case established the principle that regulation concerning the use of property is valid and will be upheld so long as the regulation is justified under the government's police power. *Police power* is generally defined as the power to legislate for the health, morals, safety, and welfare of the community. The power of the government to protect the public health, safety, and welfare is found in the federal and state constitutions and is generally construed very broadly by the courts. Nevertheless, a land use regulation that bears no rational relationship to the police power to protect general public health, safety, and welfare will be held unconstitutional and unenforceable.

The environmental protection purposes and implications of zoning must thus fit within the state police power. Those that do not would be invalid. For example, zoning to reduce the market value of land so that government can acquire it cheaply would be invalid. However, because states are given broad power and discretion to zone, it is relatively easy to show that such regulations are proper applications of the state police power.

In the following case, the plaintiffs wanted to operate a landfill on a site in West Virginia's panhandle country near North Mountain. Geo-Tech Reclamation Industries (GRI) had obtained an option to purchase a 331-acre site and subsequently filed an application for a landfill operating permit. Its application was denied by the director of the Department of Natural Resources on the ground that the proposed landfill had engendered "adverse public sentiment." A second plaintiff, LCS, acquired an option to purchase the site in 1987, and its application to operate a solid waste disposal facility there was also rejected. The West Virginia Water Resources Board affirmed the director's decision on the basis of adverse public sentiment. The plaintiffs brought a declaratory judgment challenging the constitutionality of the state statute, arguing that it violated due process by impermissibly delegating legislative authority to local citizens and that the statute exceeded the state's police power. The district court found the statute unconstitutional, and the state appealed.

Geo-Tech Reclamation Industries, Inc. v. Hamrick

886 F.2d 662 (4th Cir. 1989)

ERVIN, Chief Judge

In this consolidated appeal, several West Virginia state environmental officials (collectively "West Virginia") and an organization known as "Citizens to Fight North Mountain Waste Site" appeal from determinations on summary judgment that a provision of West Virginia's Solid Waste Management Act ... is facially unconstitutional. Because we find that the statutory language in question bears no rational relation "to the public health, safety, morals or general welfare," we must affirm the decision below.

... West Virginia, like many other states, has enacted a statutory scheme governing solid waste

disposal.... The [Solid Waste Management] Act flatly prohibits the operation of open dumps and requires landfill operators to obtain a permit from the Department before construction, operating, or abandoning any solid waste disposal facility.... Among the various reasons for which a permit may be denied,

> the director may deny the issuance of a permit on the basis of information in the application or from other sources including public comment, if the solid waste facility may cause adverse impacts on the natural resources and environmental concerns under the director's purview in chapter twenty of the Code, destruction of aesthetic values, destruction

(Continued)

or endangerment of the property of others or is significantly adverse to the public sentiment of the area where the solid waste facility is or will be located.

… It is the final clause of this section—giving the Director authority to deny a permit solely because it is "significantly adverse to the public sentiment"—which is at issue in this case.…

* * *

We see no reason, however, to decide whether [the statute] works an impermissible delegation of power to local residents because the statute suffers from a more profound constitutional infirmity. It is well settled that land-use regulations "must find their justification in some aspect of the police power, asserted for the public welfare." *Euclid v. Ambler Realty Co.*, 272 U.S. 365, 387, 47 S.Ct. 114, 118, 71 L.Ed. 303 (1926). West Virginia strenuously argues that it acts well within the broad confines of its police power in regulating the development of solid waste disposal facilities. With this we certainly agree. No one would question the state's power to impose a broad array of restrictions on an activity, such as the operation of a landfill, which was recognized as a nuisance even by the early common law.

West Virginia also argues that within this broad array of restrictions, the state may legislate to protect its communities against not only such tangible effects as increased traffic, noise, odors, and health concerns, but also against the possibility of decreased community pride and fracturing of community spirit that may accompany large waste disposal operations. Here again, we do not quarrel with the state's position. "The concept of the public welfare is broad and inclusive. The values it represents are spiritual as well as physical, aesthetic as well as monetary." … West Virginia may undoubtedly regulate the siting and operation of solid waste disposal facilities so as to eliminate or at least alleviate the deleterious effects of such facilities on more inchoate community values.

The question raised in this case, however, is whether [the West Virginia statute] does in fact further this laudable purpose or whether it is instead "arbitrary and capricious, having no substantial relation" to its purported goal.… The state argues that the statute's adverse public sentiment clause promotes its stated purpose by allowing citizens to comment upon a proposed landfill's impact on community pride, spirit, and quality

of life. But, with commendable candor, the state also recognizes that many who may speak out against a landfill will do so because of self-interest, bias, or ignorance. These are but a few of the less than noble motivations commonly referred to as the "Not-in-My Backyard" syndrome.

… "Where property interests are adversely affected by zoning, the courts generally have emphasized the breadth of municipal power to control land use and have sustained the regulation if it is rationally related to legitimate state concerns.… But an ordinance may fail even under that limited standard of review." … Nothing in the record suggests, nor can we conceive, how unreflective and unseasoned public sentiment that "a dump is still a dump" is in any way rationally related to the otherwise legitimate goal of protecting community spirit and pride.

* * *

… [W]e find that [the West Virginia statute's] clause authorizing the Director to reject permits that are "significantly adverse to the public sentiment" bears no substantial or rational relationship to the state's interest in promoting the general public welfare. The district court's decision is therefore
AFFIRMED.

Questions for Discussion

1. Do you agree with the court in *Geo-Tech Reclamation* that there is no rational relationship between the statute's inclusion of "public sentiment" and legitimate state interests?
2. In *Young v. City of Simi Valley*,[2] the Ninth Circuit characterized the statute in question in *Geo-Tech Reclamation* as giving "local residents de facto veto power over the landfill permitting process." Should legislative bodies have the right to delegate authority to citizens? Why or why not?
3. Who should make land use decisions? If you believe that private owners should have complete authority to make decisions about how their land is used, what mechanisms could protect the general welfare of a society that wishes to live in a clean, aesthetically pleasing environment? If you believe that government should be able to regulate how private landowners use their land, what mechanisms exist (or should exist) to check government power?

---

[2] 216 F.3d 807, 820 (9th Cir. 2000).

Compare the court's reasoning in *Geo-Tech Reclamation Industries* with the following case, *Phoenix Development, Inc. v. Woodinville.* In the *Phoenix* case, the Washington State Supreme Court heard an appeal from parties concerning a dispute about rezoning. The City of Woodinville denied an application for rezoning made by the owner of land, who wished to develop the land more densely than permitted by the current zoning. At issue was the City of Woodinville's ordinance.

Phoenix Development, Inc., et al. v. City of Woodinville
171 Wash. 2d 820, 256 P.3d 1150 (2011)

J.M. Johnson, J.

In 2007, the city council of Woodinville (City) unanimously denied two applications submitted by Phoenix Development Inc. to rezone undeveloped property in northeast Woodinville.... We ... uphold the City's decision, thus affirming the trial court.

Facts and Procedural History

Phoenix owns two undeveloped properties in northeast Woodinville, referred to as the Wood Trails proposal and the Montevallo proposal. The properties have been zoned as R-1 (one dwelling per acre) since Woodinville's incorporation in 1993.

In June 2004, Phoenix asked the City to amend the zoning map for these two properties. Phoenix asked the City to rezone each from R-1 to R-4 (four dwellings per acre) and submitted preliminary plat applications for approval. Phoenix planned to build 66 houses on 38.7 acres at Wood Trails (1.7 dwellings per acre) and 66 houses on 16.48 acres at Montevallo (4.005 dwellings per acre)....

City staff engaged in two years of environmental review and analyzed whether the proposals complied with Woodinville's comprehensive plan and the City's criteria for a rezone under Woodinville Municipal Code (WMC) 21.44.070. [Fn. by the court:

WMC 21.44.070 states:

A zone reclassification shall be granted only if the applicant demonstrates that the proposal is consistent with the Comprehensive Plan *and* applicable functional plans at the time the application for such zone reclassification is submitted, *and* complies with the following criteria:

(1)   There is a demonstrated need for additional zoning as the type proposed.

(2)   The zone reclassification is consistent and compatible with uses and zoning of the surrounding properties.

(3)   The property is practically and physically suited for the uses allowed in the proposed zone reclassification. (Emphasis added by the court)]

The staff concluded that both proposals were consistent with the purpose statements for R-4 zones ... and stated that two of the three criteria required to rezone were met, WMC 21.44.070(2) and (3). The staff report did not make a recommendation with respect to the first criterion—the "demonstrated need" requirement of WMC 21.44.070(1)—stating that this criterion "'ultimately requires an objective judgment by the hearing examiner and city council based upon relevant City plans, policies, goals, and timeframes.'" ... City staff recommended approval of the requested rezones if the "demonstrated need" requirement was met.

Public hearings were held in March and April 2007. The hearing examiner considered extensive testimony and documentary evidence, including the "Final Environmental Impact Statement" and a 2,144 page analysis of the proposals submitted by the Concerned Neighbors of Wellington (CNW). On May 16, 2007, the hearing examiner recommended that the City approve the rezones from R-1 to R-4. The hearing examiner also recommended approval of the preliminary plat applications subject to numerous conditions. CNW appealed to the City.

The City unanimously denied the rezone requests and preliminary plat applications after conducting a closed record review of the hearing examiner's recommendation and holding a public meeting. Among other things, the City found that there was no "demonstrated need" to rezone the properties, that rezoning was inappropriate because of deficient facilities and services (other than sewer), and that rezoning would be inconsistent with the comprehensive plan.... [T]he City stated that it was acting in its "legislative capacity" when it found that the R-1 zone was appropriate for the properties....

(Continued)

Phoenix [sought] reversal of the City's decision, approval of the Wood Trails and Montevallo proposals, and at least $5,000,000 in damages. The superior court dismissed the petition ....

... The Court of Appeals reversed and remanded to the City for reconsideration of Phoenix's preliminary plat applications.... Both the City and CNW petitioned for review, which was granted....

Standard of Review

The denial of a site-specific rezone is a land use decision....

* * *

Analysis

The Court of Appeals reversed the City's land use decision for four reasons [two of which have been omitted from this excerpt]: (1) substantial evidence does not support the City's decision that the proposed rezones are not needed; ... (3) the City engaged in an unlawful legislative procedure during a quasijudicial decision-making process, and such error was not harmless .... Accordingly, the court reversed the City's land use decision and remanded for consideration of the plat applications.... We address the Court of Appeals' holdings in turn.

A. Substantial Evidence Supports the City's Decision that the Proposed Rezones Are Not Needed

1. We defer to the City's Interpretation of What Constitutes a "Demonstrated Need" Under WMC 21.44.070(1)

When construing an ordinance, a "'reviewing court gives considerable deference to the construction of' the challenged ordinance 'by those officials charged with its enforcement.'" ... Although this is not a Growth Management Act (GMA) ... case, ... to the extent that the GMA is implicated, we note that the GMA does not prescribe a single approach to growth management.... Instead, the legislature specified that "'the ultimate burden and responsibility for planning, harmonizing the planning goals of [the GMA], and implementing a county's or city's future rests with that community.'" ... Thus, the GMA acts exclusively through local governments and is to be construed with the requisite flexibility to allow local governments to accommodate local needs.... These principles of deference apply to a local government's site-specific land use decisions where the GMA considerations play a role in its ultimate decision.

WMC 21.44.070 states that a zone reclassification "shall be granted only if ... (1) [t]here is a demonstrated need for additional zoning as the type proposed." The City interpreted the "demonstrated need" criterion under WMC 21.44.070(1) to require "an objective judgment by the City Council based upon plans, goals, policies and timeframes." ... To this end, the City found that "the proposed rezone is not 'needed' at this time" because current property zoning is consistent with its comprehensive plan,... the City is on target to meet its growth targets for 2022, ... the City currently has a diversity of housing to allow for a wide variety of housing types, incomes, and living situations, ... and because the City has prioritized development of the downtown area to implement the GMA, "Vision 2020" (a long-range growth and transportation strategy for the Puget Sound region), and relevant King County-wide planning policies.... We defer to the City's determination of what constitutes "demonstrated need" under WMC 21.44.070(1) and hold that the City properly interpreted its own ordinance to require a showing that a rezone is needed to achieve larger policy objectives.

* * *

D. The City Did Not Engage in an Unlawful Procedure

Phoenix argues that the City engaged in an unlawful procedure by invoking its legislative authority during a quasijudicial proceeding, allegedly "adopt[ing] a new policy rather than applying existing policies and regulations." ... Because the City is bound to follow its own ordinances governing rezone applications, we agree with Phoenix that a city's decision to rezone is a quasijudicial act.... However, we also hold that the City's action was not legislative, although it was mischaracterized as such.

An action is legislative if it declares or prescribes a new law, policy, or plan.... [The City's finding of fact] does not declare or prescribe a new law, policy or plan or even modify existing standards. Rather, it makes statements that are directly tied to existing policies, and to the general rules governing rezone applications.... If anything, [the City's finding of fact] is a restatement of the evidence in the record supporting its ultimate conclusions, not an unlawful procedure.

However [the City's finding of fact] is characterized, it is not fatal.... ([A]n unlawful procedure error may be harmless). Substantial evidence in the record supports the City's conclusion that a "demonstrated need" for a rezone was not shown—a required element to approve Phoenix's application.

(Continued)

Questions for Discussion

1. Is there an appreciable difference between the local actions taken in the *Phoenix Development v. Woodinville* case and the local actions taken in *Geo-Tech Reclamation Industries, Inc. v. Hamrick*? If not, which of the courts' opinions do you favor? Why? If there is a difference and the cases can be distinguished, why did local opinion override the developer's interests in the *Phoenix Development* case but not in the *Geo-Tech Reclamation* case? Can this be explained merely by jurisdictional differences? (*Geo-Tech Reclamation* is a West Virginia case, whereas *Phoenix Development* is a Washington State case.) How might regional differences in values, customs, and aesthetics be reflected in judicial opinions and common law?

2. After reviewing *Phoenix Development* and *Geo-Tech Reclamation*, do you believe that public participation in government procedures related to land use is worthwhile? Discuss.

■ *ACTIVITY BOX   NIMBY*

As you read above, the court in *Geo-Tech Reclamation Services v. Hamrick* referred to the "not in my backyard" syndrome. The "not in my backyard" syndrome, often known by its acronym NIMBY, generally refers to the attitude of people who believe that something is perhaps necessary, but do not want that thing in their own neighborhood. For example, a landfill or a waste incinerator might be recognized as a necessary land use, but people do not want to live near such things and will fight proposed siting within their area.

Research NIMBY issues in your community—or issues in your community that seem to generate NIMBY-type sentiment, regardless of whether there is an organized opposition movement—and answer the following questions:

1. Consider how zoning regulations can be used to support or to defeat NIMBY-related concerns, and how politics and law intersect to shape land use regulations. Do you believe that NIMBY-ism will defeat the project that you have identified through your research? Why or why not?

2. If NIMBY-ism defeats the project that you have identified, how or where will those needs be met? If they will not be met, what type of alternative has been developed to satisfy the need that would have been met by the project if it had been approved?

3. Who should decide how land is used? The owner of the land, members of the community where the land exists, or some central authority? How does your response reflect your culture?

Establishing Planning Authority

Zoning involves the legitimate exercise of the government's police power to regulate land use. A plan for development is a first step in the zoning process. The municipality first undertakes a study of the area to be regulated to project future growth and public needs. This study results in the adoption of a **master plan**, a planning "constitution" in the sense that zoning ordinances and rezoning decisions must conform to it. A local government's authority to adopt a master plan derives from state laws. In adopting its master plan and local zoning ordinance, the municipality must comply with these state zoning-enabling statutes, based in most cases on a standard state zoning-enabling act.

The following case illustrates that land use authority is granted by statute and may not be circumvented judicially.

master plan: Community plan for land use required by state legislation enabling zoning.

Coffey v. City of Walla Walla

145 Wash. App. 435, 187 P.3d 272 (2008)

Korsmo, J.

Appellants asked the Walla Walla County Superior Court, through a land use petition act (LUPA) ... filing, to overturn a Walla Walla City Council decision to amend the city's comprehensive plan governing the property at issue here. We conclude that the superior court lacked subject matter jurisdiction over the amendment to the comprehensive plan. The proper method to challenge the decision was to raise a complaint to the Growth Management Hearings Board (GMHB)....

The land in question is a nearly 50 acre location that is undeveloped; it is surrounded on three sides by single family residences, most of which are acre-sized parcels, and by a highway on the other side. The property owner and a developer originally sought to have Walla Walla County amend its comprehensive plan and the zoning ordinance governing the property to permit both commercial and high density residential uses. The County Board of Commissioners denied the request.

The City of Walla Walla promptly annexed the area and the applicants renewed their request to have the comprehensive plan amended and, by subsequent filing, to have the area rezoned from residential to commercial. The City Planning Commission conducted a hearing solely on the original proposal to amend the comprehensive plan. Contrary to staff recommendation, the Planning Commission recommended that the application be denied. The City Council, however, voted in favor of the plan amendment. The ordinance adopting that decision expressly indicated that it was not changing the land's zoning status.

Appellants, neighbors opposed to the development, then filed a land use petition with the Walla Walla County Superior Court, contending that the plan amendment violated countywide planning practices and was not supported by the evidence. The City of Walla Walla, joined by the owner and developer, moved to dismiss the petition on several theories, including lack of subject matter jurisdiction. The court found that the ordinance was legislative in nature and that the petitioners had not established that the City Council acted in an arbitrary or capricious manner in adopting the ordinance. The petition was therefore dismissed. The neighbors appealed to this court.

Analysis

The Growth Management Act (GMA) ... was adopted by the Washington Legislature in 1990. The GMA required, *inter alia*, that certain counties and cities jointly plan for future development. To that end it directed that local areas adopt comprehensive plans and accompanying development regulations to implement the plans.... Growth was to be steered into existing areas and sprawl discouraged. Cities and counties were to coordinate their planning with each other and identify areas where growth was to be channeled.... The legislation also created a Growth Management Hearings Board to consider challenges to legislative decisions of local jurisdictions, including allegations of failure to live up to the obligations imposed by the GMA.... Challenges to zoning ordinances and other actions affecting specific pieces of property were to be filed in superior court under a land use petition.... This two-headed approach largely replaced the former process of seeking judicial review by statutory writ....

In 1990, Walla Walla County opted to plan under the GMA. The county and the City of Walla Walla adopted county-wide planning policies in 1993, and the city adopted a comprehensive plan in 1997. As part of its GMA implementation, the city adopted "Level V" review criteria under its municipal code to guide decision-making. The review criteria, set out in Walla Walla Municipal Code 20.48.040, mandate consideration of various factors such as available infrastructure, compliance with the comprehensive plan, and the suitability of the land for the proposed rezoning.

The appellants filed a LUPA action with the superior court, which found that the legislative judgment of the city council was appropriate. Appellants then appealed to this court, contending that the comprehensive plan amendment was flawed by the failure of the city council to consider the Level V criteria when it adopted the ordinance amending the plan as to this property. In their view, the GMHB would not have authority to consider compliance with local planning requirements not imposed by the GMA. The city vigorously argues that the Level V criteria apply only to rezone decisions and are not applicable to comprehensive plan amendments. We do not decide whether the city ordinance makes Level V review applicable to comprehensive plan amendments.... Whether or not the city code requires compliance with Level V review in

(Continued)

this context, LUPA is not the appropriate method of challenging a comprehensive plan amendment.

The GMA sets up a basic dichotomy: review of political decisions regarding the broad nature of local area planning is by the GMHB, which is responsible for ensuring the decisions are consistent with state law; review of land use actions relating to specific property is by the superior court, which must confirm that statutory and constitutional processes have been followed. The former category involves decisions that are essentially legislative in character; the procedural focus of the latter category is largely judicial in character. The division of authority between the GMHB and the courts reflects the different character of decisions being reviewed.

[The statute] expressly states that the land use petition "replaces the writ of certiorari for appeal of land use decisions and shall be the exclusive means of judicial review of land use decisions." A "land use decision," in turn, means a local jurisdiction's "final determination" on "an application for a project permit or other governmental approval ... excluding applications for legislative approvals such as area-wide rezones and annexations." ... While the definition does not expressly list comprehensive plan amendments as a "legislative approval," that list is illustrative rather than exclusive. The case law, however, has long recognized that comprehensive plan amendments are legislative in nature....

Consistently, RCW 36.70A.280(1)(a) expressly gives jurisdiction to the GMHB over petitions alleging that a local jurisdiction "is not in compliance with the requirements of this chapter." Chapter 36.70A RCW is the chapter that imposes comprehensive plan requirements on local jurisdictions. Similarly, RCW 36.70A.290(2) expressly sets forth the time period in which a challenge to a comprehensive plan amendment must be brought before the GMHB.... The GMA, then, clearly contemplates that challenges to comprehensive plan amendments must be brought before the GMHB.

Appellants' attempt to use the LUPA process to challenge the amendment was not statutorily authorized. The superior court lacked subject matter jurisdiction to consider the claim since the GMHB had exclusive authority to do so. While the trial court reached the correct result in dismissing the petition, it should have done so for the reason that it lacked authority to hear the claim.

It is not uncommon for those hoping to develop property to seek both a comprehensive plan amendment and a rezone of property in the same proceeding.

Anyone seeking to challenge both aspects of a ruling granting both requests would by statute have to appeal to two entities: the GMHB for the comprehensive plan amendment and superior court for the rezone. While the two-front appeal process could be burdensome, we can imagine that trial courts would be inclined to stay proceedings pending the Board's determination of the comprehensive plan challenge.

Here, appellants were notified by the city ordinance that any appeal would have to be made to the GMHB and filed within 60 days. Similarly, when the City answered the petition and asserted that there was no subject matter jurisdiction, there was still time to file before the Board. Appellants did not do so. Without deciding the issue, it may have been possible for appellants to have pursued a writ to force the City Council to have followed the Level V criteria. Statutory and constitutional writs still have some role in the overall land use process....

The superior court lacked subject matter jurisdiction to consider a comprehensive plan amendment under a land use petition. The decision to dismiss the petition is affirmed.

Questions for Discussion

1. What benefit to society is derived by limiting the scope authority for land use planning?
2. After you read this case, describe the role the judicial and legislative branches play in land use planning in Washington State. If you were creating a land use regulatory scheme in your state, would you follow this model? Why or why not?
3. Do you think that comprehensive master plans encourage or discourage people from participating in land use governance? Explain.
4. In *Triple G. Landfills, Inc. v. Board of Commissioners of Fountain County, Indiana,*[3] the court held that local governmental bodies were prohibited from enacting a zoning ordinance in the absence of a comprehensive zoning plan. Because the county in which the land use was disputed had not enacted a plan, the zoning ordinance was held invalid under state law. Do you think that laws with which average persons may not be familiar should be able to block or override a local community's ability to protect its land from uses inconsistent with how its residents wish to live? Why or why not?

---

[3] 977 F.2d 287 (7th Cir. 1992).

Regulating Land Use

Once the government entity has adopted a master plan, the bodies subject to that plan adopt ordinances establishing and regulating various types of land uses, and establishing rules and regulations to enforce it. Within such plans, zoning categories usually include broad terms, such as residential, commercial, industrial, or agricultural. Those terms can be further refined. For example, in Grays Harbor County, Washington State, "RR" signifies rural residential, minimum 1 acre; "R-2" signifies residential general, minimum 10,000 square feet.[4]

■ Applied Problem: A State's Growth Plan

An example of a planning scheme can be seen in Washington State. The Growth Management Act[5] is a state statute that requires almost all counties and cities to create a comprehensive master plan and development regulations. The comprehensive master plans set forth urban growth areas, designate natural resources lands (i.e., forest lands, agriculture lands, and mineral resource lands), and identify critical areas (i.e., wetlands, geological hazards, frequently flooded areas, fish and wildlife habitat, and aquifer discharge areas). Other state statutes also govern land use, but the statutes are supposed to work in tandem with each other rather than at odds with each other. For example, the Washington State Environmental Policy Act serves as a gap filler for land use regulations where such a gap filler is needed.[6] Another state statute regulating land use is the Shoreline Management Act, which seeks to protect the state's fragile shorelines[7] while also protecting private property owners' constitutional rights.[8]

One interesting aspect of zoning as it relates to the Growth Management Act is that it absolutely relies upon public involvement. If local planning legislation (e.g., a zoning ordinance) violates the comprehensive master plan, but no one appeals it within 60 days, then the zoning is valid, even though it may be unlawful under the Growth Management Act.[9]

Questions for Discussion

1. Identify your state's growth management plan. How is the authority to regulate land use between state and local government allocated? Should state government or local government have the final authority to make land use decisions? Why?

2. Do you think a statute can really balance the protection of fragile environmental attributes, such as shorelines, with a private property owner's rights to use his or her land, and do so in a manner that does not result in a regulatory taking? Why or why not? (See the discussion of takings later in this chapter.)

3. Are there building activities in your neighborhood or community that seem out of place? Do you think that more restrictive zoning laws might help create a community that better reflects the type of environment you prefer to live in? What are the drawbacks to restrictive zoning laws? Also, who should be able to decide what an appropriate use of land is?

---

[4] *Zoning.* Retrieved June 15, 2013, from http://www.co.grays-harbor.wa.us/info/pub_svcs /GHCCode/pdf/GHC17.pdf

[5] WASH. REV. CODE § 36.70A.

[6] *Id.* § 43.21C.240.

[7] *Id.* § 90.58.020. *See also Biggers v. City of Bainbridge Island*, 124 Wash. App. 858, 103 P.3d 244 (2004).

[8] WASH. ADMIN. CODE § 173-26-186(5).

[9] WASH. REV. CODE §§ 36.70A.280, 36.70A.290(2).

Under statutory growth management schedules, local government entities—such as cities or counties—may generally establish zoning regulations as they wish, provided they are consistent with the state statute, such as the state's growth management plan. Amendment of zoning ordinances, such as a change in the ordinance's text or a rezoning, is regulated by state and local law. Rezoning of a single parcel, known as *spot zoning*, is generally not permitted.

Today's zoning plans often take into account critical or sensitive areas, such as wetlands and wildlife habitat. Laws related to those specific areas are addressed in subsequent chapters.

Exceptions from Zoning Regulations

Most zoning schemes allow for exceptions to the zoning regulations in particular areas, as long as those exceptions are in keeping with the master plan. These exceptions are called **variances**. A variance requires permission from the appropriate zoning authority and usually involves modest deviations from the requirements of the zoning ordinance.

A petitioner who applies for a variance usually must show (1) that he or she would suffer an undue hardship if the ordinance is enforced, and (2) that the granting of the variance will not excessively disrupt the surrounding land or the master plan. The grant of a variance may be given to alleviate a situation in which uniform zoning burdens one parcel more than others, or to make an ordinance that would be unconstitutional as applied constitutional.

Alternatively, a special permit may grant an exception to the zoning code provided certain requirements are met. The decision to grant a variance or special permit rests with the administrative board specified by the relevant state statute or local ordinance. Denial of a variance or special permit may be challenged on the grounds that the decision was arbitrary, the application process or consideration of the application was procedurally flawed, or amounted to an unconstitutional taking of property without just compensation.

A **nonconforming use** is an activity or structure on the property that is prohibited by a zoning ordinance passed after the use existed. Such uses are generally immune from new zoning ordinances. However, the nonconforming activity or structure cannot be expanded, and the ability to maintain or continue the "grandfathered" use may be lost if the activity is abandoned or the building is destroyed. Courts have also declared some nonconforming uses to be nuisances and have eliminated them under that theory. For example, a nonconforming-use landfill in a residential area might be enjoined as a nuisance.

Consider the following case, in which a major alteration to a billboard, which in its former state had been a nonconforming use, was declared a nuisance and ordered to be removed.

variance: Exception to or waiver of a requirement of the zoning code; to get a variance, the petitioner typically is required to show that (1) it would suffer undue hardship if the ordinance is enforced, and (2) granting of the variance will not excessively disrupt the surrounding land or master plan.

nonconforming use: Use of property that is allowed, even though it does not conform to the zoning ordinance, because the zoning ordinance was adopted after the use began.

Township of Blair v. Lamar OCI North Corp.

No. 296661, 2011 Mich. App. LEXIS 1920 (2011) (unpublished opinion)

Before: STEPHENS, P.J., and SAWYER and K. F. KELLY, JJ.

Per Curiam.

In this action to abate an alleged nuisance per se, defendant Lamar OCI North Corporation appeals as of right the trial court's judgment in favor of plaintiff Blair Township. We affirm, and lift the stay previously imposed.

Defendant leases property known as 468 US 31 South and 273 US 31 South on which it maintains

(Continued)

commercial billboards. A billboard located on 468 US 31 was a "double decker" billboard, i.e., a two-level sign, installed prior to enactment of the relevant ordinances in the Blair Township Zoning Ordinance (BTZO) in 2005. The billboard was a non-conforming use under the BTZO because the display area exceeded 300 square feet, its height exceeded 30 feet, and it was located closer than 2,640 feet from another billboard.

In December 2008 defendant removed the upper portion of the sign and installed an LED display face on the remaining board. While these changes eliminated the nonconformities in display area, the double decker face, and height, the distance between the billboard and other signs did not change. Defendant did not contact plaintiff before making changes to the billboard.

Plaintiff filed suit claiming that the billboard, which was a pre-existing nonconforming use, constituted a nuisance per se. Defendant filed a counter complaint alleging that the spacing requirement between signs violated the First Amendment, and that the BTZO did not set forth the standards that controlled the zoning administrator's decision to approve or deny a request for a permit to change a nonconforming sign.

The trial court found in favor of plaintiff. The trial court noted that defendant's billboard pre-existed the relevant BTZO and did not conform in three ways: the sign surface was too large, the height exceeded that allowed, and the billboard was located within 500 feet of other signs. The trial court found that the new billboard complied with the BTZO as to display surface area and height, but still violated the ordinance in terms of proximity to other billboards. The trial court found that a portion of section 20.08.2 was facially invalid under the First Amendment as the standards it set out for the exercise of discretion were too vague. Applying the BTZO severance clause, section 1.07, the trial court struck the final sentence of 20.08.2 from the ordinance. The trial court noted that cost of the changes and modernizations to defendant's billboard exceeded 30 percent of the replacement cost of the old billboard. For that reason, and because the changes did not remove all nonconformities, the trial court held the billboard violated the zoning ordinance.

The trial court entered a judgment finding defendant's billboard to be a nuisance per se, and ordering defendant to remove it within 21 days. The judgment provided that if defendant sought appellate relief the billboard could remain in place and need only be turned off pending resolution of the appeal. The trial court dismissed defendant's counterclaim with prejudice....

Defendant first argues that Michigan law prohibits plaintiff from restricting the modification of a nonconforming use that reduces its nonconformities. We disagree.

We review the trial court's ruling on a constitutional challenge to a zoning ordinance de novo.... The interpretation of a township zoning ordinance is question of law which we also review de novo.... "The general principles of statutory construction apply to the interpretation of zoning ordinances." ...

Plaintiff regulates signs, including billboards, under Article 20 of the BTZO. Section 20.01 sets forth the purpose of Article 20 as follows:

> The purpose of this Article is to regulate the size, placement, and general appearance of all privately owned signs and billboards in order to promote the public health, safety, and general welfare, to enhance the aesthetic desirability of the environment, and reduce hazards to life and property in Blair Township.

The BTZO limits the display area of a billboard to 300 square feet, and the height to 30 feet. The minimum spacing required between billboards is one-half mile. Nonconforming signs, such as the one at issue in this case, are regulated by Section 20.08 of the BTZO. That section provides in pertinent part:

> If the face, supports, or other parts of a nonconforming sign or billboard is structurally changed, altered, or substituted in a manner that reduces the nonconformity, the Zoning Administrator may approve the change. [Section 20.08.2.]
>
> Nothing in this Section shall prohibit the repair, reinforcement, alteration, improvement, or modernization of a lawful nonconforming sign or billboard, provided that such repair, reinforcement, alteration, improvement, and modernizing do not exceed an aggregate cost of thirty (30) percent of the appraised replacement cost of the sign or billboard, as determined by the Zoning Administrator, unless the subject sign or billboard is changed by such repair, reinforcement, alteration, improvement, or modernization to a conforming structure. Nothing in this shall prohibit the periodic change of message on any billboard. [Section 20.08.3.]

"A prior nonconforming use is a vested right in the use of particular property that does not conform to zoning restrictions, but is protected because it lawfully existed before the zoning regulation's effective date." ... A zoning ordinance permitting the continuation of a nonconforming use is meant to avoid the imposition of a hardship upon the property owner. However, the limitation on nonconforming uses

(Continued)

contemplates the gradual elimination of the noncon-forming use.... The construction of new nonconform-ing buildings or additions to existing nonconforming uses is not permitted....

Defendant's argument that case law prohibits a township from barring modernization of a noncon-forming use if it reduces the nonconformity is without merit.... [The case law upon which defendant relies] hinged on language within the ordinances which pro-hibited "structural alteration" of a nonconforming use. Neither alteration/modernization constituted a "structural change" within the respective ordinances. It does not follow that modernization of a noncon-forming use is allowed carte blanche regardless of the facts and the applicable zoning ordinance. This is particularly true in a case like this where the ordi-nance specifically controls the extent of modifications and repairs allowed.

* * *

Contrary to defendant's assertion, [the case law relied upon by defendant] does not hold that modifications of a nonconforming use are to be allowed if it reduces its nonconformities.... Here, the BTZO in no way pre-vents a billboard from being used or the investment destroyed.

More analogous to the present situation is the case of *Austin v Older*, 283 Mich 667; 278 NW 727 (1938), in which a gasoline station was a nonconforming use within an area zoned residential. The property owner was denied a permit to expand the structure in order to better compete with other gas stations. Our Supreme Court held that the denial was proper as "structural changes" were prohibited by the zoning ordinance even though normal business competition could, though the denial of the permit, eventually cause the plaintiff's property to be of little or no value for the sale of gasoline. The owner was still able to use the property for purposes permitted by the zoning ordinance....

The BTZO does not prohibit an owner from using, modernizing, or maintaining a billboard, but rather prevents modernization only if the proposed improve-ments exceed 30 per cent of the replacement value. While the improvement in *Austin* was denied because the owner wished to expand the nonconforming use by making structural changes prohibited by the zoning ordinance, the *Austin* Court found no fault with the potential for the permit denial to ultimately lead to the business closing as the property owner was still able to use the property for purposes permitted by the zoning ordinance. Section 20.08.3 of the BTZO still allows a property owner to maintain, modernize, and use the billboard.... Consequently, defendant is not entitled to relief.

Defendant's next argument relates to the trial court's determination that section 20.08.2 of the BTZO is an unconstitutional prior restraint on free speech. Defendant does not challenge the trial court's decision that a portion of section 20.08.2 of the BTZO is constitu-tionally invalid as it grants unbridled discretion to grant or deny permits for modifications to nonconforming bill-boards which do not bring those billboards into full com-pliance. However, defendant asserts that the trial court's remedy for the violation, i.e., the striking of the second sentence from section 20.08.2 and finding defendant in non compliance with section 20.08.3 of the BTZO, con-stitutes reversible error. We disagree.

Section 20.08.2 of the BTZO provides:

> The faces, supports, or other parts of any noncon-forming sign or billboard shall not be structurally changed, altered, substituted, or enlarged unless the resultant changed, altered, substituted, or enlarged sign or billboard conforms to the provision of this Article for the district in which it is located, except as otherwise provided in this Section.
>
> If the face, supports, or other parts of a non-conforming sign or billboard is structurally changed, altered, or substituted in a manner that reduces the nonconformity, the Zoning Administrator may approve the change.

The trial court applied the severance clause, section 1.07, and then determined that the final sentence of sec-tion 20.08.2 was invalid as the standards used to exercise discretion were too vague. Consequently, the trial court struck the offending sentence from the act. The trial court then noted that the cost of the changes and moder-nizations to the billboard exceeded 30 percent of the replacement cost of the old billboard. For that reason, and because the changes did not remove all nonconformi-ties, the trial court held that defendant's billboard violated section 20.08.3 and ordered the nuisance be abated.

In *Jott, Inc v Charter Twp of Clinton*, 224 Mich App 513; 569 NW2d 841 (1997), this Court stated:

> The doctrine of severability holds that statutes should be interpreted to sustain their constitutionality when it is possible to do so. Whenever a reviewing court may sustain an enactment by proper construction, it will uphold the parts which are separable from the repugnant provisions. To be capable of separate enforcement, the valid portion of the statute must be independent of the invalid sections, forming a complete act within itself. After separation of the valid parts o[f] the enactment, the law enforced

(Continued)

must be reasonable in view of the act as originally drafted. One test applied is whether the law-making body would have passed the statute had it been aware that portions therein would be declared to be invalid and, consequently, excised from the act....

The final sentence of section 20.08.2 can be severed from the ordinance in order to remove the portion which is unconstitutional. There is no evidence that any other section relied upon section 20.08.2. The removal of this sentence does not defeat the goal of eventually eliminating nonconforming uses. Standards remain in place for allowing modernization and repair of billboards. The valid portion of the ordinance can be read and enforced independently of the invalid portion and remains reasonable in view of the act as originally drafted....

Defendant argues that rather than severing the offending sentence, the trial court should have eliminated the need for discretionary permission from the zoning administrator, and left intact the ability to make any changes to a nonconforming billboard that reduce nonconformities. This argument is without merit. In making its argument, defendant erroneously relies on *Shuttlesworth v. Birmingham*, 394 US 147 ... (1969), to assert that the remedy for an unconstitutional permit scheme is to ignore it. In *Shuttlesworth*, 52 African-Americans were led out of a church by three ministers. The group marched down a street in an orderly fashion to protest the alleged denial of civil rights in the city. The police stopped and arrested the marchers for violation of an ordinance prohibiting demonstrations without a permit. The ordinance conferred upon the city commission practically unbridled discretion to prohibit any parade or demonstration guided by its own ideas of "public welfare, peace, safety, health, decency, good order, morals or convenience." ... The *Shuttlesworth* Court reversed the marchers' convictions, holding that it was clear to the leaders that under no circumstances would the group be allowed to demonstrate. In so holding, the Court noted:

> It is settled by a long line of recent decisions of this Court that an ordinance which, like this one, makes the peaceful enjoyment of freedoms which the Constitution guarantees contingent upon the uncontrolled will of an official—as by requiring a permit or license which may be granted or withheld in the discretion of such official—is an unconstitutional censorship or prior restraint upon the enjoyment of those freedoms." ... And our decisions have made clear that a person faced with such an unconstitutional licensing law may ignore it and engage with impunity in the exercise of the right of free expression for which the law purports to require a license. "The Constitution can hardly be thought to deny to one subjected to the restraints of such an

ordinance the right to attack its constitutionality, because he has not yielded to its demands." ...

Shuttlesworth is distinguishable on the facts. The BTZO places no restriction on the content of the speech; defendant is able to advertise all lawful commercial speech. Moreover, unlike in *Shuttlesworth* where the city commission made it clear a permit would never be issued, defendant here never sought a permit to modernize its billboard. *Shuttlesworth* cannot be interpreted as allowing defendant the right to ignore the ordinance requirements.

Finally, defendant challenges the requirement in section 20.07.3 that billboards be located 2,640 feet apart as constitutionally invalid. The trial court found that the enumerated purpose of the ordinance, to enhance the aesthetic desirability of the environment and reduce hazards to life and property in the township, satisfied the constitutional protections afforded commercial speech. We agree with the trial court's holding.

"The First Amendment, as applied to the States through the Fourteenth Amendment, protects commercial speech from unwarranted governmental regulation." ... A restriction on protected commercial speech is reviewed under a four-prong test:

> (1) The First Amendment protects commercial speech only if that speech concerns lawful activity and is not misleading. A restriction on otherwise protected commercial speech is valid only if it (2) seeks to implement a substantial governmental interest, (3) directly advances that interest, and (4) reaches no further than necessary to accomplish the given objective....

The burden of justifying a restriction on commercial speech is on the party seeking to uphold it....

In *Metromedia, Inc*, advertising companies filed suit to enjoin enforcement of the defendant's ordinance related to billboard advertising. The ordinance prohibited outdoor advertising display signs in order to "eliminate hazards to pedestrians and motorists brought about by distracting sign displays" and "to preserve and improve the appearance of the City[.]" ... The *Metromedia, Inc* Court found no issue with the first, second, and fourth prongs of the test, holding that the stated purposes of the ordinances, traffic safety and aesthetics, were substantial governmental goals.... The Court further noted that the defendant went no further than necessary to achieve its objectives and did not prohibit billboards outright but allowed onsite billboards and other specifically exempted signs. The Court determined that the ordinance directly advanced the governmental interests in traffic

(Continued)

safety and aesthetics, pointing out that "billboards are real and substantial hazards to traffic safety." ... Accordingly, the ordinance was found to directly advance the governmental interests of the defendant....

Applying the four-prong test set forth in *Metromedia, Inc*, it is clear that the BTZO's 2,640 foot spacing requirement passes constitutional muster. First, lawful commercial speech is involved. Second, the BTZO's goals of promoting aesthetic desirability of the environment and reducing hazards to life and property in Blair Township are of substantial governmental interest. Finally, the restrictions directly advance those interests and go no further than necessary to accomplish those objectives. Indeed, the requirements are less severe than those affirmed in *Metromedia, Inc*, as Blair Township does not ban billboards outright but rather restricts them based on size, placement, and general appearance. Defendant asserts that the record is devoid of proof that the distance requirement serves any aesthetic or public safety purpose. However, our courts have found as a matter of law that billboards are a substantial hazard to traffic safety.... Moreover, aesthetics alone have been found to be a sufficient reason to justify billboard regulations.... The trial court properly determined that the BTZO's spacing requirement was valid.

Judgment affirmed ....

Questions for Discussion

1. Do you think that nonconforming uses should be allowed to continue, so long as the use in question is not substantially altered? Should they be allowed to continue even if they are substantially altered? Why or why not?

2. How do billboards detract from the ability to engage with the natural environment? Should all interests be equally balanced? Why or why not?

3. Do you agree with this court that commercial speech is distinguishable from civil rights speech? Why or why not?

4. An exception to the zoned use is permitted on the condition that certain restrictions or conditions are met. These are special permit/conditional uses, and these exceptions are built into the original zoning ordinance. In contrast, nonconforming uses are generally grandfathered into the zoning code. *Derby Refining Co. v. City of Chelsea*[10] illustrates the rule that a valid nonconforming use does not lose that status merely because it is improved and made more efficient. How does *Township of Blair v. Lamar OCI North Corp.* differ from that rule?

5. *Department of Transportation v. Shiflett*[11] involved the Outdoor Advertising Control Act of 1971, which prohibited outdoor advertising within 660 feet of interstate and primary highways where visible from the road. When the Department of Transportation ordered the removal of the plaintiff's signs, the plaintiff claimed that the act unconstitutionally violated his freedom of expression. The court held that the act was constitutional because it sought to implement a substantial government interest. The legislative determination that billboards near highways diminished safety and the recreational value of public travel was rational, and the remedy was not more extensive than necessary to serve the government's interest. As billboards are commonly considered a nuisance that mars the landscape, why not use tort claims to remove billboards, instead of enacting a statutory scheme?

---

subdivision: Parcel of land divided into units.

planned unit development (PUD): A land development project that mixes land uses within the development.

Subdivision Regulations

A **subdivision** is a parcel of land that has been divided into two or more units. A **planned unit development** (**PUD**) is a development project that permits mixed uses or different types of housing within the same development. The developer needs to get local planning approval of the subdivision or PUD at the beginning

---

[10] 555 N.E.2d 534 (Mass. 1990).
[11] 310 S.E.2d 509 (Ga. 1984).

of the project, in a process that usually requires presentation of on-site plans for streets, sidewalks, and sewers, and possibly other items as well.

Deteriorating public infrastructure and explosive suburban growth have created tremendous fiscal problems for cities. Local governments must continue to maintain existing streets, water and sewage facilities, parks, and schools, and must provide for expanding development. Taxpayers expect the local government to provide these services, yet they resist property tax increases to fund these projects. For this reason, many municipalities rely on municipal exactions to fund off-site capital improvements and services. An **exaction** is a traditional construction, dedication, or in-lieu fee payment for site-specific needs such as streets, sidewalks, and drainage.

The benefits to local governments notwithstanding, subdivisions are difficult for developers to pursue in many jurisdictions. The permitting process can be very expensive and can take a very long time, and there is no guarantee to investors that such a project will be successful. The costs associated with developing land as a subdivision typically include environmental assessments, for example. Depending on the results of those assessments, a developer may simply choose not to move forward. Even if the results indicate that moving forward is feasible, the project may still meet with great opposition from neighboring property owners who are loathe to see another subdivision, particularly when it is located on presently undeveloped land.

exaction: A construction or dedication requirement, or in-lieu fee payment for site-specific needs (such as streets, sidewalks, and drainage) as a condition of approval in a development plan.

▪ ▪ ▪ REVIEW AND STUDY QUESTIONS

1. What is zoning? How is it an important tool for planners?
2. Describe the relationship between local and state governments in land use regulation schemes.
3. What is state police power? What types of things can state governments regulate through the use of this power?
4. What are the drawbacks of allowing private landowners unfettered use of their land? What are the drawbacks of allowing government to have too much authority over the use of privately held land?
5. Identify an issue in your community that relates to a land use proposal. Do you support the proposal or oppose it? How could you get involved in the process to block or to support the project?
6. Identify the different types of zoning in your community. Can you think of any use of land that the current zoning scheme does not permit?
7. How do zoning laws restrict our abilities to understand our environment? How do they expand those ideas?
8. Identify a nonconforming use in a particular zoning scheme in your community. Do you think that the nonconforming use should be grandfathered in (allowed to continue), or do you think that it should be removed entirely? Who are the stakeholders? Explain your position by comparing the benefits and drawbacks to allowing the nonconforming use to continue versus requiring it to be stopped or removed.
9. What is the difference between a variance and spot zoning? Do you think that variances should be allowed if spot zoning is not? Why or why not?
10. Identify a subdivision and a PUD in your community. Which do you believe is more environmentally friendly? Explain your reasoning.

▪ Constitutional Issues in Land Use Regulation

Historically, land use regulation has been a matter of local control. However, the environmental consequences of land development are not limited to one small jurisdictional unit. As a result, regional, state, and federal agencies have become increasingly involved in the approval of environmentally sensitive projects. The constitutional validity of agreements among such government entities may be tested in court through arguments based on a variety of theories, including takings, equal protection, due process, and separation of powers. Despite the fact that there is a trend toward regional or state planning, however, most planning and land use controls are still essentially local matters.

Zoning and Discrimination

Zoning ordinances are by definition discriminatory because they create distinctions based on classifications. A zoning ordinance may specify that certain uses require a minimum area, such as a one-acre lot in certain residential zones. Courts have looked to factors such as minimizing overcrowding, reducing the burden on public facilities like schools and water and sewer systems, and preserving the rural character of the area to support such classifications. However, if there is no relationship between the area requirements and a reasonable exercise of the police power, a court will find that the zoning is exclusionary and serves only private interests.

A difficult legal issue may arise when a zoning ordinance excludes certain kinds of uses altogether, such as commercial and industrial uses. Some courts have upheld such ordinances, but others have held that the local government unit must provide adequately for all types of uses within its confines. In Pennsylvania, the courts have taken the position that a township may not refuse to permit waste disposal facilities and quarrying operations altogether.[12]

An owner may also challenge a zoning ordinance on the grounds that the zoning ordinance was discriminatory as applied to that particular owner. In *Anderson v. Douglas County*,[13] a landowner brought suit against the county and zoning administrator, under federal civil rights statutes, claiming that their denial of permission to "thin spread" petroleum-contaminated soil violated his equal protection and due process rights. (*Thin-spreading* is a method of soil treatment by which petroleum-contaminated soil is incorporated into healthy, native soil to biodegrade the petroleum.) The district court granted the county's motion for summary judgment, and the landowner appealed. The agency's approval of thin-spreading in *Anderson* had been contingent on compliance with applicable zoning ordinances and approval by local authorities. The county planning and zoning commission had refused to issue a conditional use permit for the defendant. In upholding the commission's decision, the appeals court said:

> A party claiming a violation of equal protection must establish that he or she is "similarly situated" to other applicants for the license, permit, or other benefit being sought, particularly with respect to the same time period. Anderson failed to establish that similarly situated persons did not have to obtain conditional use permits.

---

[12] *See, e.g., Exton Quarries v. Zoning Board of Adjustment*, 425 Pa. 43, 228 A.2d 169 (1967).
[13] 4 F.3d 574 (8th Cir. 1993).

The court also found that the county's decision to require a conditional use permit for thin-spreading was not irrational because it was clearly related to public health, safety, or welfare concerns.

Historical Viewpoint: *Racial Discrimination and Restrictive Covenants*

Go to the website "Racial Restrictive Covenants" at www.depts.washington.edu/civilr/covenants.htm, to accompany this discussion.

Discrimination on the basis of race has been prohibited by law for decades. However, there are substantial historical instances in which racial discrimination occurred regularly. The Racial Restrictive Covenants website describes "racial restrictions" in housing. These restrictions (and any restrictions like them) would be absolutely illegal today, because they would violate both federal and state law.

Some people allege that racial discrimination still occurs in contracts. You can find a story related to racial discrimination in the mortgage industry at www.nytimes.com/2009/06/07/us/07baltimore.html

Questions for Discussion

1. If the latter story is true and actual discriminatory practices were occurring, what should the remedy be?

2. Are you surprised to learn about racial restrictive covenants? Should reparations be made to persons who were affected by such covenants? What about to those persons' descendants? Why or why not?

3. View the Seattle neighborhood database from the Racial Restrictive Covenants website. Reflect on how our law or legal system can be used to promote or to hinder civil society.

Land Use Regulation and the "Takings" Issue

One common legal issue in property law is the appropriate relationship between the rights of private property owners and the obligation of government to regulate land use for the protection of the public good. This is an important matter to environmentalists, property owners, public officials, and society in general.

The government can control land use in different ways. Most obviously, the government itself owns and controls a vast amount of the nation's total acreage. It can create growth plans and, in tandem with local governments, create zoning restrictions, as discussed previously in this chapter. Additionally, the government can acquire privately owned land through its power of eminent domain, one of the major powers of sovereignty.

The desire to protect environmentally sensitive areas like wetlands, floodplains, and beachfront property has led to the adoption of state and federal regulations to limit development in such areas. Private property owners sometimes challenge such environmental laws by claiming an unconstitutional **taking** of their property in violation of the Fifth Amendment to the United States Constitution (which applies to the states through the Fourteenth Amendment). The word *taking* comes from the Fifth Amendment, which states: ["No person shall be …] deprived of life, liberty, or property, without due process of law; nor shall private property be taken for public use, without just compensation."

taking: Government seizure or regulation of property that deprives the property owner of all economic value from the property.

Fifth Amendment Requirements

The Fifth Amendment recognizes that a basic characteristic of government is its power to protect the health, safety, and general welfare of its citizens.

Under the language of the amendment, a government can take title to private property in order to use it for a public purpose (for example, a park or a school). This power, which is called the power of **eminent domain**, is also established in various state constitutions. Legal actions brought under the power of eminent domain are called **condemnation proceedings**. A condemnation proceeding is the legal process by which government exercises its right of eminent domain and acquires private land for a public use. No specific procedure is dictated by due process, and condemnation procedures vary from state to state.

The government must meet the requirements of the Fifth Amendment in order to validly exercise its power of eminent domain. First, the government must establish that the taking is necessary for a public use. In general, the public use requirement is rarely a problem in takings cases because the courts have consistently interpreted it broadly. Indeed, the courts understand *public use* to mean *public purpose*. The government's action must also be rationally related to a legitimate public purpose. As some of the remaining cases in this chapter illustrate, the understanding of what constitutes a public use has undergone tremendous expansion, and the exact definition of the term is elusive.

When it exercises its power of eminent domain under the Fifth Amendment, the government must pay just compensation for the property taken. However, for government to be required to pay a landowner compensation under the doctrine of eminent domain, it must be established that the government has actually taken the property, as opposed to merely regulating it.

When the government takes title to a piece of property under its eminent domain power, courts usually use a test of fair market value at the time of the taking to determine just compensation. (*Fair market value* is what a willing buyer would pay in cash to a willing seller.) If the courts find that a taking has occurred in a regulatory takings case, the question of just compensation may raise difficult valuation problems. Should courts consider the diminished value of the regulated portion of the property only or consider the value of the parcel as a whole? Should ecological values to the public be considered in determining just compensation to the private landowner in such cases?

Regulatory Takings

The requirements of the Fifth Amendment apply only in cases where there has been a taking of property; this is seldom an issue when a government exercises its traditional power of eminent domain and actually takes title to private property. In some cases, however, a property owner may argue that the government's regulation so deprives the owner of the use and value of the property that it constitutes a taking for purposes of the Fifth Amendment, even though the government has not taken ownership.

The idea that government regulation could constitute a compensable taking developed in the 20th century. In 1922, the Supreme Court considered the problem in *Pennsylvania Coal Co. v. Mahon*.[14] In that case, a coal company challenged a state law forbidding the mining of anthracite coal in such a way that would cause the subsidence of surface structures. In that case, Justice Holmes stated the often-cited maxim: "The general rule at least is that while property may be regulated to a certain extent, if regulation goes too far it will be recognized as a taking."

eminent domain: The power of the government to take property for public use; requires the payment of just compensation to the owner of the property taken.

condemnation proceeding: The legal process by which a government exercises the right of eminent domain and acquires private land for public use.

---

[14] 260 U.S. 393 (1922).

The difficulty—one that has not been satisfactorily resolved by the courts—is how to establish rules to identify when a regulation has gone "too far." In *Village of Euclid*, the landmark zoning case discussed previously, the Supreme Court held that "mere regulation" of property does not constitute a taking for purposes of the Fifth Amendment. Nevertheless, some regulations may effectively deprive an owner of all economic value of its property and thus constitute a taking.

The courts continue to struggle to establish standards for determining when a taking, as opposed to "mere regulation," has occurred. It seems settled that a regulation may cause substantial diminution in the value of land, but still not constitute a taking if the owner can still use the land for some economic benefit. However, a regulation that totally deprives the owner of any economic use of its property will likely constitute a taking. At what point does government's regulation of private property so deprive an owner of the value and use of its property that the government action constitutes a taking of property under the Fifth Amendment (Figure 6.1)?

The question arises in challenges to land use regulations (either on their face or as applied to a particular landowner) that substantially diminish the value of property by limiting or prohibiting use or development. Zoning and floodplain regulations, permit requirements for wetlands development, and floodplain building restrictions are but a few examples of the kinds of restrictions that may give rise to a takings challenge.

In the following case, property owners challenged a decision of the California Coastal Commission because it had imposed a condition that the owners grant public access to the beachfront before it would grant permission for the owners to rebuild their beach house. The owners, the Nollans, appealed the commission's ruling, and the California Court of Appeals rejected their claim that the condition violated the takings clause. The U.S. Supreme Court agreed to review the case. As you will read, the U.S. Supreme Court held that the state's imposition of the condition of an easement on the granting of a building permit constituted a taking for which it had to compensate the landowners, because the condition placed on the building permit was unrelated to the state's purposes of reducing obstacles to public viewing and use of beaches.

■ **FIGURE 6.1**   *The Balance between Regulatory Taking and Regulation*

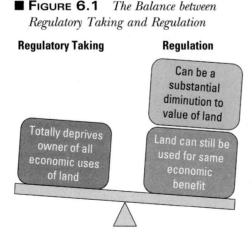

Regulatory Taking

Regulation

Can be a substantial diminution to value of land

Totally deprives owner of all economic uses of land

Land can still be used for same economic benefit

Nollan v. California Coastal Commission

483 U.S. 825 (1987)

JUSTICE SCALIA Delivered the Opinion of the Court

* * *

The Nollans own a beachfront lot in Ventura County, California. A quarter-mile north of their property is Faria County Park, an oceanside public park with a public beach and recreation area. Another public beach area, known locally as "the Cove," lies 1,800 feet south of their lot. A concrete seawall approximately eight feet high separates the beach portion of the Nollans' property from the rest of the lot. The historic mean high tide line determines the lot's oceanside boundary.

The Nollans originally leased their property with an option to buy. The building on the lot was a small bungalow, totaling 504 square feet, which for a time they rented to summer vacationers. After years of rental use, however, the building had fallen into disrepair, and could no longer be rented out.

The Nollans' option to purchase was conditioned on their promise to demolish the bungalow and replace it. In order to do so, ... they were required to obtain a coastal development permit from the California Coastal Commission. On February 25, 1982, they submitted a permit application to the Commission in which they proposed to demolish the existing structure and replace it with a three-bedroom house in keeping with the rest of the neighborhood.

The Nollans were informed that ... the Commission staff had recommended that the permit be granted subject to the condition that they allow the public an easement to pass across a portion of their property bounded by the mean high tide line on one side and their seawall on the other side. This would make it easier for the public to get to Faria County Park and the Cove. The Nollans protested imposition of the condition, but the Commission overruled their objections and granted the permit subject to their recordation of a deed restriction granting the easement....

* * *

Had California simply required the Nollans to make an easement across their beachfront available to the public on a permanent basis in order to increase public access to the beach, rather than conditioning their permit to rebuild their house on their agreeing to do so, we have no doubt there would have been a taking. To say that the appropriation of a public easement across a landowner's premises does not constitute the taking of a property interest but rather (as Justice Brennan contends) "a mere restriction on its use," ... is to use words in a manner that deprives them of all their ordinary meaning. Indeed, one of the principal uses of the eminent domain power is to assure that the government be able to require conveyance of just such interests, so long as it pays for them....

* * *

Given, then, that requiring uncompensated conveyance of the easement outright would violate the Fourteenth Amendment, the question becomes whether requiring it to be conveyed as a condition for issuing a land use permit alters the outcome. We have long recognized that land use regulation does not effect a taking if it "substantially advance[s] legitimate state interests" and does not "den[y] an owner economically viable use of his land ... ." Our cases have not elaborated on the standards for determining what constitutes a "legitimate state interest" or what type of connection between the regulation and the state interest satisfies the requirement that the former "substantially advance" the latter.... They have made clear, however, that a broad range of governmental purposes and regulations satisfies these requirements.... The Commission argues that among these permissible purposes are protecting the public's ability to see the beach, assisting the public in overcoming the "psychological barrier" to using the beach created by a developed shorefront, and preventing congestion on the public beaches. We assume, without deciding, that this is so—in which case the Commission unquestionably would be able to deny the Nollans their permit outright if their new house (alone, or by reason of the cumulative impact produced in conjunction with other construction) ... would substantially impede these purposes, unless the denial would interfere so drastically with the Nollans' use of their property as to constitute a taking....

The Commission argues that a permit condition that serves the same legitimate police power purpose as a refusal to issue the permit should not be found to be a taking if the refusal to issue the permit would not constitute a taking. We agree. Thus, if the Commission attached to the permit some condition that would have protected the public's ability to see the beach notwithstanding construction of the new house—for example, a height limitation, a width restriction, or a ban on fences—so long as the Commission could have

(Continued)

exercised its police power (as we have assumed it could) to forbid construction of the house altogether, imposition of the condition would also be constitutional. Moreover (and here we come closer to the facts of the present case), the condition would be constitutional even if it consisted of the requirement that the Nollans provide a viewing spot on their property for passersby with whose sighting of the ocean their new house would interfere. Although such a requirement, constituting a permanent grant of continuous access to the property, would have to be considered a taking if it were not attached to a development permit, the Commission's assumed power to forbid construction of the house in order to protect the public's view of the beach must surely include the power to condition construction upon some concession by the owner, even a concession of property rights, that serves the same end. If a prohibition designed to accomplish that purpose would be a legitimate exercise of the police power, rather than a taking, it would be strange to conclude that providing the owner an alternative to that prohibition which accomplishes the same purpose is not.

The evident constitutional propriety disappears, however, if the condition substituted for the prohibition utterly fails to further the end advanced as the justification for the prohibition. When that essential nexus is eliminated, the situation becomes the same as if California law forbade shouting fire in a crowded theater, but granted dispensations to those willing to contribute $100 to the state treasury.... [T]he lack of nexus between the condition and the original purpose of the building restriction converts that purpose to something other than what it was. The purpose then becomes, quite simply, the obtaining of an easement to serve some valid governmental purpose, but without payment of compensation. Whatever may be the outer limits of "legitimate state interests" in the takings and land use context, this is not one of them. In short, unless the permit condition serves the same governmental purpose as the development ban, the building restriction is not a valid regulation of land use but "an out and out plan of extortion." ...

The Commission claims that it concedes as much, and that we may sustain the condition at issue here by finding that it is reasonably related to the public need or burden that the Nollans' new house creates or to which it contributes. We can accept, for purposes of discussion, the Commission's proposed test as to how close a "fit" between the condition and the burden is required, because we find that this case does not meet even the most untailored standards. The Commission's principal contention to the contrary essentially turns on

a play on the word "access." The Nollans' new house, the Commission found, will interfere with "visual access" to the beach. That in turn (along with other shorefront development) will interfere with the desire of people who drive past the Nollans' house to use the beach, thus creating a "psychological barrier" to "access." The Nollans' new house will also, by a process not altogether clear from the Commission's opinion but presumably potent enough to more than offset the effects of the psychological barrier, increase the use of the public beaches, thus creating the need for more "access." These burdens on "access" would be alleviated by a requirement that the Nollans provide "lateral access" to the beach.

Rewriting the argument to eliminate the play on words makes clear that there is nothing to it. It is quite impossible to understand how a requirement that people already on the public beaches be able to walk across the Nollans' property reduces any obstacles to viewing the beach created by the new house. It is also impossible to understand how it lowers any "psychological barrier" to using the public beaches, or how it helps to remedy any additional congestion on them caused by construction of the Nollans' new house. We therefore find that the Commission's imposition of the permit condition cannot be treated as an exercise of its land use power for any of these purposes....

* * *

[The judgment is] Reversed.

Questions for Discussion

1. In this case, the Court said that there must be an "essential nexus" between a regulation and its purpose, and that in *Nollan* this "essential nexus" was not met. According to Justice Scalia, the commission found that the Nollans' new house would interfere with "visual access" to the beach; but it was impossible to understand how a requirement that people already on the public beach be able to walk across the Nollans' property would reduce any obstacles to viewing the beach created by the new house. Do you agree with Justice Scalia? Why or why not?

2. In his dissent in *Nollan*, Justice Brennan wrote:

   > The Commission's determination that certain types of development jeopardize public access to the ocean, and that such development should be conditioned on preservation of access, is the essence of responsible land use planning. The Court's use of an unreasonably demanding standard for determining the rationality of state regulation in this area

(Continued)

thus could hamper innovative efforts to preserve an increasingly fragile national resource.

What public policy concerns underlie the debate between the majority and dissent in this case? Do you agree that the Nollans should be compensated in this case under a takings theory? What are the implications of your answer?

3. In *Dolan v. City of Tigard*,[15] a city planning commission conditioned approval of the petitioner's application to expand her store and pave her parking lot upon her compliance (1) with dedication of land for a public greenway along a nearby creek to minimize flooding that would be exacerbated by her development and (2) for a pedestrian/bicycle pathway intended to relieve traffic congestion in the central business district. The petitioner appealed, alleging that the land dedication requirements were not related to the proposed development and therefore constituted an uncompensated taking of her property

under the Fifth Amendment. The U.S. Supreme Court held that the city's dedication requirements constituted an uncompensated taking of property. Justice Rehnquist, writing for the majority, said that the government may not require a person to give up a constitutional right in exchange for a discretionary benefit conferred by the government where the property sought has little or no relationship to the benefit, and that under *Nollan v. California Coastal Commission*, there was no essential nexus between a legitimate state interest and the permit condition. (The *Nollan* and *Dolan* cases are often referred to together.)

Do you agree with this decision? How can a government entity protect environmental attributes and encourage environmentally friendly behavior (such as bicycling), when the takings clause requires just compensation to property owners when such demands are made?

Takings Analysis: When Does a Taking Occur?

Rather than formulating precise rules for determining when a regulatory taking occurs, the courts have chosen to make an ad hoc factual inquiry in each such case. The Supreme Court has identified the following factors to be used in determining whether a regulation is a taking:

1. The economic impact of the regulation, with particular regard to the extent to which the regulation "has interfered with distinct investment backed expectation"
2. The character of the public activity; for example, a physical invasion will more readily be identified as a taking than a regulation that merely adjusts "the benefits and burden of economic life to promote the common good"
3. The history of sustaining reasonable police-power regulations that destroyed or adversely affected recognized real property interests, and that have been viewed as permissible government action (for example, zoning cases)[16]

In 2012, the U.S. Supreme Court discussed when a taking occurs in *Arkansas Game & Fish Commission v. United States*.[17] Justice Ginsburg explained:[18]

The Takings Clause is "designed to bar Government from forcing some people alone to bear public burdens which, in all fairness and justice, should be borne by the public as a whole."[19] And "[w]hen the government physically takes possession of an interest in property for some public purpose, it has a categorical duty to compensate the former owner."[20] These guides are fundamental in our Takings Clause jurisprudence. We have recognized, however, that no magic formula

[15] 512 U.S. 374 (1994).
[16] *Penn Central Transportation Co. v. New York City*, 438 U.S. 104 (1978).
[17] 568 U.S. ___, 133 S. Ct. 511, 184 L. Ed. 2d 417 (2012).
[18] Citations within this quoted material have been removed to footnotes.
[19] "... *See also Penn Central Transp. Co. v. New York City*, 438 U.S. 104, 123–125 (1978)."
[20] "*Tahoe-Sierra Preservation Council, Inc. v. Tahoe Regional Planning Agency*, 535 U.S. 302, 322 (2002) (citing *United States v. Pewee Coal Co.*, 341 U.S. 114, 115 (1951))."

enables a court to judge, in every case, whether a given government interference with property is a taking. In view of the nearly infinite variety of ways in which government actions or regulations can affect property interests, the Court has recognized few invariable rules in this area.

True, we have drawn some bright lines, notably, the rule that a permanent physical occupation of property authorized by government is a taking.[21] So, too, is a regulation that permanently requires a property owner to sacrifice all economically beneficial uses of his or her land.[22] But aside from the cases attended by rules of this order, most takings claims turn on situation-specific factual inquiries.[23]

Temporary Takings versus Moratoria on Development

In 1987, in *First English Evangelical Lutheran Church of Glendale v. County of Los Angeles*,[24] a majority of the Supreme Court held that the church was entitled to damages for a temporary taking when Los Angeles County adopted an ordinance prohibiting the church's campsite structures within a flood protection area. The Court held that the ordinance, which denied the church of "all use of its property" for a period of years, required the government to compensate the church for this loss. Several justices dissented in this case on the ground that the decision was a "loose cannon" that would ignite a litigation explosion. The Court remanded the case to the California Court of Appeals, which subsequently found that the ordinance did not deny the appellant *all* use of its property and was a "reasonable moratorium for a reasonable period of time."

In 2002, in *Tahoe-Sierra Preservation Council, Inc. v. Tahoe Regional Planning Agency*,[25] the U.S. Supreme Court held that a regulatory moratorium on development did not constitute a taking at all. In that case, a regional planning council issued a moratorium prohibiting residential development in the fragile environment at issue until a comprehensive development plan could be completed.

In *Lucas v. South Carolina Coastal Council*,[26] a majority of the U.S. Supreme Court reaffirmed its holding in *First Evangelical Church*. In *Lucas*, the South Carolina legislature had enacted a law requiring a landowner to obtain a permit before developing any coastal land located within a "critical area" designated by the act. In 1986, Lucas had purchased two residential lots that he intended to develop. He paid $975,000 for the lots. At that time, neither was located in the "critical area" and so no permit was required. In 1988, however, the state legislature enacted the Beachfront Management Act, which expanded the "critical area" covered by the act; the new act thus prohibited construction of any occupiable improvements on Lucas's lots.

In his lawsuit, Lucas claimed that the act denied him all economically viable use of his property and thus constituted a taking. The trial court agreed, and awarded him compensation in the amount of $1,232,387.50. The government appealed and the South Carolina Supreme Court reversed, because in its opinion no compensation was required for a land use regulation designed to prevent serious public harm. Lucas, the landowner, appealed to the U.S. Supreme Court.

---

[21] "*Loretto v. Teleprompter Manhattan CATV Corp.*, 458 U.S. 419, 426 (1982)."
[22] "*Lucas v. South Carolina Coastal Council*, 505 U.S. 1003, 1019 (1992)."
[23] "See *Penn Central*, 438 U.S., at 124."
[24] 482 U.S. 304 (1987).
[25] 535 U.S. 302 (2002).
[26] 505 U.S. 1003, 112 S. Ct. 2886 (1992).

Lucas v. South Carolina Coastal Council
505 U.S. 1003 (1992)

* * *

Prior to Justice Holmes' exposition in *Pennsylvania Coal Co. v. Mahon*, 260 U.S. 393 (1922), it was generally thought that the Takings Clause reached only a "direct appropriation" of property, ... or the functional equivalent of a "practical ouster of [the owner's] possession." ... Justice Holmes recognized in *Mahon*, however, that if the protection against physical appropriations of private property was to be meaningfully enforced, the government's power to redefine the range of interests included in the ownership of property was necessarily constrained by constitutional limits.... If, instead, the uses of private property were subject to unbridled, uncompensated qualification under the police power, "the natural tendency of human nature [would be] to extend the qualification more and more until at last private property disappear[ed]." ... These considerations gave birth in that case to the oft-cited maxim that, "while property may be regulated to a certain extent, if regulation goes too far it will be recognized as a taking." ...

Nevertheless, our decision in *Mahon* offered little insight into when, and under what circumstances, a given regulation would be seen as going "too far" for purposes of the Fifth Amendment. In 70-odd years of succeeding "regulatory takings" jurisprudence, we have generally eschewed any "'set formula'" for determining how far is too far, preferring to "engag[e] in ... essentially ad hoc, factual inquiries." ... We have, however, described at least two discrete categories of regulatory action as compensable without case-specific inquiry into the public interest advanced in support of the restraint. The first encompasses regulations that compel the property owner to suffer a physical "invasion" of his property. In general (at least with regard to permanent invasion), no matter how minute the intrusion, and no matter how weighty the public purpose behind it, we have required compensation....

The second situation in which we have found categorical treatment appropriate is where regulation denies all economically beneficial or productive use of land.... As we have said on numerous occasions, the Fifth Amendment is violated when land-use regulation "does not substantially advance legitimate state interests *or denies an owner economically viable use of his land*" [emphasis by the Court]....

* * *

The trial court found Lucas's two beachfront lots to have been rendered valueless by respondent's enforcement of the coastal-zone construction ban.... Under Lucas's theory of the case, which rested upon our "no economically viable use" statements, that finding entitled him to compensation. Lucas believed it unnecessary to take issue with either the purposes behind the Beachfront Management Act, or the means chosen by the South Carolina Legislature to effectuate those purposes. The South Carolina Supreme Court, however, thought otherwise. In its view, the Beachfront Management Act was no ordinary enactment, but involved the exercise of South Carolina's "police powers" to mitigate the harm to the public interest that petitioner's use of his land might occasion....

It is correct that many of our prior opinions have suggested that "harmful or noxious uses" of property may be proscribed by government regulation without the requirement of compensation. For a number of reasons, however, we think the South Carolina Supreme Court was too quick to conclude that that principle decides the present case....

* * *

Where the State seeks to sustain regulation that deprives land of all economically beneficial use, we think it may resist compensation only if the logically antecedent inquiry into the nature of the owner's estate shows that the proscribed use interests were not part of his title to begin with.... This accords, we think, with our "takings" jurisprudence, which has traditionally been guided by the understandings of our citizens regarding the content of, and the State's power over, the "bundle of rights" that they acquire when they obtain title to property. It seems to us that the property owner necessarily expects the uses of his property to be restricted, from time to time, by various measures newly enacted by the State in legitimate exercise of its police powers; "[a]s long recognized, some values are enjoyed under an implied limitation and must yield to the police power." ... In the case of land,... we think the notion pressed by the Council that title is somehow held subject to the "implied limitation" that the State may subsequently

(Continued)

eliminate all economically valuable use is inconsistent with the historical compact recorded in the Takings Clause that has become part of our constitutional culture....

* * *

The "total taking" inquiry we require today will ordinarily entail (as the application of state nuisance law ordinarily entails) analysis of, among other things, the degree of harm to public lands and resources, or adjacent private property, posed by the claimant's proposed activities,... the social value of the claimant's activities and their suitability to the locality in question,... and the relative ease with which the alleged harm can be avoided through measures taken by the claimant and the government ....

It seems unlikely that common-law principles would have prevented the erection of any habitable or productive improvements on petitioner's land; they rarely support prohibition of the "essential use" of land .... The question, however, is one of state law to be dealt with on remand.... South Carolina must identify background principles of nuisance and property law that prohibit the uses [Lucas] now intends in the circumstances in which the property is presently found. Only on this showing can the State fairly claim that, in proscribing all such beneficial uses, the Beachfront Management Act is taking nothing....

* * *

The judgment is reversed, and the case is remanded ....

Questions for Discussion

1. Two categories of takings identified by the Supreme Court in *Lucas* are physical taking of property, such as a requirement by the government that a property owner create a physical refuge for endangered species; and regulatory deprivation of all economic uses, which is a form of inverse condemnation. Can you give a hypothetical example of each?

2. The "public purpose" in *Lucas* was protection of the coastal zone area. Did the Supreme Court challenge the state's power to pass the Beachfront Management Act under its police power? Why or why not?

3. Police-power regulations are presumably valid if they leave the owner with some "economically viable" use of the land. Justice Blackmun's dissent

noted that "[the majority] creates its new takings jurisprudence based on the trial court's finding that the property had lost all economic value. This finding is almost certainly erroneous. Petitioner still can enjoy other attributes of ownership, such as the right to exclude others, 'one of the most essential sticks in the bundle of rights that are commonly characterized as property.' ... Petitioner can picnic, swim, camp in a tent, or live on the property in a movable trailer. State courts frequently have recognized that land has economic value where the only residual economic uses are recreation or camping.... Petitioner also retains the right to alienate the land, which would have value for neighbors and for those prepared to enjoy proximity to the ocean without a house." Isn't Justice Blackmun correct? Couldn't Lucas pitch a tent on his property and camp? How should *economic viability* be defined?

4. In some cases, the question of economic viability turns on whether the loss is measured by determining the loss for the entire parcel of property, or only the regulated portion. For example, in *Keystone Bituminous Coal Association v. Pennsylvania*[27] (another case involving a Pennsylvania statute requiring coal companies to provide underground support for the surface), the Supreme Court said that the takings test should be based on an entire coal field owned by petitioners and not just the coal pillars the companies were not allowed to mine.

5. One very important aspect of the *Lucas* case is its acceptance of a "nuisance exception." This, presumably, is an exception that permits the government to prevent a misuse or illegal use of property without the government action constituting a taking. In other words, a regulation may still survive a takings challenge if the proposed uses of the property contravene traditional notions and limitations found in state property law. A fundamental concern about the nuisance exception is the fact that it is based retroactively on state law. How should *nuisance* be defined? If this is purely a matter of state law, does nuisance refer only to acts recognized as nuisances in the past? Should a law that prohibited a person from killing all wildlife and flora and fauna on his land constitute a taking, or would it fall under a nuisance exception?

(Continued)

---

[27] 480 U.S. 470 (1987).

Note that Justice Kennedy concurred in the *Lucas* judgment but disagreed with the nuisance exception. He concluded that the test should be whether the "deprivation is contrary to the property owner's reasonable, investment-backed expectations."

Note also that, on remand, the South Carolina State Supreme Court concluded that there was no common law basis on which to restrain Lucas's desired use, and therefore it remanded the case to the trial court for the purpose of determining damages as a result of the state's temporary taking of the property.

6. The valuation of property in regulatory takings cases raises some significant policy problems.

Some courts, when looking at the diminution in value of the property, follow the theory that if the owner's ability to profit from the property has been severely diminished, the landowner is entitled to compensation. The issue of just compensation has been addressed by some proposed bills in Congress, which would compensate private property owners for regulatory takings for a particular percentage loss in the value of their property. How should property be valued in regulatory takings cases in which the landowners retain a fee simple absolute interest (if that is what they originally had) in the property, but are simply prohibited from using the property as they might have wished to?

Regulatory taking problems are tricky. Points of view differ depending on how a person weighs private property rights vis-à-vis public rights. One option would be for the Court to declare that land use regulation never constitutes a taking if the regulation is reasonably related to a valid public purpose. An opposing viewpoint is that concept of private property is sacred, and that the law should not authorize any violation of those rights.

Another interesting question is the extent of public rights vesting. If certain public rights—such as the protection of habitat for wildlife, or the protection of shoreline or wetlands—vest in the public, then a private property owner could not sue for a "taking" of a right that it never actually had. These rights might be developed or recognized under the **public trust doctrine**, for example. The public trust doctrine is an ancient concept which recognizes that certain property or resources are held for the public and states that the government may not convey those properties or resources to other parties (especially private parties). The government must hold them for the benefit of the public.

Factors that figure into any takings analysis include the public interest, the public harm, the interest of the landowner, the severity of loss to the landowner, and whether the regulation is a valid exercise of police power. In the following case, landowners who wished to build residential homes on their property, which was located in a fragile ecosystem, brought a claim against the government for a taking alleged to have occurred when the government imposed a moratorium on residential development while a comprehensive land use plan was created. The U.S. Supreme Court disagreed that regulations imposing a moratorium on building was a taking per se; it held that the determination of whether a taking had occurred depended upon several factors, including the landowners' expectations and the importance of the public interests involved. To adopt a rule that made any deprivation of all economic uses a compensable taking would "impose unreasonable financial obligations on governments for the normal delays involved in processing land use applications."

public trust doctrine: Legal theory stating that a government may not convey property or resources held for the public to private parties.

Tahoe-Sierra Preservation Council, Inc. v. Tahoe Regional Planning Agency

535 U.S. 302, 122 S. Ct. 1465 (2002)

Justice Stevens Delivered the Opinion of the Court

The question presented is whether a moratorium on development imposed during the process of devising a comprehensive land-use plan constitutes a *per se* taking of property requiring compensation under the Takings Clause of the United States Constitution.... This case actually involves two moratoria ordered by respondent Tahoe Regional Planning Agency (TRPA) to maintain the status quo while studying the impact of development on Lake Tahoe and designing a strategy for environmentally sound growth.... As a result of these two directives, virtually all development on a substantial portion of the property subject to TRPA's jurisdiction was prohibited for a period of 32 months. Although the question we decide relates only to that 32-month period, a brief description of the events leading up to the moratoria and a comment on the two permanent plans that TRPA adopted thereafter will clarify the narrow scope of our holding.

... All agree that Lake Tahoe is "uniquely beautiful,"... that President Clinton was right to call it a "'national treasure that must be protected and preserved,'" ... and that Mark Twain aptly described the clarity of its waters as "'not *merely* transparent, but dazzlingly, brilliantly so,'" ... (quoting M. Twain, Roughing It 174–175 (1872)).

Lake Tahoe's exceptional clarity is attributed to the absence of algae that obscures the waters of most other lakes. Historically, the lack of nitrogen and phosphorous, which nourish the growth of algae, has ensured the transparency of its waters. [Fn. by the Court: According to a Senate Report: "Only two other sizable lakes in the world are of comparable quality—Crater Lake in Oregon, which is protected as part of the Crater Lake National Park, and Lake Baikal in the [former] Soviet Union. Only Lake Tahoe, however, is so readily accessible from large metropolitan centers and is so adaptable to urban development." S. Rep. No. 91-510, pp. 3–4 (1969).] Unfortunately, the lake's pristine state has deteriorated rapidly over the past 40 years; increased land development in the Lake Tahoe Basin (Basin) has threatened the "'noble sheet of blue water'" beloved by Twain and countless others.... As the District Court found, "dramatic decreases in clarity first began to be noted in the 1950's/early 1960's, shortly after development at the lake began in earnest." ... The lake's unsurpassed beauty, it seems, is the wellspring of its undoing.

The upsurge of development in the area has caused "increased nutrient loading of the lake largely because of the increase in impervious coverage of land in the Basin resulting from that development." ...

"Impervious coverage—such as asphalt, concrete, buildings, and even packed dirt—prevents precipitation from being absorbed by the soil. Instead, the water is gathered and concentrated by such coverage. Larger amounts of water flowing off a driveway or a roof have more erosive force than scattered raindrops falling over a dispersed area—especially one covered with indigenous vegetation, which softens the impact of the raindrops themselves." ...

Given this trend, the District Court predicted that "unless the process is stopped, the lake will lose its clarity and its trademark blue color, becoming green and opaque for eternity."[Fn. by the Court: The District Court added: "Or at least, for a very, very long time. Estimates are that, should the lake turn green, it could take over 700 years for it to return to its natural state, if that were ever possible at all." ...]

* * *

... [Regulatory and judicial acts] prohibited new construction on sensitive lands in the Basin. As the case comes to us, however, we have no occasion to consider the validity of those provisions.

... The petitioners ... purchased their properties ... primarily for the purpose of constructing "at a time of their choosing" a single-family home "to serve as a permanent, retirement or vacation residence" .... When they made those purchases, they did so with the understanding that such construction was authorized provided that "they complied with all reasonable requirements for building." ...

* * *

... In our view the answer to the abstract question whether a temporary moratorium effects a taking is neither "yes, always" nor "no, never"; the answer depends upon the particular circumstances of the case....

The text of the Fifth Amendment itself provides a basis for drawing a distinction between physical takings and regulatory takings. Its plain language requires the payment of compensation whenever the government

(Continued)

acquires private property for a public purpose, whether the acquisition is the result of a condemnation proceeding or a physical appropriation. But the Constitution contains no comparable reference to regulations that prohibit a property owner from making certain uses of her private property.[Fn. by the Court: In determining whether government action affecting property is an unconstitutional deprivation of ownership rights under the Just Compensation Clause, a court must interpret the word "taken." When the government condemns or physically appropriates the property, the fact of a taking is typically obvious and undisputed. When, however, the owner contends a taking has occurred because a law or regulation imposes restrictions so severe that they are tantamount to a condemnation or appropriation, the predicate of a taking is not self-evident, and the analysis is more complex.] Our jurisprudence involving condemnations and physical takings is as old as the Republic and, for the most part, involves the straightforward application of *per se* rules. Our regulatory takings jurisprudence, in contrast, is of more recent vintage and is characterized by "essentially ad hoc, factual inquiries," *Penn Central*, 438 U.S. at 124, designed to allow "careful examination and weighing of all the relevant circumstances." ...

When the government physically takes possession of an interest in property for some public purpose, it has a categorical duty to compensate the former owner,... regardless of whether the interest that is taken constitutes an entire parcel or merely a part thereof. Thus, compensation is mandated when a leasehold is taken and the government occupies the property for its own purposes, even though that use is temporary.... Similarly, when the government appropriates part of a rooftop in order to provide cable TV access for apartment tenants, *Loretto v. Teleprompter Manhattan CATV Corp.*, 458 U.S. 419 [102 S. Ct. 316, 473 L. Ed. 2d 868] (1982); or when its planes use private airspace to approach a government airport, *United States v. Causby*, 328 U.S. 256 [66 S. Ct. 1062, 90 L. Ed. 1206] (1946), it is required to pay for that share no matter how small. But a government regulation that merely prohibits landlords from evicting tenants unwilling to pay a higher rent, *Block v. Hirsh*, 256 U.S. 135 [41 S. Ct. 458, 65 L. Ed. 865] (1921); that bans certain private uses of a portion of an owner's property, *Village of Euclid v. Ambler Realty Co.*, 272 U.S. 365 [47 S. Ct. 114, 71 L. Ed. 303] (1926); ... or that forbids the private use of certain airspace, *Penn Central Transp. Co. v. New York City*, 438 U.S. 104 [98 S. Ct. 2646, 57 L. Ed. 2d 631] (1978), does not constitute a categorical taking. "The first category of cases requires courts to apply a clear rule; the second

necessarily entails complex factual assessments of the purposes and economic effects of government actions." ...

This longstanding distinction between acquisitions of property for public use, on the one hand, and regulations prohibiting private uses, on the other, makes it inappropriate to treat cases involving physical takings as controlling precedents for the evaluation of a claim that there has been a "regulatory taking," ... and vice versa. For the same reason that we do not ask whether a physical appropriation advances a substantial government interest or whether it deprives the owner of all economically valuable use, we do not apply our precedent from the physical takings context to regulatory takings claims. Land-use regulations are ubiquitous and most of them impact property values in some tangential way—often in completely unanticipated ways. Treating them all as *per se* takings would transform government regulation into a luxury few governments could afford. By contrast, physical appropriations are relatively rare, easily identified, and usually represent a greater affront to individual property rights.... "This case does not present the 'classi[c] taking' in which the government directly appropriates private property for its own use" ... ; instead the interference with property rights "arises from some public program adjusting the benefits and burdens of economic life to promote the common good," *Penn Central*, 438 U.S., at 124.

... [Petitioners] rely principally on our decision in *Lucas v. South Carolina Coastal Council*, 505 U.S. 1003 [112 S. Ct. 2886, 120 L. Ed. 2d 798] (1992)—a regulatory takings case that, nevertheless, applied a categorical rule—to argue that the *Penn Central* framework is inapplicable here. A brief review of some of the cases that led to our decision in *Lucas*, however, will help to explain why the holding in that case does not answer the question presented here.

As we noted in *Lucas*, it was Justice Holmes' opinion in *Pennsylvania Coal Co. v. Mahon*, 260 U.S. 393 [43 S. Ct. 158, 67 L. Ed. 322] (1922), that gave birth to our regulatory takings jurisprudence. In subsequent opinions we have repeatedly and consistently endorsed Holmes' observation that "if regulation goes too far it will be recognized as a taking." ... Justice Holmes did not provide a standard for determining when a regulation goes "too far," but he did reject the view expressed in Justice Brandeis' dissent that there could not be a taking because the property remained in the possession of the owner and had not been appropriated or used by the public.... After *Mahon*, neither a physical appropriation nor a public use has

(Continued)

ever been a necessary component of a "regulatory taking."

In the decades following that decision, we have "generally eschewed" any set formula for determining how far is too far, choosing instead to engage in "'essentially ad hoc, factual inquiries.'" *Lucas*, 505 U.S., at 1015 (quoting *Penn Central*, 438 U.S., at 124). Indeed, we still resist the temptation to adopt *per se* rules in our cases involving partial regulatory takings, preferring to examine "a number of factors" rather than a simple "mathematically precise" formula.… Justice Brennan's opinion for the Court in *Penn Central* did, however, make it clear that even though multiple factors are relevant in the analysis of regulatory takings claims, in such cases we must focus on "the parcel as a whole" ….

… [I]n *First English* … we identified two reasons why a regulation temporarily denying an owner all use of her property might not constitute a taking. First, we recognized that "the county might avoid the conclusion that a compensable taking had occurred by establishing that the denial of all use was insulated as a part of the State's authority to enact safety regulations." … Second, we limited our holding "to the facts presented" and recognized "the quite different questions that would arise in the case of normal delays in obtaining building permits, changes in zoning ordinances, variances, and the like which [were] not before us." …

* * *

[Fn. 31 by the Court: Petitioners fail to offer a persuasive explanation for why moratoria should be treated differently from ordinary permit delays.…] …

The interest in facilitating informed decisionmaking by regulatory agencies counsels against adopting a *per se* rule that would impose such severe costs on their deliberations. Otherwise, the financial constraints of compensating property owners during a moratorium may force officials to rush through the planning process or to abandon the practice altogether. To the extent that communities are forced to abandon using moratoria, landowners will have incentives to develop their property quickly before a comprehensive plan can be enacted, thereby fostering inefficient and ill-conceived growth.…

* * *

We would create a perverse system of incentives were we to hold that landowners must wait for a taking claim to ripen so that planners can make well-reasoned decisions while, at the same time, holding that those planners must compensate landowners for the delay.

Indeed, the interest in protecting the decisional process is even stronger when an agency is developing a regional plan than when it is considering a permit for a single parcel. In the proceedings involving the Lake Tahoe Basin, for example, the moratoria enabled TRPA to obtain the benefit of comments and criticisms from interested parties, such as the petitioners, during its deliberations.… Since a categorical rule tied to the length of deliberations would likely create added pressure on decisionmakers to reach a quick resolution of land-use questions, it would only serve to disadvantage those landowners and interest groups who are not as organized or familiar with the planning process. Moreover, with a temporary ban on development there is a lesser risk that individual landowners will be "singled out" to bear a special burden that should be shared by the public as a whole. *Nollan v. California Coastal Comm'n*, 483 U.S. 825, 835 [107 S. Ct. 3141, 97 L. Ed. 2d 677] (1987). At least with a moratorium there is a clear "reciprocity of advantage," *Mahon*, 260 U.S., at 415, because it protects the interests of all affected landowners against immediate construction that might be inconsistent with the provisions of the plan that is ultimately adopted.…

It may well be true that any moratorium that lasts for more than one year should be viewed with special skepticism. But given the fact that the District Court found that the 32 months required by TRPA to formulate the 1984 Regional Plan was not unreasonable, we could not possibly conclude that every delay of over one year is constitutionally unacceptable.… Formulating a general rule of this kind is a suitable task for state legislatures.… In our view, the duration of the restriction is one of the important factors that a court must consider in the appraisal of a regulatory takings claim, but with respect to that factor as with respect to other factors, the "temptation to adopt what amount to *per se* rules in either direction must be resisted." …

Questions for Discussion

1. Why isn't a moratorium on development the same thing as a temporary taking? When would a moratorium on development constitute a taking requiring just compensation?

2. What dangers to protection of our natural environment are associated with allowing takings claims to be broadly construed?

In a politically explosive case, *Kelo v. City of New London*, the U.S. Supreme Court held that a development plan designed to rejuvenate the economy served a public purpose and that the government could rightfully use the power of eminent domain to implement the plan through condemnation proceedings. In that case, several homeowners refused to sell their homes to the city, and the city exercised its rights under eminent domain to condemn their property. The development project itself, however, was to be undertaken by Pfizer, a private corporation. The plan would have included mixed uses, including new housing. The homeowners were outraged that their homes were to be taken by the government so that a corporation could develop new houses exactly where their houses had been. The Court was sharply split in its decision. A dissent was written by Justice O'Connor, in which three other Justices joined. Please note that this is a dissent, rather than the majority opinion.

Kelo v. City of New London
545 U.S. 469 (2005)

JUSTICE O'CONNOR, with whom THE CHIEF JUSTICE, JUSTICE SCALIA, and JUSTICE THOMAS Join, Dissenting

Over two centuries ago, just after the Bill of Rights was ratified, Justice Chase wrote:

> "An Act of the Legislature (for I cannot call it a law) contrary to the great first principles of the social compact, cannot be considered a rightful exercise of legislative authority.... A few instances will suffice to explain what I mean.... [A] law that takes property from A. and gives it to B: It is against all reason and justice, for a people to entrust a Legislature with such powers; and, therefore, it cannot be presumed that they have done it." *Calder v. Bull*, [3 U.S. 386,] 3 Dall.[as] 386, 388[, 1 L. Ed. 648] (1798) ....

Today the Court abandons this long-held, basic limitation on government power. Under the banner of economic development, all private property is now vulnerable to being taken and transferred to another private owner, so long as it might be upgraded—*i.e.*, given to an owner who will use it in a way that the legislature deems more beneficial to the public—in the process. To reason, as the Court does, that the incidental public benefits resulting from the subsequent ordinary use of private property render economic development takings "for public use" is to wash out any distinction between private and public use of property—and thereby effectively to delete the words "for public use" from the Takings Clause of the Fifth Amendment....

Petitioners are nine resident or investment owners of 15 homes in the Fort Trumbull neighborhood of New London, Connecticut. Petitioner Wilhelmina Dery, for example, lives in a house on Walbach Street that has been in her family for over 100 years. She was born in the house in 1918; her husband, petitioner Charles Dery, moved into the house when they married in 1946. Their son lives next door with his family in the house he received as a wedding gift, and joins his parents in this suit....

In February 1998, Pfizer Inc., the pharmaceuticals manufacturer, announced that it would build a global research facility near the Fort Trumbull neighborhood. Two months later, New London's city council gave initial approval for the New London Development Corporation (NLDC) to prepare the development plan at issue here. The NLDC is a private, nonprofit corporation whose mission is to assist the city council in economic development planning. It is not elected by popular vote, and its directors and employees are privately appointed. Consistent with its mandate, the NLDC generated an ambitious plan for redeveloping 90 acres of Fort Trumbull in order to "complement the facility that Pfizer was planning to build, create jobs, increase tax and other revenues, encourage public access to and use of the city's waterfront, and eventually 'build momentum' for the revitalization of the rest of the city." ...

Petitioners own properties in two of the plan's seven parcels—Parcel 3 and Parcel 4A. Under the plan, Parcel 3 is slated for the construction of research and office space as a market develops for such space. It will also retain the existing Italian Dramatic Club (a private cultural organization) though the homes of three plaintiffs in that parcel are to be demolished. Parcel 4A is slated, mysteriously, for "'park support.'" ... At oral

(Continued)

argument, counsel for respondents conceded the vagueness of this proposed use, and offered that the parcel might eventually be used for parking....

To save their homes, petitioners sued New London and the NLDC, to whom New London has delegated eminent domain power. Petitioners maintain that the Fifth Amendment prohibits the NLDC from condemning their properties for the sake of an economic development plan. Petitioners are not holdouts; they do not seek increased compensation, and none is opposed to new development in the area. Theirs is an objection in principle: They claim that the NLDC's proposed use for their confiscated property is not a "public" one for purposes of the Fifth Amendment. While the government may take their homes to build a road or a railroad or to eliminate a property use that harms the public, say petitioners, it cannot take their property for the private use of other owners simply because the new owners may make more productive use of the property.

* * *

The Fifth Amendment to the Constitution, made applicable to the States by the Fourteenth Amendment, provides that "private property [shall not] be taken for public use, without just compensation." When interpreting the Constitution, we begin with the unremarkable presumption that every word in the document has independent meaning, "that no word was unnecessarily used, or needlessly added." ... In keeping with that presumption, we have read the Fifth Amendment's language to impose two distinct conditions on the exercise of eminent domain: "[T]he taking must be for a 'public use' and 'just compensation' must be paid to the owner." ...

These two limitations serve to protect "the security of Property," which Alexander Hamilton described to the Philadelphia Convention as one of the "great obj[ects] of Gov[ernment]." ... Together they ensure stable property ownership by providing safeguards against excessive, unpredictable, or unfair use of the government's eminent domain power—particularly against those owners who, for whatever reasons, may be unable to protect themselves in the political process against the majority's will.

While the Takings Clause presupposes that government can take private property without the owner's consent, the just compensation requirement spreads the cost of condemnations and thus "prevents the public from loading upon one individual more than his just share of the burdens of government." ... The public use requirement, in turn, imposes a more basic limitation, circumscribing the very scope of the eminent domain power: Government may compel an individual to forfeit her property for the *public's* use, but not for the benefit of another private person. This requirement promotes fairness as well as security....

Where is the line between "public" and "private" property use? We give considerable deference to legislatures' determinations about what governmental activities will advantage the public. But were the political branches the sole arbiters of the public-private distinction, the Public Use Clause would amount to little more than hortatory fluff. An external, judicial check on how the public use requirement is interpreted, however limited, is necessary if this constraint on government power is to retain any meaning....

Our cases have generally identified three categories of takings that comply with the public use requirement, though it is in the nature of things that the boundaries between these categories are not always firm. Two are relatively straightforward and uncontroversial. First, the sovereign may transfer private property to public ownership—such as for a road, a hospital, or a military base.... Second, the sovereign may transfer private property to private parties, often common carriers, who make the property available for the public's use—such as with a railroad, a public utility, or a stadium.... But "public ownership" and "use-by-the-public" are sometimes too constricting and impractical ways to define the scope of the Public Use Clause. Thus we have allowed that, in certain circumstances and to meet certain exigencies, takings that serve a public purpose also satisfy the Constitution even if the property is destined for subsequent private use....

This case returns us for the first time in over 20 years to the hard question of when a purportedly "public purpose" taking meets the public use requirement. It presents an issue of first impression: Are economic development takings constitutional? I would hold that they are not. We are guided by two precedents about the taking of real property by eminent domain. In *Berman*, we upheld takings within a blighted neighborhood of Washington, D. C. The neighborhood had so deteriorated that, for example, 64.3% of its dwellings were beyond repair.... It had become burdened with "overcrowding of dwellings," "lack of adequate streets and alleys," and "lack of light and air." ... Congress had determined that the neighborhood had become "injurious to the public health, safety, morals, and welfare" and that it was necessary to "eliminat[e] all such injurious conditions by employing all means necessary and appropriate for the purpose," including eminent domain.... Mr. Berman's department store was not itself blighted. Having approved of Congress' decision

(Continued)

to eliminate the harm to the public emanating from the blighted neighborhood, however, we did not second-guess its decision to treat the neighborhood as a whole rather than lot-by-lot. ...

In *Midkiff*, we upheld a land condemnation scheme in Hawaii whereby title in real property was taken from lessors and transferred to lessees. At that time, the State and Federal Governments owned nearly 49% of the State's land, and another 47% was in the hands of only 72 private landowners. Concentration of land ownership was so dramatic that on the State's most urbanized island, Oahu, 22 landowners owned 72.5% of the fee simple titles.... The Hawaii Legislature had concluded that the oligopoly in land ownership was "skewing the State's residential fee simple market, inflating land prices, and injuring the public tranquility and welfare," and therefore enacted a condemnation scheme for redistributing title....

In those decisions, we emphasized the importance of deferring to legislative judgments about public purpose. Because courts are ill equipped to evaluate the efficacy of proposed legislative initiatives, we rejected as unworkable the idea of courts' "'deciding on what is and is not a governmental function and ... invalidating legislation on the basis of their view on that question at the moment of decision, a practice which has proved impracticable in other fields.'" ...

Yet for all the emphasis on deference, *Berman* and *Midkiff* hewed to a bedrock principle without which our public use jurisprudence would collapse: "A purely private taking could not withstand the scrutiny of the public use requirement; it would serve no legitimate purpose of government and would thus be void." ...

The Court's holdings in *Berman* and *Midkiff* were true to the principle underlying the Public Use Clause. In both those cases, the extraordinary, precondemnation use of the targeted property inflicted affirmative harm on society—in *Berman* through blight resulting from extreme poverty and in *Midkiff* through oligopoly resulting from extreme wealth. And in both cases, the relevant legislative body had found that eliminating the existing property use was necessary to remedy the harm.... Thus a public purpose was realized when the harmful use was eliminated. Because each taking *directly* achieved a public benefit, it did not matter that the property was turned over to private use. Here, in contrast, New London does not claim that Susette Kelo's and Wilhelmina Dery's well-maintained homes are the source of any social harm. Indeed, it could not so claim without adopting the absurd argument that any single-family home that might be razed to make way for an apartment building, or any church

that might be replaced with a retail store, or any small business that might be more lucrative if it were instead part of a national franchise, is inherently harmful to society and thus within the government's power to condemn.

In moving away from our decisions sanctioning the condemnation of harmful property use, the Court today significantly expands the meaning of public use. It holds that the sovereign may take private property currently put to ordinary private use, and give it over for new, ordinary private use, so long as the new use is predicted to generate some secondary benefit for the public—such as increased tax revenue, more jobs, maybe even esthetic pleasure. But nearly any lawful use of real private property can be said to generate some incidental benefit to the public. Thus, if predicted (or even guaranteed) positive side effects are enough to render transfer from one private party to another constitutional, then the words "for public use" do not realistically exclude *any* takings, and thus do not exert any constraint on the eminent domain power.

* * *

Any property may now be taken for the benefit of another private party, but the fallout from this decision will not be random. The beneficiaries are likely to be those citizens with disproportionate influence and power in the political process, including large corporations and development firms. As for the victims, the government now has license to transfer property from those with fewer resources to those with more. The Founders cannot have intended this perverse result. "[T]hat alone is a *just* government," wrote James Madison, "which *impartially* secures to every man, whatever is his *own*." ...

Questions for Discussion

1. Why do judges and justices write dissenting opinions? The dissent is not "law," so why bother?
2. In *Midkiff*, the Hawaii land redistribution case that Justice O'Connor referred to, the land redistribution program did not work as intended by the legislative body. Instead, once land ownership was shifted to other private owners, foreign investors entered the market and bid the prices much higher, thereby exacerbating the problem of affordability of land for residents. Under what circumstances do you think that government-sanctioned economic rejuvenation programs should be the catalyst for government exercise of the power of eminent domain?

(Continued)

3. The land acquired by condemnation in the *Kelo* aftermath was never developed as planned. The developer subsequently withdrew from the project. The homeowners moved their homes elsewhere (actually moved their houses), and the lands that those homes once occupied continue to sit vacant. What lessons can other communities that might be struggling with economic challenges learn about the events in the City of New London that led to the *Kelo* case?

4. In the aftermath of *Kelo*, President George W. Bush issued an executive order restricting the use of federal eminent domain powers so that they cannot be used merely for economic development purposes. Several state legislatures also passed statutes similarly restricting the powers of eminent domain. Would you argue that this saga is an example of government checks and balances working properly? Explain.

Table 6.1 illustrates some important developments in land use regulation.

▪ **TABLE 6.1** *Some Important Points in Legal History Related to Modern Land Use Regulation in the United States*

1916: New York City enacts Comprehensive Zoning Ordinance
1922: Department of Commerce develops initial draft of the Standard State Zoning Enabling Act
1922: U.S. Supreme Court hears *Pennsylvania Coal Co.* v. *Mahon;* Justice Holmes recognizes the possibility of regulatory takings when regulation "goes too far"
1926: U.S. Supreme Court upholds comprehensive zoning in *Village of Euclid v. Ambler Realty Co.*
1978: U.S. Supreme Court, in *Penn Central Transportation Co. v. New York City,* finds that most takings claims are situation-specific factual inquiries, rather than bright-line rule types of cases
1982: U.S. Supreme Court holds, in *Loretto v. Teleprompter Manhattan CATV Corp.,* that permanent physical occupation of property authorized by government is a taking
1987: U.S. Supreme Court holds, in *First English Evangelical Lutheran Church of Glendale v. County of Los Angeles,* that a temporary taking requires just compensation
U.S. Supreme Court holds, in *Nollan v. California Coastal Commission,* that imposition of a condition of easement on the grant a building permit constitutes a taking for which landowners must be compensated under the Fifth Amendment
1992: U.S. Supreme Court holds, in *Lucas v. South Carolina Coastal Council,* that a regulation that permanently deprives landowner of all economically beneficial uses of land is a taking
2002: U.S. Supreme Court holds, in *Tahoe-Sierra Preservation Council, Inc. v. Tahoe Regional Planning Agency,* that a regulation imposing a temporary moratorium on development does not constitute a taking; it states that "[a]fter *Mahon*, neither a physical appropriation nor a public use has ever been a necessary component of a "regulatory taking"
2005: U.S. Supreme Court holds, in *Kelo v. City of New London,* that development plans designed to rejuvenate the economy serve a public purpose and government can exercise its powers of eminent domain to acquire private property in furtherance of that activity
After 2005: A federal executive order is issued, and several states enact legislation, to prohibit the use of eminent domain solely for purposes of economic development

▓ Final Thoughts

Land use regulation continues to be a contentious issue. Landowners often believe that they should have the absolute right to do with their land as they wish. However, the social benefit of maintaining a clean, healthy environment for humans and all other species is increasingly being recognized as paramount. This overwhelming public interest requires land use regulations to ensure that people are not living next to (or in the middle of) toxic waste sites, by virtue of their neighbors deciding to engage in harmful activities, and it requires the government to exercise its power to protect fragile areas from development.

Consider, too, that there are entirely different perspective about how human beings can (and have) related to the land. C.J. Weeramantry, former vice president of the International Court of Justice, noted:

> In most Western legal systems land is a commodity to be bought and sold by the rules of the market place. It is a matter between buyer and seller and the sale of land is little different from the sale of an item of merchandise. The highest bidder succeeds, he gets a whole bundle of rights to do what he will with his property and he can if he chooses cut it up into little parcels as he would with a piece of cake.

* * *

> The broader perspectives of the community's interest in the land and its right to be protected from the effects of its misuse, tend ... to be ignored in Western legal systems.... Western legal systems began to be sensitized to [the deleterious effects of environmental devastation] by thinkers such as Albert Schweitzer who discussed "reverence for life" in 1915 and L.H. Bailey who in the same year spoke ... of the respect due to the "holy earth." Such perspectives were ... not entirely absent from Western thought, but had been crowded out of the Western philosophical and economic agenda by the industrial revolution, and legal systems followed suit. The downgrading of nature was helped further by the apparently limitless power of science and the belief it induced that man had the power to tame nature to his will. Lawyers, likewise, shaped their discipline according to the belief in man's power over nature, and legal systems grew increasingly regardless of nature and its traditional protections.[28]

Elsewhere, Weeramantry wrote:

> There is [an] aspect of modern day monetarism which has great significance for ... environmental law. [This is] the belief that money can purchase anything—even things that are part of the common heritage of humanity and are not anybody's to sell. In particular there is the belief that land is a commodity that can be bought like an article that one purchases over the counter. If value is paid for it one can become its owner and do with it what one pleases because the purchaser is its lord and master. The result has been the ruthless exploitation of land.[29]

* * *

> Such an attitude is anathema to traditional ways of looking at land, as something to be looked upon with reverence. If the land prospers, the people proper; if the

---

[28] C.G. Weeramantry, Universalising International Law (Martinus Nijhoff Publishers 2004), pp. 189–190.
[29] *Id.* at 85.

land withers and dies, the people wither and die.... [T]oday [buying and selling land as though it were merchandise] is possible because of modern land law which ... gives its owner all sorts of rights over it, even to the extent of denuding it and rendering it unusable ... for generations.[30]

Consider how Weeramantry's words might be used to question our viewpoint of what land is and how or whether it should be used. In the system that we have, is it enough to say that regulations must be fair and reasonable? After all, when such assertions are made, concerns are generally limited to human interests.

The current state of our law instructs that land use regulations must be applied in a nondiscriminatory fashion and must not deprive an owner of all economic use of its property. If land use regulations deprive an owner of its property either in fact or by regulation, then that is a taking and the owner must be compensated for it.

Of course, such a requirement has a chilling effect on government attempts to protect the environment. If a taking occurs because the government wishes to impose a regulation prohibiting development, that means the government will have to pay the landowners. Not many governments could afford such claims as a consequence of regulating land use. Therein lies the rub. How do we protect fragile environmental attributes without engaging in takings that require compensation? How do we protect private property rights while still protecting the environment? Justice Weeramantry's words on this point might lead the way to future rethinking of our very relationship to the land. In the meantime, we are left with a somewhat murky area of law that provides no party with absolute satisfaction.

Ultimately, land use law raises fundamental policy questions about the appropriate balance between private property rights and the government's power to regulate land use to protect the environment.

■ ■ ■ REVIEW AND STUDY QUESTIONS

1. Should land use decisions be made locally or by a centralized (distant) decision maker? What are the benefits and drawbacks to the environment for each type of model?

2. Zoning laws discriminate between different types of land uses. Why aren't zoning laws that discriminate between residential, agricultural, and industrial uses considered illegally discriminatory?

3. Takings are relatively common for projects such as road-widening projects. If you or your family have ever experienced a taking, did you (or your family) believe that you were justly compensated? Why or why not?

4. The government has the power of eminent domain, so how can individuals ever feel secure in their ownership rights? Are ownership rights merely illusory? What public policy considerations support the government's power of eminent domain?

5. Identify a project that you believe would justify the government's use of eminent domain power to take private property. Identify a project that you believe would pass legal muster but would seem unjust. What is the difference?

6. What is the difference between a regulatory taking and a mere regulation?

7. What is the difference between a temporary taking and a moratorium on development?

8. Use the Internet to learn about the aftermath of the *Kelo* case. Do you believe that economic rejuvenation programs such as the one proposed in the *Kelo* case justify use of the government's power of eminent domain? Would your answer change if the economic rejuvenation project was undertaken solely by government, rather than by a government-sanctioned corporate project?

---

[30] *Id.* at 94.

■ *ACTIVITY BOX*   *Transferable Development Rights*

Transferable development rights (TDRs) allow the transfer of rights to develop property to other parcels. Read the paper, "Transferable Development Rights 'Post-Zoning'?" by Vicki Been and John Infranca, which can be downloaded for free: http://papers.ssrn.com/sol3/papers.cfm?abstract_id=2144808

Review Seattle's Transferable Development Rights program at http://www.seattle.gov/housing/incentives/TDRbonus.htm

Questions for Discussion

1. Are TDRs more effective than zoning regulations to control land use?
2. How can TDRs be used in tandem with zoning laws to create good environments for people and for nature?
3. What are the benefits and drawbacks of TDRs?
4. Explore your city, county, or region's land use laws and programs. Are TDRs used there? If not, how can an individual encourage their use? If so, have they been used to good effect? Provide examples.

Constitutional Law and the Environment

Learning Objectives

After reading this chapter, you will have an understanding of the concept of some important constitutional law issues as they relate to the environment. You will understand how different systems of government work in a system of federalism. You will examine the Commerce Clause, the Supremacy Clause, and the Property Clause. Specifically, after reading this chapter, you should be able to answer the following questions:

1. What is federalism, and why does it matter in environmental law?
2. What are the Commerce Clause, the Supremacy Clause, and the Property Clause, and how do they relate to environmental law?

Here's a good idea!
This is a "bare bones" outline of the chapter. Expand this outline with more detailed notes as you read the chapter. This will allow you to create a study guide as you work. This good study habit will help you to learn the material, retain important points, and make efficient use of your time.

■ Introduction

This chapter continues the discussion of constitutional law by examining issues primarily related to **federalism**, or the relationships between laws made by the federal and state governments as they pertain to the environment. In Chapter 6, we explored the Fifth Amendment to the U.S. Constitution and some constitutional issues that arise with respect to land use. Specifically, we investigated the concepts of takings, just compensation, and discrimination. We also examined the question of First Amendment rights with respect to zoning and commercial speech (billboards). This chapter broadens the discussion of constitutional issues and the environment by looking directly at certain clauses within the Constitution itself, rather than the amendments to the Constitution.

In the United States, federalism describes the relationship between the federal government and the governments of the states. In a more general sense, *federalism* refers to any system of government where power is shared or divided among multiple governmental entities. Under the U.S. federal system, individual states formed a union and subordinated their respective powers to that of the federal

federalism: A system of government in which power is divided between subordinate governments and a central government.

government. In the United States, both the federal government and the states possess certain powers, including the power to make and enforce laws.

The powers of the federal government are those expressly granted to it by the U.S. Constitution. Those powers not expressly (or impliedly) granted to the federal government by the Constitution are reserved to the states. Quite simply, this means that if the U.S. Constitution did not "take" a power for or assign a power to the federal government, then the states have that power instead. Therefore, we have a federal government with constitutionally limited powers, and we have state governments with quite a vast range of powers.

The important concept of **cooperative federalism** refers to a legislative scheme whereby the federal government allows the states to establish their own programs within the guidelines of federal minimum requirements. If a state cannot or will not do that, the federal government imposes its authority within the state to satisfy those requirements. In this chapter, we investigate how the Supreme Court has helped to define the extent of congressional power, under the Commerce Clause, to enact environmental legislation affecting private property.

The relationship between the powers and responsibilities of the state and federal governments is complex, and it was probably inevitable that conflicts would arise in environmental cases. In cases concerning the importation of hazardous waste, for example, a significant legal question is the extent to which one state may regulate to effectively protect its own environment without unconstitutionally interfering with other states' rights to engage in interstate commerce. (**Interstate commerce** is simply commerce that occurs between parties in different states.) Another important issue is the extent to which federal laws supersede or preempt state laws. The term **preemption** refers federal law taking priority over state law. This chapter examines some of these issues.

The final section of this chapter examines the federal government's power to regulate government property under the Property Clause of the U.S. Constitution. The federal government owns a vast amount of property within the United States, and the Constitution gives Congress the power to enact rules and regulations governing this property. These federally owned tracts contain much of the remaining national wilderness lands.

cooperative federalism: A legislative scheme whereby the federal government allows the states to establish or lead programs within their own borders, as long as those programs meet federal minimum guidelines for compliance.

interstate commerce: Commerce between states.

preemption: The priority of federal law over state law.

Tenth Amendment: Amendment to the U.S. Constitution that reserves to the states those powers not delegated to the federal government.

Supremacy Clause: Article VI of the U.S. Constitution; declares the Constitution and laws of the United States (federal laws) the "supreme law of the land."

◼ The Commerce Clause

A basic premise of American law is that the federal government has only limited, delegated powers. The main source of the enumerated powers of Congress is Article I, § 8, of the U.S. Constitution. For example, this section gives Congress the power to coin and borrow money, regulate commerce with foreign nations, create post offices, and regulate copyrights and patents, among other things. The Constitution does not specifically set out the powers of the states (although state constitutions sometimes list the powers that state legislatures may exercise), but the **Tenth Amendment** specifically reserves those powers not delegated to the federal government by the Constitution, nor prohibited by it, to the states or to the people. The U.S. Constitution does place limits on the powers of the states. Most significantly, Article VI of the Constitution establishes the principle of federal supremacy. This **Supremacy Clause** declares the U.S. Constitution and laws of the United States made thereunder to be the "supreme law of the land." State laws that conflict with federal laws are thus void and unenforceable under the principle of federal supremacy.

The relative power of the federal and state governments is a political question of great significance. Congress may address the appropriate balance of state and federal power to adopt environmental laws and regulations by expressly authorizing or by expressly prohibiting state action in some areas.

One of the powers expressly delegated to Congress in Article I of the Constitution is the power to regulate interstate commerce (commerce among the states). This power is called the *commerce power*. Section 8 of Article I states: "Congress shall have power ... to regulate Commerce ... among the several States." The drafters of the Constitution believed that this power was necessary to limit the protectionist state restrictions on interstate trade that were common after the American Revolution.

The **Commerce Clause** is not just a source of congressional power to enact laws protecting the environment. It also limits a state's powers to pass state laws if those laws unreasonably burden interstate commerce. The Commerce Clause indirectly limits the states' abilities to regulate, tax, or burden interstate commerce. Of course, the meaning and scope of the Commerce Clause have been refined by the courts over the years. As a result, two different and important legal doctrines have emerged. First, the Commerce Clause is a source of congressional regulatory power. Second, the Commerce Clause acts as an independent check on state regulation that unduly restricts interstate commerce.

The Commerce Clause as a Source of Federal Regulatory Power

The literal language of the Commerce Clause gives Congress the power to regulate commerce among the states. This power has been very broadly construed by the courts. The courts have also interpreted the Commerce Clause to apply to **intrastate commerce** that has any appreciable effect on interstate commerce. Thus, the Commerce Clause permits Congress to regulate both interstate and intrastate matters that may affect interstate commerce. The Supreme Court has upheld federal legislation advancing noncommercial police power purposes. In interpreting upon the power to regulate interstate commerce, the courts have recognized a broad congressional power to regulate for the public health, safety, and welfare.

In a complex, interdependent society such as ours, few activities do *not* affect interstate commerce. This is especially true of activities affecting the environment, as environmental effects and problems do not follow political boundaries. The federal government's power to enact laws protecting the environment and regulating land use within the states has been affirmed by the courts as part of its power to regulate interstate commerce.

In *Hodel v. Virginia Surface Mining & Reclamation Association*, the plaintiffs challenged the constitutionality of the Surface Mining Control and Reclamation Act of 1977. The lower court (the U.S. District Court) rejected the plaintiff's challenge that the law violated the Commerce Clause, but it held that the act violated the Tenth Amendment because it "displaced the States' freedom to structure operations in areas of traditional function." The district court also held that various provisions of the Act amounted to an uncompensated taking of private property in violation of the Fifth Amendment. The government appealed. Justice Marshall, writing for the majority of the U.S. Supreme Court, noted that the Surface Mining

Commerce Clause: Article I, § 8, of the U.S. Constitution; gives Congress the power to regulate commerce among the states.

intrastate commerce: Commerce within a single state.

Control and Reclamation Act "establishes a program of cooperative federalism that allows the States, within limits established by federal minimum standards, to enact and administer their own regulatory programs, structured to meet their own particular needs."[1]

Hodel v. Virginia Surface Mining & Reclamation Association, Inc.
452 U.S. 264 (1981)

JUSTICE MARSHALL Delivered the Opinion of the Court

* * *

The Surface Mining Act is a comprehensive statute designed to "establish a nationwide program to protect society and the environment from the adverse effects of surface coal mining operations ... [The law] establishes a two-stage program for the regulation of surface coal mining.... Under the permanent phase, a regulatory program is to be adopted for each State, mandating compliance with the full panoply of federal performance standards, with enforcement responsibility lying with either the State or Federal Government.

* * *

On October 23, 1978, the Virginia Surface Mining and Reclamation Association, Inc., an association of coal producers engaged in surface coal mining operations in Virginia, 63 of its member coal companies, and 4 individual landowners filed suit in Federal District Court seeking declaratory and injunctive relief against various provisions of the Act.... Plaintiffs' challenge was primarily directed at [the Act's] performance standards....

* * *

On cross-appeal, appellees argue that the District Court erred in rejecting their challenge to the Act as beyond the scope of congressional power under the Commerce Clause. They insist that the Act's principal goal is regulating the use of private lands within the borders of the States and not, as the District Court found, regulating the interstate commerce effects of surface coal mining. Consequently, appellees contend that the ultimate issue presented is "whether land *as such* is subject to regulation under the Commerce Clause, *i.e.*, whether land can be regarded as 'in commerce.'" ... In urging us to answer "no" to this question, appellees emphasize that the Court has recognized that land-use regulation is within the inherent police powers of the States and

their political subdivisions, ... and argue that Congress may regulate land use only insofar as the Property Clause grants it control over federal lands.

We do not accept either appellees' framing of the question or the answer they would have us supply. The task of a court that is asked to determine whether a particular exercise of congressional power is valid under the Commerce Clause is relatively narrow. The court must defer to a congressional finding that a regulated activity affects interstate commerce, if there is any rational basis for such a finding....

Judicial review in this area is influenced above all by the fact that the Commerce Clause is a grant of plenary authority to Congress.... This power is "complete in itself, may be exercised to its utmost extent, and acknowledges no limitations, other than are prescribed in the constitution." ... Moreover, this Court has made clear that the commerce power extends not only to "the use of channels of interstate or foreign commerce" and to "protection of the instrumentalities of interstate commerce ... or persons or things in commerce," but also to "activities affecting commerce." ... As we explained in *Fry v. United States*, 421 U.S. 542, 547 (1975), "[e]ven activity that is purely intrastate in character may be regulated by Congress, where the activity, combined with like conduct by others similarly situated, affects commerce among the States or with foreign nations." ...

Thus, when Congress has determined that an activity affects interstate commerce, the courts need inquire only whether the finding is rational. Here, the District Court properly deferred to Congress' express findings, set out in the Act itself, about the effects of surface coal mining on interstate commerce. Section 101(c), 30 U.S.C. § 1201(c) ... recites the congressional finding that

"many surface mining operations result in disturbances of surface areas that burden and adversely affect commerce and the public welfare by destroying or diminishing the utility of land for commercial, industrial, residential, recreational, agricultural, and forestry purposes, by causing erosion and landslides,

(Continued)

---

[1] 452 U.S. 264, 289 (1981).

by contributing to floods, by polluting the water, by destroying fish and wildlife habitats, by impairing natural beauty, by damaging the property of citizens, by creating hazards dangerous to life and property by degrading the quality of life in local communities, and by counteracting governmental programs and efforts to conserve soil, water, and other natural resources."

The legislative record provides ample support for these statutory findings....

* * *

The denomination of an activity as a "local" or "intrastate" activity does not resolve the question whether Congress may regulate it under the Commerce Clause. As previously noted, the commerce power "extends to those activities intrastate which so affect interstate commerce, or the exertion of the power of Congress over it, as to make regulation of them appropriate means to the attainment of a legitimate end, the effective execution of the granted power to regulate interstate commerce." ... This Court has long held that Congress may regulate the conditions under which goods shipped in interstate commerce are produced where the "local" activity of producing these goods itself affects interstate commerce.... Appellees do not dispute that coal is a commodity that moves in interstate commerce. Here, Congress rationally determined that regulation of surface coal mining is necessary to protect interstate commerce from adverse effects that may result from that activity. This congressional finding is sufficient to sustain the Act as a valid exercise of Congress' power under the Commerce Clause.

[Accordingly, the Court affirmed the judgment of the District Court upholding the Surface Mining Act against the Commerce Clause attack, and it reversed the judgment below insofar as the District Court held various provisions of the Act unconstitutional.]

Questions and Comments for Discussion

1. The Supreme Court in *Hodel v. Virginia Surface* rejected the argument that the surface coal mining act violated the constitutional limitation on the commerce power imposed by the Tenth Amendment. The district court had relied on a 1976 Supreme Court decision (*National League of Cities v. Usery*, 426 U.S. 833) in concluding that the Act contravened the Tenth Amendment because it interfered with the states' "traditional governmental function" of regulating land use. The Supreme Court in *Hodel* reexamined *National League of Cities*

and said that the Tenth Amendment challenge must fail. According to the Court, nothing in *National League of Cities* suggested that the Tenth Amendment shields the states from preemptive federal regulation of private activities affecting interstate commerce.

The Tenth Amendment served as a basis of important federalism rulings before Roosevelt's New Deal, but it has subsequently been considered to be nothing more than a truism stating that "all is retained which has not been surrendered." After *National League of Cities*, there was some confusion about the limits of congressional power under the Tenth Amendment. Later Supreme Court cases, however, have rejected Tenth Amendment challenges to other important environmental laws. If an amendment has "lost power," or never attained the power that its original promoters intended it to have, what could be done to strengthen it?

2. In *Hodel v. Virginia Surface Mining*, the Court also held that the Act did not result in an uncompensated taking of private property in violation of the Fifth Amendment's "just compensation" clause. Neither appellees nor the Court identified any property in which appellees had an interest that had allegedly been taken by operation of the Act. As you will recall from the discussion of regulatory takings in Chapter 6, to establish a taking in this case, the plaintiffs would have had to prove that the regulation deprived them of all economic value of the property and that they were entitled to just compensation as a result. In *Hodel*, how might the landowner have proved a regulatory taking?

3. In *Hodel v. Indiana*, 452 U.S. 314 (1981), a companion case, the Supreme Court rejected another attack on the same statute. In the *Indiana* case, the district court had held unconstitutional certain provisions of the Surface Mining Control and Reclamation Act that attempted to protect prime farm land. (Provisions included a requirement that an applicant obtain a permit for mining on prime farm land to show that it had the capacity to restore the land, and a requirement that surface mine operators remove topsoil separately and preserve it for use during reclamation.) The district court found that only 0.006% of the total prime farm land in the nation was affected annually by mining, and that mining on farm land had only an "infinitesimal" impact on interstate commerce. However, the Supreme Court rejected this argument, noting that the grain production from the

(Continued)

land affected would still be in the neighborhood of $56 million per year.

4. In a concurring opinion in *Hodel v. Virginia Surface Mining,* Justice Rehnquist warned: "[I]t would be a mistake to conclude that Congress' power to regulate pursuant to the Commerce Clause is unlimited. Some activities may be so private or local in nature that they simply may not be in commerce. Nor is it sufficient that the person or activity reached had some nexus with interstate commerce. Our cases have consistently held that the regulated activity must have a substantial effect on interstate commerce." In light of the majority decisions in *Hodel v. Virginia Surface Mining and Reclamation Association* and *Hodel v. State of Indiana,* how "substantial" must the effect on interstate commerce be? How likely is it that a court would find that a local activity that even minimally affects the environment can be regulated by Congress under the Commerce Clause?

The problem of how substantial the effect on interstate commerce must be is a difficult one, to be sure. The U.S. Supreme Court in *United States v. Lopez*[2] made it more difficult for Congress to meet this test, issuing a decision that signaled a seemingly important shift in Commerce Clause cases. In *Lopez,* the Supreme Court ruled that Congress had overstepped its powers under the Commerce Clause when it banned gun possession near public schools. The petitioner in that case had challenged the federal Gun-Free School Zones Act of 1990, which made it a federal offense "for any individual knowingly to possess a firearm at a place that the individual knows, or has reasonable cause to believe, is a school zone."

Justice Rehnquist, writing for the majority of the Supreme Court in the case, began with what he called "first principles":

The Constitution creates a Federal Government of enumerated powers.... As James Madison wrote, "[t]he powers delegated by the proposed Constitution to the federal government are few and defined. Those which are to remain in the State governments are numerous and indefinite.

He continued,

The commerce power "is the power to regulate; that is, to prescribe the rule by which commerce is to be governed. This power, like all others vested in Congress, is complete, in itself, may be exercised to its utmost extent, and acknowledges no limitations, other than are prescribed in the constitution."

The majority opinion then reviewed three broad categories that Congress may regulate under its commerce power: regulation of the use of the channels of interstate commerce; regulation of the instrumentalities of interstate commerce; and regulation of those activities having a substantial relation to interstate commerce.

According to the majority opinion, the difficulty in the final category is that case law has not clearly delineated whether an activity must "affect" or "*substantially* affect" interstate commerce in order to fall within Congress's power to regulate under the Commerce Clause. Turning to the criminal statute at issue in the case, the Court said that by its terms the statute had nothing to do with "commerce" or any sort of economic enterprise, nor was it an essential part of a larger regulation of economic activity. Further, the Court said the law contained no jurisdictional element by which to ensure, through case-by-case inquiry, that the firearm possession affected interstate commerce. According to the majority opinion in *Lopez,* the determination of congressional power under the Commerce Clause is ultimately

[2] 514 U.S. 549 (1995).

one of degree. The Court admitted that determining whether an intrastate activity is commercial or noncommercial may in some cases result in legal uncertainty. But in this case, the majority said:

> To uphold the Government's contentions here, we would have to pile inference upon inference in a manner that would bid fair to convert congressional authority under the Commerce Clause to a general police power of the sort retained by the States. Admittedly, some of our prior cases have taken long steps down that road, giving great deference to congressional action.... The broad language in these opinions has suggested the possibility of additional expansion, but we decline here to proceed any further. To do so would require us to conclude that the Constitution's enumeration of powers does not presuppose something not enumerated, ... and that there never will be a distinction between what is truly national and what is truly local.... This we are unwilling to do.

At the least, the Supreme Court's opinion in *Lopez* suggests that a majority of the Court is willing to take another look at the appropriate balance between federal and state powers in Commerce Clause cases.

Some commentators see the *Lopez* case as an important step in reevaluating the federal government's exercise of control over traditional state functions. Others do not think it will have much effect, in part because four justices dissented and there were clear differences among the five justices forming the majority opinion in *Lopez*. For example, Justice Thomas, in a separate concurring opinion, called for a thorough reevaluation of Commerce Clause jurisprudence. His opinion criticized the "substantial effects" test. Justice Kennedy, in contrast, along with Justice O'Connor, noted that "the Court as an institution and the legal system as a whole have an immense stake in the stability of our Commerce Clause jurisprudence as it has evolved to this point."[3] Kennedy also wrote that Congress is entitled to assume "that we have a single market and a unified purpose to build a stable national economy."[4] Nevertheless, the reasoning in the *Lopez* decision casts some uncertainty on the outcome of environmental cases.

In *Solid Waste Agency of Northern Cook County v. U.S. Army Corps of Engineers*,[5] (*SWANCC*), in a 5-4 opinion, the majority pointed out that *Lopez* had affirmed that congressional power under the Commerce Clause was broad, but not unlimited. In *SWANCC*, the U.S. Supreme Court invalidated the so-called Migratory Bird Rule. During the many years prior to *SWANCC*, the Clean Water Act had been interpreted by the Army Corps of Engineers to apply to isolated wetlands not otherwise connected to waterways traditionally understood to be "waters of the United States," as defined by the Clean Water Act. In short, the Army Corps of Engineers had been regulating isolated wetlands under the Clean Water Act and doing so under an interpretation that Congress had intended for the Clean Water Act to apply to isolated wetlands under its Commerce Clause authority. The Migratory Bird Rule recognized the importance of isolated inland wetlands to migratory birds, and that migratory birds were matters of interstate commerce for tourists and recreational travelers. *SWANCC* seems to implicitly—though not expressly—limit congressional authority under the Commerce Clause. However, the four-member dissent had much to say about the Commerce Clause.

---

[3] 514 U.S. 549, 574 (1995).
[4] *Id.*
[5] 531 U.S. 159 (2001).

Solid Waste Agency of Northern Cook County v. Army Corp. of Engineers

531 U.S. 159 (2001)

[Dissent by] Justice Stevens, with Whom Justice Souter, Justice Ginsburg, and Justice Breyer Join, Dissenting

* * *

Contrary to the Court's suggestion, the Corps' interpretation of the statute does not "encroac[h]" upon "traditional state power" over land use.... The CWA is not a land-use code; it is a paradigm of environmental regulation. Such regulation is an accepted exercise of federal power. *Hodel v. Virginia Surface Mining & Reclamation Ass'n, Inc.,* 452 U.S. 264, 282[, 101 S. Ct. 2352, 69 L. Ed. 2d 1] (1981).

It is particularly ironic for the Court to raise the specter of federalism while construing a statute that makes explicit efforts to foster local control over water regulation. Faced with calls to cut back on federal jurisdiction over water pollution, Congress rejected attempts to narrow the scope of that jurisdiction and, by incorporating § 404(g), opted instead for a scheme that encouraged States to supplant federal control with their own regulatory programs.... The Corps' interpretation of the statute as extending beyond navigable waters, tributaries of navigable waters, and wetlands adjacent to each is manifestly reasonable and therefore entitled to deference....

Because I am convinced that the Court's miserly construction of the statute is incorrect, I shall comment briefly on petitioner's argument that Congress is without power to prohibit it from filling any part of the 31 acres of ponds on its property in Cook County, Illinois. The Corps' exercise of its § 404 permitting power over "isolated" waters that serve as habitat for migratory birds falls well within the boundaries set by this Court's Commerce Clause jurisprudence.

In *United States v. Lopez,* ... this Court identified "three broad categories of activity that Congress may regulate under its commerce power": (1) channels of interstate commerce; (2) instrumentalities of interstate commerce, or persons and things in interstate commerce; and (3) activities that "substantially affect" interstate commerce.... The migratory bird rule at issue here is properly analyzed under the third category. In order to constitute a proper exercise of Congress' power over intrastate activities that "substantially affect" interstate commerce, it is not necessary that each individual instance of the activity substantially affect commerce; it is enough that, taken in the aggregate, the *class of activities* in question has such an effect....

The activity being regulated in this case (and by the Corps' § 404 regulations in general) is the discharge of fill material into water. The Corps did not assert jurisdiction over petitioner's land simply because the waters were "used as habitat by migratory birds." It asserted jurisdiction because petitioner planned to *discharge fill* into waters "used as habitat by migratory birds." Had petitioner intended to engage in some other activity besides discharging fill (*i.e.,* had there been no activity to regulate), or, conversely, had the waters not been habitat for migratory birds (*i.e.,* had there been no basis for federal jurisdiction), the Corps would never have become involved in petitioner's use of its land. There can be no doubt that, unlike the class of activities Congress was attempting to regulate in ... *Lopez,* ... the discharge of fill material into the Nation's waters is almost always undertaken for economic reasons....

Moreover, no one disputes that the discharge of fill into "isolated" waters that serve as migratory bird habitat will, in the aggregate, adversely affect migratory bird populations.... Nor does petitioner dispute that the particular waters it seeks to fill are home to many important species of migratory birds, including the second-largest breeding colony of Great Blue Herons in northeastern Illinois ... and several species of waterfowl protected by international treaty and Illinois endangered species laws.... [Fn. by Justice Stevens: Other bird species using petitioner's site as habitat include the "Great Egret, Green-backed Heron, Black-crowned Night Heron, Canada Goose, Wood Duck, Mallard, Greater Yellowlegs, Belted Kingfisher, Northern Waterthrush, Louisiana Waterthrush, Swamp Sparrow, and Red-winged Blackbird." ...]

In addition to the intrinsic value of migratory birds, ... it is undisputed that literally millions of people regularly participate in birdwatching and that those activities generate a host of commercial activities of great value. [Fn. by Justice Stevens: ... More than 100 million Americans spent almost $14.8 billion in 1980 to watch and photograph fish and wildlife.... Of 17.7 million birdwatchers, 14.3 million took trips in order to observe, feed, or photograph waterfowl, and 9.5 million took trips specifically to view other water-associated birds, such as herons like those residing at petitioner's site....] The causal connection between the filling of wetlands and the decline of commercial activities associated with migratory birds is ... direct and concrete....

(Continued)

Finally, the migratory bird rule does not blur the "distinction between what is truly national and what is truly local." ... Justice Holmes cogently observed in *Missouri v. Holland* that the protection of migratory birds is a textbook example of a *national* problem.... [when he wrote:] ("It is not sufficient to rely upon the States [to protect migratory birds]. The reliance is vain ...")…. The destruction of aquatic migratory bird habitat, like so many other environmental problems, is an action in which the benefits (*e.g.*, a new landfill) are disproportionately local, while many of the costs (*e.g.*, fewer migratory birds) are widely dispersed and often borne by citizens living in other States. In such situations, described by economists as involving "externalities," federal regulation is both appropriate and necessary.... Identifying the Corps' jurisdiction by reference to waters that serve as habitat for birds that migrate over state lines also satisfies this Court's expressed desire for some "jurisdictional element" that limits federal activity to its proper scope....

The power to regulate commerce among the several States necessarily and properly includes the power to preserve the natural resources that generate such commerce.... Migratory birds, and the waters on which they rely, are such resources. Moreover, the protection of migratory birds is a well-established federal responsibility. As Justice Holmes noted in *Missouri v. Holland*, the federal interest in protecting these birds is of "the first magnitude." ... Because of their transitory nature, they "can be protected only by national action." ...

Whether it is necessary or appropriate to refuse to allow petitioner to fill those ponds is a question on which we have no voice. Whether the Federal Government has the power to require such permission, however, is a question that is easily answered. If, as it does, the Commerce Clause empowers Congress to regulate particular "activities causing air or water pollution, or other environmental hazards that may have effects in more than one State," [citing *Hodel*] ... , it also empowers Congress to control individual actions that, in the aggregate, would have the same effect.

Questions for Discussion

1. Why do you suppose that the majority declined to address constitutional issues raised in *SWANCC*, instead relying only on statutory construction to reach its decision that the Migratory Bird Rule was not within congressional intent?
2. Do you agree with Justice Stevens's dissenting opinion that migratory birds are matters of interstate commerce? If so, was it ethical for the majority to decline to decide the issue based upon the Commerce Clause issue?
3. Discuss what a 5-4 opinion of the U.S. Supreme Court means. Why is such a split significant? How might a dissenting opinion be used in future cases?

The debate about the appropriate role of federal regulation to protect the environment as a matter of public policy will surely continue. One scholar studied U.S. Supreme Court decisions related to environmental regulation and concluded that the Court is hostile to environmental regulation, and interprets Commerce Clause challenges differently depending upon the thing being regulated. She refers to congressional power under the Commerce Clause as "affirmative commerce clause" power, and she compares the affirmative commerce clause power to the dormant commerce clause power (examined in the next section of this chapter). She noted that:

This study has uncovered a subtle inconsistency between the Court's affirmative and dormant commerce clause analyses. In particular, when the federal government has sought to regulate the use of water and land under the affirmative commerce clause, the Court has emphasized the natural, noncommercial nature of the protected resources rather than the commercial nature of the regulated activity. In the absence of commercial or economic activity, therefore, the federal government lacks commerce clause regulatory authority under the rationale of *Lopez*. Simultaneously, when the states have attempted to regulate the use of land, water, or fish, the Court has treated such things as market commodities rather than natural resources. As a result, the Court has invalidated those state regulations under the dormant commerce clause as constituting an undue interference with commodities in the flow of interstate commerce.[6]

If this assertion is accurate, then any environmental regulation would have a very difficult time in surviving Commerce Clause scrutiny. Let's examine the so-called dormant commerce clause to round out our understanding of the government's Commerce Clause powers and its limitations on the states' abilities to regulate within their own borders.

The "Dormant Commerce Clause"

On its face, the Commerce Clause is a grant of power to Congress, not a restriction on the state's power to legislate. Since the early 19th century, however, the Supreme Court has also construed the Commerce Clause to prevent certain kinds of state legislation that discriminate against interstate commerce. As U.S. Supreme Court Justice Thomas noted in *Oregon Waste Systems, Inc. v. Department of Environmental Quality of the State of Oregon*,[7] though the Commerce Clause is "phrased as a grant of regulatory power to Congress, the Clause has long been understood to have a 'negative' aspect that denies the States the power unjustifiably to discriminate against or burden the interstate flow of articles of commerce."[8] Under this theory, courts invalidate state laws that unduly burden interstate commerce on the ground that they are inconsistent with the power to regulate interstate commerce granted to the federal government. Courts have used the Commerce Clause to invalidate state laws in cases where Congress has failed to legislate. Such cases rely upon the **dormant commerce clause** theory.

Courts use two tests to invalidate state laws that unconstitutionally impede the flow of commerce. The first test governs state laws that discriminate against interstate commerce on their face. Such legislation is virtually per se unconstitutional. The second test subjects nondiscriminatory state legislation to a balancing test, weighing the impact of a statute on interstate commerce against the state's justification for the statute. Additionally, if the state acts as a market participant rather than a regulator, a law that might otherwise fall to a dormant commerce clause objection will be allowed to stand. We now examine these three issues.

Facially Discriminatory Laws

A common example of the application of the dormant commerce clause arises in cases involving state laws that discriminate against the importation of out-of-state waste. Under both tests—the discrimination against out-of-state actors test and the balancing test— state laws restricting or financially discriminating against the importation of hazardous waste from outside the state have been held invalid by the Supreme Court.

The problem of out-of-state waste is significant for many states. Concerns arise from states and the people who live in those states about whether there is room to dispose of waste products within their borders. Additionally, people do not like the idea of importing "someone else's" waste, particularly when it is hazardous waste. However, from the perspective of the party that wishes to dispose of the waste, the cost of dumping such waste has increased to the point that it is often cheaper to transport it hundreds of miles away to states where dumping is less expensive.

dormant commerce clause: Constitutional theory that the Commerce Clause also prevents state legislation that discriminates against or interferes with interstate commerce.

---

[6] Christine A. Klein, *The Environmental Commerce Clause*, 27 Harv. Envtl L. Rev. 1, 4-5 (2003); quoted abstract available at http://scholarship.law.ufl.edu/facultypub/6
[7] 511 U.S. 93, 98 (1994).
[8] *Id.*

Several states have attempted to minimize, restrict, or completely ban the flow of such waste from other states. Almost all such attempts have been defeated under the dormant commerce clause theory.

Notably, not all U.S. Supreme Court Justices agree that the dormant commerce clause should invalidate state laws to the extent that it has done so in the past. Justice Scalia, in a separate concurring opinion in *United Haulers Association v. Oneida-Herkimer Solid Waste Management Authority,* wrote that "the so-called 'negative' Commerce Clause is an unjustified judicial invention, not to be expanded beyond its existing domain.... The historical record provides no grounds for reading the Commerce Clause to be other than what it says—an authorization for Congress to regulate commerce."[9]

Notwithstanding some contemporary Justices' reservations about the dormant commerce clause, it has been and continues to be used to defeat laws that ban the flow of waste from other states. In the first U.S. Supreme Court decision addressing this issue, *City of Philadelphia v. New Jersey,*[10] the Supreme Court struck down a New Jersey statute that prohibited the importation into the state of most solid or liquid waste that originated or was collected outside its territorial limits. The parties in the case disagreed about the purpose of the legislation. Plaintiffs who challenged the law argued that although the statute was cloaked "in the currently fashionable garb of environmental protection," it was actually a legislative effort to suppress competition and stabilize the cost of solid waste disposal for New Jersey residents. The state, however, cited the purpose of the statute as set out in the statute itself:

> The Legislature finds and determines that ... the volume of solid and liquid waste continues to rapidly increase, that the treatment and disposal of these wastes continues to pose an even greater threat to the quality of the environment of New Jersey, that the available and appropriate land fill sites within the State are being diminished, that the environment continues to be threatened by the treatment and disposal of waste which originated or was collected outside the State, and that the public health, safety and welfare require that the treatment and disposal within this State of all wastes generated outside of the State be prohibited.

The U.S. Supreme Court said that it was not necessary to resolve the dispute about the ultimate legislative purpose of the act. In the Court's opinion, Justice Stewart wrote, "Contrary to the evident assumption of the state court and the parties, the evil of protectionism can reside in legislative means as well as legislative ends. Thus, it does not matter whether the ultimate aim of [the statute] ... is to reduce the waste disposal costs of New Jersey residents or to save remaining open lands from pollution, for we assume New Jersey has every right to protect its residents' pocketbooks as well as their environment...."[11] However, according to the Court, whatever New Jersey's ultimate purpose in enacting the law, that purpose could not be accomplished by discriminating against articles of commerce coming from outside the state unless there was some reason, apart from their origin, to treat them differently. The Court held that, both on its face and in its effect, the act violated the Commerce Clause:

> The New Jersey law at issue in this case falls squarely within the area that the Commerce Clause puts off limits to state regulation. On its face, it imposes on

---

[9] 550 U.S. 330, 348 (2007).

[10] 437 U.S. 617 (1978).

[11] 437 U.S. 617, 626 (1978).

out-of-state commercial interests the full burden of conserving the State's remaining landfill space. It is true that in our previous cases the scarce natural resource was itself the article of commerce, whereas here the scarce resource and the article of commerce are distinct. But that difference is without consequence. In both instances, the State has overtly moved to slow or freeze the flow of commerce for protectionist reasons. It does not matter that the State has shut the article of commerce inside the State in one case and outside the State in the other. What is crucial is the attempt by one State to isolate itself from a problem common to many by erecting a barrier against the movement of interstate trade.[12]

The Supreme Court in *City of Philadelphia* said there was a difference between laws banning the importation of hazardous waste and state quarantine laws; the latter have been upheld in the face of Commerce Clause challenges. The Court distinguished cases upholding quarantine laws on the basis that in these cases, the "very movement" of the articles risked contagion and other evils. According to the Court, in quarantine cases the state does not discriminate against interstate commerce as such, but simply prevents the traffic of noxious articles, whatever their origin.

Since its decision in *City of Philadelphia*, the Court has consistently refused to permit states to discriminate against out-of-state waste in order to protect state landfill space. Not only is this a significant environmental issue, it also raises important policy questions about a state's ability to control other resources within its boundaries.

In the following case, petitioners challenged an Alabama law that imposed a disposal fee on hazardous wastes generated outside of the state and disposed of at a commercial facility in Alabama. The fee did not apply to such waste that came from within Alabama. The Alabama State Supreme Court held that the fee advanced legitimate local purposes that could not be adequately served by reasonable nondiscriminatory alternatives and was therefore valid under the Commerce Clause. The petitioners appealed to the U.S. Supreme Court.

Chemical Waste Management, Inc. v. Hunt
504 U.S. 334 (1992)

JUSTICE WHITE delivered the Opinion of the Court

Petitioner, Chemical Waste Management, Inc., a Delaware corporation with its principal place of business in Oak Brook, Illinois, owns and operates one of the Nation's oldest commercial hazardous waste land disposal facilities, located in Emelle, Alabama. Opened in 1977 and acquired by petitioner in 1978, the Emelle facility is a hazardous waste treatment, storage, and disposal facility operating pursuant to permits issued by the Environmental Protection Agency (EPA) under the Resource Conservation and Recovery Act of 1976

(RCRA), ... and by the State of Alabama.... Alabama is 1 of only 16 States that have commercial hazardous waste landfills, and the Emelle facility is the largest of the 21 landfills of this kind located in these 16 States....

The parties do not dispute that the wastes and substances being landfilled at the Emelle facility "include substances that are inherently dangerous to human health and safety and to the environment. Such waste consists of ignitable, corrosive, toxic and reactive wastes which contain poisonous and cancer causing chemicals and which can cause birth defects, genetic damage, blindness, crippling and death." ... Increasing amounts

(Continued)

---
[12] *Id.* at 628.

of out-of-state hazardous wastes are shipped to the Emelle facility for permanent storage each year. From 1985 through 1989, the tonnage of hazardous waste received per year has more than doubled, increasing from 341,000 tons in 1985 to 788,000 tons by 1989. Of this, up to 90% of the tonnage permanently buried each year is shipped in from other States.

Against this backdrop Alabama enacted Act No. 90-326 [the Act].... Among other provisions, the Act ... imposes the "additional fee" at issue here, which states in full:

> "For waste and substances which are generated out-side of Alabama and disposed of at a commercial site for the disposal of hazardous waste or hazardous substances in Alabama, an additional fee shall be levied at the rate of $72.00 per ton."....

* * *

II.

No State may attempt to isolate itself from a problem common to the several States by raising barriers to the free flow of interstate trade....

* * *

The Act's additional fee facially discriminates against hazardous waste generated in States other than Alabama, and the Act overall has plainly discouraged the full operation of petitioner's Emelle facility.... Such burdensome taxes imposed on interstate commerce alone are generally forbidden....

The State, however, argues that the additional fee imposed on out-of-state hazardous waste serves legitimate local purposes related to its citizens' health and safety. Because the additional fee discriminates both on its face and in practical effect, the burden falls on the State "to justify it both in terms of the local benefits flowing from the statute and the unavailability of nondiscriminatory alternative adequate to preserve the local interests at stake." ... "At a minimum such facial discrimination invokes the strictest scrutiny of any purported legitimate local purpose and of the absence of nondiscriminatory alternatives." ...

The State's argument here does not significantly differ from the Alabama Supreme Court's conclusions on the legitimate local purposes of the additional fee imposed, which were: ... (1) protection of the health and safety of the citizens of Alabama from toxic substances; (2) conservation of the environment and the state's natural resources; (3) provision for compensatory revenue for the costs and burdens that out-of-state waste generators impose by dumping their hazardous waste in Alabama; (4) reduction of the overall flow of wastes traveling on the state's highways, which flow creates a great risk to the health and safety of the state's citizens." ...

These may all be legitimate local interests, and petitioner has not attacked them. But only rhetoric, and not explanation, emerges as to why Alabama targets *only* interstate hazardous waste to meet these goals....

Ultimately, the State's concern focuses on the volume of the waste entering the Emelle facility.... Less discriminatory alternatives, however, are available to alleviate this concern, not the least of which are a generally applicable per-ton additional fee on *all* hazardous waste disposed of within Alabama, ... or a per-mile tax on *all* vehicles transporting hazardous waste across Alabama roads, ... or an evenhanded cap on the total tonnage landfilled at Emelle, ... which would curtail volume from all sources.... To the extent Alabama's concern touches environmental conservation and the health and safety of its citizens, such concern does not vary with the point of origin of the waste, and it remains within the State's power to monitor and regulate more closely the transportation and disposal of all hazardous waste within its borders. Even with the possible future financial and environmental risks to be borne by Alabama, such risks likewise do not vary with the waste's State of origin in a way allowing foreign, but not local, waste to be burdened.... In sum, we find the additional fee to be "an obvious effort to saddle those outside the State" with most of the burden of slowing the flow of waste into the Emelle facility.... "That legislative effort is clearly impermissible under the Commerce Clause of the Constitution." ...

Questions and Comments for Discussion

1. The majority in *Chemical Waste Management v. Hunt* distinguished other court decisions holding that state quarantine laws do not violate the Commerce Clause. (A *quarantine law* is one banning the importation or sale of articles that pose a risk of contagion or other evils.) The Court in *Hunt* said the additional fee in the Alabama act could not legitimately be deemed a quarantine law because Alabama permitted both the generation and land-filling of hazardous waste within its borders and the importation of still more hazardous waste subject to payment of the additional fee. The Court specifically distinguished *Maine v. Taylor*,[13] 477 U.S.

(Continued)

---

[13]477 U.S. 131 (1986).

131 (1986), in which it had upheld a Maine statute banning the importation of out-of-state baitfish into the state of Maine. According to the Court, "Maine there demonstrated that the out-of-state baitfish were subject to parasites foreign to in-state baitfish. This difference posed a threat to the state's natural resources, and absent a less discriminatory means of protecting the environment—and none was available—the import of baitfish could properly be banned. To the contrary, the record establishes that the hazardous waste at issue in this case is the same regardless of its point of origin."

The Supreme Court has thus conceded that some quarantine laws are not forbidden by the Commerce Clause even though they discriminate against out-of-state commerce. But it has distinguished state quarantine laws like that in *Maine v. Taylor* from those banning the importation of hazardous waste into the state. Are there any similarities in the issues posed by these two cases? In what way do they differ? Do different policies underlie the Alabama and Maine legislation?

2. Congress has expressly not authorized states to enact legislation like that in *Chemical Management v. Hunt* and *City of Philadelphia.* Should it do so? What are the political, environmental, and legal implications of your answer?

3. Justice Rehnquist dissented in *Chemical Management v. Hunt.* According to his dissent, "[t]axes are a recognized and effective means for discouraging the consumption of scarce commodities—in this case the safe environment that attends appropriate disposal of hazardous wastes.... I therefore see nothing unconstitutional in Alabama's use of a tax to discourage the export of this commodity to other States...." What is the commodity at issue in this case? Is it landfill space, or is it hazardous waste? What difference does or should this distinction make? If the commodity is hazardous waste, then it is a product in interstate commerce and presumably states cannot discriminate against buying and selling it. If the product is land, the issue may be viewed as land use regulation, which is an area traditionally within the states' police powers to regulate.

The Balancing Test

As the earlier out-of-state waste cases illustrate, state laws that discriminate on their face against out-of-state commerce rarely survive a challenge under the Commerce Clause. Generally, challenges attack laws that are not discriminatory on their face but have the effect of burdening out-of-state commerce. Most state legislation challenged under the dormant commerce clause falls within this category. In these cases, courts use a balancing test between the burden imposed on interstate commerce and the state's interests in passing the legislation. State legislation attacked as a burden on commerce must be rationally related to a legitimate state purpose. Courts consider a wide range of factors in determining whether the state's interest outweighs the federal interest in the free flow of interstate trade, such as the importance of the state interest, the degree to which it restricts the federal interest, and the degree to which the state regulatory scheme actually advances the purpose of the federal legislation.

An example of application of this balancing test is found in *United Haulers Association v. Oneida-Herkimer Solid Waste Management Authority.*[14] In that case, the U.S. Supreme Court considered counties' ordinances that required all solid waste generated within those counties to be delivered to a specific state-created public benefit corporation, rather than somewhere else. If the ordinances had favored a private business, then they would have violated the dormant commerce clause. However, because the ordinances in question benefited a public business while treating all private companies the same, it was not a Commerce Clause violation.

---

[14] 550 U.S. 330 (2007).

Another example of the balancing test in action occurred in the mid to late 20th century over the use of phosphates in detergents. What became scientifically apparent during those years was that phosphates, though excellent at killing germs, were very bad for the environment. Discharge of phosphates into wastewater streams can result in excessive algal blooms in rivers and streams, resulting in catastrophic loss of life and habitat in aquatic environments. In *Proctor & Gamble Co. v. Chicago*,[15] the plaintiffs, who manufactured phosphate detergents, challenged a City of Chicago ordinance that banned the use of detergents containing phosphates. The plaintiffs demonstrated that the ordinance had an adverse effect upon their businesses, which were national in scope. Because of warehousing methods used in the industry, the Chicago ordinance would effectively restrict sales of the plaintiffs' products in a wide geographic area that included Wisconsin, Indiana, and Michigan.

The City of Chicago introduced evidence of the harmful effect of phosphates in contributing to the eutrophication of rivers and lakes. *Eutrophication* is a process whereby a body of water becomes overnourished with nutrient elements that cause an overgrowth of green plants or algae. The city ordinance was designed to counteract eutrophication on the Illinois Waterway, which contained a high percentage of phosphorus, and Lake Michigan, which is the source of Chicago's water supply.

The trial court initially held that the ordinance was unconstitutional, finding that the ordinance resulted in increased manufacturing and distribution costs to the plaintiffs and that the ordinance burdened interstate commerce. The trial court also found that the city's justifications for the ordinance were not sufficient to outweigh the interference with interstate commerce.

The Seventh Circuit, however, reversed the trial court and decided that the ordinance was constitutional under the balancing test. The court said:

> Where the statute regulates evenhandedly to effectuate a legitimate local public interest, and its effects on interstate commerce are only incidental, it will be upheld unless the burden imposed on such commerce is clearly excessive in relation to the putative local benefits.[16]

Under the balancing test applied in *Proctor & Gamble Co. v. Chicago*, the court considered the burden imposed on interstate commerce by the ordinance, and found that the ordinance was not actually a burden on interstate commerce but merely a "burden" on a company with interstate distribution facilities. According to the court, there was no impairment of the company's ultimate ability to transport its product in interstate commerce. There was also no evidence of actual conflict between the Chicago ordinance and laws of other jurisdictions that might inhibit the uniformity necessary for national manufacture and distribution of detergents. Even though the ordinance had the effect of preventing potential purchasers in other states from obtaining a detergent formula that manufacturers might legally sell in those states, it was an incidental burden on commerce, and one that the City Council could not control. The court concluded that under the balancing test, the burden imposed by the ordinance was slight compared to the important purpose of the ordinance. Under this analysis, the ordinance was constitutional.

---

[15] 509 F.2d 69 (7th Cir. 1975).

[16] 509 F.2d at 75, citing *Pike v. Bruce Church, Inc.*, 397 U.S. 137, 142 (1970).

■ Applied Problem

The issue of phosphates in detergents presents a particularly good example of two different strategies for addressing an environmental problem. One strategy is for government to create laws that ban a particular practice, such as including phosphates in detergent. A different strategy is for manufacturers of a particular good to voluntarily agree not to do something, such as a voluntary industry agreement not to include phosphates in detergent.

Today, more than 17 states have banned the use of phosphates in detergent. However, as the discussion concerning *Proctor & Gamble Co. v. Chicago* illustrates, much litigation surrounded the passage of such statutes and ordinances, because manufacturers had a financial stake in being able to continue to make their products. Of course, litigation takes time and money, and lawmakers had to commit both to defense of the restrictions enacted on businesses. Moreover, the laws had to overcome the plaintiffs' Commerce Clause objections—which they eventually did.

A voluntary ban on phosphates in detergents is also in effect. In 2010, the American Cleaning Institute, a trade organization that represents the cleaning supply manufacturers, issued a voluntary ban on the use of phosphates in dishwasher detergents.

1. If the voluntary ban had gone into effect before laws were enacted to ban phosphate use, would the laws have been necessary? Which would a manufacturer prefer: laws that expressly proscribe or permit certain conduct, or voluntary bans that have no legal penalties if not adhered to? What are the benefits and drawbacks to each scheme?

2. Eco-labels allow a company to receive certification from a neutral third party that its practices meet some environmental standard. Shoppers can make purchasing decisions based upon those labels, if they choose to do so. In comparison, command-and-control laws that require certain practices by companies do not give companies or consumers any choice in the matter. Such laws simply set forth requirements to achieve the environmental goal of concern. Consider the difference between eco-labels and laws. Is there any compelling reason to enact laws to protect the environment if eco-labels already exist?

Some judges and scholars have criticized the use of a balancing test in cases like *Proctor & Gamble v. Chicago*. First, the application of a balancing test is often unpredictable. Second, critics claim that courts should not second-guess state legislatures about the balance between a statute's costs and benefits. They argue that those decisions should properly be made within the political process and that unwise or unsound decisions can also be addressed through that process.

Despite these criticisms, however, use of the balancing test has led some courts to uphold certain state environmental laws. For example, in *Minnesota v. Clover Leaf Creamery Co.,*[17] the U.S. Supreme Court used the balancing test to hold that a Minnesota state law banning nonreturnable plastic containers for milk did not violate the Commerce Clause, because the law applied to all sellers alike, regardless of whether they were in-state or out-of-state sellers or producers of milk or containers, and because the burden on interstate commerce was minor and the law met a substantial government interest in maintaining the natural environment.

[17] 449 U.S. 456 (1981).

State laws that restrict the importation of certain items of commerce into the state have also been upheld under a balancing test. In *Maine v. Taylor* (discussed earlier), the Supreme Court upheld the constitutionality of a state law that banned the importation of baitfish into the state. Experts had testified that live baitfish imported into the state posed two significant threats to Maine's unique and fragile fisheries. First, Maine's population of wild fish—including its own indigenous gold shiners—would be placed at risk by parasites prevalent on out-of-state baitfish. Second, non-native species inadvertently included in shipments of baitfish could disturb Maine's aquatic ecology. There was no satisfactory way to inspect shipments of live baitfish for parasites or commingled species.

A majority of the Supreme Court said that the state merely needed to demonstrate that the statute served a legitimate local purpose and that this purpose could not be served as well by available nondiscriminatory means. In holding that the statute did not violate the Commerce Clause, the Court said, "As long as a State does not needlessly obstruct interstate trade or attempt to 'place itself in a position of economic isolation,' … it retains broad regulatory authority to protect the health and safety of its citizens and the integrity of its natural resources."[18] According to the Court, this was not a case of arbitrary discrimination against interstate commerce. The record suggested that Maine had legitimate reasons, apart from their origin, to treat out-of-state baitfish differently.

■ *ACTIVITY BOX*   *Banning Plastic Bags*

Find a story online concerning bans on plastic bags, such as this one: http://www.latimes.com/local/lanow/la-me-ln-plastic-bags-20130618,0,6576624.story

Plastic bags are very harmful to wildlife, causing many to suffer horrific deaths. Moreover, plastic is a major source of pollution, both on land and in our waterways, including our oceans.

1. Research online to find a city that has banned or plans to ban plastic bags. Develop a legal argument that the ban does not violate the Commerce Clause.

2. Does your city ban plastic bags? How could an individual set into motion the banning of plastic bags in your city? Write a plan to organize a movement that would result in a city or county ordinance to ban plastic. How would the ordinance have to be written to avoid a successful Commerce Clause challenge?

The State as a "Market Participant"

The courts have held that state regulation may be insulated from attack under the Commerce Clause if the state acts as a "market participant." Under this theory, if a state is not exercising a regulatory function but has itself entered the market, traditional concerns underlying the dormant commerce clause theory do not apply. For example, in *Swin Resource Systems, Inc. v. Lycoming County*,[19] the operator of a solid waste processing facility sued a county that operated a landfill. Swin challenged regulations that gave the county residents preference in use of the landfill. The court of appeals said that the county was acting as a market participant rather

---

[18] 477 U.S. 131, 151 (1986).
[19] 883 F.2d 245 (3d Cir. 1989).

than a market regulator in deciding the conditions under which Swin could use its landfill. The court said:

> No court, to our knowledge, has ever suggested that the commerce clause requires city-operated garbage trucks to cross state lines in order to pick up the garbage generated by residents of other states. If a city may constitutionally limit its trucks to collecting garbage generated by city residents, we see no constitutional reason why a city cannot also limit a city-operated dump to garbage generated by city residents.... With respect to municipal garbage trucks and municipal garbage dumps, application of the market participant doctrine enables "'the people [acting through their local government] to determine as conditions demand ... what services and functions the public welfare requires.'"[20]

■ ■ ■ REVIEW AND STUDY QUESTIONS

1. Identify an example of a law in which the concept of federalism plays an important role. If either the state or the federal government was not involved in regulation of the issue that is the subject of the law you identified, how would that change things? For the better? For the worse?

2. How does Congress use the Commerce Clause to enact laws that affect the environment? How does the Commerce Clause restrict states' rights to enact environmental laws?

3. Identify examples of intrastate commerce. How might intrastate commerce of the type you identified affect interstate commerce? Should Congress have the right to regulate intrastate commerce based upon its "ripple effect" into interstate commerce? Why or why not?

4. Do you agree that state laws should not be permitted to treat those from out-of-state differently? For example, do you agree that states should not be permitted to charge higher rates for hazardous waste disposal when the hazardous waste comes from out of state? Why would a state want to charge higher rates for such services when the materials originate from out of state?

5. Does the *Lopez* decision make federal land use regulation more tenuous? Why or why not?

6. Summarize Justice Scalia's criticism of the dormant commerce clause. Do you agree or disagree with his position? Why or why not?

7. Identify constitutional issues that lawmakers must take into consideration when enacting legislation to protect the environment.

■ The Supremacy Clause: Federal Preemption of State Laws Affecting the Environment

If a state law conflicts with a federal law enacted by Congress under its constitutional powers, the federal law takes priority and the state law is unenforceable. In such cases, state law is said to be preempted by federal law. The doctrine of preemption is based on the Supremacy Clause of Article VI of the U.S. Constitution, which provides:

> This Constitution, and the Laws of the United States which shall be made in Pursuance thereof; and all Treaties made, or which shall be made, under the Authority of the United States, shall be the supreme Law of the Land; and the Judges in every State shall be bound thereby, any Thing in the Constitution or Laws of any State to the Contrary notwithstanding.

---

[20] *Id.* at 251.

In contrast, the Tenth Amendment protects the power of states. The potential conflict between federal supremacy and state authority is reconciled by a presumption that regulation by both the federal and state governments is valid. However, Congress can forbid states from regulating in a particular area of national interest, and may do so either by expressly preempting state authority, or by implying preemption from the scope and range of its action.

In cases where state law clearly conflicts with federal law, and it is impossible to follow both, federal law will control. However, the presence of a conflict between federal and state law is not always so clear. In cases where state law does not expressly conflict with federal law, but is "incompatible" with federal law, federal law also controls.

The courts have recognized four circumstances in which federal law will preempt state action:

1. Express preemption by Congress
2. Congressionally implied preemption, where state law interferes with the policy objectives of the federal law
3. Conflict preemption, where compliance with both federal and state laws (dual compliance) is impossible
4. Field preemption, where Congress intends to remove an entire area from state legislation; field preemption is often understood to be a type or subset of conflict preemption

Every preemption case is unique, but they usually raise questions of statutory interpretation because the courts must determine whether Congress intended to preempt state law when it adopted particular laws. Consequently, the issue of whether state law is preempted by federal law or regulation is decided on a case-by-case basis.

Express (Manifest) Intention to Preempt State Law

If it wishes to do so, Congress can expressly forbid the states from legislating in an area that Congress has been given the power to regulate; this constitutes **express preemption**. In some cases, congressional intention to occupy a particular field is overtly stated in federal legislation. In the following case, *Kinley Corp. v. Iowa Utilities Board*, the plaintiff sought to invalidate a state statute regulating the transportation of hazardous liquids by pipeline within the state. A federal trial court held that the state law was expressly preempted by federal law, and the state appealed. Pay particular attention to the four types of preemption described by the court.

express preemption: Status arising when Congress expressly forbids the states from legislating in a particular area.

Kinley Corp v. Iowa Utilities Board
999 F.2d 354 (8th Cir. 1993)

McMILLIAN, Circuit Judge

The underlying facts are not disputed. Appellee Kinley Corp. owns and operates an interstate hazardous liquid pipeline extending some 13 miles from an Amoco Oil Co. terminal facility located near Council Bluffs, Iowa, to Offutt Air Force Base in Bellevue, Nebraska. The pipeline is 4 inches in diameter and transports aviation jet fuel. Aviation jet fuel is a petroleum product and thus a "hazardous liquid" for purposes of the [Hazardous Liquid Pipeline Safety Act of 1979,] HLPSA,

(Continued)

49 U.S.C.App. § 2001(2)(A). The pipeline was constructed in April 1968 and was purchased by Kinley after construction had begun but before it was completed. Neither the company that constructed the pipeline nor Kinley ever applied for a Chapter 479 state pipeline permit until 1988. Chapter 479 establishes a comprehensive state program supervising the intrastate and interstate transportation by pipeline of solid, liquid or gaseous substances, with the exception of water and interstate natural gas, ... in order to protect the safety and welfare of the public. In July 1987, [the Iowa Utilities Board] IUB, formerly the Iowa State Commerce Commission, became aware of the existence of the pipeline ... and in August 1987 IUB inspected the pipeline....

In June 1989 IUB issued an administrative order directing Kinley to show cause why civil penalties should not be assessed for noncompliance with Chapter 479 and IUB's administrative regulations. In April 1990 IUB denied Kinley's application for a state pipeline permit and ordered Kinley not to operate the pipeline in Iowa or to replace portions thereof, and assessed civil penalties.

* * *

Appellants acknowledge that the safety provisions of Chapter 479 were preempted by the HLPSA.... However, they argue that the non-safety provisions, specifically the financial responsibility provisions designed to protect the state's farmland and topsoil from damage due to construction, operation and maintenance of pipelines and to guarantee payment of property and environmental damages, were not preempted....

"The Supremacy Clause, U.S. Const. Art. VI, cl. 2, invalidates state laws that 'interfere with, or are contrary to,' federal law." ... Congressional intent is the critical question in any preemption analysis....

Under the Supremacy Clause, federal law may supersede state law in several different ways. First, when acting within constitutional limits, Congress is empowered to pre-empt state law by so stating in express terms. In the absence of express pre-emptive language, Congress' intent to pre-empt all state law in a particular area may be inferred where the scheme of federal regulation is sufficiently comprehensive to make reasonable the inference that Congress "left no room" for supplementary state regulation. Pre-emption of a whole field also will be inferred where the field is one in which "the federal interest is so dominant that the federal system will be assumed to preclude enforcement of state laws on the same subject."

Even where Congress has not completely displaced state regulation in a specific area, state law is nullified to the extent that it actually conflicts with federal law. Such a conflict arises when "compliance with both federal and state regulation is a physical impossibility," or when state law "stands as an obstacle to the accomplishment and execution of the full purposes and objectives of Congress." *Hillsborough County v. Automated Medical Laboratories, Inc.*, 471 U.S. at 713....[Fn. by the court: Preemption traditionally comes in four "flavors": (1) "express preemption," resulting from an express Congressional directive ousting state law ... ; (2) "implied preemption," resulting from an inference that Congress intended to oust state law in order to achieve its objective ... ; (3) "conflict preemption," resulting from the operation of the Supremacy Clause when federal and state law actually conflict, even when Congress says nothing about it ... ; and (4) "field preemption," resulting from a determination that Congress intended to remove an entire area from state regulatory authority.... The present case involves express preemption.]

In the present case, we need look no further than the express statutory language. The HLPSA contains the following express preemption provision: "No State agency may adopt or continue in force any safety standards applicable to *interstate* pipeline facilities or the transportation of hazardous liquids associated with such facilities." We agree with the district court that this is a case involving express preemption and that Congress has expressly stated its intent to preempt the states from regulating in the area of safety in connection with interstate hazardous liquid pipelines. For this reason, the state cannot regulate in this area and Chapter 479 is invalid to the extent it purports to do so....

[W]e note that the legislative history of the HLPSA, especially when considered with the Natural Gas Pipeline Safety Act (NGPSA), ... further demonstrates Congress's intent to preempt state safety regulation of interstate hazardous liquid pipelines. In 1979, at the same time the NGPSA was amended to cover liquefied natural gas, Congress also enacted the HLPSA. The HLPSA established federal safety regulation over the transportation of hazardous liquids by pipeline and defined "hazardous liquid" to include petroleum and petroleum products.... In enacting the HLPSA, Congress intended to "establish a statutory framework similar to the NGPSA to regulate transportation of hazardous liquids by pipeline." ...

* * *

Accordingly, we affirm the judgment of the district court.

(Continued)

Questions and Comments for Discussion

1. In *Kinley*, the state also argued that Chapter 479 was valid because it was a gap-filling state regulation. The state argued that transportation of a hazardous liquid through pipelines that operate at a stress level of 20% or less of the specified minimum yield strength of the line pipe is exempt from federal safety and accident reporting requirements, and that Chapter 479 permissibly fills this gap in the federal regulatory scheme. The court of appeals disagreed, and said that the Department of Transportation's decision to exempt certain pipelines from federal regulation did not necessarily mean that a state can step in and impose its own regulations: "[A] federal decision to forego regulation in a given area may imply an authoritative federal determination that the area is best left *unregulated*, and in that event would have as much pre-emptive force as a decision to regulate."[21] According to the court, Congress granted exclusive authority to regulate interstate hazardous liquid pipelines to the secretary of the Department of Transportation. This congressional grant of authority precluded state decision making in this area altogether and left no regulatory room for the state either to establish its own safety standards or to supplement the federal safety standards. If the public disagrees, and believes that an area should be regulated, and if the state lacks the authority to regulate, what steps can the public take to ensure regulation?

2. What are the four "flavors" of federal preemption identified by the court? Why does the federal government recognize four different types of preemption? Do you think that this interpretation of the Supremacy Clause is consistent with our Founding Fathers' intentions?

The federal government can also waive its preemptive rights if it chooses to do so. Congress made statutory allowances for this very reason when California desired to enact stricter regulations than required by the EPA regarding tailpipe emissions of greenhouse gases. After a statutory waiver of preemption was enacted, California then requested that the EPA waive its preemption rights so that the state could impose stricter tailpipe emission standards than the Clean Air Act and its associated regulations required. Though the EPA initially denied the waiver, President Obama asked the EPA to reconsider the request; after reconsideration, it granted the waiver. As the U.S. District Court for the Eastern District of California explained in *Central Valley Chrysler-Jeep, Inc. v. Witherspoon* before the waiver was actually granted:

> The federal Clean Air Act, 42 U.S.C., section 7543(a), generally preempts state regulation of motor vehicle emissions. Section 7543(b)(1) provides that California, at the discretion of the director of the Environmental Protection Agency ("EPA") may be granted a waiver to impose standards more stringent than those imposed by the Clean Air Act, if enumerated criteria are met. Although other states may not request waivers for standards they develop, the other states may adopt standards that are set by California and for which waivers are granted by EPA.
>
> * * *
>
> Put simply and directly … the Clean Air Act prevents the enforcement of California's proposed regulations absent a waiver of preemption by EPA. There is no contention that California does not have the right under the Clean Air Act to develop regulations regulating tailpipe emissions and to apply to EPA for waiver of federal preemption. It is also self-evident that if and when EPA waives preemption

---

[21] 999 F.2d at 359 (quoting *Arkansas Electric Cooperative Corp. v. Arkansas Public Service Commission*, 461 U.S. at 384 (1983)).

under the Clean Air Act pursuant to 42 U.S.C., section 7543(b)(1), then California's proposed standards will not be preempted by the Clean Air Act. Thus, if EPA ever does issue a waiver of preemption under the Clean Air Act, California will be empowered to implement its regulations so far as the Clean Air Act is concerned under conditions specified by EPA in the waiver.[22]

In the case of California's tailpipe emissions standards for greenhouse gases, Congress chose to allow the state to apply for a waiver from the appropriate regulatory agency so that, if permitted, California's state laws could essentially be more stringent than the federal Clean Air Act and its associated regulations.

Implied Preemption of State Law

Where Congress has not expressly stated an intention to preempt state regulation, Congressional intention to preempt may nonetheless be implied. Courts faced with the question of **implied preemption** may examine legislative history to determine legislative intent. Courts may also find that federal regulation is so pervasive that it manifests congressional intent to preempt the field. Congressional purpose in enacting regulation may also be relevant to the determination of preemption.

There are important constitutional considerations and implications underlying whether federal law preempts state law in a given field. In implied preemption cases, courts sometimes balance state and federal interests in a way similar to commerce theory analysis. Some preemption cases also raise burden-on-commerce issues. The difference is that in burden-on-commerce cases, courts are concerned with the policy implications of the Commerce Clause. In preemption cases, courts rely on the Supremacy Clause and focus on whether Congress intended to dominate an area of regulation.

However, as noted earlier, some states may want to enact environmental standards that are more stringent than the federal standards, and Congress may permit them to do so. For example, the Resource Conservation and Recovery Act (RCRA) expressly provides:

> [N]o State or political subdivision may impose any requirements less stringent than those authorized under this subchapter respecting the same matter.... [However, n]othing in this chapter shall be construed to prohibit any State or political subdivision thereof from imposing any requirements, including those for site selection, which are more stringent than those imposed by such regulations.[23]

Relying on this section, in *LaFarge Corp. v. Campbell*[24] a federal district court held that RCRA did not preempt a state statute that prohibited the burning of hazardous waste-derived fuel within one-half mile of an established residence. The court said that Congress obviously did not intend RCRA to preempt all state law governing the disposal of hazardous waste.

implied preemption: Status arising when Congress intends (though does not expressly state) to override, supersede, or avoid state legislative activity.

The court in *LaFarge* also pointed out that state laws and regulations concerning health and safety are historically a matter of local concern, and it noted that other courts have reached the same conclusion: If application of the law or regulation does not result in an absolute prohibition of a type of technology or totally prohibit importation of hazardous waste, federal law does not preempt it. The

[22] 2007 U.S. Dist. LEXIS 3002 (E.D. Cal. 2006).
[23] 42 U.S.C. § 6929.
[24] 813 F. Supp. 501 (W.D. Tex. 1993).

court noted that although ordinances prohibiting the storage, treatment, or disposal of "acute hazardous waste" within a state's jurisdiction are preempted by RCRA, siting prohibitions have been upheld. In the case of the siting ordinance at issue in *LaFarge*, the court said that the purposes of the statute were rational and within the purview of the legislature's authority to regulate hazardous waste management as anticipated by Congress.

As noted earlier, challenges to state laws under a preemption theory frequently involve Commerce Clause challenges as well. In *LaFarge*, the plaintiff also argued that the siting prohibition was invalid under the Commerce Clause because it did not regulate "even-handedly." However, the court said that the state statute applied evenhandedly to in-state and out-of-state companies and had only an incidental impact on interstate commerce.

According to the court, the relevant inquiry was whether or not the siting prohibition effected a legitimate public interest, and if it did, whether the burden on interstate commerce was clearly excessive in relation to the local benefits of the act. Under this test, the court held that the siting prohibition did not violate the Commerce Clause.

However, despite the preemption doctrine's slant toward allowing states to regulate matters of state and local concern, where state police powers have traditionally enabled states to regulate, in *Engine Manufacturers Association v. South Coast Air Quality Management District*[25] the U.S. Supreme Court held that some of the rules promulgated by California's South Coast Air Quality Management District were preempted by the federal Clean Air Act. The local emission rules in question established standards aimed at purchasers rather than manufacturers. However, the majority said these rules were nevertheless not permissible. To this, Justice Souter wrote a dissent to express problems with the majority's interpretation of the Clean Air Act as preempting local laws:

Engine Manufacturers Association v. South Coast Air Quality Management District

541 U.S. 246, 124 S. Ct. 1756 (2004)

JUSTICE SOUTER, Dissenting

The Court holds that preemption by the Clean Air Act … prohibits one of the most polluted regions in the United States … from requiring private fleet operators to buy clean engines that are readily available on the commercial market. I respectfully dissent and would hold that the South Coast Air Quality Management District Fleet Rules are not preempted by the Act. [Fn. by Justice Souter: … [T]he Los Angeles South Coast Air Basin is the only region in the country that has been designated an ozone "'extreme' nonattainment" area as defined by the Act.] …

So far as it concerns this case, [the Clean Air] Act provides that "[n]o State or any political subdivision thereof shall adopt or attempt to enforce any standard relating to the control of emissions from new motor vehicles or new motor vehicle engines…." The better reading of this provision rests on two interpretive principles the majority opinion does not address.

First, "[i]n all pre-emption cases, and particularly in those [where] Congress has legislated … in a field which the States have traditionally occupied, we start with the assumption that the historic police powers of the States were not to be superseded by the Federal Act

(Continued)

---

[25] 541 U.S. 246, 124 S. Ct. 1756 (2004).

unless that was the clear and manifest purpose of Congress." … The pertinence of this presumption against federal preemption is clear enough from the terms of the Act itself: [The Clean Air Act] § 101 states that "air pollution prevention (that is, the reduction or elimination, through any measures, of the amount of pollutants produced or created at the source) and air pollution control at its source is the primary responsibility of States and local governments." … [S]ee *Huron Portland Cement Co. v. Detroit*, 362 U.S. 440, 442[, 80 S. Ct. 8, 134 L. Ed. 2d 852] (1960) ("Legislation designed to free from pollution the very air that people breathe clearly falls within the exercise of even the most traditional concept of what is compendiously known as the police power"). The resulting presumption against displacing law enacted or authorized by a State applies both to the "question whether Congress intended any pre-emption at all"….

Second, legislative history should inform interpretive choice, and the legislative history of this preemption provision shows that Congress's purpose in passing it was to stop States from imposing regulatory requirements that directly limited what manufacturers could sell. During the hearings leading up to the 1967 amendments, "[t]he auto industry … was adamant that the nature of their manufacturing mechanism required a single national standard in order to eliminate undue economic strain on the industry." … Auto manufacturers sought to safeguard "[t]he ability of those engaged in the manufacture of automobiles to obtain clear and consistent answers concerning emission controls," and to prevent "a chaotic situation from developing in interstate commerce in new motor vehicles." … Congress was not responding to concerns about varying regional appetites for whatever vehicle models the manufacturers did produce; it was addressing the industry's fear that States would bar manufacturers from selling engines that failed to meet specifications that might be different in each State. [Fn. by Justice Souter: In fact, Congress allowed California to adopt its own specification standards [in the Clean Air Act] … but only California was so indulged….]

Section 209(a) can easily be read to give full effect to both principles. As amended in 1967, § 202 of the [Clean Air] Act authorized federal regulators to promulgate emissions standards for "any class or classes of new motor vehicles or new motor vehicle engines." … The 1967 amendments in turn defined "new motor vehicle" as "a motor vehicle the equitable or legal title to which has never been transferred to an ultimate purchaser," and a "new motor vehicle engine" as "an engine in a new motor vehicle or a motor vehicle engine the equitable or legal title to which has never been transferred to the ultimate purchaser." … [The relevant section of the Clean Air Act], in other words, is naturally understood as concerning itself with vehicles prior to sale and eligible to be sold….

On this permissible reading of the 1967 amendments, [the relevant section of the Clean Air Act] has no preemptive application to South Coast's fleet purchase requirement. The National Government took over the direct regulation of manufacturers' design specifications addressing tailpipe emissions, and disabled States (the California exception aside …) from engaging in the same project. The "standards" that the [relevant section of the Clean Air Act] preempts, accordingly, are production mandates imposed directly on manufacturers as a condition of sale. [The relevant section of the Clean Air Act] simply does not speak to regulations that govern a vehicle buyer's choice between various commercially available options.

This is not to say that every conceivable purchase restriction would be categorically free from preemption. A state law prohibiting any purchase by any buyer of any vehicle that failed to meet novel, state-specified emissions criteria would have the same effect as direct regulation of car manufacturers, and would be preempted … as an "attempt to enforce [a] standard relating to the control of emissions from new motor vehicles." … But that fantasy is of no concern here, owing to a third central point that the majority passes over: South Coast's Fleet Rules require the purchase of cleaner engines only if cleaner engines are commercially available…. If no one is selling cleaner engines, fleet owners are free to buy any vehicles they desire. The manufacturers would, of course, understand that a market existed for cleaner engines, and if one auto maker began producing them, others might well be induced to do the same; but that would not matter under the Act, which was not adopted to exempt producers from market demand and free competition. So long as a purchase requirement is subject to a commercial availability proviso, there is no basis to condemn that kind of market-based limitation along with the state command-and-control regulation of production specifications that prompted the passage of [the relevant section of the Clean Air Act.]

In sum, I am reading "standard" in a practical way that keeps the Act's preemption of standards in tune with Congress's object in providing for preemption, which was to prevent the States from forcing manufacturers to produce engines with particular characteristics as a legal condition of sale. The majority's approach eliminates this consideration of legislative purposes, as

(Continued)

well as the presumption against preemption, by acting as though anything that could possibly be described as a standard must necessarily be a "standard" for the purposes of the Act: a standard is a standard is a standard....

* * *

These objections to the Court's interpretation ... call attention to untidy details, and rightly understood legislation can be untidy: statutes can be unsystematic, redundant, and fuzzy about drawing lines. As a purely textual matter, both the majority's reading and mine have strengths and weaknesses. The point is that the tie breakers cut in favor of sustaining the South Coast Fleet Rules. My reading adheres more closely to the legislative history of [the relevant section of the Clean Air Act]. It takes proper account of the fact that the Fleet Rules with this commercial availability condition do not

require manufacturers, even indirectly, to produce a new kind of engine. And, most importantly, my reading adheres to the well-established presumption against preemption.

Questions for Discussion

1. What reasoning does Justice Souter use to argue that the California rule should not be preempted by the Clean Air Act?
2. Consider Justice Souter's arguments concerning market responses to demand for cleaner engines. Do you believe that the market should be trusted to lead to the development of cleaner products through demand created by command-and-control legislation at issue here? Are there some areas of environmental protection where this is a particularly attractive option, and other areas of environmental protection where it is not? Why?

Conflict Preemption of State Law

Conflict preemption occurs when compliance with both state and federal law is not possible, even when Congress has said nothing about the issue in question. If compliance with both state and federal law is impossible, or if state law obstructs federal regulations, courts will hold that federal law preempts state law.

In *Florida Lime & Avocado Growers*, a case challenging California law that excluded certain out-of-state avocados from being sold in state, the U.S. Supreme Court found that conflict preemption did not exist, because compliance with both the California law in question and the relevant federal law (specifically, the Agricultural Adjustment Act) was not impossible.

conflict preemption:
Status arising when state and federal law actually conflict, even if Congress is silent on the issue.

Florida Lime & Avocado Growers, Inc. v. Paul

373 U.S. 132, 83 S. Ct. 1210 (1963)

Mr. JUSTICE BRENNAN Delivered the Opinion of the Court

Section 792 of California's Agricultural Code, which gauges the maturity of avocados by oil content, prohibits the transportation or sale in California of avocados which contain "less than 8 per cent of oil, by weight ... excluding the skin and seed." [Fn. by the court: Avocados not meeting this standard may not be sold in California.... Substandard fruits are "declared to be a public nuisance"....] In contrast, federal marketing orders approved by the Secretary of Agriculture gauge

the maturity of avocados grown in Florida by standards which attribute no significance to oil content.... This case presents the question of the constitutionality of the California statute insofar as it may be applied to exclude from California markets certain Florida avocados which, although certified to be mature under the federal regulations, do not uniformly meet the California requirement of 8% of oil.

* * *

We consider first appellants' challenge ... under the Supremacy Clause. That the California statute and the

(Continued)

federal marketing orders embody different maturity tests is clear. However, this difference poses, rather than disposes of the problem before us. Whether a State may constitutionally reject commodities which a federal authority has certified to be marketable depends upon whether the state regulation "stands as an obstacle to the accomplishment and execution of the full purposes and objectives of Congress".... By that test, we hold that [the California statute] is not such an obstacle; there is neither such actual conflict between the two schemes of regulation that both cannot stand in the same area, nor evidence of a congressional design to preempt the field.

We begin by putting aside two suggestions of the appellants which obscure more than aid in the solution of the problem. First, it is suggested that a federal license or certificate of compliance with minimum federal standards immunizes the licensed commerce from inconsistent or more demanding state regulations.... That no State may completely exclude federally licensed commerce is indisputable, but that principle has no application to this case.

Second, it is suggested that the coexistence of federal and state regulatory legislation should depend upon whether the purposes of the two laws are parallel or divergent.... The test of whether both federal and state regulations may operate, or the state regulation must give way, is whether both regulations can be enforced without impairing the federal superintendence of the field, not whether they are aimed at similar or different objectives.

The principle to be derived from our decisions is that federal regulation of a field of commerce should not be deemed preemptive of state regulatory power in the absence of persuasive reasons....

* * *

A holding of federal exclusion of state law is inescapable and requires no inquiry into congressional design where compliance with both federal and state regulations is a physical impossibility for one engaged in interstate commerce.... That would be the situation here if, for example, the federal orders forbade the picking and marketing of any avocado testing more than 7% oil, while the California test excluded from the State any avocado measuring less than 8% oil content. No such impossibility of dual compliance is presented on this record, however.... Florida varieties marketed in California "attain or exceed 8% oil content while in a prime commercial marketing condition," even though they may be "mature enough to be acceptable prior to the time that they reach that content...." Thus the present record demonstrates no inevitable collision between the two schemes of regulation, despite the dissimilarity of the standards.

* * *

The issue under the head of the Supremacy Clause is narrowed then to this: Does either the nature of the subject matter, namely the maturity of avocados, or any explicit declaration of congressional design to displace state regulation, require [the California statute] to yield to the federal marketing orders? The maturity of avocados seems to be an inherently unlikely candidate for exclusive federal regulation. Certainly it is not a subject by its very nature admitting only of national supervision....

On the contrary, the maturity of avocados is a subject matter of the kind this Court has traditionally regarded as properly within the scope of state superintendence. Specifically, the supervision of the readying of foodstuffs for market has always been deemed a matter of peculiarly local concern....

... Federal regulation by means of minimum standards of the picking, processing, and transportation of agricultural commodities, however comprehensive for those purposes that regulation may be, does not of itself import displacement of state control over the distribution and retail sale of those commodities in the interests of the consumers of the commodities within the State. Thus, while Florida may perhaps not prevent the exportation of federally certified fruit by superimposing a higher maturity standard, nothing ... forbids California to regulate their marketing. Congressional regulation of one end of the stream of commerce does not, ipso facto, oust all state regulation at the other end. Such a displacement may not be inferred automatically from the fact that Congress has regulated production and packing of commodities for the interstate market. We do not mean to suggest that certain local regulations may not unreasonably or arbitrarily burden interstate commerce.... Here we are concerned only whether partial congressional superintendence of the field (maturity for the purpose of introduction of Florida fruit into the stream of interstate commerce) automatically forecloses regulation of maturity by another State in the interests of that State's consumers of the fruit.

Questions for Discussion

1. Why wasn't California's statute preempted by federal law?
2. Besides conflict preemption, what other types of preemption might have been relevant in this case?

(Continued)

3. In *Marsh v. Rosenbloom*, the Second Circuit Court of Appeals cited the U.S. Supreme Court to note that "[a]bsent clear congressional intent to the contrary, federal preemption of state law is not favored, ... especially in areas of law traditionally occupied by the states."[26] In which areas of law would federal preemption not be favored? Which areas of law might be subject to federal preemption if a state attempted to legislate in that area?

When state laws interfere with policy objectives of federal law, preemption may be found. If a federal agency licenses a private activity as part of a resource management program, for example, it may be argued that the federal government has authorized that activity. Thus, a state law restricting that activity would conflict with federal law.

In one such case, the Federal Energy Regulatory Commission (FERC), as a part of its licensing process, granted an applicant a license for a hydroelectric facility in California. The license prescribed minimum stream flows from the plant, but the minimum flow under the FERC standard permitted stream flows to decline to less than a third of the state's proposed minimum requirements. The State of California sought to impose its own, more environmentally protective stream flow requirements, but the FERC concluded that the task of setting such rates rested within its exclusive jurisdiction. The court of appeals affirmed the FERC's decision. On appeal, the Supreme Court held that the FERC's minimal standards controlled. Justice O'Connor, writing for the majority, summarized the reasoning as follows:

> A state measure is "pre-empted to the extent it actually conflicts with federal law, that is, when it is impossible to comply with both state and federal law, or where the state law stands as an obstacle to the accomplishment of the full purposes and objectives of Congress." ... As Congress directed in [the Federal Power Act (FPA) section] 10(a), FERC set the conditions of the license, including the minimum stream flow, after considering which requirements would best protect wildlife and ensure that the project would be economically feasible, and thus further power development.... Allowing California to impose significantly higher minimum stream flow requirements would disturb and conflict with the balance embodied in that considered federal agency determination.[27]

Field Preemption

Field preemption occurs when Congress has announced or demonstrated an intention to dominate an entire area or field; state laws regulating the same area are impliedly preempted. Field preemption is often understood to be a type of conflict preemption, rather than a separate category. An example of field preemption is the federal nuclear power regulatory scheme. In a number of cases challenging state regulation of nuclear materials and nuclear power plants, courts have upheld claims that Congress intended to preempt the field of radiation safety and power plant construction.

field preemption: Status arising when Congress intends to remove an entire area from state legislative authority.

---

[26] 499 F.3d 165, 177 78 (2d Cir. 2007).
[27] *California v. Federal Energy Regulatory Commission*, 495 U.S. 490, 506 (1990).

There are arguably strong policy reasons why there should be uniformity in setting nuclear radiation standards. Variation in radiological emissions, standards and design, and licensing requirements would result in expensive and unique designs for each plant. State governments argue that the health, safety, and welfare of their residents are essentially matters of state concern. However, state attempts to require safer and lower levels of radiation emissions have not met with success. Even in this area, though, the states retain some latitude to act.

Silkwood v. Kerr-McGee Corp.[28] was brought by the father of Karen Silkwood, a laboratory analyst at a Kerr-McGee plant that fabricated plutonium fuel pins for use in nuclear power plants. After she was contaminated by plutonium from the plant, she died in an automobile accident. Karen's father sued Kerr-McGee as administrator of her estate to recover for the contamination to Karen's person and property under Oklahoma tort law. The jury awarded Mr. Silkwood $505,000 in actual damages and $10 million in punitive damages. The court of appeals reversed the punitive damages award and other portions of the trial court decision, finding that the award was preempted by federal law. Silkwood appealed to the U.S. Supreme Court.

The Supreme Court recognized that the statutory scheme and legislative history of the federal Atomic Energy Act had convinced the lower court that Congress intended for the federal government to regulate the radiological safety aspects of construction and operation of a nuclear plant. Kerr-McGee argued that because the state-authorized award of punitive damages punished and deterred conduct related to radiation hazards in this case, the punitive damage award was preempted. The Court, however, said that its review of the legislative history of the federal law, coupled with an examination of Congress's actions with respect to other portions of the Act, convinced it that the preempted field did not extend as far as Kerr-McGee maintained. It said:

> No doubt there is tension between the conclusion that safety regulation is the exclusive concern of the federal law and the conclusion that a State may nevertheless award damages based on its own law of liability. But ... Congress [apparently] intended to stand by both concepts and to tolerate whatever tension there was between them. We can do no less. It may be that the award of damages based on the state law of negligence or strict liability is regulatory in the sense that a nuclear plant will be threatened with damages liability if it does not conform to state standards, but that regulatory consequence was something that Congress was quite willing to accept.[29]

The Supreme Court reversed the court of appeals judgment with respect to punitive damages and returned the case to the court of appeals for proceedings consistent with its opinion. Subsequently, the lower court's opinion was superseded by federal statute.

In the following case, Washington State adopted laws governing oil tankers, specifically related to navigation watch procedures, English-language skills of the crew members, training, and casualty reporting. The U.S. Supreme Court held that the area regulated by the state law had been preempted by Congress.

---

[28] 464 U.S. 238 (1984).
[29] *Id.* at 256.

United States v. Locke
529 U.S. 89, 120 S. Ct. 1135 (2000)

JUSTICE KENNEDY Delivered the Opinion of the Court

The maritime oil transport industry presents ever-present, all too real dangers of oil spills from tanker ships, spills which could be catastrophes for the marine environment. After the supertanker *Torrey Canyon* spilled its cargo of 120,000 tons of crude oil off the coast of Cornwall, England, in 1967, both Congress and the State of Washington enacted more stringent regulations for these tankers and provided for more comprehensive remedies in the event of an oil spill.…

In 1989, the supertanker *Exxon Valdez* ran aground in Prince William Sound, Alaska, and its cargo of more than 53 million gallons of crude oil caused the largest oil spill in United States history. Again, both Congress and the State of Washington responded. Congress enacted new statutory provisions, and Washington adopted regulations governing tanker operations and design. Today we must determine whether these more recent state laws can stand despite the comprehensive federal regulatory scheme governing oil tankers.… [W]e hold that some of the State's regulations are pre-empted.…

* * *

The State of Washington embraces some of the Nation's most significant waters and coastal regions. Its Pacific Ocean seacoast consists, in large part, of wave-exposed rocky headlands separated by stretches of beach. Washington borders as well on the Columbia River estuary, dividing Washington from Oregon. Two other large estuaries, Grays Harbor and Willapa Bay, are also within Washington's waters. Of special significance in these cases is the inland sea of Puget Sound, a 2,500 square mile body of water consisting of inlets, bays, and channels. More than 200 islands are located within the sound, and it sustains fisheries and plant and animal life of immense value to the Nation and to the world.

Passage from the Pacific Ocean to the quieter Puget Sound is through the Strait of Juan de Fuca, a channel 12 miles wide and 65 miles long which divides Washington from the Canadian Province of British Columbia. The international boundary is located mid-channel. Access to Vancouver, Canada's largest port, is through the strait. Traffic inbound from the Pacific Ocean, whether destined to ports in the United States or Canada, is routed through Washington's waters;

outbound traffic, whether from a port in Washington or Vancouver, is directed through Canadian waters.…

In addition to holding some of our vital waters, Washington is the site of major installations for the Nation's oil industry and the destination or shipping point for huge volumes of oil and its end products. Refineries and product terminals are located adjacent to Puget Sound in ports including Cherry Point, Ferndale, Tacoma, and Anacortes. Canadian refineries are found near Vancouver on Burrard Inlet and the lower Fraser River. Crude oil is transported by sea to Puget Sound. Most is extracted from Alaska's North Slope reserve and is shipped to Washington on United States flag vessels. Foreign-flag vessels arriving from nations such as Venezuela and Indonesia also call at Washington's oil installations.

The bulk of oil transported on water is found in tankers, vessels which consist of a group of tanks contained in a ship-shaped hull, propelled by an isolated machinery plant at the stern.… [T]he average vessel size increased from 16,000 tons during World War II to 76,000 tons in 1966. (The term "tons" refers to "deadweight tons," a way of measuring the cargo-carrying capacity of the vessels.) Between 1955 and 1968, the world tanker fleet grew from 2,500 vessels to 4,300.… By December 1973, 366 tankers in the world tanker fleet were in excess of 175,000 tons … and by 1998 the number of vessels considered "tankers" in the merchant fleets of the world numbered 6,739.…

The size of these vessels, the frequency of tanker operations, and the vast amount of oil transported by vessels with but one or two layers of metal between the cargo and the water present serious risks. Washington's waters have been subjected to oil spills and further threatened by near misses. In December 1984, for example, the tanker ARCO Anchorage grounded in Port Angeles Harbor and spilled 239,000 gallons of Alaskan crude oil. The most notorious oil spill in recent times was in Prince William Sound, Alaska, where the grounding of the *Exxon Valdez* released more than 11 million gallons of crude oil and, like the *Torrey Canyon* spill before it, caused public officials intense concern over the threat of a spill.

Washington responded by enacting the state regulations now in issue. The legislature created the Office of Marine Safety, which it directed to establish standards for spill prevention plans to provide "the best achievable protection [BAP] from damages caused by

(Continued)

the discharge of oil." Wash. Rev. Code § 88.46.040(3) (1994). The Office of Marine Safety then promulgated the tanker design, equipment, reporting, and operating requirements now subject to attack by petitioners....

If a vessel fails to comply with the Washington rules, possible sanctions include statutory penalties, restrictions of the vessel's operations in state waters, and a denial of entry into state waters....

Petitioner International Association of Independent Tanker Owners (Intertanko) is a trade association whose 305 members own or operate more than 2,000 tankers of both United States and foreign registry. The organization represents approximately 80% of the world's independently owned tanker fleet; and an estimated 60% of the oil imported into the United States is carried on Intertanko vessels. The association brought this suit seeking declaratory and injunctive relief against state and local officials responsible for enforcing the BAP regulations. Groups interested in environmental preservation intervened in defense of the laws. Intertanko argued that Washington's BAP standards invaded areas long occupied by the Federal Government and imposed unique requirements in an area where national uniformity was mandated. Intertanko further contended that if local political subdivisions of every maritime nation were to impose differing regulatory regimes on tanker operations, the goal of national governments to develop effective international environmental and safety standards would be defeated.

Although the United States declined to intervene when the case was in the District Court, the governments of 13 ocean-going nations expressed concerns through a diplomatic note directed to the United States. Intertanko lodged a copy of the note with the District Court. The concerned governments represented that "legislation by the State of Washington on tanker personnel, equipment and operations would cause inconsistency between the regulatory regime of the US Government and that of an individual State of the US. Differing regimes in different parts of the US would create uncertainty and confusion. This would also set an unwelcome precedent for other Federally administered countries." ...

* * *

The State of Washington has enacted legislation in an area where the federal interest has been manifest since the beginning of our Republic and is now well established. The authority of Congress to regulate interstate navigation, without embarrassment from intervention of the separate States and resulting difficulties with foreign nations, was cited in the Federalist Papers as one of the reasons for adopting the Constitution.... In 1789, the First Congress enacted a law by which vessels with a federal certificate were entitled to "the benefits granted by any law of the United States." ... The importance of maritime trade and the emergence of maritime transport by steamship resulted in further federal licensing requirements enacted to promote trade and to enhance the safety of crew members and passengers.... In 1871, Congress enacted a comprehensive scheme of regulation for steam powered vessels, including provisions for licensing captains, chief mates, engineers, and pilots....

The Court in *Cooley v. Board of Wardens of Port of Philadelphia ex rel. Soc. for Relief of Distressed Pilots* ... (1852), stated that there would be instances in which state regulation of maritime commerce is inappropriate even absent the exercise of federal authority.... Where Congress had acted, however, the Court had little difficulty in finding state vessel requirements were preempted by federal laws which governed the certification of vessels and standards of operation. *Gibbons v. Ogden*, [22 U.S. 1,]9 Wheat. 1[, 6 L. Ed. 23] (1824), invalidated a New York law that attempted to grant a monopoly to operate steamboats on the ground it was inconsistent with the coasting license held by the vessel owner challenging the exclusive franchise. And in *Sinnot v. Davenport*, [63 U.S. 227,]2 How. 227[, 16 L. Ed. 243] (1859), the Court decided that the federal license held by the vessel contained "the only guards and restraints, which Congress has seen fit to annex to the privileges of ships and vessels engaged in the coasting trade." ... The Court went on to explain that in such a circumstance, state laws on the subject must yield: "In every such case, the act of Congress or treaty is supreme; and the law of the State, though enacted in the exercise of powers not controverted, must yield to it." ...

Against this background, Congress has enacted a series of statutes pertaining to maritime tanker transports and has ratified international agreements on the subject.... [The court articulated how some of the Washington laws were field-preempted by federal laws.]

* * *

We have determined that Washington's regulations regarding general navigation watch procedures, English language skills, training, and casualty reporting are preempted....

* * *

When one contemplates the weight and immense mass of oil ever in transit by tankers, the oil's proximity to coastal life, and its destructive power even if a spill

(Continued)

occurs far upon the open sea, international, federal, and state regulation may be insufficient protection. Sufficiency, however, is not the question before us. The issue is not adequate regulation but political responsibility; and it is, in large measure, for Congress and the Coast Guard to confront whether their regulatory scheme, which demands a high degree of uniformity, is adequate. States, as well as environmental groups and local port authorities, will participate in the process....

Questions for Discussion

1. Should federal law preempt state law? If federal law could not preempt state law, what would the consequences be to our society?
2. Would it be possible for Washington State (or any state) to write a law that protected its environmental interests while at the same time not being subject to federal preemption? If so, how?

Despite the fact that the courts have articulated several tests to determine whether federal law preempts state law, every preemption case is unique. In each case, courts focus on the question of whether Congress intended to preempt state power to regulate in the same area. This is generally a question of statutory construction and thus requires the courts to interpret the language of the federal statute, its legislative history, and its purpose. In the absence of an express intention to preempt, the courts may infer preemption in cases where Congress has comprehensively regulated a field, when its interest is so dominant that the federal scheme is presumed to preclude enforcement of state laws, when the purpose of the federal law is obstructed by state law, or when state law actually conflicts with federal law. These rules are not precise guidelines, however, and each case turns on its own specific facts and peculiarities. Moreover, there are no bright lines separating the different categories of preemption; instead, the categories often blur together. Hence, one or more types of preemption may be found in the same case, or a particular case may not be a perfect example of any particular type of preemption.

Finally, state law may also preempt local laws. Though that issue has not been addressed in this section, the principles are largely the same, with the authority for the state's supremacy over conflicting local ordinances seated in the state constitutions.

■ ■ ■ REVIEW AND STUDY QUESTIONS

1. What are the four types of federal preemption? Identify an area that you believe should be preempted by federal law. Is it? If not, why not? If so, what are the local consequences of federal preemption?
2. Why might Congress not expressly state its intention in the case of preemption policy? Consider the realities of politics, including lawmakers' intentional deference to courts, and why such a course of action might be wise from a lawmaker's point of view.
3. Do you believe that the Supremacy Clause is necessary to our system of government? Describe how our society and systems of government might differ if the U.S. Constitution did not contain the Supremacy Clause.
4. What importance do the Commerce Clause and the Supremacy Clause have in cases in which a state government has enacted a statute or promulgated a regulation to regulate in an area where federal law already exists?

▦ The Property Clause: Federal Public Lands Laws

Another important federal power arises from the **Property Clause** of the U.S. Constitution. Article IV, § 3, provides that "Congress shall have the Power to dispose of and make all needful Rules and Regulations respecting the Territory or other property belonging to the United States." This expressly vests Congress with power to regulate federal land.

The federal government owns many millions of acres of public land, and many of those are reserved for national forests and parks. Vast tracts of public land contain many of the nation's resources. Federal lands produce some of the nation's oil and natural gas. In addition, the federal government owns large amounts of commercial forest land.

Historically, the federal government has tried to divest itself of public lands by transferring ownership to private parties. However, increasing interest in preserving national areas, especially wilderness and coastal areas, led Congress to enact laws designed to both preserve and protect public lands while capitalizing upon those resources.

Protecting Wildlife on Federal Lands

Property Clause: Article IV, § 3, of the U.S. Constitution; gives Congress the power to make rules and regulations concerning property that belongs to the United States.

The Property Clause of the Constitution gives Congress the power to manage and—if it chooses to do so—to protect these lands. In the following case, the Supreme Court addressed the scope of congressional power to regulate federal property under the Property Clause. In this case, the State of New Mexico challenged the constitutionality of the Wild Free-Roaming Horses and Burros Act. The district court held the act unconstitutional and enjoined its enforcement; the federal government appealed.

Kleppe v. State of New Mexico
426 U.S. 529 (1976)

Mr. JUSTICE MARSHALL Delivered the Opinion of the Court

At issue in this case is whether Congress exceeded its powers under the Constitution in enacting the Wild Free-roaming Horses and Burros Act.

The Wild Free-roaming Horses and Burros Act [Act] ... was enacted ... to protect "all unbranded and unclaimed horses and burros on public lands of the United States" ... from "capture, branding, harassment, or death." ... The Act provides that all such horses and burros on the public lands administered by the Secretary of the Interior through the Bureau of Land Management (BLM) or by the Secretary of Agriculture through the Forest Service are committed to the jurisdiction of the respective Secretaries, who are "directed to protect

and manage [the animals] as components of the public lands ... in a manner that is designed to achieve and maintain a thriving natural ecological balance on the public lands." ... If protected horses or burros "stray from public lands onto privately owned land, the owners of such land may inform federal officials, who shall arrange to have the animals removed...."

* * *

[The State of New Mexico, its Livestock Board and director, and the purchaser of three unbranded burros seized by the Board (pursuant to state law) on federal lands, and sold at public auction, brought this suit for declaratory judgment that the Act is unconstitutional.]

* * *

(Continued)

The Property Clause of the Constitution provides that "Congress shall have Power to dispose of and make all needful Rules and Regulations respecting the Territory or other Property belonging to the United States." ... In passing the Wild Free-roaming Horses and Burros Act, Congress deemed the regulated animals "an integral part of the natural system of the public lands" of the United States, ... and found that their management was necessary "for achievement of an ecological balance on the public lands." ... According to Congress, these animals, if preserved in their native habitats, "contribute to the diversity of life forms within the Nation and enrich the lives of the American people." ... Indeed, Congress concluded, the wild free-roaming horses and burros "are living symbols of the historic and pioneer spirit of the West." ... Despite their importance, the Senate Committee found:

> "[These animals] have been cruelly captured and slain, and their carcasses used in the production of pet food and fertilizer. They have been used for target practice and harassed for 'sport' and profit. In spite of public outrage, this bloody traffic continues unabated, and it is the firm belief of the committee that this senseless slaughter must be brought to an end."

... For these reasons, Congress determined to preserve and protect the wild free-roaming horses and burros on the public lands of the United States. The question under the Property Clause is whether this determination can be sustained as a "needful" regulation "respecting" the public lands. In answering this question, we must remain mindful that, while courts must eventually pass upon them, determinations under the Property Clause are entrusted primarily to the judgment of Congress....

Appellees argue that the Act cannot be supported by the Property Clause. They contend that the Clause grants Congress essentially two kinds of power: (1) the power to dispose of and make incidental rules regarding the use of federal property; and (2) the power to protect federal property. According to appellees, the first power is not broad enough to support legislation protecting wild animals that live on federal property, and the second power is not implicated, since the Act is designed to protect the animals, which are not themselves federal property, and not the public lands. As an initial matter, it is far from clear that the Act was not passed in part to protect the public lands of the United States ... or that Congress cannot assert a property interest in the regulated horses and burros superior to that of the State.... But we need not consider whether the Act can be upheld on either of these grounds, for

we reject appellees' narrow reading of the Property Clause.

* * *

[A]ppellees have presented no support for their position that the Clause grants Congress only the power to dispose of, to make incidental rules regarding the use of, and to protect federal property. This failure is hardly surprising, for the Clause, in broad terms, gives Congress the power to determine what are "needful" rules "respecting" the public lands.... And while the furthest reaches of the power granted by the Property Clause have not yet been definitively resolved, we have repeatedly observed that "[t]he power over the public land thus entrusted to Congress is without limitations." ...

The decided cases have supported this expansive reading. It is the Property Clause, for instance, that provides the basis for governing the Territories of the United States.... And even over public land within the States, "[t]he general Government doubtless has a power over its own property analogous to the police power of the several States, and the extent to which it may go in the exercise of such power is measured by the exigencies of the particular case." *Canfield v. United States* ... 167 U.S. [518,]525 [(1897)]. We have noted, for example, that the Property Clause gives Congress the power over the public lands "to control their occupancy and use, to protect them from trespass and injury and to prescribe the conditions upon which others may obtain rights in them...." ... And we have approved legislation respecting the public lands "[i]f it be found to be necessary for the protection of the public, or of intending settlers [on the public lands]." ... In short, Congress exercises the powers both of a proprietor and of a legislature over the public domain.... Although the Property Clause does not authorize "an exercise of a general control over public policy in a State," it does permit "an exercise of the complete power which Congress has over particular public property entrusted to it." ... In our view, the "complete power" that Congress has over public lands necessarily includes the power to regulate and protect the wildlife living there....

* * *

[For this and other reasons discussed in the opinion,] the judgment of the District Court is reversed, and the case is remanded for further proceedings consistent with this opinion.

Questions and Comments for Discussion

1. In *Kleppe*, New Mexico argued that if the Court approved the Wild Free-Roaming Horses and Burros

(Continued)

Act as a valid exercise of Congress's power under the Property Clause, then it would sanction "an impermissible intrusion on the sovereignty, legislative authority and police power of the State and ... wrongly infringe[] upon the State's traditional trustee powers over wild animals." The Supreme Court rejected this argument, saying, "Absent consent or cession, a State undoubtedly retains jurisdiction over federal lands within its territory, but Congress equally surely retains the power to enact legislation respecting those lands pursuant to the Property Clause.... And when Congress so acts, the federal legislation necessarily overrides conflicting state laws under the Supremacy Clause." According to the Court, "a different rule would place the public domain of the United States completely at the mercy of state legislation."[30] Which areas in your state are U.S. property, but are under the jurisdiction of the state unless or until Congress creates legislation that would override any conflicting state laws?

2. The state's concern expressed in *Kleppe* is another example of the tension between the powers of the state and federal governments to regulate land use within a federal system. In *Kleppe*, the state also expressed concern that the Act at issue violated traditional state power over wild animals. The Court agreed that the states have "broad trustee and police powers over wild animals within their jurisdictions." But the Court said, "[T]hose powers exist only 'insofar as [their] exercise may not be incompatible with, or restrained by, the rights conveyed to the Federal government by the Constitution.'"[31] How might conflicting federal and state policies related to animals and their habitats manifest in your own state?

3. Reconsider the traditional common law property rule regarding capture of wild animals discussed in Chapter 3. How does the federal law in this case and the Court's opinion upholding the provisions of that law reflect a change from traditional common law principles? What are the policy reasons underlying congressional action in this case? Would it make a difference if Congress were to enact a law to permit hunting and killing of wild burros and horses on public lands rather than a law protecting them from such activities?

Exercise of Federal Power over Nonfederal Land or Conduct via the Property Clause

Although the Property Clause gives Congress the power to make rules and regulations governing property belonging to the United States, the Supreme Court has held that this is not necessarily an exclusive power. An important question is the extent to which the Property Clause gives the federal government regulatory power over private lands adjoining public lands. Some courts have interpreted the Property Clause to give Congress the power to prevent activities on private lands that would interfere with the congressional purpose of protecting public lands. After *Kleppe*, some appellate courts have held that the Property Clause gives the federal government the right to regulate conduct that affects federal land even when that conduct does not occur on federal land.[32] Moreover, the Property Clause has been held to allow Congress to regulate private property interests, such as easements, on federal lands.[33]

In *Cappaert v. United States*,[34] the question before the Supreme Court was whether the reservation of Devil's Hole (a deep limestone cavern in Nevada) as a national monument also reserved federal water rights in unappropriated water at

---

[30] 426 U.S. at 543.

[31] *Id.* at 545.

[32] *Duncan Energy Co. v. United States Forest Service*, 50 F.3d 584, 589 (8th Cir. 1995).

[33] *Burlison v. United States*, 533 F.3d 419 (6th Cir. 2008).

[34] 426 U.S. 128 (1976).

the site. Recall from Chapter 3 that water rights in the Western states are based on a doctrine called the prior appropriation doctrine. Under this doctrine, "first to use the water in time is first in right."

The *Cappaert* petitioners owned a 12,000-acre ranch near Devil's Hole, 4,000 acres of which were used for growing crops and grazing more than 1,700 head of cattle. The federal proclamation designating Devil's Hole a national monument was made in January 1952. In 1968, the Cappaerts began pumping groundwater on their ranch and were the first to appropriate groundwater from an aquifer that was also the source of the water in Devil's Hole.

The question before the Supreme Court was whether the federal government intended to reserve unappropriated and available water in its federal reservation of public land. The Court said that the district court had correctly determined that the level of the pool (within the cave) could be permitted to drop to the extent that the drop did not impair the scientific value of the pool as the natural habitat of the species sought to be preserved. Under the doctrine of implied reservation of water, the Court said an amount of water necessary to fulfill the purpose of the monument reservation was impliedly reserved by the government.

▦ ▦ ▦ REVIEW AND STUDY QUESTIONS

1. What are some examples of cooperative federalism between federal and state governments related to an environmental issue that interests you?
2. What is the difference between the Commerce Clause and the dormant commerce clause?
3. What is the relationship between the Supremacy Clause and federal preemption?
4. How can the Property Clause be used to protect wildlife on private lands that adjoin public lands?

▦ Conclusion

The federal government derives its power from the U.S. Constitution. This chapter has provided an overview of some of the most powerful and constraining constitutional issues that arise in environmental law. The federal and state governments work in a system of federalism, or cooperative federalism, to address issues of mutual concern. Jurisdictional disputes commonly arise when the states regulate areas that affect interstate commerce, or regulate in areas that the federal government has preempted. Legal issues arising under such disputes often involve the Commerce Clause or the Supremacy Clause—and often both. Congress manages the federal government's vast tracts of land under the Property Clause, which gives the federal government the right to manage not only the lands, but also the wildlife upon those lands and conduct on nonfederal land that affects federal land. Other constitutional issues involve the amendments to the Constitution, such as takings and free speech. Those issues were addressed in Chapter 6. Threshold issues of litigation, such as timing of judicial review and standing, are also constitutional issues. The concept of standing was introduced in Chapter 1. Chapter 8 further addresses the issue of standing, along with other threshold issues.

Chapter 7 Case Study Activity: Water in Plastic Bottles Banned

Would you support a ban on plastic water bottles? Concord, Massachusetts, enacted such a ban (http://newsfeed.time .com/2013/01/04/massachusett-town-bans-plastic-water-bottles/). So did the Grand Canyon (http://www.reuters.com/article /2012/02/08/us-grandcanyon-bottles-idUSTRE8171K020120208)

Environmentalists hope that the ban on plastic water bottles will reduce pollution and the use of fossil fuels in the production of plastic bottles. However, not all beverages in plastic bottles are banned. Soft drinks, for example, are still allowed to be sold. Some believe that the ban will have no effect on the environment, restricts commerce unnecessarily, and will simply encourage consumers to go elsewhere.

Take one of the following positions:

1. Imagine that you supported such a ban in your community. Anticipate the constitutional challenges that might be made to such a law. Write a memo to identify the constitution-based legal challenges that will be made to your proposed ban, and address how to rebut or avoid those problems.

2. Imagine that you oppose such a ban in your community. Write a memo to identify the constitutional arguments that you will make to oppose this ban. Develop the arguments as if to inform a policy maker about the strength of your position.

Regardless of which side you have taken, couple these questions with a consideration of the political environment that you are navigating. What will determine if the ban will be successfully enacted into law or not?

CHAPTER EIGHT

Administrative Law

Learning Objectives

After reading this chapter, you will have an understanding of the role of administrative law. You will explore the delegation doctrine and the several powers held by administrative agencies. Specifically, after reading this chapter, you should be able to answer the following questions:

1. How does administrative law relate to environmental law?
2. What is the delegation doctrine and why is it important?
3. What powers do administrative agencies have?
4. What limitations exist on administrative agency power?

Here's a good idea!

This is a "bare bones" outline of the chapter. Expand this outline with more detailed notes as you read the chapter. This will allow you to create a study guide as you work. This good study habit will help you to learn the material, retain important points, and make efficient use of your time.

■ Introduction

This chapter focuses on administrative law, which is one of the most significant areas of law affecting the environment. **Administrative law** refers to the law related to the powers, duties, and procedures of administrative agencies.

The decision to address environmental issues through regulatory policy administered by government agencies emerged in the 20th century. President Nixon created the Environmental Protection Agency (EPA) by executive order in 1970. Since then, several major pieces of federal environmental legislation have been passed. The responsibility for many important environmental laws falls to various federal agencies, including the EPA. With jurisdiction over air pollution, water pollution, drinking water, hazardous waste disposal, pesticides, and toxic substances, the EPA is one of the most powerful regulatory agencies in the federal government. Furthermore, all the states have enacted state environmental protection laws, in some cases more stringent than those at the federal level, and have created state agencies with the power to administer and enforce those environmental laws within their jurisdictions.

Federal and state agencies play a central role in rule making, adjudication, and enforcement of the various provisions of federal and state environmental laws. In many cases, principles of administrative law are critical in resolving environmental disputes. In cases where there are scientific data supporting both sides of a dispute, the most important issues turn out to be the burden of proof,

administrative law: Area of law related to the powers, duties, and procedures of administrative agencies.

whether the administrative agency's decision was within the scope of its authority, or whether the agency's procedure was consistent with legal requirements.

As is true with any law or legal analysis, an important first step is to identify and verify the authority of the law or lawmaking body itself. With administrative law, a useful inquiry is to ask from whence administrative agencies draw their power and what the limits of those powers are. Unlike the three branches of government, federal administrative agencies were neither created nor given power by the U.S. Constitution. However, their existence is ubiquitous and their power vast. Moreover, unlike the legislative and executive branches of government, the people do not have a role in staffing or electing administrative agency heads. Essentially, administrative agencies are unelected creators, enforcers, and adjudicators of public law. Let's examine the source of their power, as well as the extent and limitation of those powers.

▪ Sources of Agency Power

The Delegation Doctrine

Nothing in the federal Constitution or most state constitutions provides for the creation of administrative agencies. However, as government's role in protecting the environment has increased, the legislative and executive branches of government have increasingly delegated some of their powers to administrative agencies. In the vast majority of instances, the legislative body delegates power to an agency by statute, and the new agency is made part of the executive branch of government (a logical step, as administrative agencies are established to carry out—*execute*—the terms of the law). The statute creating an administrative agency is called **enabling legislation**.

Agencies typically are given powers with characteristics of each of the three branches of government:

1. Many agencies have the *legislative* power to issue rules and regulations that have the force of law and may impose civil or criminal penalties for violation.

2. Most agencies have *executive* power to enforce provisions of the statute and agency rules and regulations. In this role, the agency is responsible for analyzing issues within its purview, and administering and enforcing laws passed by the legislative body.

3. Finally, agencies often have *judicial* power to hold hearings and adjudicate individual disputes involving questions arising under agency rules and regulations.

enabling legislation: A statute that establishes an administrative agency.

delegation doctrine: Legal doctrine addressing the question of whether a branch of government may constitutionally assign some of its powers or delegate some of its duties to an administrative agency.

A fundamental principle of administrative law is that the powers and duties of the administrative agencies are derived from the statutes that created and assigned those powers. An agency only has the power and authority that the legislature expressly or impliedly delegated to it through the enabling legislation. Under the **delegation doctrine**, the courts examine such questions as whether the legislature and chief executive could constitutionally delegate a particular power to the agency or whether the statutory language in the enabling legislation is too broad or too vague to adequately define the agency's power. Consider former Chief Justice Rehnquist's words on this matter:

The many [Supreme Court] decisions that have upheld congressional delegations of authority to the Executive Branch have done so largely on the theory that

Congress may wish to exercise its authority in a particular field, but because the field is sufficiently technical, the ground to be covered sufficiently large, and the Members of Congress themselves not necessarily expert in the area in which they choose to legislate, the most that may be asked under the separation-of-powers doctrine is that Congress lay down the general policy and standards that animate the law, leaving the agency to refine those standards, "fill in the blanks," or apply the standards to particular cases. These decisions, to my mind, simply illustrate the … principle stated more than 50 years ago by [former] Mr. Chief Justice Taft that delegations of legislative authority must be judged "according to common sense of the inherent necessities of the governmental co-ordination."[1]

In the first part of the 20th century, the courts took a narrow view of Congress's ability to delegate constitutional powers to administrative agencies. However, after a series of cases challenging Franklin D. Roosevelt's "New Deal" legislation in the 1930s, courts have generally recognized that Congress and the executive branch can constitutionally delegate some of their powers to administrative agencies. As a result, delegation of legislative authority to administrative agencies has led to increasing government regulation through agency rulemaking.

Because an agency's powers are limited to those powers expressly and impliedly authorized by its enabling legislation, if a court determines that an agency's action exceeded the agency's authority under its enabling legislation, the action is illegal and unenforceable.

The Administrative Procedure Act

If its enabling legislation specifically requires the agency to follow certain procedures in decision making, the agency must act in accordance with those procedures. Absent specific requirements in its enabling legislation, a federal agency's actions are governed by the provisions of the **Administrative Procedure Act (APA)**,[2] a federal statute that establishes the basic framework for federal agency action. Congress has enacted other regulatory statutes that may supplement or supersede provisions of the APA, and judicial interpretation of enabling legislation and APA provisions in the context of specific statutes has refined the general principles of law governing agency procedure. Presidents have also imposed procedural requirements on agency rulemaking by executive order.

The APA acts as a blueprint of modern administrative law. It establishes minimum procedural requirements for many types of agency actions, specifically rulemaking and adjudication. *Adjudication* refers to case-by-case decision making by the agency in a hearing with trial-like procedures. The APA also provides a framework for judicial review of administrative decision making. It addresses the availability of review of agency action, the scope of judicial review, and court review of agency inaction. Because states have generally modeled state administrative procedure legislation on the APA, its principles also govern judicial decision making at the state level.

An administrative agency may exercise different kinds of powers as long as its enabling legislation expressly or impliedly authorizes it to do so. Important powers addressed by the APA are rulemaking and adjudication. An agency makes policy through rulemaking by issuing legislative-like rules and regulations. Policy making through adjudication occurs when the agency acts like a judicial body and applies

Administrative Procedure Act (APA): Congressional legislation that establishes the basic framework of administrative law governing agency action.

---

[1] *Industrial Union Department, AFL-CIO v. American Petroleum Institute*, 448 U.S. 607, 675 (1980) (concurring opinion).
[2] 5 U.S.C. §§ 551-59, 701-06, 1305, 3105, 3344, 5372, 7521.

legal standards set out by statute or regulation to the facts of a particular case in an administrative hearing.

■ Examples of Federal Administrative Agencies of Interest in Environmental Law

Name of Department or Administrative Agency	Areas of Focus Related to Environmental Law
Bureau of Land Management	Administers millions of acres of public lands
Bureau of Ocean Energy Management	Manages oil, gas, and renewable energy interests
Bureau of Reclamation	Administers dams, manages water resources, power plants, canals
Department of Energy	Oversees renewable energy, energy efficiency, nuclear energy
Environmental Protection Agency	Implements and enforces major federal legislation related to air, water, endangered species, hazardous waste, and land (e.g., wilderness, conservation)
Fish and Wildlife Service	Manages fish, wildlife, and natural habitats
Forest Service	Administers national forests and grasslands
Geological Survey	Studies natural resources of the United States
National Marine Fisheries Service	Manages marine habitat
National Park Service	Manages national parks
Office of Surface Mining	Implements and enforces the Surface Mining Control and Reclamation Act of 1977

Most agencies have the power to enforce their own rules or findings through sanctions like civil and criminal penalties. Most agencies also have other important powers, including the power to investigate complaints, to advise businesses and individuals on matters of concern to the agency, to conduct studies, and to issue permits and licenses when authorized to do so by statute. The courts have recognized that an agency may formulate policy through several different means as long as it is authorized to do so by its enabling legislation.[3]

There are benefits in implementing environmental policy by rulemaking rather than adjudication. Rulemaking may be fairer to the class of persons affected by the rule because of the wider notice provisions and opportunity for participation under the APA. Rulemaking is prospective rather than retroactive. In other words, it imposes consequences for future conduct rather than past conduct or

---

[3] *SEC v. Chenery Corp.*, 332 U.S. 194 (1947).

present status. Creation and application of a rule provide greater clarity and greater likelihood of uniform enforcement than creating policy through adjudication. Rulemaking is also more efficient, because it eliminates the need for a case-by-case adjudication each time the issue arises.

Nevertheless, there are some advantages to policy making through adjudication. First, the high procedural complexity of rulemaking, as a result of rulemaking process requirements (such as paperwork reduction provisions and impact statements), may make case adjudication swifter in some situations. Second, it is easier to modify specific rules through adjudication; therefore, it may be simpler to change agency policy through adjudication. Furthermore, because adjudicatory decisions are specific to the particular circumstances of the case, the rule that emerges through adjudication is also less likely to be over- or underinclusive in its impact.

In general, however, policy with the widest application is more often created through administrative rule than through adjudication, and most agencies use rulemaking to develop legislative policy rules. Most major pieces of environmental legislation adopted by Congress since the 1960s delegate to federal agencies—often the EPA—the power to implement the legislation through rulemaking. A number of environmental statutes explicitly authorize the agency to promulgate legislative rules, and some agencies are required by their enabling legislation to issue rules on certain issues and in certain areas. For example, the EPA was required to promulgate performance standards for the treatment, storage, or disposal of certain hazardous wastes within 18 months of the enactment of RCRA in 1976.

The next section considers the various powers of administrative agencies, including rulemaking, enforcement, and adjudicative powers.

■ Powers of Agencies

Rulemaking

Under the APA, a *rule* is defined as: "The whole or a part of an agency statement of general or particular applicability and future effect designed to implement, interpret, or prescribe law or policy or describing the organization, procedure, or practice requirements of an agency ...."[4] Types of administrative rules include:

1. **Substantive rules**. These rules prescribe law or policy and are legally enforceable in court. A rule requiring safety measures for certain kinds of activities is an example of a substantive rule. Substantive rules must meet the rulemaking requirements of the APA.

   substantive rules: Rules establishing or prescribing law or policy.

2. **Procedural rules**. An agency may create rules governing its organization, procedure, or practice. These rules are often exempt from some of the requirements of the APA.

   procedural rules: Rules governing the organization, procedure, or practice of an agency or other governmental entity.

3. **Interpretive rules**. An agency may issue statements to present the agency's understanding of the meaning of the language in its regulations or in the statutes it administers. An example of an interpretive rule is the EPA's statement on the meaning of "stationary source" under the Clean Air Act (CAA), which was at issue in *Chevron v. NRDC*. An excerpt of this case appears on page 245.

   interpretive rules: Statements that present an agency's understanding of the meaning of language in statutes or in its regulations.

The distinction between substantive, procedural, and interpretive rules is not always clear. For example, the EPA had difficulty characterizing its lender liability

---

[4] 5 U.S.C. § 551(4).

rule under Comprehensive Environmental Response, Compensation, and Liability Act (CERCLA) as interpretive or legislative. The difference may be important because agencies need statutory authority to adopt legislative rules; this power may be either express or derived from a general grant of authority. However, agencies may issue interpretive rules without such authority.

The APA does not require that all administrative rulemaking follow a single fixed approach. Rather, there are three basic procedures for rulemaking under the APA: informal rulemaking, formal rulemaking, and hybrid rulemaking.

Formal rulemaking procedures are required only when a statute other than the APA requires a rule to be made "on the record after opportunity for an agency hearing." Formal ("on the record") rulemaking is governed by §§ 556 and 557 of the APA. These sections require that the agency support its rule with substantial evidence in an exclusive rulemaking record, and that there be an oral hearing presided over by agency members or an administrative law judge. The parties are granted certain trial-like procedural rights, including the right to conduct cross-examination and to submit proposed findings and conclusions for agency consideration. Formal rulemaking is the exception in agency rulemaking, and these procedures are seldom used except in rate-making and food additive cases.

Most agency rulemaking is **informal rulemaking**, sometimes called *notice-and-comment rulemaking*. Informal rulemaking is governed by § 553 of the APA. Unless exempted by another provision of the APA, rulemaking under this section requires:

1. Notice of the proposed rulemaking published in the *Federal Register*. The *Federal Register* is the official government publication in which agency statements of organization, procedural rules, and public notices must be printed. The notice must include a statement of time, place, and nature of the proceedings; a reference to the legal authority under which the rule is proposed; and terms or a description of the issues to be addressed by the proposed rule.

2. Opportunity for interested persons to submit written data, views, or arguments on the proposal. The agency may or may not allow oral presentations.

3. A concise general statement of the basis and purpose of the final rule.

4. Publication of the final rule not less than 30 days before its effective date.

Some agency rules are exempt from these requirements, and the APA authorizes agencies to dispense with notice-and-comment requirements for "good cause." However, these exemptions are narrowly construed by the courts.

An agency makes rules to fulfill its statutory responsibilities, and Congress may require by statute that the agency undertake specific rulemaking actions within a particular time. Congress may also precipitate agency rulemaking by "recommending" or "urging" action by the agency. Under § 553(e) of the APA, the public may also generate rulemaking by the agency. Under this section, agencies are required to give interested persons "the right to petition for the issuance, amendment, or repeal of a rule." The president and Office of Management and Budget also play an important role in reviewing agency rulemaking decisions and setting priorities for agency rulemaking.

In some environmental statutes, Congress has established a "hybrid" form of rulemaking procedure. **Hybrid rulemaking** describes rulemaking requirements contained in specific pieces of legislation that combine notice-and-comment procedures with formal rulemaking procedures. Statutes like the Occupational Safety and Health Act[5] and the Mine Safety and Health Act,[6] for example, are considered hybrid

formal rulemaking: A rule made on the record after opportunity for an agency hearing.

informal rulemaking: Notice-and-comment rulemaking.

Federal Register: Daily publication of federal agency actions and proposed actions, produced by the federal government.

hybrid rulemaking: Rulemaking procedure that combines formal and information rulemaking requirements.

[5] 29 U.S.C. § 651 *et seq.*
[6] 30 U.S.C. § 801 *et seq.*

rulemaking statutes because they combine elements of both formal and informal rulemaking. In some statutes, Congress may mandate requirements such as a public hearing prior to rulemaking, the ability to cross-examine witnesses appearing at the hearing, and more extensive statements of justification for the agency rule. Congress may also seek to control agency rulemaking by imposing statutory deadlines for completion of rulemaking. For example, the Asbestos Hazard Emergency Response Act of 1986[7] required the EPA to publish final rules within 360 days.

When persons challenge agency action in court, a hugely important question is the extent to which courts should defer to the agency's interpretation of the statutes it administers. This is not only a legal question but also a significant public policy question. As a practical matter, the language in enabling legislation is often broad and subject to interpretation. The question of who should decide the meaning of the statutory language is significant because it goes to the scope of the agency's power and the relationship between the powers of the agency and of the three branches of government.

In the following case, the U.S. Supreme Court addressed the appropriate standard of review for an agency's interpretation of a statute. This case involved interpretation of the CAA Amendments of 1977, which required nonattainment states (states that had not met earlier requirements of the CAA) to establish a permit program for certain new sources of air pollution within the states. The case question centered on the appropriate definition of the term "stationary source" used in the CAA. The EPA by administrative rule permitted the states to adopt a plant-wide definition of "stationary source." Under the EPA definition, an existing plant that contained several pollution-emitting devices could install or modify one piece of equipment without meeting permit conditions if the alteration would not increase the total emissions from the plant.

Environmental groups filed a petition for review of the EPA regulation in the D.C. Circuit Court of Appeals, and the court of appeals set aside the regulations. Chevron U.S.A. and others appealed to the Supreme Court. The question before the Court was whether the EPA's rule permitting states to treat all pollution-emitting devices within the same industrial grouping as though they were encased within a single "bubble" was based on a reasonable construction of the term "stationary source" in the CAA. The *Chevron* decision requires courts to defer to an agency's interpretation of the language in the statute it is authorized to administer.

Chevron U.S.A., Inc. v. Natural Resources Defense Council

467 U.S. 837 (1984)

JUSTICE STEVENS Delivered the Opinion of the Court.

***

When a court reviews an agency's construction of the statute which it administers, it is confronted with two questions. First, always, is the question whether Congress has directly spoken to the precise question at issue. If the intent of Congress is clear, that is the end of the matter; for the court, as well as the agency, must give effect to the unambiguously expressed intent of Congress…. If, however, the court determines Congress has not directly addressed the precise question at issue, the court does not simply impose its own construction on the statute, … as would be necessary in the absence of an administrative interpretation. Rather, if the

(Continued)

---

[7] 15 U.S.C. § 2641 *et seq.*

statute is silent or ambiguous with respect to the specific issue, the question for the court is whether the agency's answer is based on a permissible construction of the statute....

"The power of an administrative agency to administer a congressionally created ... program necessarily requires the formulation of policy and the making of rules to fill any gap left, implicitly or explicitly, by Congress." ... If Congress has explicitly left a gap for the agency to fill, there is an express delegation of authority to the agency to elucidate a specific provision of the statute by regulation. Such legislative regulations are given controlling weight unless they are arbitrary, capricious, or manifestly contrary to the statute.... Sometimes the legislative delegation to an agency on a particular question is implicit, rather than explicit. In such a case, a court may not substitute its own construction of a statutory provision for a reasonable interpretation made by the administrator of an agency....

We have long recognized that considerable weight should be accorded to an executive department's construction of a statutory scheme it is entrusted to administer, ... and the principle of deference to administrative interpretations

> has been consistently followed by this Court whenever [a] decision as to the meaning or reach of a statute has involved reconciling conflicting policies, and a full understanding of the force of the statutory policy in the given situation has depended upon more than ordinary knowledge respecting the matters subject to agency regulations.... If this choice represents a reasonable accommodation of conflicting policies that were committed to the agency's care by the statute, we should not disturb it unless it appears from the statute or its legislative history that the accommodation is not one that Congress would have sanctioned....

In light of these well-settled principles, it is clear that the Court of Appeals misconceived the nature of its role in reviewing the regulations at issue. Once it determined, after its own examination of the legislation, that Congress did not actually have an intent regarding the applicability of the bubble concept to the permit program, the question before it was not whether, in its view, the concept is "inappropriate" in the general context of a program designed to improve air quality, but whether the Administrator's view that it is appropriate in the context of this particular program is a reasonable one. Based on the examination of the legislation and its history ..., we agree with the Court of Appeals that Congress did not have a specific intention on the applicability of the bubble concept in

these cases, and conclude that the EPA's use of that concept here is a reasonable policy choice for the agency to make.

***

... [T]he Administrator's interpretation represents a reasonable accommodation of manifestly competing interests, and is entitled to deference: the regulatory scheme is technical and complex, ... the agency considered the matter in a detailed and reasoned fashion, ... and the decision involves reconciling conflicting policies.... Congress intended to accommodate both interests, but did not do so itself on the level of specificity presented by these cases. Perhaps that body consciously desired the Administrator to strike the balance at this level, thinking that those with great expertise and charged with responsibility for administering the provision would be in a better position to do so; perhaps it simply did not consider the question at this level; and perhaps Congress was unable to forge a coalition on either side of the question, and those on each side decided to take their chances with the scheme devised by the agency. For judicial purposes, it matters not which of these things occurred.

Judges are not experts in the field, and are not part of either political branch of the Government. Courts must, in some cases, reconcile competing political interests, but not on the basis of the judges' personal policy preferences. In contrast, an agency to which Congress has delegated policymaking responsibilities may, within the limits of that delegation, properly rely upon the incumbent administration's views of wise policy to inform its judgments. While agencies are not directly accountable to the people, the Chief Executive is, and it is entirely appropriate for this political branch of the Government to make such policy choices—resolving the competing interests which Congress itself either inadvertently did not resolve, or intentionally left to be resolved by the agency charged with the administration of the statute in light of everyday realities.

When a challenge to an agency construction of a statutory provision, fairly conceptualized, really centers on the wisdom of the agency's policy, rather than whether it is a reasonable choice within a gap left open by Congress, the challenge must fail. In such a case, federal judges—who have no constituency—have a duty to respect legitimate policy choices made by those who do. The responsibilities for assessing the wisdom of such policy choices and resolving the struggle between competing views of the public interest are not judicial ones: "Our Constitution vests such responsibilities in the political branches." ...

(Continued)

We hold that the EPA's definition of the term "source" is a permissible construction of the statute which seeks to accommodate progress in reducing air pollution with economic growth. "The Regulations which the Administrator has adopted provide what the agency could allowably view as ... [an] effective reconciliation of these twofold ends...." ...

The judgment of the Court of Appeals is reversed.

Questions and Comments for Discussion

1. The two-part test used by the Court to determine whether the EPA's interpretation of its statutory language should be upheld in this case is as follows: First, if the intention of Congress is clear, the court must give effect to the unambiguously expressed intent of Congress. Next, if the court determines that Congress has not directly addressed the question, the court should defer to the agency's construction if it is based on a permissible construction of the statute. How can the court determine whether congressional intent is clear when interpreting a statute? If it cannot determine congressional intent, how can the court determine whether the agency's construction of the statute is a permissible construction of the statute?

2. Under the holding in this case, courts are required to determine whether congressional intention was clearly stated in the agency's enabling legislation. Doesn't this require the courts to first interpret the statute before deciding whether to defer to agency interpretation? As a practical matter, the line between deference to agency interpretation and the court's primary responsibility to interpret statutory law is a hazy one.

3. This case involved the bubble concept in the interpretation of "stationary source" of air pollution under the Clean Air Act. What is the bubble concept? How might a bubble result in cleaner air despite lowering air quality standards in some cases?

4. Despite the principle of deference stated in this case, courts may avoid deferring to agency interpretations of law if they find that the "plain meaning" of the statute differs from the agency's opinion.[8] As a general rule, courts appear more likely to defer to agency interpretation when the legislative scheme is very technical and implementation details are delegated to the agency's expertise. What are the benefits and drawbacks of judicial deference to administrative agency interpretations of law?

5. There are important public policy issues underlying the *Chevron* decision. Some argue that courts should defer to administrative agencies like the EPA because of the agencies' scientific expertise in determining how best to implement public policy. However, many perceive that the regulatory agency entrusted with environmental protection is "captured" by or otherwise beholden to the industry it regulates, and thus too often defers to the concerns of business and industry. To what extent do you think courts should defer to agency expertise? What are the implications of your answer?

■ *Proactive Environmental Lawmaking*

Congress has imposed additional requirements on agency rulemaking through other legislation. Presidents have also issued various executive orders related to rulemaking. Examples of laws affecting administrative agency rulemaking include:

1. The Regulatory Flexibility Act (RFA), 5 U.S.C. §§ 601-612, which requires agencies to consider the potential impact of regulations on small business.

2. President George W. Bush's Executive Order 13272, which enhanced the RFA by requiring "[e]ach agency [to] establish procedures and policies to promote compliance with the Regulatory Flexibility Act ... (the 'Act'). Agencies shall thoroughly review draft rules to assess and take appropriate account of the potential impact on small businesses, small governmental jurisdictions, and

(Continued)

---

[8] *See, e.g., Hercules v. EPA*, 938 F.2d 276 (D.C. Cir. 1991).

small organizations, as provided by the Act."

3. The Paperwork Reduction Act of 1980, 44 U.S.C. §§ 3501-3520, which assigns to the Office of Management and Budget (OMB) the responsibility for coordinating federal information policy.

4. The National Environmental Policy Act (NEPA), 42 U.S.C. §§ 4321-4347, which directs agencies to consider the potential environmental impact of major federal actions significantly affecting the quality of the human environment. (NEPA requirements are discussed in Chapter 9 of this text.)

5. The Federal Advisory Committee Act, 5 U.S.C. App., Pub. L. No. 92-463, 86 Stat. 770, which regulates the formation and operation of advisory committees by federal agencies.

6. The Negotiated Rulemaking Act of 1990, 5 U.S.C. § 561 *et seq.*, which establishes a statutory framework for negotiated rulemaking to formulate proposed regulations. Under negotiated rulemaking, representatives of the agency and various affected interest groups negotiate the text of a proposed rule.

7. The Federal Register Act, 44 U.S.C. § 1501 *et seq.* The APA requires publication in the *Federal Register* of agency statements of organization, procedural rules, and public notices mandated for formal and informal rulemaking.

8. President Obama's Executive Order 13563, which set forth new principles to guide regulatory decision making. These include the following directions to agencies:

   a. Promote public participation, through transparency of process, and to engage the public before rulemaking has begun
   b. Reduce "redundant, inconsistent, or overlapping requirements"
   c. Identify and consider flexible approaches to regulatory problems, which may "reduce burdens and maintain flexibility and freedom of choice for the public"
   d. Promote scientific integrity
   e. Produce plans to revisit existing significant regulations to determine whether they should be modified, streamlined, expanded, or repealed

It's useful to keep in mind that the procedures for rulemaking do not exist in a void. The Constitution establishes basic procedural principles. These include the Fifth Amendment, which provides that no person shall "be deprived of life, liberty, or property, without due process of law." Of course, the Fifth Amendment is applicable to the states through the Fourteenth Amendment. These requirements mean that official government action must meet minimum standards of fairness.

Threshold issues include what and how much process is "due." This depends, in part, on the rights affected. Therefore, due process rights can vary, depending on the context, the issue, and whether a property or a liberty interest has been affected. These procedural due process guarantees are primarily applicable in agency adjudicative action rather than agency rulemaking. With that in mind, let us now turn to other powers of administrative agencies.

Enforcement

Administrative agencies have the power to enforce the laws that they are charged with implementing. Because the EPA is the administrative agency most often involved with environmental issues, this discussion is confined to its abilities to enforce environmental laws and regulations.

The EPA engages in several different enforcement programs and types of actions. It brings civil actions against polluters. It assists in the criminal prosecution of persons or businesses accused of violating environmental laws. It also engages in cleanup enforcement, by locating parties responsible for the contamination of sites and ordering them to conduct and/or pay for the cleanup. Additionally, the EPA engages in federal facilities enforcement, ensuring that federal buildings and other federal facilities meet the requirements of federal environmental law.

In carrying out its duties, the EPA can take action through civil administrative actions, including issuing a notice of violation or issuing an administrative order to do something (e.g., to comply with the law or to refrain from violating it). The EPA can also litigate. It can bring civil lawsuits—which are filed through the Department of Justice on its behalf—in court against defendants for failing to comply with the law, failing to comply with an administrative order, or failing to pay for a cleanup for which the party is responsible. The EPA can also take enforcement actions against a party in criminal matters by assisting in the prosecution of serious, willful, or knowingly committed violations.

Administrative agencies can issue subpoenas, conduct searches, seize property, and make inspections, providing they comply with constitutional protections against illegal searches and seizures. Primarily, this means that in most instances, an agency must obtain a warrant before a search is conducted.

■ ACTIVITY BOX   EPA Enforcement Activity

Visit the Environmental Protection Agency's Enforcement and Compliance History Online by visiting http://www.epa.gov/enforcement/data/index.html

Click on "Enforcement and Compliance History Online (ECHO)." In the search box, enter your city, state, or zip code. Click "search."

Answer the following questions:

1. How many enforcement and compliance actions appeared in the map? You may wish to scroll down to the bottom of the page and look at the list, rather than the map. (If none, choose another zip code, such as a nearby city, or "zoom out" on the map until some sites appear.)

2. Were you aware of the enforcement and compliance activities in this area? If so, how did you become aware of them? If not, should this information have been made more public somehow? Why?

3. What activities led to the enforcement and compliance actions that appear on the map? Are the activities still occurring? If not, who should pay for cleanup of these activities?

4. Go back to the Enforcement and Compliance History Online page where you first entered your zip code. Explore the other resources on that page. What other information can you learn about your environment from that database? Do you agree that public funds should be used to support the collection and dissemination of this information? Why or why not?

Adjudicative Powers

Administrative agencies also have adjudicative powers. Administrative law judges (ALJs) hear cases that they are authorized to hear under the APA and/or the agency's enabling statute. An ALJ will hear disputes concerning the powers exercised by the agency by which he or she is employed. Some agencies, such as the EPA, also have an appeals board. The Environmental Appeals Board (EAB) is the final decision maker in that agency and routinely hears appeals related to permits, civil penalties, cleanup costs, and regulatory decisions involving the federal environmental statutes that the EPA administers.

An important concept related to administrative law and dispute resolution is **exhaustion of administrative remedies**. In essence, this doctrine requires a party to seek all possible relief from the agency itself—exhausting the administrative remedies—before seeking review by the courts. The requirement of exhaustion gives the agency the opportunity to correct any errors that may have occurred at an earlier stage in the proceedings. Practically speaking, this means that an aggrieved party cannot bring a claim to court without first undertaking all available administrative agency avenues for relief. At the EPA, this would mean bringing the matter before an ALJ and then appealing to the EAB. Once that process has concluded, if the result is still unsatisfactory, the party may bring the claim to court, although the bases for challenge may be limited. The concept of exhaustion is discussed more fully later in this chapter, in the consideration of judicial restraints on administrative agency action.

Critics argue that the exhaustion doctrine creates great time and cost hurdles, because a party that must exhaust all administrative agency remedies before bringing a case to court may have to spend a tremendous amount of time and resources in doing so. There is also a perception that agencies often have little incentive to deal efficiently and fairly with claims and challenges, and instead use their ponderous internal remedy processes to literally "exhaust" a party's resources and motivation. Proponents of administrative agency law point out that such requirements preserve judicial time, which is already overburdened, and the procedures allow the agency a thorough opportunity to correct problems before the issue goes to litigation.

Threshold issues to litigation are discussed in the next section, in the material related to judicial review of agency action.

exhaustion of administrative remedies: Legal doctrine providing that a party must seek all possible relief from an administrative body before a court will grant review of the contested agency action.

■ ■ ■ ■ REVIEW AND STUDY QUESTIONS

1. During the past 80 years or so, a great many administrative agencies have been created. List as many different kinds of agencies as you can think of. Are these state or federal agencies? How does each of these agencies affect your life and your current or intended professional life?

2. Advantages of agency policy making include the fact that this provides more flexibility in decision making by specialized staff with expertise in the regulated area, and that regulatory procedures can be designed to address specific problems. Disadvantages include the facts that agency power has fewer checks and balances on it than other government entities, and that agency expertise may lead to rigidity in point of view. Additionally, as Justice Douglas pointed out in *Sierra Club v. Morton*, agencies may be unduly influenced or "captured" by the groups that they are created to

regulate. Write an essay arguing that agencies have either too much or too little power and propose a solution supportable within our legal system to address the problem(s) you identified.

3. What are the three major powers of administrative agencies? How do these powers mimic the tripartite system of government created by the U.S. Constitution?

4. What are the three types of rulemaking that an agency may engage in? Identify benefits and drawbacks to each type of rulemaking.

5. Review Box 8.1. Identify an additional statute or executive order related to federal agency rulemaking. What is the purpose of that statute or executive order? Does it lessen the regulatory burden, or does it add to a regulatory burden? Explain.

▪ Limitations on Agency Power

Although administrative agencies are very powerful, as they are able to conduct legislative, judicial, and executive functions "in house," there are important checks on their power as well. The judicial, legislative, and executive branches all exert important limitations on agency power. Additionally, the public and the administrative agencies themselves place limitations on agency power. Let's look at each of these sources of restraints on agency power.

Judicial Review

Judicial review occurs when a court reviews an agency's final action. Issues concerning judicial review include: (1) whether court review of the agency action is available at all; (2) if it is, what the appropriate standard of judicial review is; and (3) what remedies, if any, are available in cases where the agency has failed to initiate or to complete rulemaking. Many of these questions require the courts to consider principles of constitutional law as well as administrative law, because they raise fundamental concerns about the appropriate relationship between the courts, the legislative and executive branches of government, and the agency.

Is Judicial Review of Agency Action Available?

The APA provides guidance as to the first question: "Is agency action subject to review?" § 701 of the APA provides that the action of "each authority of the Government of the United States" is subject to judicial review, except where "statutes preclude judicial review" or "where agency action is committed to agency discretion by law."

In the following case, the Supreme Court considered this presumption of reviewability in determining whether the petitioners were entitled to judicial review of the Secretary of Transportation's approval of federal funds to build a road through a park.

judicial review: Court review of an agency's final decision.

Citizens to Preserve Overton Park, Inc. v. Volpe
401 U.S. 402 (1971)

**Opinion of the Court by
Mr. JUSTICE MARSHALL....**

The growing public concern about the quality of our natural environment has prompted Congress in recent years to enact legislation ... designed to curb the accelerating destruction of our country's natural beauty. We are concerned in this case with ... the Department of Transportation Act of 1966 ... and the Federal-Aid Highway Act of 1968.... These statutes prohibit the Secretary of Transportation from authorizing the use of federal funds to finance the construction of highways through public parks if a "feasible and prudent" ... alternative route exists. If no such route is available, the statutes allow him to approve construction through

parks only if there has been "all possible planning to minimize harm" ... to the park.

Petitioners, private citizens as well as local and national conservation organizations, contend that the Secretary has violated these statutes by authorizing the expenditure of federal funds ... for the construction of a six-lane interstate highway through a public park in Memphis, Tennessee. Their claim was rejected by the District Court ... and the Court of Appeals for the Sixth Circuit affirmed.... We now reverse the judgment below and remand for further proceedings in the District Court.

Overton Park is a 342-acre city park located near the center of Memphis. The park contains a zoo, a

(Continued)

nine-hole municipal golf course, an outdoor theater, nature trails, a bridle path, an art academy, picnic areas, and 170 acres of forest. The proposed highway, which is to be a six-lane, high-speed, expressway, ... will sever the zoo from the rest of the park. Although the roadway will be depressed below ground level except where it crosses a small creek, 26 acres of the park will be destroyed....

[The Court noted that the highway project had been approved by various federal agencies, including approval of the route and design by the Secretary of Transportation.] Neither announcement approving the route and design ... was accompanied by a statement of the Secretary's factual findings. He did not indicate why he believed there were no feasible and prudent alternative routes or why design changes could not be made to reduce the harm to the park.

***

A threshold question—whether petitioners are entitled to any judicial review—is easily answered. § 701 of the Administrative Procedure Act ... provides that the action of "each authority of the Government of the United States," which includes the Department of Transportation, ... is subject to judicial review except where there is a statutory prohibition on review or where "agency action is committed to agency discretion by law." In this case, there is no indication that Congress sought to prohibit judicial review and there is most certainly no "showing of 'clear and convincing evidence' of a ... legislative intent" to restrict access to judicial review....

Similarly, the Secretary's decision here does not fall within the exception for action "committed to agency discretion." This is a very narrow exception.... The legislative history of the Administrative Procedure Act indicates that it is applicable in those rare instances where "statutes are drawn in such broad terms that in a given case there is no law to apply." ...

§ 4(f) of the Department of Transportation Act and § 138 of the Federal-Aid Highway Act are clear and specific directives. Both the Department of Transportation Act and the Federal-Aid Highway Act provide that the Secretary "shall not approve any program or project" that requires the use of any public parkland "unless (1) there is no feasible and prudent alternative to the use of such land, and (2) such program includes all possible planning to minimize harm to such park...." ... This language is a plain and explicit bar to the use of federal funds for construction of highways through parks—only the most unusual situations are exempted.

***

Congress clearly did not intend that cost and disruption of the community were to be ignored ... by the Secretary.... But the very existence of the statutes ... indicates that protection of parkland was to be given paramount importance. The few green havens that are public parks were not to be lost unless there were truly unusual factors present in a particular case or the cost or community disruption resulting from alternative routes reached extraordinary magnitudes. If the statutes are to have any meaning, the Secretary cannot approve the destruction of parkland unless he finds that alternative routes present unique problems.

Plainly there is "law to apply" and thus the exemption for action "committed to agency discretion" is inapplicable....

Questions for Discussion

1. The question of judicial review involves a complex and overlapping set of doctrines. These rules involve fundamental questions about the appropriate relationship between courts and administrative agencies. Should the courts be able to review (and strike down) administrative agency actions? Why or why not?

2. In *Overton Park*, the Supreme Court stated that when a plaintiff makes a credible argument that an agency has violated the Constitution, a statute, or a binding regulation, that action is subject to judicial review under the APA. Is undue emphasis placed on whether a court *can* review an administrative agency action, rather than whether it *should* review the action? Why or why not?

Additional issues related to whether a particular agency action is reviewable involve whether a party has standing, and questions of timing, including the exhaustion of administrative agency remedies and ripeness. The decision to grant judicial review of an agency decision upon the petition of an aggrieved party raises important questions: Who should be the final decision maker in determining environmental policy—the courts or the administrative agency? What role should the public play in environmental policy making? To what extent should agency decision making be protected from judicial review because it is legislative power protected from court review by the separation-of-powers doctrine of the U.S. Constitution?

As you may recall from Chapter 1, **standing** is the legal status conferring on a person or legal entity the right to challenge an action in the courts. (Standing must be shown in cases that are not related to administrative agency actions, too.) The issue of standing in environmental cases has become important because challenges to agency rules and decisions are often brought by environmental organizations like the Environmental Defense Fund and National Wildlife Federation. To prove that it has standing to bring a claim, a party generally is required to demonstrate (1) actual or threatened injury (2) that is fairly traceable to the defendant's conduct and (3) that is redressable by the court.

In *Scenic Hudson Preservation Conference v. Federal Power Commission,*[9] the Second Circuit recognized aesthetic injury as giving a party standing. In that case, the Federal Power Commission had approved plans to build a hydroelectric plan on Storm King Mountain. The Scenic Hudson Preservation Conference, an interest group that opposed the project, argued that the project would cause aesthetic harm. This was an important case, because it was the first time that a federal court recognized aesthetic harm as injury-in-fact to create standing.

In Chapter 1 of this text you read excerpts from *Sierra Club v. Morton.*[10] In that case, the Supreme Court first addressed the important issue of standing in environmental cases and controversies. In *Sierra Club v. Morton,* environmental groups had challenged the Forest Service's approval of a $35 million development project in the Mineral King Valley of California. The issue before the Court was whether the plaintiff environmental groups had standing to challenge the agency's approval. Sierra Club relied on § 702 of the APA, which reads: "A person suffering legal wrong because of agency action, or adversely affected or aggrieved by agency action within the meaning of a relevant statute, is entitled to judicial review thereof." In *Sierra Club v. Morton,* the Supreme Court stated the rule that a person has standing to obtain judicial review of federal agency action under this section if the action caused him or her "injury in fact," and the alleged injury was an interest "arguably within the zone of interests to be protected or regulated" by the statute. The Court recognized that injury to aesthetics or ecology could constitute legal injury, but it said that the party seeking review must allege facts showing that he himself was adversely affected by the agency action.

Subsequently, the Court clarified these requirements in an expansive interpretation of standing. In *United States v. Students Challenging Regulatory Agency Procedures* (SCRAP I),[11] students challenged a federal agency's approval of a railroad rate increase because it would discriminate against recycled goods. In SCRAP I, the court held that the plaintiff students had standing, even though the injury they alleged was minimal.

The Supreme Court appears to have retreated from its earlier expansive interpretations of the standing requirement since 1990, limiting standing for such

standing: Legal question regarding whether a person or a legal entity has the right to be heard on a legal matter.

---

[9] 354 F.2d 608 (2d Cir. 1965).
[10] 405 U.S. 727 (1972).
[11] 412 U.S. 669 (1973).

organizations. For example, in 1990, in *Lujan v. National Wildlife Federation*,[12] the Court denied the National Wildlife Federation standing to obtain review of the Bureau of Land Management's administration of the Federal Land Policy and Management Act of 1976. The issue in that case was whether the Bureau had properly fulfilled its duties under the Act in deciding to permit previously withdrawn federal lands to be opened up to mining activities.

Justice Scalia, writing for the majority, found that the Federation was a proper representative of individual members' interests and that those interests were within the zone of interests established by the statute. However, because the facts alleged in the affidavits of individual members did not establish that their interests would be affected by the government action, the Court held that the plaintiff organization lacked standing. In 1992, Justice Scalia, again writing for the majority, concluded that an environmental organization lacked standing to challenge an agency decision even though the environmental statute at issue contained a provision authorizing citizen suits.

The Endangered Species Act requires federal agencies, in consultation with the Secretary of the Interior, to ensure that agency action is not likely to jeopardize a threatened or endangered species. In *Lujan v. Defenders of Wildlife*, the plaintiffs challenged a joint regulation by the Fish and Wildlife Service and National Marine Fisheries, which provided that consultation was required only for actions taken in the United States or on the high seas. The plaintiffs' concern was that international development projects funded in part by the U.S. government posed a threat to endangered species abroad.

The initial question before the Court was whether the plaintiff environmental groups had standing to challenge the agency rule. The court of appeals had held that the environmental groups did have standing under a specific citizen suit provision in the statute. The Supreme Court disagreed. It held that the plaintiffs lacked standing because they had suffered no concrete injury as required by Article III of the Constitution. A portion of the Court's opinion in that case follows.

Lujan v. Defenders of Wildlife
504 U.S. 555 (1992)

Justice Scalia Delivered the Opinion of the Court....

This case involves a challenge to a rule promulgated by the Secretary of the Interior interpreting § 7 of the Endangered Species Act of 1973 (ESA), ... in such fashion as to render it applicable only to actions within the United States or on the high seas. The preliminary issue, and the only one we reach, is whether the respondents here, plaintiffs below, have standing to seek judicial review of the rule.

***

Respondents' claim to injury is that the lack of consultation with respect to certain funded activities abroad "increas[es] the rate of extinction of endangered and threatened species." ... Of course, the desire to use or observe an animal species, even for purely esthetic purposes, is undeniably a cognizable interest for purpose of standing.... "But the 'injury in fact' test requires more than injury to a cognizable interest. It requires that the party seeking review be himself among the injured." ... To survive the Secretary's summary judgment motion, respondents had to submit affidavits or other evidence showing, through specific facts, not only that listed

(Continued)

---

[12] 497 U.S. 871 (1990).

species were in fact being threatened by funded activities abroad, but also that one or more of respondents' members would thereby be "directly" affected apart from their "'special interest'" in th[e] subject." ...

With respect to this aspect of the case, the Court of Appeals focused on the affidavits of two Defenders' members—Joyce Kelly and Amy Skilbred. Ms. Kelly stated that she traveled to Egypt in 1986 and "observed the traditional habitat of the endangered nile crocodile there and intend[s] to do so again, and hope[s] to observe the crocodile directly," and that she "will suffer harm in fact as a result of [the] American ... role ... in overseeing the rehabilitation of the Aswan High Dam on the Nile ... and [in] develop[ing] ... Egypt's ... Master Water Plan." ... Ms. Skilbred averred that she traveled to Sri Lanka in 1981 and "observed th[e] habitat" of "endangered species such as the Asian elephant and the leopard" at what is now the site of the Mahaweli Project funded by the Agency for International Development ..., although she "was unable to see any of the endangered species"; "this development project," she continued, "will seriously reduce endangered, threatened, and endemic species habitat including areas that I visited ... [, which] may severely shorten the future of these species"; that threat, she concluded, harmed her because she "intend[s] to return to Sri Lanka in the future and hope[s] to be more fortunate in spotting at least the endangered elephant and leopard." ...

We shall assume for the sake of argument that these affidavits contain facts showing that certain agency-funded projects threaten listed species—though that is questionable. They plainly contain no facts, however, showing how damage to the species will produce "imminent" injury to Mses. Kelly and Skilbred. That the women "had visited" the areas of the projects before the projects commenced proves nothing.... And the affiants' profession of an "inten[t]" to return to the places they had visited before—where they will presumably, this time, be deprived of the opportunity to observe animals of the endangered species—is simply not enough. Such "someday" intentions—without any description of concrete plans, or indeed even any specification of *when* the someday will be—do not support a finding of the "actual or imminent" injury that our cases require....

Besides relying upon the Kelly and Skilbred affidavits, respondents propose a series of novel standing theories. The first, inelegantly styled "ecosystem nexus," proposes that any person who uses *any part* of a "contiguous ecosystem" adversely affected by a funded activity has standing even if the activity is located a great distance away. This approach, as the Court of Appeals correctly observed, is inconsistent with our opinion in *National Wildlife Federation*, which held that a plaintiff claiming injury from environmental damage must use the area affected by the challenged activity and not an area roughly "in the vicinity" of it....

Respondent's other theories are called, alas, the "animal nexus" approach, whereby anyone who has an interest in studying or seeing the endangered animals anywhere on the globe has standing; and the "vocational nexus" approach, under which anyone with a professional interest in such animals can sue. Under these theories, anyone who goes to see Asian elephants in the Bronx Zoo, and anyone who is a keeper of Asian elephants in the Bronx Zoo, has standing to sue because the Director of the Agency for International Development (AID) did not consult with the Secretary regarding the AID-funded project in Sri Lanka. This is beyond all reason. Standing is not "an ingenious academic exercise in the conceivable," ... but as we have said requires, at the summary judgment stage, a factual showing of perceptible harm. It is clear that the person who observes or works with a particular animal threatened by a federal decision is facing perceptible harm, since the very subject of his interest will no longer exist. It is even plausible—though it goes to the outermost limit of plausibility—to think that a person who observes or works with animals of a particular species in the very area of the world where that species is threatened by a federal decision is facing such harm, since some animals that might have been the subject of his interest will no longer exist.... It goes beyond the limit, however, and into pure speculation and fantasy, to say that anyone who observes or works with an endangered species, anywhere in the world, is appreciably harmed by a single project affecting some portion of that species with which he has no more specific connection....

Questions and Comments for Discussion

1. Standing is an important threshold question in many environmental cases. The doctrine determines the kinds of challenges that courts will entertain in environmental rulemaking cases. Do you think that environmental groups like the plaintiffs in *Lujan v. Defenders of Wildlife* should be able to challenge an agency rule under the facts in this case? To what extent does your answer depend on whether you think the courts, the administrative agency, or the legislative branch should determine the appropriate geographic scope of the ESA?

(Continued)

2. The standing doctrine in environmental litigation has undergone vast changes since the Court's opinion in *Sierra Club v. Morton*. Of particular importance to environmentalists in *Lujan v. Defenders of Wildlife* was the Supreme Court's rejection of the plaintiff's argument for procedural standing based on the express citizen suit provision of the Endangered Species Act. Citizen suit provisions permit members of the public to bring suit against government agencies to enforce provisions of a law. These provisions originated with the Clean Air Act Amendments of 1970 and have been a component of environmental enforcement ever since.

The ESA citizen suit provision provided: "[A]ny person may commence a civil suit on his own behalf … to enjoin any person, including the United States and any other governmental instrumentality or agency … who is alleged to be in violation of any provision of this chapter." However, the majority of the Supreme Court in *Lujan*

v. Defenders concluded that this citizen suit provision did not create an automatic procedural right in all citizens to challenge the secretary's inaction. It said that the plaintiffs' "raising only a generally available grievance about government, claiming harm that is indistinguishable from the public at large," did not satisfy the Article III requirement for a case or controversy. The constitutional basis for standing is Article III, § 2, of the Constitution. The "case or controversy" limitation seeks to ensure sufficient opposition between parties to make the adversary system operate properly, and it is intended to help keep the judiciary within its proper role.

Most view the *Lujan* opinion as having serious negative long-term consequences for environmental protection. Find current cases initiated by environmental groups. Would you say that *Lujan* has limited efforts to protect the public interests by protecting the environment? Why or why not?

Other legal doctrines may also be relevant in determining whether the courts will grant judicial review in a particular case. Under Article III of the Constitution, federal court jurisdiction is limited to "cases or controversies." This means that there must be a **live case or controversy**, rather than a speculative or hypothetical case, controversy, or injury. Courts in the United States do not issue mere advisory opinions.

Agency action must be final to be reviewable by the courts. The requirement of **finality** derives from § 704 of the APA, which provides that "agency action made reviewable by statute and final agency action for which there is no other adequate remedy in a court are subject to judicial review." The requirement of finality prevents waste of judicial resources by consideration of an agency position that may be changed. However, it is not always a simple matter to determine whether an agency action is final, especially in situations where the agency's failure to act is challenged.

As noted earlier, a party must also exhaust all administrative remedies, seeking all possible relief from the agency itself, before seeking review by the courts. Like the requirement of finality, the requirement of exhaustion gives the agency the opportunity to correct any errors that may have occurred earlier.

Lastly, judicial review is appropriate only when the issues are "fit for judicial decision" and when delaying review will cause hardship for the challenging party. These requirements are generally treated under the judicial doctrine of **ripeness**.

The doctrines of standing, live case or controversy, finality, exhaustion of administrative remedies, and ripeness are closely interrelated, and are used to limit court review of agency action in cases where such review would be premature. These are threshold issues that must be addressed before judicial review is granted.

If Judicial Review Is Available, What Is the Standard of Review?

After determining that agency action is subject to judicial review, a court must turn to the second question: "What is the appropriate standard of judicial review?"

live case or controversy: Actual adversarial dispute or contested issue.

finality: Requirement that an agency decision be final before judicial review of the decision may be granted.

ripeness: Doctrine declaring that before judicial review is granted, legal issues must be presented that are appropriate for judicial decision making.

The *standard of review* is the way in which the courts judge the validity of the agency action. The courts' review of agency action or inaction provides relief for persons harmed by that action or decision. The function of judicial review is to require agencies to make decisions that are rationally based on facts and appropriate evidence. To answer this second question, we look again to the APA, as well as to the enabling statute, if it happens to specify the standard of review.

§ 706 of the APA governs the scope of judicial review. It provides:

> To the extent necessary to decision and when presented, the reviewing court shall decide all relevant questions of law, interpret constitutional and statutory provisions, and determine the meaning or applicability of the terms of an agency action. The reviewing court shall—
>
> (1) compel agency action unlawfully withheld or unreasonably delayed; and
> (2) hold unlawful and set aside agency action, findings, and conclusions found to be—
>
> > (A) arbitrary, capricious, an abuse of discretion, or otherwise not in accordance with law;
> > (B) contrary to constitutional right, power, privilege, or immunity;
> > (C) in excess of statutory jurisdiction, authority, or limitations, or short of statutory right;
> > (D) without observance of procedure required by law;
> > (E) unsupported by substantial evidence in a case subject to §§ 556 and 557 of this title or otherwise reviewed on the record of an agency hearing provided by statute; or
> > (F) unwarranted by the facts to the extent that the facts are subject to [**trial de novo**] by the reviewing court.
>
> In making the foregoing determinations, the court shall review the whole record or those parts of it cited by a party, and due account shall be taken of the rule of prejudicial error.

In this subsection, we review two of these standards: the arbitrary and capricious standard, and the lack of substantial evidence standard. Additionally, we will discuss judicial review in the event that an agency fails to act.

The standard of review traditionally applied by the courts in reviewing agency action is the **arbitrary and capricious** test of § 706(2)(A). In determining whether agency action avoids this characterization, courts generally examine whether the rulemaking record supports the agency's conclusions, whether the agency met procedural requirements imposed by law or public policy, and whether the agency's conclusions were reasonable in light of the evidence before it.

At this point, we return to the *Overton Park* case discussed in a previous section of this chapter. You may recall that in that case, environmental groups challenged the Secretary of Transportation's approval of federal funds for construction of a highway through a park. The Supreme Court first determined that the secretary's decision was subject to review. In the following portion of the case, the Supreme Court addressed the question of the appropriate scope of judicial review of the secretary's decision. (You may want to review the facts of *Overton Park v. Volpe* set out earlier in this chapter before proceeding with this portion of the opinion.)

trial de novo: A full new trial before the court, not limited to review of earlier proceedings.

arbitrary and capricious: A standard of judicial review specified by APA § 706(2)(A); essentially examines whether the agency had a reasonable, rational basis for its decision or action.

Citizens to Preserve Overton Park, Inc. v. Volpe
401 U.S. 402 (1971)

***

[T]he existence of judicial review is only the start: the standard for review must also be determined. For that we must look to § 706 of the Administrative Procedure Act, ... which provides that a "reviewing court shall ... hold unlawful and set aside agency action, findings and conclusions found" not to meet six separate standards.... In all cases agency action must be set aside if the action was "arbitrary, capricious, an abuse of discretion, or otherwise not in accordance with law" or if the action failed to meet statutory, procedural, or constitutional requirements.... In certain narrow, specifically limited situations, the agency action is to be set aside if the action was not supported by "substantial evidence." And in other equally narrow circumstances the reviewing court is to engage in a *de novo* review of the action and set it aside if it was "unwarranted by the facts." ...

***

Even though there is no *de novo* review in this case and the Secretary's approval of the route of I-40 does not have ultimately to meet the substantial-evidence test, the generally applicable standards of § 706 require the reviewing court to engage in a substantial inquiry. Certainly, the Secretary's decision is entitled to a presumption of regularity.... But that presumption is not to shield his action from a thorough, probing, in-depth review.

The court is first required to decide whether the Secretary acted within the scope of his authority.... Congress has specified only a small range of choices that the Secretary can make. Also involved in this initial inquiry is a determination of whether on the facts the Secretary's decision can reasonably be said to be within that range. The reviewing court must consider whether the Secretary properly construed his authority to approve the use of parkland as limited to situations where there are no feasible alternative routes or where feasible alternative routes involve uniquely difficult problems. And the reviewing court must be able to find that the Secretary could have reasonably believed that in this case there are no feasible alternatives or that alternatives do involve unique problems.

Scrutiny of the facts does not end, however, with the determination that the Secretary has acted within the scope of his statutory authority. § 706(2)(A) requires a finding that the actual choice made was not "arbitrary, capricious, an abuse of discretion, or otherwise not in accordance with law." ... To make this finding the court must consider whether the decision was based on a consideration of the relevant factors and whether there has been a clear error of judgment.... Although this inquiry into the facts is to be searching and careful, the ultimate standard of review is a narrow one. The court is not empowered to substitute its judgment for that of the agency.

The final inquiry is whether the Secretary's action followed the necessary procedural requirements. Here the only procedural error alleged is the failure of the Secretary to make formal findings and state his reason for allowing the highway to be built through the park.

Undoubtedly, review of the Secretary's action is hampered by his failure to make such findings, but the absence of formal findings does not necessarily require that the case be remanded to the Secretary. Neither the Department of Transportation Act nor Federal-Aid Highway Act requires such formal findings. Moreover, the Administrative Procedure Act requirements that there be formal findings in certain rulemaking and adjudicatory proceedings do not apply to the Secretary's action here.... And, although formal findings may be required in some cases in the absence of statutory directives when the nature of the agency action is ambiguous, those situations are rare.... Plainly, there is no ambiguity here; the Secretary has approved the construction of I-40 through Overton Park and has approved a specific design for the project.

***

... [W]e do not believe that [prior case law] compels us to remand for the Secretary to make formal findings.... [T]here is an administrative record that allows the full, prompt review of the Secretary's action that is sought without additional delay which would result from having a remand to the Secretary.

That administrative record is not, however, before us. The lower courts based their review on the litigation affidavits that were presented. These affidavits were merely "*post hoc*" rationalizations, ... which have traditionally been found to be an inadequate basis for review.... And they clearly do not constitute the "whole record" compiled by the agency: the basis for review required by § 706 of the Administrative Procedure Act....

Thus it is necessary to remand this case to the District Court for plenary review of the Secretary's decisions. That review is to be based on the full administrative record that was before the Secretary at the time he made his decision.... But since the bare

(Continued)

record may not disclose the factors that were considered or the Secretary's construction of the evidence it may be necessary for the District Court to require some explanation in order to determine if the Secretary acted within the scope of his authority and if the Secretary's action was justifiable under the applicable standard.

The court may require the administrative officials who participated in the decision to give testimony explaining their action. Of course, such inquiry into the mental processes of administrative decisionmakers is usually to be avoided.... And where there are administrative findings that were made at the same time as the decision, ... there must be a strong showing of bad faith or improper behavior before such inquiry may be made. But here there are no such formal findings and it may be that the only way there can be effective judicial review is by examining the decisionmakers themselves....

The District Court is not, however, required to make such an inquiry. It may be that the Secretary can prepare formal findings ... that will provide an adequate explanation for his action. Such an explanation will, to some extent, be a "*post hoc* rationalization" and thus must be viewed critically. If the District Court decides that additional explanation is necessary, that court should consider which method will prove the most expeditious so that full review may be had as soon as possible.

Questions and Comments for Discussion

1. The Court applied the arbitrary and capricious standard of review in this case. The Court said that to make this finding, it must investigate whether the decision was based on a consideration of the relevant factors and whether there was a clear error of judgment. What evidence would or could a court use to determine that a decision by an administrative agency was arbitrary and capricious?

2. The Court sent the *Overton Park* case back to the district court for further proceedings, which were to be based on the full administrative record that was before the secretary at the time he made the decision. Does judicial review waste time? Why or why not?

3. *Overton Park* is an important case not only for its discussion of the appropriate scope of judicial review of agency action under the APA, but also because of its emphasis on the need for the agency to compile a record for review. Although this case involved an adjudicatory decision rather than rulemaking, it has prompted agencies to develop adequate and sometimes extensive records in informal rulemaking cases. What costs and benefits are associated with greater recordkeeping burdens? Who should pay for these costs? Who does pay?

4. In *Motor Vehicle Manufacturers Association v. State Farm Mutual Automobile Insurance Co.*,[13] the Court clarified the test by stating that a rule or action would be found arbitrary and capricious if the agency "has relied on factors which Congress has not intended it to consider, entirely failed to consider an important aspect of the problem, offered an explanation for its decision that runs counter to the evidence before the agency, or is so implausible that it could not be ascribed to a difference in view or product of agency expertise." Why would an agency make a decision that was arbitrary and capricious?

5. To what extent does the Court appear to defer to agency decision making in the *Overton Park* case? To what extent does the Court's language in this case intrude on agency expertise in decision making? How would you strike the appropriate balance in this case?

6. Following the Court's ruling in *Overton Park*, the case was returned to the lower courts. The agency held new hearings and prepared an environmental impact statement. Secretary Volpe announced in 1973 that he could find no feasible and prudent alternative to going through the park, and in a challenge by the Tennessee Department of Transportation, the court of appeals upheld the secretary's ruling. Today the original interstate highway corridor abruptly ends at the edge of the park and a bypass to the north carries I-40 traffic. On what basis might this outcome be criticized? How might this outcome have been prevented?

In cases subsequent to *Overton Park*, the Supreme Court has continued to refine the arbitrary and capricious test. For example, in *Baltimore Gas & Electric Co. v. Natural Resources Defense Council*,[14] the Supreme Court upheld a series of

---

[13] 463 U.S. 29, 43 (1983).
[14] 462 U.S. 87 (1983).

rules issued by the Nuclear Regulatory Commission (NRC) that evaluated the environmental effects of a nuclear power plant's fuel cycle. The Court said that a reviewing court "must generally be at its most deferential" when examining agency predictions that are "within its area of special expertise, at the frontiers of science." According to the Court, the NRC's conclusions were within the bounds of "reasoned decisionmaking," and it found that the agency had considered the relevant factors and articulated a rational connection between the facts and the choice made. Once an agency meets those requirements, the Court said, "it is not our task to determine what decision we, as Commissioners, would have reached."

Besides the arbitrary and capricious standard, APA § 706 also specifies that a court will hold unlawful and set aside agency action that is found to be unsupported by **substantial evidence**. If there is substantial evidence to support the agency's decision or action, the court will defer to the agency's determination on appeal.

You might recall from Chapter 6 that the government is required to apply zoning and other land use regulations in a fair and nondiscriminatory manner. At a minimum, due process requires that a property owner be given notice of action affecting its property, that the owner have an opportunity to be heard at the hearing, and that the decision be a rational one based on the evidence. However, courts do not reweigh the evidence on appeal.

substantial evidence: A standard of judicial review specified by APA § 706(2)(E); essentially examines whether the agency had sufficient evidence to support its decision or action.

In re Quechee Lakes Corp.

154 Vt. 543, 580 A.2d 957 (1990)

ALLEN, Chief Justice

Quechee Lakes Corporation appeals from an Environmental Board decision requiring substantial modifications in its already-constructed Ridge condominium project. We affirm.

In 1981, Quechee Lakes Corporation (Quechee) obtained [a] land-use permit to build a twenty-eight-unit condominium project on a high ridge overlooking the Quechee valley. During the course of construction, a number of revisions to the architectural plans were made without additional permit procedures. The external changes included the addition of skylights, the enlargement of sliding glass doors, the addition of clerestory and other windows, a fourteen-foot increase in the depth of three of the six buildings, the addition of four-foot overhangs and wrap-around decks, a reduction of roof pitches, and the relocation of some buildings.

Only after construction had been completed did Quechee file an application for an amended land use permit, seeking to bring its original permit into conformity with the project as built. By this time, most of the condominium units had been sold.

The District Environmental Commission held hearings on the alterations and approved them in many respects. Certain of the changes were found to be objectionable, however, and the Commission conditioned the amended permit on four mitigating actions: the removal of the skylights, the installation of nonglare glass, the addition of tree plantings, and the installation of a barrier on the access road....

Quechee appealed to the Environmental Board, objecting only to the skylight removal condition and the Commission's denial of its motion for reconsideration.... After a de novo hearing and two site visits, the Board found that the condominium buildings are "one of the most visually prominent features in the valley." The Board found further that, taking the skylights and additional glazing together, approximately two-thirds more glass was visible than was approved under the original plans; that light from the windows and skylights is visible from many points in the valley at night; and that reflective glare from these sources results in a significant visual impact even during cloudy days. The Board also found that some of the other construction changes increased the perceived mass of the project.

(Continued)

***

Quechee … asks this Court to disregard the evidence produced through its own witnesses and from the Board's site visits and instead to focus upon the evidence actually introduced by the parties opposing the application. Quechee argues that this latter evidence, taken alone, was insufficient to establish that the project would have an adverse aesthetic impact. Since [the statute] places the burden of proof on the parties opposed to the permit where aesthetic impact is at issue, Quechee contends that the Board erred in concluding that the project would have such an impact….

***

Where the sufficiency of the evidence is questioned on appeal from a decision of the Board, this Court employs a deferential standard of review…. The legislature has mandated that "[t]he findings of the board with respect to questions of fact, if supported by substantial evidence on the record as a whole, shall be conclusive." … This Court has defined "substantial evidence" to mean "such relevant evidence as a reasonable mind might accept as adequate to support a conclusion." … After reviewing the record as a whole, we conclude that the Board's findings and conclusions are supported by substantial evidence.

***

Where a conflict in the evidence develops, its resolution falls within the Board's jurisdiction, for the Board is the proper trier of fact. The trier of fact has the right to believe all of the testimony of any witness, or to believe it in part and disbelieve it in part, or to reject it altogether. Thus, it is not for this Court to reweigh conflicting evidence, reassess the credibility or weight to be given certain testimony, or determine on its own whether the factual decision is mistaken…. Instead, our focus is upon the evidence supporting the Board's findings and the question whether that evidence is adequate.

***

[Judgment affirmed.]

Questions and Comments for Discussion

1. In *In re Quechee*, the developer argued that the board erred in making two site visits to the Quechee Valley during the course of the proceedings, and that its findings of fact and conclusions of law were based in part on observations made during those visits. The developer argued that the board's personal observations were not evidence and that, in any event, the board had failed to put its observations on the record. The court disagreed. This was a **question of first impression** in Vermont. This case raises the problem of whether members of municipal planning and zoning boards, who are often not lawyers, would be likely to be influenced by otherwise inadmissible or irrelevant evidence. What are the arguments in favor of permitting site visits? What are some arguments against permitting this kind of evidence in administrative hearings?

2. *In re Quechee Lakes Corp.* is a good example of the power of an administrative agency and the procedural issues that may arise in administrative adjudications. Quechee Lakes Corp. relied on the doctrine of **res judicata**, arguing under that doctrine that subsequent action on this particular issue should be barred because it had already been decided in a prior action. Earlier, the commission had issued an amended land use permit involving the project. This amended permit approved changes in the project's landscaping plans. But the Court said that the agency's subsequent decision was not barred by res judicata: "[R]es judicata applies only where a party seeks to relitigate the identical issues already decided…. Here, because of the unauthorized changes in the construction of the project, the landscaping issue was no longer identical to that decided by the Commission in the first permit amendment proceedings, and res judicata does not apply."[15] Why is the doctrine of res judicata important in our legal system? Why should it not apply in a case like this?

What Remedies Are Available When the Agency Has Failed to Make Rules?

Courts are sometimes asked to review agency inaction. Judicial review of an agency's failure to act is also authorized under APA § 706(1), which provides that a reviewing court may "compel agency action unlawfully withheld or unreasonably delayed." § 559(b) of the APA states that "within a reasonable time, each agency shall proceed to conclude a matter presented to it."

question of first impression: An issue before the court of a particular jurisdiction for the first time.

res judicata: A doctrine that bars a court from deciding a matter that has already been decided by a court.

---

[15] 580 A.2d at 966.

The courts have generally applied a highly deferential standard of review in such cases, recognizing that the agency is in the best position to determine its own priorities. In one case, *Heckler v. Chaney*,[16] the Supreme Court said that the Food and Drug Administration's decision not to initiate an enforcement action against a party was not reviewable, in part because the agency had to evaluate factors within its expertise in setting priorities, and in part because the agency's failure to act provided no "focus for judicial review."

Cases in which plaintiffs have challenged an agency's failure to initiate rulemaking or an unreasonable delay in initiating such proceedings often raise issues of ripeness and finality. In *Sierra Club v. Thomas*, the D.C. Circuit Court of Appeals held that EPA's delay in concluding rulemaking as to whether to place strip mines on its list of pollutant sources under the CAA was not unreasonable. The court said, "Because 'a court is in general ill-suited to review the order in which an agency conducts its business,' we are properly hesitant to upset an agency's priorities by ordering it to expedite one specific action, and thus to give it precedence over others."[17]

Courts are especially reluctant to order environmental agencies to expedite rulemaking in cases where the rule involves the evaluation of highly technical and scientific data.[18] However, when an agency refuses to engage in rulemaking despite its statutory mandate, a court can review the decision.

Massachusetts v. Environmental Protection Agency
549 U.S. 497 (2007)

Justice Stevens Delivered the Opinion of the Court

***

The scope of our review of the merits of the statutory issues is narrow. As we have repeated time and again, an agency has broad discretion to choose how best to marshal its limited resources and personnel to carry out its delegated responsibilities.... That discretion is at its height when the agency decides not to bring an enforcement action. [In an earlier case,] we held that an agency's refusal to initiate enforcement proceedings is not ordinarily subject to judicial review. Some debate remains, however, as to the rigor with which we review an agency's denial of a petition for rulemaking.

There are key differences between a denial of a petition for rulemaking and an agency's decision not to initiate an enforcement action.... In contrast to nonenforcement decisions, agency refusals to initiate rulemaking "are less frequent, more apt to involve legal as opposed to factual analysis, and subject to special formalities, including a public explanation." ... They moreover arise out of denials of petitions for rulemaking which (at least in the circumstances here) the affected party had an undoubted procedural right to file in the first instance. Refusals to promulgate rules are thus susceptible to judicial review, though such review is "extremely limited" and "highly deferential." ...

EPA concluded in its denial of the petition for rulemaking that it lacked authority under [the Clean Air

(Continued)

[16] 470 U.S. 821 (1985).
[17] 828 F.2d 783, 797 (D.C. Cir. 1987).
[18] For example, *U.S. Steelworkers of America v. Rubber Manufacturers Association*, 783 F.2d 1117 (D.C. Cir. 1986), in which the court refused to order OSHA to expedite its rulemaking on benzene.

Act] to regulate new vehicle emissions because carbon dioxide is not an "air pollutant" as that term is defined in [the statute]. In the alternative, it concluded that even if it possessed authority, it would decline to do so because regulation would conflict with other administration priorities.... [T]he Clean Air Act expressly permits review of such an action.... We therefore "may reverse any such action found to be ... arbitrary, capricious, an abuse of discretion, or otherwise not in accordance with law." ...

On the merits, the first question is whether § 202 (a)(1) of the Clean Air Act authorizes EPA to regulate greenhouse gas emissions from new motor vehicles in the event that it forms a "judgment" that such emissions contribute to climate change. We have little trouble concluding that it does. In relevant part, § 202(a)(1) provides that EPA "shall by regulation prescribe ... standards applicable to the emission of any air pollutant from any class or classes of new motor vehicles or new motor vehicle engines, which in [the Administrator's] judgment cause, or contribute to, air pollution which may reasonably be anticipated to endanger public health or welfare." ... Because EPA believes that Congress did not intend it to regulate substances that contribute to climate change, the agency maintains that carbon dioxide is not an "air pollutant" within the meaning of the provision.

The statutory text forecloses EPA's reading. The Clean Air Act's sweeping definition of "air pollutant" includes "*any* air pollution agent or combination of such agents, including *any* physical, chemical ... substance or matter which is emitted into or otherwise enters the ambient air...." ... (emphasis added). On its face, the definition embraces all airborne compounds of whatever stripe, and underscores that intent through the repeated use of the word "any." ... Carbon dioxide, methane, nitrous oxide, and hydrofluorocarbons are without a doubt "physical [and] chemical ... substance[s] which [are] emitted into ... the ambient air." The statute is unambiguous....

Rather than relying on statutory text, EPA invokes postenactment congressional actions and deliberations it views as tantamount to a congressional command to refrain from regulating greenhouse gas emissions. Even if such postenactment legislative history could shed light on the meaning of an otherwise-unambiguous statute, EPA never identifies any action remotely suggesting that Congress meant to curtail its power to treat greenhouse gases as air pollutants. That subsequent Congresses have eschewed enacting binding emissions limitations to combat global warming tells us nothing about what Congress meant when it amended

§ 202(a)(1) in 1970 and 1977.... And unlike EPA, we have no difficulty reconciling Congress' various efforts to promote interagency collaboration and research to better understand climate change ... with the agency's pre-existing mandate to regulate "any air pollutant" that may endanger the public welfare. See 42 U.S.C. § 7601 (a)(1). Collaboration and research do not conflict with any thoughtful regulatory effort; they complement it....

***

The alternative basis for EPA's decision—that even if it does have statutory authority to regulate greenhouse gases, it would be unwise to do so at this time—rests on reasoning divorced from the statutory text. While the statute does condition the exercise of EPA's authority on its formation of a "judgment," ... that judgment must relate to whether an air pollutant "cause[s], or contribute[s] to, air pollution which may reasonably be anticipated to endanger public health or welfare," .... Put another way, the use of the word "judgment" is not a roving license to ignore the statutory text. It is but a direction to exercise discretion within defined statutory limits.

If EPA makes a finding of endangerment, the Clean Air Act requires the agency to regulate emissions of the deleterious pollutant from new motor vehicles.... [cited case] (stating that "[EPA] shall by regulation prescribe ... standards applicable to the emission of any air pollutant from any class of new motor vehicles"). EPA no doubt has significant latitude as to the manner, timing, content, and coordination of its regulations with those of other agencies. But once EPA has responded to a petition for rulemaking, its reasons for action or inaction must conform to the authorizing statute. Under the clear terms of the Clean Air Act, EPA can avoid taking further action only if it determines that greenhouse gases do not contribute to climate change or if it provides some reasonable explanation as to why it cannot or will not exercise its discretion to determine whether they do.... To the extent that this constrains agency discretion to pursue other priorities of the Administrator or the President, this is the congressional design.

EPA has refused to comply with this clear statutory command. Instead, it has offered a laundry list of reasons not to regulate....

Although we have neither the expertise nor the authority to evaluate these policy judgments, it is evident they have nothing to do with whether greenhouse gas emissions contribute to climate change. Still less do they amount to a reasoned justification for declining to form a scientific judgment....

(Continued)

Nor can EPA avoid its statutory obligation by noting the uncertainty surrounding various features of climate change and concluding that it would therefore be better not to regulate at this time…. If the scientific uncertainty is so profound that it precludes EPA from making a reasoned judgment as to whether greenhouse gases contribute to global warming, EPA must say so. That EPA would prefer not to regulate greenhouse gases because of some residual uncertainty … is irrelevant. The statutory question is whether sufficient information exists to make an endangerment finding.

In short, EPA has offered no reasoned explanation for its refusal to decide whether greenhouse gases cause or contribute to climate change. Its action was therefore "arbitrary, capricious, … or otherwise not in accordance with law." … We hold only that EPA must ground its reasons for action or inaction in the statute.

Questions for Discussion

1. Why was the EPA's inaction in deciding whether greenhouse gases caused or contributed to climate change deemed arbitrary and capricious? What is the consequence of such a finding?

2. The *Massachusetts v. EPA* case also involved standing: Massachusetts and its fellow plaintiffs were found to have standing. How can a state have standing in an environmental dispute? Apply the test for standing to determine what a state would have to show in order to have standing.

3. "The Court held that the Administrator must determine whether or not emissions of greenhouse gases from new motor vehicles cause or contribute to air pollution which may reasonably be anticipated to endanger public health or welfare, or whether the science is too uncertain to make a reasoned decision."[19] The administrator subsequently entered an endangerment and cause or contribute finding, which stated "that the combined emissions of these greenhouse gases from new motor vehicles and new motor vehicle engines contribute to the greenhouse gas air pollution that endangers public health and welfare."[20] This was a prerequisite for the greenhouse gas emissions standards for vehicles that were subsequently implemented. Consider the judicial review of administrative agency action in *Massachusetts v. EPA*. How does the judicial branch check administrative agency action? Are there enough judicial checks on administrative agency action? Too few? What are the dangers with too few or too many checks on administrative agency action?

Congressional Restraints

The APA limits an administrative agency's powers to those granted to it by Congress.[21] Congress can thus limit or restrain administrative agency action through its enabling legislation. If an agency is not empowered with jurisdiction over a particular area, then it lacks the legal authority to promulgate rules, engage in enforcement, or adjudicate in that area. Both the APA and an agency's enabling legislation are important when considering whether an agency is acting in excess of its statutory jurisdiction.

Under § 706(2)(C) of the APA, an agency action that exceeds the authority delegated to it by statute is illegal and unenforceable. As the *Chevron* decision illustrates, cases challenging agency action under this theory raise important questions about the appropriate scope of the agency's power to determine how best to implement its legislative mandate.

This policy question is especially important in environmental rulemaking cases. Most environmental laws contain language mandating agency action under

[19] Endangerment and Cause or Contribute Findings for Greenhouse Gases under § 202(a) of the Clean Air Act. Retrieved July 12, 2013, from http://www.epa.gov/climatechange/endangerment/

[20] *Id.*; http://www.epa.gov/climatechange/Downloads/endangerment/Federal_Register-EPA-HQ-OAR-2009-0171-Dec.15-09.pdf

[21] APA § 555.

circumstances defined in general terms; for example, when "reasonably necessary to protect the public health or safety." While the enabling language of major environmental acts may be broad and indefinite, the agency often must resolve precise and technical issues in order to issue a particular regulation, such as when setting limits on the amount of a particular pollutant that may be expelled or released into the air or water.

Legal, factual, and policy issues are often entangled in such cases. For example, in *Industrial Union Department, AFL-CIO v. American Petroleum Institute*,[22] the Occupational Safety and Health Administration (OSHA) had issued a rule regulating the level of the carcinogen benzene in the workplace to a level of one part benzene per million parts of air. OSHA had set its standard on the basis of a policy judgment that in regulating carcinogens, no exposure level could be considered safe. Thus, it set the standard at the lowest technologically feasible level that would not impair the viability of regulated industries.

Several industries challenged the rule. The court of appeals held that in setting the 1 ppm exposure limit, OSHA had exceeded its standard-setting authority because it had not been shown that the 1 ppm exposure limit was "reasonably necessary or appropriate to provide safe and healthful employment" as required by the statute. According to the court, the statute did not give OSHA unbridled discretion to adopt standards designed to create absolutely risk-free workplaces regardless of cost.

On appeal, the Supreme Court, in a plurality opinion, agreed with the court of appeals and vacated the OSHA standard. According to Justice Sevens, OSHA failed to show by substantial evidence that benzene constituted a "significant risk" at the current level of exposure. The Court relied on the statutory definition of "occupational safety and health standard" as a standard that is "reasonably necessary or appropriate to provide safe or healthful employment." The Court interpreted this provision as requiring a finding of significant health risk before OSHA was authorized to regulate. Justice Stevens wrote:

> By empowering the Secretary to promulgate standards that are "reasonably necessary or appropriate to provide safe or healthful employment and places of employment," the Act implies that, before promulgating any standard, the Secretary must make a finding that the workplaces in question are not safe. But "safe" is not the equivalent of "risk-free."[23]

Agency rulemaking that exceeds the agency's authority violates the delegation doctrine and will be unenforceable. The courts can and do reject agency interpretations by finding that congressional intent is clear. A court of appeals decision striking down the EPA's "lender liability" rule under CERCLA illustrates this point.

In this case, the petitioners challenged an EPA rule limiting the liability of lenders for CERCLA cleanup costs. As potential litigants, the petitioners did not want to be foreclosed from recovering costs from lenders exempted from CERCLA liability. Following a series of conflicting court decisions interpreting the scope of a CERCLA exemption, the EPA adopted a final administrative rule specifying the range of activities that secured lenders could undertake or engage in without incurring CERCLA liability. Following is a portion of the court of appeals' opinion holding that the EPA lacked the authority to define lender liability under CERCLA by administrative rule.

---

[22] 448 U.S. 607 (1980).

[23] 448 U.S. at 642.

Kelley v. EPA
15 F.3d 1100 (D.C. Cir. 1994)

SILBERMAN, Circuit Judge

Petitioners challenge an EPA regulation limiting lender liability under CERCLA. We hold that EPA lacks statutory authority to restrict by regulation private rights of action arising under the statute and therefore grant the petition for review.

***

CERCLA ... authorizes private parties and EPA to bring civil actions independently to recover their costs associated with the cleanup of hazardous wastes from those responsible for the contamination.... § 107 of CERCLA generally imposes strict liability on, among others, all prior and present "owners and operators" of hazardous waste sites.... Congress created a safe harbor provision for secured creditors, however, in the definition of "owner or operator," providing that "[s]uch term does not include a person, who, without participating in the management of a vessel or facility, holds indicia of ownership primarily to protect his security interest in the vessel or facility." ...

Conflicting judicial interpretations as to the scope of this secured creditor exemption opened the possibility that lenders would be held liable for the cost of cleaning up contaminated property that they hold merely as collateral. Lenders lacked clear guidance as to the extent to which they could involve themselves in the affairs of a facility without incurring liability and also as to whether they would forfeit the exemption by exercising their right of foreclosure, which could be thought to convert their "indicia of ownership"—the security interest—into actual ownership.... In *United States v. Fleet Factors Corp.*, 901 F.2d 1550 (11th Cir. 1990), ... the court, although adhering to the settled view that Congress intended to protect the commercial practices of secured creditors "in their normal course of business," ... nevertheless stated that "a secured creditor will be liable if its involvement with the management of the facility is sufficiently broad to support the inference that it could affect hazardous waste disposal decisions if it so chose." ...

This language, portending as it did an expansion in the scope of secured creditor liability, caused considerable discomfort in financial circles....

EPA, responding to the understandable clamor from the banking community and in light of the federal government's increasing role as a secured creditor after taking over failed savings and loans, instituted a rulemaking proceeding ... to define the secured creditor exemption when legislative efforts to amend CERCLA failed.... In April 1992, EPA issued the final regulation, which employs a framework of specific tests to provide clearer articulation of a lender's scope of liability under CERCLA....

[The Court first analyzed and then rejected the EPA's argument that various specific sections of CERCLA expressly or impliedly delegated authority to the agency to define lender liability by rule.]

***

There remains the question of whether the regulation can be sustained as an interpretative rule. The preamble to the final regulation suggests that EPA attempted to straddle two horses—issuing the rule as a legislative regulation but asserting in the alternative that as an interpretative rule, it would still be entitled to judicial deference and therefore affect private party litigation.... Although we have admitted that the distinction between legislative and interpretative rules is "enshrouded in considerable smog," ... it is commonly understood that a rule is legislative if it is "based on an agency's power to exercise its judgment as to how best to implement a general statutory mandate," ... and has the binding force of law.... By contrast, an interpretative rule "is based on specific statutory provisions," ... and represents the agency's construction of the statute that is—while not binding—entitled to substantial judicial deference under *Chevron U.S.A. Inc. v. Natural Resources Defense Council, Inc.*....

The rule bears little resemblance to what we have traditionally found to be an interpretative regulation. EPA does not really define specific statutory terms, but rather takes off from those terms and devises a comprehensive regulatory regimen to address the liability problems facing secured creditors. This extensive quasi-legislative effort to implement the statute does not strike us as merely a construction of statutory phrases....

In any event, the same reason that prevents the agency from issuing the rule as a substantive regulation precludes judicial deference to EPA's offered "interpretation." If Congress meant the judiciary, not EPA, to determine liability issues—and we believe Congress did—EPA's view of statutory liability may not be given deference. "A precondition to deference under *Chevron* is a congressional delegation of administrative authority." ... *Chevron*, which sets forth the reigning rationale for judicial deference to agency interpretation of statutes, is premised on the notion that Congress implicitly

(Continued)

delegated to the agency the authority to reconcile reasonably statutory ambiguities or to fill reasonably statutory interstices. Where Congress does not give an agency authority to determine (usually formally) the interpretation of a statute in the first instance and instead gives the agency authority only to bring the question to a federal court as the "prosecutor," deference to the agency's interpretation is inappropriate.... As we have explained, that is all that EPA can do regarding liability issues. Moreover, even if an agency enjoys authority to determine such a legal issue administratively, deference is withheld if a private party can bring the issue independently to federal court under a private right of action.... Petitioners ... wish to preserve the right to sue lenders when, in petitioners' view, a lender's behavior transgresses the statutory test—whether or not EPA would regard the lender as liable. As we read the statute, Congress intended that petitioners' claim in such an event should be evaluated by the federal courts independent of EPA's institutional view....

***

We well recognize the difficulties that lenders face in the absence of the clarity EPA's regulation would have provided. Before turning to this rulemaking, EPA sought congressional relief and was rebuffed. We see no alternative but that EPA try again. The petition for review is granted and the regulation is hereby vacated.

Questions and Comments for Discussion

1. Concerns by lenders prompted the EPA's lender liability rule. Specifically, these concerns arose when a federal court held that a secured lender could be considered an "owner or operator"—that is, a potentially responsible party under CERCLA—if it participated in the day-to-day management of a facility. This alarmed lending institutions and created a disincentive for them to become involved in financing projects that might lead to liability under hazardous waste law.

    Given this background as an example, describe how administrative rules and regulations can create environmental policy.

2. The court said that a rule is legislative if it is based on an agency's power to exercise its judgment as to how best to implement a general statutory mandate, but that an rule is interpretative if it is based on specific statutory provisions and represents the agency's construction of the statute that is entitled to judicial deference under *Chevron*. Why does the classification of a rule as legislative or interpretative matter?

3. CERCLA subjects four classes of parties to potential liability for hazardous waste cleanup costs, including a current owner or operator of the site. The secured lender exemption under CERCLA provides that a person "who, without participating in the management of a vessel or facility, [holds] indicia of ownership primarily to protect [its] security interest ... is exempted from owner/operator liability."[24] Under what circumstances might a lender become an owner or operator for the purposes of CERCLA?

4. The court said that Congress should clarify the secured lender exemption rule. Congress eventually did clarify the rule when it essentially codified the EPA lender liability rule in the Asset Conservation, Lender Liability, and Deposit Insurance Protection Act of 1996.[25] What concerns of lenders prompted this change?

Congress also holds override power over administrative agency rules. For example, under the Congressional Review Act of 2001, Congress may override an agency rule in an expedited fashion. Additionally—or alternatively—it may also enact new legislation effectively barring or rendering moot the need for a new rule, or it may hold hearings to pose questions to administrative agency head officers.[26] Furthermore, Congress controls the federal budget. It may therefore

---

[24] 42 U.S.C. § 9601(20)(A).
[25] Pub. L. No. 104-208, Title II, subtitle E.
[26] *A Guide to the Rulemaking Process.* Retrieved July 13, 2013, from https://www.federalregister.gov/uploads/2011/01/the_rulemaking_process.pdf#page=10

impose funding restrictions on administrative agencies. Without proper funding, agencies cannot do the work that they were created to do.

■ *Examples: State Rules Related to Invasive Species*

Here are some examples of how state administrative agencies work to control or eradicate invasive species. Check out the USDA's website concerning Introduced, Invasive, or Noxious Plants: http://plants.usda .gov/java/noxComposite?stateRpt=yes

Click on the link for your state. What types of administrative rules exist in your state related to invasive species? Do these rules seem to be working? How do you know?

Why is controlling invasive species a matter for state lawmakers?

Executive Restraints

Agencies are either executive agencies or independent agencies. The president can appoint (and remove) an executive agency's officers. However, independent agencies' officers serve for a fixed term and cannot be removed without just cause. Thus, an executive agency is more liable to be influenced by the president's positions, initiatives, and desires than an independent agency.

Agency Restraints

Agency action is also restrained by the agency's own procedures. Under § 706(2)(D) of the APA, a court will set aside an agency rule if the agency failed to follow the procedures required by law. Rules challenged on this basis are generally informal requirements formulated under the APA or other statutes that contain rule-making procedures.

In the 1970s, some courts began to impose procedures beyond those required by the APA, either to improve the record of the proceeding or to ensure an added degree of fairness in agency decision making. The question of the courts' authority to impose these additional requirements on agency procedures ultimately reached the Supreme Court in *Vermont Yankee Nuclear Power Corp v. Natural Resources Defense Council.*[27] The controversy in that case involved the procedures used in a rulemaking hearing by the Atomic Energy Commission. The Commission had broad regulatory authority over the development of nuclear energy under the Atomic Energy Act of 1954. Under that Act, a utility seeking to construct and operate a nuclear power plant was required to obtain a separate permit or license at both the construction and operation stages of the project. Vermont Yankee was granted a permit to build a nuclear power plant in Vernon, Vermont, and applied for an operating license. Following a hearing on Vermont Yankee's application to the licensing board, the Commission instituted proceedings and adopted a rule addressing the hazards of fuel reprocessing or disposal.

Plaintiff environmental groups challenged the Commission's rule and its decision to grant Vermont Yankee an operating license. The court of appeals for the district circuit determined that the rulemaking procedures used by the agency were inadequate and hence overturned the rule. Vermont Yankee appealed.

---

[27] 435 U.S. 519 (1978).

Vermont Yankee Nuclear Power Corp. v. Natural Resources Defense Council, Inc.

435 U.S. 519 (1978)

MR. JUSTICE REHNQUIST Delivered the Opinion of the Court

In 1946, Congress enacted the Administrative Procedure Act, which as we have noted elsewhere was not only "a new, basic and comprehensive regulation of procedures in many agencies," … but was also a legislative enactment which settled "long-continued and hard-fought contentions, and enacted a formula upon which opposing social and political forces have come to rest." … Interpreting [§ 4 of the APA] …, we held that generally speaking this section of the Act established the maximum procedural requirements which Congress was willing to have the courts impose upon agencies in conducting rulemaking procedures…. Agencies are free to grant additional procedural rights in the exercise of their discretion, but reviewing courts are generally not free to impose them if the agencies have not chosen to grant them. This is not to say necessarily that there are no circumstances which would ever justify a court in overturning agency action because of a failure to employ procedures beyond those required by the statute. But such circumstances, if they exist, are extremely rare.

***

It is in the light of this background of statutory and decisional law that we granted certiorari to review two judgments of the Court of Appeals for the District of Columbia Circuit because of our concern that they had seriously misread or misapplied this statutory and decisional law cautioning reviewing courts against engrafting their own notions of proper procedures upon agencies entrusted with substantive functions by Congress…. We conclude that the Court of Appeals has done just that in these cases, and we therefore remand them to it for further proceedings….

***

In prior opinions we have intimated that even in a rulemaking proceeding when an agency is making a "'quasi-judicial'" determination by which a very small number of persons are "'exceptionally affected, in each case upon individual grounds,'" in some circumstances additional [trial-type] procedures may be required in order to afford the aggrieved individuals due process…. It might also be true, although we do not think the issue is presented in this case and accordingly do not decide it, that a totally unjustified departure from well-settled agency procedures of long standing might require judicial correction….

But this much is absolutely clear. Absent constitutional constraints or extremely compelling circumstances the "administrative agencies 'should be free to fashion their own rules of procedure and to pursue methods of inquiry capable of permitting them to discharge their multitudinous duties.'" …

***

Respondent NRDC argues that § [553] of the Administrative Procedure Act … merely establishes lower procedural bounds and that a court may routinely require more than the minimum when an agency's proposed rule addresses complex or technical factual issues or "Issues of Great Public Import." … We have, however, previously shown that our decisions reject this view…. We also think the legislative history … does not bear out its contention….

***

… Congress intended that the discretion of the *agencies* and not that of the courts be exercised in determining when extra procedural devices should be employed.

There are compelling reasons for construing § [553] in this manner. In the first place, if courts continually review agency proceedings to determine whether the agency employed procedures which were, in the court's opinion, perfectly tailored to reach what the court perceives to be the "best" or "correct" result, judicial review would be totally unpredictable. And the agencies, operating under this vague injunction to employ the "best" procedures and facing the threat of reversal if they did not, would undoubtedly adopt full adjudicatory procedures in every instance. Not only would this totally disrupt the statutory scheme, through which Congress enacted "a formula upon which opposing social and political forces have come to rest," … but all the inherent advantages of informal rulemaking would be totally lost….

Secondly, it is obvious that the court in these cases reviewed the agency's choice of procedures on the basis of the record actually produced at the hearing, … and not on the basis of the information available to the agency when it made the decision to structure the proceedings in a certain way. This sort of Monday morning quarterbacking not only encourages but

(Continued)

almost compels the agency to conduct all rulemaking proceedings with the full panoply of procedural devices normally associated only with adjudicatory hearings.

Finally, and perhaps most importantly, this sort of review fundamentally misconceives the nature of the standard for judicial review of an agency rule. The court below uncritically assumed that additional procedures will automatically result in a more adequate record because it will give interested parties more of an opportunity to participate and contribute to the proceedings. But informal rulemaking need not be based solely on the transcript of a hearing held before an agency. Indeed the agency need not even hold a formal hearing…. Thus, the adequacy of the "record" in this type of proceeding is not correlated directly to the type of procedural devices employed, but rather turns on whether the agency has followed the statutory mandate of the Administrative Procedure Act or other relevant statutes. If the agency is compelled to support the rule which it ultimately adopts with the type of record produced only after a full adjudicatory hearing, it simply will have no choice but to conduct a full adjudicatory hearing prior to promulgating every rule. In sum, this sort of unwarranted judicial examination of perceived procedural shortcomings of a rulemaking proceeding can do nothing but seriously interfere with that process prescribed by Congress.

***

In short, nothing in the APA, … the circumstances of this case, the nature of the issues being considered, past agency practice, or the statutory mandate under which the Commission operates permitted the court to review

and overturn the rulemaking proceeding on the basis of the procedural devices employed (or not employed) by the Commission so long as the Commission employed at least the statutory *minima*, a matter about which there is no doubt in this case.

Questions and Comments for Discussion

1. Since this case, federal courts have followed the Supreme Court's ruling in *Vermont Yankee* and have not imposed procedural requirements on agencies beyond those required by the APA. This Supreme Court case substantially halted the development of judge-made common law of rulemaking procedure. But *Vermont Yankee* has not displaced case law concerning the requirements of notice, opportunity to comment, and adequacy of the agency's statement for the rule under the APA. Should the courts have a greater role in agency rulemaking procedure? Why or why not?

2. There were advantages to the Commission's resolving safety and radiation waste disposal questions by rulemaking rather than adjudication in this particular case. Once the rule was published as a regulation, it could be incorporated by reference in future licensing hearings without the need to relitigate the issue. What are the disadvantages of resolving such issues by rule rather than adjudication? Should environmental groups be able to challenge an agency's decisions regarding safety requirements on a case-by-case basis, or is rulemaking the more efficient and better decision-making device?

Public Restraints

In 1962, Congress passed the Freedom of Information Act (FOIA), to provide greater public access to documents held by administrative agencies. Some exemptions exist that permit the agency not to release records. These include records related to national security, internal personnel records, trade secrets, and other records that are not appropriate to release to the public. Despite the exemptions, FOIA has made many agency deliberations, procedures, and rulemaking efforts considerably more transparent and open to public scrutiny. This accountability enhances the public's ability to restrain and otherwise influence agency action.

■ *ACTIVITY BOX*   *Rules for Habitat Conservation*

Review the report, *Conservation in America: State Government Incentives for Habitat Conservation. A Status Report,* from Defenders of Wildlife, at http://www.defenders.org /sites/default/files/publications/state_government_incentives_for_habitat_conservation.pdf
Answer the following questions:

1. In the report, locate information about your state. How do administrative agency actions work to conserve wildlife habitat? Without these programs, what other incentives would landowners have to conserve habitat?

2. Describe why a state government would wish to implement programs related to wildlife habitat conservation.

▓ Conclusion

Basic principles of administrative law underlie the legal and policy issues in environmental cases and controversies. Environmental regulatory policies are increasingly set, administered, and enforced by agencies like the EPA.

The administrative portion of government has continued to grow since the late 19th century. In the 1930s, Congress passed laws to ensure fairness and minimal due process protections in agency proceedings. These include the Federal Register Act, which mandated a daily record of administrative activities, and the APA.

Absent requirements in the agency's enabling legislation or other relevant statutes, the APA establishes minimum requirements for agency proceedings. The APA recognizes different kinds of agency procedures, including formal adjudication, formal rulemaking, informal adjudication, and informal rulemaking. Formal rulemaking is seldom used; most rulemaking is informal rulemaking, which is also called notice-and-comment rulemaking. The APA also addresses agency adjudications, which vary from relatively informal oral hearings to structured proceedings resembling formal trials.

This chapter reviewed some of the basic principles of administrative law, focused on informal rulemaking under the APA, and examined some of the constraints on agency power, including judicial, congressional, executive, agency, and public restraints.

Cases challenging environmental rulemaking and adjudication often question the appropriate balance between agency expertise and political accountability: To what extent should the courts defer to an agency's interpretation of its own enabling legislation? When is agency action "final" for purposes of judicial review? What constitutes an arbitrary and capricious action or abuse of discretion by an administrative agency? These issues highlight the role of the courts in reviewing agency action. In later chapters of this text we will examine specific federal environmental laws. Administrative law issues are often at the heart of cases and controversies involving the appropriate interpretation and enforcement of statutory and regulatory mandates under these major environmental acts.

■ ■ ■ REVIEW AND STUDY QUESTIONS

1. What restraints exist on administrative agency power? Are these restraints effective checks on administrative agency power?

2. What are the threshold issues regarding litigation of an administrative agency action?

3. How might an environmental group show that it has standing to challenge an administrative agency action?

4. If an administrative agency action is reviewable by a court, what standard of review might be used? How do you know? What does *standard of review* mean?

5. Why would Congress wish to maintain override power of administrative agency action, when Congress created the administrative agencies in the first place?

6. Exercise your rights under the FOIA. Visit the FOIA website (http://www.foia.gov/). What information can you find on this website? What information could you request?

Chapter 8 Case Study Activity: Administrative Rules and Food Labeling

Display of the label "organic" on food products is a regulated activity. Review the resources on the USDA's National Organic Program at the following link: http://www.ams.usda.gov/AMSv1.0/NOSB

Then, click on "Consumer Information" on the right side of the page. Scroll down to see the "What About Other Labels?" section, where several commonly used labels are discussed. Some labels are regulated by the USDA and others are not. The National List is a list, maintained by the USDA, of items that are allowed to be used or included in organic food. Many critics of the "organic" label on food products point to several items currently on the National List that they believe should not be permitted.

Consider the power of a food label. If consumers wish to spend money on a particular type of product and rely on the label to convey information that helps them discern whether that product meets their criteria for purchase, how can consumers know whether the label conveys what they think it conveys?

Describe the extent to which you or your family rely on labels when making purchasing decisions. If no regulations exist to regulate the label that you rely upon, what does the label mean? How might you find out? If regulations exist to govern the use of the label that you rely on, then what do you think the label "means"? After reviewing the information on the USDA's National Organic Program's website, are you confident that the label means what you thought it meant? Why or why not?

CHAPTER NINE

Major Federal Environmental Statutes Part I: NEPA, Animals, and Federal Public Lands

Here's a good idea!
This is a "bare bones" outline of the chapter. Expand this outline with more detailed notes as you read the chapter. This will allow you to create a study guide as you work. This good study habit will help you to learn the material, retain important points, and make efficient use of your time.

Learning Objectives

After reading this chapter, you will have an understanding of the major federal environmental statutes related to federal environmental policy, animals, and federal public lands. Specifically, after reading this chapter, you should be able to answer the following questions:

1. What is NEPA, and how does it limit administrative agency action?
2. How does a federal statute protect threatened or endangered species?
3. What are wilderness areas?
4. How do federal statutes related to environmental policy, animals, or federal public lands work with state statutes?

▮ Introduction

This chapter focuses on major federal environmental statutes related to federal environmental policy, animals, and federal public lands. These acts are part of the backbone of the federal regulatory scheme related to the environment, giving rise to the administrative rules and regulations that implement those statutes. Each statute is vast and complicated, and not without shortcomings. As we examine the federal statutory scheme, consider why the statute was originally enacted and whether you believe that it has succeeded in accomplishing the goals Congress intended it to reach.

■ Federal Environmental Policy

The National Environmental Policy Act (NEPA), enacted in 1970, is a federal stat-ute that seeks to ensure that federal agencies give the same consideration to envi-ronmental factors as to other factors in making decisions. NEPA compels the government to administer federal programs in the most environmentally sound fashion. An agency must consider the impact of any action significantly affecting the human environment.

NEPA established the Council on Environmental Quality (CEQ) within the exec-utive office of the president. The CEQ's duties include advising the president on environmental issues and interpreting NEPA provisions for agencies and the public.

Environmental groups have used NEPA to challenge many agency actions. These challenges have delayed, modified, and in some cases permanently halted proposed government projects. Conflicts in such cases bring into question the appropriate policy balance between environmental protection and land develop-ment and the use of natural resources.

It is important to remember that NEPA affects only agencies of the federal government; state governments and agencies are not within its purview. However, after NEPA was enacted, several states enacted their own NEPA-like acts, often called "mini-NEPAs," which do control state action.

In 1970, when NEPA was first enacted, it was considered the most important and far-reaching environmental and conservation measure ever enacted by Congress.[1] NEPA contains three important elements. The first is found in § 1 of the Act, which contains a declaration of national environmental policies and goals. The second is found in § 2, which contains several action-forcing provisions requiring federal agen-cies to implement those policies and goals. The third is found in Title II of the Act, which establishes the executive-branch Council on Environmental Quality.

Declaration of National Environmental Policies and Goals

In § 101 of NEPA, Congress declared that the federal government has the continu-ing responsibility

> to use all practicable means, consistent with other essential considerations of national policy, to improve and coordinate federal plans, functions, programs, and resources to the end that the nation may:
>
> 1. fulfill the responsibilities of each generation as trustee of the environment for succeeding generations;
> 2. assure for all Americans safe, healthful, productive, and aesthetically and culturally pleasing surroundings;
> 3. attain the widest range of beneficial uses of the environment without degra-dation, risk to health or safety, or other undesirable and unintended consequences;
> 4. preserve important historic, cultural and natural aspects of our national heritage, and maintain, wherever possible, an environment which supports diversity and variety of individual choice;

---

[1] 115 CONG. REC. 40,416 (1969) (statement of Sen. Jackson).

5. achieve a balance between population and resource use which will permit high standards of living and a wide sharing of life's amenities; and

6. enhance the quality of renewable resources and approach the maximum attainable recycling of depletable resources.

Note that § 101 of NEPA requires the federal government to use all practicable means to administer federal programs in the most environmentally sound fashion. NEPA does not give the environment greater priority than other national goals, but it does commit to protecting and promoting environmental quality. It also requires federal agencies to consider the environmental consequences of their actions.

Council on Environmental Quality

Title II of NEPA created the CEQ in the executive office of the president. The CEQ is composed of three members appointed by the president and confirmed by the Senate. The CEQ was required by statute to assist and advise the president in the preparation of an annual environmental quality report. The reports were issued through 1997, but are no longer required, per the Federal Reports Elimination and Sunset Act.

Under CEQ regulations, NEPA and other planning requirements are integrated by the agencies as early as possible to ensure that those plans reflect environmental values.[2] CEQ regulations also define key words in NEPA § 102(2)(C), which mandates that agencies prepare a formal EIS under certain circumstances.

Action-Forcing Provisions of NEPA

Section 102 of NEPA contains provisions intended to force agencies of the federal government to consider the environmental consequences of their actions in light of the broad policy goals of § 101. Section 102(1) contains a broad directive that, "to the fullest extent possible," federal policies, public laws, and regulations should be interpreted and administered in accordance with the policies set forth in NEPA.

Section 102(2) of NEPA contains a mandate to perform certain procedures to ensure that agencies utilize a systematic, interdisciplinary approach in planning and in decision making that may have an impact on the human environment. This section contains provisions that may form a basis for judicial intervention, the most significant of which is § 102(2)(C). The crucial language of this section reads:

[All agencies of the federal government shall—] ...
(C) include in every recommendation or report on proposals for legislation and other major federal actions significantly affecting the quality of the human environment, a detailed statement by the responsible official on—

i. the environmental impact of the proposed action,
ii. any adverse environmental effects which cannot be avoided should the proposal be implemented,
iii. alternatives to the proposed action,
iv. the relationship between local short-term uses of man's environment and the maintenance and enhancement of long-term productivity, and
v. any irreversible and irretrievable commitments of resources which would be involved in the proposed action should it be implemented.

---

[2] 40 C.F.R. § 1501.2 (1978).

The requirement that an **environmental impact statement** (**EIS**) accompany proposals for legislation and federal actions significantly affecting the quality of the human environment has been the focus of most of the litigation surrounding NEPA. The meaning of nearly every word in this section ("major," "federal," "significantly affecting," "human environment") has been litigated extensively.

Shortly after NEPA was passed, a lawsuit was brought to clarify the fundamental compliance requirements of the act. In one of the most important decisions to date interpreting NEPA, Judge Skelly Wright of the D.C. Circuit Court of Appeals wrote a crucial opinion in which the court made it clear that the language of the statute established a "strict standard of compliance."

The petitioners in that case argued that the rules adopted by the Atomic Energy Commission (AEC) to govern consideration of environmental matters in agency decision making failed to satisfy the requirements of NEPA. The AEC, in turn, argued that the NEPA mandate was vague and gave agencies much discretion in complying with the broad scope of the Act. But the court held that NEPA was a "good deal clearer and more demanding" than the commission contended and that § 102(2)(C) of NEPA created "judicially enforceable duties." A portion of the court's opinion in that case follows.

environmental impact statement (EIS): A requirement of NEPA for legislative and federal action proposals that significantly affect the quality of the human environment.

Calvert Cliffs' Coordinating Committee v. United States Atomic Energy Commission

449 F.2d 1109 (D.C. Cir. 1971)

* * *

The sort of consideration of environmental values which NEPA compels is clarified in Section 102(2)(A) and (B). In general, all agencies must use a "systematic, interdisciplinary approach" to environmental planning and evaluation "in decisionmaking which may have an impact on man's environment." In order to include all possible environmental factors in the decisional equation, agencies must "identify and develop methods and procedures ... which will insure that presently unquantified environmental amenities and values may be given appropriate consideration in decisionmaking along with economic and technical considerations." ... "Environmental amenities" will often be in conflict with "economic and technical considerations." To "consider" the former "along with" the latter must involve a balancing process. In some instances environmental costs may outweigh economic and technical benefits and in other instances they may not. But NEPA mandates a rather finely tuned and "systematic" balancing analysis in each instance....

To ensure that the balancing analysis is carried out and given full effect, Section 102(2)(C) requires that responsible officials of all agencies prepare a "detailed

statement" covering the impact of particular actions on the environment, the environmental costs which might be avoided, and alternative measures which might alter the cost-benefit equation. The apparent purpose of the "detailed statement" is to aid in the agencies' own decision making process and to advise other interested agencies and the public of the environmental consequences of planned federal action. Beyond the "detailed statement," Section 102(2)(D) requires all agencies specifically to "study, develop, and describe appropriate alternatives to recommended courses of action in any proposal which involves unresolved conflicts concerning alternative uses of available resources." This requirement, like the "detailed statement" requirement, seeks to ensure that each agency decision maker has before him and takes into proper account all possible approaches to a particular project (including total abandonment of the project) which would alter the environmental impact and the cost-benefit balance. Only in that fashion is it likely that the most intelligent, optimally beneficial decision will ultimately be made. Moreover, by compelling a formal "detailed statement" and a description of alternatives, NEPA provides evidence that the mandated decision

(Continued)

making process has in fact taken place and, most importantly, allows those removed from the initial process to evaluate and balance the factors on their own.

Of course, all of these Section 102 duties are qualified by the phrase "to the fullest extent possible." We must stress as forcefully as possible that this language does not provide an escape hatch for footdragging agencies; it does not make NEPA's procedural requirements somehow "discretionary." Congress did not intend the Act to be such a paper tiger. Indeed, the requirement of environmental consideration "to the fullest extent possible" sets a high standard for the agencies, a standard which must be rigorously enforced by the reviewing courts.

Unlike the substantive duties of Section 101(b) which require agencies to "use all practicable means consistent with other essential considerations," the procedural duties of Section 102 must be fulfilled to the "fullest extent possible." ...

* * *

[T]he Section 102 duties are not inherently flexible. They must be complied with to the fullest extent, unless there is a clear conflict of statutory authority.... Considerations of administrative difficulty, delay or economic cost will not suffice to strip the section of its fundamental importance.

We conclude, then, that Section 102 of NEPA mandates a particular sort of careful and informed decision-making process and creates judicially enforceable duties. The reviewing courts probably cannot reverse a substantive decision on its merits, under Section 101, unless it be shown that the actual balance of costs and benefits that was struck was arbitrary or clearly gave insufficient weight to environmental values. But if the decision was reached procedurally without individualized consideration and balancing of environmental factors—conducted fully and in good faith—it is the responsibility of the courts to reverse. As one District Court has said of Section 102 requirements: "It is hard to imagine a clearer or stronger mandate to the courts." ...

Questions and Comments for Discussion

1. In the beginning of his opinion, Judge Skelly Wright wrote: "These cases are only the beginning of what promises to become a flood of new litigation—litigation seeking judicial assistance in protecting our natural environment. Several recently enacted statutes attest to the commitment of the Government to control, at long last, the destructive engine of material 'progress.' ... But it remains to be seen whether the promise of this legislation will become a reality. Therein lies the judicial role."

   Judge Skelly Wright believed that it was the court's duty to "see that important legislative purposes, heralded in the halls of Congress, are not lost or misdirected in the vast hallways of the federal bureaucracy." Legislative history is one tool of statutory interpretation. In this case, the Court relied on "plain meaning" and congressional intent in determining that NEPA mandates a careful and informed decision-making process and creates judicially enforceable duties. Should it matter that NEPA's legislative history is sparse and that there were several versions of NEPA, and that after minimal debate, the Senate agreed to a conference report on the bill by voice vote?

2. Consistent with the court's opinion in this case, most consider NEPA to be a "procedural statute." Compliance with its provisions calls for planning and analysis to demonstrate that environmental considerations and alternatives to the proposed action have been fully considered and documented. As the court says, NEPA requires that the agency fully consider the environmental impact of its proposed action and alternatives to that action. However, if the agency meets those procedural requirements, it should be able to proceed with the proposed action. Only under circumstances where the agency's decision to proceed with a proposed action is "arbitrary and capricious" will a court intervene. NEPA requires an agency to take a "hard look" at the environmental effects of a proposed action. The proper standard for review of whether the agency did so is the arbitrary and capricious test. Under what circumstances might an agency's decision to proceed be considered "arbitrary and capricious," as discussed in Chapter 8 of this text (on administrative law)?

As a result of the court's decision in this case, preparation of an EIS became a formal legal requirement—and one that has significantly influenced federal agency decision making. Further, an agency's failure to comply with the requirements of NEPA is subject to judicial review by the courts.

■ *Threshold Requirements for EIS: A Flowchart Approach?*

Threshold question: Does the agency need to prepare an EIS?

1. Is there federal action? If yes, continue to next question. If no, then no EIS required.
2. Is the federal action major? If yes, continue to next question. If no, then no EIS required.

3. Will the action significantly affect the human environment? This question requires further consideration of the following:
   a. What is significant?
   b. What is environment?

If the answer to question 3 is yes, then an EIS required. If no, then no EIS is required.

Threshold Requirements for the EIS

NEPA § 102(2)(C) requires that an EIS be included in every recommendation or report on proposals for legislation and other major federal actions significantly affecting the quality of the human environment. The language of this section is critical in determining whether a federal agency must prepare an EIS. Is the agency's plan a "proposal"? Is the proposal for a "major" federal action? Will it "significantly affect the human environment?" Key terms in this statement are defined in the CEQ regulations and have been the subject of much litigation.

These are called *threshold requirements* because they determine whether an agency must prepare an EIS for a project. An EIS is often costly and time-consuming, and failure to prepare an EIS is an action subject to judicial review by the courts. Thus, the agency's decision to prepare an EIS is an important one.

Under CEQ regulations, an **environmental assessment (EA)** is used as a screening device to determine whether an agency must prepare an EIS or make a **Finding of No Significant Impact (FONSI)**. The EA is a public document that discusses the need for the proposal and alternatives as required by § 102(2)(E) of NEPA. If the agency determines no EIS is required, it prepares a FONSI. The FONSI briefly presents the reasons why an action will not have a significant effect on the human environment, and it must include a summary of the EA. Under some limited circumstances, the agency must make its FONSI determination available for public review.

Three criteria must be met under the statute before an EIS is required: The action must be federal, qualify as "major," and have a significant environmental impact. In many cases, the "federal" requirement does not pose much difficulty, because policies, plans, programs, and projects proposed by federal agencies meet this definition. State and local actions that are regulated, licensed, permitted, or approved by federal agencies are also considered "federal" for the purposes of NEPA. Whether federal assistance to a nonfederal project also triggers the requirements of NEPA generally depends on the extent of control that the federal agency may assert over the project.

The requirements that the project be "major" and that it "significantly" affect the environment have been the subject of some discussion. A substantial commitment of resources qualifies the project as "major," and CEQ regulations have defined *significantly* by requiring consideration of both the "context" and "intensity" (the severity of impact) of the action.

The requirement of "environmental impact" raises another important question. How broadly should the term *environment* be defined? To define

environmental assessment (EA): A screening tool used to analyze whether an EIS is required under NEPA.

Finding of No Significant Impact (FONSI): A statement presenting a determination that an action will have no significant impact on the human environment, and consequently, no EIS is required.

"environmental impact," the statute speaks of the need to assure all Americans "safe, healthful, productive, and aesthetically and culturally pleasing surroundings." Courts have agreed that NEPA is not limited to the natural environment (wilderness, rivers, etc.), but may also include impact on the urban environment.

The CEQ regulations define the *human environment* as the natural and physical environment and the relationship of people with that environment. Under the CEQ definition, economic or social effects by themselves do not require preparation of an EIS. When an EIS is prepared and economic or social and natural or physical environmental effects are interrelated, then the EIS should discuss all of those effects on the human environment.[3]

The EIS and the EIS process are the focal point of NEPA. The EIS ensures that the agency will have available and carefully consider detailed information concerning significant environmental impacts of the proposed action, and guarantees that relevant information will be made available to the public so that the public can play a role in the decision-making process. As the U.S. Supreme Court noted in *Robertson v. Methow Valley Citizens Council*, "Publication of an EIS ... serves a larger information role. It gives the public the assurance that the agency 'has indeed considered environmental concerns in its decisionmaking process,' ... and, perhaps more significantly, provides a springboard for public comment."[4] The EIS also provides a record for a court to review in determining whether the agency has made a good faith effort to take environmental values into account.

■ ACTIVITY BOX   EA, EIS, and ROD for Exploring Outer Space

Visit the NASA webpage related to NEPA activities (http://www.nasa.gov/directorates/heo/library/nepa/). Then, answer the following questions:

1. Do you think that an EIS should have been required for the Constellation Program (CxP)? An EIS was prepared, but was one necessary? Why or why not? (Hint: Use Box 9.1 to help answer this question.)

2. Since the Constellation Program was cancelled, NASA plans to focus on deep space exploration. Should it be able to substitute the EIS and ROD that it prepared for CxP for the new programs? Why or why not?

Scope and Timing of the EIS

Once the decision has been made to prepare an EIS, a number of legal issues may arise concerning that preparation. The questions of its scope (what the EIS must address) and timing (when it must be prepared) become critical, because failure to analyze the required environmental effects or include alternatives may result in a court declaring the EIS inadequate.

Scope

Judicial review of agency decision making under NEPA is governed by the Administrative Procedure Act. The "arbitrary and capricious" test is the standard of review. The questions of scope and timing have been addressed by the courts in a

---

[3] 40 C.F.R. § 1508.14.
[4] 490 U.S. 332, 349 (1989).

number of cases. The CEQ regulations contain detailed procedural requirements for the entire EIS process. The process begins with an EA, which, as noted earlier, is a brief analysis of the need for an EIS. If the agency decides to prepare an EIS, the first step in the process is called *scoping*. The agency must publish a notice of intent to prepare the EIS in the *Federal Register*, a daily publication of federal agencies' proposed regulations. In the scoping process, the agency invites participation by the public and affected agencies, determines the scope of the EIS, and decides which issues are significant and should be examined in depth. It may also determine, as lead agency, whether to prepare the entire EIS itself or to allocate some responsibility to other agencies as well.

Determining the proper scope of the EIS is very important. One way to defeat the purposes of NEPA is to "segment" a project so that each stage of the project is considered separately. By segmenting a project, an agency may avoid addressing the overall environmental costs and countervailing benefits of the project as a whole. It is a means of evading NEPA. In *Scientists' Institute for Public Information, Inc. v. Atomic Energy Commission*,[5] Judge Skelly Wright considered this issue and held that an EIS covering the whole program was required.

Timing

The question of timing of the EIS is also significant. NEPA requires that the EIS be included in "every recommendation or report on proposals for legislation and other major federal actions." Under the language of this section, an agency is not required to comply with NEPA until a proposal exists, but an agency may not recommend a proposal or proceed with a major action until an EIS and record of decision have been prepared. The CEQ regulations require agencies to begin preparation of an EIS early in the proposal process. Once the proposal is made, the EIS must accompany the proposal through the decision-making process. The CEQ guideline on timing reads in part:

> An agency shall commence preparation of an environmental impact statement as close as possible to the time the agency is developing or is presented with a proposal so that preparation can be completed in time for the final statement to be included in any recommendation or report on the proposal. The statement shall be prepared early enough so that it can serve practically as an important contribution to the decisionmaking process and will not be used to rationalize or justify decisions already made.

In a 1975 decision, the Supreme Court used a relatively mechanical test in determining the timing of the EIS. It said, "[T]he time at which the agency must prepare the final 'statement' is the time at which it makes a recommendation or report on a proposal for federal action."[6] Subsequently, in *Kleppe v. Sierra Club*,[7] the Supreme Court more fully addressed the scope and timing issues of the EIS. In that case, the Court deferred to the agency's expertise in determining whether a comprehensive EIS for the entire region was necessary.

As critics have pointed out, though, if courts have to wait until a federal action is proposed before they issue an order to prepare an adequate impact statement,

Federal Register: Daily government publication of federal agency actions and proposed actions.

---

[5] 481 F.2d 1079 (D.C. Cir. 1973).
[6] *Aberdeen & Rockfish Railroad Co. v. Students Challenging Regulatory Agency Procedures*, 422 U.S. 289, 320 (1975).
[7] 427 U.S. 390 (1976).

this will do little to further the consideration of environmental factors. This sort of timing also appears to subvert the CEQ regulations and rationale.

Contents of the EIS

NEPA requires that an EIS describe:

1. The environmental impacts of the proposed action
2. Any adverse environmental impacts that cannot be avoided should the proposal be implemented
3. The reasonable alternatives to the proposed action
4. The relationship between local short-term uses of the human environment and the maintenance and enhancement of long-term productivity
5. Any irreversible and irretrievable commitments of resources that would be involved in the proposed action should it be implemented

CEQ regulations provide a recommended format for EIS preparation.

Agencies generally prepare a draft EIS and a final EIS. If the agency makes substantial changes in its proposed action, or if significant new circumstances or information exist that are relevant to the environmental concerns of the proposed action, the EIS may be supplemented. An agency decision not to prepare a **supplemental EIS** may also be challenged in the courts. For example, in the battle over protecting the northern spotted owl in the Pacific Northwest, several challenges to agency action were based on failure to prepare and file a supplemental EIS (SEIS) in light of new information available to the federal agency. The Supreme Court has held that the appropriate standard of review in cases where agencies have failed to prepare a SEIS is whether the agency acted "arbitrarily or capriciously" in deciding not to prepare the supplemental statement.[8]

The agency files the draft EIS with the EPA and announces its availability to the public in the *Federal Register*. A waiting period is mandated by law to provide all interested persons, organizations, and agencies time to comment on the agency's compliance. The final EIS is subsequently circulated to all interested parties. The final action in the process is preparation of a **record of decision** (**ROD**), which identifies and explains the decision, identifies the alternatives considered by the agency, and specifies the alternatives that were chosen as environmentally preferable. The record must state whether the agency has taken "all practicable" means to avoid or minimize environmental harm from the alternative selected.

The public comment procedures mandated by NEPA are an essential part of the NEPA review process. Agencies with jurisdiction over a proposed action or agencies with relevant special expertise must comment on relevant EISs. The purpose of the EIS is to ensure that agency decisions are based on an understanding of environmental consequences and the reasonable alternatives available, so the alternatives section is the heart of the EIS. The agency must consider a reasonable range of alternatives but is not required to consider every possibility that might be conjectured. Also, as a general rule, the agency must discuss the alternative of "no action" to provide a basis for comparing the environmental effects of the other alternatives. In addition, the EIS must discuss the environmental effects of each of the alternatives. Because the consequences of agency action are highly uncertain, due to lack of scientific

supplemental EIS (SEIS): An addition to an EIS that may be required under NEPA if the agency makes substantial changes in a proposed action, if significant new circumstances arise, or if new information becomes available.

record of decision (ROD): Formal statement identifying and explaining an agency decision.

---

[8] *Marsh v. Oregon Natural Resources Council*, 490 U.S. 360 (1989).

certainty, some courts have held that a "worst-case" discussion is required by NEPA, though the Supreme Court has rejected that requirement.

A leading case on the question of what alternatives must be included in the EIS is *Natural Resources Defense Council v. Morton*.[9] In that case, the court of appeals held that the agency must discuss all reasonable alternatives to action by any part of the federal government. It also held that the agency must discuss the environmental effects of those alternatives in the EIS. The court of appeals said that the NEPA requirement of discussion of reasonable alternatives does not require a "crystal ball" inquiry. According to the court: "Where the environmental aspects of alternatives are readily identifiable by the agency, it is reasonable to state them." However, the court said, "There is reason for concluding that NEPA was not meant to require detailed discussion of the environmental effects of 'alternatives' … when these effects cannot be readily ascertained and the alternatives are deemed only remote and speculative possibilities."[10] The court concluded that "the functions of courts and agencies, rightly understood, are not in opposition but in collaboration, toward achievement of the end prescribed by Congress.… So long as the officials and agencies have taken the 'hard look' … at environmental consequences mandated by Congress, the court does not seek to impose unreasonable extremes or to interject itself within the area of discretion of the executive as to the choice of the action to be taken."[11] The "rule of reason" test was subsequently approved by the Supreme Court in *Vermont Yankee Nuclear Power Corp. v. NRDC*.[12]

■ *Summary of EIS Content Requirements*

The requirements for the content of an EIS can be briefly summarized as follows, based on statutory language and CEQ regulations interpreting NEPA:

1. *Alternatives requiring discussion:* NEPA requires agencies to consider and discuss two types of alternatives in the EIS. The agency must consider alternatives to the proposed action, and the agency must study, develop, and describe appropriate alternatives to recommended courses of action in any proposal where unresolved conflicts concerning alternative uses of available resources exist.

2. *Range of alternatives:* An agency must consider reasonable alternatives, but the range of those alternatives is subject to a rule of reason, and depends on the nature and timing of the proposed action. As a general rule, the agency must discuss the alternative of no action, or of maintaining the status quo. This provides a basis for comparing environmental effects of the alternative courses of action.

3. *Environmental effects:* An agency must discuss the environmental impact of the proposed action, any adverse environmental effects that cannot be avoided if the proposal is implemented, the relationship between local short-term uses of the human environment and the maintenance and enhancement of long-term productivity, and any irreversible and irretrievable commitments of resources that would be made to the proposed action should it be implemented. All significant environmental effects, including cumulative effects, must be considered.

4. *Mitigation:* Mitigation measures must be discussed in sufficient detail to ensure

(Continued)

---

[9] 458 F.2d 827 (D.C. Cir. 1972).

[10] *Id.* at 837–38.

[11] *Id.* at 838.

[12] 435 U.S. 519 (1978).

and demonstrate that environmental consequences have been fairly evaluated, though there is no requirement for an agency to formulate and adopt a complete mitigation plan.

5. *Cost-benefit analysis:* An EIS must contain some form of balancing or informal cost-benefit analysis. The analysis must be sufficient to provide the public and decision maker with sufficient information to permit a reasoned evaluation and decision. However, under NEPA, environmental costs are not entitled to more weight than other costs and benefits.

Evaluation of NEPA

The preceding discussion has focused on some of the requirements of NEPA and some of the issues that may arise in court cases brought under provisions of that Act. A more important policy question is whether NEPA has been successful in achieving its stated purpose "to improve and coordinate federal plans, functions, programs, and resources to preserve and maintain the environment."

The Supreme Court has taken the view that NEPA is purely procedural and that the statement of environmental policies in § 101 of the act is "prefatory." According to the Supreme Court, "[I]f the adverse environmental effects of the proposed action are adequately identified and evaluated, the agency is not constrained by NEPA from deciding that other values outweigh the environmental costs.... NEPA merely prohibits uninformed—rather than unwise—agency action."[13] Even if substantive review were allowed, the arbitrary and capricious test would require only that the agency present a reasoned explanation for its decision.

But this does not mean that NEPA has been unsuccessful in compelling agencies to achieve its stated goals. The EIS process should ensure that an agency, in reaching its decision, will carefully consider the significant environmental impacts of the proposal. The EIS requirement also ensures that all relevant information will be made available to the public so that the public—including environmental organizations—may also play a role in both the decision-making process and the implementation of that decision. The EIS as a means for disseminating information to the public about the environmental impacts of agency decision making gives the public the assurance that the agency has indeed considered environmental concerns in its decision-making process. It "provides a springboard for public comment."[14]

Very few federal projects have been halted by permanent injunction under NEPA. However, NEPA litigation has caused substantial delays in a number of federal projects and modification or abandonment of others. Certainly there are cases where agencies have avoided taking controversial actions because of potential NEPA litigation. Whether the benefits attained under NEPA outweigh the expense and delay to federal projects depends to some extent on one's point of view about the project in dispute. The cost of preparing an EIS is usually substantial. However, remember from the *Overton Park* case that the decision not to prepare an EIS is reviewable. Thus, it is often simpler just to go ahead and prepare the EIS. Some consider NEPA an example of "red tape" that adds time and costs to a project. Additionally, it permits a small number of people to tie up and delay a big project. However, those complaints seem minor when considering the environmental impact of projects that are significant to the human environment. After all, the

---

[13] *Robertson v. Methow Valley Citizens Council*, 490 U.S. 332, 350–51 (1989).
[14] *Id.* at 349.

EIS requirement is very easy for agencies to meet. Indeed, one criticism of the EIS requirement is that an agency can make virtually any project "look good."

Likewise, whether NEPA has made a major contribution to preserving the environment depends on one's point of view. Some have suggested that the Supreme Court, which has never upheld a NEPA claim on the merits, has evidenced little support for the statute, and this attitude has diminished NEPA's effectiveness. Others see NEPA as a cornerstone of environmental law, the mandates of which are becoming more fully integrated into the decision-making process of federal agencies. Whatever the ultimate verdict on NEPA may be, it is clear that in some cases it is a potent device for focusing the public's attention on environmental concerns. The value of NEPA is the requirement that agencies take a "hard look" at the environmental impact of its decisions. It also brings in the public and other government agencies. Decision making tends to be more careful when someone is looking over your shoulder.

■ ■ ■ REVIEW AND STUDY QUESTIONS

1. What is the federal environmental policy of the United States? How do you know? The Supreme Court has declared § 101 of NEPA "prefatory." What does that mean? Does that lessen the importance of the environmental policy declared in NEPA?

2. How does NEPA work? Why is it considered only procedural, rather than substantive?

3. What action does NEPA force? How do you know?

4. How does an agency know whether it needs to create an EIS?

5. What is the CEQ?

6. What is the *Federal Register*? What role does the *Federal Register* play in public involvement with federal administrative agency action?

7. What must be included in an EIS? Find an EIS online and identify its strengths and shortcomings.

8. What impact does NEPA have on federal agency decision making?

9. NEPA imposes procedural requirements on agencies. Does it impose substantive requirements as well? What is the difference?

10. On balance, are the costs and delays that NEPA compliance adds to a project worth it? Why?

11. Is there any judicial remedy under NEPA if a project is clearly environmentally unsound but the EIS is perfect and the agency meets all the procedural requirements of NEPA?

■ Federal Statutes Related to Animals

Animals are an important part of our lives. Likewise, they are an important part of our environment. Sadly, animals are often separated from discussions of environmental law—or, if they are discussed within the context of environmental law, they are often simply classified as a "natural resource," like a tree or a waterway. Of course, animals have very particular and unique qualities that make such reductionist labeling ill-fitted and inappropriate, especially when laws that might afford protection and conservation of them and their habitats are focused on economics rather than well-being. This section provides a brief sketch of some major federal statutes related to animals and the environment, although it certainly does not address all law related to animals. Animal law is a vast and growing field in itself.

Of course, other types of laws exist that are related to animals. For example, both common law and treaties have been developed regarding animals. However, because this chapter focuses on statutory law, we will confine the discussion hereto federal statutory law.

Furthermore, many statutes related to animals are not related to the environment per se. For example, the Adoption of Military Animals[15] act allows military animals (dogs and horses) to be adopted, rather than euthanized, after their service. The Pets Evacuation and Transportation Standards Act of 2006[16] authorizes federal disaster assistance to rescue pets. However, because these laws—and many other laws related to animals—do not directly relate to the environment, discussion of those statutes has been omitted.

Endangered Species Act

The Endangered Species Act (ESA) contains both substantive and procedural requirements intended to protect **endangered species** from government—and in some instances private—actions. "Taking" an endangered species is prohibited by the ESA. Unlike NEPA, which only requires procedural compliance, the ESA contains a substantive prohibition on activity, thereby providing protection for listed animals and plants. This discussion focuses primarily on animals.

The ESA places the highest priority on the protection of endangered species. It prohibits government agencies from authorizing, funding, or carrying out any activities that might harm an endangered species or its habitat. The Act also prohibits private individuals from taking an endangered species. The meaning of the word *taking* has been the subject of much litigation and is the source of much controversy. *Taking* may be so broadly defined that it can be construed to prohibit virtually any activity that might result in harm to a protected species.

Under the ESA, a determination that a species is endangered or threatened is to be made "solely on the basis of the best scientific and commercial data available to [the Secretary.]"[17] Section 7 of the Act protects endangered species from federal agency action without regard to the economic consequences of protection. Section 9 prohibits any person from taking an endangered species, except in very limited circumstances. That section contains substantive, specific, and mandatory provisions protecting an endangered species and its habitat regardless of cost.

One of the most important and famous cases interpreting the ESA, *Tennessee Valley Authority v. Hill,* was decided in 1978. That case, interpreting ESA § 7, involved a classic environmental conflict arising from a federal agency's decision to build a dam, called the Tellico Dam, on a last remaining segment of the Little Tennessee River. A citizens' coalition that sought to block the project had obtained an injunction under NEPA. The NEPA injunction lasted two years but was subsequently dissolved in 1973 when the Tennessee Valley Authority (TVA) produced an adequate EIS. That same year, an ichthyologist at the University of Tennessee discovered a small endangered fish, the snail darter, living in the project area. The plaintiffs filed another lawsuit, arguing that the dam project would destroy the habitat of the snail darter in violation of the ESA. The trial court agreed with the plaintiffs but declined to issue an injunction in the case. The court of appeals granted the injunction and the U.S. Supreme Court granted a petition for review.

endangered species: Any species in danger of extinction.

---

[15] 10 U.S.C. § 2583.

[16] Pub. L. No. 109-308 (codified as 42 U.S.C. §§ 5170b(a)(3)(J), 5196(e)(4), 5196(j)(2), and 5196b(g)).

[17] 16 U.S.C. § 1533(b)(1)(A).

Tennessee Valley Authority v. Hill
437 U.S. 153 (1978)

MR. CHIEF JUSTICE BURGER delivered the opinion of the Court.

The questions presented in this case are (a) whether the Endangered Species Act of 1973 requires a court to enjoin the operation of a virtually completed federal dam—which had been authorized prior to 1973—when, pursuant to authority vested in him by Congress, the Secretary of the Interior has determined that operation of the dam would eradicate an endangered species; and (b) whether continued congressional appropriations for the dam after 1973 constituted an implied repeal of the Endangered Species Act, at least as to the particular dam.

* * *

Until recently the finding of a new species of animal life would hardly generate a cause celebre. This is particularly so in the case of darters, of which there are approximately 130 known species, 8 to 10 of these having been identified only in the last five years.… The moving force behind the snail darter's sudden fame came some four months after its discovery, when the Congress passed the Endangered Species Act of 1973 (Act)…. This legislation, among other things, authorizes the Secretary of the Interior to declare species of animal life "endangered" … and to identify the "critical habitat" … of these creatures.

[The Court focused on § 7 of the Act, which requires federal departments and agencies to "tak[e] such action necessary to insure that actions authorized, funded, or carried out by them do not jeopardize the continued existence of such endangered species and threatened species or result in the destruction or modification of habitat of such species" ….]

* * *

We begin with the premise that operation of the Tellico Dam will either eradicate the known population of snail darters or destroy their critical habitat. Petitioner does not now seriously dispute this fact…. [T]he Secretary [of the Interior] promulgated regulations which declared the snail darter an endangered species whose critical habitat would be destroyed by creation of the Tellico Reservoir. Doubtless petitioner would prefer not to have these regulations on the books, but there is no suggestion that the Secretary exceeded his authority or abused his discretion in issuing the regulations.…

It may seem curious to some that the survival of a relatively small number of three-inch fish among all the countless millions of species extant would require the permanent halting of a virtually completed dam for which Congress has expended more than $100 million.… We conclude, however, that the explicit provisions of the Endangered Species Act require precisely that result.

One would be hard pressed to find a statutory provision whose terms were any plainer than those in § 7 of the Endangered Species Act. Its very words affirmatively command all federal agencies "to *insure* that actions *authorized, funded*, or *carried out* by them do not *jeopardize* the continued existence" of an endangered species or "*result* in the destruction or modification of habitat of such species …." This language admits of no exception. Nonetheless, petitioner urges, as do the dissenters, that the Act cannot reasonably be interpreted as applying to a federal project which was well under way when Congress passed the Endangered Species Act of 1973. To sustain that position, however, we would be forced to ignore the ordinary meaning of plain language. It has not been shown, for example, how TVA can close the gates of the Tellico Dam without "carrying out" an action that has been "authorized" and "funded" by a federal agency. Nor can we understand how such action will "*insure*" that the snail darter's habitat is not disrupted.… Accepting the Secretary's determinations, as we must, it is clear that TVA's proposed operation of the dam will have precisely the opposite effect, namely the *eradication* of an endangered species.

Concededly, this view of the Act will produce results requiring the sacrifice of the anticipated benefits of the project and of many millions of dollars in public funds.… But examination of the language, history, and structure of the legislation under review here indicates beyond doubt that Congress intended endangered species to be afforded the highest of priorities.

* * *

As it was finally passed, the Endangered Species Act of 1973 represented the most comprehensive legislation for the preservation of endangered species ever enacted by any nation. Its stated purposes were "to provide a means whereby the ecosystems upon which endangered species and threatened species depend may be conserved," and "to provide a program for the conservation of such … species…." … In furtherance of these goals, Congress expressly stated in § 2(c) that "all Federal departments and agencies *shall* seek *to conserve endangered species* or threatened species … to the point at which the measures provided pursuant to this chapter

(Continued)

are no longer necessary." … Aside from § 7, other provisions indicated the seriousness with which Congress viewed this issue: Virtually all dealings with endangered species, including taking, possession, transportation, and sale, were prohibited, … except in extremely narrow circumstances….

[After further discussion, the court affirmed the decision of the court of appeals that the project should be enjoined under the ESA.]

Questions and Comments for Discussion

1. Justices Powell and Blackmun filed a dissent in *TVA v. Hill.* They argued that the opinion of the majority "adopts a reading of section 7 of the Act that gives it a retroactive effect and disregards 12 years of consistently expressed congressional intent to complete the Tellico Project…. Moreover, it ignores established canons of statutory construction."[18] The dissenters expected Congress to amend the Endangered Species Act to "prevent the grave consequences made possible by today's decision." According to the dissenters, "Few, if any, Members of that body will wish to defend an interpretation of the Act that requires the waste of at least $53 million, … and denies the people of the Tennessee Valley area the benefits of the reservoir that Congress intended to confer…. There will be little sentiment to leave this dam standing before an empty reservoir, serving no purpose other than a conversation piece for incredulous tourists."[19]

   In 1978, Congress amended the Endangered Species Act to provide flexibility by creating a Cabinet-level review board (called the "God Squad" or "God Committee") which could grant an exemption if it found by special majority that:

   1. The federal project is of regional or national significance;
   2. There is no "reasonable and prudent alternative"; and
   3. The project as proposed "clearly outweighs the alternatives."

   The amendment creating this exemption was passed following a torrent of criticism leveled against the act following the snail darter decision in the Tellico Dam case. However, on January 23, 1979, the "God Committee" unanimously denied an exemption for Tellico on economic grounds. According to the committee, the project was ill-conceived and uneconomic in the first place and deserved to be killed on its own merits.

   The project ultimately went forward when Senator Baker and Congressman Duncan of Tennessee added a rider to a House appropriations bill that explicitly overrode the decision as it applied to the Tellico project. Should the so-called "God Squad" be permitted to override protections afforded to threatened or endangered species? Why or why not?

2. After the Tellico Dam case, many argued that a statute should not be applied if it would lead to an "absurd" or "extreme" result. The Supreme Court held in *TVA v. Hill* that even when a statute leads to what a court might think is an absurd result, the statute is to be applied as it is written. Do you agree that it is the function of a court to apply the law "as written" regardless of the consequences in a particular case? Why or why not?

3. Unlike earlier species protection acts, the ESA does not permit the Secretary of the Interior to consider the economic impact of listing a species as endangered under the Act. Should economic costs be considered in making that determination? In formulating your answer to this policy question, consider the reasons why species protection may have value. Many have argued that the environment has instrumental value to humans—be it aesthetic, religious, or economic—and thus there is value in preserving species for present and future human beings. However, consider a species value other than value placed on it by human beings. Any species—including the snail darter—has inherent value even if human beings do not recognize its value. As the snail darter controversy suggests, whether economic costs should be considered in protecting endangered species (the "cost-benefit" controversy) is tied to an ethical, ecological, and political debate about how, when, and what environmental values human beings should protect, and at what cost.

The ESA contains several important sections designed to implement its species protection policies. Section 4 sets out the procedure for listing of an endangered or threatened species under the Act. This is perhaps the most important section of the Act, because the ESA's protections are contingent upon the listing process.

[18] 437 U.S. at 202.
[19] *Id.* at 210.

The Secretary of the Interior (and in some cases the Secretary of Commerce) has authority to list an endangered or threatened species under the ESA.

Section 4 provides that "the Secretary shall by regulation ... determine whether any species is an endangered species or a threatened species because of any of the following factors:

(A) the present or threatened destruction, modification, or curtailment of its habitat or range;

(B) overutilization for commercial, recreational, scientific, or educational purposes;

(C) disease or predation;

(D) the inadequacy of existing regulatory mechanisms; or

(E) other natural or manmade factors affecting its continued existence."

The determination that a species is endangered excludes consideration of the economic impact of that decision. Section 4(b)(1)(a) states: "The Secretary shall make determinations required by subsection (a)(1) [of this section] solely on the basis of the best scientific and commercial data available to him after conducting a review of the status of the species...."

Once a species is listed as endangered or threatened, it is protected at all costs. The rule that "all federal departments and agencies shall seek to conserve all endangered and threatened species" is strictly construed. When a species is listed, the Secretary must designate its **critical habitat** within a year of the listing. *Critical habitat* is defined as the geographical area with the physical or biological features essential to the survival of the species. In designating critical habitat, the Secretary is required to take into consideration the economic impact, and any other relevant impact, of specifying any particular area as critical habitat. The Secretary may exclude an area if the benefits of exclusion outweigh the benefits of designating an area as critical habitat, unless the Secretary determines, "based on the best scientific and commercial data available, that the failure to designate [an] area as critical habitat will result in the extinction of the species concerned."[20] **Recovery plans**, which are biological blueprints for actions needed to bring about the recovery of a species, also must be created under this section.

The definition of *species* under the ESA is very broad, as it includes any subspecies of fish, wildlife, or plants.[21] An *endangered species* is further defined as "any species which is in danger of extinction throughout all or a significant portion of its range other than a species of the Class Insecta determined ... to constitute a pest...."[22] A **threatened species** is defined as a species that, while not yet endangered, is likely to become so in the foreseeable future.[23]

The endangered species program is administered by the U.S. Fish and Wildlife Service (FWS) and the National Marine Fisheries Service (NMFS). A state or federal agency, individual, or any other entity may petition either of these two agencies to list a species. If there is sufficient biological data, the species is named an official candidate, and after publication of notification in the *Federal Register*, the species is added to the list of endangered or threatened species.

critical habitat: The geographical area with the physical or biological features essential to survival of the species.

recovery plans: Document setting forth the actions necessary to bring about the recovery of a species.

threatened species: Any species likely to become endangered in the foreseeable future.

---

[20] 16 U.S.C. § 1533(b)(2).
[21] ESA § 3(16); 16 U.S.C. § 1532(16).
[22] ESA § 3(6); 16 U.S.C. § 1532(6).
[23] ESA § 3(20); 16 U.S.C. § 1532(20).

The determination to list or not list a species is subject to judicial review. Despite prompting from various concerned groups, only a fraction of the endangered and threatened species known to be eligible have been listed.

Section 7 of the ESA is entitled "Interagency Cooperation." Like NEPA, this section is directed at federal agencies. Section 7 contains the following mandate:

> Each Federal agency shall, in consultation with and with the assistance of the Secretary, insure that any action authorized, funded, or carried out by such agency ... is not likely to jeopardize the continued existence of any endangered species or threatened species or result in the destruction or adverse modification of habitat of such species which is determined by the Secretary, after consultation as appropriate with affected States, to be critical....[24]

This section was the focus of the Supreme Court's discussion and opinion in *Tennessee Valley Authority v. Hill.* Section 7 also establishes the Endangered Species Committee. This **"God Squad"** may grant an exemption from the requirements of § 7. (This committee's function was discussed after the *Tellico Dam* case in the text.)

The application of § 9 of the Act is much broader than that of § 7 because it applies to "any person," not just actions of federal agencies. Section 9(1) applies to "any endangered species of fish or wildlife listed under" the ESA. It makes it unlawful for any person to:

(A) import any such species into, or export any such species from the United States;

(B) take any such species within the United States or the territorial sea of the United States;

(C) take any such species upon the high seas;

(D) possess, sell, deliver, carry, transport, or ship, by any means whatsoever, any such species taken in violation of subparagraphs (B) and (C);

(E) deliver, receive, carry, transport, or ship in interstate or foreign commerce, by any means whatsoever and in the course of a commercial activity, any such species;

(F) sell or offer for sale in interstate or foreign commerce any such species; or

(G) violate any regulation pertaining to such species or to any threatened species of fish or wildlife listed pursuant to [§1533 of this title] and promulgated by the Secretary pursuant to authority provided by this Act.

A separate provision of this section addresses endangered plants. Sections 9(a) (B) and (C) prohibit the taking of any endangered species, and imposes heavy criminal sanctions on the act of killing or capturing endangered animals. In the context of the ESA, the word *taking* should be distinguished from the concept of taking under the Fifth Amendment as discussed in earlier chapters. **Taking** an endangered species in violation of the ESA is defined in that Act as "harass, harm, pursue, hunt, shoot, wound, kill, trap, capture, or collect, or attempt to engage in any such conduct." The meaning of the word *take* as used in the ESA has been the subject of much litigation. This focus raises questions about the appropriate balance between the rights of a property owner to develop its property and the government's interest in protecting endangered species' habitats.

Critics of the ESA argue that the sweep of the Act is too broad, and that an expansive definition of the takings prohibitions of the ESA effectively prevents

"God Squad": Cabinet-level review board created by the ESA to provide flexibility under the Act; the Endangered Species Committee has the power to grant exemptions under the Act.

taking: Under the ESA, action to "harass, harm, pursue, hunt, shoot, wound, kill, trap, capture, or collect, or attempt to engage in any such conduct."

---

[24] ESA § 7(a)(2); 16 U.S.C. § 1536.

activities on public or private lands that would otherwise be considered a reasonable economic use of the property. The ESA can halt development projects if that project potentially threatens a listed species.

This section cannot and does not provide a comprehensive view of ESA litigation. However, it does provide a discussion of some of the best-known cases in this area that have shaped our understanding of the law itself. In a series of well-known ESA cases, landowners, logging companies, and families dependent on the forest products industries in the Pacific Northwest and in the Southeast challenged the Fish and Wildlife Service definition of the word *harm* in the ESA.

The agency had defined the word *harm* in the statutory definition of "take" as follows:

> Harm in the definition of "take" in the Act means an act which actually kills or injures wildlife. Such act may include significant habitat modification or degradation where it actually kills or injures wildlife by significantly impairing essential behavioral patterns, including breeding, feeding or sheltering.[25]

Two federal appeals courts were divided on whether the agency's definition of *harm* in the taking prohibition of the ESA was a permissible one. In *Sweet Home Chapter of Communities for a Great Oregon v. Babbitt*,[26] the D.C. Circuit Court of Appeals determined that the FWS definition exceeded the scope of § 9's taking prohibition. The Ninth Circuit Court of Appeals, however, had upheld the definition in another case.[27] Because of this split in the circuits, the Supreme Court agreed in 1995 to address the issue. A portion of the Court's analysis upholding the agency definition of *harm* is set out here.

Babbitt v. Sweet Home Chapter of Communities for a Great Oregon
515, U.S. 687, 115 S. Ct. 2407 (1995)

JUSTICE STEVENS delivered the opinion of the Court.

* * *

Because this case was decided on motions for summary judgment, we may appropriately make certain factual assumptions in order to frame the legal issue. First, we assume respondents have no desire to harm either the red cockaded woodpecker or the spotted owl; they merely wish to continue logging activities that would be entirely proper if not prohibited by the ESA. On the other hand, we must assume *arguendo* that those activities will have the effect, even though unintended, of detrimentally changing the natural habitat of both

listed species and that, as a consequence, members of those species will be killed or injured.... The Secretary ... submits that the §9 prohibition on takings, which Congress defined to include "harm," places on respondents a duty to avoid harm that habitat alteration will cause the birds unless respondents first obtain a permit pursuant to §10.

The text of the [Endangered Species] Act provides three reasons for concluding that the Secretary's interpretation is reasonable. First, an ordinary understanding of the word "harm" supports it. The dictionary definition of the verb form of "harm" is "to cause hurt or damage to: injure." ... In the context of the ESA, that definition naturally encompasses habitat modification

(Continued)

---

[25] 50 C.F.R. § 17.3.
[26] 17 F.3d 1463 (D.C. Cir. 1994).
[27] The Ninth Circuit Court of Appeals stated in dicta that the FWS regulation defining *harm* was consistent with the ESA. *Palila v. Hawaii Department of Land & Natural Resources*, 649 F. Supp. 1070 (D. Haw. 1986), *aff'd*, 852 F.2d 1106 (9th Cir. 1988).

that results in actual injury or death to members of an endangered or threatened species.

Respondents argue that the Secretary should have limited the purview of "harm" to direct applications of force against protected species, but the dictionary definition does not include the word "directly" or suggest in any way that only direct or willful action that leads to injury constitutes "harm." … Moreover, unless the statutory term "harm" encompasses indirect as well as direct injuries, the word has no meaning that does not duplicate the meaning of other words that §3 uses to define "take." A reluctance to treat statutory terms as surplusage supports the reasonableness of the Secretary's interpretation.…

Second, the broad purpose of the ESA supports the Secretary's decision to extend protection against activities that cause the precise harms Congress enacted the statute to avoid.… As stated in §2 of the Act, among its central purposes is "to provide a means whereby the ecosystems upon which endangered species and threatened species depend may be conserved…." …

* * *

Third, the fact that Congress in 1982 authorized the Secretary to issue permits for takings that §9(a)(1)(B) would otherwise prohibit, "if such taking is incidental to, and not the purpose of, the carrying out of an otherwise lawful activity," … strongly suggests that Congress understood §9(a)(1)(B) to prohibit indirect as well as deliberate takings.… Congress' addition of the §10 permit provision supports the Secretary's conclusion that activities not intended to harm an endangered species, such as habitat modification, may constitute unlawful takings under the ESA unless the Secretary permits them.

* * *

When it enacted the ESA, Congress delegated broad administrative and interpretive power to the Secretary.… The task of defining and listing endangered and threatened species requires an expertise and attention to detail that exceeds the normal province of Congress. Fashioning appropriate standards for issuing permits under §10 for takings that would otherwise violate §9 necessarily requires the exercise of broad discretion. The proper interpretation of a term such as "harm" involves a complex policy choice. When Congress has entrusted the Secretary with broad discretion, we are especially reluctant to substitute our views of wise policy for his.…

* * *

The judgment of the Court of Appeals is reversed.

Questions and Comments for Discussion

1. Courts use the following steps to interpret statutes. First, what is the plain meaning of the words? Second, what are the legislative intent and history of the statute? Third, what is the public policy underlying the statute? The court of appeals and the dissenting Justices relied in part on the maxim *noscitur et sociis* ("words are known by the company they keep"). What techniques of statutory interpretation did the majority use in determining whether the agency's interpretation of the word *harm* was a reasonable one?

2. Whether habitat modification constitutes a "taking" of a protected species under the ESA is a question of significance to both environmentalists and landowners. Section 7's prohibition against jeopardizing a species or modifying critical habitat only applies to federal agencies. Section 9, however, applies to all persons. If this includes intentional disruption of habitat, as occurs during land development, the statute's prohibitions of "harm" as interpreted by the Fish and Wildlife Service may have a significant effect on private property rights. Do you think that government should have the right to restrict a landowner's use of real property? What are the benefits and drawbacks of such restrictions?

3. As discussed in this case, in 1982 Congress authorized the Secretary to issue permits for takings that would otherwise be prohibited under § 9. Section 10 of the ESA provides that the Secretary may permit, under terms and conditions he prescribes, a taking otherwise prohibited by § 9 if the taking is "incidental to, and not the purpose of, the carrying out of an otherwise lawful activity." This section permitting incidental takings requires that the applicant submit a conservation plan, including steps for minimizing and mitigating such impacts. If the Secretary finds, after opportunity for public comment, that the taking will be incidental, and will not appreciably reduce the likelihood of the survival and recovery of the species in the wild, the Secretary may issue a permit for the activity. This section is presumably designed to minimize the economic impact of the ESA on private property development that may affect habitat of an endangered or threatened species. Which is more important: the economic interests of landowners, or the interests of individual species otherwise protected under the ESA?

(Continued)

4. The Endangered Species Act also closes down the United States market to endangered wildlife. The market for endangered species actually encourages species extinction by raising the value of an animal as it approaches extinction. The ESA attempts to eliminate the pressures on endangered animals in other parts of the world by closing down the lucrative and major U.S. market for such species.

Foreign species protected under the Act include leopards, turtles, rare birds (for feathers), and elephants (for ivory). For obvious reasons, species protection acts like the ESA outweigh individual rights to purchase and sell personal property and to develop real property. What are the political, economic, and environmental implications of such laws?

Standing under the ESA is yet another important consideration. In *Bennett v. Spear*,[28] Oregon irrigation districts and ranches challenged a biological opinion issued by the FWS concerning the operation of the Klamath Irrigation Project by the Bureau of Reclamation. The Klamath Project is a series of lakes, rivers, dams, and irrigation canals in northern California and southern Oregon. In 1992, the Bureau of Reclamation, which administers the project, notified the FWS that operation of the project might affect the Lost River Sucker and Shortnose Sucker, species of fish that were listed as endangered in 1988. The FWS issued a Biological Opinion concluding that long-term operation of the project was likely to jeopardize the continued existence of the endangered fish, and identified as a reasonable and productive alternative the maintenance of minimum water levels on Clear Lake and Gerber Reservoirs. The petitioners, two districts that received Klamath Project water and the operators of two ranches within those districts, filed an action against the FWS and the Secretary of the Interior. The petitioners claimed a competing interest in the water that the agency had declared necessary for the preservation of the fish. They argued, among other things, that there was no scientifically or commercially available evidence indicating that the populations of endangered suckers in the lake and reservoirs had declined, were declining, or would decline as a result, and that there was no commercially or scientifically available evidence indicating that the restrictions on lake levels imposed in the Biological Opinion would have any beneficial effect on populations of the endangered species. The question before the court was whether the petitioners had standing to seek judicial review of the Biological Opinion under the citizen suit provisions of the ESA and the APA. The U.S. Supreme Court, in a unanimous opinion, held that the districts' and ranches' economic and related interests fell within the zone of interest protected by the ESA, because the Act's citizen suit provision provides that "any person" may file civil suit under the Act. In short, this means that anyone, not just environmental groups or people concerned about wildlife or habitat for the benefit of the wildlife, has standing to bring claims under the ESA.

The courts have also considered the ESA's position vis-à-vis other federal statutes, when those statutes conflict. In *National Association of Home Builders v. Defenders of Wildlife*,[29] the U.S. Supreme Court considered a case in which application of the law might create a conflict between the Clean Water Act and the ESA. In that case, Arizona proposed to exercise its own authority over the permitting system required by the National Pollution Discharge Elimination System, which a state is entitled to do if it meets the criteria set forth by the Clean Water Act. However, the EPA was concerned that such a transfer would result in the taking of endangered species. In the majority opinion, the Court held that the ESA did not apply, even if a state's Clean Water Act permitting system does not protect endangered species,

[28] 520 U.S. 154 (1997).
[29] 551 U.S. 644 (2007).

because the EPA must only consider the criteria set forth by the Clean Water Act, rather than other criteria not required by the statute. After the EPA transferred the authority to the state, the Defenders of Wildlife sued, arguing that the ESA imposed authority on the EPA to exercise its judgment independently. The dissent argued that *TVA v. Hill* requires the ESA considerations to take priority.

Evaluation of the Endangered Species Act

Some scholars have argued that subsequent cases have rendered the *TVA v. Hill* holding somewhat flimsy. The Court in *Lujan v. Defenders of Wildlife, Babbitt v. Sweet Home Chapter of Communities for a Great Oregon, Bennett v. Spear,* and *National Association of Home Builders v. Defenders of Wildlife* have each lessened, to some degree, the sweeping ESA victory enjoyed in *TVA v. Hill*.[30] Others do not see such damning defeat in these cases. After all, *TVA v. Hill* is still good law.

Perhaps most importantly, whether the ESA has been effective in actually saving species is a question of central concern. Listing a species as either endangered or threatened takes a great deal of time—which is something that species in this predicament do not have—and it takes a great deal of perseverance. Once listed, there is no guarantee that a species will recover, despite the great costs that might be incurred in developing and implementing a plan to do so.

Other concerns have arisen regarding the ESA's power to take private property through extensive regulation of land use. Regulatory takings (discussed in Chapter 6) may occur if the government regulates the use of private property in such a way as to deprive the owner of all its economic value. In some instances, an owner that is prohibited from developing its property because doing so may destroy the critical habitat of an endangered species may argue that the law has deprived it of the use and value of the property without just compensation, in violation of the Fifth Amendment.

Despite these concerns, however, the ESA's implementation process often encourages collaboration and coordination, rather than stringent prohibitions.

▪ **Historical Viewpoint: *Scientific Uncertainty and the Case of the Spotted Owl***

Consider also the case of the northern spotted owl. Environmental groups used the EIS requirements of NEPA (specifically challenging the necessity for and adequacy of the EIS), the ESA, and provisions of federal forestry management laws in a series of lawsuits designed to halt logging in the old-growth forests of the Pacific Northwest. Once the spotted owl was listed as an endangered species, the plaintiffs argued that agreements between the National Forest Service and the timber industry, which permitted logging in the forests of Olympic National Park and Forest, threatened the critical habitat of the owl and must be halted under the ESA. The plaintiffs sought primarily to preserve the ancient, old-growth forests of the Pacific Northwest; the owl became the vehicle for forest protection by providing a legal basis on which environmental groups could challenge the Forest Service's management plans. For many, the spotted owl has also become a symbol of conflicting points of view between loggers, environmentalists, the timber industry, the government, and members of the scientific community.

Using the Internet, research the conflict between the northern spotted owl and the ESA on the one hand, and the halting of logging of old-growth forests in the Pacific Northwest on the other.

1. How can NEPA and an EIS work to protect the environment?

2. Who were the stakeholders in the spotted owl controversy? What role does the law (or should the law) play in such controversies?

---

[30] *See, e.g.,* J. B. Ruhl, *The Endangered Species Act's Fall from Grace in the Supreme Court,* 36 HARV. ENVTL. L. REV. 487 (2012).

Other Animal-Related Federal Statutes

In addition to the ESA, Congress has created several federal statutes related to animals. Some of these statutes exist in support of international treaties to which the United States is a signatory to prohibit trade in certain species, or to provide protection for certain species. The table below provides a summary of some federal statutes related to animals.

■ Federal Statutes Related to Animals and the Environment[31]

Statute	Description
The Marine Mammal Protection Act (MMPA), 16 U.S.C. § 1361	Makes it unlawful, except as specifically permitted under statute or treaty, to take, possess, or trade a marine mammal or marine mammal product, or to use a method of commercial fishing that violates the MMPA regulations
Protection of Bald and Golden Eagles, 16 U.S.C. § 668 *et seq.*	Makes it a criminal offense to possess, take, or trade a bald or golden eagle
The National Wildlife Refuge System (NWRS) Administration Act, 16 U.S.C. §§ 668dd-668ee	Establishes a National Wildlife Refuge System and limits the transfer or disposal of such lands; makes it illegal to knowingly disturb, remove, or destroy property in the NWRS
The Migratory Bird Treaty Act, 16 U.S.C. §§ 703-712	Makes it unlawful to pursue, hunt, take, capture, kill, possess, trade, or transport any migratory bird or bird part, nest, or egg included in the terms of international agreements between the United States and Mexico, Japan, and the former Soviet Union
Wild Free-Roaming Horses and Burros Act, 16 U.S.C. §§ 1331-1340	Protects unbranded and unclaimed horses and burros on public lands of the United States from capture, branding, harassment, or death; provides that such animals on public lands administered by the BLM or USFS shall be protected and managed as components of the lands, in a manner designed to achieve and maintain a thriving natural ecological balance
Lacey Act, 18 U.S.C. §§ 41-43 and amendments of 1981, 16 U.S.C. §§ 3371-3378	Makes it unlawful to willfully disturb or kill any bird, fish, or wild animals, or eggs or nests of any bird or fish on any lands or waters set apart or reserved under federal law as sanctuaries, refuges, or breeding grounds; makes it unlawful to import species of wild animals, birds, or fish that may be injurious to interests of human beings or wildlife; makes it unlawful to use aircraft or motor vehicles to hunt or to pollute a watering hole of any wild horse or burro running at large on any public lands Amendment makes it unlawful to engage in commerce of any fish or wildlife or plant in violation of any treaty or federal or state law; exceptions exist for zoos, circuses, research facilities, sanctuaries, etc.

(Continued)

---

[31] Information from this table was drawn from H. COHEN, BRIEF SUMMARIES OF FEDERAL ANIMAL PROTECTION STATUTES (Congressional Research Service, 2008).

Statute	Description
Fish and Wildlife Conservation Act, 16 U.S.C. §§ 2901-2911	Authorizes the Secretary of the Interior to approve state conservation plans for nongame fish and wildlife and to undertake research and conservation activities concerning population trends and effects of environmental changes and human activities on migratory nongame birds
African Elephant Conservation Act, 16 U.S.C. §§ 4201-4246	Imposes criminal and civil penalties against persons that import raw ivory from any country where a moratorium is in effect or from the United States
Fur Seal Act of 1966, 16 U.S.C. §§ 1151-1187	Prohibits the taking of fur seals in the North Pacific Ocean or on any lands or waters under U.S. jurisdiction, or to engage in commerce in fur seals' skins taken contrary to this law or the Interim Convention on the Conservation of North Pacific Fur Seals
Great Ape Conservation Act of 2000, 16 U.S.C. §§ 6301-6305	Establishes the Great Ape Conservation Fund to be used for projects that conserve great apes
International Dolphin Conservation Act, Pub. L. No. 105-42 (1997)	Prohibits certain tuna harvesting practices; amends the MMPA
Marine Turtle Conservation Act of 2004, 16 U.S.C. §§ 6601-6607	Created to assist in conservation of marine turtles and nesting habitats of marine turtles in foreign countries
Rhinoceros and Tiger Conservation Act of 1994, 16 U.S.C § 5306 et seq.	Establishes the Rhinoceros and Tiger Conservation Fund to provide financial assistance for conservation of those species
Shark Finning Prohibition Act, Pub. L. No. 106-557 (16 U.S.C. § 1822 note)	Makes it unlawful to remove the fins of any shark and discard the carcass at sea; amends Magnus-Stevens Fishery Conservation and Management Act (16 U.S.C. §§ 1801-1884)
Salmon and Steelhead Conservation and Enhancement Act of 1980, 16 U.S.C. §§ 3301-3345	Authorizes cooperative program between Indian Tribes, Washington State, Oregon, and the United States, to manage salmon and their habitat
United States-Russia Polar Bear Conservation and Management Act of 2006, 16 U.S.C. §§ 1423-1423h	Makes it unlawful to take any polar bear in violation of existing international agreements, or to engage in commerce of any polar bear or parts of polar bears; amendment to the MMPA

(Continued)

Statute	Description
Whale Conservation and Protection Study Act, 16 U.S.C. §§ 917-917d	Directs the Secretary of Commerce to undertake comprehensive studies of all whales found in the waters of the United States
Wild Bird Conservation Act of 1992, 16 U.S.C. §§ 4901-4916	Promotes conservation of exotic birds
Whaling Convention Act of 1949, 16 U.S.C. § 916	Prohibits whaling and commerce in whale products in violation of the International Whaling Convention for the Regulation of Whaling or any whaling regulation

■ ■ ■ REVIEW AND STUDY QUESTIONS

1. Besides statutory law, what other types of law can be created to protect animals and preserve their habitats?

2. What are the benefits and the drawbacks of the ESA? Do you think that the ESA provides enough protection for endangered or threatened animals and plants? If not, how could more protection be provided? Discuss the appropriateness and implications of humans selecting which species will be protected under the ESA.

3. How can judicial review act as a check on administrative agency action related to the ESA?

4. Should animals have standing on their own? If animals had standing to bring claims on their own—through a guardian ad litem, for example—how might that change the need for the ESA? What if rights to own property were recognized as belonging to animals?

5. Given scientific uncertainty related to the status of a species' continuation or its extinction, how certain must we be before providing protection for a species that might be endangered or threatened? It is very difficult to determine the number of members of an endangered species, like owls, within a certain geographical area, and the impact of a particular activity like logging on that particular species. Who should bear the cost of such scientific studies?

6. Preserving species is important to human survival. Why?

7. Species have inherent value independent of value placed on them by human beings. How can human law be drafted or applied to animals and plants so that those interests are accounted for, rather than only human interests?

■ Federal Public Lands

Federal Land Policy and Management Act

In 1976, Congress enacted comprehensive legislation governing public lands, entitled the Federal Land Policy and Management Act (FLPMA).[32] The

---

[32] 43 U.S.C. §§ 1701-1787.

FLPMA declares that the policy of the United States is that public lands will be managed to:

- Protect scientific, scenic, historical, ecological, and environmental values
- Preserve certain public lands in their natural condition
- Provide wildlife habitats and outdoor recreation for humans

The FLPMA promotes the concept of multiple use and sustained yield on public lands. **Multiple use** means a combination of balanced and diverse uses that will best meet the needs of present and future generations of Americans, including recreational, range, timber, mineral, watershed, fish and wildlife, and natural, scenic, or scientific values. **Sustained yield** means the maintenance of a high-level output of various renewable resources on public lands, consistent with the principle of multiple use.

The Bureau of Land Management (BLM) has authority to manage public lands under the FLPMA. The BLM develops and maintains land use plans for public lands. It is authorized to acquire public lands and may sell tracts of public land (except for designated wilderness areas, wild and scenic rivers, or national trails) if it makes certain statutory findings. The FLPMA also authorizes the BLM to withdraw public lands from sale or disposition and directs it to review certain areas within the public domain for their suitability as wilderness.

National Forest Management Act

The National Forest Management Act (NFMA)[33] establishes procedures for management of the national forests. Authority to manage national forests is vested in the U.S. Forest Service (USFS). The USFS maintains a Renewable Resource Program for the protection, management, and development of the National Forest System, and it must manage the renewable resources in a way that is consistent with the concepts of multiple use and sustained yield. Under the NFMA, the USFS develops and maintains land and resource management plans within the National Forest System. Among other things, these plans must:

- Consider the environment
- Provide for plant and animal diversity
- Ensure that watershed conditions will not be irreversibly damaged and that harvested lands can be restored within five years
- Ensure that water resources will be protected
- Restrict clear-cutting and similar management practices

In the NFMA, Congress recognized the complexity of managing the nation's renewable forest resources by mandating a continuous analysis of the Renewable Resource Program.

multiple use: Under the FLPMA, a combination of diverse uses, including recreational, ranger, timber, mineral, watershed, habitat, nature, scenic, or scientific.

sustained yield: Maintenance of high-level output of renewable resources on public lands.

---

[33] Pub. L. No. 94-588.

Surface Mining Control and Reclamation Act of 1977

Congress enacted the Surface Mining Control and Reclamation Act[34] in 1977. Congress recognized that coal mining operations contribute "significantly to the nation's energy requirements" but simultaneously recognized concern over surface mining operations that, for example:

> destroy[ed] or diminish[ed] the utility of land for commercial, industrial, residential, recreational, agricultural, and forestry purposes, by causing erosion and landslides, by contributing to floods, by polluting the water, by destroying fish and wildlife habitats, by impairing natural beauty, by damaging the property of citizens, by creating hazards dangerous to life and property, by degrading the quality of life in local communities, and by counteracting governmental programs and efforts to conserve soil, water, and other natural resources.[35]

The Act regulates the environmental effects of strip mining and the surface effects of underground mining. It is administered by the Office of Surface Mining (OSM). The law provides minimum environmental performance standards for strip mining, and establishes an Abandoned Mine Land Reclamation Fund to, among other things:

- Reclaim and restore land and water resources affected by past mining
- Seal and fill abandoned deep mine entries and voids
- Control water pollution and prevent coal mine subsidence

The Act also encourages states to regulate strip mining within their borders, and directs the OSM to establish a federal program in any state that does not have an approved strip mining regulatory program.

Coastal Zone Management Act

In 1972, Congress adopted the Coastal Zone Management Act (CZMA).[36] In adopting the CZMA, Congress recognized the "increasing and competing demands upon the lands and waters of our coastal zone occasioned by population growth and economic development," and found a "national interest in the effective management, beneficial use, protection, and development of the coastal zone." The Act establishes a structure providing for the active involvement of coastal states, the development of coastal zone management plans, a process for state input into the development of federally approved plans, and an ultimate decision by the Secretary of Commerce as to whether a proposed activity deemed inconsistent by the states is permissible.

The CZMA stands as an excellent example of federalism, because it requires states to develop coastal zone management plans that meet the requirements of the federal law. Each state administers its own plans, unless it has not developed a plan consistent with the CZMA.

---

[34] 30 U.S.C. §§ 1201-1328.
[35] 30 U.S.C. § 1201.
[36] 16 U.S.C. §§ 1451-1466.

Wild and Scenic Rivers Act

The Wild and Scenic Rivers Act[37] preserves U.S. rivers that have outstanding scenic, recreational, geologic, fish and wildlife, historic, cultural, or other important values. Under the Act, rivers can be classified as wild, scenic, or recreational. This law preserves these rivers, keeping them safe from development, such as hydroelectric dam projects, that would destroy their valuable characteristics.

Wilderness Act of 1964

The Wilderness Act of 1964[38] establishes the national Wilderness Preservation System, which consists of wilderness lands designated by Congress. Such areas are to be administered in a way that leaves them unimpaired for future generations. No commercial enterprises or permanent roads in such areas are permitted except in specific and limited instances. The areas may be used recreationally, but not by motorized or mechanized vehicles or equipment, including bicycles. Packhorses are also subject to permitting. As the following case illustrates, permits for pack animals must also be limited, if the use of pack animals subordinates the character of the wilderness area to that of recreational use. In *High Sierra*, the court found that the USFS had failed to issue regulations appropriately reflecting this need.

High Sierra Hikers Association v. Blackwell
390 F.3d 630 (9th Cir. 2004)

I. Background

Encompassing over 800,000 acres, the John Muir and Ansel Adams Wilderness Areas provide some of the most beautiful and picturesque natural wonders in the world. Stretching north to Mammoth Lakes and over 100 miles south to Lone Pine, California, the John Muir Wilderness Area includes elevations ranging from 4,000 to 14,497 feet, the summit of Mt. Whitney, the highest point in the lower 48 states. Embracing unique geologic and natural areas, the Ansel Adams Wilderness Area represents one of the most beautiful alpine regions in the Sierra Nevada range. Both wilderness areas provide users recreational opportunities such as hiking, camping, fishing, and some of the finest mountain climbing in the world. Packstock, including horses and mules, have traditionally been used to access the wilderness areas.... Commercial packstock operators provide the public with the opportunity to take guided trips into the wilderness areas, transport equipment for backcountry visitors, and enable access for people who would otherwise not be able to hike in these areas.

The John Muir and Ansel Adams Wilderness Areas are located within the Inyo and Sierra National Forests. Each National Forest contains some portion of each wilderness area. In 1979, the Forest Service adopted a management plan for both the John Muir and Ansel Adams Wilderness Areas. In 1988 and 1992, the Forest Service adopted a Land Resource Management Plan ("Management Plan") for the Inyo National Forest and Sierra National Forest, respectively, and prepared an environmental impact statement ("EIS") for each Management Plan.

The Forest Service regulates the usage of the wilderness areas by the issuance of permits. Members of the general public must obtain a "wilderness permit" for an overnight visit. The Forest Service limits the number of these wilderness permits by specific trailheads. Some trailheads have daily quotas that are determined by capacity limits for wilderness zones. Commercial outfitters and guides, including those with livestock, who operate commercial services must obtain a "special-use permit." The amount of wilderness use the commercial operators are allowed is dictated by "service day

(Continued)

---

[37] 16 U.S.C. §§ 12711287.
[38] 16 U.S.C. §§ 11311136.

allocations." A "service day" equals "one person being assisted by an outfitter or guide and using the wilderness for one day." ...

* * *

[III]C. Wilderness Act

Congress enacted the Wilderness Act "to assure that an increasing population, accompanied by expanding settlement and growing mechanization, does not occupy and modify all areas within the United States and its possessions, leaving no lands designated for preservation and protection in their natural condition...." ... The Act established a National Wilderness Preservation System composed of "wilderness areas" which "shall be administered for the use and enjoyment of the American people in such manner as will leave them unimpaired for future use and enjoyment as wilderness...." ... The Act defines wilderness "in contrast with those areas where man and his own works dominate the landscape ... as an area where the earth and its community of life are untrammeled by man, where man himself is a visitor who does not remain." ...

The agency charged with administering a designated wilderness area is responsible for preserving its wilderness character.... Regulations provide that the wilderness areas will be administered "to meet the public purposes of recreational, scenic, scientific, educational, conservation, and historical uses; and it shall also be administered for such other purposes for which it may have been established in such a manner as to preserve and protect its wilderness character." ... The Forest Service, in resolving potential conflicts in resource use, must find that "wilderness values will be dominant to the extent not limited by the Wilderness Act." ...

The Wilderness Act generally prohibits commercial enterprises in the wilderness areas, ..., but authorizes commercial services within wilderness areas "to the extent necessary for activities which are proper for realizing the recreational or other wilderness purposes of the areas." ... The Forest Service has interpreted this provision to allow the agency to "permit temporary structures and commercial services within the National Forest Wilderness to the extent necessary for realizing the recreational or other wilderness purposes, which may include, but are not limited to, the public services generally offered by packers, outfitters, and guides." ...

* * *

It is clear that the statutory scheme requires, among other things, that the Forest Service make a finding of "necessity" before authorizing commercial services in wilderness areas. The Forest Service did so in its Needs Assessment for the John Muir and Ansel Adams Wilderness Areas, in which it found that commercial packstock operations were "necessary." The Wilderness Act is framed in general terms and does not specify any particular form or content for such an assessment; therefore the finding of "necessity" requires this court to defer to the agency's decision under the broad terms of the Act. The shortcomings and oversights in the 2001 Wilderness Act and Needs Assessment do not require us to conclude that the agency failed to fulfill its mandate to determine the necessity of commercial services in designated wilderness areas. Under the broad terms of the Act, a finding that packstock was needed to provide access to those people who would otherwise not be able to gain access for themselves or their gear, can support a finding of necessity.

However, under the terms of the Wilderness Act, a finding of necessity is a necessary, but not sufficient, ground for permitting commercial activity in a wilderness area. The finding of necessity required by the Act is a specialized one. The Forest Service may authorize commercial services only "to the *extent* necessary." ... Thus, the Forest Service must show that the number of permits granted was no more than was necessary to achieve the goals of the Act. Nowhere in the Wilderness Plan of the 2001 Needs Assessment does the Forest Service articulate why the *extent* of such packstock services authorized by the permits is "necessary."

The limitation on the Forest Service's discretion to authorize commercial services only to "the extent necessary" flows directly out of the agency's obligation under the Wilderness Act to protect and preserve wilderness areas. When administering a wilderness area, the Forest Service must balance many competing interests. The administering agency is charged with maintaining the wilderness character of the land, providing opportunities for wilderness recreation, managing fire and insect risk, and even facilitating mineral extraction activities....

When the Forest Service completed the Needs Assessment it examined independently three topics related to the need for commercial services: the types of activities for which commercial services are needed, the extent to which current permits are being used, and the amount of use the land can tolerate. All of these are relevant factors to consider when determining how much, if any, commercial activity is appropriate in a wilderness area. However, at some point in the analysis, the factors must be considered in relation to one another. If complying with the Wilderness Act on one factor will impede progress toward goals on another factor, the administering agency must determine the most important value and make its decision to protect that

(Continued)

value. That is what the Forest Service failed to do in this case. At best, when the Forest Service simply continued preexisting permit levels, it failed to balance the impact that that level of commercial activity was having on the wilderness character of the land. At worst, the Forest Service elevated recreational activity over the long-term preservation of the wilderness character of the land.

The question now confronting us is what level of deference is due to the Forest Service's determination that preserving the wilderness character of the land is not the ultimate interest of the Wilderness Act. If the Forest Service is not due deference for its decision to grant the permits, then summary judgment [by the lower court] was inappropriate on this issue. Although we believe that Congress intended to enshrine the long-term preservation of wilderness areas as the ultimate goal of the Act, the diverse, and sometimes conflicting list of responsibilities imposed on administering agencies renders Congress's intent arguably ambiguous.

Where the statute is ambiguous, the agency deserves *Chevron* deference only if it is acting with the force of law.... The Forest Service was not acting with the force of law in this case because it was granting permits, not acting in a way that would have precedential value for subsequent parties.... Therefore, the agency's determination is due only "'respect' based on the persuasiveness of the decision." ...

When applying this level of review, we look to the process the agency used to arrive at its decision.... Among the factors we are to consider are the "interpretation's thoroughness, rational validity, and consistency with prior and subsequent pronouncements ... the logic[] and expertness of an agency decision, the care used in reaching the decision, as well as the formality of the process used." ... The Forest Service's determination does not meet this standard.

The Wilderness Act twice states its overarching purpose. In Section 1131(a) the Act states, "and [wilderness areas] shall be administered for the use and enjoyment of the American people *in such a manner as will leave them unimpaired for future use and enjoyment as wilderness, and so as to provide for the protection of these areas, the preservation of their wilderness character.*" ...

(emphasis added). Although the Act stresses the importance of wilderness areas as places for the public to enjoy, it simultaneously restricts their use in any way that would impair their future use as *wilderness*. This responsibility is reiterated in Section 1133(b), in which the administering agency is charged with preserving the wilderness character of the wilderness area.

The Forest Service's decision to grant permits ... in the face of documented damage resulting from overuse does not have rational validity. In its Needs Assessment, the Forest Service listed the trailheads showing damage from overuse, but it did not take the next step to actually protect those areas by lowering the allowed usage. Given the Wilderness Act's repeated emphasis of the administering agency's responsibility to preserve and protect wilderness areas, this decision cannot be reconciled with the Forest Service's statutory responsibility.... Because the Forest Service made its decision to grant the permits without ... consideration of the impact its decision would have on its ultimate responsibilities under the Wilderness Act, we hold that the Forest Service was not within its statutory discretion when it granted the permits and that the district court was incorrect to grant summary judgment on the Wilderness Act claims.

Questions for Discussion

1. A NEPA claim was also brought in this case, alleging failure to prepare an adequate EIS for multiyear special-use permits for pack animals, because the USFS failed to account for the cumulative effects of the use of pack animals in its EIS. Describe how the procedural statute NEPA works in tandem with the substantive requirements of the Wilderness Act to achieve environmental preservation.

2. What is the difference between the administrative agency's view of an area as a wilderness area and its view of an area as a recreational area? How might regulations affecting use of that area differ, depending upon which use the agency allows?

3. How is administrative agencies' creation of rules and regulations restrained by Congress? How did the USFS fall short of its statutory mandate in this case?

National Park Service Organic Act

The National Park Service Organic Act[39] created the National Park Service. This federal statute also requires conservation of scenery, natural and historical objects,

---

[39] 16 U.S.C. §§ 1-18f-3.

and wildlife. In addition, it requires that these resources be enjoyed in a manner that leaves them unimpaired for future generations.[40]

Common conflicts regarding how park resources should be used arise concerning use of off-road vehicles such as snowmobiles. Off-road vehicles are damaging to the ecosystem, create noise pollution that severely affects other human visitors and wildlife, and have a strong negative impact on air quality. Parks create rules related to off-road vehicles after completing NEPA processes, and each park can establish different rules. Criticism of the NPS's apparent inability to address this problem in a manner reflective of congressional statutory mandate and good science has led to calls for Congress to simply step in and ban off-road vehicle usage in certain parks, such as Yellowstone.[41]

Federal and state land management issues are complex, and it is often difficult to bring together diverse groups and interests. Nevertheless, if we are to preserve land and resources for future generations, it is essential that natural resources be managed in an intelligent and environmentally sensitive manner. Because of these concerns, it is likely that comprehensive land management, perhaps in coordinated state-federal schemes, will continue to be the focus of environmental policies in the United States.

▓ ▓ ▓ REVIEW AND STUDY QUESTIONS

1. Which species are protected by federal statutes? Why aren't all plants and animals protected by federal statute?

2. What are the major federal statutes related to federal public lands? How do these laws work to protect public lands?

3. What challenges related to its legal mandate does the National Park Service face when parks are overused to the point of degradation? How can the Park Service meet the needs of the present generation while maintaining its charge into perpetuity?

▓ Conclusion

This chapter presented an overview of major federal environmental statutes related to federal environmental policy, animals, and federal public lands. These laws have substantially shaped the way that federal agencies make decisions affecting the environment. NEPA and the ESA, for example, specifically provide a basis on which government proposals may be challenged if it is believed that the agency has not adequately considered the environmental impact or harm to a threatened or endangered species. NEPA and the ESA have been used to attack significant government proposals and costly development projects in a number of important lawsuits.

As cases arising under NEPA and the ESA clearly illustrate, there are no easy answers to the problem of striking an appropriate balance between land development and conservation or preservation of natural resources. These statutes require

---

[40] 16 U.S.C. § 1.
[41] J.M. Hooper, *Blowing Snow: The National Park Service's Disregard for Science, Law, and Public Opinion in Regulating Snowmobiling in Yellowstone National Park*, ENVTL. L. RE P. 10975 (2004). Retrieved from http://elr.info/news-analysis/34/10975/blowing-snow-national-park-services-disregard-science-law-and-public-opinion

administrative agencies to consider the implications and alternatives of their actions and to comply with the substantive mandates of the acts.

Laws enacted to protect and preserve national lands and wildlife reflect society's changing perspectives over the years. Informed land management and protections necessary to protect wildlife have become important and hotly debated issues at all levels of government.

People have different ideas about how land should be managed and used. The courts ultimately become involved in resolving many of these disputes because it is their function to interpret and apply the language of the statutes, and to ensure that decision making by federal agencies meets the requirements of these laws.

Chapter 9 Case Study Activity: The Roadless Rule

Roads are generally not permitted in wilderness areas. See Daniel L. Timmons's 2013 article on the spate of cases related to roadless rules at http://www.martenlaw.com /newsletter/20130211-roadless-rule-litigation

1. Should the federal government or the individual state governments have authority to govern whether an area remains roadless or not? How do the separate concepts of federalism and the Property Clause influence your answer?

2. Why should a wilderness area remain roadless? What are the benefits of and the drawbacks to this policy?

3. Wilderness areas are not accessible to all people. Discuss the public policy consequences of this fact.

Major Federal Environmental Statutes Part II: Air and Water Pollution Control

Here's a good idea!

There are many vocabulary words in this chapter. Make flashcards for each section. This will help you learn the words, which will make studying the concepts easier.

Learning Objectives

After reading this chapter, you will have an understanding of the major federal statutes related to air and water pollution control. You will understand the Clean Air Act's key concepts, including the National Ambient Air Quality Standards, state implementation plans (SIPs), and permitting programs. You will understand the key concepts of the Clean Water Act (CWA), including its applicability, the CWA permit system, and the National Pollutant Discharge Elimination System. Specifically, after reading this chapter you should be able to answer the following questions:

1. What are the major federal environmental statutes related to air, and how do they work?
2. What are major federal environmental statutes related to water, and how do they work?

▆ Introduction

This chapter focuses on major federal environmental statutes related to pollution control. Just like the statutes studied in Chapter 9, these acts constitute the foundation of the federal regulatory scheme related to the environment, which gives rise to the administrative rules and regulations implementing those statutes. The complexities of each statute are beyond the scope of this book. However, we will examine each statute in general, so that by the time you have finished studying this chapter, you should have a good understanding of how each works. Consider each of these statutes critically to determine whether you believe that they have accomplished the goals set forth by Congress when it enacted them.

Air

Though it is impossible to summarize all of the provisions of the Clean Air Act (CAA)—the actual statute runs hundreds of pages—this section will provide a basic understanding of the structure of the Act. Focus on the goals of the law and the means of implementing those goals.

Air, essential to life, consists of a thin band of gases that shields the earth from the sun's radiation, supports the process by which green plants convert water and carbon dioxide into oxygen, and provides water in the form of precipitation. Consider the costs of air pollution and the benefits of pollution control. Dirty or polluted air harms natural resources; affects crops, lakes, forests, and wildlife; leads to health problems in people, animals, plants, and crops; corrodes bridges and buildings; and devastates entire ecosystems. Air pollution comes from many sources, including cars and trucks, petroleum refineries, smelters, iron foundries, wood stoves, incinerators, open-burn dumps and landfills, and combustion of fossil fuels to heat homes and generate power. Can you identify more sources of air pollution?

The cost of cleaning up or preventing air pollution is significant. Costs may force taxes higher, increase utility bills, and drive prices of consumer goods and services higher. Air pollution is also a political issue. Often, environmental interests and business interests are pitted against each other in such debates, as are state and federal governments, and different regions of the country. Moreover, air pollution can be an **environmental justice** issue as well. When certain demographic portions of our society are more heavily affected by polluted air, serious questions about fairness arise related to the negative externality of air pollution. The Environmental Protection Agency (EPA) considers environmental justice issues as part of its oversight duties.

Air pollution is not a recent phenomenon. Natural decomposition of organic matter, volcanic eruptions, and forest fires all contaminate the air. However, one of the major changes caused by the Industrial Revolution was a dramatic increase in air pollution. In fact, the popular vision of a 19th-century industrialized city is one obscured by smog and plumes of smoke. In the 20th century, the expansion of the chemical and petroleum industries and the widespread domination of the automobile have added to air pollution and increased concerns about the risks of dirty air. In the 21st century, many of these problems persist as more societies become further industrialized without adopting cleaner air technology.

In the United States, the problem of air pollution was first addressed through common law nuisance or trespass suits brought by injured plaintiffs against polluters. These common law remedies were generally inadequate to address the broader problems of air pollution. Lawsuits between an injured party and a polluter might result in damages for the plaintiff, but do little or nothing to improve the general air quality for everyone, unless a permanent injunction is entered. Furthermore, damages for common law torts are only awarded after the injury has occurred. Because judicial decision making occurs case by case in common law, it does not lend itself to formation of a comprehensive regulatory scheme that can address the problem of air pollution across a broad geographic area or industry.

environmental justice: Concern about the fair treatment of all people vis-à-vis environmental hazards such as pollution.

Timeline of Clean Air Laws

The first air pollution ordinances in the United States were passed in 1881 by the cities of Chicago and Cincinnati; their laws were intended to control smoke and soot from furnaces and locomotives. Federal clean air legislation was first enacted in 1955 with the Air Pollution Control Act. In 1963, Congress enacted the CAA, which included the first federal regulation of motor vehicles and fuels; 1965 saw the passage of the Motor Vehicle Pollution Control Act, which permitted the federal government to set emissions standards for new motor vehicles. In 1967, Congress passed the Air Quality Act, which required states to establish air quality control regions and the federal government to identify viable pollution control techniques that states could use to attain air quality standards. When it became clear that the states were making scant progress toward meeting clean air standards, Congress enacted the CAA Amendments of 1970, which created the basic statutory framework of the CAA. The 1977 amendments to the act constituted a midcourse correction of the law. In 1990, Congress dramatically expanded regulatory requirements for both stationary and mobile sources, and addressed problems like acid rain and toxic **pollutants**. Later, the Energy Policy Act of 2005 and the Energy Independence and Security Act of 2007 were enacted.

Overview of the Clean Air Act

The Clean Air Act (CAA)[1] invested the federal government with substantial authority and responsibility for addressing and controlling air pollution throughout the nation. It established a federal-state partnership for regulating the sources of air pollutants. In general, the federal government—specifically the EPA—sets requirements, which are then administered by the states.

This section addresses the CAA as a whole, without identifying which amendment added or changed earlier versions of the CAA. This approach allows readers to gain an overview of the current CAA as it functions today, without confusing bygone requirements with the current state of the law. Accordingly, the law is referred to as "the CAA," without explicit reference to the amendments that created many of the programs and features of the law today.

The CAA regulates stationary sources of pollutants, such as industrial facilities and power plants, as well as mobile sources like automobiles and trucks. The definition of a **stationary source** within the CAA is broad and includes "any building, structure, facility, or installation which emits or may emit any air pollutant."[2]

Under the CAA, the EPA is required to establish primary and secondary **National Ambient Air Quality Standards (NAAQSs)** for air pollutants that endanger public health, including the health of sensitive populations such as the elderly and children, and to protect the public welfare by regulating pollutants that affect visibility or cause damage to animals, crops, or buildings. In addition to **ambient air** quality standards, the CAA requires the establishment of limits for mobile sources of emissions, standards for new pollution sources, and standards for hazardous air pollutants, including emissions that cause acid rain. The CAA establishes a comprehensive permit system for major sources of air pollution. It also addresses pollution prevention, and it works to protect the stratospheric

pollutant: Contaminating substance discharged into the environment; often is a hazardous or toxic waste, chemical, or other substance, but the term is not limited to those categories. As used in the Clean Water Act, includes most types of industrial, municipal, or agricultural waste discharged into water.

stationary source: Non-mobile source that emits or may emit air pollution.

National Ambient Air Quality Standards (NAAQSs): National clean air standards set at a level of air quality necessary to protect the public health and welfare; divided into primary and secondary standards.

ambient air: Outdoor air.

---

[1] 42 U.S.C. § 7401 *et seq.*
[2] 42 U.S.C. § 7411(a)(3).

ozone layer. Additionally, it requires identification of nonattainment areas.[3] The following sections examine these provisions of the CAA.

National Ambient Air Quality Standards (NAAQSs)

National **primary standards** are set to achieve and maintain a level of air quality necessary to protect the public health, including the health of sensitive populations such as asthmatics, children, and the elderly. National **secondary standards** are set at levels that will provide protection of public welfare (e.g., to avoid decreased visibility and harm to animals, crops, and buildings).

The federal government's standards are minimum and national; the states have the primary responsibility for developing plans that will realize those standards. In imposing national standards for ambient air quality in the CAA, Congress recognized that air quality in one area will ultimately affect air quality in other regions. States cannot use looser or lesser standards, though they can impose stricter standards. The courts have held that cost and technological capability must be subordinated to protection of the public health when NAAQSs are set under the Act.

The CAA directs the EPA to establish primary and secondary NAAQSs for any air pollutant that has an adverse impact on the public health or welfare. Accordingly, the CAA requires the EPA to establish NAAQSs for six **criteria pollutants**: ground-level ozone, particulate matter, carbon monoxide, nitrogen oxides, sulfur dioxide, and lead. The EPA has identified the first two—ground-level ozone and particulate matter—as the two most widespread threats to human health.

Ground-level ozone is distinguished from the "good" ozone high in the atmosphere that protects the earth. Ground-level ozone is "bad" ozone. It is a principal ingredient in smog and can severely impair people with heart and lung diseases. It causes eye irritation and reduces resistance to infection. At low altitudes, ozone is a pollutant formed when nitrogen oxides react with oxygen in the presence of sunlight. Because ozone is not emitted, ozone is measured by determining the concentration of ozone in the air. Ozone pollution is a widespread and stubborn problem in major cities. The CAA specifically addresses ozone nonattainment areas by adopting five categories of nonattainment—marginal, moderate, serious, severe, and extreme—and imposing stringent controls on sources within those areas.

Particulate matter consists of solid or liquid particles suspended in the air that carry poisons and irritants into the lungs. Many industrial processes, including steel mills, power plants, smelters, and cement plants, contribute particulate matter to the air. Other activities and sources, such as industrial and construction work and wood-burning fireplaces, also produce particulate matter. Depending on the size and shape of the particles, such matter can damage lungs and lead to respiratory damage. Some particulates are carcinogenic.

Carbon monoxide is a deadly colorless and odorless gas; it is emitted primarily as an exhaust byproduct from combustion of fuels in mobile sources such as cars and trucks. Wood stoves, incinerators, and some industrial processes also contribute to carbon monoxide pollution. In addition to presenting health risks to human, carbon

primary standards: NAAQSs set at a level of air quality necessary to protect the public health.

secondary standards: NAAQSs set at a level of air quality necessary to protect the public welfare.

criteria pollutants: A pollutant for which a NAAQS has been set by the EPA. Criteria pollutants include ground-level ozone, particulate matter, carbon monoxide, nitrogen oxides, sulfur dioxide, and lead.

ground-level ozone: A criteria pollutant and contributor to smog.

particulate matter: A criteria pollutant; broad class of diverse substances existing as discrete particles in the air, including liquid droplets or solids.

carbon monoxide: A criteria pollutant; a colorless, odorless toxic gas.

---

[3] For a summary of the Clean Air Act, see James E. McCarthy, Larry B. Parker, Linda-Jo Schierow, & Claudia Copeland, *Clean Air Act*, in ENVIRONMENTAL LAWS: SUMMARIES OF MAJOR STATUTES ADMINISTERED BY THE ENVIRONMENTAL PROTECTION AGENCY (David M. Bearden, Claudia Copeland, Linda Luther, James E. McCarthy, Linda-Jo Schierow, & Mary Tiemann, eds.) (Congressional Report Service 7-5700, RL30798) (2010).

monoxide contributes to the *greenhouse effect*, trapping heat close to the ground. The greenhouse effect occurs when the sun's energy passes through the air and is absorbed by the earth. The earth then reradiates the energy into the air. Polluted air permits the passage of light but not of heat, so the heat is trapped near the earth's surface, creating an effect similar that in a greenhouse. This absorption and trapping of reradiated heat energy is magnified by pollutants or contaminants in the atmosphere.

Nitrogen oxides are a group of compounds containing nitrogen and oxygen that form highly reactive gasses. Nitrogen oxides are emitted from natural sources, such as decomposing organic matter. Nitrogen oxides are also produced when emissions from burning fuel react with nitrogen in the air. Nitrogen oxides are a key ingredient in the formation of ground-level ozone, smog, and the brown discoloration of the air and sky. They are active in the acidification of rain and depletion of the protective high ozone layer. They also contribute substantially to the creation of particulate matter pollution. Their primary health effect is damage to the lungs and respiratory tract.

Sulfur dioxide, a poisonous gas emitted during the burning of coal and oil, is highly corrosive and may bond to particles of smoke and dust. When attached to particulates, it may travel long distances. The primary danger to health posed by sulfur dioxide is lung and respiratory damage. Sulfur dioxide is a primary ingredient in acid rain.

Airborne **lead** poses a serious health risk, especially to the neurological systems and kidneys of fetuses and children. Formerly, the principal source of airborne lead was combustion of the leaded gasoline used in cars and trucks. Today, primary sources of lead pollution are lead smelters and aircraft that still use on leaded fuels.

The EPA is required to fix the NAAQSs at levels necessary to protect the public health and public welfare. It must also periodically review and revise the NAAQSs. In establishing NAAQSs, the EPA is not permitted to consider the economic or technological feasibility of attaining the standards. Generally, a court will defer to the administrative agency's decision regarding NAAQSs.

State Implementation Plans

As noted earlier, each state has primary responsibility for ensuring that air quality within its borders meets the EPA standards. Native American tribes may also implement and enforce CAA rules related to their lands. States submit **state implementation plans (SIPs)** to the EPA to specify the manner in which air quality standards will be achieved and maintained. A state that fails to achieve its **attainment** goals may be subject to a series of sanctions; if it still fails to achieve compliance thereafter, a federal implementation plan (FIP) is put into place in lieu of the inadequate (or nonexistent) SIP. Federal funding for transportation projects is tied to attainment, so the states have significant incentive to reach the goals and maintain attainment. **Nonattainment areas** are classified into groups reflecting their levels of nonattainment; depending upon the classification, the state is given a certain amount of time to bring these areas into compliance.

After the NAAQSs were established for pollutants, states were required to develop SIPs for implementation, attainment, maintenance, and enforcement of those standards. In its SIP, a state establishes source-specific requirements for achieving the primary and secondary air quality standards under the CAA. Although the state is required to meet the minimum standards for regulated pollutants, it may also adopt an implementation plan designed to exceed the national

nitrogen oxides: Criteria pollutants; specific highly reactive gasses containing nitrogen and oxygen.

sulfur dioxide: A criteria pollutant; a poisonous gas.

lead: A criteria pollutant; a neurotoxic metal.

state implementation plan (SIP): Plan submitted by a state to the EPA that details how the state will attain and maintain established air quality standards.

attainment: Designation indicating that a particular area meets a NAAQS for a pollutant.

nonattainment areas: Areas that exceed any NAAQS for a pollutant.

standards. When reviewing a SIP for approval, the EPA administrator is not permitted to consider claims of economic and technological infeasibility.[4]

The SIP document must continually be updated to meet federal requirements. Although their SIPs must be submitted to the EPA for approval, the states are generally free to choose from any available control methods as long as those methods are sufficient to meet the EPA standards.

Nonattainment Areas

As noted, *nonattainment areas* are areas that exceed any NAAQS for a pollutant. Some areas of the United States still do not meet one or more of the NAAQSs. The most widespread and difficult problem is ground-level ozone. The CAA imposes additional requirements for SIPs regarding nonattainment areas, which include specific provisions on criteria pollutants and **volatile organic compounds (VOCs)**.

Nonattainment-area SIPs must mandate reasonably available control technology (RACT) for existing sources of pollution and must require permits for the construction and operation of new or modified major stationary sources anywhere within the nonattainment area. Such sources are required to meet the lowest achievable emission rate (LAER).

Serious sanctions may apply to areas that remain in nonattainment status. Failure to submit a SIP that meets the requirements of the law can lead to a complete construction ban in the affected area and withholding of federal clean air grant funds.

Limits for Mobile Sources of Emissions

The CAA established mobile source emissions standards and established fuel-related programs designed to reduce motor vehicle emissions. The mobile source emissions standards affect sources such as cars, airplanes, and trucks. The Energy Policy Act of 2005 and the Energy Independence and Security Act of 2007 require increasing use of renewable fuel sources for motor fuel. As noted in an earlier chapter, California was granted leave to develop its own vehicle emission standards, providing that those standards were at least as strict as those imposed by the CAA. Since then, many other states have been permitted to adopt the stricter standards established by California. The California program encouraged the development and use of innovative technology to lower emissions.

New Pollution Source Performance Standards

The costs of retrofitting existing sources with state-of-the-art technology are often prohibitive. Consequently, Congress required the highest levels of technological performance for new sources, which have more flexibility in design and location. New stationary sources are subject to the technology-forcing requirement that the **best available control technology (BACT)** be installed to meet a specified limit on pounds of pollutants that can be emitted per unit of plant input or output. The EPA is required to establish **New Source Performance Standards (NSPSs)** that will limit emissions from a new stationary source if that source causes or contributes significantly to air pollution that may reasonably be anticipated to endanger public health or welfare. The EPA has set NSPSs for most major industrial processes. These standards establish a minimum level of control required at new or modified sources.

volatile organic compounds (VOCs): Petroleum-based organic compounds that mix with other substances in the air to form ozone.

best available control technology (BACT): A technology standard for new stationary sources of air pollution.

New Source Performance Standard (NSPS): Emission limitations for specific new or modified sources based on the BACT.

---

[4] *See, e.g., Union Electric Co. v. EPA,* 427 U.S. 246 (1976).

In *Chevron U.S.A., Inc. v. Natural Resources Defense Council*,[5] the Supreme Court addressed whether the EPA could permit a state to adopt a plant-wide definition of the term "stationary source" as used in the CAA. This definition, called the **bubble theory**, treats various components of an industrial complex as a single source for regulatory purposes. Under the bubble theory, increases in emissions from one component may be offset by decreases in emissions from another component, so long as the net effect does not increase total emissions. In *Chevron*, the Supreme Court upheld the EPA's decision to permit states to treat all of the pollution-emitting devices within the same industrial grouping as though they were encased within a single "bubble."

■ *ACTIVITY BOX Air Quality*

Visit http://airnow.gov/ to determine the air quality in a particular region. Do you think that the air quality index (AQI) is used effectively to help people? Why or why not?

Hazardous Air Pollutants

The CAA names several hazardous air pollutants that must be controlled through the application of technological standards based on the **maximum achievable control technology (MACT)**. If those controls fail to reduce the risks to public health or the environment, further health-based standards are required. The EPA also regulates to control and prevent accidental releases of regulated hazardous pollutants or other hazardous substances. Owners and operators of facilities where such substances are present must prepare risk management plans for each substance that exceeds a threshold level. The CAA also established a Chemical Safety and Hazard Investigation Board to investigate accidental releases and make recommendations to avoid such releases.

Acid Rain Provisions

Acid rain refers to increased acidity (as measured in reduced pH levels) in ambient moisture or precipitation. Acid rain harms fish and other aquatic life, trees, manmade structures, and human lungs. The CAA mandates permanent capping of electric utility emissions of sulfur dioxide and a reduction in nitrogen oxide, both of which are precursors of and contributors to acid rain. Under the acid rain program, electric utility sources of sulfur dioxide are assigned allowances under a statutory formula. An *allowance* is an authorization to emit one ton of sulfur dioxide. A plant's annual sulfur dioxide emissions cannot exceed the allowances allocated to it, or otherwise acquired by it, for a given calendar year. The allowances can be limited, revoked, or modified. Allowances may be saved (also called **banking**) to be used at a later date and are fully transferable. The EPA auctions allowances annually.

Comprehensive Permit System for Major Sources of Air Pollution

The CAA requires each state to develop and implement an operating permit program for major sources of air pollution. Facilities that are major sources of pollution must apply to the state authority for permits. These sources must also develop compliance plans. Permit approval depends on whether the source is located in an

bubble theory: Concept that an imaginary structure ("bubble") covers existing and/or neighboring pollution sources; used to define areas rather than single sources in determining the source of emissions for purposes of the CAA.

maximum achievable control technology (MACT): Emission rate based on best demonstrated control technology or practices; applies to air toxins under the CAA.

acid rain: Precipitation containing a high concentration of acids produced by sulfur dioxide, nitrogen oxide, and other substances emitted during the combustion of fossil fuel.

banking: Process by which an emission source may "save" sulfur dioxide emission allowances by making reductions that exceed regulatory requirements; the banked allowance may be used later or transferred.

---

[5] 467 U.S. 837 (1984).

area that has attained the NAAQSs for the pollutant in question. For example, in nonattainment areas, the SIP must require that a proposed new or modified source offset its potential to emit nonattainment pollutants through reductions in emissions by other facilities in the area.

The permits are for a fixed term that cannot exceed five years, and states collect fees from permittees to cover the costs of operating the program. The source must apply for renewal of the permit as needed. The permit system allows facilities to change their operations and emissions without revision to the permit, as long as the changes do not result in an increase of emissions above the permit limitations.

The public has a right to participate in the permitting process at the state level and to seek EPA action to oppose issuance of a permit. Under the CAA, the public is also allowed to access periodic reports of emissions monitoring results, including evidence of noncompliance by a source.

Prevention of Significant Deterioration

One of the major goals of the CAA is to protect and enhance the quality of the nation's air. To that end, it is important to ensure that air quality in attainment areas—those areas that meet or exceed federal standards—does not deteriorate. Protection and improvement of the quality of air that is already "clean" (that is, air that already meets or exceeds the NAAQSs) is an important focus of the Prevention of Significant Deterioration (PSD) program.

A new pollution source (including a "major modification" of an existing major stationary source) in an area that has attained the NAAQSs is required to install the BACT, as well as undertake other important steps such as completion of an air quality analysis, additional impacts analysis, and public involvement. Major emitting sources must undergo a preconstruction review before beginning operations in attainment areas. The PSD program also sets ceilings for certain pollutants in those areas.

Three kinds of PSD areas, and increment standards for sulfur dioxide and particulate matter levels for each area, have been established. Class I, which includes most large national parks and wilderness areas, has the most stringent increment levels. Class II includes areas where deterioration occurring through moderate and controlled growth is insignificant. In Class III areas, the increment standard is the least stringent because a greater amount of deterioration is considered insignificant. Most PSD areas are Class II areas. Under the PSD program, any major emitting facility under construction must obtain a permit, which will mandate that the emitter utilize the BACT for each pollutant subject to regulation.

Stratospheric Ozone Protection

The stratospheric ozone layer is a thin layer of triatomic oxygen high above the earth; it protects life by blocking the sun's ultraviolet radiation. Ozone-depleting chemicals do not break down in the atmosphere, but rather migrate slowly into the stratosphere. When they finally break apart, they free chlorine and bromine radicals that react with stratospheric ozone molecules, forming new compounds and thereby depleting stratospheric ozone concentrations. Scientists believe that a decrease in the stratospheric ozone layer has led to more ultraviolet radiation reaching the surface of the earth, which has resulted in an increased incidence of skin cancers, cataracts, and harm to crops and aquatic life.

The production and importation of ozone-depleting chemicals have already been phased out. New uses of hydrochlorofluorocarbons are banned as of January

2015. These phaseouts and bans are based on the Montreal Protocol, an international agreement signed in 1987 by the United States and most other industrial nations.

Greenhouse Gas Emissions

The EPA also addresses greenhouse gas emission standards under the CAA. Rules or proposed rulemakings exist for several issues of concern. The EPA's actions include programs or proposed rules to reduce carbon pollution (related to EPA's Greenhouse Gas Endangerment Findings), a reduction in permissible greenhouse gas emissions for new mobile sources, renewable fuel programs, proposed regulations for stationary pollution sources, oil and natural gas pollution standards, geologic sequestration of carbon dioxide, and waste energy regulations. However, the EPA did not begin to address greenhouse gas emissions until after a U.S. Supreme Court ruling in 2007.

Massachusetts v. EPA
127 S. Ct. 1438 (2007)

Justice STEVENS delivered the opinion of the Court.

A well-documented rise in global temperatures has coincided with a significant increase in the concentration of carbon dioxide in the atmosphere. Respected scientists believe the two trends are related. For when carbon dioxide is released into the atmosphere, it acts like the ceiling of a greenhouse, trapping solar energy and retarding the escape of reflected heat. It is therefore a species—the most important species—of a "greenhouse gas."

Calling global warming "the most pressing environmental challenge of our time," … a group of States, … local governments, … and private organizations … alleged in a petition for certiorari that the Environmental Protection Agency (EPA) has abdicated its responsibility under the Clean Air Act to regulate the emissions of four greenhouse gases, including carbon dioxide. Specifically, petitioners asked us to answer two questions concerning the meaning of § 202(a)(1) of the Act: whether EPA has the statutory authority to regulate greenhouse gas emissions from new motor vehicles; and if so, whether its stated reasons for refusing to do so are consistent with the statute.

* * *

Section 202(a)(1) of the Clean Air Act, as added by Pub. L. 89-272, § 101(8), 79 Stat. 992, and as amended by, *inter alia*, 84 Stat. 1690 and 91 Stat. 791, 42 U.S.C. § 7521(a)(1), provides:

"The [EPA] Administrator shall by regulation prescribe (and from time to time revise) in accordance with the provisions of this section, standards applicable to the emission of any air pollutant from any class or classes of new motor vehicles or new motor vehicle engines, which in his judgment cause, or contribute to, air pollution which may reasonably be anticipated to endanger public health or welfare …." …

The Act defines "air pollutant" to include "any air pollution agent or combination of such agents, including any physical, chemical, biological, radioactive … substance or matter which is emitted into or otherwise enters the ambient air." § 7602(g). "Welfare" is also defined broadly: among other things, it includes "effects on … weather … and climate." § 7602(h).

* * *

II

On October 20, 1999, a group of 19 private organizations … filed a rulemaking petition asking EPA to regulate "greenhouse gas emissions from new motor vehicles under § 202 of the Clean Air Act." …

* * *

On September 8, 2003, EPA entered an order denying the rulemaking petition. 68 Fed. Reg. 52922. The Agency gave two reasons for its decision: (1) … the Clean Air Act does not authorize EPA to issue mandatory regulations to address global climate change, see *id.*, at 52925-52929; and (2) that even if the agency had the authority to set greenhouse gas emission standards, it would be unwise to do so at this time.…

(Continued)

In concluding that it lacked statutory authority over greenhouse gases, EPA observed that Congress "was well aware of the global climate change issue when it last comprehensively amended the [Clean Air Act] in 1990," yet it declined to adopt a proposed amendment establishing binding emissions limitations....

* * *

... EPA concluded that climate change was so important that unless Congress spoke with exacting specificity, it could not have meant the agency to address it.

Having reached that conclusion, EPA believed it followed that greenhouse gases cannot be "air pollutants" within the meaning of the Act....

* * *

VI

On the merits, the first question is whether § 202(a)(1) of the Clean Air Act authorizes EPA to regulate greenhouse gas emissions from new motor vehicles in the event that it forms a "judgment" that such emissions contribute to climate change. We have little trouble concluding that it does. In relevant part, § 202(a)(1) provides that EPA "shall by regulation prescribe ... standards applicable to the emission of any air pollutant from any class or classes of new motor vehicles or new motor vehicle engines, which in [the Administrator's] judgment cause, or contribute to, air pollution which may reasonably be anticipated to endanger public health or welfare." 42 U.S.C. § 7521(a)(1). Because EPA believes that Congress did not intend it to regulate substances that contribute to climate change, the agency maintains that carbon dioxide is not an "air pollutant" within the meaning of the provision.

The statutory text forecloses EPA's reading. The Clean Air Act's sweeping definition of "air pollutant" includes "*any* air pollution agent or combination of such agents, including *any* physical, chemical ... substance or matter which is emitted into or otherwise enters the ambient air ... ." § 7602(g) (emphasis added). On its face, the definition embraces all airborne compounds of whatever stripe, and underscores that intent through the repeated use of the word "any." ... Carbon dioxide, methane, nitrous oxide, and hydrofluorocarbons are without a doubt "physical [and] chemical ... substance[s] which [are] emitted into ... the ambient air." The statute is unambiguous....

Rather than relying on statutory text, EPA invokes postenactment congressional actions and deliberations it views as tantamount to a congressional command to refrain from regulating greenhouse gas emissions. Even if such postenactment legislative history could shed light on the meaning of an otherwise-unambiguous statute, EPA never identifies any action remotely suggesting that Congress meant to curtail its power to treat greenhouse gases as air pollutants. That subsequent Congresses have eschewed enacting binding emissions limitations to combat global warming tells us nothing about what Congress meant when it amended § 202(a)(1) in 1970 and 1977.... And unlike EPA, we have no difficulty reconciling Congress' various efforts to promote interagency collaboration and research to better understand climate change with the agency's preexisting mandate to regulate "any air pollutant" that may endanger the public welfare. See 42 U.S.C. § 7601(a)(1). Collaboration and research do not conflict with any thoughtful regulatory effort; they complement it....

* * *

... Prior to the order that provoked this litigation, EPA had never disavowed the authority to regulate greenhouse gases, and in 1998 it in fact affirmed that it *had* such authority.... There is no reason, much less a compelling reason, to accept EPA's invitation to read ambiguity into a clear statute.

EPA ... argues that it cannot regulate carbon dioxide emissions from motor vehicles because doing so would require it to tighten mileage standards, a job (according to EPA) that Congress has assigned to DOT.... But that DOT sets mileage standards in no way licenses EPA to shirk its environmental responsibilities. EPA has been charged with protecting the public's "health" and "welfare," 42 U.S.C. § 7521(a)(1), a statutory obligation wholly independent of DOT's mandate to promote energy efficiency.... The two obligations may overlap, but there is no reason to think the two agencies cannot both administer their obligations and yet avoid inconsistency.

While the Congresses that drafted § 202(a)(1) might not have appreciated the possibility that burning fossil fuels could lead to global warming, they did understand that without regulatory flexibility, changing circumstances and scientific developments would soon render the Clean Air Act obsolete. The broad language of § 202(a)(1) reflects an intentional effort to confer the flexibility necessary to forestall such obsolescence.... Because greenhouse gases fit well within the Clean Air Act's capacious definition of "air pollutant," we hold that EPA has the statutory authority to regulate the emission of such gases from new motor vehicles.

VII

* * *

If EPA makes a finding of endangerment, the Clean Air Act requires the agency to regulate emissions

(Continued)

of the deleterious pollutant from new motor vehicles. [42 U.S.C. 7521(a)(1)] (stating that "[EPA] shall by regulation prescribe ... standards applicable to the emission of any air pollutant from any class or classes of new motor vehicles"). EPA no doubt has significant latitude as to the manner, timing, content, and coordination of its regulations with those of other agencies. But once EPA has responded to a petition for rulemaking, its reasons for action or inaction must conform to the authorizing statute. Under the clear terms of the Clean Air Act, EPA can avoid taking further action only if it determines that greenhouse gases do not contribute to climate change or if it provides some reasonable explanation as to why it cannot or will not exercise its discretion to determine whether they do.... To the extent that this constrains agency discretion to pursue other priorities of the Administrator or the President, this is the congressional design.

EPA has refused to comply with this clear statutory command. Instead, it has offered a laundry list of reasons not to regulate....

In short, EPA has offered no reasoned explanation for its refusal to decide whether greenhouse gases cause or contribute to climate change. Its action was therefore "arbitrary, capricious, ... or otherwise not in accordance with law." 42 U.S.C. § 7607(d)(9)(A). We need not and do not reach the question whether on remand EPA must make an endangerment finding, or whether policy concerns can inform EPA's actions in the event that it makes such a finding. Cf. *Chevron U.S.A. Inc. v. NRDC*, 467 U.S. 837, at 843-844, 104 S. Ct. 2778, 81 L. Ed. 2d 694 (1984). We hold only that EPA must ground its reasons for action or inaction in the statute.

Questions and Comments for Discussion

1. Why did the EPA initially decline to engage in rulemaking related to greenhouse gas emissions?

2. Why did the Supreme Court review the EPA's decision instead of deferring to agency expertise?

3. Do you think that the EPA's regulation of greenhouse gas emissions will have a measurable impact on global climate change? If so, how? If not, should cost be a factor in deciding whether the EPA should apply the CAA to greenhouse gas emissions?

Wrap-Up of Clean Air Act

Today there is a general consensus that air pollution poses a significant risk to the health of humans and other life, as well as to natural resources. However, there is continuing debate about how best to address those problems, such as to what extent the government should intervene to limit pollution discharge through command and control regulation rather than discouraging pollution through market incentive schemes. To what extent should air pollution control decisions be centralized and to what extent should those decisions be left to the states? What threshold limits of various pollutants should be imposed to protect the public health? What are the costs and benefits of controlling air pollution through command and control regulatory policy? How should those costs and benefits be balanced in determining regulatory policy?

Before passage of the CAA, attempts to address the problems of air pollution through local ordinances and nuisance laws had been less than successful. State permitting systems operating prior to that date had also encountered problems; notable issues included the difficulty of setting and enforcing pollution standards and the difficulty of interpreting and applying technical scientific and engineering data. The determination of the amount of a pollutant that can be assimilated into the air without causing harm is a difficult and complex scientific question that understaffed state agencies lacked the funds and expertise to address. In addition, political and economic issues at the state level, especially concern by the states over industrial flight (that is, losing industry to other states with less stringent pollution requirements), made it difficult for states to adopt and enforce strict pollution control standards.

The CAA addressed some of these problems by establishing a state-federal partnership for controlling air pollution. Through these partnerships, the EPA establishes maximum permissible concentrations of criteria air pollutants. The federal agency sets primary standards protecting human health and secondary standards if health-based standards are insufficient to protect nonhealth values such as protection of agricultural products and exposed materials. Under the CAA, the EPA must set those standards at levels that provide an adequate margin of safety.

By establishing NAAQSs that all areas of the country must meet, the CAA made it more difficult for industries to avoid locating in states with stricter pollution standards than other states. But the decision to impose national uniform standards also means that all areas of the country are locked into the same national standards, regardless of the costs of control, the quality of air, or the geographic or climatic conditions of the particular area. Further, the law requires the EPA to set primary air quality standards to provide an "adequate margin of safety," without consideration of economic or technological feasibility. In doing so, Congress apparently took the position that there were indeed "safe" levels for common air pollutants; however, there is debate about whether that is indeed true—that is, whether there are any safe levels for some pollutants.

As their part of the federal–state partnership, the states have primary responsibility for ensuring that these national standards are met. By permitting the states to develop SIPs to determine how best to achieve the national standards, the CAA implicitly recognized that the states are subject to differing political and economic realities, and that they are in the best position to determine within their specific jurisdictions how best to achieve the national goals. The law also recognized that controlling pollution falls under the state's traditional function and authority regarding protection of public health and safety. Of course, there are political and economic limits on the states' willingness to impose strict pollution controls within their jurisdictions—a situation complicated by the fact that air pollution does not stop at state boundaries.

■ ■ ■ REVIEW AND STUDY QUESTIONS

1. Describe the federal-state cooperative scheme under the Clean Air Act. Should regulation under the CAA be primarily a state issue or primarily a federal issue? Why?

2. Write an email to a friend to describe the Clean Air Act and how it works. Write it in plain language, using your own words, so that your friend can understand it.

3. Identify one way in which air pollution has negatively affected your community or members of your community. What has been done or is being done to minimize the damage or remediate the damage? What more can be done? What types of costs were or will be incurred for cleaning up the air in that situation?

4. What are the National Ambient Air Quality Standards? How do state implementation plans relate to the NAAQSs?

5. Read *The Plain English Guide to the Clean Air Act* on the EPA's website (http://www.epa.gov/air/peg/index.html). Discuss other ways that the EPA might disseminate information about the Clean Air Act. Do you think that this way is effective? Why or why not?

6. Do tradeable emissions permits encourage the adoption of cleaner technology to a greater extent than statutory requirements that set limits on pollution? Explain your position. What are some downsides of such programs?

■ Water

Water covers most of the Earth's surface, and it is essential to life. An adequate water supply is also essential for the economic, industrial, and agricultural development of human society. In the United States, irrigation has transformed deserts like the

Imperial Valley in California into fertile land that yields billions of dollars in agricultural products. In the western United States, aggressive programs to divert and dam rivers and tap into groundwater have allowed cities to grow and thrive on essentially arid land.

Despite its value, water is often taken for granted, especially in parts of the world where it is a common resource. In the early development of the eastern part of this country, there was little concern about excessive water use or water pollution. In the latter part of the 20th century, however, alarm over shrinking water resources and water health and safety led to demands for laws to protect this valuable resource. The federal response was passage of laws that included the Clean Water Act (CWA), the Safe Drinking Water Act (SDWA), and the Oil Pollution Act (OPA).

Water resource management, not directly addressed here, has historically been a matter of state, rather than federal, law. State laws (both statutory and common) generally regulate the use of water within the state by treating individuals' water rights as property rights. As one might expect, laws establishing water rights have evolved differently in states where water is a plentiful resource from those where water resources are scarce. Although federal law generally governs water pollution and state law generally regulates water management, policy issues involved in protecting water quality and managing water resources are interrelated.

Timeline of Water Pollution Laws

Regulation and control of water use directly affects the health, welfare, and economic resources of every person within the United States. Initially, though, federal water pollution control law concentrated on protecting the nation's navigable waters by controlling the discharge of pollutants into rivers, streams, and other waterways. The first federal law regulating discharge of pollutants into the nation's waterways was the Rivers and Harbors Appropriations Act of 1899, designed to protect navigation.

In the 1940s, public concern over drinking water contamination led to the establishment of federal programs to assist states in constructing waste treatment plants. In 1948, Congress passed the Federal Water Pollution Control Act (FWPCA), which permitted courts to order pollution abatement after considering the practicability and economic feasibility of such abatement.

In 1965, Congress passed the Water Quality Act, under which the federal government assisted states in establishing and enforcing water quality standards. Before 1972, standards were generally set by the states. These laws usually established permissible concentrations of pollutants, which were used to formulate individualized permit limitations for dischargers.

The 1965 act was generally ineffective because of its limited scope, awkward enforcement mechanisms, and state inaction and inattention. In addition, the establishment of pollutant parameters for a body of water created problems in determining when a particular discharge violated applicable standards. In response to these problems, in 1972 Congress passed a comprehensive revision and recodification of the FWPCA, which became known as the Clean Water Act (CWA). In later amendments, Congress specifically addressed the problem of toxic pollutants, established new water quality requirements for areas where compliance was insufficient to meet national goals, and addressed the problem of stormwater discharges.

Just as with our discussion of the CAA, the focus here will be on the CWA as a whole, without identifying which amendment added to or changed the law. This approach allows readers to gain an overview of the current CWA as it functions today, without confusing bygone provisions with the current state of the law. Accordingly, the law is primarily referred to as the CWA, without explicit reference to the amendments that established many of the current programs and features of the law.

Overview of the Clean Water Act

The CWA, like other federal environmental statutes, was enacted by Congress through its commerce clause authority. Its goals include "restor[ation] and main-tain[ance of] the chemical, physical, and biological integrity of the Nation's waters."[6] Like the CAA, the CWA sets goals without regard to costs. National goals of the CWA include achievement of a level of water quality that "provides for the protection and propagation of fish, shellfish and wildlife" and "for recreation in and on the water"; it also aims for the elimination of discharge of pollutants into surface waters and the prohibition of discharge of toxic pollutants. The CWA goals have not been met.

The CWA establishes the basic framework of current federal water pollution control law. The Act requires the EPA to set nationwide effluent standards, on an industrywide basis, for discharge of pollutants into waters of the United States. "New source" direct dischargers are subject to even more stringent standards of performance. To implement these requirements, the CWA establishes the National Pollutant Discharge Elimination System (NPDES). Under this system, the EPA issues permits for the discharge of any pollutant or combination of pollutants into public waterways based on technology and water quality-based standards of the Act. Discharge from a point source without a permit or in violation of permit requirements can result in criminal and/or civil liability.

The CWA contains specific provisions governing federal and state coordination in administration of the Act. States can administer the permit program if the states meet the legal requirements for doing so. The Act requires states to set EPA-approved water quality standards and develop plans to achieve those standards. The EPA provides technical support and guidance to the states. Most states have assumed the responsibility for permitting under these provisions, but federal rules and interpretations continue to dominate application of the law at the state and local levels. The CWA leaves enforcement primarily to states, albeit with oversight by the EPA. It also allows citizen suits.

The CWA requires industries that discharge indirectly to publicly owned water treatment works (POTWs) to meet pretreatment standards under the Act. The law also contains specific provisions governing oil spills and discharge of toxic sub-stances. Section 404 of the CWA gives the Army Corps of Engineers the authority to issue permits for the discharge of dredged or fill material to waters of the United States. However, the CWA does not set or establish ground or surface water quality standards.

Pollution Discharge Prohibition

The statute prohibits the discharge of any pollutant by any person into navigable waters, except in compliance with the CWA's permit requirements. The discharger bears the burden of proving compliance.

---

[6] 33 U.S.C. § 1251(a).

The CWA defines *discharge of a pollutant* to mean "any addition of any pollutant to navigable waters from any point source...."[7] The wording used in this section has generated much litigation. The term "navigable waters" in particular has generated a great deal of litigation. This is because the federal permitting system is somewhat controversial, in the sense that jurisdiction of the Clean Water Act remains vague as to who might need to obtain a permit to discharge. If the discharge will be made into something other than "navigable waters," then no permit is necessary. However, if the waters are within the jurisdiction of the Clean Water Act, and identified as such by the definition of *navigable waters,* then a permit is required. For example, in 2008, the United States District Court for the District of Columbia, in *American Petroleum Institute v. Johnson,*[8] held that a current EPA regulation defining "navigable waters" was arbitrary and capricious; this decision resulted in a 1973 regulatory definition being reinstated.

The definition of *pollutant* under the CWA has been broadly interpreted to include virtually all waste material, whether or not it has value at the time it is discharged. For example, in *Hudson River Fishermen's Association v. Arcuri*[9] the court held that owners and developers of an abandoned construction site were liable under the FWPCA for discharging pollutants without a permit. The court said that solid waste, including wrecked, discarded equipment, garbage, rock, sand, and dirt, that was discharged from the site into a tributary of the Hudson River constituted a pollutant under the Act. Bombs dropped on a naval target range[10] and dead fish and fish parts discharged by a power plant[11] have also been held to be pollutants under this definition.

One of the more difficult issues under the CWA is the meaning of the term **point source**, which is defined to include "any discernible, confined and discrete conveyance ... from which pollutants are or may be discharged."[12] The courts have tended to interpret the definition of point source very broadly to achieve the policies underlying the CWA. There are, however, some discharges that are expressly exempted as point sources under the Act. These include irrigation return flows, discharge of sewage from vessels (including cruise ships) regulated under other sections of the Act, and certain agricultural and silvicultural discharges.

Citizen Suit Provision

The citizen suit section of the CWA[13] authorizes any person to bring a civil action either against a discharger for violation of the act or against the EPA for failing to enforce the Act's provisions. The Act encourages citizen suits by specifically providing for the payment of attorney and expert witness fees when appropriate. National environmental groups like the Sierra Club have used this section to enforce provisions of the CWA. Courts have generally held that members of these environmental groups have standing under the language of this section.

point source: As defined in CWA § 502, "Any discernible, confined and discrete conveyance ... from which pollutants are or may be discharged."

---

[7] 33 U.S.C. § 1362(12).
[8] 571 F. Supp. 2d 165 (D.D.C. 2008).
[9] 862 F. Supp. 73 (S.D.N.Y. 1994).
[10] *Weinberger v. Romero-Barcelo*, 456 U.S. 305 (1982).
[11] *National Wildlife Federation v. Consumers Power Co.*, 675 F. Supp. 989 (W.D. Mich. 1987), *rev'd on other grounds*, 862 F.2d 580 (6th Cir. 1988).
[12] 33 U.S.C. § 1362(14).
[13] 33 U.S.C. § 1365(a).

Most major federal environmental protection laws contain citizen suit provisions (important exceptions are FIFRA and NEPA). Because the NPDES program under the CWA requires that dischargers file routine discharge monitoring reports, it is relatively easy for citizens to discover and prove violations under the NPDES program. For this reason, more citizen suits have been filed under the CWA than under any other federal environmental law.

Permit Program

The NPDES permit system serves two primary functions. First, an NPDES permit establishes specific levels of performance each discharger is required to meet; second, the law requires the discharger to monitor and report compliance to the appropriate agency. Effluent limitations include technology-based limitations on discharge and water quality-based limitations on discharge. Technology-based limitations are industry specific and based on technological and economic capability. Water quality-based limitations are more stringent and are imposed to protect the quality of the receiving water. Technological and economic capabilities are not factored in during development of these latter effluent standards.

Sometimes it is difficult to determine whether something is or is not a point source. If it is not a point source, then no NPDES permit is required. However, if it is a point source, then a permit application is required. One example of where such a dilemma exists is a concentrated animal feeding operation (CAFO). In 2005, the Second Circuit Court of Appeals held, in *Waterkeeper Alliance, Inc. v. EPA*,[14] that only CAFOs that actually discharge into waters of the United States need to apply for an NPDES permit. If a CAFO merely has a potential to discharge, there is not enough to trigger the requirement to apply for a permit. This interpretation was later echoed in the Fifth Circuit's 2011 decision in *National Pork Producers Council v. EPA*.[15] In that case, the court held that a proposed discharge is not enough to trigger the permit requirement; there must be actual discharge.

Monitoring and Reporting Requirements

The self-monitoring requirements of the NPDES program are critical in assuring compliance with the CWA requirements. The EPA may require the owner or operator of any point source to maintain specific records; install, use, and maintain monitoring equipment; and identify pollutant parameters that must be sampled. The agency may also impose other requirements necessary to assure accurate sampling and reporting of effluent discharge. Records must be maintained for a specified length of time, and annual reporting is required. The data are open to the public (though information protected as trade secret is excluded).

Effluent Limitations: Technology-Based Limitations

One issue in the NPDES regulatory process is the determination of effluent discharge limitations. The CWA uses three methods to establish discharge limitations: (1) technology-based effluent limitations, which establish the baseline for treatment requirements; (2) water quality-based effluent limitations, which are more stringent requirements imposed to achieve water quality standards; and (3) limits on toxic discharges as necessary to protect public health.

---

[14] 399 F.3d 486 (2d Cir. 2005).
[15] 635 F.3d 738 (5th Cir. 2011).

Technology-based effluent limitations are based on the performance of pollution control technologies. These limitations take several factors into consideration, including the technological and economic feasibility of the pollution control technology. The law does not, however, require a discharger to use a specific pollution control technology; as long as it can satisfy the applicable discharge limits, the discharger can choose and use any technology it wishes.

The CWA provided for the establishment of technology-based effluent limitations on an industry-by-industry basis. Technology standards were to be phased in so that by July 1, 1977, effluent limitations would be governed by best practicable control technology (BPT) standards and by 1983, effluent limitations would be governed by the best available technology (BAT) economically achievable standards. Generally, BPT limitations represent "the average of the best" treatment technology in an industrial category. In setting BPT standards, the EPA considers the total cost of the technology in relation to effluent benefits, the age of equipment, engineering aspects, nonwater quality environmental impact, and other relevant factors.[16]

BAT was originally based on the single best performer within an industry, rather than on an average of exemplary plants. Under the original Act, the EPA was to consider factors similar to BPT factors, except that determination of BAT involved consideration of the cost of achieving the pollution reduction rather than a comparative cost-benefit analysis. The BAT definition was essentially unchanged by 1977 and 1987 amendments, but its date for attainment was extended. The 1977 amendments created a new standard: the best conventional pollutant control technology (BCT), which applies to conventional pollutants.

In implementing the CWA, the EPA set technology-based effluent limitations by categories. Industrial categories were based on the products manufactured and subcategories of the processes or raw materials used in the production process. BPT and BAT criteria were applied to these categories and subcategories and were formulated to contain maximum daily and monthly average limitations. Following lawsuits by industry and confusion in the courts, the Supreme Court upheld this approach, but required the EPA to develop a variance procedure for plants that did not fit into a particular subcategory. Congress subsequently amended the Act to incorporate this fundamentally different factors (FDF) variance.

Much of the dramatic improvement in water quality in recent decades has been credited to reductions in discharges of some pollutants forced by these technology-based limits. This approach has also been credited for helping to ensure a market for the development of water pollution control technology. However, a technology-based approach to regulating effluent discharge has also been criticized as being costly to industry, because the standards are set without reference to the receiving waters.

Water Quality Standards

Water quality standards, unlike technology-based standards, are performance standards based on the impact of a discharge on the receiving waters. Water quality requirements are designed to achieve a certain level of quality and to ensure that the level of quality is consistent with both public water supply, recreation, industrial, or agricultural uses and the protection of fish and wildlife. Water quality standards are adopted by the states and approved by the EPA. They include

---

[16] *Rybachek v. EPA*, 904 F.2d 1276 (9th Cir. 1990).

(1) the designated use or uses of a body of water, (2) the water quality criteria necessary to protect those uses, and (3) an antidegradation statement.

Water quality goals for a particular body of water serve as a basis for imposing treatment controls beyond the minimum required by the CWA. Although the Act relies on a technology-based standard approach, water quality limitations are to be imposed when achievement of technology-based standards will not result in reaching water quality goals.

Limits on Toxic Discharges

The EPA's toxicant strategy developed following failure to establish a workable program to control the discharge of toxic pollutants. As a result of a lawsuit filed by the Natural Resources Defense Council (NRDC) against the EPA,[17] the EPA and the NRDC developed a policy for identifying the pollutants that would be the primary subject of regulation, the industries to be regulated, and the methods of regulating toxic discharges. The agreement was approved by the court in a settlement decree and incorporated into subsequent amendments of the CWA.

The consent decree and subsequent amendments to the CWA have directed attention away from a few conventional pollutants toward overall effluent toxicity. As a result of the increasing focus on toxic pollutants, water quality standards may become increasingly important, because they impose more stringent limitations on the discharger.

Congress also created a third class of "nonconventional" pollutants that includes nontoxic, nonconventional pollutants such as ammonia, chlorine, colors and dyes, iron, and total phenols. These substances are subject to the BAT effluent limits, but dischargers are entitled to cost-based and harm-based variances.

New Source Performance Standards (NSPS)

The CWA requires all new pollution sources in an industry (including major modifications of existing sources) to meet standards reflecting "the greatest degree of effluent reduction … achievable through application of the best available demonstrated control technology." These New Source Performance Standards (NSPS) are equally or more stringent than the BAT standard, though in most cases they are equivalent to BAT. In setting these requirements, the EPA considers not only pollution control techniques, but also alternative production processes and methods. In addition, costs are less important in establishing an NSPS than in establishing BAT, in part because new sources can incorporate the most efficient processes and treatment systems during plant designs.

Variances

The CWA permits a facility that is "fundamentally different" from those on which effluent guidelines are based to seek a variance from a BAT, BCT, or pretreatment standard for existing sources (PSES) technology-based effluent limitation. The FDF variance must be submitted within 180 days of establishment of the guideline, and the cost of controlling pollutants by the industry may not be considered. The law also recognizes a few other instances in which the EPA may grant variances from BAT limitations, but in general these instances are rare and the variances are almost never granted.

---

[17] *NRDC v. Train*, 545 F.2d 320 (2d Cir. 1976).

Pretreatment and Indirect Dischargers

In many instances, industrial facilities do not discharge directly into surface water. Instead, they discharge into publicly owned treatment works (POTWs), owned by a state or municipality.

Discharges by industry into POTWs are not regulated as direct discharges under the NPDES system, but rather are regulated by **pretreatment standards** adopted under CWA § 307(b). The CWA requires the EPA to promulgate pretreatment standards that will (1) protect the POTW operation and (2) prevent discharge from the POTW without adequate treatment. Discharges by POTWs into U.S. waters must meet the requirements of the NPDES system.

General pretreatment regulations prohibit discharge into a POTW of any pollutant that would cause a "pass-through," which is defined as a discharge that exits the POTW in quantities or concentrations that would constitute a violation of the POTW's NPDES permit. General pretreatment regulations also prohibit specific discharges of pollutants that would create a fire or explosion hazard; cause corrosive structural damage to the POTW; obstruct the flow; heat the water and thereby inhibit biological activity in the POTW; contain oil; or produce toxic gases. The discharger is required to notify the POTW of any discharge of hazardous waste.

The EPA has established categorical pretreatment regulations for specific quantities or concentrations of pollutants; these rules focus on industries and toxic pollutant categories specified in the NRDC consent decree. Generally, the facility must meet the same requirements for pretreatment as for discharge into surface water.

Pretreatment requirements are enforced by the EPA and the states that have the authority to issue permits. Pretreatment regulations also include reporting and monitoring requirements to ensure compliance.

Protecting Wetlands

Wetlands is a general term describing certain types of areas where land meets water. It may include marshes, fens, bogs, wet meadows, and swamps. Because wetlands are transitional zones between water and dry land, they are unique habitats for a variety of fish and wildlife. Under EPA regulations, *wetlands* are those areas that are inundated or saturated by surface water or groundwater with a frequency and duration sufficient to support, and that under normal circumstances do support, a prevalence of vegetation typically adapted for life in saturated soil conditions.

In the past, wetlands were often considered nuisances because they were sources of insects and unpleasant odors. People drained and converted wetlands to farm land, or filled them to support residential and industrial development. As a result, more than half of America's original wetlands have been destroyed. Today, however, the value of these natural resources is well recognized. Wetlands help improve water quality, reduce flood and storm damage, and provide essential habitats for many species. Increased understanding of the importance of wetlands to ecological processes has led to increased protection of wetlands. The EPA is responsible for restoring and maintaining the integrity of the nation's waters, and thus has jurisdiction over wetlands.

Section 404 of the CWA establishes a permit program to regulate the discharge of dredged or fill materials into waters of the United States. This means that permits are required if anyone wishes to dredge and fill wetlands that are governed by the CWA. Section 404 extends to all U.S. waters, including wetlands.

pretreatment standards: Standards for treating industrial discharges into a publicly owned treatment works.

wetlands: A general term for marshes, swamps, bogs, and similar areas where land meets water.

Section 404 authorizes the Army Corps of Engineers to designate disposal areas and issue permits for discharge of dredged and fill material. Section 404 permits are not subject to the general permit program under the CWA and differ both substantively and procedurally from the NPDES program. The U.S. Fish and Wildlife Service and National Marine Fisheries Service have important advisory roles in the permit review process, which is jointly administered by the U.S. Army Corps of Engineers and the EPA.

Under § 404, any individual, company, corporation, or government entity planning construction or fill activities in wetlands must first obtain a permit from the Corps. These activities include:

- Placement of fill (rock, soil, or sand) necessary for the construction of structures or impoundments
- Site development fills
- Fills for causeways, roads, dams, dikes, and the like
- Fills for construction of ponds or intake or outlet pipes

The CWA permitting process may delay development significantly, or even forbid it entirely. Projects for the construction of refineries, highways, and shopping centers have been halted by the Act.

Jurisdiction of the § 404 permit program depends on the definition of "waters of the United States." In 1977, the Corps issued regulations extending § 404 jurisdiction to all "wetlands" that are "adjacent" to traditionally navigable waters, all tributaries of traditionally navigable waters, and all interstate waters and adjacent wetlands. Despite this expansion in jurisdiction from coastal and riparian waters to inland isolated areas, the CWA's jurisdiction has since contracted. The arc of this expansion and contraction of jurisdiction is fairly easy to trace. In 1985, the U.S. Supreme Court held, in *United States v. Riverside Bayview Homes, Inc.*,[18] that intrastate wetlands were subject to jurisdiction of the federal government under the CWA. In the preamble to the 1986 rules to implement the Clean Water Act, the so-called Migratory Bird Rule was presented, which also stated that isolated waters fell under ambit of the CWA. For purposes of the Migratory Bird Rule, jurisdiction was believed to exist if the waters were used by birds protected by migratory bird treaties, used as habitat by other migratory birds that cross state lines, used by species that are protected by the Endangered Species Act, or used to irrigate crops sold in interstate commerce. However, in 2001, the U.S. Supreme Court, in *Solid Waste Agency of Northern Cook County v. Army Corps of Engineers* (*SWANCC*),[19] invalidated the Migratory Bird Rule. Isolated wetlands were held not to be within the jurisdiction of the CWA. Later, in *Rapanos v. United States*, the Court further narrowed federal jurisdiction by suggesting that the link between navigable waters and wetlands must be more substantial than the rather vague standard the federal government had been using. Essentially, *Rapanos* greatly narrowed the *Riverside Bayview* holding. In *Rapanos*, the Court specified that a significant nexus must exist for wetlands to be considered waters of the United States and therefore under the jurisdiction of the CWA. This test had existed prior to *Rapanos*, but the *Rapanos* Court indicated that a narrowing of federal jurisdiction was warranted.

---

[18] 474 U.S. 121 (1985).
[19] 531 U.S. 159 (2001).

Rapanos v. United States

547 U.S. 715 (2006)

Justice SCALIA announced the judgment of the Court ...

In April 1989, petitioner John A. Rapanos backfilled wetlands on a parcel of land in Michigan that he owned and sought to develop. This parcel included 54 acres of land with sometimes-saturated soil conditions. The nearest body of navigable water was 11 to 20 miles away. ... Regulators had informed Mr. Rapanos that his saturated fields were "waters of the United States," ... that could not be filled without a permit. Twelve years of criminal and civil litigation ensued.

The burden of federal regulation on those who would deposit fill material in locations denominated "waters of the United States" is not trivial. In deciding whether to grant or deny a permit, the U.S. Army Corps of Engineers (Corps) exercises the discretion of an enlightened despot.... The average applicant for an individual permit spends 788 days and $271,596 in completing the process, and the average applicant for a nationwide permit spends 313 days and $28,915—not counting costs of mitigation or design changes.... In this litigation, for example, for backfilling his own wet fields, Mr. Rapanos faced 63 months in prison and hundreds of thousands of dollars in criminal and civil fines....

The enforcement proceedings against Mr. Rapanos are a small part of the immense expansion of federal regulation of land use that has occurred under the Clean Water Act—without any change in the governing statute—during the past five Presidential administrations. In the last three decades, the Corps and the Environmental Protection Agency (EPA) have interpreted their jurisdiction over "the waters of the United States" to cover 270-to-300 million acres of swampy lands in the United States—including half of Alaska and an area the size of California in the lower 48 States. And that was just the beginning. The Corps has also asserted jurisdiction over virtually any parcel of land containing a channel or conduit—whether man-made or natural, broad or narrow, permanent or ephemeral—through which rainwater or drainage may occasionally or intermittently flow. On this view, the federally regulated "waters of the United States" include storm drains, roadside ditches, ripples of sand in the desert that may contain water once a year, and lands that are covered by floodwaters once every 100 years. Because they include the land containing storm sewers and desert washes, the statutory "waters of the United States" engulf entire cities and immense arid wastelands. In fact, the entire land area of the United States lies in some drainage basin, and an endless network of visible channels furrows the entire surface, containing water ephemerally wherever the rain falls. Any plot of land containing such a channel may potentially be regulated as a "water of the United States."

* * *

For a century prior to the CWA, we had interpreted the phrase "navigable waters of the United States" in the Act's predecessor statutes to refer to interstate waters that are "navigable in fact" or readily susceptible of being rendered so. ... After passage of the CWA, the Corps initially adopted this traditional judicial definition for the Act's term "navigable waters." ... After a District Court enjoined these regulations as too narrow, ... the Corps adopted a far broader definition. ... The Corps' new regulations deliberately sought to extend the definition of "the waters of the United States" to the outer limits of Congress's commerce power. ...

[However], on its only plausible interpretation, the phrase "the waters of the United States" includes only those relatively permanent, standing or continuously flowing bodies of water "forming geographic features" that are described in ordinary parlance as "streams[,] ... oceans, rivers, [and] lakes." ... The phrase does not include channels through which water flows intermittently or ephemerally, or channels that periodically provide drainage for rainfall. The Corps' expansive interpretation of the "the waters of the United States" is thus not "based on a permissible construction of the statute." ...

Questions and Comments for Discussion

1. What are the consequences for landowners of narrowing federal jurisdiction under the CWA? What are the consequences for wetlands and living beings that rely upon wetlands for survival?

2. Do you think that the Commerce Clause should allow the CWA to extend its jurisdiction to inland wetlands that are not obviously connected to larger waterways? Why or why not?

3. What are the consequences to the natural environment when privately owned inland wetlands are filled? Do you think that the states should have sole authority to determine whether this type of activity is permitted? If 50 different states had 50 different approaches to this issue, should that be acceptable? Why or why not?

No Net Loss Policy

In 1977 amendments to the Clean Water Act, Congress authorized the states to establish a permit program for dredge and fill activities in nonnavigable waters. The amendments also authorized the Corps of Engineers (or a state with an approved program) to issue "general" permits for certain activities that have minimal adverse effects. The general permit program is designed to reduce the regulatory burden for activities involving incidental dredge or fill work. Section 404(f) provides for exemptions from the regulation if the operator avoids specific effects on navigable waters.

In 1989, the Corps of Engineers and the EPA signed a Memorandum of Agreement (MOA) endorsing a "no net loss" policy for the nation's wetlands. Under the memorandum, the Corps is to avoid adverse impacts in permit decisions whenever possible and is required to choose the least environmentally damaging alternative. Mitigation policy under the MOA endorses a national goal of no overall net loss of the nation's remaining wetlands base. Each president since has reaffirmed a commitment to the no net loss policy.

Nonpoint Source Pollution

The NPDES permit system, which is a cornerstone of the CWA, only addresses point source pollution. In fact, a substantial amount of the pollution of the nation's waterways is a result of **nonpoint source pollution**. Nonpoint source pollution is caused by diffuse sources, such as those associated with agriculture, silviculture, urban runoff, precipitation, atmospheric deposition, or percolation. Conveyance of runoff through a mechanism such as a pipe or a trench may be treated as a point source.

Nonpoint source pollution is most easily addressed through land use planning. This approach was adopted by the 1972 CWA amendments, which established a planning and regulatory program for controlling nonpoint source pollution. Under this amended section, states must identify and address nonpoint source pollution through an area-wide planning process.

In 1987, Congress amended the CWA to further address the problem, authorizing funding for nonpoint source pollution programs and requiring each state to prepare a management program for controlling it. States must also identify water bodies that fail to meet standards for toxic pollutants. Congress also created the voluntary National Estuary Program, under which states plan and implement additional controls on sources of pollutants to estuaries. In addition, Congress established an Environmental Quality Incentives Program to improve water quality and address some environmental issues posed by agricultural production.

Stormwater Discharge

Stormwater discharge is another difficult-to-regulate but substantial challenge to water quality. The problem with stormwater runoff is that it includes pollutants from developed land, such as pesticides. Most runoff cannot be easily controlled or monitored using point source or "end-of-pipe" technology. However, in many instances stormwater runoff is discharged through storm sewers or other conveyances, and thus can be considered a point source discharge. The 1987 CWA amendments required the EPA to regulate five categories of municipal or stormwater discharges. These include discharges covered by NPDES permits, discharges associated with industrial activity, discharges from municipal storm sewers meeting criteria under the Act, and other discharges that "contribute to a violation of a

nonpoint source pollution: Water pollution resulting from sources that are not point sources, such as runoff.

water quality standard or [are] a significant contributor of pollutants to waters of the United States."[20]

Stormwater regulations do not apply to all discharges by industry, only those associated with industrial activity. The EPA defines *stormwater* to include stormwater runoff, snowmelt runoff, and surface runoff and drainage. Agricultural stormwater discharges are specifically excluded by statute.

Oil and Hazardous Substance Spills

Section 311 of the CWA addresses water pollutant discharges resulting from accidental releases and spills. This section addresses spill planning and prevention, reporting responsibilities, and response authority. Discharges in compliance with an NPDES permit are not considered spills for purposes of § 311. Releases of hazardous substances into water are also addressed under CERCLA, as briefly discussed later in this chapter.

The CWA specifically prohibits the discharge of oil or hazardous substances into or upon *designated waters*, defined to include navigable waters, adjoining shorelines, the contiguous zone, and waters beyond the contiguous zone containing or supporting natural resources. Section 311 requires the person in charge of the vessel or facility to report the discharge to the appropriate agency as soon as he or she has knowledge of the spill. Reports filed according to this provision cannot be the basis for any criminal action against the person reporting.

The Oil Pollution Act (OPA) was adopted in 1990 in response to the damage caused by the *Exxon Valdez* oil spill in Alaska. Among other things, the OPA expanded the CWA's requirements for prevention and preparedness requirements, imposed legal liability on shippers and oil companies for the cost of spills, and established a liability trust fund. The law also extensively amended § 311 of the CWA.

The OPA authorizes the president to arrange for removal of an actual or threatened discharge of oil or a hazardous substance and requires such removal to be done in accordance with the National Contingency Plan (established by the EPA under CERCLA). The owner and operator is liable for the actual costs of removal, but § 311 limits that liability based on the type of vessel or facility involved.

The CWA also provides for the development and implementation of spill prevention, control, and countermeasure (SPCC) plans for owners and operators of certain nontransportation-related onshore facilities. An SPCC plan must describe previous spills and response and prevention measures to be taken regarding future spills. Containment equipment and structures and other physical plant requirements may be mandated.

Ocean Dumping

Except for oil spills and ocean outfalls, ocean dumping is regulated under the Marine Protection, Research, and Sanctuaries Act (MPRSA) of 1972.[21] EPA regulations prohibit the issuance of a permit for ocean discharge unless the discharge will not cause unreasonable degradation of the environment. The MPRSA imposes conditions on the issuance of ocean dumping permits and prohibits the dumping of radiological, chemical, and biological warfare agents or high-level radioactive

---

[20] 33 U.S.C. § 1342(2).
[21] 33 U.S.C. § 1401 *et seq.*

waste. Since 1991, it has also specifically prohibited the dumping of sewage sludge and industrial wastes, except in emergencies as defined by the Act. The Secretary of the Army may issue permits for dumping of dredged material into ocean waters if appropriate findings made in a process are similar to that required by the EPA. Ocean incineration is considered ocean dumping and consequently requires a permit.

Enforcement of the Clean Water Act

The 1987 amendments to the CWA substantially strengthened its criminal penalty provisions, and the 1990 OPA extended those penalties to oil and hazardous waste spills. Negligent and "knowing" violations are subject to criminal penalties, including fines and imprisonment. The law created the offense of "knowing endangerment" and allows imposition of substantial fines and/or imprisonment on a person who knowingly violates a permit requirement and knowingly places another person in imminent danger of death or serious bodily injury thereby. The law also enhanced the penalties for filing false reports or tampering with any monitoring device or method.

Problems with the CWA

Despite the many amendments made to it over the years, several important terms in the Clean Water Act remain notoriously ambiguous. Consider Justice Alito's concurrence in the following opinion.

Sackett v. EPA

566 U.S. _____, 132 S. Ct. 1367 (2012)

Justice SCALIA delivered the opinion of the Court.

We consider whether Michael and Chantell Sackett may bring a civil action under the Administrative Procedure Act, 5 U.S.C. § 500 *et seq.*, to challenge the issuance by the Environmental Protection Agency (EPA) of an administrative compliance order under § 309 of the Clean Water Act, 33 U.S.C. § 1319. The order asserts that the Sacketts' property is subject to the Act, and that they have violated its provisions by placing fill material on the property; and on this basis it directs them immediately to restore the property pursuant to an EPA work plan.

I

The Clean Water Act prohibits, among other things, "the discharge of any pollutant by any person," § 1311, without a permit, into the "navigable waters," § 1344—which the Act defines as "the waters of the United States," § 1362(7). If the EPA determines that any person is in violation of this restriction, the Act directs the agency either to issue a compliance order or to initiate a civil enforcement action. § 1319(a)(3). When the EPA prevails in a civil action, the Act provides for "a civil penalty not to exceed [$37,500] per day for each violation." ... § 1319(d). And according to the Government, when the EPA prevails against any person who has been issued a compliance order but has failed to comply, that amount is increased to $75,000—up to $37,500 for the statutory violation and up to an additional $37,500 for violating the compliance order.

The particulars of this case flow from a dispute about the scope of "the navigable waters" subject to this enforcement regime. Today we consider only whether the dispute may be brought to court by challenging the compliance order—we do not resolve the dispute on the merits. The reader will be curious, however, to know what all the fuss is about. In *United States v. Riverside Bayview Homes, Inc.*, 474 U.S. 121 ... (1985), we upheld a regulation that construed "the navigable waters" to include "freshwater wetlands," ... themselves not actually navigable, that were adjacent to navigable-in-fact waters. Later, in *Solid Waste Agency of Northern Cook Cty. v. Army Corps of Engineers*, 531 U.S. 159 ... (2001), we held that an abandoned sand and gravel

(Continued)

pit, which "seasonally ponded" but which was not adjacent to open water ... was not part of the navigable waters. Then most recently, in *Rapanos v. United States*, 547 U.S. 715 ... (2006), we considered whether a wetland not adjacent to navigable-in-fact waters fell within the scope of the Act. Our answer was no, but no one rationale commanded a majority of the Court. In his separate opinion, THE CHIEF JUSTICE expressed the concern that interested parties would lack guidance "on precisely how to read Congress' limits on the reach of the Clean Water Act" and would be left "to feel their way on a case-by-case basis." ...

The Sacketts are interested parties feeling their way. They own a 2/3-acre residential lot in Bonner County, Idaho. Their property lies just north of Priest Lake, but is separated from the lake by several lots containing permanent structures. In preparation for constructing a house, the Sacketts filled in part of their lot with dirt and rock. Some months later, they received from the EPA a compliance order. The order contained a number of "Findings and Conclusions," including the following:

> "1.4 [The Sacketts' property] contains wetlands within the meaning of 33 C.F.R. § 328.4(8)(b); the wetlands meet the criteria for jurisdictional wetlands in the 1987 'Federal Manual for Identifying and Delineating Jurisdictional Wetlands.'
> "1.5 The Site's wetlands are adjacent to Priest Lake within the meaning of 33 C.F.R. § 328.4(8)(c). Priest Lake is a 'navigable water' within the meaning of section 502(7) of the Act, 33 U.S.C. § 1362(7), and 'waters of the United States' within the meaning of 40 C.F.R. § 232.2.
> "1.6 In April and May, 2007, at times more fully known to [the Sacketts, they] and/or persons acting on their behalf discharged fill material into wetlands at the Site. [They] filled approximately one half acre.
> ...
> "1.9 By causing such fill material to enter waters of the United States, [the Sacketts] have engaged, and are continuing to engage, in the 'discharge of pollutants' from a point source within the meaning of sections 301 and 502(12) of the Act, 33 U.S.C. §§ 1311 and 1362(12).
> ...
> "1.11 [The Sacketts'] discharge of pollutants into waters of the United States at the Site without [a] permit constitutes a violation of section 301 of the Act, 33 U.S.C. § 1311." ...

On the basis of these findings and conclusions, the order directs the Sacketts, among other things, "immediately [to] undertake activities to restore the Site in accordance with [an EPA-created] Restoration Work Plan" and to "provide and/or obtain access to the Site ... [and] access to all records and documentation related to the conditions at the Site ... to EPA employees and/or their designated representatives." ...

The Sacketts, who do not believe that their property is subject to the Act, asked the EPA for a hearing, but that request was denied. They then brought this action in the United States District Court for the District of Idaho, seeking declaratory and injunctive relief. Their complaint contended that the EPA's issuance of the compliance order was "arbitrary [and] capricious" under the Administrative Procedure Act (APA), 5 U.S.C. § 706(2)(A), and that it deprived them of "life, liberty, or property, without due process of law," in violation of the Fifth Amendment. The District Court dismissed the claims for want of subject-matter jurisdiction, and the United States Court of Appeals for the Ninth Circuit affirmed, 622 F.3d 1139 (2010). It concluded that the Act "preclude[s] pre-enforcement judicial review of compliance orders," ... and that such preclusion does not violate the Fifth Amendment's due process guarantee .... We granted certiorari....

II

The Sacketts brought suit under Chapter 7 of the APA, which provides for judicial review of "final agency action for which there is no other adequate remedy in a court." 5 U.S.C. § 704. We consider first whether the compliance order is final agency action. There is no doubt it is agency action, which the APA defines as including even a "failure to act." §§ 551(13), 701(b)(2). But is it *final*? It has all of the hallmarks of APA finality that our opinions establish....

* * *

We conclude that the compliance order in this case is final agency action for which there is no adequate remedy other than APA review, and that the Clean Water Act does not preclude that review. We therefore reverse the judgment of the Court of Appeals and remand the case for further proceedings consistent with this opinion.

It is so ordered.

* * *

[Concurrence]

Justice ALITO, concurring.

The position taken in this case by the Federal Government—a position that the Court now squarely rejects—would have put the property rights of ordinary Americans entirely at the mercy of Environmental Protection Agency (EPA) employees.

The reach of the Clean Water Act is notoriously unclear. Any piece of land that is wet at least part of

(Continued)

the year is in danger of being classified by EPA employees as wetlands covered by the Act, and according to the Federal Government, if property owners begin to construct a home on a lot that the agency thinks possesses the requisite wetness, the property owners are at the agency's mercy. The EPA may issue a compliance order demanding that the owners cease construction, engage in expensive remedial measures, and abandon any use of the property. If the owners do not do the EPA's bidding, they may be fined up to $75,000 per day ($37,500 for violating the Act and another $37,500 for violating the compliance order). And if the owners want their day in court to show that their lot does not include covered wetlands, well, as a practical matter, that is just too bad. Until the EPA sues them, they are blocked from access to the courts, and the EPA may wait as long as it wants before deciding to sue. By that time, the potential fines may easily have reached the millions. In a nation that values due process, not to mention private property, such treatment is unthinkable.

The Court's decision provides a modest measure of relief. At least, property owners like petitioners will have the right to challenge the EPA's jurisdictional determination under the Administrative Procedure Act. But the combination of the uncertain reach of the Clean Water Act and the draconian penalties imposed for the sort of violations alleged in this case still leaves most property owners with little practical alternative but to dance to the EPA's tune.

Real relief requires Congress to do what it should have done in the first place: provide a reasonably clear rule regarding the reach of the Clean Water Act. When Congress passed the Clean Water Act in 1972, it provided that the Act covers "the waters of the United States." 33 U.S.C. § 1362(7). But Congress did not define what it meant by "the waters of the United States"; the phrase was not a term of art with a known meaning; and the words themselves are hopelessly indeterminate. Unsurprisingly, the EPA and the Army Corps of Engineers interpreted the phrase as an essentially limitless grant of authority. We rejected that boundless view, see *Rapanos v. United States*, 547 U.S. 715 … (2006) (plurality opinion); *Solid Waste Agency of Northern Cook Cty. v. Army Corps of Engineers*, 531 U.S. 159 … (2001), but the precise reach of the Act remains unclear. For 40 years, Congress has done nothing to resolve this critical ambiguity, and the EPA has not seen fit to promulgate a rule providing a clear and sufficiently limited definition of the phrase. Instead, the agency has relied on informal guidance. But far from providing clarity and predictability, the agency's latest informal guidance advises property owners that many jurisdictional determinations concerning wetlands can only be made on a case-by-case basis by EPA field staff. …

Allowing aggrieved property owners to sue under the Administrative Procedure Act is better than nothing, but only clarification of the reach of the Clean Water Act can rectify the underlying problem.

Questions and Comments for Discussion

1. What does Justice Alito believe should be done to remedy the ambiguity of the Clean Water Act?

2. Why does the Court reject the idea that property rights should be at the mercy of the EPA employees?

3. Do you agree or disagree with the sentiments expressed by Justice Alito? Describe the differing interests appearing in this case.

■ *ACTIVITY BOX   Test Your Water "Sense" at the EPA*

Take the "water sense" quiz found at the EPA website (http://www.epa.gov/watersense /test_your_watersense.html).

How well did you do? What did you learn? What did you already know?

The Safe Drinking Water Act

The federal Safe Drinking Water Act (SDWA)[22] protects the nation's drinking water supply. Its goals are twofold: first, to ensure that tap water is fit to drink; and second, to prevent the contamination of groundwater. The states may assume primary authority for oversight and enforcement, providing they meet certain requirements. Most states have taken primary authority.

---

[22] 42 U.S.C. §§ 300f–300j-9.

The Act applies to public water systems (PWSs). The law defines a *public water system* as any system "for the provision of piped water for human consumption" that has at least 15 service connections or that serves at least 25 individuals; a PWS does not have to be publicly owned. "Water for human consumption" includes not only drinking water, but also water for bathing and showering, cooking and dishwashing, and maintaining oral hygiene.

There are two types of PWSs: community and noncommunity. The distinction is based on the assumption that systems serving residential populations should be designed to protect against long-term adverse effects of chronic exposure to contaminants. The SDWA requires the EPA to establish national primary and secondary drinking water regulations for particular contaminants. Primary drinking water standards are designed to protect against adverse health effects, whereas secondary standards address contaminants that may adversely affect the odor or appearance of water. Primary standards are based on maximum contaminant level goals (MCLGs). Once a standard is set, the EPA must specify a maximum contaminant level (MCL) for drinking water that is as close as feasible to the MCLG. For some contaminants, such as lead, the MCL measured at the water source will not protect public health, because levels of lead often depend more on the condition of indoor plumbing than on the lead content of the water source. Given these circumstances, the EPA has prescribed treatment techniques (such as additives) to control lead in drinking water. The SDWA also requires any pipe, solder, or flux used in installation or repairs to be free of lead. The SDWA specifically addresses lead hazards by requiring states to test for lead contamination in their schools' drinking water.

The SDWA also requires the EPA to establish and regulate state underground injection programs. This program most affects wells used for the disposal of hazardous waste, and the injection or reinjection of fluids to aid in extraction of certain minerals in oil and gas production. Hydraulic fracturing (fracking) is exempt from regulation under the SDWA, because it is excluded from the definition of the term *underground injection*, though other regulations may apply (e.g., CWA, state regulations, or regulations related to the use of diesel fuel as an injecting agent).

The Act also protects aquifers that are the sole or principal source of drinking water. Most of New Jersey, all of Staten Island, Cape Cod, and Nantucket Island are examples of designated sole-source aquifers (SSAs). The law bars federal assistance for projects that might contaminate an SSA. Local governments can seek federal assistance in designing "comprehensive management plans" for protection of an aquifer. The SDWA encourages states to establish programs to protect wellhead areas, surrounding waters, and wells or well fields, and it establishes minimum requirements and authorizes federal assistance for such programs.

The 1996 amendments to the SDWA gave regulators more flexibility regarding monitoring of contaminants, and created a grant and loan fund to pay for water system improvements. The law contains a "right to know" provision, under which large water systems are required to provide customers with annual reports on water contaminants and the health effects of those contaminants.

In 2002, the Public Health Security and Bioterrorism Preparedness and Response Act amended the SDWA. Under this amendment, vulnerability assessments must be conducted by community water systems.

The law currently requires the EPA to use risk assessment and cost-benefit analysis in setting new standards for contaminants, but such an analysis cannot be used to weaken existing standards or to set standards for certain contaminants.

◼ ◼ ◼ REVIEW AND STUDY QUESTIONS

1. What are the arguments in defense of command and control legislation? What shortcomings do you recognize in this approach to environmental regulation?

2. An alternative to command and control regulation is market-based environmental regulation. Such a system might include taxes on environmentally harmful practices, and provide for tradeable pollution rights. However, there are challenges associated with such approaches. In some situations, for example, it would be prohibitively expensive to set up a market to address an environmental problem affecting large numbers of people (e.g., automobile pollution). Some people object to the idea of licensing pollution at all, as the effects on health and the environment may be unclear. Identify areas where market-based environmental regulation seems to make sense. Why would such an approach be better than command and control legislation?

3. If hydraulic fracturing and clean water are "choices"—one presumably representing greater oil and energy independence and the other representing basic human needs—should hydraulic fracturing be excluded from regulation under the SDWA? Why or why not?

4. Consider the BP Gulf oil spill (the Deepwater Horizon oil spill). Do laws protecting water and water quality adequately address such incidents? Why or why not? If you were a lawmaker and had the power to create a law to protect against such events, what would your law require? If your law existed to address such incidents after they had already occurred, what would your law require? Do those two goals require different types of laws? If so, what are the differences?

5. What roles exist for businesses in the control of nonpoint source pollution?

Chapter 10 Case Study Activity: Big Business and Local People Working Together

View the video at http://bp.concerts.com/gom/natural_resource_damage_assessment_coast_survey_092710.htm Then, address the following questions:

1. Identify the opportunities for a multinational corporation that caused an environmental harm to work with local stakeholders to implement the cleanup and to negotiate the real or potential disputes related to the local economy. Which party should have the most influential voice in setting forth a plan for cleanup? Why?

2. What should the legal consequences be to a corporation that causes an environmental harm that damages or destroys the natural environment and substantially interferes with local people's abilities to earn a living from their environment?

3. Identify an environmental harm in your state that occurred as a result of the actions of a corporation. If the harm has been remedied, what role did the local people have in creating that remedy? If the harm has not been remedied, what role should the local people have in creating that remedy? Why?

Here's a good idea!

There are many vocabulary words in this chapter. Make flashcards for each section. This will help you learn the words, which will make studying the concepts easier.

Major Federal Environmental Statutes Part III: Toxic Substances

Learning Objectives

After reading this chapter, you will have an understanding of the major federal statutes related to toxic substances. You will understand the key concepts of the TSCA and FIFRA, as well as the similarities and differences between these two statutes. Specifically, after reading this chapter you should be able to answer the following questions:

1. What are the major federal environmental statutes related to toxic substances, and how do they work?

2. How do the major federal environmental statutes related to toxic substances differ from each other, and how are they similar?

■ Toxic Substances

Major federal laws that address risks associated with pesticides and other chemical substances include the Toxic Substances Control Act (TSCA); the Federal Insecticide, Fungicide, and Rodenticide Act (FIFRA); and the Federal Food, Drug, and Cosmetic Act (FDCA), as amended by the Food Quality Protection Act of 1996.

The EPA regulates pesticides under two statutes. FIFRA gives the EPA the authority to regulate the use and safety of pesticides, a class of substances that includes insecticides, rodenticides, and herbicides, produced and used in the United States. The FDCA requires the EPA to set tolerance levels for pesticide residues in food. Costs and benefits of pesticide use are considered by the EPA when regulating pesticide usage.

The Toxic Substances Control Act (TSCA) was adopted in 1976 to fill a void left by other environmental statutes and regulations. Unlike other federal laws regulating chemical pollutants that have already entered the environment, TSCA gives the EPA the authority to review and regulate the manufacture, use, and distribution of chemical substances before they are introduced into commerce.

Other pollution laws adopted in the 1970s, especially the CAA and the CWA, are also chemical control laws. In addressing such air and water toxicants through technology-based "command and control" legislation, these federal antipollution laws prohibit or severely limit the use or discharge of certain chemicals and toxic substances used in the industrial process. Though they apply in almost all areas, these constraints especially affect the manufacturing processes of the steel, auto, and chemical industries.

The CWA and the CAA require regulatory decisions to be based on technological availability or margins of safety, and they limit agency consideration of economic factors in setting regulatory policy. TSCA and FIFRA differ from the CAA and the CWA in that they adopt a risk-cost balancing approach to the regulation and use of toxic substances. TSCA and FIFRA also differ from these laws because they address the way chemicals and pesticide products are manufactured and used, rather than focusing primarily on the residual problems to human health and the environment resulting from the use of such products.

▪ The Federal Insecticide, Fungicide, and Rodenticide Act

Our ability to understand the relative costs and benefits of pesticide use is complicated by our lack of understanding of the environmental side effects and cost to human health of the widespread use of chemicals. The issue of pesticides is a particularly environmentally sensitive one because it directly affects the safety of the human food supply and the health of agricultural workers.

One of the earliest toxic chemical problems to gain widespread public attention was the effects of chemical pesticides. In 1962, Rachel Carson's *Silent Spring* sparked enormous public concern about the potential environmental and health effects of chemical pesticides.

The first pesticide law, adopted in 1910, was a labeling law that prohibited the manufacture of insecticides or fungicides that were adulterated or misbranded. In 1947, Congress enacted the original version of FIFRA, which was at that time still primarily a labeling statute. In 1954, Congress gave the Food and Drug Administration (FDA) the authority to establish pesticide residue tolerances for food and animal feed. In 1964, FIFRA was amended to strengthen it, but in practice very few pesticide registrations were actually cancelled, and no sanctions were available for a consumer's application of chemicals.

Amid growing concern about the effects of pesticides and other chemicals, Congress adopted major amendments to FIFRA in 1972. Those amendments established the basic structure of the present law, although FIFRA has been further amended many times since then. Under FIFRA, the EPA gained expanded authority over the use of pesticides and more flexibility in controlling their use. The law now requires that all pesticides be registered with the EPA before shipment, delivery, or sale in the United States can be undertaken. Before registering a pesticide under FIFRA, the EPA must evaluate the risks to the environment posed by that pesticide.

Overview of FIFRA

FIFRA has the following purposes:

1. It establishes a registration system by which the EPA evaluates the risks posed by pesticides. Under this system, pesticides are also classified and certified for specific uses in order to control exposure.
2. It permits the EPA to suspend, cancel, or restrict pesticides that pose a risk to the environment.
3. It authorizes the EPA to enforce the requirements of FIFRA through inspections, labeling notices, and regulation by state authorities.

A pesticide cannot be legally shipped or sold in the United States unless it is registered under FIFRA. The EPA can refuse to register a pesticide that it determines is unreasonably hazardous. The EPA can also impose conditions or restrictions to control or reduce the hazard, and it may only permit the use of toxic or carcinogenic pesticides under certain limited conditions. FIFRA, like TSCA, authorizes the EPA to require manufacturers to submit test data that the agency can use to determine whether to register a particular pesticide. This is an important provision, because testing of even a single new active ingredient in a pesticide can cost millions of dollars.

▪ ACTIVITY BOX   *Read the Label First*

Go to the "Read the Label First" page at the EPA, available at the EPA website (http://www.epa.gov/opp00001/label/). This is an interactive tool to help people understand the information required on pesticide labels.

Click on the label graphic under the instructions: "Click and explore the generic label. It will help you understand the different parts of a product label." Move your pointer over each part of the label to learn about each section.

1. Do you think that consumers generally understand the parts of a pesticide label? If not, how might the label be simplified or clarified for a consumer who might not be familiar with scientific terms, legal terms, or labeling requirements?

2. After reviewing this sample label, do you believe that pesticide labels contain all necessary information? What additional information might be included to help consumers make informed choices about whether or to what extent they will use a pesticide?

Cost-Benefit Analysis under FIFRA

Under the system established by FIFRA, the EPA may not approve a pesticide's introduction into commerce unless the EPA administrator finds that the pesticide will not generally cause unreasonable adverse effects on the environment. FIFRA requires the EPA to consider the risks posed by a pesticide, as well as its economic, social, health, and environmental benefits.

Pesticide Registration

A company that wants to manufacture, formulate, import, or distribute a pesticide in the United States must register that substance in accordance with the requirements of FIFRA. This obligation applies both to newly discovered chemicals and to new combinations or mixtures of already registered pesticides. To register a new pesticide, the registrant must submit the complete formula, a proposed label, and a description of the tests made and the results of those tests to the EPA.

Registration of pesticides under the Act is very specific, and designates the crops and insects to which they may be applied. The EPA may require the party to provide additional data supporting the safety of the product. After 1972, the increased stringency of the newer EPA health and safety testing requirements created a double standard, because older pesticides (those registered by the FDA under prior law) could continue to be marketed even though test data demonstrated that they did not meet current standards. Consequently, in amendments to FIFRA, Congress directed the EPA to review and reregister all older pesticides as quickly as possible, to ensure that all pesticides were evaluated according to the new product testing requirements. In 1988, FIFRA was amended again to speed up this reregistration process. To help pay for the testing required for the reregistration program, a maintenance fee was assessed on manufacturers of each active ingredient during the reregistration program. The Food Quality Protection Act of 1996 reauthorized and increased user fees for the pesticide reregistration program.

The law requires the EPA to periodically review pesticide registrations with the goal of establishing a 15-year cycle. The law also contains a provision designed to expedite review of safer pesticides so that they can reach the market sooner and replace older, more dangerous chemicals; furthermore, it established new requirements to expedite review and registration of antimicrobial pesticides. The EPA may suspend a pesticide registration immediately in an emergency. In 2004, the Pesticide Registration Improvement Act of 2004 amended FIFRA to reauthorize annual maintenance fees and extend the deadline for reregistration. Another amendment by the same name (Pesticide Registration Improvement Act of 2007) modified the fee payment process and the subject matter of fee applicability.

■ ACTIVITY BOX   EPA's Consumer Labeling Initiative

Review the EPA's Consumer Labeling Initiative at its website (http://www.epa.gov /pesticides/regulating/labels/consumer-labeling.htm).

1. Using your knowledge of the legal environment and liability, critique the benefits and/or drawbacks of the Consumer Labeling Initiative's "label changes that have resulted from the CLI" for manufacturers of products subject to FIFRA's labeling requirements.

2. Can you identify any products used in your household whose manufacturers appear to have participated in the CLI? If so, how have they participated? If not, why do you think that some product manufacturers have not participated in the CLI?

Trade Secrets and Use of Data

The generation and submission of pesticide test data are major costs in the development and marketing of a new pesticide. To minimize this cost, FIFRA permits the EPA to use test data supplied by one manufacturer to register the product of another manufacturer if the new product contains all or some of the same ingredients. However, the later registrant must compensate the earlier producer for the use of its data, to minimize financial advantage-taking. Moreover, FIFRA allows a 10-year "exclusive use" period for a registrant of a new pesticide that submits data in support of its original registration.

FIFRA permits the release of scientific data generated in the registration process to the public under some circumstances, when necessary to carry out the provisions of the statute. Additionally, information relating to formulas of products acquired by authorization of FIFRA may be revealed to any federal agency consulted and may be revealed at a public hearing or in findings of fact issued by the administrator.

The question of how the EPA may use data that may constitute a trade secret has become an important and thorny issue in the pesticide regulatory process. A company can have a property interest in such data under state law if the company reasonably expects that its secrets will not be disclosed to or used by other companies, even with adequate compensation.

Special Registrations

FIFRA also provides a number of limited registration or exemption mechanisms. For example, the EPA has used conditional registration under the 1978 amendments to reduce the regulatory advantage enjoyed by older products. If a product is substantially similar in ingredients and proposed use to an already registered pesticide, the agency may conditionally reregister the product and not require the submission of a full set of test data until registrants of the older products are required to submit such data under the reregistration program. Another use of conditional registration occurs in instances when an applicant has not had time to complete the long-term toxicological studies required for new products. In some cases, when a product contains new active ingredients, the EPA may register the product on the condition that the registrant complete the testing and submit data within a reasonable period of time.

A state government may permit additional uses of a pesticide to combat a pest limited to a specific area or crop. This is called *special local need registration.* The EPA also has authority to exempt federal or state agencies from the provisions of FIFRA under emergency situations. The agency may grant an emergency registration exemption allowing the use of pesticides for unregistered uses when there is no alternative means to control a serious outbreak or to prevent the introduction or spread of a foreign pest. The agency may also permit experimental use of pesticides for the development of data needed for registration of a new product or a new use.

Classification and Certification

The EPA may classify a pesticide for either general use or restricted use. The latter class is available only to "certified applicators," who are trained and certified through federal and state programs. In 1975, Congress amended the law to exempt from the examination requirement for certification farmers and their employees who apply pesticides to their own land.

Criteria for the classification of pesticides vary depending on the type of use (for example, domestic, nondomestic, indoor, or outdoor use). Most pesticides receive general use classification. If a pesticide is unusually toxic or presents a special hazard to human health or the environment, it is classified for restricted use. The EPA establishes the specific requirements that apply to such products by regulations, and other types of use restrictions are imposed through labeling requirements. Using a product in a way that violates its labeling restrictions is a violation of FIFRA.

Minor Use Registrations

Minor use registrations of pesticides are potentially available for those substances for which product sales do not justify the costs of developing and maintaining EPA registrations. The Food Quality Protection Act increases incentives for the development and maintenance of minor use registrations. These provisions do not apply, however, if the minor use might pose unreasonable risks or the lack of data would significantly delay EPA decision making.

Removal of Pesticides from the Market

The EPA may suspend, cancel, or restrict a pesticide registration to prevent an unreasonable risk to humans or the environment. *Suspension* is an emergency procedure under which the EPA may suspend the registration of a pesticide immediately. Under FIFRA, the EPA is required to suspend registration of a pesticide when a product constitutes an "imminent hazard" to humans or the environment. Suspension permits the agency to suspend registration of a pesticide while cancellation proceedings continue.

A *cancellation action* is initiated if a substance is suspected of posing a substantial risk to humans or the environment. The cancellation order is final if not challenged within 30 days, but the process is often protracted, sometimes for years. The process typically includes public hearings, a decision from an administrative law judge, review by the EPA administrator, and judicial review.

The complicated procedural requirements and criteria applied by the EPA in cancellation and suspension proceedings under FIFRA are illustrated by the EPA's decision to cancel the registration for the pesticides aldrin and dieldren. In *Environmental Defense Fund, Inc. v. Environmental Protection Agency,*[1] environmental groups challenged the EPA's failure to suspend registrations for these pesticides after initiating proceedings to cancel their registration. In a lengthy opinion, the court determined that the EPA's findings as to the benefits of the pesticides were deficient and returned the case for further EPA proceedings. The court also distinguished a suspension order from cancellation of registration; according to the court, the function of the suspension decision is to make a preliminary assessment of evidence and probabilities, not to ultimately resolve the difficult issues addressed in the cancellation proceeding.

Because of the cumbersome and lengthy cancellation procedure, the EPA has not frequently used the process. Cancellation has been initiated for DDT, aldrin/dieldrin, 2,4,5-T/Silvex, Kepone, mirex, ethylene dibromide, and Compound 1080. In general, however, the agency tends to address the problems of hazardous pesticides through the review process, which may result in cancellation of some registered uses or reclassification of the product to impose new regulatory restrictions on its use.

In the following case, a manufacturer challenged the EPA's decision to cancel registration of the pesticide diazinon for use on golf courses and sod farms on the ground that it "generally causes unreasonable adverse effects on the environment."

---

[1] 465 F.2d 528 (D.C. Cir. 1972).

Ciba-Geigy Corp. v. United States EPA
874 F.2d 277 (5th Cir. 1989)

ALVIN B. RUBIN, Circuit Judge:

* * *

The EPA issued a Notice of Intent to cancel the registrations of pesticide products containing diazinon for use on golf courses and sod farms because of concern about the effects of diazinon on birds. After extensive public hearings, the EPA's Chief Administrative Law Judge concluded that diazinon should be classified for "restricted use" by licensed applicators only and that its label should be amended, but that its registration for use on golf courses and sod farms should not be cancelled. The EPA staff appealed to the Administrator, who, after a careful analysis of the record, ordered diazinon banned from use on golf courses and sod farms. The Administrator accepted many of the Administrative Law Judge's findings and conclusions, but rejected his balancing of the risks and benefits of diazinon use. The Administrator also specifically rejected Ciba-Geigy's argument ... that because FIFRA § 6(b) authorizes cancellation of the registration of products that "generally cause[] unreasonable adverse effects on the environment," ... cancellation is justified only if a product causes unreasonable adverse effects most of the time it is used. The Administrator stated:

> FIFRA § 6(b) requires compliance with all other provisions of the statute, including FIFRA § 3(c)(5)(C) which prohibits unreasonable adverse effects on the environment without regard to whether such effects are caused "generally." Moreover, Ciba-Geigy's reading of the word "generally" as meaning "most of the time" is unnatural. In light of the basic statutory standard in FIFRA § 2(bb), which requires consideration of a broad range of factors, "generally" is more appropriately read as meaning "with regard to an overall picture".... It is simply untenable to suggest that FIFRA requires continued registration where a pesticide causes unreasonable adverse effects in less than 51 percent of the cases in which it is used.

In the Administrator's view, FIFRA authorizes him to cancel registration of a pesticide whenever he finds that it causes any unreasonable risk, irrespective of the frequency with which that risk occurs.

Urging that FIFRA requires the EPA to conclude that diazinon "generally" causes unreasonable adverse effects to birds before it can cancel its registration, Ciba-Geigy petitions this court to set aside the Administrator's order.

II

The Administrative Law Judge concluded that bird kills due to diazinon may be an "unusual occurrence." Ciba-Geigy asserts, therefore, that even if diazinon sometimes causes adverse environmental effects, it does not do so "generally" as the statute requires.

Ciba-Geigy's argument focuses on a single word in the statutory phrase, ignoring the meaning of the phrase as a whole. FIFRA provides that the Administrator may cancel the registration of a pesticide if it appears to him that, "when used in accordance with widespread and commonly recognized practice, [it] generally causes unreasonable adverse effects on the environment." ... The statute defines "unreasonable adverse effects on the environment" to mean "any unreasonable risk to man or the environment, taking into account the ... costs and benefits." ...

Neither the statute nor its legislative history explains the word "generally," but, as the numerous dictionary definitions that the parties have quoted to us make clear, it means "usually," "commonly," or "with considerable frequency," though not necessarily "more likely than not." Interpreting the statutory standard as a whole, therefore, the Administrator may cancel a registration if it appears to him that the pesticide commonly causes unreasonable risks.

Because FIFRA defines "adverse effects" as "unreasonable risks," the Administrator need not find that use of a pesticide commonly causes undesirable consequences, but only that it commonly creates a significant probability that such consequences may occur. FIFRA therefore does not oblige the Administrator to maintain the registration of a pesticide that might not generally have adverse effects but, say, killed children on 30% of the occasions on which it was used. A 30% risk that children might be killed is plainly an "unreasonable risk" more than sufficient to justify cancellation of the noxious pesticide.... Similarly, a significant risk of bird kills, even if birds are actually killed infrequently, may justify the Administrator's decision to ban or restrict diazinon use.

Nevertheless, the Administrator improperly read the word "generally" out of FIFRA § 6(b). The word is not superfluous: it requires the Administrator to determine that the use of a pesticide in a particular application creates unreasonable risks, though not necessarily actual adverse consequences, with

(Continued)

considerable frequency, and thus requires the Administrator to consider whether he has defined the application he intends to prohibit sufficiently narrowly. If the use of diazinon creates an unreasonable risk of killing birds on only 10% of the golf courses on which it is used, for example, the Administrator should define the class of golf courses on which its use is to be prohibited more narrowly. Without attempting to interpret the vast administrative record ourselves, therefore, we grant Ciba-Geigy's petition to the extent of remanding this case to the Administrator for application of the correct legal standard.

* * *

... [T]he order cancelling the registration of diazinon for use on golf courses and sod farms is set aside, and the case is REMANDED to the Administrator for further proceedings consistent with this opinion.

Questions and Comments for Discussion

1. Why did the EPA cancel the registration of the pesticide diazinon for use on golf courses and sod farms?

2. Based on the language of this section, why did the manufacturer argue that the EPA had improperly cancelled the registration of the pesticide?

3. How did the court interpret the meaning of the word "generally" as used in this section of FIFRA? What was the court's ruling in this case?

Effect of Cancellation of Registration

What happens to a product already in commercial use if the product's registration is cancelled or suspended? In several cases, the EPA has ordered product recalls. However, for practical reasons, the EPA has usually permitted newly banned pesticides to be used until existing supplies are exhausted.

EPA regulations also establish approved methods for storage and disposal of pesticides under FIFRA, including incineration, soil injection, and other means of disposal. Obviously, disposal methods that do not degrade the environment or pose risks of harm to humans are the aim here.

State Authority to Regulate Pesticides

FIFRA and the Food, Drug, and Cosmetic Act (FDCA) preempt state authority to regulate issues already regulated by FIFRA or the FDCA. However, FIFRA generally permits the states to administer pesticide applicator certification programs, issue experimental use permits, register pesticides to meet special local needs, enforce federal pesticide laws, and regulate pesticides in ways not specifically prohibited by FIFRA.

Although enforcement of the federal law is primarily carried out by the states, states may not permit the sale or use of pesticides prohibited under FIFRA, and they may not impose labeling or packaging requirements that differ from the requirements of FIFRA or the FDCA. The following case illustrates federal preemption of FDCA regarding labeling. Though the case does not factually address pesticides, the FDCA is implicated through its labeling requirements associated with generic drugs.

Enforcement and Penalties

Sale of unregistered, adulterated, or misbranded pesticides; use of a registered pesticide in a manner inconsistent with its labeling; and production of pesticides in an unregistered facility are all violations of FIFRA. The EPA may inspect production

Mutual Pharmaceutical Co., Inc. v. Bartlett
570 U.S. ___, 133 S. Ct. 2466 (2013)

Justice ALITO delivered the opinion of the Court.

We must decide whether federal law pre-empts the New Hampshire design-defect claim under which respondent Karen Bartlett recovered damages from petitioner Mutual Pharmaceutical, the manufacturer of sulindac, a generic nonsteroidal anti-inflammatory drug (NSAID). New Hampshire law imposes a duty on manufacturers to ensure that the drugs they market are not unreasonably unsafe, and a drug's safety is evaluated by reference to both its chemical properties and the adequacy of its warnings. Because Mutual was unable to change sulindac's composition as a matter of both federal law and basic chemistry, New Hampshire's design-defect cause of action effectively required Mutual to change sulindac's labeling to provide stronger warnings. But ... federal law prohibits generic drug manufacturers from independently changing their drugs' labels. Accordingly, state law imposed a duty on Mutual *not* to comply with federal law. Under the Supremacy Clause, state laws that require a private party to violate federal law are pre-empted and, thus, are "without effect." ...

... [W]e hold that state-law design-defect claims that turn on the adequacy of a drug's warnings are pre-empted by federal law....

I

Under the Federal Food, Drug, and Cosmetic Act (FDCA), ... drug manufacturers must gain approval from the United States Food and Drug Administration (FDA) before marketing any drug in interstate commerce.... In the case of a new brand-name drug, FDA approval can be secured only by submitting a new-drug application (NDA)....

The process of submitting an NDA is both onerous and lengthy.... In order to provide a swifter route for approval of generic drugs, Congress passed the Drug Price Competition and Patent Term Restoration Act of 1984, ... popularly known as the "Hatch-Waxman Act." Under Hatch-Waxman, a generic drug may be approved without the same level of clinical testing required for approval of a new brand-name drug, provided the generic drug is identical to the already-approved brand-name drug in several key respects.

First, the proposed generic drug must be chemically equivalent to the approved brand-name drug: it must have the same "active ingredient" or "active ingredients," "route of administration," "dosage form," and "strength" as its brand-name counterpart.... Second, a proposed generic must be "bioequivalent" to an approved brand-name drug.... That is, it must have the same "rate and extent of absorption" as the brand-name drug.... Third, the generic drug manufacturer must show that "the labeling proposed for the new drug is the same as the labeling approved for the [approved brand-name] drug." ...

Once a drug—whether generic or brand-name—is approved, the manufacturer is prohibited from making any major changes to the "qualitative or quantitative formulation of the drug product, including active ingredients, or in the specifications provided in the approved application." ... Generic manufacturers are also prohibited from making any unilateral changes to a drug's label. See [Hatch-Waxman] §§ 314.94(a)(8)(iii), 314.150(b)(10) (approval for a generic drug may be withdrawn if the generic drug's label "is no longer consistent with that for [the brand-name] drug").

II

In 1978, the FDA approved a nonsteroidal anti-inflammatory pain reliever called "sulindac" under the brand name Clinoril. When Clinoril's patent expired, the FDA approved several generic sulindacs, including one manufactured by Mutual Pharmaceutical.... In a very small number of patients, NSAIDs—including both sulindac and popular NSAIDs such as ibuprofen, naproxen, and Cox2-inhibitors—have the serious side effect of causing two hypersensitivity skin reactions characterized by necrosis of the skin and of the mucous membranes: toxic epidermal necrolysis, and its less severe cousin, Stevens-Johnson Syndrome....

In December 2004, respondent Karen L. Bartlett was prescribed Clinoril for shoulder pain. Her pharmacist dispensed a generic form of sulindac, which was manufactured by petitioner Mutual Pharmaceutical. Respondent soon developed an acute case of toxic epidermal necrolysis. The results were horrific. Sixty to sixty-five percent of the surface of respondent's body deteriorated, was burned off, or turned into an open wound. She spent months in a medically induced coma, underwent 12 eye surgeries, and was tube-fed for a year. She is now severely disfigured, has a number of physical disabilities, and is nearly blind.

(Continued)

At the time respondent was prescribed sulindac, the drug's label did not specifically refer to Stevens-Johnson Syndrome or toxic epidermal necrolysis, but did warn that the drug could cause "severe skin reactions" and "[f]atalities." ... However, Stevens-Johnson Syndrome and toxic epidermal necrolysis were listed as potential adverse reactions on the drug's package insert.... In 2005—once respondent was already suffering from toxic epidermal necrolysis—the FDA completed a "comprehensive review of the risks and benefits, [including the risk of toxic epidermal necrolysis], of all approved NSAID products." ... As a result of that review, the FDA recommended changes to the labeling of all NSAIDs, including sulindac, to more explicitly warn against toxic epidermal necrolysis....

Respondent sued Mutual in New Hampshire state court, and Mutual removed the case to federal court. Respondent initially asserted both failure-to-warn and design-defect claims, but the District Court dismissed her failure-to-warn claim based on her doctor's "admi[ssion] that he had not read the box label or insert." ... After a 2-week trial on respondent's design-defect claim, a jury found Mutual liable and awarded respondent over $21 million in damages.

The Court of Appeals affirmed.... As relevant, it found that neither the FDCA nor the FDA's regulations pre-empted respondent's design-defect claims. It distinguished *PLIVA, Inc. v. Mensing*, ...—in which the Court held that failure-to-warn claims against generic manufacturers are pre-empted by the FDCA's prohibition on changes to generic drug labels—by arguing that generic manufacturers facing design-defect claims could simply "choose not to make the drug at all" and thus comply with both federal and state law. We granted certiorari....

III

The Supremacy Clause provides that the laws and treaties of the United States "shall be the supreme Law of the Land ... any Thing in the Constitution or Laws of any State to the Contrary notwithstanding." ...

Even in the absence of an express pre-emption provision, the Court has found state law to be impliedly pre-empted where it is "impossible for a private party to comply with both state and federal requirements." ...

In the instant case, it was impossible for Mutual to comply with both its state-law duty to strengthen the warnings on sulindac's label and its federal-law duty not to alter sulindac's label. Accordingly, the state law is pre-empted.

A

We begin by identifying petitioner's duties under state law....

B

That New Hampshire tort law imposes a duty on manufacturers is clear.... New Hampshire requires manufacturers to ensure that the products they design, manufacture, and sell are not "unreasonably dangerous." ...

... New Hampshire imposes design-defect liability only where "the design of the product created a defective condition unreasonably dangerous to the user." ... To determine whether a product is "unreasonably dangerous," the New Hampshire Supreme Court employs a "risk-utility approach" under which "a product is defective as designed if the magnitude of the danger outweighs the utility of the product." ... That risk-utility approach requires a "multifaceted balancing process involving evaluation of many conflicting factors." ...

While the set of factors to be considered is ultimately an open one, the New Hampshire Supreme Court has repeatedly identified three factors as germane to the risk-utility inquiry: "the usefulness and desirability of the product to the public as a whole, whether the risk of danger could have been reduced without significantly affecting either the product's effectiveness or manufacturing cost, and the presence and efficacy of a warning to avoid an unreasonable risk of harm from hidden dangers or from foreseeable uses." ...

In the drug context, either increasing the "usefulness" of a product or reducing its "risk of danger" would require redesigning the drug: A drug's usefulness and its risk of danger are both direct results of its chemical design and, most saliently, its active ingredients....

In the present case, however, redesign was not possible for two reasons. First, the FDCA requires a generic drug to have the same active ingredients, route of administration, dosage form, strength, and labeling as the brand-name drug on which it is based.... Consequently, ... "Mutual cannot legally make sulindac in another composition." ... Indeed, were Mutual to change the composition of its sulindac, the altered chemical would be a new drug that would require its own NDA to be marketed in interstate commerce.... Second, because of sulindac's simple composition, the drug is chemically incapable of being redesigned....

Given the impossibility of redesigning sulindac, the only way for Mutual to ameliorate the drug's

(Continued)

"risk-utility" profile—and thus to escape liability—was to strengthen "the presence and efficacy of [sulindac's] warning" in such a way that the warning "avoid[ed] an unreasonable risk of harm from hidden dangers or from foreseeable uses." ... Thus, New Hampshire's design-defect cause of action imposed a duty on Mutual to strengthen sulindac's warnings.

* * *

[However, a]s *PLIVA* made clear, federal law prevents generic drug manufacturers from changing their labels.... Thus, federal law prohibited Mutual from taking the remedial action required to avoid liability under New Hampshire law.

D

... When federal law forbids an action that state law requires, the state law is "without effect." ... Because it is impossible for Mutual and other similarly situated manufacturers to comply with both state and federal law, New Hampshire's warning-based design-defect cause of action is pre-empted with respect to FDA-approved drugs sold in interstate commerce....

V

The dreadful injuries from which products liabilities cases arise often engender passionate responses.... But sympathy for respondent does not relieve us of the responsibility of following the law.

* * *

This case arises out of tragic circumstances. A combination of factors combined to produce the rare and devastating injuries that respondent suffered: the FDA's decision to approve the sale of sulindac and the warnings that accompanied the drug at the time it was prescribed, the decision by respondent's physician to prescribe sulindac despite its known risks, and Congress' decision to regulate the manufacture and sale of generic drugs in a way that reduces their cost to patients but leaves generic drug manufacturers incapable of modifying either the drugs' compositions or their warnings. Respondent's situation is tragic and evokes deep sympathy, but a straightforward application of pre-emption law requires that the judgment below be reversed.

It is so ordered.

Questions and Comments for Discussion

1. How could the holding in *Mutual Pharmaceutical Co. v. Bartlett* be applied to pesticide manufacturers and their products?

2. What are the benefits and drawbacks of federal preemption of state law?

3. When injuries are as egregious as those suffered by Bartlett, do you think the court should offer some remedy for the plaintiff? Why or why not?

---

facilities and examine and test pesticides, impose fines or criminal penalties for violation of the Act, and stop the sale of and seize products that are in violation of the law. FIFRA gives state governments primary authority to enforce the law, and authorizes funding assistance to state enforcement programs.

The Interrelationship of FIFRA with Other Laws

The Federal Food, Drug, and Cosmetic Act   Under the federal Food, Drug, and Cosmetic Act (FDCA), the EPA establishes **tolerances**, which are maximum legally permissible levels for pesticide residues in food or animal feed. To register a pesticide, an applicant must obtain a tolerance for that pesticide. Thus, the applicant is required to provide evidence showing the level of residues likely to result and the data necessary to establish safe residue levels.

The authority for setting of tolerances for pesticide residues in food is derived from the FDCA. The EPA sets tolerances "to protect the public health" and to give appropriate consideration "to the necessity for the production of an adequate, wholesome and economical food supply." The Food Quality Protection Act of 1996 set the applicable standard as "a reasonable certainty of no harm."

tolerances: Maximum legally permissible levels for pesticide residues in food or animal feed.

Under limited circumstances, the new FDCA law permits tolerances to remain in effect that would not otherwise meet the standard. This provision, however, is subject to a number of limitations on risk, and all tolerances must be consistent with the special provisions for infants and children. The law requires the EPA to consider specific factors in setting tolerances in addition to special provisions for infants and children, and requires that all existing tolerances be reviewed within 10 years.

The FDCA also prohibits the sale of food that is adulterated. **Adulterated food** is defined as food containing any unsafe food additive. Prior to 1996, a specific clause in the FDCA called the *Delaney clause*[2] prohibited the use of any food additive in processed foods that was found to induce cancer.

Before 1988, EPA regulations permitted the use of benomyl, mancozeb, phosmet, and trifluralin as food additives. In 1988, however, the EPA found these pesticides to be carcinogens. In *Les v. Reilly*,[3] the petitioners sought judicial review of a final order of the EPA and challenged on the ground that the order violated the Delaney clause. However, the EPA refused to revoke the earlier regulations, reasoning that, although the chemicals posed a measurable risk of causing cancer, that risk was de minimis. The court in *Les v. Reilly* disagreed with the EPA's refusal to revoke the regulations permitting the use of the four pesticides as food additives, finding those rules contrary to the provisions of the Delaney clause prohibiting carcinogenic food additives. For this reason, the *Les* court set aside the EPA's final order.

The Food Quality Protection Act of 1996 and Repeal of the Delaney Clause   The Food Quality Protection Act of 1996 amended both the FDCA and FIFRA to establish a health-based safety standard for pesticide residues in all foods, and to establish a more consistent, protective regulatory scheme for pesticides. The new law repealed the Delaney clause and substituted the standard of "a reasonable certainty of no harm" for both processed foods and raw agricultural commodities. This standard applies to all risks, not just cancer risks. In setting the standard, the EPA must consider all nonoccupational sources of exposure to pesticides, including drinking water, and exposure to similar pesticides.

The 1996 Act contains a special provision requiring an explicit determination that tolerances are safe for children, and places specific limits on the consideration of pesticide benefits when setting tolerances. It also incorporates provisions for endocrine testing, and enhances enforcement of standards by permitting the FDA to impose civil penalties for tolerance violations. In addition, it contains a "right to know" provision requiring distribution of a brochure on the health effects of pesticides.

Other Pesticide Regulation   Pesticides in the air may be regulated under the Clean Air Act as hazardous air pollutants, and may be regulated under the Clean Water Act when released as effluents into a body of water. In addition, the EPA and the Department of Labor share responsibility under FIFRA and the Occupational Safety and Health Act (OSHA) for protecting agricultural workers from hazardous pesticides.

adulterated food: Food containing any unsafe additive.

---

[2] 21 U.S.C. § 834(c)(3).
[3] 968 F.2d 985 (9th Cir. 1992).

▦ ▦ ▦ REVIEW AND STUDY QUESTIONS

1. The EPA sets maximum allowable residue limits on pesticides in food to ensure that exposure to the ingredient will be "safe." "Safe" means a level at which there is "a reasonable certainty of no harm" from exposure. How certain should this determination be? If most people do not have ill effects from a level of exposure, but some people do, should that be safe enough? Why or why not?

2. Locate a pesticide at the store and read the label required by FIFRA. Do you understand the label? What parts of the label are unclear? What does "inert" mean? What potential liability exists for products that are labeled in a manner that is consistent with the law but difficult for most people to understand? How can a business minimize its liability exposure through labeling?

3. Consider whether substances should be classified as pesticides under FIFRA based on claims made about them and their "intended use." What are the benefits and drawbacks to businesses that produce substances that could be used as pesticides in claiming that the intended use is as a pesticide? What risks exist to society in relying upon "intended use" claims?

4. What is the process for registering a pesticide? What finding must the EPA make to approve registration of a pesticide?

5. How might pesticide registration be cancelled or suspended?

▦ The Toxic Substances Control Act

Fueled by an overall expansion of the economy and a demand for new products, the U.S. chemical industry grew rapidly after World War II. In the decades following the war, however, concerns about the effects of particular chemicals led to increased concern about the health risks and environmental effects of the production and dispersion of natural and synthetic materials in general. In the 1950s, an association between exposure to asbestos and cancer first began to be reported, and further studies only heightened public concern about asbestos exposure. Carson's *Silent Spring* generated great public concern about the adverse effects of synthetic pesticides such as DDT, and the ability of these chemicals to persist and accumulate in biological organisms. Vinyl chloride, organic mercury compounds, and polychlorinated biphenyls (PCBs) are other substances that have generated public concern, as evidence of their toxic effects on the environment and public health continue to be documented.

In response to mounting concern about the toxic effects of PCBs and other chemical substances, in 1976 Congress passed TSCA. TSCA is a gap-filling statute that permits the EPA to control or ban substances that cause harm to health or the environment, and that are not regulated by other federal environmental laws. Before the passage of TSCA, there was no way to ban the manufacture of PCBs or control their use, even though PCB molecules were found to contaminate river and lake sediment. In response to this concern, TSCA specifically includes a ban on the manufacture of PCBs.

TSCA gives the Environmental Protection Agency the authority to:

1. Screen new chemicals
2. Require testing of chemicals that may present a significant risk to human health or the environment
3. Gather information about the adverse health or environmental effects of existing chemicals
4. Limit or prohibit the manufacture, use, distribution, and disposal of chemicals posing such risks

Title I of TSCA establishes the basic framework for the control of toxic substances. Subsequent amendments to the law have added Title II, the Asbestos Hazard Emergency Response Act; Title III, the Indoor Radon Abatement Act; Title IV, the Lead-Based Paint Exposure Reduction Act; Title V, Energy Independence and Security Act of 2007; and Subtitle E—Healthy High-Performance Schools (Reducing Risks in Schools). Additionally, in 2008, the Mercury Export Ban Act was added as an amendment.

TSCA gives the EPA broad authority to regulate chemicals, but it requires the agency to balance the risks and costs of doing so. In deciding whether to regulate a particular chemical, the EPA must consider the benefits of the substance to society's economic and social welfare, the availability and risks from alternative substances, and the health or economic risks resulting from regulation of the substance. Thus, TSCA does not mandate regulation of all chemicals that present a risk to human health or the environment; it only regulates chemicals that present an unreasonable risk.

Another important part of TSCA makes industry responsible for providing information about the chemicals it manufactures and distributes. Under TSCA, a *manufacturer,* which is defined broadly to include importers and extractors of chemical substances, has the responsibility for providing data to the EPA on the health and environmental effects of new and existing substances and mixtures.

Screening New Chemicals

TSCA establishes a Premanufacture Notification Program. Under this program, the EPA assesses the safety of new chemicals before they are manufactured. Any person who intends to manufacture or import a new chemical substance must file a **premanufacture notice (PMN)** with the EPA before undertaking manufacture or importation. Existing chemicals, chemicals used solely for research and development, and chemicals regulated under other laws (e.g., pesticides regulated under FIFRA) are exempt from the PMN review. The EPA receives many notifications every year from manufacturers who want to make or import new chemicals into the U.S. market.

The question of whether or when a manufacturer of chemical substances is required to file a PMN turns on the distinction between "new" chemicals (and "significant new uses of existing chemicals" for which a PMN is required) and "existing" chemicals. Under TSCA, the EPA keeps and publishes a current list of all chemical substances manufactured or processed for commercial purposes in the United States. This list is known as the **TSCA inventory**, and it is the basis on which EPA distinguishes between existing and new chemicals that require a premanufacture notification. The EPA continuously adds new chemicals that have been cleared through the TSCA premanufacture notice review to the inventory, and it also periodically removes or "delists" chemicals not currently manufactured or imported for commercial purposes.

If a chemical is not already listed on the TSCA inventory, or does not fall within an exemption, a company must submit a PMN to the EPA for review before beginning manufacture of the chemical. The PMN must include:

1. The common or trade name of the substance
2. The chemical identity and molecular structure of the substance
3. The estimated production levels for the substance

premanufacture notice (PMN): A filing required by TSCA by a person who intends to manufacture or import a new chemical substance.

TSCA inventory: A current list of all chemical substances manufactured or processed for commercial purposes in the United States; published by the EPA.

4. The proposed use of the chemical and method of disposal

5. The estimated levels of exposure in the workplace and number of workers involved

6. The byproducts, impurities, and other related products

7. The available test data on health and environmental effects related to manufacture if the data are within the manufacturer's possession and control

8. A description of known or reasonably ascertainable test data

A manufacturer is not expressly required to undertake or produce specific tests for a PMN. TSCA does not require the manufacturer to provide a minimum set of premarket data on a new chemical as part of the premanufacture review process. Additionally, TSCA prohibits promulgation of regulations that would require testing of all new chemicals, in the interest of not stifling innovation.

Approval of the PMN

TSCA requires the EPA to review a PMN within 90 days of its submission. After reviewing the notice, the agency publishes a notice in the *Federal Register* advertising the date the PMN was received and the date the 90-day review period ends. During the review period, the EPA evaluates the risks posed by the new chemical. If the EPA takes no regulatory action within the 90-day period, the company may begin commercial manufacture or importation without further agency approval. The manufacturer or importer must, however, file a Notice of Commencement (NOC) of Manufacture or Import within 30 days of beginning such action. After it receives the NOC, the EPA adds the PMN substance to the TSCA inventory, and it then becomes an existing chemical under TSCA.

If the EPA has questions about a substance submitted for premanufacture review, TSCA allows the EPA to prevent, delay, or limit the manufacture of a new chemical after the 90-day period expires. Additionally, the agency may delay manufacture for an additional 90 days for "good cause." It may also issue a proposed order to limit or prohibit manufacture of the chemical if the agency determines that the available information is "insufficient to permit a reasoned evaluation." The agency may approve a new chemical but condition that approval on the manufacturer's providing further data on its uses and effects by adding the chemical to a list of existing substances.

The EPA may also act immediately to limit or delay the manufacture of a chemical substance if the agency concludes that such manufacture "presents or will present an unreasonable risk of injury to health or the environment." The EPA is permitted to take immediate action to ban such a chemical from commercial manufacture, distribution, processing, and use while it undertakes a rulemaking action. The scope of judicial review of the EPA's orders depends on the kind of action taken.

Rather than issuing such orders, the EPA may choose to enter into a consent agreement with the manufacturer. Under this legally binding agreement, the manufacturer agrees to restrict production, use, disposal, or exposure of the new chemical. The agency then issues a significant new use rule (SNUR) which extends those restrictions to all subsequent manufacturers or importers of the substance.

Testing Requirements

TSCA authorizes the EPA to require manufacturers and processors to develop data about the health and environmental effects of their products. The EPA may require manufacturers and processors to test chemical substances that are already on the market or are about to be produced.

The EPA is required to make a risk determination of both toxicity and exposure before it can order testing. The agency uses several factors in determining the possible unreasonable risk of a substance:

- Knowledge of the physical and chemical properties of the substance
- Structural relationships to other chemicals with demonstrated adverse effects
- Data from inconclusive tests
- Case history data

Testing required by the Act must be specific with respect to the type of effects to be evaluated; the agency must also specify the standards to be used and the time period for submitting test results to the EPA. TSCA requires the EPA administrator to undertake formal rulemaking to mandate testing by the manufacturer of the chemical or mixture.

The Interagency Testing Committee (ITC), composed of representatives of eight federal agencies, makes recommendations to the EPA administrator in respect to the chemical substances and mixtures to which the administrator should give priority consideration. TSCA requires the ITC to give priority to substances suspected of causing or contributing to cancer, gene mutations, or birth defects. Within one year after the ITC designates a chemical, the EPA must propose a test rule or publish reasons why testing is not required.

In reviewing the agency's rulemaking decision to require testing under § 4 of TSCA, a court reviews the rulemaking record to determine whether the agency's factual findings were supported by substantial evidence. In the following case, the petitioners—the Chemical Manufacturers Association and four companies that manufactured chemicals—sought to set aside a rule promulgated by the EPA which required toxicological testing to determine the health effects of the chemical 2-ethyhexanoic acid (EHA), and which placed on exporters of EHA a duty to file certain notices with the agency. An important issue in the case was the EPA's determination that the substance presented an "unreasonable risk of injury to human health or the environment" under TSCA § 4.

Chemical Manufacturers Association v. U.S. EPA

859 F.2d 977 (D.C. Cir. 1988)

WALD, Chief Judge

Petitioners, Chemical Manufacturers Association and four companies that manufacture chemicals ... seek to set aside a rule promulgated by the Environmental Protection Agency.... This Final Test Rule was promulgated under section 4 of the Toxic Substances Control Act.... The Final Test Rule required toxicological testing to determine the health effects of the chemical 2-ethylhexanoic acid ("EHA") and it continues to impose on exporters of EHA a duty to file certain notices with EPA.

We uphold EPA's interpretation of TSCA as empowering the Agency to issue a test rule on health grounds where it finds a more-than-theoretical basis for suspecting that the chemical substance in question presents an "unreasonable risk of injury to health." This, in turn, requires the Agency to find a more-than-theoretical basis for concluding that the substance is sufficiently toxic, and human exposure to it is sufficient in amount, to generate an "unreasonable risk of injury to health." We hold, further, that EPA can establish the existence and amount of human exposure on

(Continued)

the basis of inferences drawn from the circumstances under which the substance is manufactured and used. EPA must rebut industry-supplied evidence attacking those inferences only if the industry evidence succeeds in rendering the probability of exposure in the amount found by EPA no more than theoretical or speculative. The probability of infrequent or even one-time exposure to individuals can warrant a test rule, so long as there is a more-than-theoretical basis for determining that exposure in such doses presents an "unreasonable risk of injury to health." Finally, we hold that the Agency correctly applied these standards in this case and that its findings are supported by substantial evidence. Consequently, we affirm the Final Test Rule.

I. Background

A. Statutory Structure

TSCA provides for a two-tier system for evaluating and regulating chemical substances to protect against unreasonable risks to human health and to the environment. Section 6 of the Act permits EPA to regulate a substance that the Agency has found "presents or will present an unreasonable risk of injury to health or the environment." ... Section 4 of the Act empowers EPA to require testing of a suspect substance in order to obtain the toxicological data necessary to make a decision whether or not to regulate the substance under section 6. The Act provides, not surprisingly, that the level of certainty of risk warranting a section 4 test rule is lower than that warranting a section 6 regulatory rule. EPA is empowered to require testing where it finds that the manufacture, distribution, processing, use or disposal of a particular chemical substance "may present an unreasonable risk of injury to human health or the environment." ... The Agency's interpretation of this statutory standard for testing is the central issue in this case.

One of the chief policies underlying the Act is that—

> adequate data should be developed with respect to the effect of chemical substances and mixtures on health and the environment and that the development of such data should be the responsibility of those who manufacture and those who process such chemical substances and mixtures. [§ 2601(b)(1).]

... The statute establishes an Interagency Testing Committee, comprised of scientists from various federal agencies, to recommend that EPA give certain chemicals "priority consideration" for testing.... Under section 4, the Agency "shall by rule require that testing

[of a particular chemical] be conducted" if three factors are present: (i) activities involving the chemical "may present an unreasonable risk of injury to health or the environment"; (ii) "insufficient data and experience" exist upon which to determine the effects of the chemical on health or environment; and (iii) testing is necessary to develop such data.... The companies that manufacture and process the substance are to conduct the tests and submit the data to the Agency.... Costs of testing are to be shared among the companies, either by agreement or by EPA order in the absence of agreement....

A test rule promulgated under section 4 is subject to judicial review in a court of appeals, pursuant to section 19(a) of TSCA.... A test rule may be set aside if it is not "supported by substantial evidence in the rulemaking record ... taken as a whole." ...

* * *

III. Statutory Interpretation

The Toxic Substances Control Act requires EPA to promulgate a test rule under section 4 if a chemical substance, inter alia, "may present an unreasonable risk of injury to health or the environment." ... The parties both accept the proposition that the degree to which a particular substance presents a risk to health is a function of two factors: (a) human exposure to the substance, and (b) the toxicity of the substance. ... They also agree that EPA must make some sort of threshold finding as to the existence of an "unreasonable risk of injury to health." The parties differ, however, as to the manner in which this finding must be made. Specifically, three issues are presented.

The first issue is whether, under section 4 of TSCA, EPA must find that the existence of an "unreasonable risk of injury to health" is more probable than not in order to issue a test rule. [The petitioner] CMA argues that the statute requires a more-probable-than-not finding. ... EPA disagrees, contending that the statute is satisfied where the existence of an "unreasonable risk of injury to health" is a substantial probability—that is, a probability that is more than merely theoretical, speculative or conjectural....

The second issue is whether, once industry has presented evidence tending to show an absence of human exposure, EPA must rebut it by producing direct evidence of exposure....

The third issue is whether the Agency has authority to issue a test rule where any individual's exposure to a substance is an isolated, non-recurrent event. CMA argues that, even if EPA presents direct evidence of exposure, the Act precludes issuance of a test rule

(Continued)

where exposure consists only of rare instances involving brief exposure.... EPA contends ... that the Act does not require in all circumstances a risk of recurrent exposure....

A. Required Finding of "Unreasonable Risk"

As to the first issue in this case, the standard of probability of an unreasonable risk to health, we find that Congress did not address the precise question in issue. Examining the EPA interpretation ... we find it to be reasonable and consistent with the statutory scheme and legislative history. Consequently, we uphold the Agency's construction of TSCA as authorizing a test rule where EPA's basis for suspecting the existence of an "unreasonable risk of injury to health" is substantial—i.e., when there is a more-than-theoretical basis for suspecting that some amount of exposure takes place and that the substance is sufficiently toxic at that level of exposure to present an "unreasonable risk of injury to health."

* * *

B. Use of Inferences Versus Direct Evidence of Exposure

The second issue in the case is whether EPA must produce direct evidence documenting human exposure in order to rebut industry-submitted evidence casting doubt on the existence of exposure.... EPA contends that it need not provide direct evidence of exposure, even in response to industry evidence rebutting its initial circumstantial case on exposure, so long as the evidence on exposure as a whole provides a more-than-theoretical basis for discerning the presence of an "unreasonable risk of injury to health." EPA concedes that exposure is a necessary component of "unreasonable risk of injury to health." ... The Agency argues, however, that it can issue a test rule where the existence of exposure is inferred from the circumstances under which the substance is manufactured and used. So long as industry evidence attacking those inferences fails to negate the Agency's more-than-theoretical basis for inferring the existence of exposure, EPA claims, a test rule is warranted. After a careful search of the legislative materials, we conclude

that Congress did not address this particular issue.... Applying the second prong of Chevron, however, we conclude that the Agency's construction of section 4 is a reasonable one and therefore uphold it.

* * *

C. Recurrent Versus Rare Exposure

The third statutory issue is whether section 4 of TSCA authorizes EPA to issue a test rule where any individual's exposure to a chemical is likely to be a rare, brief event. CMA contends that only recurrent exposure warrants a test rule. EPA maintains that it can issue a test rule in the absence of recurrent exposure, where there is a more-than-theoretical basis for suspecting that infrequent or single-dose exposure presents an "unreasonable risk of injury to health." We find no indication in the statute or its history that Congress addressed this particular issue, but once again turning to the second prong of Chevron, we deem reasonable the Agency's construction of section 4 as permitting a test rule even where exposure is not recurrent.

[The court concluded that the EPA had "presented substantial relevant evidence of exposure and toxicity so as to justify the promulgation of a test rule" and that its "findings as to exposure, subchronic toxicity, and developmental toxicity [were] supported by substantial evidence on the record viewed as a whole." It therefore denied the petition for review.]

Questions and Comments for Discussion

1. Who sued whom in this case? Why?
2. What three issues did the court address in this case? How did the court resolve those issues?
3. The court relied on the holding in *Chevron* in reviewing the EPA's interpretation of the statutory language of TSCA. What is the *Chevron* test of statutory interpretation as set out by the court in this case?
4. This case provides a good example of the importance of burden of proof in rulemaking. According to the court, who has the burden of proof in this case? What is the standard of proof?

The EPA may require testing if a chemical substance is produced in substantial quantities, if it is reasonably expected to be released into the environment in substantial quantities, if there is or may be significant or substantial human exposure, or if data are insufficient and testing is necessary to develop the data. When the agency requires a chemical to be tested, all manufacturers and processors participate, but the law permits them to agree to have one laboratory perform the tests and share the costs of testing.

TSCA also contains a provision mandating that the EPA take regulatory action when a chemical poses "a significant risk of serious or widespread harm to human beings." This provision has been triggered for formaldehyde, for example.

Information Gathering and Reporting

The EPA is authorized to collect general information on chemicals it may regulate. TSCA also establishes requirements for the collection, recording, and submission of information to the EPA by chemical manufacturers and processors. Such information includes data on chemical production, use, exposure, and disposal, as well as records of allegations of significant adverse reactions, adverse effects on human health or the environment, and unpublished health and safety studies.

TSCA requires manufacturers, processors, and distributors to keep records of significant adverse health reactions and environmental effects alleged to have been caused by a chemical substance or mixture they manufacture, process, or distribute. The EPA has limited mandatory adverse-effect allegation recording and reporting to those effects that substantially impair activity, are long-lasting, or are irreversible. A person who manufactures, processes, or distributes a chemical substance or mixture is required to submit to the EPA lists and copies of health and safety studies conducted by, known to, or ascertainable by that person. This includes unpublished studies.

Chemical manufacturers, processors, and distributors must report substantial risks associated with chemicals. Data required include toxicology tests or results of animal studies indicating adverse health effects. The purpose of TSCA's reporting requirements is to provide the EPA with information so that it can make reasoned judgments about the safety or hazards of the chemicals it regulates. Some of the information collected under TSCA may be trade secrets and confidential commercial or financial information. TSCA does not prohibit the disclosure of health and safety studies or the release of information to federal officials, but it does provide that the EPA may not release any information that is exempt from mandatory disclosure under the Freedom of Information Act. EPA regulations under TSCA are designed to permit industry to submit information to the agency without fear that confidential trade information will be released to competitors.

Regulation of Existing Chemicals

TSCA authorizes the EPA to regulate existing chemicals that present an unreasonable risk to health or the environment. The EPA may control, restrict, or ban the manufacture, use, processing, disposal, or distribution of such chemicals. To determine whether a risk is unreasonable, the EPA must conduct a risk assessment and is required to consider:

1. The effects on health and the environment
2. The magnitude of exposure to humans and the environment
3. The benefits of the substance and the availability of substitutes
4. The reasonably ascertainable economic consequences of the rule

Once the EPA has found an unreasonable risk, it must impose the least burdensome restrictions necessary to control the risk.

The EPA has attempted to regulate only a few chemical substances under this section. They include asbestos, chlorofluorocarbons, dioxins, hexavalent chromium, certain metalworking fluids, and polychlorinated biphenyls.

In 1989, after more than 10 years of effort, the EPA issued a final rule under TSCA § 6 to ban the manufacture, import, processing, and distribution of asbestos products. Exposure to asbestos fibers has been associated with pulmonary fibrosis (asbestosis), lung cancer, and other cancers and diseases. In a hard-fought case, industry challenged the EPA's asbestos regulations on a number of grounds. Among other things, they claimed that the EPA's rulemaking procedure was flawed and that the rule was not promulgated based upon substantial evidence. Others contended that the rule was invalid because it conflicted with international trade agreements.

In 1991, the case reached the U.S. Court of Appeals for the Fifth Circuit. Portions of the opinion in which the court discusses the TSCA "substantial evidence" standard and its requirement that the agency adopt the "least burdensome alternative" appear in the following case.

Corrosion Proof Fittings v. EPA
947 F.2d 1201 (5th Cir. 1991)

JERRY E. SMITH, Circuit Judge:

The Environmental Protection Agency (EPA) issued a final rule under section 6 of the Toxic Substances Control Act (TSCA) to prohibit the future manufacture, importation, processing, and distribution of asbestos in almost all products. Petitioners claim that the EPA's rulemaking procedure was flawed and that the rule was not promulgated on the basis of substantial evidence.... Because the EPA failed to muster substantial evidence to support its rule, we remand this matter to the EPA for further consideration in light of this opinion.

I. Facts and Procedural History

Asbestos is a naturally occurring fibrous material that resists fire and most solvents. Its major uses include heat-resistant insulators, cements, building materials, fireproof gloves and clothing, and motor vehicle brake linings. Asbestos is a toxic material, and occupational exposure to asbestos dust can result in mesothelioma, asbestosis, and lung cancer.

The EPA began these proceedings in 1979, when it issued an Advanced Notice of Proposed Rulemaking announcing its intent to explore the use of TSCA "to reduce the risk to human health posed by exposure to asbestos." ...

An EPA-appointed panel reviewed over one hundred studies of asbestos and conducted several public meetings. Based upon its studies and the public comments, the EPA concluded that asbestos is a potential carcinogen at all levels of exposure, regardless of the type of asbestos or the size of the fiber. The EPA concluded in 1986 that exposure to asbestos "poses an unreasonable risk to human health" and thus proposed at least four regulatory options for prohibiting or restricting the use of asbestos....

Over the next two years, the EPA updated its data, received further comments, and allowed cross-examination on the updated documents. In 1989, the EPA issued a final rule prohibiting the manufacture, importation, processing, and distribution in commerce of most asbestos-containing products. Finding that asbestos constituted an unreasonable risk to health and the environment, the EPA promulgated a staged ban of most commercial uses of asbestos. The EPA estimates that this rule will save either 202 or 148 lives, depending upon whether the benefits are discounted, at a cost of approximately $450-800 million, depending upon the price of substitutes. ...

* * *

IV. The Language of TSCA

A. Standard of Review

Our inquiry into the legitimacy of the EPA rulemaking begins with a discussion of the standard of review governing this case. EPA's phase-out ban of most

(Continued)

commercial uses of asbestos is a TSCA § 6(a) rulemaking. TSCA provides that a reviewing court "shall hold unlawful and set aside" a final rule promulgated under § 6(a) "if the court finds that the rule is not supported by substantial evidence in the rulemaking record ... taken as a whole." ...

Substantial evidence requires "something less than the weight of the evidence, and the possibility of drawing two inconsistent conclusions from the evidence does not prevent an administrative agency's finding from being supported by substantial evidence." ... This standard requires (1) that the agency's decision be based upon the entire record, ... taking into account whatever in the record detracts from the weight of the agency's decision; and (2) that the agency's decision be what "a reasonable mind might accept as adequate to support [its] conclusion." ... Thus, even if there is enough evidence in the record to support the petitioners' assertions, we will not reverse if there is substantial evidence to support the agency's decision....

Contrary to the EPA's assertions, the arbitrary and capricious standard found in the APA and the substantial evidence standard found in TSCA are different standards, even in the context of an informal rulemaking. ... Congress specifically went out of its way to provide that "the standard of review prescribed by paragraph (2)(E) of section 7806 [of the APA] shall not apply and the court shall hold unlawful and set aside such rule if the court finds that the rule is not supported by substantial evidence in the rulemaking record ... taken as a whole." ... "The substantial evidence standard mandated by [TSCA] is generally considered to be more rigorous than the arbitrary and capricious standard normally applied to informal rulemaking," ... and "afford[s] a considerably more generous judicial review" than the arbitrary and capricious test.... The test "imposes a considerable burden on the agency and limits its discretion in arriving at a factual predicate." ...

* * *

The recent case of *Chemical Mfrs. Ass'n v. EPA*, 899 F.2d 344 (5th Cir. 1990), provides our basic framework for reviewing the EPA's actions. In evaluating whether the EPA has presented substantial evidence, we examine (1) whether the quantities of the regulated chemical entering into the environment are "substantial" and (2) whether human exposure to the chemical is "substantial" or "significant." ... An agency may exercise its judgment without strictly relying upon quantifiable risks, costs, and benefits, but it must "cogently explain why it has exercised its discretion in a given manner"

and "must offer a 'rational connection between the facts found and the choice made.'" ...

We note that in undertaking our review, we give all agency rules a presumption of validity, and it is up to the challenger to any rule to show that the agency action is invalid.... The burden remains on the EPA, however, to justify that the products it bans present an unreasonable risk, no matter how regulated.... Finally, as we discuss in detail *infra*, because TSCA instructs the EPA to undertake the least burdensome regulation sufficient to regulate the substance at issue, the agency bears a heavier burden when it seeks a partial or total ban of a substance than when it merely seeks to regulate that product....

B. The EPA's Burden Under TSCA

TSCA provides, in pertinent part, as follows:

(a) Scope of regulation—If the Administrator finds that there is a *reasonable basis* to conclude that the manufacture, processing, distribution in commerce, use, or disposal of a chemical substance or mixture, or that any combination of such activities, presents or will present an *unreasonable risk* of injury to health or the environment, the Administrator shall by rule apply one or more of the following requirements to such substance or mixture to the extent necessary *to protect adequately* against such risk using the *least burdensome requirements* [emphasis added by the court].

... As the highlighted language shows, Congress did not enact TSCA as a zero-risk statute.... The EPA, rather, was required to consider both alternatives to a ban and the costs of any proposed actions and to "carry out this chapter in a reasonable and prudent manner [after considering] the environmental, economic, and social impact of any action." ...

We conclude that the EPA has presented insufficient evidence to justify its asbestos ban. We base this conclusion upon two grounds: the failure of the EPA to consider all necessary evidence and its failure to give adequate weight to statutory language requiring it to promulgate the least burdensome, reasonable regulation required to protect the environment adequately. Because the EPA failed to address these concerns, and because the EPA is required to articulate a "reasoned basis" for its rules, we are compelled to return the regulation to the agency for reconsideration.

1. Least Burdensome and Reasonable.

TSCA requires that the EPA use the least burdensome regulation to achieve its goal of minimum reasonable risk. This statutory requirement can create problems

(Continued)

in evaluating just what is a "reasonable risk." Congress's rejection of a no-risk policy, however, also means that in certain cases, the least burdensome yet still adequate solution may entail somewhat more risk than would other, known regulations that are far more burdensome on the industry and the economy. The very language of TSCA requires that the EPA, once it has determined what an acceptable level of non-zero risk is, choose the least burdensome method of reaching that level.

In this case, the EPA banned, for all practical purposes, all present and future uses of asbestos—a position the petitioners characterize as the "death penalty alternative," as this is the *most* burdensome of all possible alternatives listed as open to the EPA under TSCA. ...

By choosing the harshest remedy given to it under TSCA, the EPA assigned to itself the toughest burden in satisfying TSCA's requirement that its alternative be the least burdensome of all those offered to it. Since, both by definition and by the terms of TSCA, the complete ban of manufacturing is the most burdensome alternative—for even stringent regulation at least allows a manufacturer the chance to invest and meet the new, higher standard—the EPA's regulation cannot stand if there is any other regulation that would achieve an acceptable level of risk as mandated by TSCA.

* * *

... While the EPA may have shown that a world with a complete ban of asbestos might be preferable to one in which there is only the current amount of regulation, the EPA has failed to show that there is not some intermediate state of regulation that would be superior to both the currently-regulated and the completely-banned world. Without showing that asbestos regulation would be ineffective, the EPA cannot discharge its TSCA burden of showing that its regulation is the least burdensome available to it.

[The court remanded the case to the EPA for further consideration in light of this opinion.]

Questions and Comments for Discussion

1. The court discussed the petitioners' procedural challenge to the EPA's rulemaking in this case. The petitioners argued, among other things, that the EPA's rulemaking procedure was flawed because it did not cross-examine the petitioners' witnesses, it did not assemble a panel of experts on asbestos disease risks, it designated a hearing officer rather than an administrative law judge to preside at the hearing, and it did not swear in witnesses who testified. Although the court did not agree with all of these procedural challenges, it did find that the EPA's failure to give notice to the public, before the conclusion of the hearings, that it intended to use "analogous exposure" data to calculate the expected benefits of certain product bans, was an abuse of discretion by the agency. According to the court, "failure to seek public comment on such an important part of the EPA's analysis deprived its rule of the substantial evidence required to survive judicial scrutiny."[4] This case also illustrates the procedural hurdles facing the EPA in a TSCA § 6 rulemaking case, and it may explain why the EPA has initiated few § 6 cases. How might the EPA have proceeded to avoid this criticism? Is your recommendation realistic? Why or why not?

2. After the court denied the EPA's petition for rehearing in this case, the Justice Department chose not to appeal the decision to the Supreme Court. In 1991, the EPA announced that it would follow OSHA in promulgating any new regulations regarding inspection of commercial buildings for friable (airborne) asbestos. Why do you suppose the agency reached this decision?

The Asbestos Hazard Emergency Response Act

The EPA regulates asbestos under several federal environmental statutes, including the CAA, the CWA, TSCA (reporting requirements), and CERCLA. In 1986, Congress amended TSCA by adding a new Title III, the Asbestos Hazard Emergency Response Act of 1986 (AHERA). This law requires the EPA to establish regulations for inspecting, managing, planning, and undertaking operations and maintenance activities for controlling asbestos-containing materials in schools.

---

[4] 947 F.2d at 1212.

Regulating PCBs

PCB regulations are specifically mandated by TSCA, which establishes a legal presumption that PCBs pose an unreasonable risk. Manufacturing, processing, or distributing PCBs in commerce in the United States is prohibited by law unless they are totally enclosed or packaged in an otherwise specifically authorized manner. The law mandates standardized PCB warning labels and limits PCB disposal methods. EPA regulations include those governing the reporting and cleanup of spills containing PCBs and those establishing a nationwide PCB manifesting system.

Radon and Lead-Based Paint

TSCA directs the EPA to develop model construction standards and techniques for controlling radon levels within new buildings. *Radon* is an odorless, colorless gas that has been associated with an increased risk of human lung cancer. TSCA also establishes a radon information clearinghouse and provides for training and grants to states to assist in the development of state radon programs.

In 1992, the Lead-Based Paint Exposure Reduction Act was signed into law. It requires the EPA and OSHA to develop lead paint abatement training and certification programs for contractors, and to identify lead-based paint hazards and safe levels of lead in various media.

Biotechnology

The EPA has also asserted authority under TSCA to regulate microbial products of biotechnology, as it considers intergenetic microorganisms to be new chemicals.

Reducing Risks in Schools

In 2007, TSCA was amended to include the Energy Independence and Security Act of 2007. This amendment is primarily concerned with state school environmental health. It expressly recognizes children's higher vulnerability to pollution and hazardous substances.

Importers and Exporters

Importers of chemical substances must comply with TSCA certification requirements. The importer is responsible for determining whether a chemical substance is on the TSCA inventory, and a manufacturer of any new chemical substance imported into the United States for commercial purposes must file a PMN unless the substance is imported as "part of an article." Imported wastes are also subject to TSCA because they are chemical substances. Even if accompanied by a hazardous waste manifest under RCRA, imported wastes must meet the certification requirements of TSCA.

Exporters of chemicals may also be subject to notification requirements under TSCA § 12. However, TSCA requirements do not apply to toxic substances distributed for export unless such activities pose an unreasonable risk of harm *within* the United States.

▪ Comparison of FIFRA and TSCA

Unlike many major environmental laws, which regulate the emission of toxicants and pollutants from a production process, TSCA and FIFRA regulate the chemical products themselves. Both FIFRA and TSCA mandate cost-benefit analysis for agency decision making regarding regulation of chemicals and pesticides, and both TSCA and FIFRA provide for review of new chemicals. These laws also give the EPA authority to address hazardous chemicals already in commerce, including authority to ban the manufacture or use of dangerous chemicals.

There are, however, significant differences between FIFRA and TSCA. TSCA, for example, does not impose up-front testing requirements for new chemicals, although the proposal must identify the chemical and its use as well as its alleged safety. After notification to the EPA, manufacture of a new chemical can begin unless the agency takes affirmative action to prevent it. In contrast, FIFRA prohibits introduction of any new chemical pesticide unless the EPA registers it.

Because the approval processes differ, the costs borne by manufacturers under the two programs also differ. Tests for a major new pesticide ingredient may cost substantially more than the costs associated with introducing a new chemical. It is also easier for the EPA to gather information under FIFRA than under TSCA because failure to provide pesticide data may result in loss of registration. Under TSCA, the EPA must issue a rule to gather such data.

In adopting TSCA and FIFRA, Congress incorporated the notion of "unreasonable risk." Thus, Congress made the policy decision to adopt cost-risk criteria for regulation of toxic chemicals under these laws—and this decision raises several important questions: To what extent can the risks associated with toxic chemicals be quantitatively evaluated? How effective is the agency's program for gathering and evaluating information about the chemicals it regulates? Considering the long time periods associated with development of disease from exposure to toxic chemicals, can the long-term environmental effects of new chemicals and pesticides be effectively determined?

Risk assessment may be defined as the process of characterizing the potentially adverse consequences of human exposure to an environmental hazard. **Risk management** is the process by which policy choices are made once those risks have been determined. One of the risks a potentially toxic substance may pose is carcinogenicity (the risk of causing cancer). The following four-step risk assessment process was first described and recommended by a committee of the National Research Council[5]:

1. *Hazard identification:* Information used at this stage includes comparisons of molecular structures, short-term studies, animal bioassay data, and epidemiological studies.

2. *Dose-response assessment:* After a hazardous substance is defined, this step determines the response of humans to various levels of exposure. Dose-response assessment usually requires assessments of animal studies.

3. *Exposure assessment:* This step determines which populations would be exposed to the chemical and the dosages to which they would be exposed.

4. *Risk characterization:* This final step involves estimating the magnitude of the risk to public health. The conclusions drawn by the assessor (that is, the EPA or other agency) are most likely to involve value judgments at this stage.

The courts' willingness to defer to agency decision making in characterizing risk means that if the agency follows an appropriate risk assessment model, the agency's decision has a stronger likelihood of being upheld.

risk assessment: The process of characterizing the potentially adverse consequences of human exposure to an environmental hazard.

risk management: The process by which policy choices are made once risks have been determined.

---

[5] Joseph V. Rodricks, Calculated Risks: Understanding the Toxicity and Human Health Risks of Chemicals in Our Environment (Cambridge, 1992).

FIFRA creates a licensing system for pesticides, under which pesticides must be registered before they can be sold. The registrant has the initial and continuing burden to demonstrate the safety of a pesticide; however, the EPA has the burden in a cancellation proceeding. Approval of a product at the premarket phase of production occurs when little information may be available about long-term effects of the chemical, and when the scheme focuses on new products and risks; however, FIFRA's reregistration system does address retroactive licensing requirements.

TSCA does not permit the EPA to require testing of every chemical. The agency must first find the possibility of a risk of extensive exposure detrimental to humans or the environment, and then require testing because more information is needed. TSCA also requires that the EPA promulgate and support test rules through notice-and-comment rulemaking.

Under TSCA, manufacture and distribution may begin if the EPA does not act to require testing before expiration of the 90-day PMN period. Whereas FIFRA presumes that a pesticide is unsafe unless the manufacturer proves otherwise, TSCA presumes safety unless the EPA can prove that a substance is unsafe. Also, TSCA's use of strict rulemaking procedures inhibits the production of health and safety data.

Because of the uncertainties of risk and the enormous economic implications of chemical regulation, the question of how best to regulate existing and new chemicals and pesticides is a policy question of substantial importance to all involved.

■ ■ ■ REVIEW AND STUDY QUESTIONS

1. Should TSCA regulate genetically engineered (or genetically modified) organisms. If so, which ones? If not, why not?
2. What is the distinction between "new chemical" and "existing chemicals"? What does the term "significant new uses" mean?
3. What burdens exist for businesses that must comply with TSCA? Be sure to consider regulatory requirements under TSCA including premanufacture notice, the TSCA inventory, the distinction between "new chemicals" and "existing chemicals," and the term "significant new uses."
4. What is the purpose of TSCA?
5. Specifically, what is regulated by TSCA? What is exempt under TSCA? What is the EPA's authority under TSCA?
6. What is the Premanufacture Notice Program? What is the TSCA inventory?

Chapter 11 Case Study: Environmental Compliance Manager

Imagine that you have been hired as an environmental compliance manager for Big AG, Inc. which is a large corporation. Big AG is a manufacturer of pesticides, agricultural fertilizer, and herbicides. You know that TSCA has been criticized as among the least effective of environmental laws because it requires the EPA to determine risk before requiring testing, and it imposes a cumbersome and difficult procedure for doing so. FIFRA, in contrast, requires the manufacturer to provide data showing that a pesticide is safe before the pesticide can be registered. Write a short memo to your supervisor to discuss these issues from the perspective of an environmental compliance manager. How might Big AG limit its liability exposure? What issues must the company consider before bringing new products to market?

Major Federal Environmental Statutes Part IV: Solid and Hazardous Wastes

Here's a good idea!

There are many vocabulary words in this chapter. Make flashcards for each section. This will help you learn the words, which will make studying the concepts easier.

Learning Objectives

After reading this chapter, you will understand CERCLA, including that statute's provisions on potentially responsible parties and defenses to liability. You will also understand RCRA's cradle-to-grave concept, and its compliance requirements for generators, transporters, and treatment, storage, and disposal facilities. You will understand the interaction of CERCLA and RCRA in the management or prevention of hazardous waste pollution. Specifically, after reading this chapter you should be able to answer the following question:

1. What are the major federal environmental statutes related to solid and hazardous waste substances, and how do they work?

▦ Introduction: Regulating Solid and Hazardous Wastes

Previous chapters examined major federal environmental legislation designed to address the problems of air and water pollution and regulation of toxic substances. This chapter focuses on another important area of federal regulation: laws governing the generation, transportation, and disposal of hazardous waste and mandating the cleanup of inactive hazardous waste sites.

Millions of tons of hazardous waste are produced in the United States each year. According to the EPA, there are 20,000 hazardous wastes generators in the country.[1] Hazardous waste disposal sites and the hazardous materials located in those sites can be difficult to identify. Complicating the problems of identifying disposal sites is the fact that, in many cases, generators of waste have hired independent transporters to dispose of wastes away from the site of generation.

In response to such concerns and the serious risks associated with hazardous waste generation and disposal, in 1976 Congress adopted the Resource Conservation and Recovery Act (RCRA)[2] to amend the Solid Waste Disposal Act of 1965; in 1980, it passed the Comprehensive Environmental Response, Compensation, and Liability Act (CERCLA),[3] known as the "Superfund" law. Since enacting these laws, Congress has passed major amendments to both acts.

RCRA was passed the same year Congress enacted the Toxic Substances Control Act (TSCA). RCRA replaced the language of the Resource Recovery Act and ordered the EPA to create a regulatory program designed to provide "cradle-to-grave" control of hazardous waste. RCRA also required the EPA to set standards for hazardous waste treatment, storage, and disposal facilities.

In 1978, buried chemicals near Love Canal, New York, began to bubble to the surface and seep into homes and yards. This event alarmed the public and mobilized the EPA and Congress. In 1980, the EPA issued the first two portions of hazardous waste rules mandated by RCRA. Also in 1980, Congress adopted CERCLA, which is designed to address the problem of abandoned, inactive hazardous waste sites.

Many CERCLA and RCRA provisions overlap. Generally, CERCLA addresses past activities and RCRA governs current activities. Another important distinction is that RCRA encourages states to develop and operate their own hazardous waste regulatory programs in lieu of EPA implementation and enforcement. For a state to exercise such jurisdiction, it must receive EPA approval, and in many states the state and federal programs are identical. In contrast, CERCLA application and enforcement cannot be delegated to the states, but it does not preempt a state from adopting an equivalent state Superfund law.

■ The Resource Conservation and Recovery Act

RCRA is primarily concerned with active waste sites, whereas CERCLA is designed to address the problem of abandoned hazardous waste sites. As first passed in 1976, RCRA was intended to address recycling and waste disposal issues.

RCRA was significantly amended in 1984 by the Hazardous and Solid Waste Amendments (HSWA). RCRA provisions regulate the generation, transportation, and storage of hazardous waste. HSWA makes it clear that Congress also intended to address the special health risks presented by the problems of hazardous waste. In its amendments to RCRA, Congress made the following policy statement:

> Congress hereby declares it to be the national policy of the United States that, wherever feasible, the generation of hazardous waste is to be reduced or eliminated as expeditiously as possible. Waste that is nevertheless generated should be

---

[1] http://www.epa.gov/osw/basic-hazard.htm
[2] 42 U.S.C. § 6901 *et seq.* (1976).
[3] 42 U.S.C. § 9601 *et seq.* (1980).

treated, stored, or disposed of so as to minimize the present and future threat to the environment.[4]

RCRA contains 10 subtitles. Significant among these are Subtitle C, which establishes a national hazardous waste management program; Subtitle D, which provides for state or regional solid waste plans; and Subtitle I, which regulates underground storage tanks.

RCRA was also amended in 1988 by the Medical Waste Tracking Act, in 1992 by the Federal Facility Compliance Act, and in 1996 by the Land Disposal Program Flexibility Act. These latter provisions are not directly discussed in this section.

Structure of the Act

As originally enacted, RCRA was designed not only to address the problems of hazardous waste, but also to control the disposal of solid wastes and promote the recovery of usable materials and the recycling of wastes. Subtitle C imposes management and recordkeeping requirements on generators and transporters of hazardous wastes as well as on owners and operators of treatment, storage, and disposal facilities. The provisions of Subtitle C are implemented through extensive regulations promulgated by the EPA. RCRA Subtitle C provisions and concerns have often overshadowed other goals of the Act.

Subtitle D addresses nonhazardous solid waste, and it directs most of the responsibility for active municipal solid waste management to state and local governments. Under the 1984 RCRA amendments, the EPA was required to revise its disposal criteria for sanitary (nonhazardous waste) landfills. The EPA's final rule added landfill construction, operation, monitoring, and closure requirements. The requirements for municipal solid waste landfills are still less stringent than those for hazardous waste landfills.

The following outline identifies the Subtitle C RCRA sections and titles more fully discussed in this chapter:

3001: Identification of hazardous waste

3002: Generators of hazardous waste

3003: Transporters of hazardous waste

3004: Standards for TSD (treatment, storage and disposal) facilities

3005: Permit requirements for TSD facilities

3006: Guidelines for state programs

7002: Citizen enforcement provisions

7003: EPA authority to seek injunctive relief

Section 3001: What Is Hazardous Waste?

Under RCRA, *hazardous waste* is a subset of "solid waste." That latter pivotal term is defined by RCRA as any "garbage, refuse, sludge from a waste treatment plant, water supply treatment plant or air pollution control facility and other discarded material, including solid, liquid, semisolid, or contained gaseous materials resulting from industrial, commercial, mining and agriculture activities and from community activities."[5]

---

[4] 42 U.S.C. § 6902(b).

[5] 42 U.S.C. § 6903(27).

Subtitle C covers those solid wastes deemed hazardous. *Hazardous waste* under RCRA is a solid waste, or combination of solid wastes, which because of its quantity, concentration, or physical, chemical, or infectious characteristics may:

- Cause or significantly contribute to an increase in mortality or an increase in serious irreversible, or incapacitating reversible illness
- Pose a substantial present or potential hazard to human health or the environment when improperly treated, stored, transported, or disposed of, or otherwise managed.

Under RCRA, solid waste refers to any discarded material, which includes material that is abandoned, recycled, or inherently waste-like.

EPA Definition of Hazardous Waste   Certain solid wastes are exempted from hazardous waste by EPA regulations. These include household waste and agricultural waste returned to the ground (such as fertilizer); industrial point-source discharges regulated under the CWA; irrigation return flows; and certain nuclear, mining, coal, and oil-drilling wastes.

Unless exempted from the definition of hazardous waste, a solid waste is deemed a hazardous waste under either of two tests: (1) it is listed as hazardous waste by the EPA, or (2) it exhibits one of the following four hazardous waste characteristics:

1. Ignitability (poses a fire hazard during routine management)
2. Corrosivity (has the ability to corrode standard containers or dissolve toxic components of other wastes)
3. Reactivity (has the tendency to explode under normal conditions, to react violently with water, or to generate toxic gasses)
4. Toxicity (exhibits the presence of one or more specified toxic materials)

If a waste is hazardous, those generating, transporting, storing, or disposing of it are subject to RCRA requirements. Generators of waste are responsible for determining if a substance is hazardous, either because it is listed by the EPA or because it exhibits the characteristics set out in the preceding list.

The EPA has published a list of specific chemicals that are defined as toxic wastes. If a generator of waste demonstrates that its waste is fundamentally different from the waste listed, it may obtain an exemption from RCRA regulations. To do so, it must provide test data showing that the specific waste does not meet EPA criteria.

mixture rule: Under RCRA, a mixture (combination) of a listed hazardous waste and solid waste is considered hazardous waste unless exempted.

derived-from rule: Under RCRA, a waste generated by the treatment, storage, or disposal of a hazardous waste is also a hazardous waste unless exempted.

contained-in rule: Under RCRA, soil, groundwater, surface water, and debris contaminated with hazardous waste are considered hazardous waste.

The EPA has adopted other rules broadly defining hazardous waste for purposes of RCRA regulation. Under the **mixture rule**, a mixture of a listed hazardous waste and solid waste is considered a hazardous waste unless it qualifies for an exemption. Under the EPA's **derived-from rule**, a waste that is generated by the treatment, storage, or disposal of a hazardous waste is also a hazardous waste, unless exempted. Finally, under the EPA's **contained-in rule**, soil, groundwater, surface water, and debris contaminated with hazardous waste are also regulated under Subtitle C.

The EPA also regulates recycling activities under RCRA. Regulated activities include (1) recycling in a manner constituting disposal, such as land application; (2) burning for energy recovery; (3) reclamation; and (4) speculative accumulation. In general, hazardous wastes destined for recycling are subject to RCRA regulations and storage facility requirements.

Any person who generates, transports, or owns or operates a treatment, storage, and disposal (TSD) facility, or who produces, markets, or burns hazardous waste-derived fuels, must file a notification form with the EPA, listing the reporting company and its location, and providing EPA identification numbers for the listed and characteristic hazardous wastes it manages.

Requirements Imposed on Generators of Waste

Sections 3002 and 3003 of RCRA govern hazardous waste generators and transporters. EPA regulations issued under authority of those sections establish the duties of generators and transporters of hazardous waste.

A **generator** is defined by EPA regulations as "any person, by site, whose act or process produces hazardous waste identified or listed in Part 261 of this chapter or whose act first causes hazardous waste to become subject to regulation."[6] Under this definition, every plant site must evaluate and comply with generator requirements. A generator of hazardous waste must:

1. Obtain an EPA identification number within 90 days of beginning operation (available from the EPA regional office with jurisdiction over the facility)
2. Obtain a permit for the facility where waste is generated if the waste is held on site for more than 90 days before disposal
3. Use shipping containers specified by the Department of Transportation that meet labeling-for-shipment requirements
4. Prepare a manifest (shipping form) to enable tracking of the waste
5. Assure that the waste reaches the designated disposal facility
6. Periodically submit a summary of hazardous waste activities to the EPA

RCRA hazardous waste generator categories are as follows:

▪ *Large quantity generator*—generates more than 1,000 kilograms/month of hazardous waste, or generates more than 1 kg/month of extremely hazardous waste. This type of generator may store hazardous wastes on site for up to 90 days, or to a maximum quantity of 6,000 kg, without obtaining a RCRA Part B permit as a storage facility.

▪ *Small quantity generator*—generates 100 to 1,000 kg/month of hazardous waste, or generates 1 kg/month or less of extremely hazardous waste. A small quantity generator may store hazardous wastes on site for up to 180 days (270 days if more than 200 miles from a TSDF facility) without obtaining a RCRA Part B permit as a storage facility. Under the 1984 amendments, generators of between 100 and 1,000 kilograms of hazardous waste per month are now covered. These small quantity generators are governed by regulations that parallel existing generator standards but exempt smaller generators from the full manifest provisions. Small generators are permitted to store wastes on site for a longer period of time and are subject to reduced requirements for emergency planning and training of employees. Small generator regulations cover small businesses such as laundries, printers, and garages.

generator: Under RCRA, a person whose act or process produces hazardous waste or whose act first causes hazardous waste to become subject to regulation.

---

[6] 40 C.F.R. § 260.10.

■ *Conditionally exempt small quantity generator*—generates less than 100 kg/month of hazardous waste and no extremely hazardous waste; may store hazardous wastes on site indefinitely, or until 100 kg is accumulated, without obtaining a RCRA Part B permit as a storage facility. When 100 kg has accumulated, the small quantity generator limitations are triggered.

The Hazardous Waste Manifest   The **Uniform Hazardous Waste Manifest** is a control and transport document that accompanies the hazardous waste at all times. The manifest must contain the generator's name, address, and EPA identification number; names and identification numbers of transporters; name and identification number of the facility designated to received the waste; description and identification number of the waste; quantity and number and type of containers; the generator's signature certifying that the waste meets EPA and Department of Transportation regulations; and a certification that the volume of waste has been minimized.

Copies of the manifest are prepared for all parties. The final copy is signed and returned to the generator by the TSD facility and must be kept by the generator for at least three years; however, because of its potential liability under CERCLA (discussed later in this chapter), generators commonly maintain RCRA manifests, and other records, much longer.

A generator that stores waste for more than 90 days is considered to be operating a waste storage facility and must obtain a TSD permit. Small quantity generators may store wastes for longer periods of time, as noted earlier.

Requirements Imposed on Transporters of Waste

Transporters of hazardous waste are governed by the EPA and Department of Transportation (DOT). A *transporter* is any person engaged in the off-site transportation of hazardous waste by air, rail, highway, or water. Transporters include both interstate and intrastate transporters. A generator that moves hazardous waste off site is a transporter for purposes of RCRA.

The EPA has promulgated standards for all transporters of hazardous wastes. These include labeling and packaging requirements, and other standards coordinated with DOT standards issued under the Hazardous Materials Transportation Act (HMTA).[7] These rules require transporters to:

1. Obtain an EPA identification number
2. Use the uniform manifest system (or shipping papers meeting DOT requirements for wastes traveling by rail or in bulk by water)
3. Deliver all wastes as specified on the manifest
4. Keep the manifest copy for three years
5. Comply with DOT requirements for reporting discharges and spills of wastes under the HMTA
6. Clean up any hazardous wastes discharged during transportation (in most cases, the discharge must also be reported to the National Response Center, which is charged with coordinating response to hazardous substance spills)

Uniform Hazardous Waste Manifest: Control and transport document required by RCRA; originates with the generator and accompanies the hazardous waste to the place of disposal.

---

[7] 49 U.S.C. § 1801.

Transporters may hold a hazardous waste for up to 10 days at a transfer facility without obtaining a RCRA storage permit. A transporter may become subject to the RCRA generator requirements if it mixes wastes by placing them in a single container or accumulates waste in a vehicle or vessel.

The Hazardous Materials Transportation Act

The HMTA became law in 1975, and it gives the Department of Transportation the authority to regulate movement of all substances within the United States that may pose a threat to health, safety, property, or the environment. This includes a broad range of substances, including RCRA hazardous wastes. Substances shipped in bulk by water are regulated separately by the U.S. Coast Guard. The HMTA regulates hazardous materials, which are subject to requirements regarding special packaging, labeling, handling, and routing. Shippers are primarily responsible for assuring compliance with the HMTA. The shipper is required to classify the shipment according to DOT requirements, select an authorized package, mark and label the package as required by law, and certify compliance with DOT regulations.

All hazardous material must be classified according to the hazard it presents. Hazards are numbered according to a classification scheme that divides hazardous materials into nine classes. A hazardous material is classified based on such factors as its flash point, boiling point, toxicity, pressure, and corrosivity.

Standards for Treatment, Storage, and Disposal (TSD) Facilities

EPA rules under RCRA governing the treatment, storage, or disposal of hazardous wastes are intended to ensure that wastes are handled safely. These EPA rules include provisions governing emergencies, manifest handling, recordkeeping, waste treatment, storage, monitoring, facility closure, and financial liability of the owner and operator.

The 1984 amendments to RCRA added several important provisions to the TSD management regulations. Among other things, the amendments banned the disposal of various liquid wastes and hazardous wastes in landfills, imposed minimum technological requirements (double liners) for surface impoundments and landfills, and added controls on the marketing and burning of hazardous wastes as fuels. Congress also mandated that the EPA make a number of regulatory decisions and set a strict timetable for EPA implementation of a land disposal ban on untreated hazardous wastes and establishment of treatment standards for such wastes.

Under EPA rule, a facility is a *treatment facility* if the operator utilizes any method, technique, or process designed to change the physical, chemical, or biological character or composition of hazardous waste. Under EPA rules, almost anything done to a hazardous waste qualifies as treatment.

A *storage facility* is one that holds hazardous waste for a temporary period. A *disposal facility* is a place where hazardous waste is intentionally placed (on land or water), and where the waste will remain after closure. Some TSD facilities are exempted by EPA regulation, including facilities disposing of hazardous waste by means of ocean disposal in conformance to a permit issued under the MPRSA; the disposal of hazardous waste by underground injection under permit issued under the Safe Drinking Water Act; publicly owned treatment works' treatment or storage of wastes delivered to the POTW; and TSD facilities regulated under a state program authorized by RCRA.

Under general RCRA requirements, owners and operators of TSD facilities must:

1. Analyze wastes entering the facility to ensure that waste identities are as specified on the manifest
2. Provide security at the site and undertake inspections monitoring safety, security, operating, and structural equipment
3. Train employees in handling emergencies and take special precautions to prevent reactions between incompatible wastes
4. Maintain emergency equipment and inform local police, fire, and emergency response teams about the facility layout and possible hazards
5. Have a written plan for responding to emergencies

The owner or operator of the TSD facility is required to sign, date, and return a copy of the manifest to the transporter and the generator of the waste. It must also keep records of the wastes received at the site and report unmanifested wastes and releases of wastes, fires, explosions, or groundwater contamination. Other TSD requirements include groundwater monitoring requirements when hazardous waste is placed onto or into the land, waste storage and treatment requirements, and financial responsibility arrangements upon closure of the facility.

Land Disposal Restrictions   The HSWA established a strong presumption against land disposal by prohibiting land disposal of hazardous wastes beyond dates specified in the law, unless the EPA determines means for such disposal to protect human health and the environment.

In RCRA, Congress stated that "reliance on land disposal should be minimized or eliminated, and land disposal, particularly landfills and surface impoundments, should be the least favored method for managing hazardous wastes."[8] *Land disposal* under EPA regulations includes any placement of hazardous waste in a landfill, surface impoundment, waste pile, injection well, land treatment facility, salt dome formation, or underground mine or cave. The EPA sets levels or methods of treatment to substantially diminish the toxicity of the waste. Wastes meeting those standards are not prohibited from land disposal.

Permit Requirements for TSD Facilities   Under RCRA, any TSD facility must obtain a permit from the EPA (or the state if the state has taken over operation of the hazardous waste program). A facility that was in existence or under construction in 1980 had to seek an interim status permit. Such facilities needed to obtain a final permit by submitting a second application within six months after EPA request. The EPA must inform the public that a request for a permit application is pending, and must meet requirements for public notice, public comment, and public hearings before granting a permit. Permits are effective for 10 years, but may be reviewed, modified, or revoked by the EPA. Under the 1984 amendments, permits must be reviewed after five years and facilities must be inspected every two years. However, a continuing issue concerns the EPA's ability to enforce these rules and conduct these reviews and inspections.

---

[8] 42 U.S.C. § 6901(b)(7).

State Hazardous Waste Programs

Congress authorized states to develop and carry out their own hazardous waste programs in lieu of RCRA if the program is "equivalent" to and "consistent" with the federal program. States must also provide adequate enforcement of the requirements of Subsection C. Because Congress believed it was important to implement the 1984 amendments quickly, EPA regulations implementing the 1984 amendments took effect in authorized states the same day they were effective for the federal program. Because the EPA implements HSWA provisions until a state takes over authority, joint permitting of a TSD facility (that is, permitting by both the EPA and the state) is often required.

Enforcement Mechanisms and Citizen Suit Provisions

The EPA, the states, and the DOT are all responsible for enforcing RCRA. The EPA may use compliance orders, administrative orders, and consent decrees to force compliance. Section 3007 authorizes the EPA to enter sites for compliance inspection, to collect samples of wastes, and to examine and copy records. Civil penalties, including suspension or revocation of the hazardous waste permit, are possible penalties for violation. In addition, it is a criminal offense to knowingly violate certain provisions of the law. Under § 3008, an individual who knowingly violates RCRA in a way that places another person in imminent danger of death or serious bodily injury is subject to a penalty of $250,000 or 15 years' imprisonment or both. A defendant organization is liable for a $1 million fine in such cases.

The RCRA citizen suit provisions permit a person to bring civil action against a violator, or against the EPA administrator for failing to perform a nondiscretionary duty. The 1984 amendments expanded the citizen suit provisions to authorize suits where past or present management or disposal of hazardous wastes has contributed to a situation presenting "imminent or substantial endangerment." A potential plaintiff must give notice to the violator, the EPA administrator, and the state in which the alleged violation occurred 60 days prior to bringing a citizen suit action.

The question of whether RCRA's citizen suit provision gives the federal courts authority to award money judgments for costs incurred in cleaning up contaminated sites has been frequently litigated. That section, 42 U.S.C. § 6972, authorizes a private cause of action

> against any person ... who has contributed or who is contributing to the past or present handling, storage, treatment, transportation, or disposal of any solid or hazardous waste which may present an imminent and substantial endangerment to health or the environment....[9]

The U.S. Supreme Court addressed this issue in *Meghrig v. KFC Western*.[10] KFC Western, after complying with a county order to clean up contamination on its property, brought an action under the citizen suit provision of RCRA, attempting to recover its cleanup costs from the Meghrigs, prior owners of the property.

The district court had held that RCRA's citizen suit provision did not authorize such damages, and the court of appeals had reversed. The Supreme Court

---

[9] 42 U.S.C. § 6972(a)(1)(B).
[10] 516 U.S. 479, 116 S. Ct. 1251 (1996).

unanimously held that RCRA's provision does not permit recovery of past cleanup costs, nor does it authorize a cause of action for the remediation of toxic waste that does not pose an "imminent and substantial endangerment" at the time the suit is filed. The court relied on its plain reading of the remedial scheme under RCRA, and the fact that provisions of CERCLA demonstrate that "Congress … demonstrated in CERCLA that it knew how to provide for the recovery of cleanup costs, and … the language used to define the remedies under RCRA does not provide that remedy."[11]

Consider the following case, in which the fines imposed against Southern Union Company for unlawfully storing mercury in contravention of RCRA requirements resulted in a large criminal fine. Here, the U.S. Supreme Court reminds us of the importance of constitutional protections.

Southern Union Co. v. United States
567 U.S. _____ (2012)

JUSTICE SOTOMAYOR delivered the opinion of the Court

The Sixth Amendment reserves to juries the determination of any fact, other than the fact of a prior conviction, that increases a criminal defendant's maximum potential sentence. *Apprendi v. New Jersey*, 530 U.S. 466 (2000); *Blakely v. Washington*, 542 U.S. 296 (2004). We have applied this principle in numerous cases where the sentence was imprisonment or death. The question here is whether the same rule applies to sentences of criminal fines. We hold that it does.

I

Petitioner Southern Union Company is a natural gas distributor. Its subsidiary stored liquid mercury, a hazardous substance, at a facility in Pawtucket, Rhode Island. In September 2004, youths from a nearby apartment complex broke into the facility, played with the mercury, and spread it around the facility and complex. The complex's residents were temporarily displaced during the cleanup and most underwent testing for mercury poisoning.

In 2007, a grand jury indicted Southern Union on multiple counts of violating federal environmental statutes. As relevant here, the first count alleged that the company knowingly stored liquid mercury without a permit at the Pawtucket facility "[f]rom on or about September 19, 2002 until on or about October 19, 2004," … in violation of the Resource Conservation

and Recovery Act of 1976 (RCRA).… A jury convicted Southern Union on this count following a trial in the District Court for the District of Rhode Island. The verdict form stated that Southern Union was guilty of unlawfully storing liquid mercury "on or about September 19, 2002 to October 19, 2004." …

Violations of the RCRA are punishable by, *inter alia*, "a fine of not more than $50,000 for each day of violation." §6928(d). At sentencing, the probation office set a maximum fine of $38.1 million, on the basis that Southern Union violated the RCRA for each of the 762 days from September 19, 2002, through October 19, 2004. Southern Union objected that this calculation violated *Apprendi* because the jury was not asked to determine the precise duration of the violation. The company noted that the verdict form listed only the violation's approximate start date (*i.e.*, "on or about"), and argued that the court's instructions permitted conviction if the jury found even a 1-day violation. Therefore, Southern Union maintained, the only violation the jury necessarily found was for one day, and imposing any fine greater than the single-day penalty of $50,000 would require factfinding by the court, in contravention of *Apprendi*.

The Government acknowledged the jury was not asked to specify the duration of the violation, but argued that *Apprendi* does not apply to criminal fines. The District Court disagreed and held that *Apprendi* applies. But the court concluded from the "content and context of the verdict all together" that the jury

(Continued)

---

[11] *Id.* at 485.

found a 762-day violation.... The court therefore set a maximum potential fine of $38.1 million, from which it imposed a fine of $6 million and a "community service obligatio[n]" of $12 million....

On appeal, the United States Court of Appeals for the First Circuit rejected the District Court's conclusion that the jury necessarily found a violation of 762 days.... But the Court of Appeals affirmed the sentence because it also held, again in contrast to the District Court, that *Apprendi* does not apply to criminal fines.... We granted certiorari to resolve the conflict ... and now reverse.

II

A

This case requires us to consider the scope of the Sixth Amendment right of jury trial, as construed in *Apprendi*. Under *Apprendi*, "[o]ther than the fact of a prior conviction, any fact that increases the penalty for a crime beyond the prescribed statutory maximum must be submitted to a jury, and proved beyond a reasonable doubt." ... The "'statutory maximum' for *Apprendi* purposes is the maximum sentence a judge may impose solely on the basis of the facts reflected in the jury verdict or admitted by the defendant." ... Thus, while judges may exercise discretion in sentencing, they may not "inflic[t] punishment that the jury's verdict alone does not allow." ...

Apprendi's rule is "rooted in longstanding common-law practice." ... It preserves the "historic jury function" of "determining whether the prosecution has proved each element of an offense beyond a reasonable doubt." ... We have repeatedly affirmed this rule by applying it to a variety of sentencing schemes that allowed judges to find facts that increased a defendant's maximum authorized sentence....

While the punishments at stake in those cases were imprisonment or a death sentence, we see no principled basis under *Apprendi* for treating criminal fines differently. *Apprendi's* "core concern" is to reserve to the jury "the determination of facts that warrant punishment for a specific statutory offense." ... That concern applies whether the sentence is a criminal fine or imprisonment or death. Criminal fines, like these other forms of punishment, are penalties inflicted by the sovereign for the commission of offenses....

* * *

This case is exemplary. The RCRA subjects Southern Union to a maximum fine of $50,000 for each day of violation.... The Government does not deny that, in light of the seriousness of that punishment, the company was properly accorded a jury trial. And the Government now concedes the District Court made factual findings that increased both the "potential and actual" fine the court imposed.... This is exactly what *Apprendi* guards against: judicial factfinding that enlarges the maximum punishment a defendant faces beyond what the jury's verdict or the defendant's admissions allow.

* * *

We hold that the rule of *Apprendi* applies to the imposition of criminal fines....

Questions and Comments for Discussion

1. How were precedents used in *Southern Union v. United States*?
2. How will the Court's decision in *Southern Union* affect future RCRA enforcement actions?
3. Why are corporations able to enjoy constitutional rights, such as the right to a jury trial?

Restraining Imminent or Substantial Endangerment to Health or the Environment

Under RCRA, the EPA is authorized to bring a suit to restrain an "imminent or substantial endangerment to health or the environment."[12]

Underground Storage Tanks   Underground storage tanks (USTs) are a major source of groundwater and soil contamination because such tanks frequently corrode or fail for structural reasons. As a result of concerns about these problems, Congress enacted Subtitle I in the 1984 amendments to RCRA to regulate underground storage tanks containing petroleum or other regulated substances.

---

[12] 42 U.S.C. § 6973(a).

The UST program affects tanks containing regulated substances. Certain residential tanks, septic tanks, and tanks regulated under other provisions of RCRA are exempted from this program. Nonexempted underground storage tanks must meet certain technical performance standards. In addition, the UST program contains notice requirements to assist the EPA in identifying existing tanks. These provisions also include requirements that manufacturers and distributors inform owners about their RCRA obligations. Failure to notify the EPA about a tank (including those out of service since 1974) may result in substantial fines.

The RCRA program also requires that releases from USTs be reported and cleaned up, and it sets financial responsibility requirements for persons who own and operate petroleum USTs. A new UST program was included in the Superfund Amendments and Reauthorization Act of 1986, requiring states to make an inventory of underground storage tanks and requiring the EPA to establish financial responsibility regulations for owners of USTs.

▪ ▪ ▪ REVIEW AND STUDY QUESTIONS

1. What is meant by RCRA's commitment to "cradle-to-grave" management of hazardous waste?

2. Do you think that RCRA is adequate for controlling hazardous wastes from "cradle to grave"? Why or why not? How might the law be improved?

3. What is hazardous waste? What is not considered hazardous waste?

4. Why are definitions of key terms important in understanding the requirements of statutes? Provide an example of how a definition might affect whether or not RCRA applies to an activity.

5. What is necessary for the disposal of hazardous waste under RCRA?

6. What requirements does RCRA impose on generators, transporters, and TSD facilities?

7. How do your state and local governments regulate solid waste (not hazardous waste)? What issues are important in the regulation of non-hazardous solid waste? Do your state and local governments address those issues sufficiently? Explain.

▪ The Comprehensive Environmental Response, Compensation, and Liability Act

In 1978, public attention suddenly focused on the serious risks posed by abandoned hazardous waste sites following the discovery of massive chemical contamination at Love Canal near Niagara Falls, New York. The CERCLA Act of 1980, also known as "Superfund," was enacted in direct response to those concerns, because many felt that existing laws did not adequately address the need to identify and clean up abandoned hazardous waste sites. CERCLA created a broad framework under which multiple parties, including past and present owners, operators, transporters, and generators, can be held jointly, severally, and strictly liable for the costs of cleaning up a contaminated site.

■ *ACTIVITY BOX   Superfund Test Your Knowledge Quiz*

Find the Superfund quiz at the EPA's website (http://www.epa.gov/superfund/students /testknow/index.htm). There are four multiple-choice quiz questions. Answers are available by clicking on "Superfund Quiz Answers."

Overview

CERCLA has four basic elements:

1. It established an information-gathering and analysis system that enables federal and state governments to develop priorities for response actions at hazardous waste sites
2. It established federal authority to respond to hazardous substance emergencies through removal and remedial actions
3. It created a Hazardous Substances Trust Fund (the *Superfund*) to pay for the costs of cleanup actions
4. It imposed liability on persons responsible for releases of hazardous substances

CERCLA requires the EPA to develop criteria for determining priorities among hazardous waste sites. Using a rating system, the EPA ranks each site with respect to priority for cleanup. The **National Priorities List (NPL)**, which is updated annually, is the EPA's record of abandoned or uncontrolled hazardous waste sites. The EPA's decision to place a site on the list is subject to notice and public comment. The sites on this list are among the most contaminated and present the greatest risks.

The **National Contingency Plan (NCP)** is a document guiding CERCLA response actions. The NCP establishes procedures that the EPA and private parties must follow in conducting cleanup response actions. The NCP was first prepared to govern responses to oil spills, but after the enactment of the Clean Water Act, it was expanded under CERCLA to emphasize procedures for responding to releases of hazardous substances.

CERCLA authorizes the federal government to pay for cleanup if the parties liable by the statute cannot be found or cannot pay. As discussed later in this section, those parties are known as *potentially responsible parties*. The requirement for a potentially responsible party to pay, if that party can be found and can pay, is an example of the "polluter pays" principle.

In 1986, Congress extensively amended CERCLA by adopting the Superfund Amendments and Reauthorization Act (SARA). SARA clarified some provisions of the original act, added new provisions such as the Emergency Planning and Community Right to Know Act (EPCRA), and increased the Superfund amount. In 1990, Congress reauthorized Superfund. The authority to collect taxes from industry to fund Superfund expired in 1995. Because the revenue from those funds was exhausted by 2003, congressional appropriation from the General Fund of the U.S. Treasury has become the primary source of funding for the Superfund Trust Fund. In 2002, Congress has also amended CERCLA by carving brownfields off from the "regular" CERCLA treatment of severely contaminated sites.

The 2002 Small Business Liability Relief and Brownfields Revitalization Act provides funding specifically for the cleanup of abandoned brownfield sites, to encourage their redevelopment. Although the EPA originally provided monies for

National Priorities List (NPL): Under CERCLA, list in which the EPA ranks each hazardous waste site with respect to priority for cleanup.

National Contingency Plan (NCP): Under CERCLA, the scheme that establishes procedures for cleanup response actions.

brownfields cleanup under Superfund authority, this amendment has provided clear authority for EPA to act on these sites even if they are not listed on the National Priorities List.

■ *ACTIVITY BOX*   *Superfund Redevelopment Videos*

Choose one video to view at the EPA's website (http://www.epa.gov/superfund/programs /recycle/info/video.html). After viewing a video, explain the benefits of using a remediated Superfund site for public purposes. What are the risks? Do you believe that such sites are safe to use? Why or why not?

CERCLA liability is broad, applying to prior and current owners, generators, and transporters of hazardous waste alike. Because of the expansive reach of liability, attachment of liability to some "responsible parties" over the years and in specific cases has seemed unfair. Because of this, Congress limited liability for certain parties. For example, certain fiduciaries and lenders have been shielded from liability under the 1996 Asset Conservation, Lender Liability, and Deposit Insurance Protection Act. Similarly, in 1999, certain generators and transporters (those handling recyclable scrap materials) were exempted providing they met certain conditions established by the Superfund Recycling Equity Act. In 2002, the Small Business Liability Relief and Brownfields Revitalization Act limited liability for contributors of minor amounts of waste, owners of property to which hazardous waste had migrated from a contiguous neighboring property, and other bona fide purchasers. The 2002 amendment also provided clarification regarding the innocent landowner defense.

Hazardous substances are broadly defined under CERCLA by incorporating definitions used in other environmental statutes. The term *hazardous waste* as used in CERCLA includes hazardous wastes under RCRA, hazardous substances and toxic pollutants under the CWA, hazardous air pollutants under the Clean Air Act, imminently hazardous substances and mixtures under the TSCA, and any additional substance the EPA designates as hazardous under CERCLA. Petroleum, including crude oil, is expressly excluded from the definition of hazardous waste under CERCLA, although petroleum contamination is addressed under RCRA. Petroleum releases are also addressed by other statutes, such as the Oil Pollution Act of 1990. Other substances, such as certain nuclear materials, are also excluded.

The vast majority of CERCLA actions involve hazardous substances, although CERCLA permits EPA response to a release or threat of release of "any pollutant or contaminant." However, only sites contaminated with hazardous substances are subject to actions for recovery of cleanup costs from private parties.

Liability under CERCLA attaches in the event of a release or substantial threat of release of a hazardous substance from a facility or vessel. The definition of *release* is very broad: "any spilling, leaking, pumping, pouring, emitting, emptying, discharging, injecting, escaping, leaching, dumping, or disposing into the environment"[13] of any quantity of hazardous waste constitutes a release under the act. The courts have also interpreted "substantial threat of a release" very broadly.

Likewise, the term *facility* is broadly defined. A facility is "any site or area where a hazardous substance has … come to be located,"[14] and includes buildings,

---

[13] 42 U.S.C. § 9601(22).
[14] 42 U.S.C. § 9601(9)(B).

structures, installations, equipment, pipes, and wells. Under this expansive definition, almost any site meets the test for being a facility.

Generally, federal lands are also required to be cleaned up under CERCLA, but federal funds do not draw upon the Superfund Trust Fund for payment of the cleanup.

CERCLA Response Actions

CERCLA authorizes the EPA to undertake two categories of response actions: removal actions or remedial actions. The statute does not specify the degree to which a site must be cleaned up; this is determined on a case-by-case basis. **Removal actions** are those that address emergency situations to promptly diminish the threat posed by a hazardous waste site. **Remedial actions** are long-term, permanent cleanups. Some take years or even decades to complete, and are significantly more complex and costly than removal actions. Because the costs of permanent cleanup are so substantial, an important issue for potentially liable parties is the process by which the EPA selects the appropriate remedial action and remedies chosen. Fewer administrative requirements are imposed on an EPA removal action than on a remedial action. For example, the courts have held that a site must be listed on the NPL before federally funded remedial action is taken.

In undertaking a cleanup, the EPA has two options. It may clean up the site itself and then seek to recover its costs from potentially responsible parties, or it can compel those parties to perform the cleanup. Before authorizing expenditure from the Superfund, the EPA usually tries to force the responsible party to clean up the site, or to get the state or local government to take responsibility for the cleanup. About 90% of all cleanup actions are performed by the responsible parties.

The EPA responds to releases on land, but the U.S. Coast Guard responds to releases in water where it has jurisdiction to do so. Federal agencies respond to their own federal facilities where releases occur, though the EPA and state governments where such facilities are located provide oversight. Additionally, citizen suits are permitted under CERCLA to challenge the adequacy of a cleanup action, providing that the action at the site has (allegedly) been completed.

Liability of Potentially Responsible Parties under CERCLA Much of the litigation under CERCLA concerns the parties who may be responsible for the costs of cleanup. Potentially responsible parties (PRPs) under CERCLA § 107(a) include:

- Owners and operators of a vessel or facility
- Any person who at the time of disposal of any hazardous substance owned or operated any facility at which such substances were disposed
- Any person who arranged for the disposal or treatment of a hazardous substance and any person who arranged for transportation of a hazardous substance for disposal
- Any person who accepts or has accepted any hazardous substance for transport to a disposal or treatment facility or other site

Person is defined in § 107(a) as any "individual, firm, corporation, association, partnership, consortium, joint venture, commercial entity, United States Government, state, municipality, commission, political subdivision of a state, or interstate body."

removal action: Short-term emergency responses under CERCLA.

remedial action: Long-term permanent cleanup responses under CERCLA.

The definition of *potentially responsible party* under CERCLA is very broad and inclusive, as the intent is to expand the pool of parties who may be liable for cleanup costs. In addition, the courts have held that CERCLA incorporates the strict liability standard utilized in the CWA. Under principles of **strict liability**, a party's claims that it was not negligent or that its actions met standard industry practices at the time of disposal are not a valid defense to liability. In most cases involving a site with multiple PRPs, liability is **joint and several**, which means that one party may be liable for the entire costs of cleanup in a case where it is difficult to apportion liability (as in the case of commingling of hazardous substances at a site). However, an individual who pays for the entire cleanup may bring an action for contribution against other responsible persons under the act.

Additionally, CERCLA is retroactive, which means that it reaches PRPs dating back to the generation, transportation, and/or disposal of the hazardous materials. As a result, owners and operators who were responsible for the release of hazardous substances long before CERCLA was passed may incur the same liability as present owners or operators of a site.

■ ACTIVITY BOX   Superfund Sites Near You

Visit http://scorecard.goodguide.com/ and "Superfund Sites Where You Live," at the EPA website (http://www.epa.gov/superfund/sites/index.htm). These web pages contain information about the locations of different Superfund sites. How many Superfund sites exist in your county?

Defenses to CERCLA Liability   Defenses are available in a CERCLA liability situation where a release was caused solely by:

1. An act of God
2. An act of war
3. An act or omission of a third party (other than an employee, agent, or party with whom there is a contractual relationship), as long as the defendant exercised due care and took precautions against foreseeable acts of the third party

Most litigation focuses on the third-party defense. If the defendant contributed to the release, the defense is unavailable because it was not "solely" caused by a third party. In many instances, the contractual-relationship exception limits the defense because the third party has a direct or indirect contractual relationship with the defendant through a lease, employment contract, hauling contract, or real estate contract.

In the 1986 SARA amendments, Congress expanded the third-party defense by creating the **innocent landowner defense**. Under this provision, a landowner who acquires contaminated property from a third party is not liable under CERCLA if the landowner acquired the property without knowledge of the contamination. For the defense to be available, the landowner must show that it undertook "all appropriate inquiries ... into the previous ownership and uses of the property consistent with good commercial or customary practice"[15] before acquiring the property. The property owner must also take "reasonable steps" to prevent contamination after

strict liability: Liability without proof of negligence.

joint and several liability: All defendants are liable for the entire amount of damages imposed by the court.

innocent landowner defense: Under CERCLA, rule that a landowner who acquired property after contamination is not liable if he or she had no knowledge of the contamination and no reason to know of the contamination.

---

[15] 42 U.S.C. § 9601(35)(b)(i).

acquiring the property. This defense has stimulated the development of an entire industry of environmental consulting firms, as purchasers conduct the due diligence investigations necessary to undergird this defense.

As noted earlier, amendments to CERCLA have limited liability for certain parties, including fiduciaries and lenders, generators and transporters of recyclable scrap materials (providing certain conditions are met), contributors of minor amounts of waste, owners of property onto which hazardous waste has migrated from a contiguous neighboring property, and other bona fide purchasers.

The question of liability under CERCLA is a critical one for lenders. Because the cleanup costs for contaminated property are often substantially greater than the market value of the property, commercial lenders are extremely wary of taking a security interest in property that may be contaminated. In 1997, Congress clarified the exemption in response to lenders' concerns. The "security interest" exemption (or defense) is now available to a person who does not participate in management of the facility or vessel, and holds ownership primarily to protect a security interest.

It is important to note that an owner who transfers contaminated property to another without disclosing its knowledge of on-site waste disposal discovered during its ownership loses the potential to claim any of these defenses. Although this provision was clearly designed to protect subsequent purchasers, it may actually have a negative impact on the discovery and cleanup of hazardous waste sites: Current owners may be wary of conducting environmental audits on their property because they would be required to disclose any information discovered during the audit to a subsequent purchaser, and anything revealed by the audit is imputed to the current owner as actual knowledge.

Recoverable Response Costs **Response costs** that may be recovered under CERCLA, include any costs associated with a response action, such as sampling and monitoring costs, costs associated with identifying and disposing of hazardous substances, and attorneys' and consultants' fees. Damage claims may also be made for "other necessary costs of response" incurred by any other person and "damages for injury to, destruction of, or loss of natural resources, including the reasonable costs of assessing such injury, destruction, or loss."[16]

SARA expanded the list of recoverable costs to include all expenses associated with Superfund cleanup activities, including the costs of health assessments and health effects. However, damages to compensate individuals for personal injury or property damage are not recoverable under CERCLA. Individual plaintiffs rely on common law remedies such as nuisance, trespass, negligence, and strict liability to recover such damages.

Most CERCLA cases are settled without trial. Settlement gives PRPs greater control over the selection and implementation of remedial actions and minimizes the costs of litigation. To encourage settlement, the SARA amendments added settlement procedures, which the EPA follows in negotiating settlement of a CERCLA response action. Settlements are ordinarily formalized in a consent decree (filed and signed by a federal court in a case involving judicial action) or consent orders (by administrative order). The U.S. Department of Justice must approve any settlement and consent order if the total response cost exceeds $500,000. The law also encourages early settlement with de minimis parties (those who have disposed of

response costs: Costs of cleanup that may be recovered under CERCLA.

---

[16] 42 U.S.C. § 9607(a)(4)(C).

relatively small quantities of hazardous substances at a site). In return for settlement payment, the EPA generally provides such parties with a covenant not to sue, which relieves those parties from the obligation to pay for future remediation at the site.

CERCLA provides two different causes of action by which a party may recover some or all of the response costs incurred: a cost recovery action and a contribution action. However, a contribution action may not be brought by a party who has never been sued for cleanup by the EPA. Review the following case for more on this.

Cooper Industries, Inc. v. Aviall Services, Inc.
543 U.S. 157 (2004)

JUSTICE THOMAS delivered the opinion of the Court

Section 113(f)(1) of the Comprehensive Environmental Response, Compensation, and Liability Act of 1980 (CERCLA) ... allows persons who have undertaken efforts to clean up properties contaminated by hazardous substances to seek contribution from other parties liable under CERCLA. Section 113(f)(1) specifies that a party may obtain contribution "during or following any civil action" under CERCLA §106 or §107(a). The issue we must decide is whether a private party who has not been sued under §106 or §107(a) may nevertheless obtain contribution under §113(f)(1) from other liable parties. We hold that it may not.

* * *

This case concerns four contaminated aircraft engine maintenance sites in Texas. Cooper Industries, Inc., owned and operated those sites until 1981, when it sold them to Aviall Services, Inc. Aviall operated the four sites for a number of years. Ultimately, Aviall discovered that both it and Cooper had contaminated the facilities when petroleum and other hazardous substances leaked into the ground and ground water through underground storage tanks and spills.

Aviall notified the Texas Natural Resource Conservation Commission (Commission) of the contamination. The Commission informed Aviall that it was violating state environmental laws, directed Aviall to clean up the site, and threatened to pursue an enforcement action if Aviall failed to undertake remediation. Neither the Commission nor the EPA, however, took judicial or administrative measures to compel cleanup.

Aviall cleaned up the properties under the State's supervision, beginning in 1984. Aviall sold the properties to a third party in 1995 and 1996, but remains contractually responsible for the cleanup. Aviall has incurred approximately $5 million in cleanup costs;

the total costs may be even greater. In August 1997, Aviall filed this action against Cooper in the United States District Court for the Northern District of Texas, seeking to recover cleanup costs. [The complaint] alleged that, pursuant to §113(f)(1), Aviall was entitled to seek contribution from Cooper, as a PRP under §107(a), for response costs and other liability Aviall incurred in connection with the Texas facilities. ...

* * *

Each side insists that the purpose of CERCLA bolsters its reading of §113(f)(1). Given the clear meaning of the text, there is no need to resolve this dispute or to consult the purpose of CERCLA at all. As we have said: "[I]t is ultimately the provisions of our laws rather than the principal concerns of our legislators by which we are governed." *Oncale v. Sundowner Offshore Services, Inc.*, 523 U.S. 75, 79 (1998). Section 113(f)(1), 100 Stat. 1647, authorizes contribution claims only "during or following" a civil action under §106 or §107(a), and it is undisputed that Aviall has never been subject to such an action.... Aviall therefore has no §113(f)(1) claim.

Questions and Comments for Discussion

1. What effect will the Court's decision in *Cooper Industries* likely have on parties who have never been sued by the EPA for a cleanup action, but who own contaminated property?

2. What did the Court say about how laws are created? Do you think that the Court should take a stronger stance on issues in its own capacity, or is the Court's reliance upon the legislative body proper? How does the structure of the U.S. government as set forth in the U.S. Constitution shape your understanding of this issue?

Community Right to Know

In addition to amending CERCLA, SARA added a new Title III, the Emergency Planning and Community Right to Know Act (EPCRA). This law was passed in response to the disaster in Bhopal, India, in December 1984, when the release of methyl isocyanate at a Union Carbide plant killed an estimated 3,000 people and injured thousands more. EPCRA requires companies that make, process, or use chemicals to meet certain emergency preparedness requirements. These include a plan developed in coordination with community groups for response to chemical emergencies, disclosure of information on hazardous chemicals used or stored at the site, and notification of releases at the plant. The law also requires companies to submit copies of Material Safety Data Sheets (MSDS) for OSHA-regulated chemicals to community groups, and to produce an annual inventory of toxic chemicals released into the environment. Under this amendment, each state has duties related to emergency planning.

■ Emergency Response Plan

Using the Internet, locate and read the emergency response plan for your local community. Evaluate the sufficiency of this plan as an emergency planning tool. Why or why not? Does it place undue burden on business? Does it place undue burden on individual members of society? Does it satisfy EPCRA's requirements? Regardless of whether you believe the plan is sufficient or not, provide two suggestions for improving it. (If you cannot locate your local emergency response plan, choose any city's plan to evaluate instead.)

■ ■ ■ REVIEW AND STUDY QUESTIONS

1. Describe liability in CERCLA. What do *joint, several,* and *retroactive* mean in this context?

2. Do you think that CERCLA is "fair" in holding so many persons to be potentially responsible parties for cleanup costs? Why or why not?

3. If a polluter cannot be found to pay for the cleanup of a contaminated site, why should taxpayers be required to pay? Are there any other options? What dangers exist in allowing contaminated sites to remain unremediated?

4. What does CERCLA authorize the EPA to do?

5. Review "Chemicals in Your Community," at http://www.epa.gov/ceppo/web/docs/chem/chem-in-comm.pdf. What responsibility do you have to know about chemicals in your community? Do you think that most people are aware of these issues? If not, whose responsibility is it to make people aware? Defend your position.

6. Review the requirements imposed by RCRA upon generators, transporters, and TSD facilities. Do you think that these requirements are sufficient to prevent the creation of future Superfund sites? Explain.

7. What are the possible defenses to CERCLA liability?

■ Conclusion

RCRA and CERCLA establish a partnership between the federal and state governments for addressing both past and present waste disposal activities. RCRA focuses on the tracking of hazardous materials and the management of active disposal sites; CERCLA was designed to address the problem of abandoned toxic waste sites. The regulatory programs established to implement and enforce these acts are intricate and complex.

Chapter 12 Case Study: RCRA and CERCLA Wrap-Up

Prepare a memo summarizing what is meant by RCRA's commitment to "cradle-to-grave" management of hazardous waste. Additionally, identify the requirements imposed by RCRA upon generators, transporters, and TSD facilities. Critique these requirements: Are they sufficient to prevent future Superfund (CERCLA) sites?

Exercises for Chapters 9, 10, 11, and 12: Major Federal Environmental Statutes

1. How can a business ensure that it complies with all environmental statutes? Create a flow chart for a business to ensure compliance with *each* of the following federal statutes:

   ESA
   CAA
   CWA
   TSCA
   FIFRA
   RCRA
   CERCLA

   You may identify a specific industry (e.g., timber products, oil and gas, etc.), or you may create a "generic" approach for a business in any industry to follow.

2. Imagine that you have been hired to work as an environmental compliance manager at an administrative agency of the federal government. Your agency has decided to plant large tracts of land with seeds that have been genetically modified to be resistant to glyphosate, a commonly used herbicide. The administrative agency's decision to use the product was not preceded by any NEPA processes.

   Imagine that a nonprofit organization sued the administrative agency because the nonprofit organization believed that the sale and planting of the genetically modified agricultural product in question would have a significant environmental impact. A federal district court judge issued an injunction to delay the planting of the product until the processes of NEPA had been completed satisfactorily. In your role as environmental compliance manager, you must decide how to proceed. Consider NEPA as you complete the rest of this exercise.

   Threshold questions when considering whether an EIS must be prepared:

   A. An EIS must be prepared if there is a _____ action.
   B. The action must be _____.
   C. The action must have a _____.

   If these three criteria are met, then an EIS must be prepared. But how will you find the answers to those questions? You will need to prepare an _____. This will lead to a finding that an EIS must be prepared, or it will lead to a _____.

   You have finally determined that an EIS must be prepared. Identify specifically what must be contained in the EIS.

   Now imagine that an EIS has been prepared. The process took three years. The EIS concluded that there was no reasonable likelihood of harm to the environment by use of the genetically modified crop. As a result, the product is (again) allowed to be sold and planted. Prepare a very brief report to the administrative agency head, who wishes to hear your thoughts on the matter. Evaluate the effectiveness of NEPA in this scenario. Consider its effectiveness, costs, delays, the value of the EIS, and the process.

International Law

Learning Objectives

After reading this chapter, you will understand the structure of the international legal environment and how it differs from domestic legal environments. You will be introduced to several contemporary international environmental challenges that laws and legal systems have attempted to address. Specifically, after reading this chapter you should be able to answer the following questions:

1. What is the difference between international law and foreign domestic law?
2. How does international law differ from domestic law?
3. Why must certain environmental concerns be addressed through international law and/or through foreign domestic law?
4. What are the sources of international environmental law?
5. What issues arise in matters related to trade and the environment?
6. When do U.S. laws apply extraterritorially?
7. Can foreign citizens use U.S. courts to sue for environmental harms?

▦ Introduction

Many nations address environmental concerns within their own borders through their domestic legal system. Additionally, many nations have worked together to create agreements to address environmental challenges of common concern. For example, pollution knows no national boundaries. It affects entire ecosystems, destroys the natural environment, and endangers the health of humans, animals, and plants. Air pollution may have long-range effects on the atmosphere, ozone layer, and the global environment. Acid rain, a kind of air pollution caused by increased sulfur emissions from the burning of fossil fuels, pollutes the atmosphere and has been shown to cause damage to the forests of many nations. Water pollution threatens aquifers, oceans, and rivers alike. Solid waste—hazardous, toxic, or simply excessive—is dangerous to all land inhabitants.

Likewise, natural resources and nonhuman beings are appropriate foci for international environmental law. For example, migratory species naturally move

Here's a good idea!

This is a "bare bones" outline of the chapter. Expand this outline with more detailed notes as you read the chapter. This will allow you to create a study guide as you work. This good study habit will help you to learn the material, retain important points, and make efficient use of your time.

across geopolitical borders. River resources often border more than one country. Sometimes species that are wholly contained within the borders of one nation may be the focus of intense international interest. Finite resources of all types might be found in limited areas, though those resources remain in demand by everyone. International law quite appropriately focuses on these and other environmental concerns.

This chapter discusses the nature of international law, and then examines some of the sources of international environmental law, as well as contemporary issues that illustrate the efforts that span national borders.

■ The Nature of International Law: A Primer

Before studying international environmental law, it is important to understand the nature and structures of international law, because international law differs substantially from domestic law in important ways. Unlike domestic law, there is no international "lawgiver" in the form of a legislature or executive with jurisdictional powers over all international matters. **Domestic law** is created, applied, and enforced by an authority recognized as exercising legitimate powers to do so, within the jurisdiction of the nation-state where it is created.

Most of this textbook has focused on U.S. domestic law. Everyone is subject to domestic law in various forms. For example, all persons in the United States are subject to both federal and state laws. This is because everyone in the United States is within the overall federal jurisdiction and within a state jurisdiction.

As a rule, the United States and all other nation-states (countries) are sovereign. **Sovereignty** of a nation-state denotes that entity's power to govern the population and territory with its own borders. Additionally, essential to the concept of sovereignty is the idea that no outside authority has the power to make decisions about the natural resources within the borders of the nation-state. "Sovereign" is thus both a political and a legal designation.

Domestic law can be conceptualized as a vertical power structure, because law is created by lawmakers and applicable to all within the jurisdiction. Likewise, disputes can be taken to an authority recognized as having the power to settle legal disputes. A shorthand way of thinking about domestic law as a vertical legal structure is that there is a "higher" legal power to which the people submit. In the United States, for example, the legislature creates law and those with legal personhood abide by those laws. If they do not, there are consequences. As you learned in Chapter 2, the legislative branch creates statutes, judges create common law, the executives create executive orders, and executive or legislative authorities create administrative agencies, which in turn create administrative rules and regulations. These governmental entities are recognized as legitimate, and the laws created by them are therefore considered legitimate rules of law. Of course, people in the United States and elsewhere have a role in their own governance. They do this by participating in elections, communicating with lawmakers, and bringing their grievances to court. Nonetheless, the domestic legal system is generally understood to be vertical in nature.

domestic law: Law created, applied, and enforced by an authority recognized within the nation-state as exercising legitimate powers.

sovereignty: A nation-state's power to govern the population and territory within its own borders.

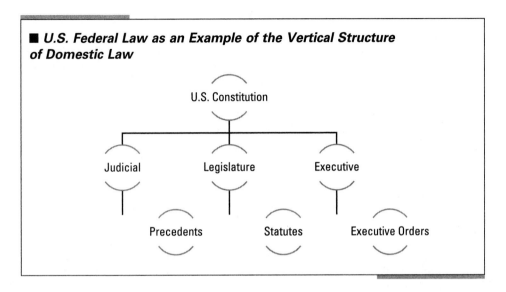

■ *U.S. Federal Law as an Example of the Vertical Structure of Domestic Law*

Compare the structure of domestic law to that of international law. Many international laws are better understood as structurally horizontal, rather than vertical. This is because in most cases, no overarching authority is recognized as having legitimate authority over sovereign states. The very fact that states are sovereign denotes that they are not subject to the power of an external authority. If sovereign states have voluntarily agreed to submit any disputes arising under an agreement to an international tribunal, for example, then the parties have created a vertical structure within their agreement. However, parties to international agreements that do not vest an outside party with lawmaking or dispute resolution power can be understood to be in a horizontal relationship. Because no external authority has the power to enforce the terms of the agreement, enforcement of international law becomes very difficult.

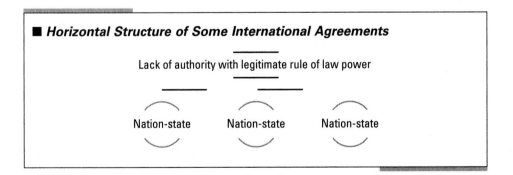

■ *Horizontal Structure of Some International Agreements*

International environmental law between nations is created by governments. However, all persons within the jurisdiction of binding international law are bound to obey the law. For example, environmental treaties that have been ratified by the United States are law for persons within the jurisdiction of the United States.

Generally speaking, international law related to the environment draws upon several sources, such as customs developed over time and recognized as having attained the status of law, bilateral or multilateral agreements, domestic law and foreign domestic law, and so-called "soft law" principles. Of course, national governments are normally reluctant to surrender their sovereign powers to any overarching body that might be developed to govern matters of international environmental importance. Likewise, governments are also reluctant to voluntarily surrender any of their sovereign power through international **conventions** and treaties. Moreover, economic implications of environmental regulation often limit a country's willingness to comprehensively address global environmental problems—or to be bound to agreements with other nations that will require a continued commitment of resources.

▓ Sources of International Environmental Law

International environmental law, like all international law, consists of principles derived from several sources. These include customary international law, resolutions and practices of international organizations, international conventions (or treaties), and judicial decisions. The Statute of the International Court of Justice (ICJ) delineates which types of laws may apply to the resolution of international disputes that come before that court. This list is useful for our study, because international environmental legal issues are matters of international law, though not all such issues are resolvable at the ICJ. This is because the ICJ, established by the United Nations Charter in 1945, is a court of general jurisdiction, established to resolve legal disputes between sovereign states (nations) and to give advisory opinions when asked to do so by the United Nations or any of its various agencies that are authorized to request such opinions. Article 38 of the International Court of Justice reads:

1. The Court, whose function is to decide in accordance with international law such disputes as are submitted to it, shall apply:

   a. international conventions, whether general or particular, establishing rules expressly recognized by the contesting states;
   b. international custom, as evidence of a general practice accepted as law;
   c. the general principles of law recognized by civilized nations;
   d. subject to the provisions of Article 59, judicial decisions and the teachings of the most highly qualified publicists of the various nations, as subsidiary means for the determination of rules of law.

2. This provision shall not prejudice the power of the Court to decide a case *ex aequo et bono*, if the parties agree thereto.[1]

convention: An international treaty or agreement.

---

[1] Statute of the International Court of Justice. Retrieved January 2, 2014, from http://www .icj-cij.org/documents/?p1=4&p2=2&p3=0#CHAPTER_II

■ **ACTIVITY BOX** *International Environmental Legal Disputes*

Visit the ICJ's website (http://www.icj-cij.org/docket/index.php?p1=3&p2=3).
   Click through several "contentious cases" to identify cases that have involved an environmental dispute, then answer the following questions:

1. Are disputes between nation-states concerning the environment rare or common?
2. Do you think an international court should exist where private parties can raise issues related to the environment? If so, why hasn't such a court been created that has jurisdiction over all persons in the world? If not, in what other ways can environmental disputes be resolved besides going to court?

Customary international law describes those guiding principles that nations generally recognize as part of international legal order. The Statute of the International Court of Justice describes *international custom* as "evidence of a general practice accepted as law."[2] For example, sovereign nations generally recognize that countries have the right to use and conserve the marine resources of their coastal waters. Nations also generally recognize a responsibility not to harm the environment of another nation, and to warn another state if an event threatens another's environment.

An example of a legal decision resting on international custom is a 1941 arbitration decision in a dispute between the United States and Canada. In the Trail Smelter Case (*U.S. v. Canada*),[3] a Canadian mining and smelting company operated a smelter plant in British Columbia. Over a 12-year period, emissions of sulfur dioxide fumes from the plant caused considerable damage in the U.S. state of Washington. The Canadian government agreed to pay damages under previous agreements and arbitration, but the United States asked the arbitration tribunal to issue an injunction barring further environmental damage to the state of Washington. In granting the injunction, the arbitration tribunal stated:

> No case of air pollution dealt with by an international tribunal has been brought to the attention of the Tribunal nor does the Tribunal know of any such case. The nearest analogy is that of water pollution. But, here also, no decision of an international tribunal has been cited or has been found.
>
> There are, however, as regards both air pollution and water pollution, certain decisions of the Supreme Court of the United States which may legitimately be taken as a guide ... where no contrary rule prevails in international law.... The Tribunal, therefore, finds that [these] decisions, taken as a whole, constitute an adequate basis for its conclusion, namely, that, under the principles of international law, ... no State has the right to use or permit the use of its territory in such a manner as to cause injury by fumes in or to the territory of another or the properties or persons therein, when the case is of serious consequence and the injury is established by clear and convincing evidence.

This arbitral decision illustrates the importance of existing law in individual countries as a guide to decision makers in international environmental disputes. It also shows how a sovereign's existing domestic law shapes international environmental law itself.

customary international law: General guiding principles recognized by nations as a source of international law.

---

[2] Art. 38(1)(b).
[3] 3 R.I.A.A. 1905 (1938/1941).

Other customary international law includes principles such as the duty to cooperate and the duty of good neighborliness. Importantly, not all agree as to which principles constitute customary international law. Because customary international law is not codified like statutory law, disagreement exists as to its meaning, extent, and application. Indeed, parties who might incur liability or whose interests might be infringed upon by application of customary law could object to application of the relevant principles of customary law. Notice that this is not unlike domestic law. When a party believes that a domestic law has been applied erroneously, that party will argue against such application.

A second source of international environmental law is resolutions and declarations of international organizations. A comprehensive list of such organization is beyond the scope of this book, although a few examples are provided for illustration purposes. The United Nations (UN) has addressed important global environmental issues. Its activities affect the environment in several important ways: First, it focuses the attention of the world community on significant environmental concerns; second, it coordinates the efforts of various nation-states through treaties and international conventions; third, it creates specialized organizations, such as the United Nations Environment Programme (UNEP), which coordinates global environmental protection initiatives; and fourth, it introduces scientific and technological systems designed to address environmental problems.

The UN has also sponsored several important international conferences on the environment, such as the 1972 Stockholm Conference on the Environment, which ended with a "Declaration on Principles of the International Law of the Environment." The Stockholm Conference has become a cornerstone of modern international environmental law. Since the Declaration of the Stockholm Conference was produced in 1972, many international conventions, treaties, and other organized efforts have been concluded under the auspices of the UN and its specialized agencies. These have addressed the preservation of wildlife; whale and seal catching; fisheries; protection of birds; conservation of living resources and plants; protection of rivers, seas, and oceans; the banning of nuclear weapons tests in the atmosphere; exploration of the seas, outer space, and celestial bodies; the banning of chemical weapons; sustainable development; and climate change. For example, the Intergovernmental Panel on Climate Change (IPCC), established by UN organizations, assesses reports concerning climate change.

Other international organizations important in establishing international environmental policy include intergovernmental organizations that formulate and encourage public and private compliance with environmental policies. Some examples are:

▪ The Organization for Economic Cooperation and Development (OECD), which has been responsible for establishing environmental policies that have led to environmental regulations adopted by international conventions.

▪ The International Law Commission, created by the UN General Assembly and charged with developing and codifying international law. The commission has proposed that willful acts of serious environmental pollution be regarded as crimes against the peace and security of humankind.

▪ The World Bank has also adopted policies addressing issues of international environmental concern. For example, it adopted a policy calling for the rejection of financing for environmentally destructive projects. However, the bank has been criticized for failing to follow this policy and instead favoring desirable economic development.

▦ The European Union (EU) has far-reaching and progressive environmental policies. The European Environment Agency is an agency of the EU.

▦ The African Union addresses environmental degradation, including climate change.

▦ The Union of South American Nations is concerned about natural resources and development.

Nongovernmental organizations (NGOs) and worldwide "green" movements have been effective in pressuring sovereign governments to strengthen global environmental protections. These movements have generated global environmental concern that has led to the passage of both domestic laws and international conventions. NGOs range widely in subject matter and/or expertise focus. For example, the International Council for Science consists of a broad-based federation of scientific organizations, some of which engage in environmental research. The members of the International Union for the Conservation of Nature (IUCN) include states, government agencies, political/economic integration organizations, and national and international NGOs. The Worldwide Fund for Nature (WWF) is a global conservation organization; one of its pioneering ideas was the "debt-for-nature" swap, which involves the purchase of an underdeveloped nation's commercial debts in exchange for that country's agreement to promote conservation.

■ *ACTIVITY BOX*

Identify an environmental issue that is important to you. Using the Internet, find three international environmental organizations (intergovernmental or NGO) that work in that area. Identify an activity or program undertaken by each of these organizations that might benefit the environmental issue you have identified. What progress has been made? What is left to be done? How might you get involved in the work of those organizations?

A third source of international environmental law is treaties and conventions. These agreements are often viewed as the clearest sources of international environmental law. These types of agreements typically contain general principles rather than specific mandates, but they serve an important function by stating environmental goals and by requiring adopting nations to record and periodically report their environmental activities to international organizations. Often, such agreements are aspirational in nature, rather than punitive. These agreements can be bilateral or multilateral.

It is not possible to list all international environmental treaties and conventions in this textbook, though a few notable and exemplary agreements are briefly discussed.

The Stockholm Declaration and Its Aftermath

The first Earth Summit occurred in 1972 at the UN Conference on the Human Environment in Stockholm, a meeting convened under the auspices of the UN. Delegations from more than 100 nations, as well as many organizations, attended the conference. At the Stockholm Conference, the global community came together to plan a framework for comprehensive environmental consideration within the UN. Among other things, the Stockholm Conference produced a "Declaration of the United Nations Conference on the Human Environment," otherwise known as the Stockholm Declaration. The Stockholm Declaration affirms human responsibility to preserve the environment and it sets forth 26 principles concerning the environment. These principles include the human right to a safe environment, the responsibility of nations to preserve natural ecosystems and wildlife, and the need to halt the release of substances and heat beyond levels consistent with human health and the earth's capacity to absorb them. The Stockholm Conference also established a basic plan for worldwide environmental assessment and created the United Nations System-wide Earthwatch, which is a program to facilitate international cooperation in research activities, monitoring, and exchange of information among nations.

Delegates at the Stockholm Conference also confronted the serious problem that a nation's level of economic development substantially affects its willingness and ability to protect the environment. Delegates at the conference asserted that sound economic development is environmentally attainable with proper international cooperation and international financial assistance. They also affirmed that each nation has the sovereign right to plan and control its economic development and the exploitation of its natural resources; however, they also recognized a nation's obligation to prevent and abate extraterritorial environmental damage. The Stockholm Conference called for financial and technical assistance for underdeveloped nations and urged national governments to develop international rules for liability and compensation for environmental damage that crosses national borders.

Following the Stockholm Conference, global and regional conferences continued to address a wide range of international environmental issues. In 1982, the UN General Assembly promulgated the "World Charter for Nature," which attempted to implement principles from the Stockholm Conference. The World Charter recognized humans' responsibility to maintain the quality of nature and to conserve the world's natural resources, and it urged nations to incorporate conservation efforts into economic planning and domestic law making.

The growing awareness of the wide differences separating developed and developing nations, and the fact that many developing nations viewed environmental protection as a threat to their economic growth, led the World Commission on Environment and Development to issue "Our Common Future," more commonly known as the Brundtland Report, in 1987. In this report, the commission stressed the importance of environmental protection for the developing world, and introduced the concept of sustainable development. As defined in the Brundtland Report, *sustainable development* is "economic development that meets the needs of the present without compromising the ability of future generations to meet their own needs."[4]

Earth Summit and Its Progeny

In June 1992, delegates from more than 150 countries, including the political leaders of more than 100 nations, more than 30,000 activists, world religious figures,

---

[4] UN Document A/42/427, Our Common Future: Report of the World Commission on Environment and Development, ch. 1, § 1. Retrieved from http://www.un-documents.net/ocf-02.htm

and corporate CEOs convened in Rio de Janeiro for the United Nations Conference on the Environment and Development (UNCED). They gathered in three primary forums: governmental, nongovernmental, and indigenous leaders. This 1992 Earth Summit gave participants the opportunity to exchange information and focused worldwide attention on environmental issues.

The conference was based on a platform of five documents. Of these five, two were legally binding and were negotiated and prepared prior to UNCED.

The United Nations Framework Convention on Climate Change (UNFCCC) was proposed in response to growing evidence that the earth is warming as a result of human activities, such as large-scale burning of fossil fuels and massive cutting of forests that absorb carbon dioxide. Scientists have warned that the effects from global warming, which include rising sea levels and changes in rainfall and evaporation patterns, will lead to drought and desertification in some parts of the world, and storms and flooding in others. Melting land ice could cause the sea to rise between three inches and a foot within the next 40 years, flooding low-lying islands and coastal regions.

In response to alarm about the impact of climate change, delegates drafting the Convention on Climate Change detailed specific actions to address the problem. This ultimately led to a dispute among nations about specific targets and timetables for reducing emissions of carbon dioxide. Japan and the EEC favored a proposal mandating the stabilization of carbon emissions at 1990 levels by the year 2000, but the United States disputed the need for legislation and pushed for voluntary adherence to this goal. Eventually, the document was signed without any set targets or timetables. The convention also addressed the need to control emissions of other greenhouse gases and the need for financial and technical aid to developing countries, especially to assist those countries in protecting their forests.

After the signing of the UNFCCC and as a consequent to it, the Kyoto Protocol, which established emissions targets, was signed by some members of UNFCCC. Notably, the United States has not ratified the Kyoto Protocol. Therefore, it is not a binding legal agreement for the United States. Similar later agreements include the Bali Action Plan of 2007, the Copenhagen Accord of 2009, the Cancun Agreements of 2010, and the Durban Platform for Enhanced Action of 2012.

The Convention on Biological Diversity is a treaty. Prior to the Rio Conference, UNEP established the Intergovernmental Negotiating Committee for a Convention on Biological Diversity (INC). INC held five sessions to negotiate an agreement satisfactory to all countries. The ultimate document outlined the need to preserve biological diversity for present and future generations and sought to guarantee that royalties for medicines derived from plants found in a developing country would go to that country in perpetuity, even if the medicines were synthesized. The Convention on Biological Diversity attracted the most media attention at the conference because the United States refused to sign it; President George Bush stated that the treaty did not adequately protect the intellectual property rights (patents) of industry. On June 4, 1993, President Clinton signed the Convention on Biological Diversity, but Congress has not ratified the agreement.

The 2000 Cartagena Protocol on Biosafety, known simply as the Biosafety Protocol, protects biological diversity from genetically modified organisms or other biotechnology.

Agenda 21 is a large document that identifies future environmental problems and describes courses of action necessary to address those problems. Although

Agenda 21 is not a legally binding instrument, it is an important statement of policy and recommendations.

The Rio Declaration is also not legally binding. However, it sets out 27 principles on how humankind can live in harmony with the earth. It outlines the rights and responsibilities of countries toward the environment, and it attempts to balance principles important to both developed and developing nations. This 1992 declaration addressed environmental concerns that had emerged since 1972—most notably, the deterioration of the environment and the interrelationship between economic progress and environmental protection. The United States disagreed with the wording of some parts of the Rio Declaration, and issued a written statement listing its formal reservations.

The Statement of Forest Principles is not legally binding, but it reflects the first global consensus on forests. It sets a policy of maintaining forests while utilizing them as an economic resource. It includes a declaration that states have, in accordance with the UN Charter and principles of international law, the sovereign and inalienable right to utilize, manage, and develop their forests in accordance with their developmental needs and level of socioeconomic development. It declares that national forest policies should recognize and support the identity, culture, and rights of indigenous people and their communities. It recognizes the important role forests play in meeting energy requirements and declares that specific financial resources should be provided to developing countries with significant forested areas. It recognizes that efforts should be taken to protect and enhance forests around the world, and that all countries, notably developed countries, should take positive action toward reforestation and forest conservation.

After the 1992 Earth Summit, the Commission on Sustainable Development was formed. In 2002, another Earth Summit was held in Johannesburg, South Africa, where sustainable development was the focus. Earth Summit 2002 produced the Johannesburg Declaration, which, unsurprisingly, focused on sustainable development.

Earth Summit 2012 was not attended by some notable world leaders, including President Obama. Sometimes referred to as Rio+20, this conference was also held in Rio de Janeiro. *The Future We Want*, a nonbinding work paper, was the outcome of this summit.

The Millennium Summit

The United Nations Millennium Summit in 2000 culminated in the United Nations Millennium Declaration. These goals are wide-reaching, but they include a commitment to attaining environmental sustainability.

■ *ACTIVITY BOX*

Using the Internet, identify relevant international environmental laws, including agreements between states, domestic law, foreign domestic law, and soft law, related to each of the following topics:

- Pesticides
- Acid rain
- Biodiversity
- Coral reefs

- Genetically modified organisms
- Climate change/global warming
- Population
- Ozone layer
- Desertification
- Dumping of hazardous waste
- Groundwater depletion
- Trade in endangered and threatened species
- Hazardous waste shipments
- Sustainable development
- Wetlands
- Oil spills
- Marine plastics
- Pollution from ships
- Transboundary nuclear waste
- Air pollution

The Vienna Conference of 1985

The Vienna Convention for the Protection of the Ozone Layer is a multilateral treaty that resulted from the Vienna Conference of 1985. One protocol of that treaty is the Montreal Protocol on Substances That Deplete the Ozone Layer (commonly referred to as the Montreal Protocol), which became effective in 1989. The ozone layer is a region of gaseous molecules 15 to 30 miles above the surface of the earth. The ozone layer absorbs and shields the earth from ultraviolet radiation. In the 1980s, scientists observed a significant "hole" developing in the ozone layer over the Antarctic each spring. Although changes in the earth's ozone shield and climate occur naturally due to natural events such as volcanic eruptions, emissions of manmade substances such as chlorofluorocarbons (CFCs) substantially aggravated these natural changes. CFCs and halons are chemicals that were widely used for air-conditioning and manufacturing of solvents, styrofoam, and spray aerosol propellants.

Parties to the Montreal Protocol agreed to freeze consumption of CFCs at 1986 levels and to cut production and consumption in half by 1999. Developing nations were given a 10-year exemption.

Following the effective date of the agreement, new scientific data indicated that CFCs were a greater threat than originally thought, and that a wider variety of chemicals than originally believed were destroying the ozone layer. In response to these new concerns, adopting countries reconvened and agreed to amendments that resulted in a more comprehensive and aggressive program to phase out CFCs. Participants also recognized the need to provide technical and financial support to developing nations and created a fund to assist developing nations in reaching the goals of the protocol. In total, the agreement has been modified seven times.

The Montreal Protocol advanced the 1985 Vienna Convention for the Protection of the Ozone Layer by establishing specific time schedules and control measures for limiting the use of ozone-depleting chemicals. In the 1990 Clean Air Act, the U.S. Congress mandated that the EPA take action in compliance with the provisions of the Montreal Protocol.

Many consider the Montreal Protocol to be the most successful international environmental initiative, for two reasons. First, its specificity assured concrete results in reducing industrial sources of ozone depletion. Second, its call for regular reassessment of the provisions of the agreement provides an opportunity for nations to quickly reconvene to address new scientific information and environmental concerns as they arise.

■ Imitating the Success of the Montreal Protocol

Review the UNEP webpage concerning the Montreal Protocol (http://ozone.unep.org /new_site/en/montreal_protocol.php). Identify three specific reasons why you believe that the Montreal Protocol can be considered a success. Then, identify three specific ways in which this success could be replicated by other international environmental treaties to achieve success in other areas of concern.

International Export of Toxic and Hazardous Wastes

The 1989 Basel Convention on the Control of Transboundary Movements of Hazardous Wastes and Their Disposal, known as the Basel Convention, resulted from a conference convened by the UNEP to address problems caused by the international export of toxic and hazardous wastes. Many feared that as developing nations struggled to improve their economic condition, these nations would become a dumping ground for the rest of the world. The Basel Convention forbids the export of hazardous waste to any country whose government does not agree in advance to accept it. The agreement establishes a notice and consent structure for wastes covered by the agreement. Both exporting and importing nations must take the necessary measures to assure environmentally safe methods of disposal of any shipped wastes.

Under the agreement, when a shipper intends to export hazardous wastes, it must first notify the export country, the import country, and any country through which the waste will be transported. Shipment cannot be made until written confirmation from those authorities is received. Further, all transboundary shipments of hazardous waste must be covered by insurance, and the convention requires an adopting nation to treat violations of its terms as criminal acts.

In 1994, at a conference on the Basel Convention in Geneva, Switzerland, all attending nations, including members of the Organization for Economic Cooperation and Development (OECD), unanimously approved a resolution calling for an immediate and total ban on hazardous waste exports to countries outside the OECD. Though it was an attendee, the United States has not ratified the Basel Convention.

The United Nations Convention on the Law of the Sea

The international UN Convention on the Law of the Sea (UNCLOS) recognizes the need for nations to address, and to harmonize efforts to combat, the problems of marine pollution and the use of marine resources. UNCLOS sets territorial limits, including the exclusive economic zone (EEZ).

The United States has not signed UNCLOS. Nevertheless, much of UNCLOS is recognized as reflecting customary international law.

Identify another environmental treaty that has not been discussed in this text. Find its Secretariat on the Internet to learn about it. For example, what is the history of the treaty? What is its purpose? How many countries have signed it? How many of those have ratified it? What barriers and obstacles hinder accomplishment of the goals of the treaty?

Foreign Domestic Law

Another source of "international" environmental law is not really international at all. Domestic laws—both foreign and U.S.—are important sources of law for matters of concern in international environmental efforts. Its existence, application, and enforcement are essential to protecting environmental resources and preventing further degradation of environmental amenities.

Foreign domestic law is the law of other nation-states. Those laws are created and enforced by the appropriate authorities in the nation-states where the laws apply. The creation and application of law may be accomplished in a manner similar to or radically different from the way domestic law is made and administered in the United States.

Imagine, for example, that an NGO based in the United States was interested in protecting polar bears. Of particular importance to that NGO would be U.S. domestic law, international treaties (specifically, the Agreement on the Conservation of Polar Bears), and foreign domestic law related to the protection of polar bears from the other countries where those animals exist. Only by viewing the entire legal scheme can the NGO determine where the laws might be strengthened. For example, if a country where polar bears exist had not yet signed or ratified a relevant treaty, the NGO might decide to focus its efforts on gaining support for that treaty in that country.

Domestic law is also an essential instrument in matters of importance to international environmental law. For example, the Endangered Species Act, a U.S. federal statute, implements the Convention on International Trade in Endangered Species of Wild Flora and Fauna (CITES). Likewise, the Migratory Bird Treaty Act, a federal statute, implements many agreements between the United States and other nation-states relating to the protection of migratory birds.

Soft Law

A final source of international environmental "law" is not really law at all. *Soft law* includes agreements, principles, resolutions, codes of conduct, and the like. Although these do not have legally binding authority, and usually are not subject to signature or ratification, they are nonetheless important in guiding behavior, shaping outcomes, and developing binding law.

■ Trade and the Environment

The impact of international trade on the natural environment is a key issue in environmental policy debates. Liberalizing world trade is often touted as indispensable to the economic welfare of all nations. However, environmental problems related to international trade have been a source of ongoing tension between nations.

Some believe that liberalizing trade between nations invites increased pollution and results in a loss of regulatory sovereignty. They see "free trade" as a synonym for anti-environmental policy making, driven by the desire for jobs and profits at the expense of the environment. They also fear that enforcement mechanisms under free trade agreements often permit obscure, unaccountable, and business-oriented control over environmental policy. In contrast, some people believe that concerns about the environment will block foreign producers from entering markets and reduce the efficiency gained from trade.

Free Trade Agreements

Free trade agreements, such as the North American Free Trade Agreement (NAFTA), are legal instruments that have been the subject of great controversy. In 1993, Congress approved NAFTA, which created a free trade market among Canada, Mexico, and the United States. NAFTA eliminated tariffs and other barriers to trade, and also established a framework for supervising and implementing the provisions of the agreement.

Throughout its approval process, NAFTA generated much debate in the United States and Canada. The debate created some strange bedfellows, as organized labor joined with environmentalists to oppose the agreement. The debate tended to focus on two important issues: the socioeconomic benefits of free trade versus job protection, and the environment. With respect to the environment, many believed that further trade liberalization between the United States and Mexico would result in incremental environmental damage, citing as evidence the environmental conditions along the 2,000-mile border between the United States and Mexico, an area contaminated by excessive air pollution, sewage in underground water, and toxic dumping. Fears that NAFTA could be used as a basis to attack state environmental standards as illegal barriers to trade were also raised.

In response to these concerns, the North American Free Trade Agreement Side Accord on the Environment (the environmental side agreement) was created. Among other things, the side agreement sets up a dispute resolution process if a NAFTA signatory persistently fails to enforce its domestic environmental laws, and it sets out a plan for coordinating and financing environmental infrastructure. The agreement also requires all parties to inform each other of domestic decisions to ban or severely restrict a pesticide or other chemical.

The NAFTA side agreement produced further controversy. Prior to congressional approval of NAFTA, several environmental groups pursued legal action in *Public Citizen v. Office of United States Trade Representative*[5] to compel the U.S. Office of the U.S. Trade Representative (OTR) to produce an EIS for NAFTA before the agreement was submitted to Congress for ratification. Preparation of an EIS could have substantially delayed ratification of the agreement.

A U.S. District Court ruled that the administration could not seek approval of NAFTA until it completed the NEPA-required environmental impact statement. The Clinton administration filed an appeal. In denying judicial review to plaintiff environmental groups, the appellate court refused to force the administration to comply with NEPA before submitting international trade agreements to Congress for ratification. NEPA is one of the most powerful environmental public disclosure laws presently on the books. Thus, some argue that the court's holding in this case substantially diminished the role of the public in the debate over the environmental implications of future trade agreements.

---

[5] 5 F.3d 549 (D.C. Cir. 1993).

Unfortunately, those concerns seemed to have been justified: During NAFTA's first 20 years, from 1993 to 2013, NAFTA countries' environmental laws have frequently been challenged by investors. *Investors* are corporations that are permitted to challenge a NAFTA country's regulations if those regulations undermine expected profits. These so-called investor-state cases have raised the ire of NAFTA opponents, especially because they often result in nondomestic tribunals awarding corporations hefty damages amounts, payable by defendant governments from taxpayer funds. Domestic environmental regulations that have been challenged by investors in NAFTA-related tribunals include zoning, toxic bans, land use rules, and forestry and water policies.

■ ACTIVITY BOX   Investor-State Cases under NAFTA

Review the list of investor-state cases under NAFTA (http://www.citizen.org/documents /investor-state-chart.pdf).

Under the U.S. Constitution, the president has the power to enter into treaties with other nations, with the advice and consent of two-thirds of the Senate. Congress has delegated authority to different executive agencies to coordinate trade regulation. The U.S. Trade Representative (USTR) is a cabinet-level post that carries the rank of ambassador. The trade representative coordinates and formulates international trade policy. The courts have broadly construed presidential treaty power and have held that this power extends to any issue involving negotiations with foreign governments, even if those issues substantially affect domestic issues.

Consider *Department of Transportation v. Public Citizen*,[6] in which the U.S. Supreme Court held that the executive branch has significant discretion to implement policy related to fair trade agreements in interpreting domestic law. The issue concerned objections by public interest groups to Mexican-based trucks being permitted to use U.S. highways under NAFTA, despite the Mexican-domiciled trucks having less stringent environmental and safety standards related to emissions and driver training. The plaintiffs brought a NEPA claim arguing that an EIS must be undertaken first. The Supreme Court disagreed.

Department of Transportation v. Public Citizen
541 U.S. 752 (2004)

Justice Thomas delivered the opinion of the Court.

In this case, we confront the question whether the National Environmental Policy Act of 1969 (NEPA) … and the Clean Air Act (CAA) … require the Federal Motor Carrier Safety Administration (FMCSA) to evaluate the environmental effects of cross-border operations of Mexican-domiciled motor carriers, where FMCSA's promulgation of certain regulations would allow such cross-border operations to occur. Because FMCSA lacks discretion to prevent these cross-border operations, we conclude that these statutes impose no such requirement on FMCSA.

I

Due to the complex statutory and regulatory provisions implicated in this case, we begin with a brief overview of the relevant statutes. We then turn to the factual and procedural background.

(Continued)

---
[6] 541 U.S. 752, 124 S. Ct. 2204 (2004).

A

1

Signed into law on January 1, 1970, NEPA establishes a "national policy [to] encourage productive and enjoyable harmony between man and his environment," and was intended to reduce or eliminate environmental damage and to promote "the understanding of the ecological systems and natural resources important to" the United States.... At the heart of NEPA is a requirement that federal agencies "include in every recommendation or report on proposals for legislation and other major Federal actions significantly affecting the quality of the human environment, a detailed statement by the responsible official on—(i) the environmental impact of the proposed action, (ii) any adverse environmental effects which cannot be avoided should the proposal be implemented, (iii) alternatives to the proposed action, (iv) the relationship between local short-term uses of man's environment and the maintenance and enhancement of long-term productivity, and (v) any irreversible and irretrievable commitments of resources which would be involved in the proposed action should it be implemented." ...

This detailed statement is called an Environmental Impact Statement (EIS). The Council of Environmental Quality (CEQ), established by NEPA with authority to issue regulations interpreting it, has promulgated regulations to guide federal agencies in determining what actions are subject to that statutory requirement.... The CEQ regulations allow an agency to prepare a more limited document, an Environmental Assessment (EA), if the agency's proposed action neither is categorically excluded from the requirement to produce an EIS nor would clearly require the production of an EIS.... If, pursuant to the EA, an agency determines that an EIS is not required under applicable CEQ regulations, it must issue a "finding of no significant impact" (FONSI), which briefly presents the reasons why the proposed agency action will not have a significant impact on the human environment....

2

... In 1970, Congress substantially amended the CAA into roughly its current form.... The 1970 amendments mandated national air quality standards and deadlines for their attainment, while leaving to the States the development of "implementation plan[s]" to comply with the federal standards....

In 1977, Congress again amended the CAA ... to prohibit the Federal Government and its agencies from "engag[ing] in, support[ing] in any way or provid[ing] financial assistance for, licens[ing] or permit[ting], or approv[ing], any activity which does not conform to [a state] implementation plan." ... The definition of "conformity" includes restrictions on, for instance, "increas[ing] the frequency or severity of any existing violation of any standard in any area," or "delay[ing] timely attainment of any standard ... in any area." [42 U.S.C.] §7506(c)(1)(B). These safeguards prevent the Federal Government from interfering with the States' abilities to comply with the CAA's requirements.

3

FMCSA, an agency within the Department of Transportation (DOT), is responsible for motor carrier safety and registration.... Importantly, FMCSA has only limited discretion regarding motor vehicle carrier registration: It must grant registration to all domestic or foreign motor carriers that are "willing and able to comply with" the applicable safety, fitness, and financial-responsibility requirements.... FMCSA has no statutory authority to impose or enforce emissions controls or to establish environmental requirements unrelated to motor carrier safety.

B

We now turn to the factual and procedural background of this case. Before 1982, motor carriers domiciled in Canada and Mexico could obtain certification to operate within the United States from the Interstate Commerce Commission (ICC).... In 1982, Congress, concerned about discriminatory treatment of United States motor carriers in Mexico and Canada, enacted a 2-year moratorium on new grants of operating authority. Congress authorized the President to extend the moratorium beyond the 2-year period if Canada or Mexico continued to interfere with United States motor carriers, and also authorized the President to lift or modify the moratorium if he determined that doing so was in the national interest.... Although the moratorium on Canadian motor carriers was quickly lifted, the moratorium on Mexican motor carriers remained, and was extended by the President.

In December 1992, the leaders of Mexico, Canada, and the United States signed the North American Free Trade Agreement (NAFTA), 32 I.L.M. 605 (1993). As part of NAFTA, the United States agreed to phase out the moratorium and permit Mexican motor carriers to obtain operating authority within the United States' interior by January 2000. On NAFTA's effective date (January 1, 1994), the President began to lift the trade moratorium by allowing the licensing of Mexican carriers to provide some bus services in the United States. The President, however, did not continue to ease the moratorium on the timetable specified by NAFTA, as

(Continued)

concerns about the adequacy of Mexico's regulation of motor carrier safety remained.

The Government of Mexico challenged the United States' implementation of NAFTA's motor carrier provisions under NAFTA's dispute-resolution process, and in February 2001, an international arbitration panel determined that the United States' "blanket refusal" of Mexican motor carrier applications breached the United States' obligations under NAFTA.... Shortly thereafter, the President made clear his intention to lift the moratorium on Mexican motor carrier certification following the preparation of new regulations governing grants of operating authority to Mexican motor carriers.

In May 2001, FMCSA published for comment proposed rules concerning safety regulation of Mexican motor carriers....

In January 2002, acting pursuant to NEPA's mandates, FMCSA issued a programmatic EA for the proposed Application and Safety Monitoring Rules.... The EA considered the environmental impact in the categories of traffic and congestion, public safety and health, air quality, noise, socioeconomic factors, and environmental justice. Vital to the EA's analysis, however, was the assumption that there would be no change in trade volume between the United States and Mexico due to the issuance of the regulations. FMCSA did note that [certain statutory] restrictions made it impossible for Mexican motor carriers to operate in the interior of the United States before FMCSA's issuance of the regulations. But, FMCSA determined that "this and any other associated effects in trade characteristics would be the result of the modification of the moratorium" by the President, not a result of FMCSA's implementation of the proposed safety regulations.... Because FMCSA concluded that the entry of the Mexican trucks was not an "effect" of its regulations, it did not consider any environmental impact that might be caused by the increased presence of Mexican trucks within the United States.

The particular environmental effects on which the EA focused, then, were those likely to arise from the increase in the number of roadside inspections of Mexican trucks and buses due to the proposed regulations. The EA concluded that these effects (such as a slight increase in emissions, noise from the trucks, and possible danger to passing motorists) were minor and could be addressed and avoided in the inspections process itself. The EA also noted that the increase of inspection-related emissions would be at least partially offset by the fact that the safety requirements would reduce the number of Mexican trucks operating in the United States. Due to these calculations, the EA concluded that the issuance of the proposed regulations would have no significant impact on the environment, and hence FMCSA, on the same day as it released the EA, issued a FONSI.

On March 19, 2002, FMCSA issued the two interim rules.... In the regulatory preambles, FMCSA relied on its EA and its FONSI to demonstrate compliance with NEPA. FMCSA also addressed the CAA in the preambles, determining that it did not need to perform a "conformity review" of the proposed regulations ... because the increase in emissions from these regulations would fall below the Environmental Protection Agency's (EPA's) threshold levels needed to trigger such a review.

In November 2002, the President lifted the moratorium on qualified Mexican motor carriers. Before this action, however, respondents filed petitions for judicial review of the Application and Safety Monitoring Rules, arguing that the rules were promulgated in violation of NEPA and the CAA. The Court of Appeals agreed with respondents, granted the petitions, and set aside the rules....

We ... reverse.

II

An agency's decision not to prepare an EIS can be set aside only upon a showing that it was "arbitrary, capricious, an abuse of discretion, or otherwise not in accordance with law." ... Here, FMCSA based its FONSI upon the analysis contained within its EA; respondents argue that the issuance of the FONSI was arbitrary and capricious because the EA's analysis was flawed. In particular, respondents criticize the EA's failure to take into account the various environmental effects caused by the increase in cross-border operations of Mexican motor carriers.

Under NEPA, an agency is required to provide an EIS only if it will be undertaking a "major Federal actio[n]," which "significantly affect[s] the quality of the human environment." ... Under applicable CEQ regulations, "[m]ajor Federal action" is defined to "includ[e] actions with effects that may be major and which are potentially subject to Federal control and responsibility." ... "Effects" is defined to "include: (a) Direct effects, which are caused by the action and occur at the same time and place," and "(b) Indirect effects, which are caused by the action and are later in time or farther removed in distance, but are still reasonably foreseeable." ... Thus, the relevant question is whether the increase in cross-border operations of Mexican motor carriers, with the correlative release of emissions by Mexican trucks, is an "effect" of FMCSA's issuance of the Application and Safety Monitoring Rules; if not, FMCSA's failure to address these effects in its EA did not violate NEPA, and so FMCSA's issuance of a FONSI cannot be arbitrary and capricious.

* * *

(Continued)

B

... [R]espondents have only one complaint with respect to the EA: It did not take into account the environmental effects of increased cross-border operations of Mexican motor carriers....

Respondents' argument, however, overlooks a critical feature of this case: FMCSA has no ability to countermand the President's lifting of the moratorium or otherwise categorically to exclude Mexican motor carriers from operating within the United States....

* * *

... Since FMCSA has no ability categorically to prevent the cross-border operations of Mexican motor carriers, the environmental impact of the cross-border operations would have no effect on FMCSA's decisionmaking—FMCSA simply lacks the power to act on whatever information might be contained in the EIS.

* * *

It would not, therefore, satisfy NEPA's "rule of reason" to require an agency to prepare a full EIS due to the environmental impact of an action it could not refuse to perform. Put another way, the legally relevant cause of the entry of the Mexican trucks is not FMCSA's action, but instead the actions of the President in lifting the moratorium and those of Congress in granting the President this authority while simultaneously limiting FMCSA's discretion.

* * *

C

We hold that where an agency has no ability to prevent a certain effect due to its limited statutory authority over the relevant actions, the agency cannot be considered a legally relevant "cause" of the effect. Hence, under NEPA and the implementing CEQ regulations, the agency need not consider these effects in its EA when determining whether its action is a "major Federal action." Because the President, not FMCSA, could authorize (or not authorize) cross-border operations from Mexican motor carriers, and because FMCSA has no discretion to prevent the entry of Mexican trucks, its EA did not need to consider the environmental effects arising from the entry....

Questions and Comments for Discussion

1. Should requirements to implement international agreements, such as NAFTA, take priority over domestic law related to the environment, when requirements to implement international agreements and domestic laws conflict? Why or why not?

2. Can an international agreement be effective without infringing on state sovereignty? Can state sovereignty be absolutely maintained by a country that is committed to an international treaty? Why or why not?

Besides NAFTA, many other free trade agreements exist or are contemplated. The International Trade Administration, an agency of the U.S. Department of Commerce, maintains a helpful website (http://trade.gov/fta/).

Trade in Endangered or Threatened Animals and Plants

Another important international agreement related to trade and the environment is the Convention on the International Trade in Endangered Species of Wild Flora and Fauna (CITES). This agreement has been ratified by 165 nation-states. The impetus for this convention was the Stockholm Conference, where much concern was expressed concerning the extinction rate of wild plants and animals, as those threats related to unregulated trade between nations. CITES entered into force in 1975.

The CITES agreement provides a framework for restrictions on international trade of endangered and threatened species. Three appendices created by CITES list species that are threatened and/or endangered. International trade in those species, parts of those species, or products made from those species, is restricted or prohibited, depending on which appendix the species is listed in. Regulation under CITES requires certificates and permits for trade in appendix-listed species. An appendix I listing denotes that a species is threatened with extinction, and trade is generally banned or severely restricted. An appendix II listing indicates that restriction of international trade in that species is necessary to avoid the decline of the species. An appendix III listing generally indicates that a species is subject to regulation within the jurisdiction of a party that asked to have the species included in appendix III, and signifies that the cooperation of other parties is needed to control trade in the species.

The CITES parties meet regularly—every two or three years—at the Conference of Parties (CoP), where appendices are adjusted to reflect new statuses of the health of populations of flora and fauna. Each party must enact domestic law in its respective nation to implement the CITES requirements. In the United States, the domestic statute known as the Endangered Species Act implements CITES.

The Emergence of the World Trade Organization

In 1944, during World War II, the United States and its allies determined that greater international cooperation and coordination would be required if future economic disasters and wars were to be prevented. As a result, they established the International Monetary Fund, the World Bank, and the International Trade Organization (ITO). Although the ITO never evolved into a viable trade organization, negotiators did establish the General Agreement on Tariffs and Trade (GATT), which was designed to assist in creating and maintaining international trade standards and tariff reductions.

GATT provides a regular mechanism for conducting multilateral trade negotiations. GATT sponsors "rounds" of negotiations, which last several years and are designed to remove global trade barriers. GATT is actually composed of approximately 200 different treaties that form a legal framework for trade relations. GATT members have conducted nine major trade rounds.

GATT has four major principles. First, trade tariffs are the only form of import protection permitted, and the system is designed to encourage reduction of import duties. Second, all members of GATT are given most-favored-nation status. This means that, with some exceptions, any privilege or benefit granted to one GATT member must be extended to all other GATT members. Third, the principle of national treatment requires that imports from a member nation, once duties and cleared from customs, may not be treated less favorably than domestic products. Finally, reduction of tariffs should occur on a reciprocal basis. Combined with most-favored-nation status, this principle helps ensure a balanced and worldwide reduction in tariffs.

If a country fails to honor its GATT obligations, a member nation may use GATT's dispute settlement procedures. Under the procedures originally established by the agreement, nations first attempt to resolve the dispute through informal negotiations. If this avenue is unsuccessful, GATT provides for a formal consultation process. If that also fails, the GATT Council appoints a panel to assist the GATT membership in resolving the dispute. Within six months the GATT panel issues a report, which is then forwarded to the GATT Council for consideration. The council's decision on the adoption of the report must be given within 15 months, and must be unanimous. The breaching nation is given a reasonable period of time to come into compliance with the council's recommendations. If it fails to do so, GATT members may permit the complaining country to suspend concessions it owes the noncompliant nation. Such suspensions are, however, extremely rare.

A major issue affecting the global environment is GATT's prohibition against excluding products of member nations. In the past, GATT has tended to enforce trade access without regard for the environmentally harmful practices of some businesses, although GATT recognizes an exception if the product directly harms the health or environment. Consequently, the businesses of an environmentally progressive importing country may be at a competitive disadvantage with regard to businesses based in countries with less aggressive environmental regulations. This policy reflects trade advocates' fear that one nation's unilateral exclusion of foreign goods for environmental reasons could create an enormous loophole that might destroy the principles of free trade.

A 1991 GATT dispute between the United States and Mexico over the importation of tuna drew worldwide attention to the problems of trade and the environment. The so-called "tuna-dolphin controversy" began when a U.S. district court issued an injunction against the importation of yellowfin tuna from Mexico. Plaintiff environmental groups had sought the injunction against the domestic sale and importation of tuna caught in "purse seine" nets, a practice prohibited in the United States under the Marine Mammal Protection Act (MMPA). The government appealed the district court's decision, which held that the practice violated the MMPA, in the following case.

Earth Island Institute v. Mosbacher

929 F.2d 1449 (9th Cir. 1991)

SCHROEDER, Circuit Judge

* * *

Congress enacted the MMPA in 1972 to address, among other problems, the tremendous number of dolphins killed by the purse seine method of fishing for yellowfin tuna in the eastern tropical Pacific Ocean. For unknown reasons, yellowfin tuna swim below schools of dolphins in that area. Thus, fishing vessels often set their purse seine nets on dolphins to catch the tuna below. The dolphins are frequently killed or maimed in this process. In the early 1970s, the United States fishing fleet was responsible for the slaughter of over 300,000 dolphins annually....

Although the Act brought about a material reduction in the number of dolphins killed by the United States fleet, dolphin slaughter by foreign nations remained a growing problem. By amendments to the Act in 1984 and 1988, Congress enacted specific standards intended to ensure that foreign tuna fishing fleets would reduce the number of dolphins killed and to protect certain endangered subspecies of dolphins. Such

subspecies included the eastern spinner dolphin which is the subject to this lawsuit. The weapon Congress chose to bring about such reductions in killings was a mandatory embargo on the importation of yellowfin tuna to be imposed upon those countries whose fleets failed to meet the standards Congress established.

The statute mandates the Secretary of the Treasury to ban imports of yellowfin tuna products from a foreign nation until the Secretary of Commerce certifies that that nation's incidental kill rate of dolphins is comparable to that of the United States. The statute specifies that the total incidental kill rate of a foreign nation shall not be found comparable unless it is no more than 2.0 times the total incidental kill rate of the United States fleet.... With respect to the eastern spinner dolphin, the statute additionally provides that the total number of eastern spinner dolphins killed by a foreign fleet cannot exceed fifteen percent of the total number of mammals killed by the fleet of that country....

[The National Marine Fisheries Service (NMFS), which was responsible for implementing the provisions

(Continued)

of the Act, had promulgated regulations implementing the requirements of the Marine Mammal Protection Act. Under its regulations, if a foreign nation had exceeded the limitations for a given year, and remained under embargo, the secretary could] nevertheless "reconsider" the embargo and certify compliance with the statute's provisions based upon data only for the first six months following the year in which the limits were exceeded....

The events giving rise to the preliminary injunction in this appeal are as follows. On June 25, 1990, Earth Island filed its first motion for a preliminary injunction in the federal district court for the Northern District of California. Earth Island sought an "interim" embargo which would enjoin the importation of yellowfin tuna products pending NMFS' issuance of the comparability findings required by the MMPA.... Earth Island argued that, by the plain terms of the MMPA, an embargo was mandatory and the agency could not authorize imports until the requisite comparability findings were made; therefore, it argued, the agency was required to impose an embargo until after the relevant data had been reviewed....

* * *

The government's primary argument is that the six-month "reconsideration" provision is within the discretion delegated by Congress to the agency for regulatory implementation of the Act. The government points to the deference the courts owe to agencies in matters of statutory interpretation. *See, e.g., Chevron,* 467 U.S. at 844, 104 S. Ct. at 2782 ("We have long recognized that considerable weight should be accorded to an executive department's construction of a statutory scheme it is entrusted to administer"). The difficulty with this position is that agencies do not have discretion to issue regulations which conflict with statutory language and congressional purpose.... This regulation clearly does.

* * *

The government also suggests that regardless of the language used in the statute, the reconsideration provision should be upheld as a matter of policy because it offers an incentive to foreign countries to speed up their efforts to meet the statutory standards. The record in this case belies the existence of any incentive effect. The record demonstrates that the six-month reconsideration allows foreign nations and NMFS to withhold the release of negative findings until they have available a subsequent set of positive findings, as occurred with the 1989–90 data for Mexico. The result in this case was that Mexico, which had exceeded MMPA standards for an entire year, was subject to embargo for less than one day. Under this regulation, foreign nations could thus continually exceed MMPA limits for part of each year, yet never be subject to the ban. Because the reconsideration regulation creates such a potential for abuse, and has in fact already been used to circumvent the intent of Congress, we reject the government's argument that the reconsideration regulation offers a more effective incentive to foreign countries to reduce dolphin kill rates.

* * *

Because the government's position is at odds with both the language and the purpose of MMPA, and the agency's intended role under it, we affirm the district court's order of October 4.

Questions and Comments for Discussion

1. Which domestic environmental law was involved in this dispute? Which agency was responsible for enforcing the law? How had the agency responsible for enforcing this law interpreted its application?

2. On what legal basis did the Court strike down the agency regulation? What were the international policy implications of that regulation and the court's ruling?

Following the decision in the *Earth Island* case, Mexico sought and obtained a GATT panel ruling that the tuna embargo violated GATT international trade rules. The panel concluded that the United States had violated GATT by instituting a ban under the MMPA; that U.S. embargoes on imports of tuna were inconsistent with U.S. GATT obligations; and that the embargoes were inconsistent with GATT's rules against prohibitions or restrictions on imports. Although GATT restrictions theoretically do not prevent nations from excluding products that are environmentally offensive, or from adopting measures necessary to protect human, animal, or plant life, the GATT panel said that this exception was not applicable here.

United States—Restrictions on Imports of Tuna
No. DS21/R, 30 I.L.M. 1594 (1991)

Dispute Settlement Panel General Agreement on Tariffs and Trade

Chairman Szepesi and Messrs. Ramsauer and Roselli:

The Panel noted that under the General Agreement, quantitative restrictions on imports are forbidden by Article XI:1 [of the General Agreement].... The Panel therefore found that the direct import prohibition on certain yellowfin tuna and certain yellowfin tuna products from Mexico and the provisions of the MMPA ... were inconsistent with Article XI:1....

* * *

The ... United States considered the prohibition of imports of certain yellowfin tuna and certain yellowfin tuna products from Mexico ... to be justified by Article XX(b) because they served solely the purpose of protecting dolphin life and health....

* * *

... The Panel recalled the finding of a previous panel that this paragraph of Article XX was intended to allow contracting parties to impose trade restrictive measures inconsistent with the General Agreement to pursue overriding public policy goals to the extent that such inconsistencies were unavoidable.... The Panel considered that if the broad interpretation of Article XX(b) suggested by the United States were accepted, each contracting party could unilaterally determine the life or health protection policies from which other contracting parties could not deviate without jeopardizing their rights under the General Agreement. The General Agreement would then no longer constitute a multilateral framework for trade among all contracting parties but would provide legal security only in respect of trade between a limited number of contracting parties with identical internal regulations.

* * *

The Panel proceeded to examine whether the prohibition on imports of certain yellowfin tuna and certain yellowfin tuna products from Mexico and the MMPA provisions under which it was imposed could be justified under the exception in Article XX(g)....

* * *

... The Panel considered that if the extrajurisdictional interpretation of Article XX(g) suggested by the United States were accepted, each contracting party could unilaterally determine the conservation policies from which other contracting parties could not deviate without jeopardizing their rights under the General Agreement. The considerations that led the Panel to reject an extrajurisdictional application of Article XX(b) therefore apply also to Article XX(g).

* * *

... [A] contracting party is free to tax or regulate imported products and like domestic products as long as its taxes or regulations do not discriminate against imported products or afford protection to domestic producers, and a contracting party is also free to tax or regulate domestic production for environmental purposes. As a corollary to these rights, a contracting party may not restrict imports of a product merely because it originates in a country with environmental policies different from its own.

[The panel found that the MMPA was inconsistent with the United States' obligations under GATT and requested that the United States modify the MMPA to make it consistent with the General Agreement.]

The United States and Mexico subsequently resolved this dispute without requesting that the panel's decision be adopted by the full GATT Council. In October 1992, the U.S. Congress enacted the International Dolphin Conservation Act. Under this law, any nation currently under embargo could have the embargo lifted if it agreed to reduce dolphin mortality and abide by a five-year moratorium on the use of purse seine nets.

Although the GATT Council never formally adopted the panel's recommendation, the now-famous "tuna-dolphin" decision alarmed many by appearing to place trade obligations on a higher plane than environmental protection. The GATT ruling raised the specter of domestic environmental laws and regulations being overridden by an obscure and environmentally insensitive international trade tribunal. The decision is viewed as evidence that GATT undermines domestic environmental protection standards, and many of the environmental concerns raised by the tuna-dolphin controversy spilled over into the debate about NAFTA, as discussed earlier concerning investor-state cases, as well as the Mexican-domiciled truck case.

In 1994, the Senate approved legislation implementing the Uruguay Round of GATT. The round included 117 participants and resulted in 28 separate accords covering, among other things, agriculture, textiles, services, intellectual property, and foreign investment. The parties also agreed to form a World Trade Organization (WTO), which is a formal international body supporting GATT.

Critics were upset that the Uruguay Round contained no provisions addressing environmental concerns. Also, concerns exist that the WTO, created to oversee the global trade pact, is too powerful, and that it has the power to override domestic environmental laws. In response to public concerns regarding the implications of WTO dispute settlement procedures, the U.S. Congress included in its approval of the Uruguay Round of GATT comprehensive requirements to ensure monitoring of WTO dispute settlement proceedings involving U.S. laws, regulations, or policies. These requirements include mandates for the executive branch to keep Congress and the public advised of any WTO dispute resolution proceeding involving a U.S. law or regulation.

Issues affecting consumers and the environment will continue to play an important role in the debate over future international trade agreements. In addition, trade and environmental issues are likely to re-emerge in future congressional debates over the president's authority to negotiate trade agreements.

■ Extraterritorial Application of U.S. Domestic Laws

The question of whether U.S. domestic environmental laws apply to the actions of the federal government or others outside the territorial United States is important for those concerned about the global environment. The U.S. Supreme Court has held that there must be clear evidence of congressional intent in order to apply a U.S. statute extraterritorially, and that Congress has the power to do so through statutory construction.[7] Absent clear intent, domestic environmental laws do not apply to the actions of American citizens or companies in other countries. Among major U.S. environmental statutes, the Clean Air Act and CERCLA both contain statutory language to indicate that in certain narrow circumstances those laws do apply extraterritorially to U.S. companies.[8] The Marine Mammal Protection Act (MMPA) applies to all persons subject to the jurisdiction of the United

---

[7] *EEOC v. Arabian American Oil Co.*, 499 U.S. 244, 248 (1991). The Court held that Title VII of the 1964 Civil Rights Act did not apply extraterritorially to regulate the employment practices of United States firms employing American citizens abroad. The decision was subsequently superseded by statute, as stated in *Stender v. Lucky Stores*, 780 F. Supp. 1302 (N.D. Cal. 1992).
[8] CAA § 115(a)-(c), 42 U.S.C. § 7415(a)-(c)(2006); CERCLA § 111(I)(4), 42 U.S.C. § 9611(I)(4)(2006).

States. The Magnuson-Stevens Act contains express language regarding its extraterritorial reach as well.[9]

In *Amlon Metals Inc. v. FMC Corp.*,[10] a U.S. district court ruled that RCRA did not apply extraterritorially to waste that presented a hazard in the United Kingdom. Amlon Metals had arranged for wastes generated by FMC Corporation in the United States to be shipped to the United Kingdom. After it discovered that the waste contained hazardous substances, Amlon sought injunctive relief and damages from FMC under RCRA's citizen suit provisions, alleging that the waste presented an "imminent and substantial danger" to workers in the United Kingdom. However, the district court ruled against Amlon in the case. It found no evidence of congressional intent to apply RCRA extraterritorially, and it noted that Congress had failed to prove a venue for citizen suits based on hazards from wastes in other countries.

In *Lujan v. Defenders of Wildlife*,[11] the U.S. Supreme Court reversed a ruling by the court of appeals that had upheld regulations promulgated by the Secretary of the Interior under the Endangered Species Act (ESA). Those regulations limited the consultation requirements of the ESA to agency actions within the United States or on the high seas. In *Lujan*, the Supreme Court held that the plaintiff environmental groups lacked standing to challenge the federal agency's decision. The Court found that the plaintiffs had failed to demonstrate a specific injury or that the injury was redressable, and therefore the plaintiffs lacked standing to challenge the agency rule.

In *Defenders of Wildlife v. Norton*,[12] the U.S. District Court for the District of Columbia held for the plaintiffs in deciding that procedural requirements of the Endangered Species Act must be met to ensure that endangered species in Mexico would not be harmed as a result of actions taken related to the lower Colorado River.

The U.S. Court of Appeals for the District of Columbia ruled that NEPA does apply to certain federal actions outside the United States. This decision is important because it suggests that environmental statutes regulating the decision-making process of federal agencies may not raise the problem of extraterritoriality at all. Under the court's reasoning in *Environmental Defense Fund, Inc. v. Massey*, an agency's decision making may be subject to the requirements of NEPA even if the actions at issue occur outside the United States.

Environmental Defense Fund, Inc. v. Massey
986 F.2d 528 (D.C. Cir. 1993)

MIKVA, Chief Judge.

The Environmental Defense Fund ("EDF") appeals the district court's order dismissing its action seeking declaratory and injunctive relief under the National Environmental Policy Act ("NEPA"). EDF alleges that the National Science Foundation ("NSF") violated NEPA by failing to prepare an environmental impact statement ("EIS") in accordance with [NEPA] Section

(Continued)

---

[9] Magnuson Stevens Act, 16 U.S.C. §§ 1801(c)(5), 1826(g) (2006). *See Blue Water Fishermen's Association v. National Marine Fisheries Service*, 158 F. Supp. 2d 118, 123 n.19 (D. Mass. 2001).
[10] 775 F. Supp. 668 (S.D.N.Y. 1991).
[11] 504 U.S. 555 (1992).
[12] 257 F. Supp. 2d 53 (D.D.C. 2003).

102(2)(C) before going forward with plans to incinerate food wastes in Antarctica. The district court dismissed EDF's action for lack of subject matter jurisdiction. The court explained that while Congress utilized broad language in NEPA, the statute nevertheless did not contain "a clear expression of legislative intent through a plain statement of extraterritorial statutory effect"....

We reverse the district court's decision, and hold that the presumption against the extraterritorial application of statutes ... does not apply where the conduct regulated by the statute occurs primarily, if not exclusively, in the United States, and the alleged extraterritorial effect of the statute will be felt in Antarctica—a continent without a sovereign, and an area over which the United States has a great measure of legislative control....

I.

As both parties readily acknowledge, Antarctica is not only a unique continent, but somewhat of an international anomaly. Antarctica is the only continent on earth which has never been, and is not now, subject to the sovereign rule of any nation. Since entry into force of the Antarctic Treaty in 1961, the United States and 39 other nations have agreed not to assert any territorial claims to the continent or to establish rights of sovereignty there.... Hence, Antarctica is generally considered to be a "global common" and frequently analogized to outer space....

Under the auspices of the United States Antarctica Program, NSF operates the McMurdo Station research facility in Antarctica. McMurdo Station is one of three year-round installations that the United States has established in Antarctica, and over which NSF exercises exclusive control. All of the installations serve as platforms or logistic centers for U.S. scientific research; McMurdo Station is the largest of the three, with more than 100 buildings and a summer population of approximately 1200.

Over the years, NSF has burned food wastes at McMurdo Station in an open landfill as a means of disposal.... [In 1991, NSF] decided to resume incineration in an "interim incinerator" until a state-of-the-art incinerator could be delivered to McMurdo Station. EDF contends that the planned incineration may produce highly toxic pollutants which could be hazardous to the environment, and that NSF failed to consider fully the consequences of its decision to resume incineration as required by the decisionmaking process established by NEPA.

* * *

As the district court correctly noted, the Supreme Court recently reaffirmed the general presumption against the extraterritorial application of statutes....

Extraterritoriality is essentially, and in common sense, a jurisdictional concept concerning the authority of a nation to adjudicate the rights of particular parties and to establish the norms of conduct applicable to events or persons outside its borders. More specifically, the extraterritoriality principle provides that "[r]ules of the United States statutory law, whether prescribed by federal or state authority, apply only to conduct occurring within, or having effect within, the territory of the United States." ... As stated by the Supreme Court ..., the primary purpose of this presumption against extraterritoriality is "to protect against the unintended clashes between our laws and those of other nations which could result in international discord."

* * *

There are at least three general categories of cases for which the presumption against the extraterritorial application of statutes clearly does not apply. First, ... the presumption will not apply where there is an "affirmative intention of the Congress clearly expressed" to extend the scope of the statute to conduct occurring within other sovereign nations....

Second, the presumption is generally not applied where the failure to extend the scope of the statute to a foreign setting will result in adverse effects within the United States....

Finally, the presumption against extraterritoriality is not applicable when the conduct regulated by the government occurs within the United States. By definition, an extraterritorial application of a statute involves the regulation of conduct beyond U.S. borders. Even where the significant effects of the regulated conduct are felt outside U.S. borders, the statute itself does not present a problem of extraterritoriality, so long as the conduct which Congress seeks to regulate occurs largely within the United States....

* * *

NEPA is designed to control the decisionmaking process of U.S. federal agencies, not the substance of agency decisions. By enacting NEPA, Congress exercised its statutory authority to determine the factors an agency must consider when exercising its discretion, and created a process whereby American officials, while acting within the United States, can reach enlightened policy decisions by taking into account environmental effects. In our view, such regulation of U.S. federal agencies and their decisionmaking processes is a legitimate exercise of Congress' territoriality-based jurisdiction and does not raise extraterritoriality concerns.

... Section 102(2)(C) binds only American officials and controls the very essence of the government function: decisionmaking. Because the decisionmaking

(Continued)

processes of federal agencies take place almost exclusively in this country and involve the workings of the United States government, they are uniquely domestic....

* * *

Antarctica's unique status in the international arena further supports our conclusion that this case does not implicate the presumption against extraterritoriality. The Supreme Court explicitly stated ... that when applying the presumption against extraterritoriality, courts should look to see if there is any indication that Congress intended to extend the statute's coverage "beyond places over which the United States has sovereignty or *some measure of legislative control.*" ... Thus, where the U.S. has some real measure of legislative control over the region at issue, the presumption against extraterritoriality is much weaker.... And where there is no potential for conflict "between our laws and those of other nations," the purpose behind the presumption is eviscerated, and the presumption against extraterritoriality applies with significantly less force....

* * *

Conclusion

Applying the presumption against extraterritoriality here would result in a federal agency being allowed to undertake actions significantly affecting the human environment in Antarctica, an area over which the United States has substantial interest and authority, without ever being held accountable for its failure to comply with the decisionmaking procedures instituted by Congress—even though such accountability, if it was enforced, would result in no conflict with foreign law or

threat to foreign policy. NSF has provided no support for its proposition that conduct occurring within the United States is rendered exempt from otherwise applicable statutes merely because the effects of its compliance would be felt in the global commons. We therefore reverse the district court's decision, and remand for a determination of whether the environmental analyses performed by NSF, prior to its decision to resume incineration, failed to comply with Section 102(2)(C) of NEPA.

* * *

Reversed and remanded.

Questions and Comments for Discussion

1. What is the principle of "extraterritoriality," as defined by the court in this case? What is the purpose of the rule? Under what circumstances will a domestic environmental law be applied extraterritorially? What are three exceptions to that rule?

2. On what basis did the court hold that NEPA applies to the NSF's actions in Antarctica? Under the court's ruling, would or should NEPA apply to federal agency decisions affecting projects in places other than Antarctica?

3. Extending NEPA's application to federal actions taking place outside the territorial limits of the United States was an important decision. Some have suggested that the decision may open the door to those who would extend NEPA's requirements to federal actions in foreign countries. What are the environmental, economic, and political ramifications of applying NEPA extraterritorially?

Although U.S. courts have narrowly construed the applicability of environmental laws abroad, U.S. environmental laws still have substantial impact outside the United States. Many domestic laws affect businesses that import goods into the United States. The U.S. courts have also ruled that they may exercise jurisdiction over foreign citizens and corporations that are responsible for violating U.S. environmental laws in the United States. In *United States v. Ivey*,[13] a federal district court in Michigan ruled that it had jurisdiction over a Canadian citizen and a Canadian corporation in a case to recover governmental costs incurred in cleaning up a Michigan Superfund site.

The United States was once considered a leader in enacting laws addressing the problems of environmental pollution, protection of wildlife and its habitat, ecosystems management, and natural resource preservation. These laws and the regulations enacted in conformance with them have provided other nations with examples of ways to approach (and perhaps some ways not to approach) similar

---

[13] 747 F. Supp. 1235 (E.D. Mich. 1990).

environmental problems within their borders. However, the failure of the United States to ratify important international environmental agreements, such as the Kyoto Protocol, have undermined its reputation as an environmental law leader, and have led many to speculate that the United States has failed in its opportunity for global influence and leadership in this area.

Legal Actions by Foreign Citizens in U.S. Courts

In some instances, U.S. courts have been willing to accept jurisdiction over environmental injury suits brought by foreign plaintiffs against American companies if they have a legal basis for doing so. In *Dow Chemical Co. v. Alfaro*,[14] a Texas statute provided:

> An action for damages of a citizen of a foreign country may be enforced in the courts of this state, although the wrongful act takes place in a foreign country, if: (1) the laws of the foreign country give a right to maintain an action for damages; (2) the action is begun in this state within the time provided by the laws of this state for beginning the action; and (3) the foreign country of which the plaintiffs are citizens has equal treaty rights with the United States on behalf of its citizens.

In *Alfaro*, 82 Costa Rican employees of Standard Fruit Company sued Dow Chemical Company in a Texas district court. They claimed that while working on a banana plantation in Costa Rica, they were required to handle DBCP, a pesticide manufactured and supplied to Standard Fruit by Dow Chemical. They alleged that exposure to DBCP caused physical and mental damage, including sterility. Dow sought to dismiss the case according to the doctrine of forum non conveniens. Under this doctrine, a court may refuse to hear a case if, for the convenience of the parties and in the interest of justice, the action should be instituted in another forum. The Texas court held that the statute applied because Costa Rica recognized the plaintiffs' claims against Dow, the lawsuit was filed in a timely manner, and Costa Rica permits U.S. citizens to brings lawsuit before its courts.[15]

Historical Viewpoint

On the nights of December 2 and 3, 1984, winds blew deadly methyl isocyanate gas from a plant operated by Union Carbide India Limited (UCIL) into densely occupied parts of the city of Bhopal, India. The result was one of the most devastating industrial disasters in history, resulting in the deaths of more than 2,000 persons and injuries to more than 200,000. UCIL was incorporated under the laws of India, with 50.9% of its stock owned by Union Carbide Corporation (UCC), an American company.

Four days after the accident, the first of some 145 consolidated personal injury actions arising out of the disaster were filed in federal district courts in the United States. The plaintiffs sought relief in the United States against UCIL and UCC. The plaintiffs' decision to bring suit in the United States was attributed in part to the fact that the Indian courts did not have jurisdiction over UCC.

UCC moved to dismiss the plaintiffs' complaints on the ground of forum non conveniens and lack of standing. The district court agreed and dismissed the lawsuits on several conditions, including that UCC consent to the Indian courts' jurisdiction, that it agree to satisfy any judgment rendered by an Indian court against it, and that it be subject to discovery under the Federal Rules of Civil Procedure of the United States.

(Continued)

---

[14] 786 S.W.2d 674 (Tex. 1990).

[15] The holding in this case was subsequently superseded by statute. *'21' International Holdings, Inc. v. Westinghouse Electric Corp.*, 856 S.W.2d 479 (Tex. App. 1993).

The Federal Court of Appeals subsequently affirmed the district court's decision, although it modified a few of its conditions. The court said:

> As the district court found, the record shows that the private interests of the respective parties weigh heavily in favor of dismissal on grounds of forum non conveniens. The many witnesses and source of proof are almost entirely located in India, where the accident occurred, and could not be compelled to appear for trial in the United States. The Bhopal plant at the time of the accident was operated by some 193 Indian nationals.... The great majority of documents bearing on the design, safety, start-up and operation of the plan, as well as the safety training of the plant's employees is located in India....
>
> The plaintiffs seek to prove that the accident was caused by negligence on the part of UCC in originally contributing to the design of the plant and its provision for storage of excessive amounts of the gas at the plant....

> [H]owever, UCC's contribution was limited and its involvement in plant operations terminated long before the accident.[16]

Litigation in India continued for two years. On February 14, 1989, the Supreme Court of India entered an order of settlement of all litigations, claims, rights, and liabilities arising from the disaster at Bhopal. Under the terms of the settlement, UCC and UCIL agreed to pay $470 million to the Registrar of the Supreme Court of India to settle claims arising from the disaster.

1. Do you think that a U.S. court should have heard the plaintiffs' claims?
2. How should U.S. companies be held responsible when they harm persons and/or environmental attributes of natural resources abroad?

International regulation may not always be a satisfactory means of addressing global environmental problems. First, customary law and general principles of law are slow to develop and slow to be recognized worldwide, and therefore they are often unable to address immediate health and environmental hazards. Second, although international agreements tend to set goals and policy, they rarely impose precise obligations on participating nations, because the principle of national sovereignty also protects nations from being forced to comply with international agreements except by consent. The International Court of Justice is the only judicial forum that may conduct international litigation, but its jurisdiction is voluntary and depends upon a nation's consent for its power to adjudicate disputes.

In addition, major polluters throughout the world tend to be individual corporations and private individuals; international law tends to address the rights and obligations of nations. There are instances in which nations have agreed to implement and enforce strict regulatory measures to address international environmental concerns—for example, amendments to the Montreal Protocol—but these instances are rare.

International environmental issues are inextricably tied to issues of political sovereignty, economic development, trade, and international business. One can only hope that, in the future, significant changes in the world's political environment and the increasing interdependence of nations through international trade and communications will also lead to an increased concern for the world's natural environment and a willingness to address those concerns.

---

[16] *In re* Union Carbide Corp. Gas Plant Disaster at Bhopal, India, December, 1984, 809 F.2d 195, 200 (2d Cir. 1987).

Chapter 13 Case Study: Ecuador v. Colombia

Environmental issues also arise in illegal trade. For example, efforts taken to curtail the illegal trade in narcotics have led to disputes between nations: A dispute arose between Ecuador and Colombia concerning the aerial eradication of illegal crops by herbicide spraying.

Illegal drug trafficking is a serious international problem. In 2008, 178 nation-states were parties to the United Nations Convention against Illicit Traffic in Narcotic Drugs and Psychotropic Substances (1988 UN Drug Convention), which is a treaty that promotes international cooperation to address the problem of illicit drugs.[17] Illegal drug use poses a "serious threat to the health and welfare of human beings and adversely affect[s] the economic, cultural and political foundations of society."[18]

One international antidrug program, Plan Colombia, used herbicides to eradicate illicit coca and opium poppy crops, the sources of cocaine and heroin, respectively. The herbicide was applied aerially by helicopters and airplanes. The Colombian government chose the areas to spray.[19]

The herbicide used in Colombia's aerial fumigation program was glyphosate,[20] an herbicide approved by the U.S. Environmental Protection Agency (EPA) in 1974 and by reregistration in 1993 for cropland, forests, residential areas, and aquatic areas. This defoliant was chosen for use in Plan Colombia in part because it could be applied to large forested areas from high altitudes; many of the targeted Colombian rural areas were not safe fly zones due to the presence of drug traffickers, guerrillas, and ongoing military-type disputes.

Despite the EPA's approval of glyphosate, some people believed that it was unsafe as used in the Colombian fumigation program. For example, many complaints originating in Colombia and in neighboring Ecuador reported adverse human health effects, environmental degradation, destruction of legal crops, and illness and death to animals as a result of its use.

Colombia and Ecuador are ecologically rich environments, and many people who lived there, as well as in the greater international community, were concerned about the effects of the chemical spraying on the area's natural diversity. In 2008, Ecuador instituted proceedings against Colombia in the International Court of Justice to ask for relief and damages resulting from the sprayings. The United States was not named as a defendant.

THE COLOMBIAN GOVERNMENT

In 1984—well before the implementation of Plan Colombia—the Colombian government convened experts to study the effects of aerial spraying.[21] These experts concluded that the spraying of herbicides—including glyphosate—was not recommended, because little was known about the toxicity to humans of these substances.[22] These experts likened the aerial eradication program to "human experimentation."[23]

Notwithstanding these findings, Colombia began aerial fumigation at least by 2000.[24] It identified illegal coca and opium poppy crops through the use of an aircraft-mounted GPS, which identified exact coordinates.[25] A computer established flight lines, but the pilots did not open the valve to release the herbicide until they had visual confirmation of the crop.[26] The Colombian target areas included the frontier region along the border of Ecuador.[27] To avoid drift, aerial fumigation missions were cancelled if wind speed

---

[17] 1988 UN Drug Convention, Resolution 2, ¶ 1. Retrieved from https://www.unodc.org/pdf/convention_1988_en.pdf

[18] 1988 UN Drug Convention, p. 1.

[19] Republica del Ecuador Ministerio de Relaciones Exteriores, Application of the Republic of Ecuador to the Registrar, International Court of Justice (2008) (hereinafter "Republica del Ecuador"), p. 1.

[20] U.S. Department of State, Bureau for International Narcotics and Law Enforcement Affairs, International Narcotics Control Strategy Report, p. 23 (March 2008). Retrieved March 13, 2014, from http://www.state.gov/documents/organization/102583.pdf

[21] Republica del Ecuador, p. 4.

[22] Republica del Ecuador, p. 5, citing Administrative Tribunal of Cundinamarca, Colombia, Second Section, Subsection B, 13/6/2003, "Claudia Sampedro y Hector Suarez v. Ministry of Environment and Others," p. 15 [hereinafter "Cundinamarca Admin. Tribunal"].

[23] Republica del Ecuador, p. 5, citing Cundinamarca Admin. Tribunal.

[24] Republica del Ecuador, p. 1.

[25] Bureau for Narcotics and Law Enforcement Affairs, Aerial Eradication of Illicit Crops: Frequently Asked Questions (March 24, 2003). Retrieved March 13, 2014, from http://2001-2009.state.gov/p/inl/rls/fs/18987.htm

[26] Id., p. 3.

[27] Republica del Ecuador, p. 2.

(Continued)

exceeded 10 mph, humidity was greater than 75%, or temperatures exceeded 90 degrees Fahrenheit.[28] In response to environmental concerns, the Colombian government contracted with an environmental auditor to review and monitor spray areas, analyze data, conduct field checks, and check on oversprays.[29]

In response to Ecuador's concerns about the spraying program, the Colombian Government answered that "Plan Colombia is ... the most effective method for protecting the fraternal country of Ecuador from the perverse effects of narcotrafficking and armed conflict, in a way that is aimed at preventing ... [drug traffickers] from continuing to get stronger and metastasizing to Ecuador."[30]

THE ECUADORIAN GOVERNMENT

In March 2008, Ecuador instituted proceedings at the International Court of Justice (ICJ) against Colombia concerning the aerial spraying of toxic herbicides.[31] Ecuador alleged that the aerial spraying "ha[d] already caused serious damage to people, to crops, to animals, and to the natural environment on the Ecuadorian side of the frontier."[32] Ecuador requested relief from the ICJ in the form of an order to "respect the sovereignty and territorial integrity of Ecuador; ... take all steps necessary to prevent the use of any toxic herbicides in such a way that they could be deposited onto the territory of Ecuador; ... prohibit [Colombia's] use, by means of aerial dispersion, of such herbicides on or near any part of its border with Ecuador; and ... indemnify Ecuador for any loss or damage caused by its internationally unlawful acts."[33]

In its application, Ecuador alleged that Colombia's aerial spraying of toxic herbicides had been conducted "near, at, and across its border with Ecuador,"[34] affecting the Ecuadorian provinces of Esmeraldas, Carchi, and Sucumbios.[35] It further alleged "serious damage to people, to crops, to animals, and to the natural environment on the Ecuadorian side of the frontier," with "grave risk of further damage over time."[36]

Ecuador alleged that Colombia sometimes breached the Ecuadorian airspace by using that airspace to turn its aircraft around, and occasionally the pilots simply kept spraying within the Ecuadorian border.[37] Additionally, the winds dispersed herbicide dropped into Colombia over the border into Ecuador.[38]

Ecuador further alleged that serious human health problems had resulted from these sprayings, including eye irritation, such as burning and itching; skin sores and lesions; respiratory problems; heart arrhythmias; temporary paralysis; temporary blindness; intestinal bleeding; and death.[39] These symptoms were said to mirror complaints made by Colombians.[40] Ecuador argued that the sprayings were carcinogenic and posed reproductive risks, citing laboratory studies as its evidence.[41]

Additionally, Ecuador alleged damage to non-target crops such as yucca, plantains, rice, coffee, hay, corn, cocoa, coffee, and fruit.[42] These problems had resulted in serious interference with Ecuadorian subsistence farmers of that region. The nonhuman toll also included illness of birds, fish, dogs, horses, and cows, as well as allegations of the deaths of "thousands of animals."[43]

Ecuador reported that it had unsuccessfully attempted diplomatic negotiations with Colombia to end the sprayings and, with Colombia, had convened bilateral scientific commissions to examine the effects of the spraying.[44] Ecuador argued that the inert ingredients used with the herbicide glyphosate were toxic, and that, together, these products had a synergistically toxic effect. Ecuador believed that the surfactant Cosmo-Flux 411f was used, and complained that

[28] Aerial Eradication, p. 3.
[29] Id., p. 2.
[30] Republica del Ecuador, p. 15.
[31] International Court of Justice, 2008.
[32] Aerial Herbicide Spraying (Ecuador v. Colombia), I.C.J. Reports 2008 (General List No. 138) (hereinafter "ICJ Order"), p. 174. Available at http://www.icj-cij.org/docket/files/138/14629.pdf
[33] ICJ Order, p. 1.
[34] Republica del Ecuador, p. 1.
[35] Id., p. 6.
[36] Id., p. 1.
[37] Id., pp. 2, 7.
[38] Id., p. 7.
[39] Id., pp. 2, 8.
[40] Id., p. 8.
[41] Id., p. 10.
[42] Id., pp. 2, 7.
[43] Id., pp. 7, 8.
[44] Id., p. 2.

Colombia refused to release proprietary information concerning Cosmo-Flux's chemical composition; consequently, "the glyphosate/Cosmoflux combination has not been subject to proper evaluations for safety to humans or ... to animals."[45] Ecuador also believed that Colombia was using polyethoxylated tallowamine (POEA) as another surfactant, which "cause[d] eye burns, skin redness and blistering, nausea and diarrhea."[46]

Ecuador argued that it was environmentally unique and vulnerable.[47] It was one of only 17 countries designated as "megadiverse" by the UN Environment Programme's World Conservation Monitoring Centre.[48] It claimed that it had the world's highest biological diversity per square kilometer than anywhere else in the world, having many species of mammals, plants, birds (including 35% of the world's hummingbirds), reptiles, amphibians, and fish. About one-quarter of its land was comprised of protected areas or national parks.[49]

Additionally, Ecuador was geographically and culturally unique, consisting of coastal, mountainous, and Amazonian jungle areas. Moreover, indigenous peoples lived there, including 3,500 Awâ, who were dependent upon the natural environment. The people of the region relied upon subsistence farming.[50] Due to the "terror induced by the sprayings," up to 50% of the local populations had fled their homelands.[51]

Between 2000 and 2007, Ecuador had initiated many diplomatic overtures to Colombia, seeking to restrict spraying along the frontier border region, and each had failed.[52] Indeed, Colombia maintained that its actions were in full conformity "with the principle of precaution enshrined in the 1992 Rio Declaration on Environment and Development."[53] Colombia further maintained that its aerial fumigation program protected Ecuador from the metastasizing effects of narcoterrorism. In effect, it argued that it was being a good neighbor by carrying out its fumigation program. In July 2007, "Ecuador informed Colombia ... that it considered the process of dialogue exhausted, and without prospects for success."[54] Ecuador then commenced proceedings at the ICJ against Colombia.

Ecuador asserted that "Colombia's conduct amounts to a dangerous ecological and toxicological experiment on a vast scale."[55] Ecuador claimed that Colombia had violated Ecuador's rights under customary and conventional international law, and "failed to meet its obligations of prevention and precaution."[56] It sought indemnification for damage to property, death or injury to humans, and environmental damage.[57] It also asked that Colombia respect its sovereignty and territorial integrity and prevent toxic herbicides from being deposited in Ecuador or near its border.[58]

THE INTERNATIONAL COMMUNITY

General concerns existed in the international community concerning Plan Colombia's effects on conventional Colombian farmers' crops, general environmental damage to wildlife and ecosystems, and potentially negative effects on waterways. For instance, Dr. Theo Colburn argued that aerial glyphosate dispersal could not be contained, and that the surfactant used enhanced the toxicity of the sprayings. She also pointed out that early studies found that glyphosate did pose risks to human health.[59] Likewise, general concerns existed with the use of glyphosate in a rainy and humid environment, because the chemicals would run into the Amazonian Basin, affecting Peru, Ecuador, and Brazil.

A report of the UN Special Rapporteur for human rights identified aerial fumigation of illicit crops as a most serious problem.[60] The Ecuadorian indigenous Awâ people had complained that their rights to food had been violated, they had been displaced from their homeland, the

---

[45] Id., p. 11.
[46] Id., p. 11.
[47] Id., p. 12.
[48] Id., p. 12, citing World Resources Institute, Ecuador Country Profile, Biodiversity and Protected Areas (available at http://earthtrends.wri.org/text/biodiversity-protected/country-profile-54.htrnl).
[49] Id., p. 12.
[50] Id., p. 11.
[51] Id., p. 18.
[52] Id., pp. 14–16.
[53] Id., p. 16.
[54] Id., p. 17.
[55] Id., p. 14.
[56] Id., p. 20.
[57] Id., p. 19.
[58] Id., p. 19.
[59] Colburn interview in Plan Colombia: Cashing in on the Drug War Failure (2003). Cinema Libre ASIN: B00074DXF8 [video]. Available from Amazon.com.
[60] Republica del Ecuador, p. 12, citing Report of the Special Rapporteur on Colombia.

(Continued)

surrounding wildlife had died, the soil was contaminated, and the waters had become polluted. Their economic and social lives had been devastated.[61]

Epilogue

In 2013, Ecuador asked the International Court of Justice to dismiss the proceedings against Colombia, as the parties had reached an out-of-court resolution on the matter.

Questions and Comments for Discussion

2. Who were the stakeholders in this case? What were their interests in the outcome of the conflict? How would each be affected if the aerial fumigation plan continued? How would each be affected if it ceased?

3. Should the protection of a rich ecological system, such as that found in Ecuador and Colombia, be considered a domestic issue subject only to domestic laws, or should it become an international issue that requires input from other nation-states?

4. What arguments support the continuation of Plan Colombia's aerial fumigation program? What arguments support rejection of it? Is there a middle ground?

5. If aerial fumigation of crops is subsequently found to be harmful to humans or the natural environment, who should bear the liability? The Colombian government? The United States? The Monsanto Company? The farmers who grow the illicit crops? Why?

6. Which international environmental law concepts bear on this case? How does resolution of a case like this differ procedurally from a case involving disputants from the same jurisdiction?

---

[61] *Id.*, pp. 12–4, citing Document A/HRC/4/32/Add.2 (28 December 2006), Powell 15-35.

Glossary

A

abandoned property Property over which the original owner has completely relinquished ownership and control.

acid rain Precipitation containing a high concentration of acids produced by sulfur dioxide, nitrogen oxide, and other substances emitted during the combustion of fossil fuel.

administrative law Area of law related to the powers, duties, and procedures of administrative agencies.

Administrative Procedure Act (APA) Congressional legislation that establishes the basic framework of administrative law governing agency action.

adulterated food Food containing any unsafe additive.

adversary system Legal framework in which opposing parties present evidence in the way that is most favorable to their respective sides.

adverse possession Means of acquiring title to land by openly taking possession of and using another's property for a certain period of time.

alternative dispute resolution (ADR) Any form of dispute resolution that is not litigation.

ambient air Outdoor air.

animal rights perspective The belief that animals have the right to live without interference by humans.

answer A pleading submitted by a defendant to admit and/or deny the allegations of a complaint.

anthropocentric view Belief that human beings are the most important species on Earth.

appellate court A court that hears appeals.

arbitrary and capricious A standard of judicial review specified by APA § 706(2)(A); essentially examines whether the agency had a reasonable, rational basis for its decision or action.

attainment Designation indicating that a particular area meets a NAAQS for a pollutant.

B

banking Process by which an emission source may "save" sulfur dioxide emission allowances by making reductions that exceed regulatory requirements; the banked allowance may be used later or transferred.

bench trial A trial before a judge but no jury.

best available control technology (BACT) A technology standard for new stationary sources of air pollution.

bequest A transfer of personal property by will; an inheritance or legacy.

beyond a reasonable doubt The burden of proof standard in a criminal case.

bill A draft of a proposed statute.

Bill of Rights The common name for the first 10 amendments to the U.S. Constitution.

brownfields Abandoned hazardous waste sites.

bubble theory Concept that an imaginary structure ("bubble") covers existing and/or neighboring pollution sources; used to define areas rather than single sources in determining the source of emissions for purposes of the CAA.

C

carbon monoxide A criteria pollutant; a colorless, odorless toxic gas.

Cartagena Protocol on Biosafety   An international agreement related to the protection of biological diversity in the face of potential risks associated with the genetic modification of organisms made possible by modern technology.

caveat emptor   "Let the buyer beware"; maxim expressing a warning and expectation that a buyer will examine or test the potential purchase before consummating the transaction."

caveat venditor   "Let the seller beware"; maxim expressing that a seller must meet its heightened legal and contractual obligations."

CERCLA   The "Superfund" statute that addresses hazardous waste sites.

chattel   An item of tangible, moveable personal property.

checks and balances   Political system in which each branch of government has specifically assigned powers and duties that constrain or limit the other branches' powers and duties; ensure that no branch becomes too powerful on its own.

CITES   An international agreement relating to trade in endangered plants and animals.

citizen suit provision   Statutory provision that allows any citizen to bring a legal action to enforce that statute or force a governmental entity to perform a nondiscretionary duty.

civil law   Law involving actions for breach of legal duties owed by private parties to other individuals. A civil lawsuit may be based on a statute or common law.

Code of Federal Regulations (CFR)   Codification of the rules and regulations promulgated by administrative agencies.

codification   The arrangement of statutes into an organized code.

command and control   Direct regulation that proscribes or permits (or mandates) certain behaviors.

Commerce Clause   Article I, § 8, of the U.S. Constitution; gives Congress the power to regulate commerce among the states.

commercial speech   Speech that is economic or commerce-related.

common law   Judge-made law or case law.

commons   A scarce resource available for use by all or many.

community property   System of property ownership by husband and wife that exists in some but not all states.

compensatory damages   Monetary awards that compensate the plaintiff for injuries.

complaint   A pleading that initiates a lawsuit.

concurrent jurisdiction   A situation in which two or more legal authorities may exercise jurisdiction.

condemnation proceeding   The legal process by which a government exercises the right of eminent domain and acquires private land for public use.

condominium   A type of shared ownership of real property.

conflict preemption   Status arising when state and federal law actually conflict, even if Congress is silent on the issue.

conservation   Stance stressing wise use of natural resources so that they continue to be available for use in the future.

constitutional law   Laws and legal doctrines drawn or derived from the U.S. Constitution.

contained-in rule   Under RCRA, soil, groundwater, surface water, and debris contaminated with hazardous waste are considered hazardous waste.

contract   A legally enforceable promise.

convention   An international treaty or agreement.

conquest   Taking possession of enemy territory through force.

cooperative federalism   A legislative scheme whereby the federal government allows the states to establish or lead programs within their own borders, as long as those programs meet federal minimum guidelines for compliance.

corporation   A legal entity separate and distinct from its shareholders (owners).

counterclaim   A pleading through which the defendant files its own complaint against the plaintiff.

courts of general jurisdiction Courts that have authority to hear all types of cases.

courts of limited jurisdiction Courts that have authority to hear only limited or specific types of cases.

covenant A contractual agreement to do or refrain from doing something that binds owners of the land subject to it.

creation The production of personal property.

criteria pollutants A pollutant for which a NAAQS has been set by the EPA. Criteria pollutants include ground-level ozone, particulate matter, carbon monoxide, nitrogen oxides, sulfur dioxide, and lead.

critical habitat The geographical area with the physical or biological features essential to survival of the species.

customary international law General guiding principles recognized by nations as a source of international law.

D

damages Compensation in money for a loss or injury.

declaratory relief A court's ruling regarding the legality of a statute or regulation.

defendant The party alleged by the plaintiff in a civil suit to be responsible for the plaintiff's injury.

delegation doctrine Legal doctrine addressing the question of whether a branch of government may constitutionally assign some of its powers or delegate some of its duties to an administrative agency.

deposition An out-of-court statement made under oath; one of several discovery mechanisms.

derived-from rule Under RCRA, a waste generated by the treatment, storage, or disposal of a hazardous waste is also a hazardous waste unless exempted.

disclaimer Contract provision whereby one party denies responsibility for certain events or occurrences.

discovery The process through which litigants acquire information relevant to the dispute.

distinguish To notice differences in the facts of a case that allow the court to change common law, apply it differently, or depart from stare decisis.

diversity jurisdiction Federal court jurisdiction that arises when citizens of different states present a substantial issue arising under the laws of the United States.

doctrine of ancient lights Doctrine that anyone who used light for an uninterrupted period of 20 years was entitled to protection of that use; historically rejected by American courts.

domestic law Law created, applied, and enforced by an authority recognized within the nation-state as exercising legitimate powers.

dormant commerce clause Constitutional theory that the Commerce Clause also prevents state legislation that discriminates against or interferes with interstate commerce.

due process Constitutional requirement for notice and opportunity to be heard, to ensure fairness in legal proceedings.

duty-based worldview Belief that one's duties to the community are of primary importance compared to individual rights to do as one wishes.

E

easement A right to use another's property.

easement appurtenant An easement that benefits a particular possessor or tract of land.

easement by prescription (prescriptive easement) An easement obtained through use and that meets statutory requirements similar to those required to establish adverse possession.

easement in gross An easement that belongs to the public regardless of whether the holder owns adjacent property.

ecosystem rights perspective The belief that the ecosystem itself has the right to exist; does not necessarily hold that individual members of the ecosystem have rights.

eminent domain The power of the government to take property for public use; requires the payment of just compensation to the owner of the property taken.

enabling legislation A statute that establishes an administrative agency.

environmental assessment (EA) A screening tool used to analyze whether an EIS is required under NEPA.

environmental impact statement (EIS) A requirement of NEPA for legislative and federal action proposals that significantly affect the quality of the human environment.

environmental justice Concern about the fair treatment of all people vis-à-vis environmental hazards such as pollution.

estate An ownership interest in real property.

estate for years A type of tenancy that has a definite beginning and ending.

exaction A construction or dedication requirement, or in-lieu fee payment for site-specific needs (such as streets, sidewalks, and drainage) as a condition of approval in a development plan.

executive order An order issued to the executive branch by the executive.

exhaustion of administrative remedies Doctrine requiring that a plaintiff use all procedural channels and seek all possible relief from an agency before seeking relief from the courts.

express easement An easement created by a specific grant.

express preemption Status arising when Congress expressly forbids the states from legislating in a particular area.

express warranty A warranty explicitly set out in words in the contract.

F

federalism A system of shared government, where power is divided between a central government and additional political units.

federal question jurisdiction Federal court jurisdiction based on a substantial issue arising under the laws of the United States.

Federal Register Daily government publication of federal agency actions and proposed actions.

fee simple absolute The most comprehensive estate in land, which conveys to the grantee complete ownership of the property.

fee simple defeasible A fee simple qualified by language that will cause the fee to end if and when a certain event happens.

field preemption Status arising when Congress intends to remove an entire area from state legislative authority.

finality Requirement that an agency decision be final before judicial review of the decision may be granted.

Finding of No Significant Impact (FONSI) A statement presenting a determination that an action will have no significant impact on the human environment, and consequently, no EIS is required.

formal rulemaking A rule made on the record after opportunity for an agency hearing.

found property Personal property that has been abandoned, lost, or mislaid by the original owner and is discovered by another.

fraud The use of deception to acquire money or property; in this context, the basis for a defense to performance of a contract.

G

Gaia hypothesis Belief or theory that the Earth is a living, self-regulating organism.

general public purpose The lawmakers' intended purpose for a law; investigated as the third step in statutory interpretation.

generator Under RCRA, a person whose act or process produces hazardous waste or whose act first causes hazardous waste to become subject to regulation.

gift A free, voluntary transfer of an ownership interest between a donor who intends to deliver the ownership interest and actually delivers the interest, and a recipient who accepts the interest.

"God Squad" Cabinet level review board created by the ESA to provide flexibility under the Act; the Endangered Species Committee has the power to grant exemptions under the Act.

grantee Person to whom a legal interest in real property is conveyed or transferred.

grantor Person who conveys an interest in real property to another.

grassroots efforts Actions organized at the community level to address a problem or concern of importance to that community.

green accounting An accounting method that attempts to include negative environmental externalities in the financial operation of a business or other institution.

ground-level ozone A criteria pollutant and contributor to smog.

H

hybrid rulemaking Rule making procedure that combines formal and information rulemaking requirements.

I

implied easement An easement that arises out of necessity.

implied-in-fact warranty A warranty not stated in words within a contract but implied by the intent and conduct of the parties.

implied-in-law warranty A warranty imposed by law; not expressly or implicitly intended by the parties.

implied preemption Status arising when Congress intends (though does not expressly state) to override, supersede, or avoid state legislative activity.

implied warranty of fitness An implied warranty that goods are suitable for a particular purpose.

implied warranty of habitability Warranty implied in law that a living structure will be habitable and fit for occupation.

implied warranty of merchantability An implied warranty that goods conform to the ordinary standard for usage (that they are "merchantable").

in rem jurisdiction Jurisdiction over property located within a state.

incidental beneficiary A third party who does not acquire the right to enforce a contract because the contract was not designed or intended to benefit the third party, even though benefit to that third party may be byproduct of the contract.

indemnification Reimbursement for costs or damages incurred.

indemnification agreement Agreement by which one person promises to reimburse another person, or hold that person harmless, for loss or damage.

inferior courts Minor courts with limited jurisdiction.

informal rulemaking Notice-and-comment rulemaking.

injunction A court order to refrain from or perform some activity.

innocent landowner defense Under CERCLA, rule that a landowner who acquired property after contamination is not liable if he or she had no knowledge of the contamination and no reason to know of the contamination.

intangible property Property that does not have a physical existence.

intellectual property Intangible personal property consisting of creations of the mind.

intent Knowledge that harm is substantially certain to follow a particular action.

intentional tort Tort resulting when a person acts with a desire to cause harm or with knowledge that such harm is substantially certain to follow as a result of those actions.

intergenerational equity The concept that the current generation owes a duty to future generations to maintain the environment in a manner that will allow those future generations to enjoy, use, and benefit from it.

interpretive rules Statements that present an agency's understanding of the meaning of language in statutes or in its regulations.

interrogatories Written questions relevant to the dispute served on the opposing party; one of several discovery mechanisms.

interstate commerce Commerce between states.

intrastate commerce Commerce within a single state.

J

joint and several liability   Liability of all responsible parties, together or independently, for the full amount of damages until the total amount is paid.

joint tenancy   Form of real property co-ownership that includes a right of survivorship.

judicial review   Court review of the action of an agency or other governmental entity.

jurisdiction   The power or authority of a court to hear a case.

jurisdictional   Relating to authority to apply or enforce a law.

L

lateral support   The upholding of land by the land next to it.

lead   A criteria pollutant; a neurotoxic metal.

lease   A contract for possession of property for a specified period of time.

legal remedy   Judicial remedy imposed by law.

legislative history   Lawmakers' record concerning why a statute was passed or the meaning of the words in the statute.

lessor   A person who leases a property to another; commonly referred to as a landlord.

limited liability company (LLC)   A distinct legal business structure that limits liability exposure of its owners, while offering favorable tax treatment and flexibility in the creation of the operating agreement.

life estate   An ownership interest in real property measured by a specified person's life.

life tenant   A person who owns a life estate.

live case or controversy   Actual adversarial dispute or contested issue.

long-arm statute   Law that gives the courts in a state personal jurisdiction over out-of-state defendants for certain acts done within the state.

lost property   Property involuntarily left where the owner is unlikely to find it.

M

market-based incentives   Regulations that encourage certain behavior through market action that rewards such behavior.

master plan   Community plan for land use required by state legislation enabling zoning.

maxim   A general statement of a rule of law.

maximum achievable control technology (MACT)   Emission rate based on best demonstrated control technology or practices; applies to air toxins under the CAA.

mislaid property   Property left in a place that the owner then forgot or could not find again, although the owner intended to be able to retrieve the item.

misrepresentation   An assertion not in accord with the facts.

mistake   A defense to performance of a contract based upon ignorance of an important fact not caused by neglect of a legal duty.

mixture rule   Under RCRA, a mixture (combination) of a listed hazardous waste and solid waste is considered hazardous waste unless exempted.

Montreal Protocol   A treaty that phases out the production of ozone depleting substances.

motion for the production of real evidence   Application to the court to allow one party to gain access to documents and other evidence in the possession of the opposing party; one of several discovery mechanisms.

multiple use   Under the FLPMA, a combination of diverse uses, including recreational, ranger, timber, mineral, watershed, habitat, nature, scenic, or scientific.

N

National Ambient Air Quality Standards (NAAQSs)   National clean air standards set at a level of air quality necessary to protect the public health and welfare; divided into primary and secondary standards.

National Contingency Plan (NCP)   Under CERCLA, the scheme that establishes procedures for cleanup response actions.

National Priorities List (NPL)   Under CERCLA, list in which the EPA ranks each hazardous waste site with respect to priority for cleanup.

negative externality   A negative impact on a third party.

negligence   Failure to maintain the standard of care in a legal duty to another (usually the duty to act with reasonable care), which results in a breach of the duty that actually and proximately causes actual injury.

negligence per se   Negligence arising from a defendant's breach of a legal duty imposed by statute, ordinance, or administrative rule or regulation, which results in injury occurring to a person whom that statute was intended to protect.

New Source Performance Standard (NSPS) Emission limitations for specific new or modified sources based on the BACT.

nitrogen oxides   Criteria pollutants; specific highly reactive gasses containing nitrogen and oxygen.

nonattainment areas   Areas that exceed any NAAQS for a pollutant.

nonconforming use   Use of property that is allowed, even though it does not conform to the zoning ordinance, because the zoning ordinance was adopted after the use began.

nonownership theory   Doctrine that a landowner does not own oil until the landowner has taken possession of the oil.

nonpoint source pollution   Water pollution resulting from sources that are not point sources, such as runoff.

normative law   What the law should be; a value-based statement about the law.

nuisance   Substantial or unreasonable interference with the plaintiff's use and enjoyment of its property.

O

obscenity   A form of speech that is not constitutionally protected; speech that appeals primarily to prurient interest.

ordinances   Local laws passed by a legislative body.

ownership in place theory   Doctrine that a landowner owns the oil beneath the landowner's land.

P

particulate matter   A criteria pollutant; broad class of diverse substances existing as discrete particles in the air, including liquid droplets or solids.

partition   A physical division of co-owned property whereby co-owners become adjoining landowners or neighbors.

partnership   An association of two or more persons formed to carry on a business for profit; examples of business forms in partnership include general partnership, a limited partnership, or a limited liability partnership (LLP).

periodic tenancy   A type of tenancy that lasts for a period of time and is automatically renewed until either party gives notice that it will end.

personal property   Tangible or intangible property that is not attached to land.

personal (in personam) jurisdiction   Jurisdiction over a person based on residency, consent, presence in a location, or a long-arm statute.

petition   A written application to a court by which a plaintiff commences a lawsuit.

plain meaning rule   Doctrine according to which a court interprets and applies a statute according to the plain, accepted meaning of the language used in that law.

plaintiff   The party who brings a civil suit.

planned unit development (PUD)   A land development project that mixes land uses within the development.

pleadings   The documents that define and limit the questions to be brought before the court; in civil litigation, the complaint, answer, counterclaim, and reply.

point source   As defined in CWA § 502, "Any discernible, confined and discrete conveyance … from which pollutants are or may be discharged."

political speech   Speech used to express opinions about government.

pollutant Contaminating substance discharged into the environment; often is a hazardous or toxic waste, chemical, or other substance, but the term is not limited to those categories. As used in the Clean Water Act, includes most types of industrial, municipal, or agricultural waste discharged into water.

polluter pays principle Holds that the actual polluter should bear the cost of pollution reduction or remediation of the damage.

positive law Human-made law that actually exists.

precautionary principle The idea that decision makers should err on the side of caution when their decisions will affect the environment.

preemption The priority of federal law over state law.

premanufacture notice (PMN) A filing required by TSCA by a person who intends to manufacture or import a new chemical substance.

preponderance of the evidence The burden of proof standard in a civil case.

preservation Stance that the environment should be protected rather than used.

pretreatment standards Standards for treating industrial discharges into a publicly owned treatment works.

pretrial conference A meeting between the opposing attorneys and the judge before the trial.

primary standards NAAQSs set at a level of air quality necessary to protect the public health.

prior appropriation doctrine Common law doctrine concerning determination of water rights which essentially declares "first in time, first in right," regardless of riparian owner status; followed primarily in states west of the Mississippi.

prior interpretations Precedents.

private nuisance Substantial interference with the right of another to the use and enjoyment of its property.

private property Property owned by an individual, group of individuals, or a business.

proactive Anticipatory; acting in advance to address an expected challenge or issue.

procedural rules Rules governing the organization, procedure, or practice of an agency or other governmental entity.

product liability Name for a group of theories used in cases where plaintiffs seek to recover for personal injury or property damage resulting from a defective product.

property A legally protected expectation of being able to draw an advantage from a thing.

Property Clause Article IV, § 3, of the U.S. Constitution; gives Congress the power to make rules and regulations concerning property that belongs to the United States.

public good A resource that is available or common to all or many (nonexcludability) and use of which by an individual does not diminish its availability to others (nonrivalrous).

public nuisance A wrong that affects a large portion of the public by interfering with their common rights.

public property Property owned by a government entity.

public trust doctrine Legal theory stating that a government may not convey property or resources held for the public to private parties.

punitive damages A monetary award designed to punish a defendant and deter it from similar actions in the future.

purchase An exchange of something of value for title to property.

Q

question of fact Question about the truth of a matter or what actually happened; evidence presented by both sides in a litigation tries to answer such questions.

question of first impression An issue before the court of a particular jurisdiction for the first time.

question of law A dispute or disagreement that requires the interpretation of law or application of a law to a specific set of facts.

quiet title action A proceeding to establish title to land by bringing into court all who have claims to the title to the property.

R

reactive   Responding to something that happened in the past.

real property   Land or immovable objects attached to the land.

reasonably prudent person standard   An objective standard of conduct against which actions are measured to determine negligence.

recklessness   Conduct demonstrating a conscious disregard for a known risk of probable harm to others.

record of decision (ROD)   Formal statement identifying and explaining an agency decision.

recovery plans   Document setting forth the actions necessary to bring about the recovery of a species.

redressable   Capable of being rectified or remedied.

regulatory taking   A regulatory restriction on an owner's use of property to the extent that all or nearly all economic value in the property is lost.

remainder   A future interest in property.

remainderman   A person who has a remainder interest in real property.

remedial action   Long-term permanent cleanup responses under CERCLA.

removal   Transfer of a case from a state to federal court, or vice versa.

removal action   Short-term emergency responses under CERCLA.

reply   A plaintiff's answer to a counterclaim.

res judicata   A doctrine that bars a court from deciding a matter that has already been decided by a court.

rescission   Cancellation of a contract and placement of party in position he was in prior to the formation of the contract cancelled.

response costs   Costs of cleanup that may be recovered under CERCLA.

restrictive covenant   A contractual promise that passes with the land.

rights-based worldview   Belief that one's individual rights to do as one wishes are of primary importance compared to any duties that one might have to the community.

right of survivorship   Interest in real property such that upon the death of a co-owner, the ownership interest of the deceased automatically vests in the other owner(s).

right of termination   Express contractual provision giving a party the right to cancel the contract upon the occurrence of some specified event.

Rio Declaration   An international agreement on principles guiding sustainable development.

riparian owner   A person who owns property adjacent to a waterway.

riparian rights doctrine   Common law doctrine concerning determination of water rights, which requires "reasonable use" and declares that only riparian owners may assert those rights; followed primarily in states east of the Mississippi.

ripeness   Doctrine declaring that before judicial review is granted, legal issues must be presented that are appropriate for judicial decision making.

risk assessment   The process of characterizing the potentially adverse consequences of human exposure to an environmental hazard.

risk management   The process by which policy choices are made once risks have been determined.

rule of capture   Doctrine holding that the first person to capture a natural resource owns that natural resource; also applies in various ways, according to state law, to oil and minerals.

S

secondary standards   NAAQSs set at a level of air quality necessary to protect the public welfare.

signing statement   A statement by the president relating to the bill being signed into law.

soft law   Rules that do not lack legal significance but are not necessarily binding.

sovereignty   A nation-state's power to govern the population and territory within its own borders.

solar easement laws Statutes that permit the execution and recognition of easements for solar access.

specific performance Remedy whereby a defendant is ordered to perform the contract according to its terms.

standing The legal right to bring a lawsuit. The federal courts require that the citizen be able to prove injury in fact, a causal connection between the conduct that is the subject of the suit and the injury, and redressability of the injury by a court decision in the plaintiff's favor.

stare decisis Literally, "let the decision stand"; doctrine requiring judges to follow precedent in their jurisdictions in similar cases.

state implementation plan (**SIP**) Plan submitted by a state to the EPA that details how the state will attain and maintain established air quality standards.

statutes Laws passed by the legislative branch of government.

statute of limitations Law prescribing time limits on the right to bring certain legal actions.

statutory interpretation The process by which a court determines the meaning of a law.

stationary source Nonmobile source that emits or may emit air pollution.

strict liability Liability resulting from activities that cause harm to others, even if no intent or negligence exists.

strict liability in tort Product liability theory that holds the manufacturer, distributor, or seller of a defective product liable for physical harm or property damage suffered by the purchaser even though the manufacturer, distributor, or seller exercised all reasonable care in the preparation and sale of the product.

subdivision Parcel of land divided into units.

subject matter jurisdiction Jurisdictional authority over a particular kind of case.

substantial evidence A standard of judicial review specified by APA § 706(2)(E); essentially examines whether the agency had sufficient evidence to support its decision or action.

substantive rules Rules establishing or prescribing law or policy.

sulfur dioxide A criteria pollutant; a poisonous gas.

summary judgment Decision issued by a court when no genuine issues of material fact exist and a party is entitled to judgment as a matter of law.

summons A notice of lawsuit served on the defendant.

Supremacy Clause Article VI of the U.S. Constitution; declares the Constitution and laws of the United States (federal laws) the "supreme law of the land."

sustainability Use of resources in a manner that does not permanently deplete them.

sustainable development "Development that meets the needs of the present without compromising the ability of future generations to meet their own needs."

sustained yield Maintenance of high-level output of renewable resources on public lands.

T

taking A government seizure of privately owned property for public use.

regulatory taking Government seizure or regulation of property that deprives the property owner of all economic value from the property.

taking (Under the ESA), action to "harass, harm, pursue, hunt, shoot, wound, kill, trap, capture, or collect, or attempt to engage in any such conduct."

tangible property Property that has a physical existence.

tenancy at sufferance A type of tenancy that arises when a person in possession refuses to leave after its right to possession has ended.

tenancy at will A type of tenancy characterized by an indefinite duration.

tenancy by the entirety Form of real property ownership by husband and wife.

tenancy in common Form of real property coownership in which the parties hold separate undivided interests in the property.

Tenth Amendment   Amendment to the U.S. Constitution that reserves to the states those powers not delegated to the federal government.

third party   One who is not party to a transaction, but might be affected by it.

third-party complaint   A complaint filed by a defendant against another person other than the plaintiff.

title   The right of ownership in property.

tolerances   Maximum legally permissible levels for pesticide residues in food or animal feed.

tort   A civil wrong or injury.

transboundary   Crossing jurisdictional boundaries.

treasure trove   A collection or cache of money or refined precious metals.

treaties   Agreements made between two or more nation-states.

trespass   Intentional, voluntary intrusion on or invasion of the tangible property of another without permission or privilege.

trespass to land   Intentional, voluntary intrusion on or invasion of the land owned by another without permission or privilege.

trial   An examination of the issues between two parties by a court with appropriate jurisdiction.

trial court   The court where evidence is submitted and questions of facts are resolved.

trial de novo   A full new trial before the court, not limited to review of earlier proceedings.

TSCA inventory   A current list of all chemical substances manufactured or processed for commercial purposes in the United States; published by the EPA.

U

U.S. Constitution   The supreme law of the United States.

U.S. district court   The trial court in the federal court system.

unconscionability   A defense to performance of a contract based on procedural and/or substantive unfairness. An unconscionable contract is one that

"no man in his senses … would make … and … no fair and honest man would accept …" [Hume v. United States, 132 U.S. 406, 10 S. Ct. 134, 33 L. Ed. 393 (1889)].

Uniform Commercial Code (**UCC**)   A model statute, which has been adopted in full or in part by most or all states, that governs certain types of contracts.

Uniform Hazardous Waste Manifest   Control and transport document required by RCRA; originates with the generator and accompanies the hazardous waste to the place of disposal.

V

variance   Exception to or waiver of a requirement of the zoning code; to get a variance, the petitioner typically is required to show that (1) it would suffer undue hardship if the ordinance is enforced, and (2) granting of the variance will not excessively disrupt the surrounding land or master plan.

venue   The particular physical location where a court exercises its jurisdiction.

voir dire   A jury selection process in which attorneys question potential jurors.

volatile organic compounds (**VOCs**)   Petroleum-based organic compounds that mix with other substances in the air to form ozone.

W

warranty   A contractual promise that an assertion or statement is true.

waste   An unlawful act or breach of duty by a tenant that results in permanent injury to the leased property.

wetlands   A general term for marshes, swamps, bogs, and similar areas where land meets water.

writ of certiorari   Discretionary writ by which the U.S. Supreme Court chooses which decisions from the state and federal appeals courts to review.

Z

zoning   Term describing local and regional land use regulations controlling the use of land within a particular jurisdiction.

Index